A CENTURY TO CELEBRATE

History of Woman's Missionary Union

Catherine Allen

Published by Woman's Missionary Union, Auxiliary to Southern Baptist Convention, P. O. Box C-10, Birmingham, Alabama 35283-0010: Marjorie J. McCullough, president; Carolyn Weatherford, executive director; Bobbie Sorrill, associate executive director, Missions Education System; Lynn Yarbrough, Publications Section director; Karen C. Simons, Products Group manager.

Contents

This will be written

for the generation to come;

That a people yet to be created

may praise the Lord.

Psalm 102:18

Preface

Shame on you if standing on the shoulders of your fathers you do not see farther.

John A. Broadus to daughter Eliza

OR 100 YEARS a neglected cause and a repressed group of people have clung together in the swirling white water rapids of Southern Baptists. The cause is missions. The people are women. Separately, they have been immersed in controversy. Together, they have risen to walk on the waters victorious.

The cause and the people tied themselves together in Woman's Missionary Union, organized in 1888 as auxiliary to the Southern Baptist Convention. The Convention did not officially throw out a lifeline to the dreaded women's union. Rather, the women inflated their own life raft, pulled the Convention's mission boards aboard, and anchored themselves in the promises of God. Instead of drowning in the watery grave of controversy, Woman's Missionary Union managed to baptize the Convention in a sea of prayer, a gush of funds, a stream of consciousness, and finally a watershed of social action.

Historians have not yet plumbed the depths of Woman's Missionary Union's significance in church and culture. In the 850 pages of the latest major history of Baptists, women and Woman's Missionary Union are mentioned on only 8 percent of the pages.

On the secular historical scene, the skies have rained for 20 years with significant women's histories and with analyses of southern religion. Yet one can scarcely find mention of the largest, most enduring, and by some measures most powerful religious women's organization of all: Woman's Missionary Union.

Why has WMU (as the organization is usually abbreviated) been ignored in the footnotes of historical writing? The answer can be found in the fact that men have been the primary writers of history. Even the experts have not yet learned their way into the archives of WMU, where an enormous body of published literature and unbroken minutes lie unmined.

Being ignored has never deterred WMU. WMU has simply commissioned and published its own histories. WMU has wielded history as a potent weapon. From the beginning WMU officers believed they were making history. They preserved history as they created it. They followed the admonition of their second president, Fannie E. S. Heck, who said, "Think long thoughts. Plan not for the year but for the years."

Heck herself was WMU's first major chronicler. Although WMU had produced numerous historical leaflets, its first book-length history was Heck's *In Royal Service*, a volume marking the 25th anniversary of WMU. It was published in 1913, the year the women nailed the last plank on their structure of age-graded organizations and rounded out a full statement of purpose and program.

In Royal Service revealed WMU at the apex of the rising tide of women as missions executives and professional missionaries. Heck's goal was to help people understand the "plant" known as WMU by exposing the "social soil" in which the plant flourished. The study of *In Royal Service* proved to WMU the power of history to inspire another generation of true believers, to raise enormous amounts of money, and to deflect critics.

The lesson was well learned and was repeated at the 50th anniversary of WMU. Ethlene Boone Cox, another president of WMU, wrote *Following in His Train*. This volume redug the roots Heck had uncovered, then piled up the powerful triumphs of WMU during the years of denominational depression, debt, and disgrace.

WMU reached its peak enrollment when women flocked to the study of *History of Woman's Missionary Union,* written for the 75th anniversary by Alma Hunt, WMU's chief executive officer. Hunt's history was built on the biographies of WMU leaders. Their accomplishments magnetically drew many women into WMU membership and out of the rumbles which quaked into the woman's liberation movement.

Hunt, like her predecessors Kathleen Mallory and Annie Armstrong, wrapped WMU in the armor of facts, figures, and faces. Mallory, at the 60th anniversary, stated that WMU "has the sanction of history." Each of these executives led with the confidence that time was on her side.

Laura D. Armstrong, another president of WMU, told her followers: "A heritage is a precious thing, not to be squandered, but to be treasured, added to, and transmitted." At the 50th anniversary celebration, Armstrong quoted Heck at the 25th: "It was good, but it is past. To be past is not, however, to have ceased to influence."

For all their reliance on history and their scrupulous honesty in transmitting it, WMU's historians have made strategic errors. Their writings have tended to be unsupported by visible footnotes, bibliographies, and societal viewpoints that would woo outside historians. And, WMU writers have refrained from claiming all the credit due them.

Perhaps they wrote too close to the glare and blare of events to state for a certainty that WMU had turned the tides of history. So, while winning the inside audience, WMU stepped into the shadows on the wider platform of social history.

With a century to celebrate, WMU must march into the spotlight. WMU stands at the center of a fascinating slice of society. WMU is the only visible evidence of the majority of members in a male-dominated denomination, the largest evangelical organization in the world. Southern Baptists have the largest missionary force among Protestants and their financial support of missions is without parallel. Southern-style religion seems to be the cradle of the nation's political mood. Who is rocking that cradle? No longer can the past be analyzed without lifting the lamp over Woman's Missionary Union. Nor can the present be comprehended nor the future estimated without acknowledging WMU as the source of much that distinguishes Southern Baptists.

History is rewritten because new questions are asked. Looking ahead to the Centennial year of WMU, its leaders again prepared to ignite the cannons of history. They commissioned a thorough re-examination of the deepening roots and widening branches of WMU. They saw the need for a book that would match WMU with the major problems of its environment and ask: Is WMU shaping society or being shaped by it? Is WMU achieving its purpose? What of the future? They wanted an inspirational volume for women inside WMU and an educational volume for outside observers.

To reach the latter audience, this volume ideally should have been written by an independent scholar and published by a university press. Because none of these have stepped foward to meet the challenge of WMU, WMU's Centennial history has an inside writer and publisher.

A Century to Celebrate: History of Woman's Missionary Union proposes to be an objective, factual, yet analytical view of how women driven by their Christian faith have done battle with the forces of church and society. The book is organized by the topics WMU has chosen to address or has been forced to address. The book is not in chronological form. A chapter may be read without dependence on what preceded.

Chapter 1 untangles the knots which restrained WMU from organizing until prosperity returned to the South after the Civil War. The chapter reveals that even without organization, women pulled the tattered threads of their churches together during Reconstruction.

Chapter 2 shows how the women saw their purpose and flexed their muscles until their organization became an institution, a business, a profession, and a power.

Chapter 3 explains the social, ethnic, and geographical spread of WMU into a worldwide sweep.

Chapter 4 pictures the operating style of women as they built a union of organizations for all ages and won the right to direct their own activities in the local congregation.

Chapters 5 and 6 add up the dollars by which WMU slowly bought a place for women at the Baptist conference tables.

Chapter 7 looks at the place where women first found their voices: in prayer. From their knees they arose to champion the right of women to serve as professional missionaries and ministers.

Chapter 8 deals with WMU as propagandist, educator, and publisher.

Chapters 9 and 10 show how WMU introduced social action into the Southern Baptist experience, with chapter 10 examining WMU's wrestling matches with the major social issues such as temperance, woman suffrage, and race.

Chapter 11 reminds this generation that it was WMU who won a place for Baptist women in theological classrooms, even owning a theological and social work school for 50 years.

Chapter 12 traces the struggle of women to gain recognition in the Southern Baptist family at the associational and national levels.

Chapter 13 traces unique leadership style of women, cleaving only to their chosen cause of missions, which has made WMU stand in purity above the occasional feuds of the SBC.

In sum, *A Century to Celebrate* shows how a few zealous women started out to save souls, detoured to save the Southern Baptist Convention on several occasions, and accidentally saved the women themselves from their state of silent submission. In the process WMU tossed into other hands many innovations that became standard equipment in Baptist life. These are listed in chapter 14.

By no means is this a complete history of WMU. The story has spilled into a companion volume, *Laborers Together with God,* which tells the personal stories of WMU's remarkable elected officers and key personalities. This book should be at hand throughout the study of *A Century to Celebrate.*

To link the topical chapters, a chronological list of historical high points, beginning on page 427, is provided. Tables showing enrollment, reported financial achievements, and other data will afford closer scrutiny of the year-by-year impact between WMU and its publics. The main officers in the national organization of WMU are listed beginning on page 442. Although most of these women hid their given names behind their husbands' identity, history nevertheless records they locked arms and walked successfully through the deep waters of their times.

If the book seems overly documented, one purpose will have been achieved: to light the way for further examination of the facts and their meaning. History is never complete; history never stands still; history will always need one more dip in the deep waters.

Many an alarmed Southern Baptist has quoted John A. Broadus to

13

prove that women should keep silence in the church. Broadus was one of the first and finest theological teachers in Southern Baptist life. In the month of WMU's formal organization, he issued a major statement to oppose women speaking in public leadership of their faith.

But history is not properly told without the later facts. Broadus had a devoted daughter, Eliza, whom he personally educated. She became a founder of WMU. Her father taught her to be a public speaker. In the face of opposition, he encouraged her by saying, "Just keep on, daughter. The stars in their courses will fight for you."[1] On another occasion he told Eliza: "Shame on you if standing on the shoulders of your fathers you do not see farther."

From the pinnacle of a century, with the luxury of a long view, isolated facts and statements take on truer meaning. Standing on the shoulders of visionary fathers, daughters can look across the rivers of years, drink new consent and blessing from the past, and swim into all the world on the uncharted seas of the future.

Measure not the work
Until the day is out and the labor done;
Then bring your gauges. If the day's work's scant,
Then call it scant; affect no compromise,
And in that they've nobly striven at least
Deal with them nobly—women though they be—
And honor them with truth if not with praise.

Quoted by Susan Tyler Pollard (Mrs. James) in "Enlistment of State Forces and Organization of Woman's Missionary Union, SBC," one of WMU's earliest historical tracts

1
Shaking the treetops

*There is a sound of shaking in the tops of the trees
and we feel abundantly persuaded the wind which is
stirring the peaceful commotion is none other than
the Spirit of the living God.*

Alice Armstrong (Ruth Alleyn),
Religious Herald, July 28, 1887

HE TREES OF tradition have always towered around
Baptist women. In the shadowy forests of Baptist history, the custom of man has often been mistaken for
the command of God. The thick trunks of Baptist habit
have staunchly withstood the winds of social change.
Only the breath of God could have peeled back the
leaves of time, permitting divine light to beam on a mustard seedling
known as Woman's Missionary Union. By faith the little seed grew to
be a gracious plant of the garden, with branches wide enough to shelter
all of God's creatures.[1]

When the modern missions movement dawned in 1792, a woman
provided the parlor and wielded the teapot. Mrs. Beeby Wallis of Kettering, England, was hostess to a group of young men who formed the
Baptist Missionary Society of Great Britain. The voluntary society sent
William Carey, an associate of Wallis's late husband, as a missionary
to India. In the senders and in the one sent, the world found inspiringly
fresh models for accomplishing what Christ had commanded about
taking the gospel to all the world.[2]

In the same year and from the same country Mary Wollstonecraft
wrote *A Vindication of the Rights of Woman*. From this pamphlet
stemmed continuing agitation for equality for females. The Widow
Wallis and Mary Wollstonecraft walked in vastly differing circles, yet
their actions would soon flow in parallel channels to change the course
of history.

The treetops of tradition next trembled in the New World. American
ideals caused citizens to organize voluntarily for common causes.[3] Not
only men, but also women formed associations. An early women's
organization was the Society for the Relief of Poor Widows with Small

Children. Woman's Missionary Union was a descendant of this group, which was formed in November 1797 in New York by Isabella Graham. A devout Presbyterian, Graham in the previous year had prompted the formation of a men's society for support of missionaries on the New York frontier.[4]

The next known women's organization in the United States was devoted to missions. It launched the first, largest, and most enduring women's movement of history.[5] In 1800 a tiny 21-year-old paralyzed woman read a missionary sermon based on this Bible text: "Be ye strong therefore, and let not your hands be weak: for your work shall be rewarded."[6] These words gave a vision to Mary ("Polly") Webb, who had recently been baptized into Second Baptist Church of Boston. She called together seven other Baptist women and six Congregationalist women to form the Boston Female Society for Missionary Purposes. Mary Webb served as secretary and treasurer. Their purposes were to pray and to collect money for missions. William Carey was one who received their aid. The Baptist members outgave the Congregationalists and ultimately took over the organization.

The earliest recorded women's missionary society in the southern states was the Wadmalaw and Edisto Female Mite Society in South Carolina. Its first reported contributions were made in 1811 for the Charleston Baptist Association's work with Indians and ministerial students. This society was encouraged by one of the first denominationally-minded pastors in the South, Richard Furman. As pastor of the oldest Baptist church in the South, First Baptist of Charleston, he had formed a Juvenile Missionary and Education Society in the 1790s.

Forty miles away from Charleston, Hephzibah Jenkins Townsend became the leader of the missionary society serving Edisto and Wadmalaw Islands. Townsend had inherited a fortune, and her huge plantation yielded profitable crops of cotton and indigo. Still, she had no money for missions. Her assets were controlled by her husband, who was not sympathetic to missions. So she directed her slaves to build a huge outdoor oven. There she baked bread and cake for sale on the streets of Charleston, a six-hour boat trip away. Her profits went to missions.[7]

No more than 20 women's missionary societies are known to have existed by 1812.[8] In that year the Boston Female Society called for other women to organize, to join them in prayer, and to correspond with them. Mary Webb wrote: "We are not ashamed to acknowledge that we pray, that we meet in praying circles . . . and though we wish ever to preserve our place as females we cannot view it inconsistent with that modesty and shamefacedness enjoined by the apostle thus openly to come out on the Lord's side." As an early reporter said of the Boston Baptist women, "They feared God more than men."[9] Such courage was duplicated around the 18 states of the US. Eventually the mother society was in touch with more than 100 different groups, including several in the South.

The assistant pastor of First Baptist Church of Richmond, Virginia, read Mary Webb's call. His wife, her sister, and other women of the church decided to form a women's praying society. Some felt that the elderly pastor, John Courtney, would forbid the society, for he had opposed Sunday Schools and hymnbooks, and the church had no organizational activity. But he said, "I never heard of praying doing anybody any harm. For my part, the sisters may pray on." So the first Female Missionary Society in Virginia began in the spring of 1813.[10] Likewise, the females of First Baptist Church, Baltimore, organized.[11] In the next year, women of Fredericksburg, Virginia, organized to help the Richmond women. They decided to join them in prayer and to forward their contributions through them.[12]

Women's societies from Maine to South Carolina were boosted when the first missionaries from America to foreign lands sailed in 1812. They went out Congregationalists, but three became Baptists as they studied en route to their permanent stations. Adoniram and Ann Hasseltine Judson were to plant the gospel in Burma, while Luther Rice, a bachelor, returned to the US to stir up support among Baptists.

In 1813-14 Rice visited his new denomination, spending most of his time galloping through the South to collect funds and to round up organizers for the first Baptist convention. On January 11, 1814, he received his first contribution from a woman, Lydia Turner of South Carolina. On January 14 he was in Charleston, where he received the first contribution from a women's organization. The Wadmalaw and Edisto Female Mite Society gave $44 and promised $100 more. Rice reported these contributions when 33 men gathered to form the Baptist General Convention, known as the Triennial Convention, May 18, 1814.[13]

The first Triennial Convention knew of 17 active Baptist women's mission societies, 8 of them in the South. By the time of the next meeting in 1817, 187 societies were reported in cooperation with the Triennial Convention, and a majority, 110, were women's societies. Luther Rice was a great favorite with women, especially Southerners, who tended to his wardrobe and indulged his taste for tea as he traveled the country.[14]

Women's mission societies sent men to organize Baptist state conventions in southern states. More than half the groups who sent delegates to and organized the Alabama Baptist State Convention in 1823 were women's groups.[15] Among the first receipts of the North Carolina Baptist State Convention was 9 cents from "Negro Amey."[16]

Before the Southern Baptist Convention was organized in 1845, more than 100 female societies had flourished in the South, in slightly more

than 2 percent of the churches. But whereas the Triennial Convention
had endorsed the societies and encouraged women to organize, the
Southern Baptist split-off did not.[17] One reason for this may have been
that women were gaining notoriety in the North because they organized
and spoke out in public in opposition to slavery. When Southerners
condemned the antislavery organizations, they condemned woman's
rights activities also. At the first regular convention meeting after organization (1849), however, a few of the delegates represented women's
societies.

Southern Baptist women's societies in the 1840s and 1850s had no
heroic missionary women to rally around. Ann Judson, inspiration for
dozens of mission societies named for her, had died. Henrietta Hall
Shuck (Mrs. J. Lewis), the first American woman in China and the darling
of Virginia Baptists, died just before the SBC formed. Her husband
became an SBC missionary, and he married a suitable new southern
wife who belonged to a mission society. But they did not inspire the
women to organize. Unlike the Triennial foreign mission board, Southern Baptists would not in the early years appoint unmarried women
as missionaries, except for one unsuccessful trial in 1849.

DAYS OF WAR AND WRATH

The Civil War brought dark clouds of death and deprivation that
threatened every vestige of Southern Baptist organization. Contributions to the Home Mission Board and the Foreign Mission Board crum-
bled to a fraction of prewar levels. The FMB conveyed limited funds
to its faraway missionaries only by means of border state Baptists and
blockade running. Foreign missionaries took secular jobs, and home
missionaries joined the Confederate army as chaplains. The American
Baptist Home Mission Society (northern), with permission of the United
States government, seized several Southern Baptist church buildings
during the war, an affront the SBC was slow to forgive. Other church
property was destroyed, damaged, or allowed to fall into disrepair.[18]
Baptist historian William Heth Whitsitt was to call the postwar years
1865-1879 the "period of poverty and peril" for the SBC.[19] Only twice
in the first 14 years after the war did foreign missions contributions
reach prewar levels. The number of home missionaries plunged to an
all-time low in 1876.[20] Missions took a temporary backseat to survival,
and the priorities were not reversed until after the federal military
occupation of the South ended in 1877.

Such gloom understandably could have quelled the growth of wom-
en's societies and of missions expansion. But poverty gave the women
a chance to prove their powers. Nobody expected women to act de-
cisively to meet the crisis, but necessity made them become nurses,

farmers, teachers, tradespersons, and church leaders. And, necessity made males accept their initiative. Analysts of women's history have suggested that times of drastic social upheaval are the best times for women to flourish in new roles. When women are outside the controlling social system, they have a creative view of opportunity and freedom to maneuver.[21] This was certainly the case for Baptist women in the Reconstruction South.

Similarly, students of women's history have suggested that American economic expansion has been the root of women's movements.[22] Not expansion, but economic destitution of the South, undoubtedly gave Baptist women a point of entry to leadership. When the old economy was wrecked and many women were left without fathers or husbands, they clearly had to make their own livings. Thoughtful Baptists were forced to encourage women to seek education, marketable skills, and equitable pay.[23] Also, women had to assume some of the financial support of their churches.

LADIES AID SOCIETIES

The desperate plight of Southern Baptists after the Civil War demanded a new kind of woman's organization. The Ladies Aid Society, also known by a variety of other names, rescued many a local congregation. Aid societies had existed before the Civil War, but afterwards their numbers increased to save the churches. The ladies aided by earning (often through sewing circles), giving, or soliciting money for local church needs. They repaired dilapidated buildings, paid off mortgages, bought stoves and lights. They paid pastors, many of whom had lived without compensation during the hardest times. They bought musical instruments, dispensed food to the hungriest, tended the sick, sheltered orphans, and befriended those who had lost their niches in society.[24] As a by-product of their efforts, they lightened the gloom of communities by the innocent entertainments they staged for fundraising.

In 1869 women of First Baptist Church of Nashville organized the Ladies' Christian Association, later known as the Ladies' Benevolent Association "to advance and foster the glorious work of Christ." They helped the poor, built up the Sunday School, cared for the sick, aided ministerial students, raised money for the organ fund, bought a piano, paid church debts, and assisted the pastor in his duties.[25]

In 1872 First Baptist Church of Greenville, Alabama, organized a ladies aid society "to aid in all church expenses."[26] In 1889 the aid society of Ruhama Baptist Church in Birmingham completed paying the back salary due a former pastor.[27] When the young First Baptist Church of Lufkin, Texas, wanted to build its own building in 1890, it turned to the Ladies Aid Society. The women staged pie and cake sales, bazaars and suppers, and dinners on court days to finance the building of the church. The story was repeated in Gainesville, Georgia, where the Baptist Aid Society members contributed one dollar each to buy cloth. Then they met each week to make bonnets and aprons to sell to summer visitors. As they sewed, the Bible was read aloud. Their profits largely built a brick church building begun in 1873.[28]

Soon after March 1861, R. C. Buckner, who would gain fame for leading Texas Baptists in missions and benevolent work, organized the first Ladies Aid Society in Texas, at Paris Baptist Church. With the society's help the house of worship was neatly finished and paid for. [29] This success story was matched throughout the state, and pastors sang women's praises.

In 1872, four years after First Baptist Church of Dallas was organized (primarily by women), the pastor resigned in desperation. Dropping by the home of Lou Beckley Williams (Mrs. W. L.) to bid farewell, he said, "If the women of the church don't organize and help, I am afraid the cause will yet fail." Williams and her friends quickly raised $500, the church obtained a pastor, and the women laid the foundation for the first Baptist church building of the city.[30]

With such achievements to their credit, Texas aiders founded the Ladies' General Aid Society in 1874 as an adjunct to the Baptist General Association of North Texas. This was the only known coalition of aid societies.[31]

When the "period of grinding poverty"[32] was over, a broader vision crept from the recesses of leading feminine minds. Mary T. Corbell Gambrell (Mrs. J. B.) of Texas chided the aid societies for "aiding the pastor to do nothing" for the wider application of the gospel.[33] She advised a pastor who wrote for help in developing a missions consciousness in the women of his church, "No aid society is apt to do much, unless you have the missionary plank in it, too, because women centered alone on their own church work grow selfish, and our Lord did not put His churches here just to do work for themselves."[34]

The earliest leaders in the postwar missions movement recognized that the ladies aids had blazed their trail. They believed that the aiding spirit now needed to advance to wider good works.[35] A woman, S. A. Chambers of Alabama, otherwise unknown in Baptist annals, said in 1882,

> Is this the "good part" which Mary chose? Our houses will crumble and decay . . .; but a single soul saved from death will shine as the stars forever. . . . We love to labor with our hands for these temples where we worship God. We love them; we want to see them rise fair and comely all over our beautiful land; we want them comfortable and decent as, alas! they are often not.

> All honor to our sisters who do their part in keeping the sanctuary of the Lord. But let us not do this and leave the other undone. We must not wait until every church is lighted with an elegant chandelier before we send the lamp of God's word to the nations that sit in darkness. [36]

After a dozen years as the financial and working backbone of the churches, aid societies were little more than the butt of jokes. Although Baptist churches were supposed to be democratically operated, women usually had no vote in business matters, except perhaps in reception of new members. Although women were subject to disciplinary actions, they had no voice for defense nor "trial" by female peers.

When sermons were over and the men of the church convened for business, "the women and children and sinners were expected to retire, and leave the whole house to a handful of male members." They had to return home without escort or wait outside shivering or stay at home. "Why should not women be permitted to attend their own church conferences?" one asked. She gained permission to observe a meeting, and was disappointed to see that the brethren huddled around the stove, chewing tobacco, doing nothing. She hoped to continue attending and to improve the meetings. "We could not make them worse," she decided. "Dear, great, wise men, in all your pride and glory, stoop down long enough to help us in this."[37]

Women may have "found their voice in public prayer" during Reconstruction, but they had no voice before the congregation, other than to give a sufficient statement of faith to gain church membership. And if silent in the local church, they were dumbstruck before the councils of churches beyond. The majority of women of the dawning New South may have been willing, "God bless them, to carry on their work grandly whether [the men] smiled or frowned at them."[38] But some of them felt the sting of injustice.

Social historians have suggested that the aid societies were simply neighbors and kinswomen who elected officers over their natural groupings. The rudimentary organization would be supplanted by the more highly structured mission society. Women would then move into civic clubs and sociopolitical organizations such as the Woman's Christian Temperance Union and the woman suffrage organizations.[39]

This ladder might have been stronger in some denominations than among Southern Baptists. When missions-minded women tried to get the aid societies to add "a missionary plank," they usually met resistance. Not until after World War I did the missions cause gain top priority and absorb the aid devotees, and probably then only because Southern Baptists had crawled out of their poverty. And, as will be seen in chapter 10, civic and political organizations never seriously tapped the missions leadership of Southern Baptist women.

WOMAN'S UNION MISSIONARY SOCIETY

To the woman who told Jesus she was eager even for the crumbs that fell from the table of faith, He granted impossible desires. "Great is your faith, woman. Be it as you wish," He said. This account from Matthew 15:21-28 became the rally cry for women's next venture into religious leadership.

In 1834 a Dutch Reformed Church missionary, David Abeel, attempted to organize women to respond to the plea of a Chinese woman. Upon hearing the gospel, she had said, "Are there no female men who can come to teach us?" Convinced that only women could successfully reach the women of the Orient, Abeel was able to organize a woman's missionary sending society in London, but in the United States he was squelched by the American Board of Commissioners for Foreign Missions (primarily serving Congregationalists). "Is the American Board afraid that the ladies will get ahead of them?" a prominent New York woman asked. The answer was that the men feared injury to their established support system if the women pulled away into their own plans.[40]

The Triennial Convention's Baptist Board of Foreign Missions on a few occasions did appoint unmarried women as missionaries, and some served with distinction. Their status was imperiled by critics among constituents and missionaries. The issue of the evangelization of women was not strategically addressed.[41]

One young woman who heard David Abeel bided her time until 1861. She was Sarah Haines Doremus (Mrs. Thomas C.) of New York. As a girl she had accompanied her mother to women's benevolent meetings conducted by America's original organization woman, Isabella Graham. Reared a Presbyterian, Sarah Doremus was now a Dutch Reformed Church member and an activist for many good causes. Spurred by a married woman missionary returned from Burma, Doremus would no longer delay. She called together women of a half-dozen denominations, including Baptists. Each was willing to act because her denomination had ignored the needs of women at home and abroad. They organized an independent, nondenominational society "to send out single women untrammelled by family cares to Christianize heathen women who cannot be reached by men missionaries."

Sarah Doremus's organization was called the Woman's Union Missionary Society. The use of *Woman* in the name was an innovation. Other organizations had been called *Female*. At its first meeting early in 1861, Doremus read the Bible from Matthew 15:20-28. The group distributed a pamphlet, "Woman's Mission to Woman," and thereby women's history broke out of the woods and into God's heavenly light.

The WUMS took over support of the first single woman missionary teacher, Sarah Hall Marston, a Baptist. She had been appointed to Burma a few months earlier by an interdenominational, Baptist-dominated women's group in Boston which tied itself into the WUMS. The next appointee was Harriet G. Brittan, a Methodist, who went to India.

Starting as it did in the morning days of the Civil War, the Woman's Union Missionary Society made no impact in the South until the dust of battle had settled. By then, the WUMS had women colleagues in the field. The Congregational Woman's Board of Missions was organized in 1868. Northern Methodist women organized in 1869, Northern Presbyterians in 1870. Each of these organizations had the purpose of appointing and supporting women missionaries. Every feature of these organizations raised a point of Southern Baptist opposition. They were women-run, outside of the proper home sphere. They were northern. They were not purely Baptist. They were competitive to the male-controlled mission boards. They were not subject to local churches.

But the breeze that blew from the turning pages of God's Word irresistibly pushed the movement south. First it swept a few inches across the Mason-Dixon line, into Baltimore.

WOMAN'S MISSION TO WOMAN OF BALTIMORE

As early as 1848 Baltimore Methodist women had organized a society to support China missions. This group was later in touch with the Woman's Union Missionary Society. From among the Methodist women emerged one who carried the seed of women's organization into Baptist ranks. A Methodist bishop said he preferred a conversation with Ann Jane Graves to the counsel of his clerical peers. She was an intellectual, a widely known author of theology and philosophy of women's roles. Well educated, well read, and well bred, she advocated education for women so they could rear competent children and manage wholesome households.

Ann Graves reared sons who chose to be Baptists. One of them, Rosewell Graves, a doctor, went to China as a Southern Baptist missionary in 1856. Not until 1868 did his mother "pursue her acquaintance with Jesus" by being baptized into First Baptist Church of Baltimore. Here she activated her vision of what a woman could and should do as a Christian. Her pastor was John W. M. Williams, who along with his wife, Corinthia, had promoted women's missionary societies from before the Civil War. Early in his pastorate in Baltimore, the church was known as First Female Baptist Church because all the active members were women, and because women were permitted to vote and serve on committees.[42]

Corinthia Williams said of Ann Graves, "She was a woman of extraordinary breadth of intellect and thorough culture of both head and heart, great decision and force of character, with the advantages of an extensive social influence. God selected this woman by a special anointing for the cause of Foreign Missions. . . . She was literally possessed by the spirit of missions."[43]

Rosewell Graves convinced his mother that only women could be missionaries to women in his China field. His Methodist aunt (undoubtedly in the Ladies China Society), his mother, and his wife provided funds for employment of a Chinese woman to distribute and read the Scripture to women in their homes. This ministry, begun in 1864, led Ann Graves in 1867 to organize an interdenominational Female Missionary Prayer Meeting for the support of native Bible women.

In 1868 the Southern Baptist Convention met in Baltimore. Ann Graves, so enraptured by the concept of Woman's Mission to Woman, took courage in hand. The Convention was strictly for men only, but a few women accompanied their husbands to town. Occasionally they were permitted to observe from the gallery. Graves invited the women to gather around. A good crowd responded. She addressed them dressed in a plain gray dress, her face shaded by a poke bonnet. Quite possibly she was at that moment still a Methodist or a very new Baptist. Her message was go home and organize. Huddled in the church balcony, the women read letters from China and they prayed.

When Harriet Brittan, the Woman's Union Missionary Society missionary, had her first furlough in 1869, Ann Graves invited her to Baltimore. Brittan thrilled a large audience, many of them Baptists, as she delivered a dynamic speech. Baptist reporters were careful to note that she spoke while demurely seated, avoiding the appearance of the evil of public speech making.[44] The result was the formation, in February 1870, of the Baltimore branch of the Woman's Union Missionary Society. Corinthia Williams was president; Ann Graves was the corresponding secretary, and women of other denominations held other offices.

Louisa Levering Lawrason, a member of one of the reigning Baptist families of Baltimore, prodded Graves and Williams to organize an exclusively Baptist missionary society. Graves thought it would be impossible to overcome the many Baptist barriers to such an organization. Said Williams, "Had this impulse been other than of divine origin, we would have yielded our purpose, when she thought our efforts would be futile. We said, 'Come and let us try.' "[45]

Woman's Mission to Woman was reorganized as an all-Baptist society in October 1871. No man had an overt role in the organization, but every upstanding pastor in Baltimore was prepared to back it. Graves continued as corresponding secretary. Williams was one of eight vice-presidents, each representing a different Baptist church. The president was Mrs. Franklin Wilson, a prominent pastor's wife. Among the officers were families who would sustain Southern Baptist missions for 50 years: Armstrong, Taylor, Levering, Pollard, Tyler, Crane, Norris.

The purpose of Woman's Mission to Woman was clearly stated: "to give light to the women that sit in darkness because of Bible destitution, by taking the gospel of Christ in their homes, through the agency of native Bible women, aided and superintended by their Christian sisters from Bible lands." They planned to rely on "mite boxes" as their means of collecting funds. Each woman would have a mite box in her home, where she would lay aside not less than two cents on the first day of each week.[46]

The founders enfolded the entire South into their arms. They expected to stimulate women's missions work throughout the area. They took the pattern of the Boston Female Society for Missionary Purposes, offering to correspond with and encourage societies at all points southward. Ann Graves issued a circular letter inviting women to form branches in each state and missions circles in each church. She promised a simple organization and thrilling work.[47]

Baltimore women saw themselves as the southern alternative to the two Northern Baptist women's societies formed earlier in 1871 to appoint women missionaries. In this role they were welcomed to the Southern Baptist scene by male leaders who feared that the Northern Baptist women would pull money out of the South. Indeed northern women did move quickly to appoint a Virginian, Kate Evans.[48] The president of the northern women occasionally met with and addressed the Baltimore group, although no hint of their financial cooperation was mentioned.

The concept of Woman's Mission to Woman seemed to erupt spontaneously in strategic points of the Southern Baptist Convention territory. In the same month that Baltimore women organized, a women's society was born at First Baptist Church of Newberry, South Carolina. The young pastor, John Stout, newly wed and newly graduated with a commitment to foreign missions, corresponded with Ann Graves. She sent him mite boxes.[49]

John and Corinthia Williams and Graves notified the Foreign Mission Board of their plans. Could Woman's Mission to Woman and the Board cooperate, or should the women work independently? The Board's longtime secretary, James B. Taylor, had exchanged many letters with Graves and the Williamses. But he had not shown any acceptance of women's input other than their money. No sooner had Woman's Mission to Woman been put on paper than Taylor died.

His successor, Henry Allen Tupper, took office in January 1872. He made the Baltimore women's proposals his first order of business. Sensitive, charming, wealthy, aristocratic, he took with him to Richmond the flavor of his Charlestonian heritage. Tupper made room for women in foreign missions. He began by leading the Foreign Mission Board to reverse its antiwoman policy. It gave approval for Lula Whilden of South Carolina to accompany her married sister and brother-in-law, Jumille Whilden and Nicholas B. Williams, to China. This stroke bonded Lula Whilden to the newly forming women's work in South Carolina.[50]

Next he gained approval of Edmonia Moon of Virginia, well connected, willing, and able to be self-supporting as a missionary in China. Using Moon as a lure, he suggested that the energetic women of Richmond churches organize in her behalf. This they did on April 4, 1872, under leadership of the brilliant hand of Mrs. Jeremiah Bell Jeter.[51]

Circumstances, certainly divinely framed, brought this flurry of progress home to Baltimore on April 17, 1872. The largest group of foreign missionaries assembled in Southern Baptist history gathered there to be dispatched to China amid tender ceremony and prayer. Among them were Edmonia Moon, Lula Whilden, and Nicholas and Julmille Williams. Ann Graves's son Rosewell had come home to find a second wife, and he had chosen none other than the recording secretary of Woman's Mission to Woman, Jane Norris. Also in the party were Jesse Boardman and Julia Jewett Hartwell. Of course in the audience were members of Woman's Mission to Woman, thrilled with the prompt success of their efforts.[52]

Also in the audience was J. B. Hartwell's sister, Ellen Hartwell Edwards of Society Hill, South Carolina.[53] Edwards was Ann Graves's guest in Baltimore. She returned home to Society Hill with a handful of mite boxes. Never did two cents a week seem a more impossible financial goal, but Edwards in her Reconstruction poverty loyally cast into the treasury a gift pleasing to the One watching. She led the women of her church to do likewise, among them Martha McIntosh. In just two years, John Stout moved to Society Hill. The women formally organized a Woman's Mission to Woman society with Ellen Edwards as president, copying their constitution from Baltimore's. This group then set Martha McIntosh and Fannie Coker Stout, the pastor's wife, on the trail of Southwide women's leadership. Ellen Edwards's little daughter Jane gave the first child's contribution to missions from South Carolina, one dollar for Lula Whilden's school in China.[54]

By the time the caravan of missionaries set sail for China, the Foreign Mission Board had promised to keep separate accounts of the women's contributions, had agreed to help the Baltimore women foster women's societies elsewhere, and had agreed to emphasize the evangelization of women. With these assurances, Baltimore began encouraging the other centers of women's work to forward their contributions straight to Tupper, instead of via Baltimore. The FMB requested Henry Allen Tupper to "do all he can to multiply these societies and to inform the

Woman's Missionary Society of Baltimore that the Board heartily approves of its objects."[55]

Women's societies continued to grow, woman to woman, through family and friend connections. The first women's society in Louisiana was founded by the mother and sister of J. B. Hartwell and Ellen Edwards—Margaret F. Hartwell and Mrs. M. H. Gibbs of Mt. Lebanon, who persuaded their pastor to call a women's meeting in 1874.[56] Ann Graves sent mite boxes to them, to Florida, Alabama, North Carolina, and probably to every other state before her death in 1878.

Meanwhile, a similar impulse had gathered strength in the border state of Missouri. Loyalties were divided between Northern and Southern Baptists in the state. Carolyn Thornton Moss (Mrs. Oliver Perry), an ardent Southerner, volunteered to be the Foreign Mission Board's agent in Missouri in 1867. She organized a women's society in Second Baptist Church of Liberty in 1869. Following the example of Virginia women, Moss formed a statewide women's foreign mission society, auxiliary to the FMB, in 1876, making it official in 1877. Privileged and independent, Moss ardently defended the Foreign Mission Board's interests in Missouri.[57] In 1872 women of several churches in St. Louis organized what is regarded as the first associational women's organization, with sympathies and funds divided between North and South.[58]

Tupper's diplomacy paid off for the Foreign Mission Board. In 1873 its contributions increased by 75 percent, the first fiscal sign of life since before the Civil War. At the 50th anniversary of the Southern Baptist Convention, he was paid tribute because: "in the gloomiest period of our suffering and privation the wise and hopeful Tupper began to encourage our women."[59]

In effect, by 1872 Southern Baptist women had as effective a foreign missions effort as any of the northern denominations, but with a uniquely Southern Baptist accent. Every corner of the Convention had a permanent women's organization, with Baltimore mothering them all. The women had plowed ground where the seedling of women's work could flourish. Instead of being independent, the work was integrated. Yet it had its own visible personality within the official SBC Foreign Mission Board. While it did not immediately grow as tall as its peers in other denominations, it branched out more lushly. For 16 years it would send down an intricate root system. By the time Woman's Mission to Woman grew into Woman's Missionary Union in 1888, it would be a sturdier, more comprehensive, more durable women's organization than any other, and its opposition would be pruned back. Even after 1888 the Baltimore women would exercise a sisterly encouragement for several struggling state women's organizations until they were permitted to affiliate with WMU.[60]

SENDING DOWN DEEP ROOTS

The women and their friends had to spade, sweat, and impatiently wait while the rootage of a unique women's organization took hold. Many stumps and stones had to be circumvented or left to decay of their own disease. These became apparent at the Southern Baptist Convention of 1872. After the glowing launch of Woman's Mission to Woman and the April send-off of missionaries, the Baltimoreans might have expected a little applause. Ann Graves herself journeyed with John and Corinthia Williams to the Convention meeting in Raleigh. There they conferred with John Stout and other sympathizers, and Graves is said to have convened the women.

John Williams, as part of the Foreign Mission Board report, asked for an endorsement of the entire Woman's Mission to Woman cycle of thought, including encouragement of women's organizations in local churches. Although his motion was finally approved, the debate was apparently caustic. Graves told him, "Do not be discouraged; you are only in advance of your brethren; in a few years they will be with you."[61] She would not live to see that day, but he would.

For the next 16 years, debates in the Southern Baptist Convention and in the denominational press were marked by active acrimony about women's missions work. Still, the Foreign Mission Board pushed cautiously onward. Each year women's work was mentioned at the SBC. Always the final vote was favorable to women missionaries, women's organizations, and women's control over the expenditure of their contributions through the FMB.

In 1874 the FMB fanned the fires of Woman's Mission to Woman by appointing central committees for women's work in each state. The Board cajoled the men to cooperate with the women thus appointed. Usually the committees were composed of prominent women, wives of pastors in harmony with the SBC, and unmarried daughters of privileged families. In some states, local opposition smothered the women.

For example, H. A. Tupper personally traveled to North Carolina in 1876 to organize a central committee. He went to the center of organized Baptist prosperity, Raleigh, and called on Mattie Callendine Heck (Mrs. J. M.). Not only did she have the backing of husband, church, neighboring Baptists, and wealth, but she had just enjoyed the singular honor of representing her state's women at the US Centennial Exposition in Philadelphia. Heck agreed to head the Central Committee for Foreign Missions, and she issued an excellent first report of increased contributions and organizations. But the men of the state Baptist convention rose up in such horror that her committee shrank away for ten years.[62]

By 1878 the FMB completed its network of central committees in most of the states.[63] In Maryland the central committee was Woman's Mission to Woman, after Tupper again guaranteed that their contributions would be spent as designated.

By 1877 and 1878 there was open talk of the need for a southwide central committee of the state central committees. Evidently this idea was too radical. The Foreign Mission Board reassured the Southern Baptist Convention that the women did not want a general organization.[64]

In 1878 the FMB happily reported increased receipts, while the Home Mission Board, which had faintly acknowledged the women in 1877, was lamenting its lowest ebb since the Civil War. Southern Baptist turf was more of a parched missions field than a source of living water. From the outside, the HMB was bitterly outmaneuvered by the American Baptist Home Mission Society of New York, which had three times as many missionaries in the South as the SBC did. From the inside, the HMB was drained by state conventions who either did their own projects or who (as four states did) formed liaisons with the American Baptist Home Mission Society. The HMB raised money through paid agents or fund-raisers whose expenses skimmed off 44 to 53 percent of the contributions. This system was wasteful and unpopular with donors. Some states prohibited the HMB from soliciting funds in their borders.[65]

The HMB timidly began to ask the women to help, but for some years it was in effect blocked by the FMB. The HMB wanted to tap into the FMB's central committees; the FMB insisted that the HMB form its own.[66] The piecemeal competition for the women's time and money left an uneasy feeling among the female leaders.

Many men went to the 1882 Southern Baptist Convention with plans to sack the Home Mission Board. Instead, the year brought three innovations: Isaac Taylor Tichenor agreed to leave the presidency of Auburn University in order to head the Board. Second, the Board moved out of the sleepy Old South town of Marion, Alabama, to the booming New South city of Atlanta. Third, Tichenor asked Annie Armstrong of Baltimore to organize the women to clothe the Indians at a HMB school her uncle had built.

Tichenor would win credit for saving not only the HMB but also the entire Southern Baptist program. He would also go down in history as a friend to the women, and they would memorialize him by raising funds for a Church Building and Loan Fund. Tichenor's wife and daughters were heavily involved in women's societies.[67]

When Tichenor took over, only 31 women's societies were remitting funds to the Home Mission Board, while the Foreign Mission Board claimed 500. Armstrong's success in clothing the Indians led to the formation of the Woman's Baptist Home Mission Society of Maryland

in 1882, with Miss Armstrong as president.[68] Although no other state
had a home mission society or home missions committee equal in
strength to its foreign missions central committee, the Maryland society
was strong enough to be pacesetter for them all. In various ways the
women worked home missions into their agenda so that they brought
a dual commitment to both home and foreign missions into Woman's
Missionary Union of 1888.

THE CLIMATE OF HOSTILITY

Defeat in the Civil War, humiliation during Reconstruction, and dev-
astation of culture left many male southerners ill-humored, and they
took their anger out on the women. The women's acclaimed powers
to preserve the mission boards seemed only to stoke the fires of hos-
tility among a large, vocal segment of the Southern Baptist Convention.
The Southern Baptist climate was too hot for unhindered development
of women's work.

The arguments varied little from year to year. They fell into three
categories: church organization, women's rights, and southern pride.

A Threat to the Church.—Some objected to the existence of a
women's organization within or attached to a local congregation. To
comprehend the fears on this point, one must recall that a slate of
activities in a typical Southern Baptist church of the 1870s and 1880s
consisted of nothing more than one to four preaching services a month,
plus periodic business meetings. Few churches had Sunday Schools,
though the SBC had recommended them. Choirs, youth activities, suppers, weekly preaching, weekly contributions, and study courses came
much later. The Landmark controversy, deeply inbred since the 1850s,
made people suspicious of any activity suggested from outside, as a
threat to local church independence.

Most church leaders imagined a women's missions organization to
be a competitor, not a helper. "What God hath joined together, let not
man—or woman—put asunder," said a committee of men who believed
the churches would fall if women organized to run their own affairs.[69]

A primal fear was economic. Some men believed that women controlled the wealth and would divert it out of the local church if they
formed their own network.[70]

The Woman Question.—At the root of most arguments against a
women's missions organization was fear that women would leave home
and enter the pulpit. The widespread dread was colorfully summed up
in 1888 by a committee of the Baptist General Association of Virginia,
determined to prevent Virginia women from joining Woman's Missionary Union:

It is to be feared that a separate and distinct organization of the women of the churches for independent mission work might have a tendency, in its ultimate results at least, to compromise that womanly reserve and modesty, and as Paul styles it, that "shamefacedness," which is, in our esteem . . . beyond all price. Not only so, but we further fear that such an independent organization of women naturally tends toward a violation of the divine interdict against women's becoming a public religious teacher and leader—a speaker before mixed assemblies, a platform declaimer, a pulpit proclaimer, street preacher, lyceum lecturer, stump orator."[71]

Another commentator noted: "The only four things any Christian can do for missions are to pray, to give, to talk, to go. . . . Three of these are open to women. . . . They may give and pray and go to their heart's content."[72]

The writer of course meant silent prayer. He gave no guidance as to the means of proper evangelization after the missionary arrived at the place she would go, if she could not talk.

Cultural Captivity.—The passion for restraining women grew not only from interpretation of the Bible, but also from the struggle to glue the shattered Southern culture back together. As Southerners gained distance from the Civil War and its aftermath, they tended to hide their humiliation under a costume of traditional pride. The glorification of "the Lost Cause," the mythological Old South, drilling in the code of chivalry and belle behavior—all tended to make Southern Baptists play roles that could not easily accommodate the Woman's Missionary Union that was growing.[73]

Each of these cherished Southern dreams was buttressed against rejected northern values. The woman's rights movement arose in the North; it was rejected. Woman suffrage arose in the North; it was spurned. The first women public lecturers were Northerners; they were ridiculed. Woman's Mission to Woman arose in the North; it was questionable. Northern Baptist women appointed their own missionaries; they were criticized. Southern Baptist men often stated that "our women" did not want change, did not want to be public speakers, did not want organization, did not want rights; only outside agitators and misguided men could have pushed such ideas.[74]

RESISTANCE TO WOMEN'S ORGANIZATIONS

Such a mood, added to the lingering mourning and poverty of the South, retarded development of all forms of women's organizations in the region. Missions organizations were the first structured groups built by southern women. Southern Baptist women were among the pioneers in their region. For example, Woman's Mission to Woman of Baltimore, which portended to be a southwide concern, was orgnized in 1871, and the Foreign Mission Board shortly was sponsoring women's groups in a comprehensive way. In that same year, 1871, the Woman's Auxiliary of the Protestant Episcopal Church was formed to serve both North and South. Also in 1871, Northern Baptist women organized for foreign missions.

Southern Methodist women developed the first centralized Southern women's group with the Woman's Board of Foreign Missions in 1878, nine years after Northern Methodist women organized. Southern Methodist women's home missions work took shape in 1886. During this period, Southern Baptist women's work remained decentralized under the management of state-level organizations.

Presbyterian women in the South did not organize until 1912, when Southern Baptist women were ready for their 25th anniversary.

On secular fronts, southern organizations emerged much later than northern forerunners. The Women's Christian Temperance Union did not successfully colonize in the South until after 1882, when the northern organization was eight years old. The woman's club movement, which began in the North in 1890, did not gain momentum in the South until after 1900. In general, southern women lagged at least a decade behind the North in perfecting organizations.

Despite obstacles and opponents, throughout Reconstruction the tides of progress pushed the women steadily toward their own formal general organization. By 1880 the southern economy was showing vitality. Even the corset trade improved.[75] Women knew they had a place in the new "science of missions."[76] A growing fraternity of sympathetic pastors, usually the most eloquent and most progressive in each state, did the women's talking for them. In 1881 the SBC recommended that the FMB employ a woman to superintend and promote women's work. The FMB declined, saying in 1882 "a false step now might entail fatal embarrassments." This the Board said while acknowledging that its comparative financial ease for two years was due to the women.

This rejection snapped some of the women into a more aggressive stance.

THE HEATHEN HELPER

The Central Committee of Kentucky decided that Woman's Mission to Woman needed its own communications medium. In November 1882 they brought out the first issue of the their monthly newspaper, the *Heathen Helper*. Contributing editors, each a top leader among women in her state, collected the contents. The editor was a competent journalist, the secretary of the Kentucky Central Committee, Agnes Osborne. She was backed financially by her brother Thomas D. Osborne, a philanthropic Baptist, who was editor of the Louisville *Ledger*.[77] Aided by Thomas's wife, Charlotte Ray Osborne, they created a cannon which blasted away obstacles to a permanent organization.

Other important denominational media were also open to women. Most of the editors were shining white knights dedicated to the women's cause. The one notable exception was T. T. Eaton, superconservative editor of the *Western Recorder* of Louisville. The women hit him with head-on competition by issuing the *Heathen Helper* right under his nose.

Missouri's paper, *Ford's Christian Repository,* was edited by S. H. and Sallie Rochester Ford, and she was to become the best-known women's leader between 1882 and 1888. The *Religious Herald* was owned by the husband of Virginia's Central Committee president, Mrs. Jeremiah Jeter. The Mississippi *Baptist Record* was edited by James B. Gambrell, whose wife, Mary, was secretary of the state's Baptist women. The *Baltimore Baptist* was owned and edited by H. M. Wharton, whose mother-in-law and wife were later officers of WMU. The young secretary of the revived North Carolina Central Committee, Sallie Bailey was daughter of the editor of the *Biblical Recorder*. The women organized in his office. As one woman wryly commented, since the ladies could not speak in church, they were fortunate indeed to be able to speak in print.[78]

Speaking in the men's media, however, they had to refight old battles and be battered by old opponents. Writing in the *Heathen Helper*, they could safely assume a readership sympathetic with missions, with women, and with cooperative efforts for missions. So they could write to resolve the fine points of organization and operation. They could share information about women missionaries and about progress of the various state organizations. For the first time, a woman could leaf through the well-edited pages of one publication and see the worldwide network that had been woven by women.

From the first issue of the *Heathen Helper*, the whole matter of women in the SBC leaped to a higher, hotter plane. The women of the *Heathen Helper* organized a steady parade of meetings in which the final form of Woman's Missionary Union would be shaped.

REACHING BEYOND WOMAN'S MISSION TO WOMAN

In the second issue of the *Heathen Helper*, the women pitched the first ball of the new game. Martha Foster Crawford (Mrs. T. P.), veteran of 21 years in China, challenged the very idea of Woman's Mission to Woman, on the grounds from which the movement grew: foreign mission strategy. "One sex cannot be Christianized without the other," she said.

One of my lifelong battles has been to break down the prejudices which keep women shut out. . . . If women say to me, "I will be baptized if you will baptize me, I cannot have a man do it," I know she is not yet a thorough Christian. We go out to teach them to observe whatsoever Christ has commanded and not to endorse heathen ideas or perpetuate heathen customs where they conflict with Christianity.

Crawford insisted that men and women must work together in mission support and in missionary delivery, "and make such division of labor as shall seem best according to circumstances." She wanted women's societies to work not only for women, but also for men's conversion.[79]

Her proposal carried weight because of her known faithfulness to the missions task. Crawford was the tenth married woman sent out by Southern Baptists. Except for one other woman, Eliza E. Moring Yates (Mrs. Matthew T.), she alone actively did the work of a missionary. In the same issue, Crawford was answered by a Kentucky Woman's Mission to Woman leader, who explained that Southern Baptist women did not really want their work to be independent; she wished for a quiet talk with Crawford.

That opportunity quickly presented itself at the Southern Baptist Convention of 1883.

THE FIRST GENERAL MEETING OF SOUTHERN BAPTIST WOMEN, 1883, WACO

Texas Baptists invited the Southern Baptist Convention to meet in Waco in 1883. Texas women, headed by Fannie Breedlove Davis (Mrs. George B.) of San Antonio, had organized in 1880. They added an invitation to women. Texans assured the SBC that Waco was a paradise where the men, their wives, and their daughters could be entertained free of charge.

Host cities for the SBC meetings customarily gave free lodging and meals to the official delegates, but women were specifically not welcomed because they were superfluous. Not so in Texas. A record crowd of 3,000 people arrived in Waco, at least 700 of them women—more than had ever attended a Baptist Convention.[80] Waco called in 1,000 cots and lined them up in churches for the men. Every woman was entertained in a home. All the surrounding Texas towns sent in wagon loads of baked bread, ham, chicken, pie, and cake.[81]

At the Southern Baptist Convention, J. W. M. Williams presented a laudatory report on women's work which was adopted without any argument. A meeting of the women was held in the Methodist Church while the Convention continued its business with only one-third of the men.

Before a packed house at the Methodist church, Sallie Rochester Ford presided. Because of her fame as a writer and because of her beauty, she always made heads turn and competing male editors write words of praise. As author of the best-selling religious novel, *Grace Truman,* and as assistant editor of *Ford's Christian Repository,* she had a large following. She was one of the few women with the nerve to speak in public, having survived a public denouncement for her belief that a woman might pray aloud and testify at church.[82] Ford was stylish and striking with black eyes and hair. The editor of the *Heathen Helper*, taking meticulous notes and glorying in the triumph of causing this meeting, estimated that Ford was about 48 years old. Actually she was 55.[83]

The audience sang "Nearer My God to Thee," Ford's husband read the Scriptures, then Sallie herself "very modestly introduced" Martha Foster Crawford. When Crawford began to speak, her face lighted up, onlookers noted, like an angel's. An anxious stir came over the audience, and the meeting seemed to halt. Never before had a woman made a speech to a crowd of Baptist men and women.

J. A. Hackett of Louisiana, whose late wife had been one of the original staff of the *Heathen Helper,* stood up and said: "Let every one keep very quiety [sic] now; this is the opportunity of our lives." Crawford relaxed the tension by commenting that this was just an informal meeting. She would only speak in a general way about China and answer questions. This she did in a subdued voice for a long time.

Then Sallie Ford introduced Mary Hollingsworth, matron of the Louisville Baptist Orphans' Home, who spoke briefly. She and Fannie Davis of Texas promoted subscriptions to the *Heathen Helper.* The men present were represented in comments by Hackett and S. H. Ford. The audience spontaneously passed several hats around to collect $200 for Crawford's missions work.

The next day, Sallie Ford convened the group again at the Methodist church. This time the men made the speeches. J. W. M. Williams advised the women to go home and organize Woman's Mission to Woman societies. "Women are the ruling power in the world. Man is the head, woman is the neck. She turns the head any way she wants to," he said. I. T. Tichenor tried to find a common ground with the women, but had no women home missionaries to report on—a situation he would shortly try to correct. J. A. Hackett told of 14 women foreign missionaries and 600 women's societies who had given more than $10,000 to the FMB that year. Martha Crawford was again called to the platform. Her presence so electrified the audience that this meeting would be referred to as "Mrs. Crawford's meeting." Also it was known as the meeting that "sent a thrill all through the South."[84] So excited were the women that Fannie Davis and Sallie Ford called an extra parley at a hotel, giving women a chance to chat and some male missionaries a chance to speak.

THE 1884 MEETING, BALTIMORE

Baltimore Woman's Mission to Woman took responsibility for organizing a meeting for women attending the Convention which met in their city in 1884. Remembering the Waco meeting, Texas women wrote to Baltimore suggesting that they make a permanent organization to be called The Woman's Missionary Union of the Southern Baptist Convention. The assembly at Baltimore agreed to make the meeting a perpetual event but stopped short of calling itself organized or named.

Lily Graves (daughter of Ann), who succeeded her mother as secretary of WMTW, wrote all the state central committees asking for reports; thus a stake was driven for the tent of a real organization.[85] The serious flurry of preparations caused the editor of the *Baltimore Baptist* to advise the Convention hospitality committee to get ready for the women. "They are coming. They are too great a power in our denominational work to be ignored, and they should have a place in our programme. They expect to hold separate meetings, we understand, but entirely in accord with our work."[86]

A large number of women did show up for a one-day meeting at Westminster Presbyterian Church. Mrs. Franklin Wilson, president of Woman's Mission to Woman of Baltimore, presided. Men were invited to attend, but the speaking was mostly by females. Reports of 12 states were read—the first serious collection of information about the state of women's work. The number of societies had grown to 642 and contributions by the women had grown by 68 percent.

Then, all grew tense as the guest speaker rose, walked to the pulpit, and spoke without a manuscript.[87] She was Adele Fielde, missionary sent to China by the American Baptist Foreign Mission Society. Fielde was famous for her remarkable work among unevangelized persons in China and for her scholarly writings, and infamous for her heretical remarks to some men who called her down for preaching. "Are you ordained?" they asked. "No, I was foreordained," she answered.[88]

Now she gave a long and fascinating address on Chinese women and "was cheered by leading members of the Convention." A reporter said, "She was heard by a large audience, and so far as I know, no one felt called upon to apologize for the performance or for being present at it."[89]

But the event set off suspicious antagonism in the nearby Southern Baptist Convention. Joshua Levering, one of the leading young men of the Convention, took the floor. Like his father, interested in home missions, he proposed that women were ready and able to evangelize the South. He asked that the Home Mission Board employ a woman to superintend and organize women's societies. During an adjournment for lunch, the opponents of the idea loaded their ammunition. J. William Jones, a beloved Confederate veteran, decried the proposal as "the entering wedge of Woman's Rights." He believed the women of the South did not want to do such work (in fact, Levering had acted on request of the women—undoubtedly led by his home missions loving cousin, Annie Armstrong).[90] Another man proposed that a woman might as well be employed to collect and disseminate information about the colored people of the South; this was intended as the ultimate insult to Levering's proposal.

J. B. Gambrell, young and fresh faced, accused the convention of being "old fogies." Seeing defeat and bad feelings rise, J. W. M. Williams moved that the proposal be referred to the Home Mission Board, where it died.[91]

The opposing sides on the question of women's work had polarized. Defeated on their request for a staff connection with the Home Mission Board, rejected in previous years by the Foreign Mission Board, and unable to effect a permanent organization, three women retreated to a hotel room for prayer. Martha Loftin Wilson (Mrs. Stainback) of Georgia, Fannie Davis of Texas, and Mrs. N. A. Bailey of Florida prayed for an hour, then agreed to pray on the morning of the first Sunday in each month for the success of women's missions work.[92] They publicized their appeal for prayer through the denominational press. Martha Crawford joined in their prayer from China.

THE 1885 MEETING, AUGUSTA

Tension mounted as the 1885 Convention in Augusta, Georgia, drew near. Some of the women believed they had a full-fledged organization aborning. They claimed the name Woman's Missionary Union of the Southern Baptist Convention and noted that "our work is not an independent one, but auxiliary to the convention."[93]

The more conservative brethren were offended by the female speechmaking before men which had made the last two meetings such spectacular events. The Georgia women, who by agreement were to plan the program for the 1885 women's meeting, decided to head off critics. They announced in advance that only men would give addresses at the women's meeting. Women might read their reports of state work, if they wished, or they might ask a man to read for them.[94]

The Foreign Mission Board feared that the women, with their own separate meeting now in place, would pull out and form their own Northern style women's board. They had the power to do it, and if so the FMB would be financially deflated by one-third.

The FMB believed the women would not want their own organization if they could have better representation in the Southern Baptist Convention itself. Since 1875 (and even earlier) several delegates to the Convention had represented women's societies. H. A. Tupper himself was the delegate of the women of Richmond.

The FMB aired the history and entire scope of the woman question in its journal of May 1885, just on the eve of the Convention. The report attempted to be progressive and sympathetic, while assuring the conservative brethren that nothing unwomanly or unscriptural would be done. Trying to please everybody, the Foreign Mission Journal managed to offend a number of people, including Lottie Moon, who shot off her resignation as a missionary to China (which was not accepted).[95]

The FMB pleaded with the convention to "give form to these meetings, as we are sure the ladies desire—else they will soon give fixed form to themselves." The FMB proposed that the women be given fuller and fairer representation on the floor of the convention, before they demanded it. The Board went to the Convention with a detailed proposal which would have made the central committees an official part of the SBC and allowed them to appoint delegates.[96]

The idea was bathed in acid when two women showed up as authorized delegates to the Convention. They were Mary Oldham Eagle (Mrs. J. P.), president of the women of Arkansas, and Margaretta Dudgeon Early (Mrs. M. D.), secretary. Each was duly authorized by the Arkansas State Convention of which J. P. Eagle was president. Margaretta Early's husband was a pastor. Both women were rugged individualists able to handle a touchy situation. The Eagles were pro-woman suffrage. J. P. Eagle would soon be the governor of Arkansas. Mary Eagle was a feisty debater, beautiful, fabulously dressed, and the joy of her childhood mentor, Sallie Ford's husband. Margaretta Early, an Irish immigrant who was widowed before her marriage to Early, had made her own way in the world as a teacher.[97]

When the women's names were presented, J. William Jones, who had defended the SBC against women's rights at the last convention, rose to protest their being seated. A committee of five hurriedly studied the situation. Three of the committee were tightly related to women prominent in the women's movement, and they reported that the constitution did not prohibit women from serving as messengers. Jones and the other committee member submitted a minority report, saying that the founders had not anticipated women delegates or they would have written more carefully. Jones insisted that "our Southern women did not desire to be members of the Convention."[98]

One man called attention to the fact that a woman had previously served as a delegate, twice in fact. She was Myra E. Graves (Mrs. H. L.), widow of the president of Baylor University and herself a future missionary to Mexico. She had registered under the name M. E. Graves in 1877 and 1882. The Convention was unmoved. Among choice bits of invective hurled at women in general was a comment by J. B. Hawthorne, whose wife had briefly headed the Alabama Central Committee. According to a reporter, Hawthorne, one of the all-time famed orators of the Convention, "loves the women but dreads them more. If ladies are admitted as delegates, they will be qualified for any office. If one should aspire to be President of the Convention [no man] would allow his name to be used for that office. The women would get all the offices. It is all wrong. We are not prepared for such a revolution. Our Southern women do not want it."[99]

Despite defenses mounted by their husbands, Mary Eagle and Margaretta Early sent up word that they were withdrawing their names. Later in the meeting, the men amended the constitution to specify that delegates must be men. The Foreign Mission Board not only did not gain representation for the women in the convention, but H. A. Tupper was soundly trounced and had to take his report on women's work back into committee. Sponsorship of the women's central committees was stripped from the mission boards and placed under management of the state conventions. There several of the committees would perish from persecution.

Such official acts and violent hall talk cast a cloud over the women's meetings in progress at St. John's Methodist Church. Sallie Ford was technically again in the chair, but scarcely another woman's voice was heard. The women were hurt by the Convention action; they were not pleased with their own meeting. As one woman reporter said, it was not a women's missions meeting, but a meeting held in the interest of women's missions work.[100] The Georgia women had turned it over to men.

J. J. D. Renfroe, a sympathetic pastor from Alabama, preached from the text, "Let Her Alone." The women liked what he said. Then S. H. Ford adjourned the meeting and asked the ladies to linger for conversation. In other words, he cleared the men out of the church so his wife could preside without criticism. She pointedly gained approval of a motion that henceforth these meetings would be restricted to women only.

The next session went by the same pattern. Husbands read their wives' reports, including M. D. Early reading the Arkansas report. Men gave sermons; the mission board secretaries tried to cheer up the women. After the men had departed, Martha Wilson, the hostess for the meeting, gained adoption of a resolution which was sent over for reading into the minutes of the Convention. Designed to be conciliatory, the motion stated that the women did not want a separate, independent organization, but wanted to work directly through the churches with representation in the SBC through the state conventions as in the past.

Under Sallie Ford's leadership the women went home determined to be in full control when they met next year.

THE 1886 MEETING, MONTGOMERY

The storm did not die but moved into the columns of the Baptist periodicals. It seemed that some men did not trust the women to hold meetings without male enforcers present; while others would not permit the women to open their mouths if a man were in earshot.[101]

J. J. D. Renfroe knew the women's viewpoint:

> True after the women were conquered they sent in a resolution of surrender; but an element of so much energy, whose work is so much blessed and so much felt, will be constantly showing itself. . . . Work for the cause of Christ with Southern women is comparatively a new thing, and yet is moving rapidly and powerfully; and to manage this influence in harmony with what is supposed to be 'the Southern idea,' and not subdue it or impede it, is one of the difficult issues now coming on.[102]

Sallie Ford held the women's fellowship together during the tense months of 1885-86. She issued a public denial that the women were plotting treason and denied the "two bugbears": that the women were planning a separate organization, and that they were profaning southern propriety by making women public speakers. "Should the women of the South ever transcend gospel limitation, it will not be through the influence of meetings for women only, but because our brethren have shunned to declare the whole gospel of our Lord Jesus Christ," she wrote.[103]

True to her word, men were barred from the women's meeting during the 1886 SBC. Sallie Ford had corresponded with the central committees and put together an entertaining all-woman program except for three invited men speakers. Few reports were released.

J. A. Hackett, one of the women's enduring friends, plus J. W. M. Williams, J. P. Eagle, N. A. Bailey, and H. M. Wharton tried to get the SBC to invite the women to attend the Convention "as visitors." The idea was rejected on the familiar basis, "The women do not want it." The *Heathen Helper* was commended only after a "breezy discussion" carried over two sessions.[104] Only five of the SBC delegates represented women's societies.

The damage was done. The state central committees were not prospering under the hand of the state conventions. The Foreign Mission Board insisted on keeping up communication with the committees, but could not gain a complete report. Receipts declined, and that problem got attention.

THE 1887 MEETING, LOUSIVILLE

By 1887 the women's contributions to the Foreign Mission Board had slipped by 33 percent and the FMB was sliding into debt. The Board had grown more dependent on women for support of certain new programs. Several men of the Convention were concerned about the realities of the situation, not to mention the feelings of the women. As in bygone days, Baltimore came to the rescue. During 1886-87 Baptist men of Baltimore agreed to back a missions literature bureau run by the women, headed by Annie Armstrong.

Sallie Rochester Ford again pulled together a program for the 1887 women's meeting. Agnes Osborne, editor of the *Heathen Helper*, again served as secretary. This time, the women came prepared to talk business. More than 300 of them met at Broadway Methodist Church. Men were excluded. Three Northern Baptist women's leaders were there in an unofficial capacity. The women examined the financial picture; they swapped ideas about how to promote the work.[105] The only special speaker was Anne Luther Bagby (Mrs. W. B.), a founder of Texas WMU, then on furlough as a missionary in Brazil.

Some felt that they should create on the spot a permanent slate of officers and ongoing program, but Martha McIntosh of South Carolina and Annie Armstrong of Maryland suggested delay. They wanted an organization formed so properly that it could not be destroyed. The group carefully planned its strategy for 1888. They asked that each central committee appoint three lady delegates to meet during the 1888 Convention to decide upon the advisability of organizing a general committee, and if so, to provide for its operation. They made sure to state that they had no desire "to interfere with the management of the existing Boards of the Convention, either in the appointment of missionaries or in direction of mission work," but "to be more efficient in collecting money and disseminating information on mission subjects."

Announcing this resolution in the Baptist newspapers was a woman named Ruth Alleyn.

> There is a sound of shaking in the tops of the trees, and we feel abundantly persuaded that the wind which is stirring the peaceful commotion is none other than the spirit of the living God. . . . With the blessing of God, with the prayers of the people, with the wisdom which comes from practical experience in affairs, with the strength resulting from union in effort, . . . we hope in the growth of the years to emulate the generosity and earnestness of our Northern sisters, retaining all the while a vital connection with the Southern Baptist Convention.[106]

Ruth Alleyn was none other than Alice Armstrong, sister of Annie.

She would flood the papers with a series of educational articles on the history and promise of women's work for missions. She stated that facts are more valuable than idealizing, theorizing, or prophesying possible evils. The facts were that the mission boards needed money and that women's organizations make money.

WOMAN'S MISSIONARY UNION AT LAST
1888, RICHMOND

To prepare the way to the Southern Baptist Convention of 1888 in Richmond, James Pollard of Baltimore, closely identified with leading women there, proposed a harmless-sounding motion at the SBC in 1887. He called for a committee of the mission boards and others to study ways the Convention might be improved. The chairman of that committee would be F. M. Ellis, pastor of the Armstrong sisters at Eutaw Place Baptist Church of Baltimore.[107] On the committee were men known to be sympathetic with organized women's work, with one exception: T. T. Eaton of the *Western Recorder* in Kentucky. Eaton editorialized prior to the 1888 meeting that if a few women thought they were wiser than all the churches, they could organize and give each one an office. He said the Convention should not and would not take notice of them and should dismiss its boards if they did.[108]

The women lined up their supporters to speak via the press and at the Convention. For their own meeting, men excluded, they prepared a program consisting of two careful study papers: "The Special Obligation of Woman to Spread the Gospel" by Alice Armstrong and "Organization" by Fanny Coker Stout (Mrs. John). Armstrong and Stout each played the role of quiet, studious lieutenant to a more activistic leader. Alice lived with Annie Armstrong and managed their home, while Stout took McIntosh into her parsonage so McIntosh would be relieved of the cares of maintaining a big mansion while leading missions business.[109]

Who should preside over this history-making meeting? It would not be Sallie Ford. Her anxiety was showing and H. A. Tupper counseled, "There is no need of disquietude with regard to the woman's work in our Southern states. There is an average common sense and piety among our people which always prevails in the end."[110] Perhaps Ford was considered too controversial (see chap. 13). Perhaps she considered herself too old at age 60. Perhaps the women looked to someone else because Ford, while a great leader on the national level, was not a working officer of the Missouri Central Committee, which group would accredit delegates to the meeting.

Some recommended another prestigious woman, Mattie Heck (Mrs. Jonathan M.) of Raleigh. But Heck was "in ill health," as she referred to her pregnancy at age 46, so she sent her second daughter, Fannie, as an observer. North Carolina men would not permit the state's women to have official delegates.[111]

Nor would Virginia women feel at ease about affiliating with the proposed organization, for the Virginia men had bitterly disbanded the Central Committee. In order to help them fulfill the courtesies of hostessing the women's meeting, the FMB took the committee back under its wing. The secretary was Mary Caldwell Tupper, daughter of the FMB secretary. She offered complimentary accommodations to the official delegates of the central committees.[112] The Virginia women decided to assign the presiding responsibilities to Mrs. Theodore Whitfield, newly arrived young pastor's wife in Richmond. At their previous pastorate at First Baptist of New Bern, North Carolina, the Whitfields had formed a women's missionary society with her as president and him as secretary. Theodore Whitfield had persuaded North Carolina men to reactivate a central committee in 1886 and had personally enlisted Fannie E. S. Heck to head it. Then he moved to Richmond. Mrs. Whitfield begged to be excused from the nerve-wracking task of presiding, but finally consented.

The stage was set and the delegates arrived in Richmond. To the stately First Baptist Church on Broad Street went 835 male delegates. To Broad Street Methodist Church just one block away went a smaller group of women, their leaders having spent a day in prayer before they deliberated.[113]

Who were the founders of Woman's Missionary Union? The official core of delegates at the meeting were 32 in number, representing 12 states. Fannie Heck was there unofficially represting North Carolina. Alabama had no delegates, but a little girl, Annie Grace Tartt, and some others were present. At least 100 Virginia ladies were on hand, including Abby Manly Gwathmey (Mrs. W. H.), a future WMU president, who had deliberately brought her ten-year-old twin daughters to see history happen. A young woman from Arkansas, Mrs. George Bottoms, who would become the greatest benefactor of Southern Baptist missions prior to the 1970s, was quietly observing. At least 200 women are known by name or category to have been present. Given the large attendance of previous meetings and the publicity surrounding this event, the number was probably much greater than that.

Only two men were on the program. John H. Eager, a missionary from Italy, would lead the devotions on the second day. The first day's leader was F. M. Ellis, dashing, youthful, a charming orator better known among Northern Baptists than in the South. Not only was he an appropriate choice for opening devotional exercises as the Armstrongs' pastor, but he was also the star of the Southern Baptist Convention then in session.

The women gathered on a rainy Friday morning, May 11, 1888. Ellis led off with "religious exercises," then launched into a pep talk. He urged the women not to magnify difficulties lying in the way, but to realize their strength. He called it absurd that some feared this was a woman's rights meeting. "All fear ought to be put aside before the overmastering thought of divine command for service," Ellis said. Then he retired, as propriety demanded. (That night the women would pack the galleries at First Baptist Church to hear him brilliantly deliver the Convention sermon on the theme of stewardship.)

Jennie Snead Hatcher (Mrs. William E.), president of the rump Central Committee of Virginia, welcomed the women and called for divine guidance, then introduced Mrs. Theodore Whitfield, the chosen presiding officer. Agnes Osborne, the editor of the *Heathen Helper,* served as secretary.

After Fanny Stout read her convincing paper on the benefits of organization, Whitfield called the roll of states to air their opinions on the subject of general organization. One by one they answered, beginning with Maryland and Annie Armstrong. The majority were strongly ready to organize. Several made challenging speeches. Fannie Davis of Texas said, "This movement is not for 'woman's rights,' though we have our rights, the highest of which is the right for service."

The Virginians, uncertain about their own proper course of action, asked that no vote be taken until after the Convention expressed its opinion. Armstrong insisted that the Convention's opinion did not matter. "The work and its attendant responsibilities are our own. The history of religious work has not shown that it could afford to wait for majorities." She had her eye on the calendar and feared that if action were delayed until later in the Convention, the women would not have time to perfect their plans. Jennie Hatcher took offense and snapped, "I deplore undue haste and urge a strict compliance with the program."[114]

In a spirit of compromise, official voting was delayed, but a committee was appointed to work out all the plans for a general organization. Clearly the women were going to organize, whether with the Convention's blessings or without.

So the program proceeded with detailed state reports. The women would not convene again until Monday, giving the Convention plenty of time to say what it would about the proposed organization. Instead on Saturday morning the women crowded into the balcony to hear the report of the committee on Convention improvements. It was chaired by F. M. Ellis.

The eloquent Ellis delivered a lengthy report recommending changes in the basis of representation, in the relation of the Convention to the state conventions, and in systematic giving. Buried in the middle was

a mild mention of women's work: a simple encouragement of missionary circles and children's bands in all the churches, using the established channels for conveying their contributions to mission boards,
who were instructed to keep separate accounts to show the women's
contributions, with the societies invited to make reports annually to
the boards through their central committees, "or otherwise." There
was commendation for the Bureau of Missionary Information in Baltimore (not mentioning that it was woman-run).

The brethren fell voraciously on the report and debated the first
section on representation for four hours. As the lunch hour was over-
due, and the debate tedious, the men suddenly wanted to vote and
leave for a reception at the governor's mansion. The president had to
send out a committee to round up the throngs who had drifted out to
smoke.[115] The entire committee report passed handsomely, with not a
word of reported debate on the women's matters.

Yet there lingered in oral accounts of the meeting a powdering of
soot from flaming threats and dark doomsaying. A tall, angular, half-
breed Indian Territory leader, J. G. Washburn, tired of the dire statements about women. He arose with a story of a little girl named Mary,
whose mother sent her to the spring down under the hill to bring milk
and butter. When Mary did not return, the mother went to see what
had happened. She found Mary weeping by the spring. "Mother, I got
to thinking that I might grow up and get married; I might have a little
daughter named Mary. I might send her to the spring and she might
fall in and get drowned." Washburn spoke dramatically and ended with
sobs, then sat down amid amusement.[116]

Another account spoke of a Kentuckian saying, "You can't overthrow
Paul and Paul said, 'If you vote for this organization, God only knows
what the women will do. Nobody on the face of this earth will be able
to manage them, and they will be in danger of wrecking the whole
business.'"

A young man watching the debate from the balcony wanted to get
a better seat. He was surrounded by the watching women, arrayed in
their long skirts and bustles. As the young man climbed over a pew,
his boot "struck one of the bustles amidships and knocked a hole in
a black silk dress 18 inches long."[117] As if the women did not have
troubles enough.

When the women reconvened on Monday, they felt the convention
had said, "Do as you please, only send us your money." (Critics were
to claim just the opposite.)[118] They had only to sing "Rock of Ages,"
hear Alice Armstrong's address, take the final vote, and set up their
organization, but not before Martha McIntosh called the women to
prayer. The constituting states were Maryland, South Carolina, Missouri,
Tennessee, Texas, Arkansas, Florida, Georgia, Louisiana, and Kentucky.

They named their general organization the Executive Committee of
Woman's Mission Societies, Auxiliary to Southern Baptist Convention.
Virginia and Mississippi refrained from affiliating because of troubles
with the men at home.

For president, the women chose Martha McIntosh of South Carolina,
graceful, quietly powerful, a proven campaigner for foreign missions
for 14 years. For corresponding secretary they chose Annie Armstrong,
sharp, forceful, tall, attractive, second generation women's leader, for
6 years the foremost female advocate for home missions.

The recording secretary was Susan Tyler Pollard (Mrs. James), a
pioneer in Woman's Mission to Woman, beautiful, and a highly literate
writer. The treasurer was Mrs. John F. Pullen, a Baltimore woman
faithful in little details of many years in Woman's Mission to Woman.
Each state had its own vice-president; some elected were not at the
meeting.

The Maryland women had come prepared with a carefully laid constitution. Before adjourning, the women established their headquarters
in Baltimore, where unofficial headquarters had been since 1871 and
space had been offered in connection with the missions information
bureau, known as Maryland Baptist Mission Rooms. There Armstrong
would set up the mechanics of running the body which now housed
the spirit of women's work for missions.

The day after official adjournment the women settled down for the
activity they liked best—hearing the missionaries who attended the
meeting. These included Sallie J. Little Holmes (Mrs. J. Landrum), in-
trepid co-worker of Martha Crawford and Lottie Moon in China; Mina
Everett of Brazil, who would soon take an office in Texas WMU; and
Lula Whilden of China, home to see the Woman's Mission to Woman
movement grown up.

Back to their home stations of service went the women, to live out
the well-laid plans. "With prayer of thanksgiving and praise for the
grand advance made, for the evident presence of God of all peace in
their midst and for strength and wisdom for the future, closed the most
memorable assemblage of Southern Baptist women."[119]

*There is in our churches a great power, which has not yet
been utilized but has remained dormant: the power and influence of woman. The lines of destiny seem to point to her
as the great power by which the gospel is to be sent to the
ends of the earth.*

F. M. Ellis, quoted
by Susan Tyler Pollard
(Mrs. James)

We the women

We, the women of the churches connected with the Southern Baptist Convention, desirous of stimulating the missionary spirit and the grace of giving among the women and children of the churches, and aiding in collecting funds for missionary purposes, to be disbursed by the Boards of the Southern Baptist Convention, and disclaiming all intention of independent action, organize . . .

Preamble
to WMU Constitution, 1888

ROBABLY NO MORE than 12 percent of Southern Baptist churches in 1888 had missions organizations. Yet the 32 voting founders of Woman's Missionary Union boldly claimed to represent all the women. Even though the voters were surrounded by approving women, their male critics scorned them as a dangerous minority of persistent sisters from only two cities.

"We, the women of the churches" should have been written, "We, the handful of the women," one critic said.[1] And what had they organized? Not a society, or a convention, or a board. Merely an Executive Committee of the Woman's Mission Societies. Even though the name Woman's Missionary Union had been informally used by the leading women for several years, they shelved it until 1890 in order to sound less threatening to the opposition. Just as the opposers suspected, this ploy was the "thin entering edge of the wedge" which would retool the face of Southern Baptist life.[2]

What was accomplished in the 1888 action? Prior to that year, each state's central committee (or committees) operated unto itself. The committees had had nothing but the *Heathen Helper*, the *Baptist Basket*, and the mission board secretaries to keep them in touch. Now they had general officers who would braid enduring ties among them. Prior to 1888, there was no central address where a woman could write for guidance. Now the Maryland Baptist Mission Rooms, which had become the main source of missions information, would also be the operational headquarters for WMU. Prior to that year, the women had no stated

purpose or program, no uniform plan of action. Now they had a constitution for a conventionwide program.

"Verily, God has guided the enterprise from its inception, laying the
foundations so wisely that no rebuilding has been necessary, the main
specifications of its Consititution . . . being as closely adhered to today
as when first promulgated," noted Annie Armstrong after 15 years of
successful operation. As years passed, the women had to edit only one
phrase out of the preamble; that defensive statement thrown in at the
last minute to comfort the fearful: "disclaiming all intention of independent action." Armstrong quipped that instead, these words should
be engraved somewhere on the WMU structure: "Womanly, wise, and
winsome," for they seemed to have conquered the enemies.[3]

Armstrong always attributed the organization structure to God's own
hand. How else could it have been so comprehensive, elastic, and
adaptable? How else could it have endured?[4] Others noted that God
had been aided in framing the constitution by such notable men as
Joshua Levering (who served on Convention boards for more than 60
years and as Convention president), Howard Kerfoot (who wrote the
rules of parliamentary procedure long used by the Convention), and
James Pollard (a noted attorney). The constitution also bore the un-
mistakable mark of Alice and Annie Armstrong.[5]

"We the women" and the 1888 statement of purpose remained virtually unchanged until 1954. The statement was copied into a growing
network of organizational constitutions. In the 1954 constitution WMU
no longer felt it necessary to identify itself as "We the women." The
modern women faithfully carried over the purpose "to promote Christian missions."[6]

WMU PURPOSES

"Stimulating the missionary spirit" and "collecting funds" for the
mission boards were the two original stated jobs for which women
organized. Through the years purpose statements have been sculpted
and recast, but they have always sprung back to the shape of missions.
Each re-statement is yet another attempt to sharpen the arrowhead of
a shaft in motion.

For 30 years the program moved so fast that the women did not
make a serious attempt to refine the purpose statement. They assumed
that such activities as praying, studying the Bible, converting non-
believers, and doing good deeds would happen normally. What needed
attention was the cause of missions: Christian activity in an alien
environment, activity that could not happen unless people worked
together.

WMU lost no time in undertaking major fund-raising projects for each mission board. Before they adjourned in 1888, the women agreed to help the Home Mission Board finance its newest missions field, Cuba. In the first executive meeting they launched a Christmas offering for China (see chaps. 4 and 5 for full discussion). WMU struck gold with the first tools they touched, so they have never laid them aside.

At the local level, women received many bids for their financial attentions. Each church, association, and state was free to respond as it wished, so that WMU dollars built colleges, aided retired preachers, sent young women to school, and operated social work institutions. On the national level, WMU seldom strayed far from the two mission boards.

How to stimulate the mission spirit was a broader topic. The women were aware that the missionary spirit was being quenched by theological controversy. The Campbellites, the Primitives, and the Hardshells used the identical language to object to missions that was used to defame WMU.[7] Throughout the Annie Armstrong administration, the women assumed that action would speak louder than words: they concentrated on projects which would attract and inspire participation in the mission spirit. Such projects ranged from packing boxes of goods for missionaries to planting gardens with proceeds dedicated to missions.

Armstrong developed a remarkable literature publishing business. Through it women's societies could get promptings for prayer and knowledge. But the organization did not see itself as an educational or devotional organization. It was assumed that mission society meetings would be too heavily laden with the important business of missions finance to be strongly instructional.

The Ideals.—The organization sailed slowly into the business of education (see chap. 8). As Fannie E. S. Heck's broader thinking began to permeate the organization in 1907, religious devotion began to gain its own place in WMU purposes. Prayer was programmed in 1908. The new wave of study and personal development began to sweep in from secular women's organizations, and with it the tide of mission study from the interdenominational mission study movement. In 1909 Heck borrowed from the social service movement and social gospel theology the makings of a program of personal service (see chaps. 9 and 10).

Heck began to speak of the Union Ideals:[8]

growth of Christian womanhood through individual and united prayer and study of God's Word;

a larger intellectual life through mission study;

the enlistment of all Southern Baptist women in mission service;

systematic monthly contributions given in sums commensurate with one's real ability and the demands of the world's needs;

direct service rendered by members of the societies for the salvation of their own neighborhoods;

the care of missionaries' children in the Margaret Home;

the recognition of the responsibility for the missions training of young women and children;

the training of young women for special service in the home church and in the home and foreign mission fields in the Woman's Missionary Union Training School.

Thus, neatly stated, WMU before its 25th year had a full-blown program which would not appreciably change. To put the comprehensive program across, WMU issued its first Year Book in 1912. Each of the Union Ideals lived on.

The Fundamentals.—In 1918 the fundamentalist movement began to chip away at foundations of Baptist cooperation. Bickering among the men of the Convention threatened to destroy missions activities that WMU lived for.[9] Although the women did not directly speak their opinions about the movement, they adroitly defended their program against it. In 1918, the same year that the World's Christian Fundamentals Association was formed under sponsorship of the Baptist-published *Watchman-Examiner*, WMU adopted the term *fundamentals* to describe these purposes:

individual and united prayer;

regular Bible and mission study;

systematic and proportionate giving;

organized personal service.[10]

With the addition of a statement of sympathies "for all the forces of righteousness" (see p. 234), and with the addition of an emphasis on soul winning in 1920, these fundamentals became WMU's test of faith.

Minnie K. James (Mrs. W. C.) promoted the fundamentals in her presidental message of 1919, explaining that their value lay in their idealism, the personal devotion of members to them, and the remaking of society because of them.[11]

The Aims.—The fundamentals were interchangeably called *chief aims* beginning in the 1920s, and this term survived the next sharpening of purposes in 1958. This was the first program draft influenced by the professional staff. The aims were stated as follows:

world awareness;

spiritual life development;

Christian witnessing;

sharing possessions;

educating youth in missions.[12]

These five aims embraced the familiar areas of mission study, prayer and Bible study, community missions and soul-winning, giving money, and sponsorship of young people's missions organizations. The major aims were augmented by three operational aims which characterized

the highly efficient organization of the 1950s and 1960s:
enlistment for missions;
leadership training;
reporting advancement.

The Tasks.—During the aims era, WMU's sister organizations in other old-line denominations underwent shock waves of change, leading to major alterations in purpose. Inside the Southern Baptist Convention, WMU's purposes were reviewed in the arena of joint planning by the church programs. All the church organizations agreed to state their purposes as tasks. Behind tasks was a dramatic shift in WMU's self-perception. In the past WMU had carried out its purposes among those who signed up as members. With tasks understood as churchwide purposes, WMU was accepting concern for every church participant.

Outside the SBC arose pressure from the woman's movement. Yet WMU resisted the major shifts that characterized other women's organizations of the times, in order to stay with the purpose of missions. WMU's tasks, first published by WMU in 1964, were these:
Teach missions.
Lead persons to participate in missions.
Provide organization and leadership for special mission projects of the church.
Provide and interpret information regarding the work of the church and the denomination.

The historic WMU purposes prevailed, but with a significant change. Whereas WMU had begun as an activistic organization, it now considered itself educational—the viewpoint, no doubt, of a new generation of WMU leaders schooled in religious education. "WMU specializes in teaching missions," said the interpreters of 1965, whereas the original WMU specialty was raising money. "WMU is one of five educational organizations in a church. . . . The other tasks of WMU grow out of its teaching task."[13]

Task statements would be slightly revised every five years. Whereas WMU had always considered its function in a church to be unique among other church activities, it came to share its task statements with a male counterpart, the Brotherhood. Together they were to teach, do, and support missions among the entire church constituency. Minor shifts in emphasis were explained in fine print. The WMU task statements to be effective beginning in the Centennial year will be as follows:
Teach missions.
Engage in mission action and personal witnessing.
Support missions.
Provide and interpret information regarding the work of the church and the denomination.

WMU training manuals explain that teaching missions includes personal spiritual development, Bible study, missions history, current mission strategy and news, world trends. The support task is defined as a many-splendored thing close to the original dreams of the founders: praying for missions, giving to missions, providing personal ministries for missionaries and their families, leading persons into missionary careers, and promoting involvement in voluntary mission service.

Perpetual Purposes.—Except for developing a woman's devotion to God, WMU has never stated a purpose related to the personal needs of women. No statement of purpose has ever hinted at woman's rights or the uplift of members. Without doubt the organization has opened every door for women that has ever been opened in Southern Baptist life. Such has been the organization's accidental by-product, not the fundamental, the aim, or the task. As stated at the 1888 meeting, "to say that this is a woman's rights movement is absurd." But to say that WMU has not gained rights for women is also absurd.

A 100-year survey of purposes shows a remarkable consistency of concern, a corporate cohesiveness that has kept WMU shooting straight for the future. Not only did its purpose hold the organization together, but it nurtured the Southern Baptist Convention into leadership among other denominations in the field of missions. By 1977, missiologists outside the Southern Baptist Convention were studying why the SBC had continued to increase its missions work while other denominations had declined. The loyalty and effectiveness of Woman's Missionary Union to its purposes was an apparent factor in SBC success. One authority told the WMU Executive Board, "The worst thing that could happen would be for you to be renamed the Southern Baptist Woman's Union, leaving missions out. You must not rest until every country has its own WMU to keep missions at the heart and soul of its work."[14]

"WE, THE WOMEN" MEAN BUSINESS

As demonstrated at its birth, Woman's Missionary Union, Auxiliary to Southern Baptist Convention, consists of women, organized, constituted, incorporated, lawfully recognized as a body with a separate existence from any other. It is most visible each year in May or June when the national Annual Meeting is held. Until 1962, the Annual Meeting consisted of authorized delegates from the state Woman's Missionary Unions who did the voting, plus hundreds of other observers. Since then, any member of a WMU organization in a local church has been considered a voting participant in the Annual Meeting. Although most of the business is carried on by an Executive Board which represents the state WMUs, that Board reports to the Annual Meeting. The Annual Meeting elects the general officers. The fact that WMU has a large, cohesive membership has given it a voice that is heard and a presence that is accommodated among groups that have sometimes been hostile.

WMU began the process of legal incorporation in the city of Baltimore in 1906. Its work was "for missionary, benevolent, and educational purposes not for profit or gain." In 1925 the organization was incorporated under Alabama laws relating to corporations not of a business character. WMU was defined a "religious or educational society."

In organizing, the women knew they would need money for literature and communications. They agreed on three principles: they would receive no missions money, but have the women send it directly to the mission boards for expenditure; the officers would receive no pay; and its expenses would be paid by the mission boards.[15] The mission boards readily agreed to this bargain. The Foreign Mission Board promised to pay more than half the expenses, because it expected to receive more than half the benefits of the women's work.[16]

For more than 66 years the process of WMU funding was commonly known as "recalling." WMU officers would incur or estimate expenses, then "recall" from the mission boards the amount they wished. Always this was done with reluctance and self-sacrifice, for the women wanted as much money as possible to go to missions fields. Neither Board ever hesitated to remit what was requested. The WMU treasurer kept meticulous records, audited each year, and reported to the Annual Meeting all the operating revenues and expenses.

In fact, the mission boards encouraged the officers to invest more money in their work. They were the first to suggest that WMU officers and staff be funded for expenses and salary. From 1895 through 1948 the Sunday School Board also contributed to the WMU budget. The Education Board and the Relief and Annuity Board, as they came onto the Southern Baptist scene, added small amounts to the operating fund for several years (see table, p. 497).

In 1906 the officers found a way to ease the financial load of their efforts. They began publishing literature for sale. The proportion of WMU operating expenses paid by mission board money began to decline. The officers prided themselves on economy of operation. For 1912 their expenses were 4.5 percent of the money they raised. This made them the most frugal of the women's missions organizations of all denominations. They vowed to bring in more money the next year so that expenses would be only 3.5 percent of collections. One of the officers, however, pointed out that a small percentage is not always a wise plan.[17] By 1928-29 the expenses had been reduced to 2.75 percent of contributions. The figure never went higher than 5 percent.

When the Union began to own property (Margaret Home for Missionary Children, Woman's Missionary Union Training School, and headquarters building), it began to build assets and investments. Headquarters office operations continued on a cash basis. Little money was in the bank except for a small cap of excess cash kept on hand for publishing new literature. This hand-to-mouth system began to change in 1944. The Southern Baptist Convention ordered its agencies to accumulate reserve funds as a hedge against debt like that of the past 20 years. Although WMU was not required to follow suit, Kathleen Mallory asked the mission boards to refund a little extra to WMU for the purpose of reserves.[18] WMU survived the 1920-44 debt era without a cent of debt.

Under the administration of Alma Hunt, WMU finances were put on a sound business basis. As membership boomed, so did publishing revenues. WMU was able to build reserve funds in larger proportion to expenses than any SBC agency. Hunt pressed toward a serious personal goal of dispensing with any mission board funds in the WMU operating budget. The mission boards did not want to clip the financial cord which tied WMU to them. Courts Redford, secretary of the Home Mission Board, told Hunt he hoped WMU would never be financially independent. "I like to feel the Home Mission Board is aiding WMU and I think the relationship is good."[19]

Still, she hoped to make WMU pay its own way by 1966. Instead, WMU suffered a financial setback, due to declining membership. This first showed itself in the sales of nonperiodical literature in 1966. Hunt wrote the mission boards that WMU would still need its appropriation.[20] The continuing membership loss, added to a complete overhaul in the WMU periodicals, led to the first operating financial loss in WMU history. Losses came in 1970, 1971, and 1972. The reserve funds set aside in previous years made up the difference.

In the late 1970s, under Carolyn Weatherford's administration, WMU began using earnings from its reserve fund investments as operating revenue. In one year investment income accounted for 17 percent of revenue. In this way the organization avoided asking for significant increases in mission board appropriations. WMU incurred its first debt in 1983 during construction of a new national office building. AmSouth Bank of Birmingham, WMU's longtime bank, gave the organization an unsecured capability to borrow up to $6,500,000. WMU held borrowing to $5,600,000. One of the bank's senior officers noted that WMU qualified for a loan on each of the "three C's" of lending: character, collateral, and capability to repay.

The operating budget for 1985-86 was $8,854,000.

"WE, THE WOMEN" ORGANIZED
The first WMU constitution provided that general officers would be

a president, a corresponding secretary, a recording secretary, and a treasurer. Following standard Baptist practice, the corresponding secretary was understood to be the main administrative officer, the head of the headquarters.

Additionally, each cooperating state would nominate a vice-president to represent it among the officers. At first the vice-president in the state where the headquarters was located was to preside in the president's absence. More recently the idea of having a super-vice-president has been discussed from time to time, but it has been rejected in favor of having all vice-presidents equal. In 1901 the vice-presidents were made members of the Executive Committee.

Prior to that time, the Executive Committee of women in the headquarters city, later known as the local committee, effectively ran the organization between Annual Meetings. The Executive Committee met monthly and gave close scrutiny to the office operations. For efficiency, the recording secretary and treasurer, as well as the corresponding secretary, had to be residents of the headquarters city. This plan, while practical and economical in a time of difficult communication and no money, vested great authority in the hands of a narrow slice of WMU constituency.

Thus arose the first serious conflict among WMU leaders. Annie Armstrong believed that the president's role was only to preside at the Annual Meeting. Fannie Heck believed that the women elected their president to be an all-year worker. The issue continued to plague the organization until Armstrong's resignation.[21]

The Heck viewpoint triumphed after mails, travel, telephone, and expense budgets made communications easier. The result is that Woman's Missionary Union is a two-headed organization. The president is indeed the president, not a board chairman; but the executive director (as the corresponding secretary is now called) supervises the headquarters office.

The presidency of Woman's Missionary Union early became a full-time volunteer career. The president has not been considered part of the national office staff, and she has usually lived in another city. As early as 1901 her travel expenses were paid by the Union, as were those of the other primary officers. The travel item grew as funds permitted, so that by the mid-1920s, the WMU president was on the road representing WMU full time. By the early 1940s the president was granted a small account to defray her personal expenses incidental to being on public display at all times. Also in that decade WMU began providing funds and equipment for secretarial assistance to the president.

Until 1957 the elective officers had no limitations on tenure, although they were subject to election every year. In the 1955 Annual Meeting,

Pauline Willingham Moore (Mrs. John Allen), a foreign missionary, proposed a constitutional amendment, duly advertised in advance, that a limit be placed on the years the president might serve. This was the only case in WMU history of a governance change being proposed from outside the executive group. The motion was defeated, but it in effect signaled criticism of the president, Olive B. Martin (Mrs. George), and she declined reelection the next year.[22] Tenure limits were set in the next constitutional revision, 1957. Since then the limit has been steadily decreased, so that in 1981 the limit was set at five years.

The offices of executive secretary and treasurer ceased being filled by annual election in the constitutional revision in 1957. The office of treasurer was dropped, its functions being handled by staff under management of the executive director.

The corresponding secretary's office was retitled executive secretary in 1937, then executive director in 1976. After 1957 she was elected by the Executive Board rather than the annual session (the Executive Committee was replaced by the Executive Board in 1954). She ceased to have a vote on the Board in 1957.

The concept of local committee was dropped in 1961. By that time the staff was large enough to carry on much detail, and transportation could quickly assemble the state representation if needed.

The WMU of 1988 will be a far more businesslike operation than the organization founded in 1888. The organizational changes of the mid-1960s required such intense office work at the national level and such inordinate amounts of time that the elected officers tended to turn increasing responsibility over to staff.

The WMU Executive Board normally meets twice a year. One meeting is prior to the Annual Meeting, the other is in mid-January in Birmingham. In 1983 the Board was reorganized to put the lay, volunteer leadership of WMU in direct touch with headquarters operations. Every member of the Board serves on one of three committees that consult with the three major operating divisions of the staff. These are Missions Education, Mission Services, and Missions Coordination. Additionally the Board has two administrative committees: finance and personnel.

The WMU program for the church and association is developed each year by an Executive Board committee called the Dated Plan work group. This is a large team of elected board officials and state WMU professionals representing all age groups and representative WMU members. Representatives from the Home Mission Board, Foreign Mission Board, and other SBC agencies consult with the Dated Plan work group in order to frame plans that will set forward the work of missions. The group continues its labor over a ten-month period.

THE WMU PROFESSIONAL

It was a point of pride and procedure that the first officers of WMU received no salary. Annie Armstrong was careful to remind the constituents of this policy at all times. The officers were well-to-do women and could afford to give their services. Accepting a salary was not appropriate to their idea of femininity. The fact that the women worked without pay gave them a moral power over the mission boards' salaried officers, who did no more work than the volunteers. And, the example of the Baltimore office workers deterred the state WMU organizations from paying their workers. Thus the missionary society members could be asked to give with assurance that their entire contribution would go to missions, not to organizational machinery.

The salary issue was quietly debated among WMU leaders for a decade. Alice Armstrong insisted that "a workman is worthy of his hire" even if said workman were a woman. Annie Armstrong insisted that everyone be free to make an offering to the Lord of his or her costly labor.[23] She even refused the free hospitality normally accorded officials attending Baptist conventions and WMU meetings.[24]

In 1900 the WMU Executive Committee wanted to pay Annie Armstrong. They were motivated out of concern for her declining personal finances as well as for the future of a growing administration.[25] Armstrong refused, but did accept travel money beginning in 1901, "for the sake of the work." The mission boards gladly paid the bills. This concession enabled her to begin spending as much as half the year on the field, meeting the women and missionaries, promoting the work.

In 1903, with the encouragement of the mission boards, the women officially attached a salary to the office of corresponding secretary. Only South Carolina's representatives, undoubtedly influenced by the early opposition of Martha McIntosh Bell (Mrs. T.P.) to salaried officers, voted against it. Bell's husband, editor of the Georgia *Christian Index* editorialized that WMU's "glory was dimmed" by paying salaries. Knowing this negative opinion, and always sensitive to criticism, Annie Armstrong refused to hold office if she were forced to accept pay. That decision earned vigorous objection from Texans. They insisted that the entire mission board concept would crumble if people could not be paid to give full time to the work. The issue was dropped until after Armstrong's retirement. From that time forward, the WMU chief executive received a salary.[26] The treasurer also was salaried from 1911, having received a small stipend from 1909 and a paid assistant from 1908.

Even before WMU was organized, occasional state central committees obtained funds to employ field workers. Florida WMU was one of the first in 1883, with a stipend provided by the Home Mission Board.

Mississippi hired a former missionary, Martha ("Mattie") J. Nelson, in 1888 to travel the state and organize societies, noting that her employment "incurs but little expense."[27]

The Home Mission Board and the Foreign Mission Board let the Baltimore WMU office know in 1889 that they wanted to furnish salary and equipment for a clerk, "the growth of the work demanding such outlay." Pressures of the work drove WMU to accept the offer in 1890. Mrs. A. C. Wroe, a former member of the Executive Committee, was the first employee.[28] Another typewriter and a second clerk joined the office in 1891. Although many volunteer hands carried the primary work load of wrapping packages and addressing thousands of pieces of mail, the clerical staff grew.

Immediately upon Annie Armstrong's retirement in 1906, Elia Brower Nimmo (Mrs. W. R.), another Executive Committee member, began to receive a small stipend for her services as chairman of the newly formed Literature Department. She was the start of a professional staff, soon joined by the salaried officers of treasurer and corresponding secretary.[29] The presence of employed staff in the office made WMU invest in telephone service in 1907.

WMU's ardent interest in promoting involvement of young women and girls led to the employment of the first full-time professional staff member other than the officers. She was Mary Faison Dixon, employed as young people's secretary in 1916 on recommendation of a 1915 commission studying the efficiency of Young Woman's Auxiliary.[30]

Meanwhile WMU was keeping an eye on the overall professional needs of the Union family. Between 1900 and 1912 almost every state WMU employed from one to three professional officers or staff. Even South Carolina had reversed its policy against paid staff by 1905 and had three on salary by 1907. Fannie Heck's 1907 presidential address urged that staffs be employed in order that the work might progress more efficiently. Usually the first state position to be salaried was that of field worker—a job that might be done part-time. Next came the demanding slot of treasurer, then corresponding secretary.

Recognizing the new professionalism, Edith Campbell Crane, the second corresponding secretary of WMU, SBC, organized the Secretaries and Field Workers Council of WMU in 1911.[31] The WMU professionals held meetings whenever they had occasion to be together, such as at Annual Meetings. They elected their own officers, and they discussed professional matters as well as WMU methodology.

This group grew so powerful that by January 1921 Minnie Kennedy James (Mrs. W. C.), then president of WMU, SBC, began the practice of having state executive secretaries and other staff meet in conjunction with the Executive Committee of WMU. In the constitution of 1954-57 state professional staffs were officially granted the privilege of voting on matters before the Executive Board which pertained to the WMU program, but not on the legal and financial business of WMU, SBC. After 1969 the only professionals granted a vote were state WMU executive secretaries.

Studies sponsored by WMU, SBC, in 1914 and 1915 revealed that only Louisiana and Maryland lacked salaried corresponding secretaries.[32] Many of the rising breed of WMU professionals came to the work by the route of volunteerism. By the 1930s, a different kind of WMU professional emerged, one with educational credentials for the job. Woman's Missionary Union Training School in Louisville and the Woman's Training School in connection with Southwestern Baptist Theological Seminary taught courses in WMU work. Along with other seminary training, women students were expected to graduate with competence to pursue a missionary career or a WMU career. WMU, SBC, encouraged state offices to employ training school students as part-time field workers. In the late 1930s and early 1940s, they were often paid from funds collected by WMU in state mission offerings and from the Annie Armstrong Offering.

WMU, SBC, employed training school students in 1941 to work during the summer in Arizona and New Mexico, where WMU experience was in short supply. Graduates were most readily hired to lead work with young people in state WMUs. This led to a new dynamic in WMU ranks, highly competent young women who were committed and fresh in their approaches. In the 1930s and 1940s, these young people's secretaries occasionally convened for professional retreats.[33] Not until 1954 were they welcomed routinely to participate in Executive Committee meetings. Although they gained official privileges of voting only in 1954-57, they have attended meetings, spoken out, served on committees, and advised their voting representatives.

In 1951 state WMUs employed 51 professionals including a number of men who led Royal Ambassadors for boys, an organization then sponsored by WMU. By 1966, after WMU had transferred the boys to management of the Brotherhood, state WMUs still had 80 professional staff members.[34] In 1986 the number was 87.

Professional leadership of youth activities corresponded with the population explosion and organizational maturity which made WMU membership mushroom in the late 1950s. The effect was quickly felt in the national WMU office. A panel of age-level experts was hired in 1955, and a management consultant was retained in 1956 by Alma Hunt, executive secretary, to advise in reorganizing the staff of 90 for modern efficiency.[35] The number of employees escalated to 123 in 1965. As Hunt retired in 1974, another set of management consultants advised on yet another reorganization. The total number of employees dropped to 98 in 1976.[36] The number grew to 143 by 1986.

Most early career WMU workers were never-married or widowed women. In the national office, the first professional staff member with husband was hired in 1964. In 1986, 48 percent of the professionals employed were married, several of them with young children.

In 1943 the first male professional joined the staff. He was J. Ivyloy Bishop, secretary of Royal Ambassadors. His presence caused some rearrangements of habits in the cramped office. Kathleen Mallory, the very proper secretary of WMU, asked Bishop to come to work late and to leave early, so the ladies would not be embarrassed by having to take off their hats before a man. Like the women, Bishop remained unmarried and lived a spartan life throughout his ten years of employment at the national office.[37]

By 1986, 10 percent of the WMU employees were men, five of these in professional or managerial slots. Each of them worked in office administration or business supporting but not determining WMU program.

The financial life of the WMU professional for the first half of the twentieth century is pictured in Kathleen Mallory. During 1909-12 she was employed as the corresponding secretary of Alabama WMU. She and her associate did "light housekeeping," meaning that their room had an improvised kitchen for making cocoa for supper.[38]

When Mallory became corresponding secretary of WMU, SBC, her salary of $1,000 a year did not improve her standard of living. By 1921 she was accepting $2,000 a year, but when she took extended leave to travel abroad in 1924 and 1926, she refused salary for the months of absence. She accepted a raise to $2,100 in 1927, but insisted on a cutback during the Great Depression, in sympathy with the reduced salaries of the mission board staffs. Her sacrifice was hardly warranted, for her subsistence pay was a mere 35 percent of that received by the Foreign Mission Board secretary.[39]

Even in postwar inflation times, Mallory never earned more than $3,000 a year. Some employees understood that she wanted her salary to be less than a missionary's. Of course, missionaries received living expense allowances in addition to cash compensation. She continued to live in a single room or a studio apartment, never owned a car, had no radio until 1936, and dined on boiled eggs, canned spinach, crackers, church suppers, and lunchroom fare.

Other national WMU professional staff made approximately the same salary as Mallory, her pay being perhaps a token $100 more than theirs. Their living arrangements were similar. The president of the WMU Training School received higher compensation than Mallory. Not until 1941 did WMU enter into a retirement program for its employees, through the SBC Relief and Annuity Board, after having refused to do so for five years.[40] Not until 1951 did WMU pay Social Security taxes for its employees, and that over the objections of some who felt this a violation of church-state separation.[41]

By 1943 Mallory was perhaps changing her viewpoint on employee compensation. She began to set up a wage scale. WMU began to comply with wage and hour law regulations concerning holidays and work weeks.[42] At that time clerks in the headquarters office were making less than maids and janitors in southern cities. Mallory and other longtime employees of her era retired on impossibly small stipends and could not have survived without personal inheritances and continued sporadic aid from WMU. In 1986 WMU was still supplementing retirement pay for employees who had labored for low pay during the 1940s and 1950s.

Alma Hunt, leaving her position as dean of women at William Jewell College in 1948 to succeed Mallory, took a cut in pay. Although committed to raising the WMU employees' standard of living, and although she put a well-planned pay scale into operation, she did not appreciably change WMU's self-sacrificing culture. She herself was paid only a few dollars more than her associates. In years of financial stringency, she turned down personal raises offered by the Executive Board. Staff members continued to live in rooming houses and small apartments. Not until 1949 did a WMU staff member own an automobile, and hers was provided by her family's generosity. In the late 1960s some staff members were able to afford to buy houses.

Annuity, insurance, and other normal employee benefit packages were considered very good by the 1970s. Still, salaries at the national WMU office were 14 percent less than those at certain SBC agencies in 1982-83. WMU compensation in many of the state offices was superior to this, because WMU pay was determined on scales set to accommodate a predominantly male staff. For WMU professionals to leave certain state jobs for more responsibility at the national office, they had to take cuts in pay. In June 1986 the WMU Executive Board set a goal for the post-Centennial year of achieving parity with other Southern Baptist employers in salaries.

With such commitment, most national and state WMU professionals have served for a lifetime. The all-time record of tenure for any Southern Baptist chief executive was Kathleen Mallory's 36 years. Some WMU professionals did leave their work for other church and denominational service. WMU has remained the best route into SBC agency work. The first woman theology professor at a Southern Baptist seminary began her career on a state WMU staff. She was Helen E. Falls, professor of missions at New Orleans Baptist Theological Seminary. The highest ranked state Baptist convention female manager is a former WMU executive. Perhaps a dozen associational WMU organizations employ professional staff.[43]

With a growing staff and increasingly complex business, WMU has never forgotten its real strength: the volunteer woman. As in Annie Armstrong's days, volunteers continue to work in the national office. A formal volunteer program was instituted in 1977. Bernice Elliott, a retired professional staff member, coordinated the program until she was succeeded by Martha Broome, a local church WMU member. In 1986, Betty Bryant, officer in a local WMU organization, headed the program. More than 1,000 hours of work were volunteered during each year of the 1980s.

A special committee worked throughout 1985 to define the roles of the Board, the officers, and the executive staff. The decision was that WMU's strength lies primarily with the members of the church democratically represented on the Executive Board. Yet the Board expects to delegate much of the national organization's work to full-time professionals. Based on the committee's report, Executive Director Carolyn Weatherford in 1986 insisted that WMU would maintain its two-headed character and its unique female style of management.

HEADQUARTERS

In its first century WMU, SBC, has called two cities home. At the founding meeting, a small committee which worked on administrative plans suggested that headquarters be located in Baltimore. The city had earned unofficial status as the WMU mecca, beginning with Ann Graves's leadership in Woman's Mission to Woman in 1871. It offered the advantage of the Maryland Baptist Mission Rooms, where Annie Armstrong and other leading women presided over a library and publishing operation. Their offices were donated rooms over the Wharton and Barron Book Store. This establishment was owned by Henry Marvin Wharton, editor of the *Baltimore Baptist*, pastor, and noted orator. Often he had crusaded on behalf of women, and now his future mother-in-law was the recording secretary of WMU. The women's new missions enterprise was sure of a hospitable welcome in his store. Not only were the offices available free of charge, but women with many years of home and foreign missions know-how were present to be the Executive Committee and volunteer workers.

The WMU and the Maryland Baptist Mission Rooms, each headed by Armstrong, continued to share the same address through several moves. Whenever Wharton and Barron Book Store moved, Armstrong packed her few desks, bookcases of literature, curio display, and even the couch on which Ann Hasseltine Judson died, and moved along to new offices.[44]

When Armstrong announced her intention to retire from office, she assumed that WMU would choose to locate the headquarters and local

Executive Committee elsewhere. She systematically closed down operations and announced that the office would move. Executive Committee members were divided in their backing of Armstrong. Apparently some of them arranged for their pastors to meet and to state in public that Baltimore wanted to retain the headquarters, indeed would be insulted if the office were moved. The secretaries of the Foreign Mission Board, Home Mission Board, and Sunday School Board hastened to Baltimore. With much to lose if WMU should not survive this major transition in leadership, the men made sure that the WMU headquarters would be safe in Baltimore.[45]

At the 1906 Annual Meeting, Fannie Heck was returned to the presidency. She announced via the press that "there shall be no lapse in the work because of the present vacancy in the office of corresponding secretary," and that the address of WMU would be unchanged.[46]

In 1909 WMU was faced with two new challenges: the need for more office space and the need to invest money. As owner of the Woman's Missionary Training School (see chap. 11), WMU was accumulating an endowment which had to be earning interest. The organization flexed its business muscles and used WMUTS endowment funds to buy a building for $11,359 at 15 West Franklin Street in Baltimore.[47] In turn, WMU rented the building to itself and to other tenants at a rate which earned interest on the investment. The new headquarters, the first the women had owned, was dedicated October 26, 1909.

The Baltimore base of WMU caused the organization to be dominated by one region for more than 30 years. When the office of president was up for keen competition in 1894, the Annual Meeting was held in Fort Worth. Passing over several brilliant Texas leaders, the women chose for president the quiet Abby Manly Gwathmey (Mrs. W. H.) of Richmond. She had probably never been West before, but she stemmed from a family prominent in the Southeast. Again and again, WMU elected officers from Virginia, the District of Columbia, North Carolina, and Baltimore. No doubt this arrangement eased the difficulties of communication and transportation, but it annoyed the leaders of other regions. Not until 1933 would a president come from west of the Mississippi.

In February 1920, at an Executive Committee meeting called in Nashville, when the Maryland local members were not present, Georgia and Alabama representatives called for the headquarters to be moved.[48] It was a deliberate move to break up the old center of power.

Mary Hill Davis (Mrs. F. S.) of Dallas, Texas, chaired the committee which studied and recommended the change. Thirteen of 17 states favored the move. Davis aired her own opinion that other states wanted to be in on the headquarters operations. She considered Baltimore too far from the psychological hub of WMU. The local committee was too far away to attend Annual Meetings. Other leaders believed that the general officers needed to be in shorter reach of the constituency. Also, the eastern leaders (really middle southerners, but seemingly far east to the typical Southern Baptist of 1921) bore the taint of affiliation with the ecumenical movement. Opponents of the move saw nothing to be gained from a change, but money to be lost in changing printers, banks, charter, and buildings.[49]

The proposal was so jarring that a decision was deferred until 1921. Four cities invited the headquarters: Atlanta, Nashville, Birmingham, and Memphis. Nashville's invitation was particularly intriguing, because the Baptist Sunday School Board, headquartered there, offered to provide offices free of charge. Birmingham also seemed to have its charms, one of which being that the SBC Education Board had recently established offices in that city. The Education Board's secretary was the husband of WMU president, Minnie James.

The officers residing in Baltimore; James; and Kathleen Mallory, the WMU corresponding secretary, abstained from voting. When the vote was counted, 203 had stood up for Nashville and 203 for Birmingham. To save James from having to cast the tiebreaking vote, the treasurer and the brand-new young people's secretary, Juliette Mather, were asked to vote. Mather looked for a cue from her elders and voted for Birmingham.[50]

Temporary offices were set up in the Baltimore home of the treasurer, Elizabeth Chapman Lowndes (Mrs. W. C.). To salve Baltimore's feelings, the incorporation, the recording secretary, and the treasurer were kept in Baltimore. But in October 1921, the rest of the operation moved to Birmingham. The office was at 1111 Comer Building (originally the Jefferson County Bank Building), then reputed to be the tallest building in the South. When the Executive Committee held its semiannual meeting there in February 1922, they watched the sun go down from the roof. One of the enlistment-minded officers said that the address should be spelled "Won one, One won." [51]

The Sunday School Board, with true grace, decided to pay the WMU rent anyway. I. J. Van Ness, the Board's secretary, promptly forwarded the first year's rent, and the SSB continued the contribution for 27 years.[52]

Mallory set up her tiny desk with cardboard accessories in 1921 and never changed it. Although WMU membership tripled, although the publication business soared, although the staff necessarily grew, she packed every activity into essentially the same suite of rooms. She knew that the offices must be enlarged, but was hampered by lack of funds resulting from her long years of frugality. In early spring 1947 she searched for new quarters to rent, then realized that they would have to be built. She wrote to one of the state leaders that one of the hardest problems she had ever had to face, keeping her awake at night, was the realization that WMU had nothing with which to secure a loan for building money.[53]

Although the 1947 WMU Annual Meeting approved her proposal that property be purchased and although she bought a lot on Birmingham's Southside, Mallory decided that her successor should bear the responsibility of leading WMU into its next home.[54]

Her successor, Alma Hunt, was confronted in the cramped, hot offices by sacks of magazine orders unopened in the corridors, stacks of magazines in the process of being mailed out. The fire marshal informed her to clear the corridors or go to jail. Each meeting of the building committee brought realization that the $100,000 fund-raising drive promised by the state WMUs in 1948 would be completely inadequate. At the January 1949 meeting of the Executive Committee, local members of the committee decorated for a luncheon. They decided to feature a model of their ideal WMU building. With no definite blueprints, they built a replica of a handsome new building that had just been completed in Birmingham. It was an insurance company's office with limestone columns, brass doors, and elegant lobby on Birmingham's main street near the houses of government.[55]

As the committee struggled with the architect to design a building both economical and as beautiful as the luncheon centerpiece, they grew discouraged about the cost. Two years later, in January 1951, the very building the women had admired became their own. At a cost of $500,000, less a $25,000 gift by the owner, WMU acquired the building at 600 North 20th Street. It was paid for by 1953 from the sale of the unused land previously purchased, from contributions raised by the state WMUs in honor of Kathleen Mallory, from cash saved from the operating budget, from small gifts from the Sunday School Board, and from a short-term loan WMU took from its own endowments.[56] Even before Alma Hunt signed the purchase contract, the Executive Committee had convened in the building's auditorium to sing "Praise God, from Whom All Blessings Flow."

The building had been purchased with knowledge that the foundation would accommodate two more floors on top of the original three. These were added in 1959-60.[57] Publications had boomed into multiples with growing circulation, necessitating more space and bringing in more revenue to pay for it. The completed building housed not only a growing staff, but also a growing collection of important artworks and interesting curios bestowed by friends and missionaries from around the world.

Despite several remodelings to make completely efficient use of space, the building was again too small by 1977. The surrounding property was sold (after the adjoining building had burned in 1974) for a high-rise office building. During 1977, WMU expanded its building into a small, rear garden plot at a cost of $500,000, paid for from funds on hand. This addition brought the building to its maximum size, approximately 41,000 gross square feet of space.

In December 1980 the literature department was moved to a warehouse two miles away at 201 North 39th Street. Space needs were again acute as numbers of publications and staff grew. In January 1981 the Executive Board voted to offer the building for sale and in June authorized a complete study of space needs. A relocation committee, chaired by Betty Collins Gilreath (Mrs. J. Frank), recording secretary of WMU, steered the resulting move. Property was purchased south of Birmingham on New Hope Mountain, just off US Highway 280. The 25-acre tract was in the middle of a fast-growing residential and office community. Contractors chopped into the woods to build WMU's own streets. WMU chose for an address 100 Missionary Ridge. The Executive Board assembled in a rare called meeting September 23, 1982, to approve plans and to break ground for the building.

During the regular Executive Board meeting of 1984, with the building under construction, the state WMUs helped to fill a large copper-lined underground vault with historical information about the organization. The cornerstone was placed over this repository. The building was occupied in April and May 1984, with the downtown building evacuated on May 25. The new building was dedicated January 16, 1985. It consists of 137,000 square feet including warehouse, conference rooms, offices, library, and expansion space.

Total cost of the property and building and new furnishings was $8,621,300. This was temporarily financed by a loan, plus funds on hand, with expectation that the indebtedness would be retired from contributions and from the completed sale of the building at 600 North 20th Street. As of September 1986 contributions totaled approximately $500,000. The WMU Executive Board in January 1986 launched a Centennial Thank Offering to help achieve the goal of making the new building debt free by the time of WMU's Centennial. Except for requesting contributions for buying the building at 600 North 20th Street, this was the only time in a century that WMU asked for money for its own purposes.

The life of Woman's Missionary Union is made up of its purpose and of the program by which we move to its attainment.

Marie Wiley Mathis (Mrs. R. L.)

3
The minority rules

Religious work has not always been advanced
by a majority.
Carey stood alone for a long time.

Annie Armstrong, 1888

F THE WMU founders had delayed until a majority joined them or approved them or even spoke kindly of them, history would still be holding its breath. But the minority went forward, never satisfied with their meager numbers, but nevertheless so potent a leaven that they made the whole lump rise. A Centennial measurement of WMU's value at any point must take into consideration that it has been a minority movement.

WMU has never wanted to be a minority. Two of its favorite words have been *enlistment* and *enlargement* with periodic campaigns by these names, and eternal optimism that next year every woman in every church will join forces. Annie Armstrong's genius was "bringing forces together," an ability she recognized as God-given. WMU's genius has been its energy to expand geographically and to include every stripe of womankind.

No photographer was present in 1888 to capture a picture of the founders of Woman's Missionary Union. If a portrait existed, it would show wealth, white skin, soft hands. Woman's Missionary Union of 1888 was a creature of the educated, enlightened, closely kin upper class.

If a photographer could capture a perfect cross section of Woman's Missionary Union after 100 years, the scene would have shifted drastically to portray rich and poor; red and yellow, black and white; tender and tough. The women of missions have achieved a union of minorities of multiple cultural backgrounds.

The Union is a blending not only of peoples, but of geographic areas. From its ten Solid South states the original WMU exported its values and its methods coast to coast. By 1963 WMU had a foot in every state.

At the heart of Southern Baptist expansion is the missions motive pumped by WMU. Culturally cohesive organizations do not usually set out to broaden themselves. In fact, many Southern Baptists have often resisted new arrivals on their scene. But WMU's leaders, beginning with

Annie Armstrong, opened their eyes quickly to a heavenly vision of
women whose devotion triumphed over diversity.

BRINGING WOMEN TOGETHER

The women who boldly proclaimed "We, the women of the churches"
in 1888 represented the aristocracy of the white South. Of the 32 official
delegates, a half dozen were wives of prominent pastors. The daughter
of the Foreign Mission Board secretary and the daughter of the Home
Mission Board secretary were among them (Mary Caldwell Tupper of
Virginia and Mary B. Tichenor Barnes of Georgia). Several, such as
Martha McIntosh and Annie Armstrong, were the daughters of wealthy
parents. One, Minnie Alfred of Louisiana, was a missionary. Another,
Mrs. L. B. Telford of Florida, was formerly a Northern Baptist missionary
in Siam. Agnes Osborne of Kentucky, independent, well educated, a
member of a brilliant family, had her own journalistic pursuits. Several
were exceptionally well educated. Adelia M. Hillman (Mrs. Walter) of
Mississippi would be a college president, and Mrs. W. E. Hatcher had
earned one of the first master's degrees awarded women in the South.
Some were married to prosperous doctors, lawyers, or planters.

These women were typical of those watching in the large audience
of the 1888 meeting. They were typical of WMU founders in each state.
The first leaders in Woman's Missionary Union were loaded with credentials or cash or both. Those not blessed with the world's goods
were rich with missionary experience. They were unanimously whites
of Anglo-Saxon parentage. Even the poorest had servants at home to
give them some freedom from washtubs and wood stoves. Since each
had to fund her own travel, her postage, her stationery, and her give-
away literature, and since none but Annie Armstrong had an office
away from her home, some personal resources were essential.

This privileged minority were a collection of denominational royalty
who could have woven themselves into an exclusive sorority. Exactly
the opposite was their intent. Their Christian beliefs and their missions
zeal overwhelmed the human tendency to hoard their blessings. The
members deliberately set out to include women from other walks of
society. Among the first to be brought into the fold of Woman's Missionary Union were women of moderate and poor financial circumstances. The national officers encouraged the state WMU organizations
to arrange funds in order to make possible leadership by women whose
talents exceeded their purses. At the turn of the century WMU at the
national level was being led by women who had excellent family connections but reduced wealth.

By the 50th anniversary of WMU, the leadership circle had greatly
expanded in number and in scope. The fourth and fifth executive sec-

retaries, Alma Hunt and Carolyn Weatherford, were self-supporting career women. The presidents from the 1940s onward were from families of moderate circumstances.[1]

The widening sweep of WMU was revealed in the literature. Early WMU publications wrote of the members as if each had servants at home. Indeed, many Southern whites did in the first 30 years of the organization. As life changed, so did literature. Women were reminded that they could dispense with costly servants in order to give more money to missions. They were encouraged to simplify their housework routines in order to have time for WMU activities.[2]

FROM SOUTH TO WEST, NORTH, AND EAST

The state WMU network has been integral to the operation and expansion of WMU. The Conventionwide organization was a collection of state WMU central organizations. These represented women's societies in the churches. By ladies' agreement, the state central committee or statewide organization served as liaison between the general organization and the local church.[3] Since each state was independent, Annie Armstrong was rejoicing over a real miracle when she could report after one year that harmony prevailed,[4] with every state fully cooperating. "Central Committees are not part of the Union but separate organizations working in harmony with it," explained one of the first histories of WMU.[5]

Yet the strong dedication of the women to each other and to the common cause of missions inevitably "brought forces together" into an organization which in many respects seems centralized. WMU slowly accommodated the varying regional styles of operation.

Of the 14 Southern Baptist states of 1888, 4 restrained their women from affiliating with the southwide organization. Women in each case quietly agitated until they were authorized to affiliate. On July 18 Adelia Hillman, president of the Mississippi Central Committee, telegraphed Baltimore, "Mississippi Baptist women wheel into line by unanimous vote."[6] In November 1888, the Virginia state general association gave its consent for the women to carry on their own auxiliary. The women, however, decided to work "under the ground" until they felt safer about affiliating with WMU, SBC. This came on March 26, 1889.[7]

Alabama's Central Committee had been rudely abolished when they requested approval to unite with the general organization. But in the fall of 1889, the state convention gave consent and appointed a new committee. Its president was Amanda Tupper Hamilton (Mrs. T. A.), daughter of the Foreign Mission Board secretary. Another officer was the daughter of the first secretary of the Home Mission Board, another was a future founder of the WMU Training School, and yet another was

Margaretta D. Early (Mrs. M. D.), who had been ejected from the Southern Baptist Convention in 1885. These competent and honored women nevertheless had to keep quiet about their affiliation with WMU, SBC, for opposition remained intense.[8]

North Carolina won consent in 1890, with Fannie E. S. Heck, the silent observer at the 1888 meeting, serving as president of a new statewide organization of women. The vice-president was Ellen H. Edwards, who had taken the first mite boxes from Baltimore to South Carolina in 1872, and who now lived in North Carolina.

As WMU, SBC, welcomed each new state into the Union, the headquarters in Baltimore began to send it shipments of literature and mite boxes. The states in return gave to the special offerings, packed boxes for needy missionaries, joined in prayer.[9]

WMU had gained a foothold, if not a victory, in every southern state. But the Union's missions nature hungered after new territory. Geographic expansion would occur because of three primary factors. One was the out-migration of Southern Baptists. Going afar to seek prosperity, they took along a preference for Southern Baptist churches, including Woman's Missionary Union. A second factor was the splintering of the Northern Baptist Convention over theological disagreement. A third dominant factor was the missions initiative of Southern Baptists, sending missionaries and backing them with all the resources of Woman's Missionary Union.

It was direct missions effort that spilled WMU out of the South in 1891. WMU members had been shipping goods to Indian Territory missionaries since 1882, and the women recipients naturally felt themselves an integral part of the Union's work. Northern Baptist missionaries were also at work in Oklahoma Territory and Indian Territory, and their women's organizations had taken an early lead in organizing the area. In 1891 a pro-Southern Baptist organization of churches was founded, with a women's central committee. WMU, SBC, without hesitation welcomed Indian Territory to the union and permitted it a vice-president on the same basis as the well-established states. In 1896 two Indian women were admitted to the WMU Annual Meeting as delegates.

Growing competition with Northern Baptist women in the territories took Annie Armstrong herself to Oklahoma in the fall of 1900. In consultation with her Northern Baptist counterpart, Mary Burdette, she guaranteed that each local women's organization could choose whether to send its contributions North or South. In the face of much opposition, Mrs. W. H. Kuykendall, the missionary who was president of the WMU affiliate, was asked to speak at the meeting of the general association in Indian Territory. She asked how many persons were enabled to be present by the help of WMU. More than 20 men (plus wives) stood, dressed in clothes from missionary boxes. The association pledged its cooperation with WMU.[10]

Armstrong continued visits to and heavy correspondence with Oklahoma and secured funding for two women missionaries who would represent WMU interests there. Her action undoubtedly helped maintain dual allegiance to South and North, until in 1914 Oklahoma decided to affiliate exclusively with the South.[11]

Next the WMU burst across the border into the District of Columbia. A southern woman, Jessie Davis Stakely (Mrs. Charles A.), moved there when her husband became pastor of First Baptist Church. She was hostess for the 1895 WMU Annual Meeting which convened in Washington. Jessie Stakely led some of the women of the District to cooperate with WMU instead of with the northern women's societies. By 1896 D.C. was functioning as a state WMU organization, with Stakely as a vice-president of the general organization. Before she moved from the District, she would be president of WMU, SBC. The District would continue dual alignment with both South and North throughout WMU's first century.[12]

Illinois women organized in 1908 with allegiance to the Northern Baptist women's work, in spite of the fact that their churches had formed a state association in protest of liberal theology they perceived in Northern Baptist bodies. The Illinois State Association sent messengers to the Southern Baptist Convention in 1910, but the women did not investigate WMU until 1911. After their delegates took a favorable report home from the WMU Annual Meeting, Illinois affiliated. They changed their name and constitution to WMU style, and thus caused some of their members to withdraw.[13]

In the same year New Mexico WMU was recognized by WMU, SBC, although neither WMU nor the state convention was formed or officially declared as Southern Baptist until 1912. The work had originally been encouraged by Northern Baptist women.[14]

The westward expansion slowed for the next 30 years. Southern Baptists and Northern Baptists in 1911 and 1912 reached a comity agreement by which the SBC did not deliberately encourage affiliates from outside the existing territory. Exceptions came in 1929 with Arizona and in the 1940s with California.

Arizona WMU, like its state convention, began with disaffection with Northern Baptist doctrine. At the same time that the SBC recognized the state convention, WMU, SBC, recognized the WMU. California WMU came into being in 1941, shortly after the state convention was organized in 1940 due to doctrinal differences with Northern Baptists. California sought and gained recognition by the SBC in 1941 and after much controversy, was admitted in 1942.[15] WMU did not welcome the new group with open arms. Northern Baptists were offended that the SBC had accepted the Californians in a way that violated the 1912 comity

agreements. Kathleen Mallory, always a meticulous rule-follower, informed the Californians that they would have to get their women's
materials from the North, apparently because she believed the SBC had
been in error in recognizing them. But by 1943, WMU permitted California to name members to its committees and probably would have
permitted a vice-president, but the Annual Meeting was not held because of wartime. In 1944 the SBC cleared up its procedure in recognizing California, and WMU elected a California vice-president.

In 1944, 1949, and 1951 the Southern Baptist Convention affirmed
that its territory was unlimited. In effect, the Northern Baptists did the
same by renaming their convention in 1950 the American Baptist Convention. The SBC prepared for more new conventions in 1946 by stating
in the bylaws that a state convention must have 25,000 members to
gain representation on Convention boards. WMU, by contrast, did not
set numerical limits until 1954. By constitutional revision in effect until
1969, a state WMU could have a vice-president of WMU, SBC, when it
had 3,000 members. However, the WMU Board voted to open its meetings to the officers of a state not yet qualifying for a vice-president.
The headquarters staff was authorized to furnish literature and render
aid to the unaffiliated new areas.[16]

Development of WMU proceeded hand in hand with development of
new state conventions. Kansas-Nebraska WMU was organized in 1948,
the same year its state convention was admitted to the SBC; WMU gave
recognition in 1949. Oregon-Washington (the Northwest Convention)
WMU was organized in 1948, and admitted to WMU, SBC, in 1950.

By this time, the post-World War II migration of southerners to
industrial centers of the North was making big business of Baptist
expansion. In 1952 WMU members were reminded to lift their horizons.
Eva Inlow, WMU secretary in New Mexico, rose in the 1952 meeting of
her sister state secretaries to remind them that the Southern Baptist
Convention was no longer exclusively southern. "Use the term *conventionwide,* not *southwide,*" she told them.[17]

In 1955 the Home Mission Board entered into a program of pioneer
missions which was formalized into a department. This program cooperated with older state conventions as they developed new state
conventions in the north central states. The Home Mission Board and
the WMUs of neighboring states projected WMU into these new areas.
Already the Kentucky state convention was fostering work in Ohio
which resulted in a new state convention in 1954. Kentucky WMU
sponsored Ohio WMU which gained immediate recognition by WMU,
SBC.

Arizona and New Mexico sponsored expansion into Colorado, Wyoming, Montana, the Dakotas, and Utah. Here began a pattern of new
WMU development that would become standard. Three WMU leaders

took these states under their wings: Lois G. Stewart (Mrs. Cecil M.), Arizona president; Gladys M. Griffin (Mrs. Charles M.), Arizona secretary; and Eva Inlow. Associational WMU organizations in Colorado and the Northern Plains states were developed as affiliates of either Arizona or New Mexico. The older states conducted leadership training conferences in the new areas. Statistics of the new states were counted in with the old. When Colorado WMU was ready to fly on its own, the established leaders set up the meeting, invited the guest dignitaries, and presided over the organizational meeting. Colorado WMU was organized November 21, 1955.[18]

In January 1956, the new Colorado WMU president, Virjama Hamilton (Mrs. John), went to Birmingham to participate in the Executive Board meeting of WMU, SBC. She was warmly welcomed and considered that she was accorded all the privileges enjoyed by the voting state representatives.[19] Colorado did not have the 3,000 WMU members required for having a vice-president on the Board until 1958. Even so, Hamilton's immediate acceptance into the WMU leadership group excited some uneasiness because other Colorado leaders were not similarly taken into the councils of SBC agencies.

HELP FOR NEW STATES

WMU had a dual interest in the manifest destiny of the SBC. First of all, WMU viewed the expansion as missions—work to be studied and supported and celebrated. Second, WMU absorbed the new areas as nourishment for its own future growth. By 1960 WMU magazines regularly featured new area expansion. Editors tried to prune southern regionalisms from their sentences and told readers that "southwide" terminology was obsolete. By 1961 Southern Baptist congregations existed in all 50 states, and full-fledged churches were established in each by 1963, Vermont being the last state to be mapped.[20]

WMU publications and studies were calculated to stimulate growth in the pioneer areas. The 1961-62 WMU emphasis was on church extension and prayer. The women supported the 1956-64 Thirty Thousand Movement, a Conventionwide campaign to establish 30,000 new congregations by the time of the 150th anniversary of the first Baptist convention. Alma Hunt and Marie Wiley Mathis (Mrs. R. L.) of WMU, SBC, had helped develop the Conventionwide goals. Women were encouraged to organize congregations themselves and to establish WMU in every new preaching point. By 1964 almost 25,000 new congregations had been begun, resulting in 6,682 new churches.[21] This tremendous boost undoubtedly contributed to a dramatic rise in WMU enrollment during the same period.

Another church extension project in the pioneer areas was Project

500. The Home Mission Board appealed to WMU to raise sufficient funds through the Annie Armstrong Easter Offering to establish 500 new congregations in the post-1940 Southern Baptist territories. The financial goals were not fully realized, nor were the church establishment goals, but 211 churches were planted in new areas during 1968-69.[22]

Another contribution of WMU to the geographic growth of the SBC was the concept of volunteer missions work. In order to assist new state WMUs, WMU leaders began volunteering their services as short-term missionaries. Susie Nabb Illingworth (Mrs. G. C.) of Birmingham volunteered her services to assist in the Colorado WMU girls camp in 1961. This example led to the adoption of short-term volunteer missionaries as an integral part of home mission strategy (see chap. 7).[23] By the 1970s thousands of volunteers were traveling to new SBC territories to help establish churches.

The older WMUs continued voluntarily to extend themselves into new areas throughout the 1980s. Illinois and Kentucky WMUs sponsored Indiana WMU, organized in 1959, and qualified immediately for WMU, SBC, representation, even before the state convention was recognized by the SBC.

Whereas most of the state-to-state relationships had been among adjacent states, Arkansas jumped over several states to aid Michigan. Michigan organized its WMU in 1958 and qualified for WMU, SBC, representation in 1961, four years before the SBC accepted the Michigan convention. Virginia, Kentucky, and Ohio sponsored work in West Virginia. The West Virginia WMU was organized in 1970 and gained representation with WMU, SBC, in 1986.

The snowball effect of work in the new areas brought many demands for assistance to the WMU headquarters. Whereas the pre-1955 state WMUs simply declared themselves organized whenever a few churches concurred, the pioneer missions process aided by the Home Mission Board required a stronger foundation.

An example of the process was the New York WMU. It began with the arrival in Manhattan of Paul S. and Ava Leach James. He had been pastor of a 3,000-member church in Atlanta. They left a five-bedroom, three-bath house for three rooms in a New York City high rise in the fall of 1957.

A small congregation was meeting in Manhattan. WMU had already organized activities for the children. Paul James served as pastor of this, the Manhattan Baptist Church, constituted January 10, 1958. Ava James began to organize the women, beginning in Chatham, New Jersey, in November 1957. One year later she pulled together a meeting of several women's groups in the New York City area, with 25 women present, some from 350 miles away. In April 1960 the work was suffi-

ciently well established for the Northeast Baptist Association to be
formed, with the associational WMU following in the summer. Ava
James served as president.[24]

Alma Hunt, executive secretary of WMU, SBC, visited the area about
that time. Ava James begged her for assistance from the national WMU
office. Although Maryland WMU, headed by its executive secretary
Josephine Norwood, was regularly bringing training teams into eastern
New York and Becie Kirkwood (Mrs. A. L.) of Ohio WMU was doing the
same in western New York, more leadership was needed. The Birmingham staff of WMU was spread too thinly to offer much help.

Hunt went to Atlanta to confer with the executive secretary of the
Home Mission Board, Courts Redford, and his assistant, Arthur B. Rutledge. The HMB agreed to provide funds for a full-time WMU staff
member to travel the pioneer areas. She would have her home base in
Birmingham under management of WMU, but would be jointly employed by the HMB and WMU. They agreed to offer the job to Bernice
Elliott, the experienced secretary for WMU young people's work in New
Mexico. In August 1961 Elliott began her work as promotion associate
in pioneer areas.[25]

New York was only one of a dozen states needing Elliott's attention.
In one five-month segment of 1964, she packed her bags for work tours
in Nebraska, Wyoming, Idaho, Oregon, Washington, Alaska, New Mexico,
Minnesota, Indiana, northern Illinois, Wisconsin, Michigan, Ohio, New
York, West Virginia, and North Carolina. She was in her office for parts
of two weeks and had one week of vacation.

In her first outing she directed a girls camp in Montana. Arriving at
a campsite she found leaders volunteering their services from Mississippi, Alabama, Texas, South Carolina, Georgia, and Montana. Thirty
girls registered, and Montana was launched into a WMU youth
program.[26]

Bernice Elliott's work began to bear fruit. New York Baptists formed
a fellowship group to prepare for SBC statehood. New York WMU was
officially constituted September 25, 1969, at a Holiday Inn in Syracuse,
with Ava James presiding and Bernice Elliott installing the new officers.
Helen Long Fling (Mrs. Robert) had just retired as president of WMU,
SBC, in order to assist her husband as he became a home missions
pastor in Westchester County, New York. Helen Fling soon became
president of the new New York WMU. She recruited Edwina Robinson,
recently retired WMU executive of Mississippi, to volunteer her services
as the interim WMU staff for New York. Together with Bernice Elliott's
continued visits, they built the New York WMU.[27] Fling returned to WMU
Executive Board meetings, but without vote. In 1969 WMU, SBC, modified its bylaws to match the SBC's recognition of new states. As of 1986
the New York convention had not yet grown to the 25,000 members

required for voting representation on the Board.

Paul James, meanwhile, had served as director of missions for the Metropolitan New York Baptist Association from 1964 to 1969. He became the first executive secretary-treasurer of the New York state convention. As he and Ava lived in Syracuse, where offices were established, he would look out each day at the Holiday Inn where WMU had been constituted. The sight reminded him that the fledgling state convention would succeed, because WMU was behind it.[28] The Jameses retired in 1975. In 1984, the New York convention named their state missions offering in honor of Paul and Ava James.

The New York story was repeated in Utah-Idaho, founded in 1964 by Arizona; the Northern Plains (Montana, Wyoming, and Dakotas), an outgrowth of Colorado, in 1967; Wyoming as a separate convention in 1983; Pennsylvania-South Jersey, developed by Ohio and Maryland, in 1970; Nevada, fostered by Arizona and California, in 1978; New England, aided by Maryland and New York until its formation, in 1983; and Minnesota-Wisconsin, sponsored by Texas and established in 1983. In each of these, formation of a separate statewide or areawide convention and WMU was preceded by several years of "fellowship" status. Iowa WMU; under direction of Missouri, in 1986 had the status of a fellowship group, anticipating state status within a few months.

Even after a new state WMU was organized it continued to receive aid from the mother and sister states. In 1972 the north central state conventions asked WMU and SBC agencies for concentrated assistance. The goal was to double Southern Baptist work by 1990. WMU, SBC, was the first SBC entity to respond with a plan for WMU leadership development and with a $25,000 grant was the first to contribute funds.[29] WMU's innovation for North Central Mission Thrust was to suggest partnerships between old, established states and north central states. Prayer partners, "share the leader" projects, and mission action training were suggested. In 1977-78 and 1980 WMU study plans featured the area.

In the 1980s, 12 of the early state WMU organizations were formally linked to newer areas, as were their state conventions. WMU officers in the well-established states sent teams of leaders, supplies of literature, and occasionally funds to assist their sister states. Formal partnerships were established as follows: Alabama with Wyoming; Arkansas with Indiana; Florida with Pennsylvania-South Jersey; Georgia with New York; Kentucky with Ohio; Louisiana with Nevada; Missouri with Iowa; North Carolina with West Virginia; South Carolina with Puerto Rico; Tennessee with Michigan; Texas with Minnesota-Wisconsin; and Virginia with New England. Mississippi had assisted WMU development in Montana and other states. The mother state of Maryland was still recovering from developing WMUs in ten states.

EASING INTO THE CIRCLE

During the WMU, SBC, presidential administration of Christine Gregory (Mrs. A. Harrison), the young state WMUs not yet qualifying to have a vice-president represent them on the Board were invited for the first time into the confidential executive sessions of the WMU Board. They were informally given the privilege of expressing their wishes on votes. Gregory and Carolyn Weatherford, WMU executive director, sought the advice of Porter Routh, executive secretary-treasurer of the SBC Executive Committee. He reminded them that WMU was free to set its own requirements for state recognition, but that perhaps relationships would be smoother within a new state if the WMU representative were treated similarly to other state leaders. Gregory decided not to pursue a bylaw change for WMU representation.[30]

Instead, the state WMU officers not qualifying for representation were given every involvement short of voting. Additionally, WMU, SBC, began to invite the officers of fellowship groups not yet constituted as state convention WMUs to attend Board meetings. Thus WMU repeatedly demonstrated its missions attitude toward the new members of the SBC family, bringing WMU into national leadership before other elements of the SBC did. In 1986 and 1987, the SBC relaxed its requirements for representation. WMU followed its lead and prepared to accept as vice-presidents those elected from states with more than 15,000 members. Thus Alaska, Nevada, New England, New York, Pennsylvania-South Jersey, and Utah-Idaho will gain votes.

Two state conventions came to the WMU circle by unusual circumstances. Hawaii WMU had been formed in 1944 under the Foreign Mission Board's ministries on the islands. When Hawaii achieved US statehood in 1959, the FMB transferred its interests in Hawaii to the Home Mission Board and to the Hawaii Baptist Convention. WMU featured Sue Saito Nishikawa (Mrs. Nobuo), the WMU executive secretary, at the 1960 Annual Meeting. Although Hawaii has not yet met the numerical requirement for voting representation, its officers participate as any other small state.

Likewise, Alaska WMU was organized in 1949. Once it achieved status as the 49th state of the Union, its officers were welcomed to WMU Board activities without benefit of vote.

WMU has been hard to confine to any set of geographic borders. The European Baptist Convention, consisting of English-language churches in several European countries, has a WMU organization closely akin to the one headquartered in Birmingham, Alabama. Under the leadership of a president and an executive officer who is a missionary of the Foreign Mission Board, the European Baptist Convention WMU follows the WMU, SBC, plans closely and subscribes to the literature from Birmingham.

As early as 1967, Florida WMU was helping develop WMU in Puerto Rico. Carolyn Weatherford, then the WMU director in Florida, was going to Puerto Rico to train leaders. After Weatherford became executive director for WMU, SBC, she welcomed Puerto Rico's first WMU executive director to the Executive Board meetings. Puerto Rico is carried on the list of state WMU organizations not yet qualified for representation on the WMU, SBC, Board.

In 1953, Woman's Missionary Union of the Northwest Baptist Convention began having affiliates in Canada. WMU membership throughout Canada in 1986 was estimated at 790, but no nationwide WMU has been established.

NEW FORCES IN THE FAMILY

The geographic expansion of WMU into all 50 states did more than redraw the map. It also repainted the face of the typical WMU member. The move into Oklahoma at the turn of the century brought Indian women into the organization.

One of the oldest associational-level WMU organizations identified with Woman's Missionary Union is an Indian union.[31] The WMU of the Choctaw-Chickasaw Association in Oklahoma was formed in 1876. A missionary, J. S. Murrow, had attended the Northern Baptist Convention and heard, for the first time, a woman make a public speech. He was so fascinated that he invited her and her husband to visit the Choctaw-Chickasaw associational meeting at Nunny Cha-ha. The guest, Mrs. C. R. Blackall, held a women's meeting, interpreted by Czarina Bond. She told the objectives of a women's mission society in foreign missions work. An Indian woman, Sallie Holston, raised her had to ask a question. "If you are doing so much to help women across the big waters, why do you not send Christian women to teach us here in your own country?" Blackall could not answer, but she organized the Indian women representing several churches into a missionary society, claimed to be the first home missionary society for women. Blackall went back north to stimulate the organization of the Northern Baptist women's home missionary societies.[32]

The Indian women's organization, headed by Holston and Bond, prospered and maintained a continuous existence. Although it was more closely identified with Northern Baptist women than Southern Baptist in its early years, it functions today in full cooperation with WMU. Other Oklahoma Indian tribes formed associational organizations as late as 1926. Annie Armstrong on her visits organized women's groups among the Indians. Along with missions information she taught them how to make food for the Lord's Supper.[33] In 1926, 106 Indian WMU organizations with 800 members were reported.[34]

State WMU organizations have strongly encouraged Indian women. Mississippi, Alabama, Florida, and New Mexico WMUs, among others, have sponsored camps and training sessions for Indians of all ages. For many Indians a language barrier exists. WMU has published no literature in Indian languages, but on a regional basis some leaders have translated certain materials for use in their own locales.

WMU, SBC, did not begin direct promotion of Indian WMU until 1973-74. With help from the Home Mission Board, Indian women were given scholarship aid to attend the WMU national conference at Glorieta, New Mexico. This experience led to development of a network of Indian women trained to lead conferences in WMU operations. As of 1985, Indian churches receiving financial assistance through the Home Mission Board reported 5,172 WMU members of all ages—a 79 percent increase in five years. This figure does not include WMUs in self-supporting Indian churches such as would predominate in the established Indian WMU associations in Oklahoma.

Hispanics.—WMU's involvement with Spanish-speaking persons in the US began in 1888. Mina Everett, who had been forced to give up her foreign missionary career because of ill health, gained appointment as a missionary to minister to the Mexicans in San Antonio, Texas. She raised funds among the women to build the first Baptist house of worship for Hispanics in the US. Simultaneously, Everett served as secretary for Texas Baptist women, and she linked them to concern for the Mexicans.

Mary C. Gambrell (Mrs. James B.) next served as secretary of Texas Baptist women. She concurrently worked as assistant to the secretary of the state mission board, her husband. Gambrell developed strong affection for the Mexican people and for a troop of Mexican missionaries she supervised. To speed their work, she learned Spanish. She battled to achieve social acceptance of Mexicans and schooling for their children. She assisted at the organization of the Texas Mexican Baptist Convention in 1910, but died before its committee on women's work could report the next year.[35] WMU, Auxiliary to the Mexican Baptist Convention of Texas, was formed in 1917.

In 1931, Hattie G. Pierson (Mrs. P. H.), missionary to Texas Hispanics, became the first field worker devoted to Hispanic women's activities. She was followed by a steady stream of women, both Anglo and Hispanic, who translated literature and published it as funds permitted. All this activity was funded by WMU appropriations from the Annie Armstrong Offering.

In 1928 WMU, SBC, gave $500 from its literature revenues to the WMU of Cuba as a memorial to Elia Brower Nimmo (Mrs. W. R.), the first manager of the literature department. Cuba WMU used this money to launch *Nosotras,* a WMU magazine in Spanish. As late as 1938 this magazine was the main item of literature used by Spanish-speaking women in the US.[36]

Translations of *Royal Service* were published in *El Bautista Mexicana*, a paper published by the Mexican Baptist Convention of Texas. Again in 1942 another Texas WMU officer, Olivia Davis, mastered Spanish in order to speak at the Mexican WMU meetings and keep the women in touch with English language WMU methods.

Finally, in February 1955, the first USA-based WMU magazine in Spanish, a condensed translation of *Royal Service*, was published under the name *Nuestra Tarea*. Esther B. Moye (Mrs. J. L.) was the first editor, followed by Martha Thomas Ellis, who was then followed by Doris Diaz, all Home Mission Board workers. The magazine was used throughout the Southwest.

In 1954 the Executive Board of WMU, SBC, invited the officers of the Hispanic WMU organizations to attend its meetings. The Spanish-language organizations of Texas, New Mexico, and Arizona had routinely reported in the WMU, SBC, Annual Report for a decade. The national WMU office thus helped keep the top Hispanic WMU leaders informed of organizational methods. Also the Birmingham WMU office dispatched early drafts of publications to the staff of *Nuestra Tarea* to enable the translations to be made in time for publication. A field worker with the Texas churches believed that the Texas-Mexican WMU adhered much more strongly to the Anglo WMU pattern than they did to Anglo models in other church activities.[37]

Alma Hunt and Arthur B. Rutledge, Home Mission Board executive secretary, agreed in 1971 for WMU, SBC, to begin coordinating ethnic WMUs. On January 1, 1972, Doris Diaz, editor of *Nuestra Tarea*, moved to the Birmingham office of WMU with her assistant and the entire portfolio of Spanish WMU management. From that date, the Home Mission Board funded and WMU directed the expansion of ethnic WMU work.

In 1969 Alma Hunt worked with HMB staff to arrange the first conference for Spanish-speaking women at Glorieta. For this occasion, two outstanding WMU officers of Mexico came to return their expertise to the land of its origin. They were Olivia S. D. de Lerin and Ana Maria Swenson. Ethnic leadership training became a standard item on WMU meeting agendas as Indians and other internationals found conference opportunities at Glorieta.

Other Ethnic Groups.—While WMU, SBC, was still aborning, its leaders were conscious of the growing ethnic population in the country. Under leadership of Lula Whilden, pioneer single woman missionary who was furloughing from China in Baltimore, several WMU founders were involved in a permanent ministry to the Chinese. This innovation in 1886 was matched in Augusta, Georgia, by the Woman's Missionary

Society of the First Baptist Church, headed by Mary Emily Wright, a future secretary of WMU.

One of the first projects of WMU, SBC, was to appoint a committee on foreign population, which functioned for 20 years. The committee's function was vague, perhaps little more than consciousness-building. In some cases WMU negotiated with the Home Mission Board for appointment of missionaries to ethnic groups (see chap. 7). Most of the Home Mission Board's initial ministries to language-culture groups were connected in some way to Woman's Missionary Union.

Concern for ethnics fell under the umbrella of personal service, a formalized phase of work instituted by WMU in 1909. The chairman, Lulie P. Wharton (Mrs. H. M.), attended nationwide conferences on immigration and stayed current on enlightened responses to the needs of immigrants.[38]

WMU's long years of missions investment in ethnic women resulted in their being harvested into the organization. This turn became clear in 1961 as Bernice Elliott began traveling the new SBC areas as the joint staff member of WMU and the Home Mission Board. On one West Coast trip in 1962 she spoke in 38 different language churches.[39]

Doris Diaz turned over much of the Spanish editing to an assistant in order to cultivate WMU contacts with other ethnic groups. Among her contacts in 1975 were Polish, Romanian, and Assyrian women. To multiply her outreach, she invited key Spanish WMU leaders to Birmingham in 1979 for intensive training. The next year, leading women of a half dozen different ethnic groups visited Birmingham for training.

WMU expanded its languages in 1980 with the first leaflets in Chinese, Japanese, Korean, Romanian, and simplified English published by Southern Baptists for use in the US. The first piece was a biographical sketch of Lottie Moon; the second was a sketch of Annie Armstrong. Next came leaflets in various languages on how to organize and maintain a WMU organization. In December 1982 WMU launched a new periodical in simplified English, a short edition of WMU periodicals used by the deaf. The new magazine was called *Our Missions World*. By 1986 its circulation had grown to 1,000. In the 1986 inventory of WMU products, more than 40 different books, pamphlets, and other literature were published in Spanish.

The ethnic presence in WMU grew so rapidly that fellowship events were staged at the 1984, 1985, and 1986 national WMU Annual Meetings. In this same period WMU, SBC, recommended that each associational WMU elect a language WMU director to encourage organizations for women and girls who prefer to work in a language other than English.

Ethnic WMU organizations appear to be growing at a faster rate than Anglo organizations. The only ethnic statistics kept are those of churches which receive financial aid of the Home Mission Board. In these 52,926 WMU members were reported in 1985, or 4.5 percent of the total WMU membership. The ethnic membership had grown 96 percent in five years, while overall membership had grown 6.2 percent. Asian WMU membership grew 393 percent in these years.

The ethnic diversity of WMU can be seen slightly in the WMU Executive Board. The first ethnic state president was Grace Peña Salazar (Mrs. Augustine), who was vice-president from California in 1979-81. Before her marriage, Salazar had worked in Birmingham as editorial assistant on *Nuestra Tarea*. The first foreign born ethnic on the national WMU Board was elected as vice-president from Ohio, beginning 1982. She was Akiko Naito Wolford (Mrs. James), who had come to this country as a serviceman's bride from Japan. WMU members befriended her, led her to profess Christianity, and promoted her through the ranks to the presidency of Ohio WMU. As her personal missions project she has taught English to Laotians, Vietnamese, and Mongolian people and constantly ministers to newly arrived Japanese nationals.

Blacks.—Only one group was restricted to the outskirts of WMU membership for most of the century. This group was black women, the daughters of the servants who had tended the home fires for the white founders of WMU. WMU women viewed black Americans as their missions field and obligation, never as prospective members, until the 1960s. (See full discussion of WMU and the race issue in chap. 10.)

Blacks came into WMU not through ministry, but through the geographic expansion of the organization. In the West and North, blacks were welcomed into organizations. Through these enrollment points, black women showed up at national conferences and conventions, and Deep South women gradually accepted them.

When WMU spread further geographically, it embraced some significant changes in cultural makeup. A WMU group organized in LeFrak City in New York City in 1975 consisted of women from Ceylon, Cuba, Haiti, Congo, Brazil, Panama, Hong Kong, Taiwan, and the USA.[40]

One veteran WMU pioneer, Becie Kirkwood (Mrs. A. L.), executive secretary of WMU in Ohio, observed that the new areas contributed these new thoughts to the WMU culture: racial openness; respect for Yankees, who were not traditionally beloved in the South; ability to evangelize all kinds of people; greater respect and visibility for WMU; salaries for WMU staff equal to male peers; wider roles for women in starting and leading churches; effectiveness in the urban environment.[41]

Urbanites and Country Women.—Along with geographic, socio-economic, and ethnic change in WMU came a change in residence. Early leaders were keenly influenced by urbanization. The Baltimore women who first led WMU had a city mind-set. Likewise, the early state WMUs were operated by committees in the major cities: Raleigh, Atlanta, Birmingham, Nashville, Jackson, New Orleans, Dallas, Richmond,

Little Rock, Louisville, and St. Louis. Only South Carolina remained in the hands of a tiny antebellum village, Society Hill. Yet the vast majority of Southern Baptists and their churches were in rural areas.

The rural-urban conflict changed the structure of WMU. Between 1895 and 1913, the rural ranks of WMU rose up. They reorganized the state WMUs to be representative of all the state, not just the city of the central committee. This approach was more feasible when transportation and funds were made available for the officers' travel.

Early WMU leaders recognized that most women's societies were in country churches with small amounts of cash available. Although some country churches were wealthy, most were poor. The only state not characterized by this reality was Maryland. Fannie Heck stated that the country churches were harder to reach than city churches and could seldom be inspired to give for special causes.[42]

City-side WMU officers realized in 1913 that they needed to concentrate on the missing rural links in the Union. Heck appointed a Commission on Rural Efficiency. It reported in 1914 that two-thirds of Southern Baptist churches were in the country, and only one-eighth of them had missionary societies. Clearly WMU was an urban phenomenon at that point. The Rural Commission listed hindrances to development of WMU in the country: loosely arranged, irregular church activities; bad roads; ignorance; antimissionary pastors and husbands; lack of servants; lack of transportation; reluctance of women to lead in prayer or program. To relieve the situation, the commission decided to recommend active officers at the district and associational level. These women would work more closely with the country churches, while state officers arranged for free literature, prayer support, and mail contacts with the churches. Unfortunately, fewer than two-thirds of the associations had associational officers and regular meetings.[43]

By contrast, the Commission on Urban Efficiency found that city churches had functioning women's societies ready for more sophisticated organization. Committees, multiple organizational units, special studies, elaborate personal service projects, and home departments were prescribed. Externally, societies were encouraged to form city-wide unions and interdenominational women's leagues.[44]

The decision to move the Conventionwide WMU headquarters from Baltimore to Birmingham might have been motivated by rural-urban struggles as much as by East-West tension (see chap. 2). The new home base of Birmingham was considered a boom town in 1921, but it was surrounded by the rural South.

By 1926, 64 percent of WMU organizations were in rural churches. Still more than half the rural churches had no WMU, nor did those churches have Sunday Schools. In 1925 and 1926, the Sunday School Board offered to match money spent by the state WMU organizations in employing women to organize women's societies in rural churches. In the first year 691 rural societies were organized and 295 revived.[45]

WMU's main response to the urbanization of the South was to establish points of personal service ministry in conjunction with mills and industries (see chap. 9). The leaders recognized that many workers moving in from the country were Baptists. These were frequently organized into women's and children's missions groups by WMU or their sponsored missionaries, and new churches resulted. Personal service approaches suggested for rural churches were different from those for small-town or urban settings.

Throughout its first century of service, Woman's Missionary Union grappled with a wide variance in sizes of churches and their WMU organizations. In the 1960s all the church program leaders felt strong pressure from the new areas of the Convention to offer a one-program simplified church organization form. WMU refused to participate, on the basis that WMUs had functioned well for years in small churches, rural and urban, without significant modifications of the suggested program. The women believed that every church, no matter how small, would function better with a full WMU program and that the women and children of every congregation needed their own weekday activities.

Several attempts at distilling the WMU program to be more easily grasped by small churches came to a head late in 1980. Six state WMU officers with expertise in working with small churches came to Birmingham. In a weekend lockup, they wrote a manual for WMU in churches with fewer than 150 members. It presented not so much a simplified program as a simple explanation of the program already known to be workable.

WMU faced a new urbanization question in 1973. A team of SBC agency staff studied Metropolitan Churches in Crisis, those whose original membership base moved to the suburbs. The agencies tried to plan a way to help such churches pour out ministry to a declining or rapidly changing neighborhood. WMU's response was to publish literature for teaching the Bible to children with no previous church background. The studies would be taught by WMU members and others in a weekday Big A Club (see chap. 9). WMU was among 11 SBC entities to sponsor the Center for Urban Church Studies from 1981-1986. The center conducted urban studies and research projects.

THE STATISTICAL STORY

Gains in territory and ethnic mix have been offset by other factors which pulled WMU membership down in the late 1960s. Without WMU's efforts to embrace new groupings, the enrollment decline might have been more severe than it was. WMU has always been a minority organization. WMU leaders have sometimes estimated that 65 percent of total church members are females. A recent study estimated female membership at 57 percent. Yet WMU never enrolled more than 15 percent of the total membership at one time. Still WMU had at times been a fast-growing body. Between 1891 and 1931 its membership grew 1,579 percent, while Sunday School (also a newly promoted activity) increased only 476 percent. Growth of WMU resulted when a tightly knit organization was perfected in the states and in each association. Growth also resulted from a full-scale campaign to enlist members. Enlistment Days in 1907, 1908, and 1909 resulted in a 26 percent increase in the number of organizations.

Not until 1929 did enrollment pass the half million mark. Not until 1950 did WMU pass 1 million members. The organization has provided for all ages, yet its enrollment was more than 50 percent adult until the mid-1960s. Then children became the majority members. This fact probably indicates the most hard-hitting strike against WMU enrollment: women flocking into the workplace. Prior to this time, WMU statistics had declined only during the world wars and the Great Depression. WMU reached its peak enrollment in 1963-64. It had been pushed to a peak by the enlistment goals of the WMU 75th anniversary celebration. That same year has come to be recognized as the dawn of the contemporary woman's liberation movement.

The more women took employment outside the home, the more WMU statistics declined, especially for adults. WMU reacted with major program adjustments to fit the schedules of modern women and children. Falling statistics were halted in 1974 by an enlistment drive called Giant Step, begun in 1972. After 1974 the enrollment remained stable.

The rate of Sunday School growth outstripped WMU's growth in the latter part of WMU's first century. Almost every church came to have a Sunday School. Yet a significant number of churches continued to report no form of WMU work. More than half the churches reported WMU shortly before World War II. Then the figure declined. After the war the majority again reported WMU and the percentage grew to a high of 73 percent during the early 1960s. The establishment of new churches outstripped the establishment of WMU. This might have been due to the number of small, struggling churches in the states newly entered by Southern Baptists.

WMU, SBC, and the state WMUs joined hands to reverse the trend in 1980. The National Enlargement Plan, nicknamed New WMU, was an effort to make personal contact with a key woman and the pastor in every church not reporting WMU. The campaign enlisted a corps of volunteer STARTEAM members who visited the churches. When the National Enlargement Plan ended in 1983, 3,133 churches had initiated

WMU activities. Enrollment showed a corresponding growth.

The changing characteristics of WMU's leading women were pictured in the election of the national president who served 1981-86. Dorothy Elliott Sample (Mrs. Richard) of Flint, Michigan, was the first president from outside WMU's original states. A PhD, ThD, psychologist, teacher, and lecturer, she typified the growing proportion of WMU members pursuing careers. As a mother, and as the wife of a pastor, she also represented WMU's traditional members.

DAUGHTERS OF MANY LANDS

WMU, SBC, has not tried to keep statistical tabs on or maintain formal ties with its descendants in foreign countries. But the emotional bonds with these groups of women are strong.

When WMU became a young woman celebrating her 25th anniversary, she began to acknowledge her daughters. The WMU hymn adopted in 1913 sang of "sisters of many lands." Women of Cuba, Brazil, Nigeria, and China sent greetings to the organization they acknowledged as their mother in the faith.

Women missionaries in attendance at the 1913 meeting offered a resolution asking WMU, SBC, to take note of women's work on foreign fields. From that day forward Woman's Missionary Union has taken a proprietary interest in seeing WMU established abroad. From 1913 through 1953 greetings or reports from foreign WMU organizations were forwarded for inclusion in the WMU Annual Report. In 1953, women's work was proliferating because of the departure of missionaries from China into other countries. Embryonic women's work was reported from Thailand, Malaya, Panama, Taiwan, Jordan, Israel, Ghana, and Rhodesia (now Zimbabwe). Because most of these countries did not have formalized organizations and collection of reports was difficult, the reports were dropped from WMU's Annual Report.

The oldest WMU abroad was formed in Brazil in 1908. Next came Cuba, in 1913, when Charlotte R. Peelman (Mrs. H. C.), executive secretary of Florida WMU, sailed across to assist in its organization. Nigeria WMU and Mexico WMU were fully organized in 1919. Japan followed with complete organization in 1920. Chile and Hungary were added in 1923; Romania in 1928. Uruguay (along with Paraguay and part of Argentina) reported organization in 1930, Italy in 1933, Yugoslavia in 1934. And so on the organizations have followed as missionary effort has matured.

According to a survey in 1986, 58 countries related to Southern Baptist missions have women organized nationwide. Of these, 47 were fostered originally by missionaries and follow the WMU, SBC, plan. The traditional WMU emblem is the model for 38 organizations, and the

Laborers Together with God watchword is used by 39. Such familiar program features as weeks of prayers and special missions offerings are followed by more than 40 countries. The pattern of children's and youth organizations has been duplicated (with modifications) in 36 countries.

Fifteen of the foreign WMU organizations have permanent offices or headquarters. Twenty publish literature. Seven own or operate campgrounds. Seven operate social work centers. Three own training schools or seminaries for women.

Some of the organizations, such as Japan, are self-supporting; others are funded in part by their members, plus aid from Southern Baptist Foreign Mission Board allocations or from the local convention budget.

The name Woman's Missionary Union or a roughly equivalent translation is used in many countries, but not all. The Foreign Mission Board has not stressed any particular form of organization, but it has encouraged the development of women as a strategy in developing Christians, churches, and missions concepts. In some countries the women's groups have appointed missionaries. Korea, for example, appointed the first missionaries known among Korean Baptists.

In 1975 Alma Hunt, retired executive secretary of WMU, SBC, began assisting the Foreign Mission Board as special consultant for women's work, traveling to 44 countries in three years. At her own insistence, she did not push the WMU, SBC, plan of organization on a country, but simply shared ideas about approaches workable in various countries. She found great emphasis on evangelism, Bible study, prayer, and—as the common thread—missions, at least in a beginning form.[46]

Alma Hunt and Marie Wiley Mathis (Mrs. R. L.) had stimulated the formation of Taiwan WMU in 1960 (organization followed their visit in 1959). Mathis was driven up and down Highway 1 in Vietnam in 1973 under fire in order to encourage the women to organize. Carolyn Weatherford was present for the organization of WMU of Togo and Barbados.

In 1985 the enrollment of WMU-type organizations abroad was 425,000.[47] Almost one-third of all Baptists affiliated with Southern Baptist missions abroad were members of these organizations.

Beginning in 1945 (as a result of the work of the Survey Committee) WMU invited the women missionaries who are involved in leading WMU in their fields of service to meet with the WMU, SBC, Executive Board during their times of furlough. Through the years, WMU has made the funding of foreign WMUs a priority in the Lottie Moon Christmas Offering allocations. The Mrs. W. J. Cox Fund, established in 1933 to honor the outgoing president of WMU, has been the means of funding WMU development in most countries entered since that time. The Fannie E. S. Heck Fund, another department of Lottie Moon Christmas Offering allocations, has given special attention to women's training schools abroad. Other allocations are made for WMU literature work, which in several countries has become self-supporting.

SISTERS OF MANY LANDS

Daughters seem more as sisters when WMU meets its counterpart organizations as peers through the Baptist World Alliance Women's Department. In the absence of any other form of ecumenical contact, WMU has put the attentions of its best leaders in the development of this fellowship.

At the first meeting of the BWA in 1904, no WMU officers made the trip to London. The only American woman taking prominent part was Nannie Helen Burroughs, the magnetic young woman Annie Armstrong had been coaching as secretary of the Woman's Convention of the National Baptist Convention.

The next BWA Congress was in Philadelphia. Edith Campbell Crane was one of the organizers of a women's meeting. Fannie E. S. Heck was a speaker. Confronted for the first time with an array of sisters from many lands, she confessed: "We have not realized you. Self-satisfied with our great numbers, our prosperity, our wealth, we have said that in America resided four-fifths of the Baptists of the world and were content. . . . Perhaps you did not realize us." She immediately put her finger on the nerve cord that has tied women psychologically through the BWA: the heroism of women who are Baptists in the face of difficulties not imaginable in the United States. "Your faith sets before us in the living reality of today new possibility of service in our own lives."[48]

Edith Crane was elected corresponding secretary of a committee formed to maintain contact among the women until the next congress. After Crane's resignation from WMU, SBC, Kathleen Mallory carried out this responsibility until World War I interrupted. The 1923 congress in Stockholm had women's meetings led by Minnie Kennedy James (Mrs. W. C.). Northern Baptist women noted that the men hovered to see whether the meeting was being properly conducted, but found their assistance unnecessary in the face of James's presiding.

At the next congress in Toronto in 1928, the women dissolved their committee because two women were named to the BWA Executive Committee. One of those first women was Ethlene Boone Cox (Mrs. W. J.). At the 1934 congress in Berlin, the women again convened, under the gavel of Laura M. Armstrong (Mrs. F. W.). Feeling too submerged in a male-dominated organization, the women revived their own international committee when the BWA met in Atlanta in 1939. That year Ethlene Cox addressed the entire BWA in an open-air assembly.

Wartime shattered the women's committee, and the pieces fell into the hands of Olive B. Martin (Mrs. George R.). She was asked to preside over a women's meeting during the 1947 Congress in Copenhagen, and she took along Blanche Sydnor White to assist. White was not pleased with the general tenor of the BWA and believed (as usual for her) that the women could excel in emphasizing unity and faith in a meeting. Olive Martin, Mrs. Ernest Brown of England, and Marion Bates (Mrs. J. Edgar) of Canada were named to the BWA women's committee. Bates and Martin chatted with Blanche White as they sailed home. White had only one pair of tattered stockings left, having given all her good ones to European women who were still unable to get them following the war.

Bates later credited White for dreaming of the Women's Department that would arise. White tapped funds from Virginia's contributions to the Lottie Moon Christmas Offering and equipped Martin to organize all the Baptist women of the world. Martin and White went back to Europe in 1948 and secured the appointment of a new BWA women's committee. This was the foundation of the Women's Department. On the spot Martin participated with the European women in forming a European Baptist Women's Union, the first in a string of continental unions she organized. Martin's key European contact was a Southern Baptist missionary in Italy, Alice Moore (Mrs. Dewey). In 1951 the second continental union, the North American Baptist Women's Union, was formed. The WMU executive head served on its executive committee from the beginning.[49]

Martin served as president (or chairman) of the Women's Department through its 1960 meeting. She was succeeded by Marion Bates, who served until 1970. Marie Mathis succeeded her and served until 1980, when Kerstin Ruden (Mrs. Erik) of Sweden became president. Edna Lee de Gutierrez (Mrs. Rolando) of Mexico became president in 1985.

The main source of funds and fellowship for the Women's Department and its continental unions has been the Baptist Women's Day of Prayer and the offering taken on that day. This event was begun in 1948 as a means of reconciliation among European Baptist women and the Women's Department made it a worldwide idea in 1950. At first the day was scheduled during the Week of Prayer for Foreign Missions so that WMU could combine the two events. Beginning in 1963 the Day of Prayer was moved to the first Monday in November, where it could have its own identity.

At the beginning the offering was not sufficient for all expenses, for the Women's Department never received any financial support from the BWA as a whole. The Lottie Moon Christmas Offering began carrying allocations for the work, including expenses of the European women's union, in 1949. When Marion Bates was elected the first president of North American Baptist Women's Union, she went home to work with an empty treasury. The next day her mail contained a check for $1,000 from Virginia WMU, with no strings attached, for her to use in launching continental communications among Baptist women.[50] From the origin of the North American Women's Union in 1951 through 1967, the Annie Armstrong Offering allocated funds to support it.

Additionally, WMU from its operating budget has provided between $1,500 and $15,000 per year for BWA women's activities. In recent years, with the BWA women raising more of their own support through the Day of Prayer, WMU's direct contribution has been $2,500 per year.[51]

WMU representatives were involved in providing staff work to the Women's Department before it established its own office in 1982 in connection with the BWA offices. Similarly, for 15 years the WMU office in Birmingham assisted the North American Baptist Women's Union with publications and promotion.

Mildred Dodson McMurry (Mrs. William) was elected president of the North American Baptist Women's Union in 1962. At her death in 1965, Alma Hunt assumed her responsibilities and presided over the continental assembly in 1967. Several WMU staff members have worked on the Baptist World Youth Committee, including Beverly Sutton who was program chairman for the 1984 Youth Conference at Buenos Aires.

WMU, SBC, officers took to heart the 1977 reminder issued them by Ralph Winter, missiologist from Fuller Theological Seminary. He recommended that one of the fastest ways to spread the gospel is to organize women to send missionaries over the border of the nearest country. Remembering this, WMU set a priority for the post-1988 era to take more initiative in fostering women's work abroad. The WMU Second Century Fund, which will be built as a permanent memorial to the Centennial celebration, will give special assistance to women's organizations in developing Baptist areas in the United States and around the world.

WMU began planning in 1984 to start its second century with a growing home base of membership. VISION 88 is a three-year enlargement campaign reaching for 2 million members in the United States by 1988.

Think what has been accomplished by our minority in past years; think what could be accomplished if we should enlist the majority!

Alma Hunt, 1952 Annual Report

4
Laborers together

*Our watchword is Union—not so much union with each
other but union with Christ.*

Fannie E. S. Heck, 1899

HAT ARE your marching orders?" Annie Armstrong
asked the delegates to the 1888 meeting of Woman's
Missionary Union.[1]

The answer was not stated in the minutes, but it was
probably the snippet of the Scriptures by which Armstrong lived her life. "Go Forward!"[2] This was God's
command to the children of Israel as they cowered on the edge of the
Red Sea. The women heard it too, through Annie Armstrong, and took
courage to organize Woman's Missionary Union. The seas of opposition
parted and the women walked through.

In the first meeting of the Executive Committee, June 9, 1888, President Martha McIntosh led the group to select a motto. Go Forward was
the first choice. Thus began the unfailing custom of Woman's Missionary Union to wrap its work in God's Word. On that same day the women
chose another verse appropriate for the first year of joined hands. From
Hebrews 10:24 they took "Let us consider one another to provoke unto
love and to good works."

Quietly, without any official action, WMU drifted into the piece of
the Scriptures which would become the permanent watchword. Women
were urged to remember that they were "laborers together with God."[3]
Annie Armstrong's New Year's greeting card for 1904 bore the message
"We are laborers together with God."[4] In Fannie E. S. Heck's 1910
address she referred to this verse from 1 Corinthians 3:9 as a motto
selected long ago.

Interestingly, the women at first did not choose mottoes from the
familiar missions commissions of the Bible. Instead they clung to operational verses. Surrounded by critics who insisted that women had
no part in building God's kingdom, and accused of heresy for organizing,
they were courageous indeed to claim to be laborers together with
God.

When the Union came to its 25th anniversary, the women felt the need of a permanent emblem. Emma Whitfield, a noted artist and historian of Richmond, Virginia, whose mother had presided at the 1888 meeting, designed the emblem. She took the shape of the fish head, early sign of trust among Christians, and doubled it. Inside she pictured the open Bible, the torch of God's spirit, and the world. On the Bible were the words, "Laborers Together with God, 1 Cor. 3:9." The adoption of this emblem made the watchword permanent and official.

For 1907 and 1908, Fannie Heck suggested themes of Larger Things and Higher Things. These themes unified the Union as it took on many new ventures. From then on, a different Bible verse was chosen annually to highlight the current emphasis of the Union.

For the 25th anniversary celebration, Heck wrote "The Woman's Hymn." It was adopted as the permanent song of the organization. In that same year the women chose their first hymn of the year. It was "Joy to the World," an appropriate choice for a year of celebration. The women had shown from the beginning their love of singing. "Jesus Shall Reign" was the opening song of the first Annual Meeting in 1889 and was frequently the annual choice throughout the century. Through the Scriptures and song the women hid God's message in their hearts and spread it on their plan. In the spirit of their 1 Corinthians watchword, they considered themselves master builders, each adding to the firm structure laid by one before her. The women creatively took the materials at hand and built a many-storied organization.

A UNION OF ORGANIZATIONS FOR ALL AGES

Woman's Missionary Union, Auxiliary to Southern Baptist Convention, began as a union of state organizations, which in turn were unions of women's societies. The term *Woman's Missionary Union* was not often used within the church until after age-graded organizations were introduced. Then WMU came to mean a union of all ages. From the first day of organization, WMU considered both women and children to be members. Woman's Missionary Societies were suggested for adults; bands were suggested for everybody else. The central tower of Woman's Missionary Union structure was until 1970 the Woman's Missionary Society. This organization was suggested for every church, complete with constitution, bylaws, officers, regular meetings, reports to the WMU officers, and a program of work.

Women of the missionary societies took 25 years to build their union of age-graded organizations. Martha McIntosh in her first presidential address admitted that the children's bands had been neglected in the rush to get WMU into running order. "We could only make the beginning in this line of work," she said.[5] The first steps were a booklet on how to conduct bands entitled *Garnered Gleanings*, and a leaflet introduced at the first Annual Meeting by Alice Armstrong, "Our Duty to Young People."

Woman's Missionary Union continued as primarily a women's organization long after the age-graded system was in place. In 1912, Fannie Heck took a strategic look at the future and urged the women to make greater effort to organize the children. She showed the women a picture of a huge house perched on a tiny foundation. This was the way 6,914 women's organizations looked on top of a slender stack of 5,000 children's organizations of assorted ages. One woman in the audience who was deeply impressed by the chart, drew it in her diary and remarked, "This house we are building is three times as large as its base. It will topple if not braced with more materials."[6]

By 1918, with many of its children lost in World War I, WMU began in earnest to promote "fully graded WMUs." They took stock of how many churches had at least one unit of each age-level organization. Less than 1 percent of the churches did. So the push was on. The women's societies were made responsible for fostering the children's groups. In 1925, Minnie Kennedy James (Mrs. W. C.) announced that the future was secure: young people's organizations outnumbered the adult groups. Not until after World War II did a significant number of churches report fully graded unions. In 1952 the percentage was 15. Fully graded Woman's Missionary Unions have not been counted in several years. A basic requirement for a top-rated WMU is that it have an organization in each level for which there are prospects.

EFFICIENCY

WMU approached its second 25 years with the battle cry of "Efficiency."[7] Southern Baptists had for the first time shown enthusiasm for organized activities in the church. Leaders sought growth through division into new units of operation. They sought efficiency through standardization. The Sunday School Board in Nashville joined WMU in the efficiency craze. Church organizations became big business and WMU leaders were proud to be good managers.

Woman's Missionary Union was on the efficiency bandwagon as early as 1911, when a Standard of Excellence was adopted.[8] The standard applied only to the Woman's Missionary Societies at first. It called for monthly meetings with devotional exercises and a definite missions program, an increase in membership, a 16 percent increase in contributions, quarterly reports rendered to the state officers, use of the calendar of prayer, a class in mission study, and two-thirds of the members in average attendance. It was a strict standard. By 1913 every age-level organization had its own Standard of Excellence, and in 1914, 16 percent of the organizations merited commendation for their progress. Only 2 percent fully met the standard.

The Standards of Excellence went through regular face-liftings. In 1956-57 they were renamed Aims for Advancement, the requirements being based on the chief aims of the organization. The Aims for Advancement allowed more flexibility than Standards of Excellence. Still, in the first year only 11 churches merited the top honor award. In 1968 the standards became Achievement Guides.The achievement guides were easier to master. By 1986, 6 percent of church WMUs (fully graded) were receiving Distinguished (the top) recognition.[9]

Throughout the remainder of the 1910-20 decade efficiency commissions surveyed methods and gained endorsement of them at WMU Annual Meetings. WMU's ideas of efficiency did not always agree with the ideas of men, notably pastors and seminary professors. The women were accustomed to making do in whatever circumstances they found themselves. Well into WMU's second quarter century, missions was still not a popular cause with pastors, or with many women for that matter, so WMU's approach was very flexible.

Many churches continued to have women's societies that were dedicated to causes other than home and foreign missions. They might be doing local missions work, or benevolence as it was often called. They might be raising money for Baptist orphanages, hospitals, and colleges. They were still building and decorating their church buildings and pastors' homes. They enjoyed getting together for social occasions and for sewing. Sometimes missionary societies of WMU competed intensely with these "aid" or "industrial" societies. Sometimes the same women belonged to several groups. WMU reached a peace with the groups in the early part of the century. Rather than head-on war against them, WMU preferred to take them over by slow persuasion. In the meantime, WMU recognized that many nonmissions societies did send occasional contributions through the WMU offerings and did support causes WMU favored.[10]

When Martha McIntosh, first president of WMU, married T. P. Bell and moved to Atlanta, she found herself starting on the bottom rung of WMU activity. The Bells joined Capitol Avenue Baptist Church, which had no missionary society, only a woman's auxiliary doing aid work. The women knew something of Martha Bell's importance as a leader, so they offered her the presidency of the group. She politely declined, but she offered to present a missions feature at each meeting. Those features got WMU, foreign missions, and home missions on the women's agenda. At first, few gave money to these causes. Bell introduced the women to the Lottie Moon Christmas Offering for Foreign Missions and the Week of Prayer and Self-denial for Home Missions. She took them to WMU Annual Meetings for the state and the association. In a few years they were a missionary society, with no feelings hurt.[11]

Men seemed to be impatient with WMU's silent strategy. They looked on the multiplicity of women's groups as confusing and threatening.[12] One point of contention seemed to be the women's groups status within the church. Woman's Missionary Union at the convention level was auxiliary to the Southern Baptist Convention—meaning not controlled by the Convention (see chap. 12). But in the local congregation, WMU was not to be an auxiliary. WMU never in any publication suggested auxiliary status for the church-level missionary society. Always the suggested constitutions simply said, "Woman's Missionary Union of the _____ Baptist Church." WMU occasionally referred to the young people's and children's organizations as auxiliaries. Their relationship was auxiliary to the women's society which cared for them. In every permissible way WMU considered itself a functioning part of the church.

By contrast, the other kinds of women's organizations often chose the name *Woman's Auxiliary,* and they meant by that an arm's length relationship to the church.

A barrier to efficiency was money. Most churches prior to the mid-1920s had no budget, no routine intake of money, no financial records, and no regular plan for funding activities locally or around the world. WMU did much to regularize church finance (see chap. 5) in its quest to stabilize funds for the Home Mission Board and the Foreign Mission Board. But WMU did little to protect its own financial needs. For these most societies charged dues. Some took up freewill offerings of loose change. Usually the societies simply relied on members to pay their own way—the secretary buying her own postage, the hostess providing the refreshments, the leader of children's activities ordering her own literature and supplies. Each individual woman bought her own subscription to the official WMU magazines.

Women's societies cooperated with the apportionment plan. WMU's original fund-raising strategy was for national officers to set financial goals for the various missions offerings each year. These goals were divided, or apportioned, among the various states according to their proven ability to pay. The states in turn apportioned the amount needed to the church societies. Each woman knew what she had to do to meet the national goal. The system worked. The women had a treasurer who collected the money and delivered it to the source designated by the donor. Similarly, state WMU operations assessed each society for a portion of its own operating expenses.

Efficiency advocates and nervous pastors wanted the church treasurer to handle all such money. WMU had always approved the idea of reporting or sending its contributions via the church treasurer with one stipulation: he must "give credit."[13] That is, the church treasurer must show in his reports that the WMU, down to individual women, gave certain amounts to certain causes. The women had good reason for insisting on recognition. First, they had to know whether they were achieving their goals. They had to report to the state and national organization. And they had to be sure that the treasurer was not re-appropriating their money. They wanted to safeguard the right of WMU to guarantee that missions activities were funded.

So serious was the concern of women in Spartan Association (Spartanburg, South Carolina) in 1921 that they suggested each WMU have a woman elected assistant church treasurer. She would then be sure that women were properly credited and that their quotas were met.[14]

The efficiency and financial issues became a hot topic in 1916 when the manual of church operating methods was to be published. The Sunday School Board enlisted a team of men to write the manual. It was to deal with WMU, but no WMU experts were invited to write. However, all the writers were friends of WMU except the lead author, S. E. Tull. Kathleen Mallory, WMU's executive secretary, appealed to the Sunday School Board to keep Tull from writing anything objectionable to WMU. Mallory and Tull argued intensely about the forms of women's organizations and financial procedures. WMU threatened to haul Tull before the Southern Baptist Convention if he did not rewrite his manuscript. The Sunday School Board tried to negotiate a compromise.[15]

The Church Organization and Methods Manual, published in 1916, ultimately worked to WMU's advantage. WMU did not like it and was prodded to publish its own manual in defense. The controversy surrounding the manual gave WMU the opportunity to take over the other kinds of women's groups. The church manual gave a needed push toward churches having a unified budget, a contributions envelope system, and a central treasurer.

The matter of local WMU finance was by no means settled. Tull vigorously objected to the women "getting credit":

> Such organizations should never have been fund-raising in the first place. Their role is educational. There is no more reason why the women of a church should know or have special credit for what they do as women than for men. . . . In the past this idea may have helped to articulate the work of the women in the church and open to them their possibilities as a class, but the time will doubtless soon come when the women themselves will brush aside these demands.[16]

Tull was far, far ahead of his times. Not until the mid-1950s did WMU stop counting every penny the members gave, though some women wanted to on several pivotal occasions (see chap. 5). Tull was also far from reality when he suggested that WMU be provided for as an expense item in the church budget.

The women were afraid to trust their plans to all-male boards of deacons and finance committees. Not until 1960 did WMU, SBC, suggest that local WMU organizations seek their own funding through the church budget. "Taking offerings [for WMU use] is not looked upon with favor. Passing of the hat can provide an embarrassment, a nuisance, and a contributor to absenteeism," said the authoritative WMU Year Book. The statement suggested that the women had not received church funding because they had not asked. A key issue in this article was the idea that the WMU budget should provide literature for the WMU organizations, just as the church provided literature for Sunday School and other organizations.

The 1960 suggestion about church budgeting for WMU was mildly stated. Not until 1971 did WMU, SBC, wholeheartedly endorse the idea.[17] That year, total circulation of WMU periodicals began to decline and continued to decline for several years. Church funding of WMU has not yet proved adequate or universally popular. As of 1986 probably no more than two-thirds the WMU literature was purchased by churches, the remainder being purchased by individual women.

As local WMU treasurers increasingly took their hands off handling the contributions, two counteractions occurred. The special missions offerings increased, as WMU treated them less as exclusive joys and more as churchwide projects. Second, operating funds disappeared for local WMU projects (such as social work) and state WMU operations (including offices, camps, and WMU-controlled mission projects).

An important factor in the changing financial scene was the unified local church budget and the Cooperative Program for state and national Baptist work. These plans frowned on women sending "nickel funds" to the state WMU office. Locally the women were able to get necessities for their organizations in the time-honored ways. But most state WMUs had to seek significant parts of their funds (if not all) from the Cooperative Program, which was allocated by males. In some states, especially newer state conventions, this in turn led to restraints on the women's freedom to innovate.[18] Even though WMU itself did not benefit from the unified budget, the women ardently promoted it beginning before 1920 as a means of getting a steady stream of support for missions.

WOMAN'S MISSIONARY SOCIETY

The first how-to book on missionary society operations was published in 1888. "Chips from Many Workshops," a small booklet, gave the basics for running a women's organization in that day: a constitution, a section on how to conduct a public meeting, encouragement to speak loudly enough to be heard, encouragement to pray aloud, simple parliamentary procedure, and techniques for fund-raising. Each society improvised from that point on, coping with opposition and opportunity in its own way.

Woman's Missionary Society methods moved toward formality in 1917 when Kathleen Mallory compiled the first major *Manual of WMU Methods*. WMU believed in offering the women several patterns by which to fashion their work—a freedom that has continued to distinguish WMU from other Southern Baptist organizational patterns to this day. But two important rules were laid down.

WMU suggested that all women's organizations of the church be centralized under one Woman's Missionary Society. Thus for all time women and the cause of missions were uniquely linked in Southern Baptist experience. Some churches, to be sure, compromised on another name for a few years. But years later scarcely any women's organization could be found outside the Woman's Missionary Union family of names.[19]

WMU accommodated the aid societies by adopting the circle plan of organization. The WMU manual suggested that the woman's society consist of multiple circles. Those interested in aid or industrial work could form a circle to pursue their interest. Then at least once a month, the entire society would meet together for business and for missions.

Or, circles might be organized according to neighborhood. Each circle was to have a monthly program including prayer for missions. Each would support financially the total missions program of the society. At least once a year it would study a missions book.

The circle plan was WMU's answer to the departmentalization of Sunday Schools. It was a religious answer to the growing woman's study club movement. Women's organizations of the other major denominations were also adopting the circle method. The circles met a social need for the women, and the women ministered to each other's spiritual need.

The absorption of aid societies broadened WMU's viewpoint and function in a church. Their benevolent work coincided with WMU's new social action program of personal service. WMU became more conscious of overall church financial needs and the wisdom of unified giving. However, WMU did not absorb the aid societies' fund-raising techniques. Instead of making and selling, WMU taught sacrificing and tithing. WMU also assumed the responsibility in an unofficial way for "woman's work" of the church—serving suppers, handling social events, beautifying the building. Never did such activities find expression in official WMU documents.

When WMU was debating the circle plan in 1917, Josephine J. Truett

(Mrs. George) proposed that the plan would enable WMU to enroll every woman in the church automatically. She insisted that a united society would be better than the three camps of women then identifiable: aide, missionary, and "nothing."[20]

Businesswomen.—The circle plan enabled WMU to take in the "nothing" women, the businesswomen whose schedules did not permit them to participate in the daytime activities that typified all women's groups. As early as 1914 the Commission on Urban Efficiency of WMU pleaded for a way to involve businesswomen, for thousands of women were moving from country to city to be employed, and women were taking jobs of men away at war.

Business Women's Circles met in the evening. When possible a representative came to the daytime meetings of the Woman's Missionary Society. But the linkage between nighttime organizations and daytime organizations was constantly broken by the businesswomen's lifestyles. Instead, the career women turned to each other. In 1923, Mrs. W. F. Robinson organized businesswomen's circles of several churches into the first Business Woman's Federation. This functioned as an arm of the Ocoee Associational WMU in Chattanooga. An interdenominational BWC also functioned there.[21]

Businesswomen's organizations tended to be independent and they constantly stimulated the main WMU organizations either to accommodate them or to lose them.[22] Nationally WMU accommodated them by issuing a pamphlet, "A Guide to Business Women's Circle" in the late 1930s. *Royal Service* carried regular promotion concerning their work from 1927 to the 1950s.

World War II gave a boost to women working outside the home and incidentally to BWC. One statistician estimated that in 1941, 2,700,000 women in SBC territory were gainfully employed. He thought that only one-ninth of them were Southern Baptist women, or 300,000. At that rate, not more than 6 percent of all Southern Baptists would have been working women.[23] WMU thought their numbers were large enough to merit a tailor-made organization plan. Between 1941, when Georgia WMU organized a Business Woman's Federation, and 1950, almost every state gained a statewide BWC organization.

In 1942 WMU sponsored the first southwide BWC conference at Ridgecrest Baptist Assembly. The women who came, largely state and associational BWC Federation officers, 190 of them, were a mature, determined lot of women. The popularity of their conference paved the way for an annual WMU conference at Ridgecrest. By 1946 perhaps 5 percent of the WMS circles were BWCs, and they were growing at a faster rate than other circles.

But the BWC movement peaked in the mid-1950s, perhaps because the federations tended to concentrate on meet-and-eat-and-give-money banquet functions rather than in-depth study and prayer as did other WMS circles. From the national office, promotion of BWC as a unique arm of WMU was phased into other WMS structures in the mid-1950s.

The Night Meeting.—In 1948 the professional WMU leaders noted a trend toward evening meetings of missionary society members who were not necessarily businesswomen. For four years they discussed this phenomenon. It was undoubtedly spurred by the shortage of servants, live-in relatives, and older siblings in the American household.[24] Throughout the 1950s WMU officers woke up to the need for women's meetings to be scheduled at a variety of times, with nursery provided, if all women were to be reached. Nighttime circles came to be commonplace. The organization was growing fast and steadily shifting to accommodate women who could not, or would not meet in the daytime.

After 1957 the circle meeting became definitely a meeting for mission study. Each circle and each society pursued a balanced diet of study, prayer, giving, and local missions. One of the most important functions of the WMS was to foster the organizations for children and youth. In 1957 Margaret Bruce, who had been the secretary of young people's work for WMU, SBC, became the first full-time specialist in Woman's Missionary Society work.

In 1960 WMS got its own identity separate from WMU in the local church. WMU was defined as a WMS plus one or more youth organizations. The WMU might, if it chose, have a set of general administrative officers totally separate from the WMS. Instead of one WMS, a WMU might have one WMS and its circles meeting in daytime and another separate set of organizations meeting at night.[25]

This move toward complexity and sophistication was offset by a move toward simplicity in 1964. A survey showed that 36.8 percent of the Woman's Missionary Societies had 15 or fewer members. Doubtless many of these were the smaller nighttime organizations. So WMU gave its OK to "societies without circles."[26]

The original concept of circles came full circle in 1965-68. In 1965 WMU launched mission action, with the suggestion that groups might be formed within the WMS for the primary purpose of doing witness and ministry in the community. In a way, the mission action group was the old concept of the benevolence circle.

In 1968 WMS "emotions ran the gamut from excitement to complete rejection,"[27] when WMS was redesigned. In keeping with the latest educational methods which were based on small-group interaction, circles were replaced by groups. A group might choose to concentrate on current missions, mission Bible study, mission action, prayer, or other options. A woman might choose to belong to several groups. Whereas WMS leaders had been accustomed to assigning women to circles, now the members were to make their own choice. Many chose to drop out of what appeared to be a bewildering array of choices. Although the number of WMS organizations did not decline, almost 100,000 members were lost in three years. More changes were ahead.

SUNBEAM BAND

Woman's Missionary Union from day one expected to encourage children's missions bands. Many women had been doing so, and many pastors had. The children's groups varied in name: Little Reapers, Gleaners, Rosebuds, Ivy Bands, but the name and the promoter most successful were the Sunbeam Band, and its leader "Cousin George."

He was George Braxton Taylor, son of early Southern Baptist missionaries to Italy, and nephew of the first secretary of the Foreign Mission Board. As a student pastor, he worked with J. W. M. Williams of Baltimore and preached in Annie Armstrong's church. In every way he was prepared to support missions in cooperation with women. An early pastorate was a substantial country church in Fairmont, Virginia. There he found a children's Sunday School class called the Sunbeams, taught by Anna L. Shepherd Elsom.

"The Mother of Sunbeams," as Elsom would later be called, was said by Taylor to be a cultured, deeply pious, lovely woman of strong character. She was tall, with black hair, good imagination, and good education. She was more than 50 years old. She came to church on horseback through a gap in the mountains. Sometimes she drove a buggy with her elderly mother. Sometimes she walked the two miles with her grown sons.[28]

In a corner of the church, without benefit of little chairs, a dividing curtain, organ, or blackboard, she and her Sunday School class formed the first Sunbeam Band. Taylor located missionary information for them. Elsom taught. This was 1886. By early 1887 George Braxton Taylor, with endorsement of the Foreign Mission Board, was speaking through the denominational papers to children across the South. They were asked to form Sunbeam Bands and to correspond with Cousin George.

The main work of the Sunbeams was to raise money, a purpose readily understood by friends of missions in those days. By 1889 Cousin George was corresponding with 284 Sunbeam Bands from Virginia to Texas, with membership of more than 8,000. During the first year the Sunbeams sent in $1,582; the second year the amount was $2,179. Virginia Sunbeams were supporting a missionary in the field.[29]

An example of Cousin George's influence can be seen in Mississippi. As soon as Alma Ratliff Gray (Mrs. B. D.) of Clinton heard of Sunbeams, she organized the first band in the state. Her own baby was the first enrollee. A pastor's wife, she soon had 50 members of her band and they contributed $25 to missions that year. She organized 30 more bands in the state. Later her husband would become secretary of the Home Mission Board.[30]

Obviously the Sunbeam movement was growing too fast for one man to handle. He had been in touch with the officers of Woman's Missionary Union from their beginning, and they had promised their cooperation.[31] So, with consent of the Foreign Mission Board, Sunbeams became the special task of WMU in 1896. The women thanked Taylor for "fostering this work to its present success." They resolved, "In the inheritance of this legacy, trusting only in God, it is the earnest hope of the Union that the work may fulfill the most cherished wishes of its founder."[32]

State WMUs elected Sunbeam leaders who organized new bands and shared tips on how to conduct them. Eliza Yoer Hyde, longtime Sunbeam promoter in South Carolina, was from a distinguished family that included Henry Allen Tupper. She was a schoolteacher and a city missionary, all the while inspiring the Sunbeams of the state. From 1897 to 1900 she suggested such Sunbeam activities as these: teaching songs, repeating catechistic questions and answers about missions, saying memorized speeches, contributing dues of one or two cents, memorizing Bible verses, hearing stories, reading from a missionary's journal, showing pictures, doing good deeds, filling mite boxes, earning money for missions.

Eliza Hyde especially encouraged the formation of Sunbeam Bands among children who worked as millhands in South Carolina. Often the bands would include as many as 60 children. Sometimes all the members were boys, but usually the bands were coeducational.

One of Hyde's correspondents reported that she usually encouraged her Sunbeams to earn their own money for missions. But as most of them worked early and late in the cotton mill to support parents, she only urged them to deny themselves chewing gum or candy in order to give. She told them stories and taught songs: "Over the ocean wave, far, far away, There the poor heathen live, waiting for the day."[33]

The Sunbeams' money-raising projects were interestingly varied. One of Mary Corbell Gambrell's (Mrs. J. B.) Sunbeam girls earned money trapping rats for her father at 25 cents each. She earned $7.50 before her father reduced the price.[34]

Sunbeams had official colors of gold and white, a pin, a song, mottoes, and a rally cry:

> Sunbeams! Sunbeams!! Sunbeams!!!
> To climb the mountains steep
> To cross the waters deep
> To carry the light
> That makes the world bright
> Sunbeams! Sunbeams!! Sunbeams!!!

As WMU added age-level organizations, the Sunbeam age span shrank to age eight and under. Preschool Sunbeams were separated from school-age children by 1942. Sunbeam Babies were not strongly emphasized until the late 1950s. By 1956 Nursery, Beginner, and Primary units were suggested within the Sunbeam organization.

The curriculum grew more educational and less oriented toward fund-raising. Yet every element of WMU was included: prayer, stewardship, community missions, telling others about Jesus, and study. The first Conventionwide Sunbeam staff specialist was Elsie Rives, employed by WMU, SBC, in 1955.

By the late 1950s WMU leaders feared that eight-year-olds were not gaining enough serious missions experience from Sunbeam Band. They renamed the eight-year-olds World Friends, with a separate emblem and promise: "I will try to be a friend and help others to know Jesus." Despite historic attachment to the name Sunbeams, many wanted to change it to something more current. That decision was delayed until after 1961, the 75th anniversary of Sunbeams, then further delayed by knowledge that changes in the WMU organizational plan were forthcoming.[35]

YOUNG WOMAN'S AUXILIARY

There were women's societies and there were children's bands, but where were the young women? Not in Woman's Missionary Union in 1904, at least not in an organized way. Eliza Broadus, head of the Kentucky Central Committee, was determined that young women would grow up able to lead in prayer and take part in a meeting, so she organized a young ladies missionary society at McFerran Church in Louisville in 1900. She supplied them literature, pointed them to a project, and left them on their own.[36]

Other key WMU leaders did the same, but the young women needed their own program. The need was discussed by WMU leaders at the 1904 Annual Meeting. Olive Board Eager (Mrs. J. H.), a returned missionary who was WMU's vice-president from Maryland, called the young women the "dropped stitch" in WMU. She called on the women's societies to organize a young women's society.[37]

Nothing more definite was planned until Fannie Heck returned to the presidency of WMU in 1906. Her first year in office was busy as she prepared to launch the Woman's Missionary Union Training School, to publish a magazine, and to pick up the "dropped stitch."

At the WMU Annual Meeting of 1907, a number of young women were present to see what would happen to the proposal for a permanent organization. Heck, who led a young women's society and worked with college students herself, was the perfect picture of a Christian woman

leader. One young woman who was present observed her keenly:
> She was a little larger than most women, though not tall. Not too
> stout, just perfect in face and figure. Her beautiful dark eyes
> reflected joy in the discussions. She was dressed in pastel pink
> or blue (as she usually was). God painted her cheeks. Her voice
> was full, strong, forceful, rich. . . . As one listened, one felt as if
> one could lay down her life for the cause she presented.[38]

Heck presented Mrs. J. W. Vesey of Alabama, chairman of a committee to plan for young women. Heck said, "We must overcome our neglect by adopting and naming our many daughters." The committee recommended naming the new organization Young Woman's Auxiliary, a name already in use in Alabama. They adopted a design for a pin, and watchword, Daniel 12:3: "They that be wise shall shine like the brightness of the firmament; and they that turn many to righteousness, as the stars forever and ever."

In 1912 the YWAs adopted the song "O Zion, Haste" as their theme. Heck not only wanted to develop the young women aged 16-25 as future WMS members, she also wanted to keep them securely in the Baptist fold as potential missionaries. This was the era of strong nondenominational student movements. The YWCA was deeply involved in missions. The Student Volunteer Movement was exciting young people to the possibility of foreign mission service. These groups offered conferences, literature, and a missionary-sending route to foreign fields. Heck issued a "rally cry" for Baptist girls to be loyal to YWA. As Willie Turner Dawson (Mrs. J. M.) said, "We must train the girls for denominationalism."[39]

YWA grew rapidly to 992 organizations in two years. The purposes of YWA were the familiar purposes of WMU, but with a more visionary statement: "To develop a symmetrical Christian young womanhood and to bind together the young women of the church for worldwide service for Christ."

College YWA.—WMU was keenly interested in the cream of the crop, "choice young women" who were in college. In 1910 a college correspondent was elected. She was Mary K. Applewhite (later Mrs. J. Killian Yates) of Raleigh, North Carolina. She was succeeded by a Baltimore woman, Susan Bancroft Tyler (later Mrs. Curtis Lee Laws). She carried on the task of corresponding with the YWAs on college campuses, particularly Baptist women's schools.

In 1910 the college YWAs were given their own name, Ann Hasseltine YWA, in memory of the first American woman missionary, Ann Hasseltine Judson (Mrs. Adoniram). The first known college missions organization among Southern Baptists was organized in 1838 at Judson College in Alabama; it was called the Ann Hasseltine Missionary Society.

After Mary Faison Dixon became the staff young people's secretary in 1916, she became college correspondent. This work also received prime attention from Juliette Mather, young people's secretary of WMU from 1921 until she took another position in 1948. She distributed a simple publication, the "College YWA Bulletin," beginning in 1921.

YWA for Nurses.—In 1923 Juliette Mather organized the first YWA for nursing students at Baptist hospitals. The earliest groups were in Alabama and Tennessee. Mather's interest in nursing was stimulated because her sister, Harriett Mather, was founder of the Mather School of Nursing at New Orleans Baptist Hospital. Juliette Mather gave the nurse YWAs their own name: Grace McBride Young Woman's Auxiliaries. Grace McBride, a graduate of the WMU Training School, was appointed a Foreign Mission Board nurse in Hwanghsien, China, in 1916. Two years later wartime needs caused her to join the Red Cross. She was sent to Siberia, where she died of typhus fever in 1918.

Until the 1920s YWA was the only Southern Baptist program on college campuses. WMU was keenly interested in making it the dominant factor in student religious life. When students at one college voted to have only one religious organization, YWA, Juliette Mather noted, "Isn't this nice. One more YWCA put out of business."[40]

In 1920 the Southern Baptist Convention, noticing an unofficial but successful Baptist Student Missionary Movement in Texas (headed among others by Crickett Keys Copass [Mrs. B. A.], who would become president of WMU of Texas) formed an Inter-Board Commission on student work. WMU's secretary, Kathleen Mallory, served on this commission along with representatives of the SBC boards. The commission projected plans for student work that might have jeopardized YWA. WMU sent a protest to the Southern Baptist Convention of 1921 that too much expense and denominational machinery were being considered. The plans were not carried out. WMU and the SBC boards continued the cooperative administration of student work until 1928, when it was turned over to the Sunday School Board. WMU continued to consult with Baptist Student Union leaders as the organization developed, and YWA flourished as a related organization.[41]

State WMUs also supported campus work. In 1939 Virginia WMU funded the first director of religious activities for Baptist students in the state.[42]

In 1965 WMU appointed a committee to study Ann Hasseltine and Grace McBride YWA. Believing that the Baptist Student Union program would handle the necessary missions emphasis among women on campus, WMU discontinued promotion of campus YWA. Instead, churches near campuses were asked to take up the work. The committee pointed out that the "ratio of participants to the potential is alarmingly low. Means must be found to reach the largest possible number of college girls." The committee considered that YWA was really designed for churches, not campuses.[43] They would reverse their opinion in a few years.

YWA was a forum for innovation in WMU. Camping was proven an effective missions education method at the YWA camp at Ridgecrest. The YWA Citation, first awarded in 1947, encouraged individual initiative in mission study and service. A southwide radio broadcast on February 11, 1932, linked together 70 banquet meetings around the country where YWAs celebrated their 25th anniversary. Ethlene Boone Cox (Mrs. W. J.) was the speaker. Another radio broadcast June 22, 1947, from YWA camp featured foreign YWA members and a young woman appointed as a missionary to China. In 1947 a color sound movie about YWA was filmed at Judson College and New Orleans Baptist Theological Seminary.[44]

ROYAL AMBASSADORS

"An Open Door: Who Will Enter It?" asked a 1901 newspaper article. "When boys grow too old for Sunbeam Band, they begin to drift. They are the future of the church. Who will provide leadership?"[45] Throughout the churches where WMU had made a beachhead, this question was asked for several years. The women tried to organize boys bands in various forms, but as a whole, WMU hesitated to walk through the open door into the forbidden kingdom of manhood. Criticism and difficulties lay ahead.[46]

One who feared not was Fannie Heck. When she resumed leadership of WMU in 1906 she had a full agenda and boys were in it. She invited a Presbyterian woman who led a boys missions band to speak to the 1907 Annual Meeting. She pleaded, "Save the boys for their own sakes and for the future of the gospel."[47] This speech set WMU to thinking. One of Heck's closest WMU friends in North Carolina, Elizabeth Briggs Pittman (Mrs. T. M.) was also thinking, because she was inspired by the singing of a song, "The King's Business": "O be ye reconciled to God." [48] Heck's imagination already saw the shape of Royal Ambassadors, with the motto "We are ambassadors for Christ" (2 Cor. 5:20).

The WMU Executive Committee met in Louisville in October 1907 to open the doors of the WMU Training School. Sitting around the dinner table of Ella Broadus Robertson (Mrs. A. T.) with the WMU officers, Heck shared her vision.[49] The others were reluctant. They hoped for somebody else to take up this work. But at the 1908 Annual Meeting, Heck turned over the presiding gavel to someone else so that she could personally bring the proposal to form the Order of Royal Ambassadors.

Women and boys everywhere seemed ready for this decision. Mrs. H. M. Evans, field worker for Tennessee WMU, soon went to a country church to form a Woman's Missionary Society. Some boys were present. The women were not ready to organize, but the boys were, and the women agreed to help them. The first RA order in Tennessee was established.[50]

Even before that, the Cary Newton RA Chapter was formed in Goldsboro, North Carolina, claiming to be the first.[51] More than 100 chapters were organized the first year.

In Arkansas, where a strong Landmark and antimission sentiment prevailed, two missions-minded pastors decided to use Royal Ambassadors to educate the next generation in missions. W. J. Hinsley of Booneville and G. L. Boles of Lonoke personally led their chapters and organized others. Boles developed a ranking system, through which boys could work their way by study and action in Christian missions. From his experience as a Mason, Boles devised a secret ritual and passwords for the boys. He invited the state WMU young people's leader from Arkansas, Una Roberts (later Mrs. Irvin Lawrence), to visit. After much deliberation, the men and boys decided to initiate her into RAs, even though she was a woman. After the impressive ceremony, she consented to help Boles spread his RA plans across the state.[52] The ritual was handed over to qualified leaders who guaranteed that they would maintain its secrecy. The ceremony and the ranking system, involving some 50 projects, were prescribed as standard by WMU, SBC. The popular organization, which took on a badge and regalia, had a distinctly missions theme. The Northern Baptist Missionary Education Department asked in 1925 for permission to adapt the program, and it flourished for several years.[53]

In 1927, 1930, 1939, 1948, and 1949, WMU asked the Brotherhood to confer about taking over some of the RA responsibility. WMU was wary about "entrusting this treasure" to another sponsorship, but would have done so if Brotherhood had guaranteed the survival and missions emphasis of RA. On the local level many men became RA leaders.[54] Meanwhile, state by state, key pastors supported the work. In 1941, Mississippi WMU employed J. Ivyloy Bishop to work part-time with RA camps. He was the first man employed by WMU for professional RA work. Soon he was jointly employed by Mississippi, Alabama, and South Carolina. In 1943 he moved to the WMU, SBC, staff in Birmingham.[55]

During Bishop's ten years as RA secretary, RA enrollment doubled. An energetic promoter and inspiring believer in missions, he involved USA RAs in fostering RA work in such countries as Korea, Brazil, and Nigeria. The camping program and a custom of state conclaves, or conventions, attracting up to 4,000 boys each, built strong enthusiasm. Several state WMUs employed male RA staff. This job proved to be the first rung on the ladder of denominational prominence for several men. Among them were Robert T. Banks, Jr., who became executive vice-president of the Home Mission Board; Jimmy Allen, who became president of the Radio and Television Commission; and Glendon McCullough, who became executive director of the Brotherhood Commission. The presence of these and other men in the official ranks of WMU opened the door to men serving as voting delegates to the WMU Annual Meeting. The first man delegate was A. T. Greene, Jr., of South Carolina, in 1944.[56]

Although WMU's top officials were enormously proud of their boys, they continued to feel uneasy about the arrangement. They were concerned because boys at age 17 graduated into nothing: Brotherhood did not provide a program for the older teens, nor was Brotherhood avowedly a missions organization at that time. The women believed that younger boys should have more male influence than they got under WMU management. One way they dealt with the uneasiness was to omit the name of Woman's Missionary Union whenever possible on letterheads and publications received by RA members. By 1949 more men than women were counselors for RA chapters. Only 42 percent of Junior chapters, 16 percent of Intermediate chapters, and 46 percent of mixed-age chapters were led by women.[57]

In 1952, W. R. White of Texas asked the Southern Baptist Convention for an endorsement of Boy Scouts as a recommended program for churches. WMU had been rejecting appeals from Boy Scouts of America for some form of liaison with RA.[58] E. R. Eller of South Carolina, whose wife was vice-president of South Carolina WMU, brought a substitute motion appointing a joint WMU and Brotherhood committee to study RA work. This substitute passed, but with White's amendment requiring it to study also Boy Scouts.

Supporters of the scouting movement implied that Scouts were already well established in SBC churches and that RA did not "develop the whole boy." Ivyloy Bishop issued a news statement that the facts were misrepresented. Thus was launched an intensive debate over a two-year period. In January 1954 the WMU Executive Committee had such an emotional discussion that the women resorted to the unusual measure of voting by secret ballot and straw polls. After long prayer, the WMU officers agreed to endorse a report by the SBC-appointed committee, chaired by Robert E. Naylor of Texas. In effect, this called for a three-year period of joint administration of RA by WMU and Brotherhood, after which Brotherhood would assume the responsibility. This proposal was approved by the SBC in 1954.[59] Meanwhile, in August 1953 the first national Royal Ambassador Congress was held in Atlanta with approximately 5,000 boys participating. Immediately afterward, Ivyloy Bishop resigned as RA secretary to pursue doctoral studies, then marriage, then a career as professor of religion at Wayland Baptist University.

WMU would not have agreed to the transfer had the Brotherhood

Commission not convinced the women that the missions purpose would be retained. Suitably convinced, WMU appropriated $10,000 per year for three years to help Brotherhood establish an RA staff and contacts. The SBC Executive Committee increased the Brotherhood's operating budget by $15,000. As of October 1, 1957, WMU transferred literature, magazine subscription lists, and 127,656 members to the Brotherhood Commission.

The transfer of Royal Ambassadors may have been the most traumatic action in the history of WMU other than the reorganization in 1970. The financial impact on the national office was significant. Some of the women doubted that the Brotherhood Commission would live up to its promises to keep missions at the forefront of RA.[60] Under Brotherhood's leadership RA enrollment more than doubled in seven years—a faster growth rate than under WMU.

As part of the grouping-grading reorganization of 1970, six-, seven-, and eight-year-old boys fell into the same age bracket as the younger Royal Ambassadors members. To lose these younger boys was also traumatic for WMU leadership. However, some associations and churches were already making similar arrangements.[61] Effective with October 1, 1970, another block of boys was transferred to Brotherhood.[62]

GIRLS' AUXILIARY

After Royal Ambassadors was organized, only one link was missing from the chain of WMU, and the women knew it. The missing link was the preteen and young teenage girl, the female equivalent of RA. WMU begin publishing literature in 1909 for Junior Auxiliaries.[63] YWAs were asked to foster these groups. They were reported beginning in the 1913 report. That year was claimed in later years as the official founding of Girls' Auxiliary, though its new name was not bestowed until 1914. The GA pin was introduced in 1915.

In 1924 GA was assigned the watchword "Arise, shine, for thy light is come" (Isa. 60:1). The hymn chosen was "We've a Story to Tell," and the colors were white and Nile green.

Juliette Mather, among her other duties as WMU's young people's secretary, developed Forward Steps in 1928. Like the RA Ranking System, Forward Steps gave individual recognition to girls who memorized assigned Scripture passages, studied denominational work, and completed other service requirements. Impressive recognition ceremonies were called coronation services, often conducted formally on the associational level. Girls wore formal dresses and were crowned, caped, and given scepters and badges to mark their progression through the ranks.

The GA Ideals were a girl-size statement of WMU purposes: "Abiding in Him through prayer, advancing in wisdom by Bible study, acknowledging my stewardship, adorning myself with good works, accepting the challenge of the Great Commission." Girls repeated this statement at their meetings, and they memorized the addresses and officers of the SBC missions agencies. Their curriculum was a study in denominational operations.

GA grew to be WMU's second largest organization, with enrollment of more than 350,000. When the 50th anniversary of GA was celebrated in 1963, a national convention was announced for Memphis. Registrations poured in at such a rate that WMU held three consecutive conventions to accommodate the total crowd of 21,533.[64]

THE ERA OF CHANGE

The late 1960s and early 1970s were tense days of despair and social rearrangement in the United States. The racial revolution and the war in Southeast Asia shattered public confidence in government and social organizations. Of added significance for members of Woman's Missionary Union was the woman's liberation movement. Generally rejected and resisted on the surface by Southern Baptists, the woman's movement nonetheless had practical and emotional impact on WMU. In daily life women found many more choices of what to do with their lives than they had previously known. WMU found itself competing with careers, classes, and social chaos for the time and loyalty of women.

By coincidence, the woman's liberation movement gained momentum at the same time Southern Baptist agencies launched a series of unprecedented changes in their recommended plans for churches. Between 1964 and 1970 WMU restated its program and redesigned its family of organizations. The times could hardly have been worse for injecting major changes in the organization. Or were the times perfect for the change? Time has not yet told whether the move was completely wise. One thing is certain: WMU could have been destroyed between 1968-71, if the majority of the members had not been fully committed to being "laborers together."

The overhaul of WMU's organization plan was influenced by an agreement reached among officers of the Sunday School Board (including programs of Sunday School, Church Training, and Church Music), WMU, and Brotherhood. They agreed to make available by September 30, 1970, suggested programs and products so that churches might develop a unified, correlated, coordinated program. For the first time, WMU planned its church activities not in isolation, but in constant consultation with the other programs.

All agreed that the church itself would be central. Task statements and program assignments were pruned to avoid duplication (see chaps. 2 and 12). In 1963 the Sunday School Board had begun planning for revised age grading which would group persons on a uniform age schedule in all church organizations. WMU appointed Billie Pate, who was to head WMU's Field Services Department, as its representative in the study. WMU organizations at that time were divided into age groups that differed from those of other church organizations. After a 1966 research project, all the program agencies agreed to four basic age groupings: preschool, children, youth, and adult.

The age ranges for each were sufficiently different from WMU's existing organizations to necessitate new organizational names and lines of operation. To accompany new organizations, WMU introduced new periodicals. All these were unveiled October 1970, simultaneously with changes in other church organizations.

This sweeping change gave WMU an opportunity to make the organizations more appealing. Enrollment had begun to decline in 1965. Recommended methods had to be educationally updated. WMU wanted to keep in step with the rest of the denomination.

THE UMBRELLA ORGANIZATION

Staff and Executive Board members considered whether to rename Woman's Missionary Union itself at this time. Some of the younger leaders favored change, but found stiff resistance from the seasoned leaders.[65] The idea was never brought to general discussion. WMU was clearly separated from WMS, however, in 1968. This was a step toward implementing the age-level organization changes in 1970.

Woman's Missionary Union was already defined as an umbrella name; now WMU in a church had its own officers. At the head was a WMU director who presided over a council of top leaders of the age-level organizations. The WMS president was responsible only for the adult organization, which was being reorganized into groups instead of circles. The separation of duties between WMU and WMS officers divided a heavy work load. WMU officers could give more attention to the younger organizations.[66]

The changes in WMU and WMS were not easily made. Staff and the Executive Board agonized over the changes. While some were reluctant, a remarkable triumvirate of top leaders ardently embraced change. Alma Hunt told the 1966 Annual Meeting: "This is Woman's Missionary Union's hour of opportunity to provide a program of missionary education for NOW—for these days of world crisis. This is WMU's hour of opportunity to give missions leadership. . . . I am glad to say we are not asleep; we are not unaware of the demands of our day."[67]

She took a look back at Fannie E. S. Heck's 1909 classic address[68] which officers often have quoted as a checklist of effectiveness: "The ultimate test of any institution is its present vitality." Then Hunt challenged the women with: "Our lane is broad, there are no roadblocks ahead."[69]

While some bemoaned change, Hunt welcomed the opportunity to strengthen WMU: "In one sentence one can say truthfully that the world is in a mess and also that the world has never been so exciting."[70]

Helen Long Fling (Mrs. Robert), president of WMU, sounded the same note in her presidential message of 1967: "There is always risk in change. But there is greater risk in standing still. Sooner or later every person comes to the time in his life when he needs a miracle. Today Southern Baptists need a miracle—the miracle of energizing faith."[71]

Two decades later, Fling analyzed the change era: "We had to change. We had to cooperate with the Sunday School Board. We couldn't resist. We either had to participate in their planning or be left out, programmed right out of existence."[72]

Marie Wiley Mathis (Mrs. R. L.), the former president, was sitting in the staff Education Division director's chair guiding the staff in a phenomenal output of planning documents. The Executive Board came to meetings and sat down with blank pieces of paper on which to draw up the future WMU structure. Mathis's counterpart at the Sunday School Board, W. L. Howse, said that 34 years of needed changes in church programs were made in 9 years.[73]

Leading up to the ultimate changes to take effect October 1, 1970, WMU magazines were heavily filled with encouragement to change. Helen Fling wrote a book, *Changes and Choices*, to encourage the women in their adjustment to the new organization (described on the following pages). After nine months of trial, a former vice-president addressed the WMU Executive Board and pleaded: No more change for a long time. Keep the average person's ability in mind. Develop strong enlistment plans. Give more stewardship plans. See that easier terminology is used.[74]

After the dust settled, WMU continued to lose members, but at a slower rate, for four years. Then figures increased slightly and stabilized. Contributions to missions were not adversely affected. The leaders had embraced change and made it work.

BAPTIST WOMEN

Most of the drastic changes had already been introduced to Woman's Missionary Society by 1968. A new name, Baptist Women, was added in October 1970. The age group for Baptist Women was 30 and above.

With this name WMU hoped to appeal to a wider range of women in the church.

One feature of the revised organization was the reduction in number of officers suggested. Within the groups, formerly known as circles, only one officer was to be formally elected, a chairman. Members of the group were to volunteer for tasks as needed. In January 1973 the recommended structure was adjusted to encourage election of more officers if desired. Also, an emphasis on spiritual growth was restored to the organization.

In 1978-79 one of the major emphases of WMU was Baptist Women Year in the Church. The purpose was to upgrade the image of the organization and to start new units. The emphasis resulted in 686 new organizations. The Baptist Women organization was hard hit by the 1970s' woman's movement and by its own organizational changes. In 1986 membership remained 267,000 less than its all-time high, but it was growing.

BAPTIST YOUNG WOMEN

In 1970 a new young adult women's organization, Baptist Young Women, was targeted for students, young career women, and others. The age range originally was 18-29; effective in 1988 BYW will include women ages 18-34.

Though originally planned only as a church organization, BYW was extended to college campuses in 1977. Campus BYW was instituted at the request of National Student Ministries, headquartered at the Sunday School Board. Out of concern for the missions emphasis among students, BYW was modified to suit campus plans. In 1986 Campus BYW was reported on 81 campuses. Even the US Military Academy at West Point had a BYW.

The first national conference for Baptist Young Women was held in 1976 in connection with the WMU Annual Meeting. More than 600 young adults registered for the event, called Kaleidoscope.

In 1985 BYW Enterprisers, a volunteer missions plan, was introduced. BYW members receive 50 hours of training before assignment by the Home Mission Board for short-term service. The first Enterpriser team of Campus BYWs from Oklahoma Baptist University served for a week in inner-city New Orleans.

ACTEENS

Acteens was launched in 1970 as the organization for girls in grades 7 through 12. Studiact is the individual achievement plan through which Acteens study and work directly in missions projects. For their efforts they are recognized in five levels of achievement including Queen, Queen with a Scepter, Queen Regent, Queen Regent in Service, and Service Aide.

With Acteens membership of more than 125,000, the organization produces many get-together activities for girls. In addition to the camping program sponsored by several state and associational WMU organizations, WMU, SBC, has sponsored four National Acteens Conventions, known as NAC. The first, in 1972, attracted a capacity of 900 girls at Glorieta Baptist Conference Center. In June 1975 in Memphis, 10,716 Acteens registered. At Kansas City in July 1979 registration was 11,500. In Fort Worth in July 1984 the registration topped 14,000. Another NAC is scheduled for San Antonio in 1989.

In 1977 WMU inaugurated the Acteens National Advisory Panel. Six girls are chosen each year from a field of several hundred applicants. They are judged for Acteens accomplishments, Christian maturity, and school and community excellence. The chosen panelists serve as pages at the national WMU Annual Meeting. Beginning in 1981 the panelists were permitted to serve as pages for the Southern Baptist Convention, the first time in Convention history that females had been able to enjoy this distinction.

Acteens have their own short-term volunteer missions program. The Acteens Activators plan was launched with a pilot team of girls in 1976. Activators must complete at least 50 hours of supervised training before going as a group to a designated spot of assistance in missions. Prior to 1986 all Acteens Activators worked in the United States under commission by the Home Mission Board. The number of participants has grown every year but one. In 1986, 65 teams of 581 persons served. The ten-year total was 270 teams with 2,354 volunteers. Acteens Activators Abroad was piloted in 1986 in cooperation with the Foreign Mission Board. Five teams went to Jamaica or the Philippines and 36 persons were involved.

GIRLS IN ACTION

The grade-school weekday missions organization continues to be WMU's most attention-getting organization for young people. The Girls in Action organization was named not only for what the name means, but in order to preserve the popular initials of GA. Membership is more than 225,000 girls in grades 1 through 6.

The individual achievement plan for Girls in Action is called Missions Adventures, involving a progression through six levels of activity. Day camping is a suggested activity to be conducted by local groupings. Some state WMUs sponsor residential camps for GAs; others sponsor statewide rallies.

MISSION FRIENDS

Mission Friends is the WMU organization launched in 1970 for preschool boys and girls. Male members of Mission Friends are the remnant of the sizable enrollment of boys formerly taught in WMU. WMU stresses that even infants may gain foundations in missions if cared for in a proper environment. Mission Friends often provides child care for the convenience of adults involved in WMU activities. Older preschoolers have regular weekly meetings of their own.

Woman's Missionary Union, not as an organization but as a force for the fulfilling of the Great Commission, is worth the investment of one's most precious gift . . . life itself.
                                    Alma Hunt, Annual Report, 1974

Mites to millions

*The widow's mite is still in circulation. Coined in the mint of
self-sacrifice, its influence is being felt today by every
member of the church of God.*

Annie Armstrong's notebook

ONEY FOR MISSIONS was the original goal of Woman's
Missionary Union. The WMU purpose in 1888 was "to
stimulate the grace of giving, . . . aiding in the collection
of funds for missionary purposes."[1] The bottom line of
the Centennial ledger shows more than 1 billion dollars
to the credit of Woman's Missionary Union (see table,
p. 495). This money reported through the conventionwide WMU treasurer is only the hem of a long and winding scarf the women wove
around the local congregation and the whole world. The treasures of
unreported sacrifice for local and state missions causes are laid up in
heaven; not half can be told from the national historical records.

Most of the millions came from sugar bowls and thin purses of women
who had little money of their own. As Southerners, most members of
Woman's Missionary Union drew their funds from a low-cash agricultural economy until recently. As women, they had the lowest paying
jobs and the least control legally over their assets, if they had paying
jobs or had inherited assets.

Yet out of their relative poverty, Woman's Missionary Union members
have cast into the treasury the greater part of the money that has fueled
Southern Baptist cooperative enterprises. For two decades they saved
the mission boards from total collapse, then they financed expansion
of the mission boards into 50 states and more than 100 countries.

THE FOUNDATION OF STEWARDSHIP

For all the wealth of Southern Baptists today, they have been slow
to lay their all on the altar. Therefore, the little mite box of the 1870s,
filled by women driven by Christian ardor, was hefty enough to tip the
scales of history.

The economic earthquake set off by the Civil War left the finances of home and church momentarily in the hands of the women. To rebuild their church buildings and to pay and house their pastors, women timidly organized themselves into ladies aid societies. Their purpose was to raise money.

Their resourcefulness quickly caught the eye of the Foreign Mission Board, destitute and virtually out of business in 1865. Its secretary, James B. Taylor, issued a survival call to the "Baptist ladies of the South." His circular letter asked that each church form a committee of ladies with the assignment of securing a freewill offering from each church member.[2]

Taylor did little to foster such committees, but Baptist women took matters into their own hands. In 1871 Ann Jane Graves organized Baltimore women to support women missionaries and looked for a way to increase and regularize funds. The mite box was the solution. Her object was to encourage women to place in the box a definite amount—at least two cents—on a weekly basis, rather than annually as most church members then gave.

Graves had paper boxes manufactured at a cost of four to six cents each. On one side was the name Woman's Gospel Mission to Woman in Foreign Lands. Among Scripture verses printed on the sides was this one: "To give light to them that sit in darkness." Tiny garnet colored mite boxes with gold lettering found their way throughout the South via family and friends. Although the collection plate was seldom passed at church on nineteenth century Sundays, the mite box was passed at home on Sunday mornings. Funds began to flow with regularity to the Foreign Mission Board. In ten years the FMB had furnished 28,520 mite boxes at a cost of $733.40 and had reaped $75,000.[3]

The theological significance of these symbolic boxes was clear to the women. They liked to point out that the only two offerings commended by Jesus were made by women: one an offering of mites brought by a poor widow into the temple; and the other a gift by a woman of means brought into a home.[4] In a day when a woman would walk a mile rather than spend two cents on a postage stamp, mite boxes were filled only by sacrifice.

Some women's societies, especially in cities, organized sewing projects so that their members might earn money to contribute. In rural and suburban areas, women raised money by sale of butter, vegetables, and poultry. Most women had chickens if they had nothing else. Eggs laid on Sunday could be sold for missions. An Illinois WMU field worker gave women a choice of signing pledge cards either for cash or for eggs. More women signed the egg cards. Egg money supported not only missionaries but also WMU operating expenses and scholarships as well. An Alabama woman hearing reports at an associational meeting said to a minister, "Why sir, an industrious missionary hen would earn more in laying eggs and hatching chickens in one year than some of these churches give to missions!"[5]

If women were limited in their earning opportunities, they could withhold cash out of their household and clothing allowances—an approach Martha McIntosh called "plainer dressing and plainer living." An early women's missions newspaper said, "Let us devise some plan to get Christian women of Missouri to quit spending money for foolish superfluities. Think of the money spent for rings, earrings, kid gloves, dress trains—those trains that the women drag around in the dirt would support ten missionaries for the year."[6]

The obligation of self-sacrifice as a Christian tenet was drilled into women's consciousness. Fannie E. S. Heck said, "To have the privilege of giving is much; to have the privilege of giving up is more." Alice Armstrong said, "It is obligatory upon every woman to do something or to do without."[7] Early WMU leaders saw no reason to let any woman, poor or rich, escape the call of stewardship. Answering criticism about asking needy frontier women to join in the support of missions, Annie Armstrong said, "The widow was called on to feed the prophet when she had only a little meal in the barrel and a little oil in the cruse. If we always took out the Lord's portion first, do you not think our experience would be the same? God would look after us."[8]

Women's beliefs and their strategies about missions money took shape in organizations. Martha McIntosh gave women's societies in South Carolina a constitution that called for each to have a president, a secretary, a treasurer, and two or more collectors. The collectors were to divide the membership list, secure regular contributions (preferably weekly) from each member assigned, and turn the funds over to the treasurer.[9]

The matter of women handling money raised questions of practicality and propriety. In the early development of WMU, it was assumed that single women knew nothing about money, so a married woman had to be elected treasurer. A woman likely had no banking opportunities, so her husband or pastor had to assist in transmitting money to the mission boards.

Some claimed that women violated scriptural teaching when they handled church funds. S. E. S. ("Miss Lily") Shankland of Tennessee said of a state missionary who opposed women's work, "Let us help to pay his salary. Good deeds are better than argument." To help a woman answer critics in her church, Mary C. Gambrell (Mrs. J. B.) of Texas spun off a list of Scripture passages showing women assisting the spread of the gospel and said, "Is it not commanded, 'Let everyone of you on the first day of the week lay by in store as the Lord has prospered so that there be no gathering when I come'? Does that not include women, are they not a part of the Lord's church, and if He prospers them, have they not a right to lay in store? Are women transgressing any command of the Scriptures when they send their contributions for missions to the Boards? Look into the Scriptures and see."[10]

The Southern Baptist Convention of 1888 struggled over the Convention's perennial problem—lack of money. F. M. Ellis, pastor of Annie Armstrong, was chairman of a committee assigned to solve the problem. He reported two solutions: systematic and proportionate giving and approval of women's missionary societies.[11]

Ellis implemented the idea by walking down the street to the Methodist church where the Baptist women were gathered and encouraging them to get organized. Before the WMU founding meeting was adjourned, the first special project was adopted. Isaac Taylor Tichenor, secretary of the Home Mission Board, asked the women to raise $5,000 for buying a new church building and cemetery in Havana, Cuba.

Annie Armstrong designed a small card picturing 20 bricks for the proposed new building. Each member was to take a card and mark off a brick for each ten cents contributed. During the first year 11,372 cards were distributed, netting several thousand dollars.[12] At the WMU Executive Committee's October 1888 meeting Armstrong brought the proposal which resulted in the Lottie Moon Christmas Offering for Foreign Missions (see chap. 6).

These attractive projects gave WMU an immediate rallying point. But the women did not intend to base their organization on spasmodic giving. Instead, they took a bedrock educational approach. WMU's first procedures manual, "Chips from Many Workshops," gave substantial attention to "how to raise money." This booklet, produced by Armstrong in 1888, stressed self-denial methods, recommended the regularity of mite box giving, and assumed that women would tithe.

The first use of the word *stewardship* came in 1889. WMU published a tract, "A Lesson in Stewardship," showing that even children could be taught to earn money to give for missions.[13] The WMU Plan of Work in that year suggested the usual self-denial and butter-and-egg money methods. It additionally stated, "We would earnestly deprecate the employment of any method that would put the cause of Christ before the world as a beggar, or one needing to secure aid from it in any way, by catering to the lower elements of human nature."

The 1890 Plan of Work became more specific: "We urge discretion, . . . that no unchristian or questionable methods be employed." The plan urged that all methods develop a permanent spirit of giving rather than temporary excitement. "Money is not the sole or chief object . . . but that we should most earnestly invoke to rest upon the mission work . . . the blessing of him who can make treasurers of influence out of widows' mites and give to weakness strength to move mountains and overturn worlds."[14]

The women were forming a principle which distinguished Woman's Missionary Union from the ladies aid societies and from counterparts in most other denominations. WMU never espoused fund-raising events such as bazaars, entertainments, and suppers. It was understood that individual women must have some way to obtain cash for missions, but the prescribed methods usually were reliance upon private effort with group encouragement. There were exceptions in actual practice. Annie Armstrong herself managed an annual boat trip and supper by which the Maryland Woman's Baptist Home Mission Society earned much of its money.[15] But such ideas never made their way into the Union's official recommendations, and they died out of WMU experience by the 1920s.

STEWARDSHIP MATURES

WMU steadily increased emphasis on stewardship education. Seeing that adults would be harder to train, the women concentrated on children. Even before the network of age-level organizations was woven, literature for children emphasized giving. WMU published a new version of the mite box entitled "Young Banker's Friend." Markings on the box helped children learn to allocate their money to giving, saving, and spending.

WMU popularized the use of offering envelopes, having distributed these for the first Christmas offering. The mission boards were quick to say that WMU's steady cash flow kept them afloat throughout the year. Most of the churches took annual collections for missions (if any) and forwarded them during the last quarter of the fiscal year after frantic pleading from the Board secretaries.

Lansing Burrows, recording secretary and statistician of the SBC, wrote that WMU's systematic giving plans constituted the "power of that portion of the church which we have wrongly designated as the weaker sex." Burrows pointed out that with a small fraction of the SBC membership, through prayer and system, WMU had provided a quarter million dollars in 1910 for missions. Victor Masters of the HMB estimated that in 1915 WMU, with 7.6 percent of SBC membership, was giving 30.6 percent of the money for home and foreign missions, not counting its support of state missions and related programs. He further remarked that this was done with quietness and modesty which had kept the "more loud-speaking brethren from understanding the bigness and blessedness of their work." A Louisiana leading man observed that in the panic of 1907 the contributions of men fell off 50 percent, while the women's did not decline. He learned that every church with a WMU organization made some contribution to missions.[16]

WMU's efforts were strongly assisted in 1907 when the SBC adopted the Layman's Missionary Movement. The laymen were able to force the issue of pressing every member to give something. They stressed that the collection plate be passed every Sunday. In 1910 the laymen formally launched the Every Member Canvass. WMU promised to co-operate by securing a pledge from every woman in the church.[17]

BOX WORK

If women did not have much cash to contribute, they did have goods. And, they had their needles. WMU members enjoyed making a suit for a missionary more than embroidering decorations to sell at a bazaar. Annie Armstrong had personally experienced the power of "box work" in attracting the interest of women. So in 1890 she led WMU to undertake the preparation of boxes of goods for frontier missionaries.

The WMU central office in Baltimore became a clearinghouse through which missionaries requested goods and through which WMU organizations secured assignments. Women made or contributed food, clothing, books, and other supplies. These were shipped in large boxes or barrels. The women reported a dollar value of the box as a contribution to home missions.[18] The women thought of every need. When it became a matter of discussion at the 1898 Annual Meeting that a missionary woman had walked six miles to borrow a needle, a missionary urged the women to slip patches, needles, thread, and pins into their boxes.[19] Packing day was a strenuous and festive one for the women; the day of unpacking the box was the same for the missionary.

In 1895, 224 missionary families were helped with goods valued at $12,871. The picture brightened in 1896 when 358 boxes valued at $21,475 were sent. On the average a box could have the effect of raising a missionary's income by one-fourth. The larger number of boxes was due in large part to a tender leaflet written by Fannie Heck in 1895 which told the story of a frontier missionary whose child died of want while awaiting the arrival of the longed-for box. The Home Mission Board issued official thanks for this tract.

But the box was not a satisfactory means of mission support. Not only did some societies fail to produce their promised boxes, but some sent worthless and bothersome discards. Mail and shipping to the frontier made communication uncertain. Perhaps the most important function of box work was to make women's societies personally informed about missionaries and their needs. WMU officers knew the missionaries as SBC leaders never did.

Not coincidentally, the same year that Armstrong launched box work, she also began trying to organize missionary societies on the frontier. Armstrong thus helped lay the foundation of Southern Baptist mission strategy: that missions fields must immediately upon birth begin to be mission supporters. Box work was a durable idea. By 1898 the box valuation added to cash contributions made WMU's contribution to home missions exceed gifts to foreign missions.

Frontier box work declined drastically when Armstrong, with her passion for frontier missions, went out of office in 1906. By 1919 many state WMUs no longer reported box valuations. But during the depression, women again packed whatever goods of value they might have and sent them to missions fields. By 1930, as desperate need swept the country, box value reached $124,448, an increase of 50 percent over 1928's figure. In 1941 WMU financial reports ceased to mention boxes.

Box work arose in a new form in 1950. It was called Christmas in August. WMU magazines suggested that members pack boxes of supplies in August to send to home missionaries for distribution at Christmas. The gifts were not for the missionary's personal needs, but for his professional use. Although adults and children participated in Christmas in August at first, the project was soon restricted to children and youth. With adult participation, the outpouring of supplies was unmanageable. In the 1980s WMU asked the Home Mission Board to assume responsibility for selecting the missionaries to be aided. The selected missionaries and their lists of needed items are advertised in magazines for youth, children, and preschoolers. Usually the requested items are toilet articles, art supplies, craft items, and health aids. After being listed in 1982, a prison chaplain in Kentucky wrote that he had received packages from 450 churches with estimated value of $15,000.[20]

CAREY CENTENNIAL

The Southern Baptist brethren of the 1890s had no trouble spotting the women's generosity. From then on, the Convention counted on the women when it wanted to raise money. The SBC voted to celebrate the centennial of William Carey's going to India as a missionary of the first Baptist mission society. The chairman of the centennial committee, T. T. Eaton of Kentucky, who was a critic of WMU, came to the WMU Annual Meeting of 1891 asking for the women's support.[21]

The women were offended by Eaton's approach. At the request of the mission boards and F. M. Ellis, however, they pumped phenomenal effort into the centennial drive. The object was to raise money for new church buildings and to support 100 new missionaries. The women set out to secure a contribution from every woman and child in Baptist churches, an unrealistic goal considering that WMU was then represented in only 11 percent of the churches. WMU distributed literature "out of their sphere" to men and children, earning criticism for themselves. They issued a certificate picturing Carey and distributed other aids to encourage contributions. Armstrong's outgoing office correspondence leaped from 4,000 pieces to 18,000. WMU contributions increased during the campaign, but the SBC fell far short of the goal. Fannie Heck said, "We have attempted great things for God. Now we are called as earnestly to fulfill the other half. Expect great things from God."[22]

NEW CENTURY MOVEMENT

The SBC's next big money-raising effort was timed to welcome the twentieth century. A New Century Committee was chaired by F. H. Kerfoot, who was Annie Armstrong's former pastor, a seminary professor, and soon to become the next secretary of the Home Mission Board. The main strategy of the movement was to link all Convention agencies in a unified campaign to provide adequate, regular support for the mission boards.

The SBC itself spoke directly to WMU for the first time, asking WMU to "induce every church to take regular collections for missions and every member to make regular contributions."[23] Considering that half the churches had given nothing to missions the previous year, and estimating that only one-tenth of the membership gave anything to missions, the campaign was desperately needed. The committee agreed that the best way to regularize contributions was to organize WMU in every church. In return, WMU agreed to help pastors conduct New Century Meetings, which were in effect missions rallies.

With her own hands and the Boards' money, Armstrong compiled the first known list of churches and church clerks, with addresses. She sent to 5,625 churches literature describing the New Century Movement and the method for organizing missionary societies in the church. Pastors responded with the names of 2,325 key women. To each she sent information about how to organize women's societies and children's bands. The result was 616 new missionary societies (an increase of 12 percent) and growth in WMU contributions of 29 percent.

CHURCH BUILDING LOAN FUND

Despite the efforts of the New Century Movement, the Southern Baptist Convention entered the 1900s without sufficient cash and without a system for getting it. Woman's Missionary Union, through the personal creativity of Annie Armstrong, set out to put Convention finances on firmer footing. One idea which she resurrected and carried to fruition was the Church Building Loan Fund.

In 1883 the Home Mission Board had attempted to establish a Church

Building Loan Fund by approaching individuals for major contributions.[24] Lacking staff and funds to do this, the HMB let the loan idea
lie dormant until 1900, when Armstrong suggested that the WMU raise
the fund.[25] She kicked off the fund by getting her travel companion,
Anna Schimp of Baltimore, to give $3,000. Mrs. M. A. Asher of Bowling
Green gave $500.[26] Armstrong wrote an appeal which compared a
church to a newborn infant needing shelter, clothing, and nurture. She
suggested that WMU women could provide those needs for a church
as well as for their own babes. Missionaries immediately peppered
"Sister Armstrong" with desperate appeals for building funds.

The fund slowly grew in 1902 and 1903 when Mary Gambrell of Texas
prompted offerings during the Annual Meeting. In 1903 WMU decided
to make an all-out effort to raise $20,000 as a memorial to I. T. Tichenor,
who had recently died, in memory of his loyalty to the women in their
struggles to get organized. The Sunday School Board helped with a
grant of $2,000, and more than $20,000 was raised. As late as 1909 the
loan fund had no assets other than those given through WMU.[27] Seventy-
five churches were assisted before the fund was expanded, but more
than 4,000 churches remained without buildings of their own.

The SBC repeatedly urged the HMB to expand the fund, and the
Board launched a Million Dollar Fund drive in 1914-15. WMU assumed
a goal of $325,000 and incorporated it into its 25th anniversary cele-
bration. The HMB published "Baptist Hall of Fame" books picturing the
donors and honorees of the fund. More than half were women. The
largest memorials listed were in honor of WMU leaders.[28]

The Home Mission Board in 1920 acknowledged that the growth of
the loan fund was due to women more than anybody else: "The mother
heart yearning to house the homeless, the mother instinct compelling
help for the helpless . . . is the foundation of the Fund."[29] Although the
financial records became unclear as the $75 Million Campaign took
center stage, WMU claimed to have paid its pledge in full.

The Church Building Loan Fund continued to grow from special
contributions, Cooperative Program allocations, and Annie Armstrong
Offering grants. Through a quarter century of severe indebtedness, the
Home Mission Board paid its staff in part from earnings on the fund.
In 1986 the value of the fund had grown to more than $90 million.

ANNUITY PLAN

Another funding plan launched by WMU was the annuity plan of
contribution. This too was the brainchild of Annie Armstrong. Her idea
was for Baptists to give their savings to the mission boards and the
Sunday School Board with guarantee of receiving a lifelong tax-free
income through the board's investment of the gift. Upon the donor's

death, all principal and interest reverted to the Board.

Again Armstrong turned to her friend, Anna Schimp. Schimp placed funds with all three Convention boards in 1899. Armstrong of course had secured consent of the boards to receive the money. Then she activated publicity about this mutually beneficial means of mission support. The boards continued occasionally to receive such contributions until 1938. At that time the Southern Baptist Convention ruled that all gift annuities must be handled through the Relief and Annuity Board of the SBC.[30]

THE $75 MILLION CAMPAIGN

WMU came out of World War I with a new awareness of its strength and of its worldwide missions opportunity. The women soon were put to the test. The Education Commission, which had become an agency of the SBC in 1917, wanted WMU's help with a $15 million fund-raising drive. In January 1919 Kathleen Mallory and Anna C. Eager (Mrs. George B.), chairman of the board of the WMU Training School, met with the commission. Eager volunteered WMU to raise $3 million for education, if the WMUTS could retain $300,000 for its endowment fund. Mallory gasped aloud at her nerve, but the idea passed. Some other concerns of the women were also to be funded because of WMU's help: the Woman's Training School at Southwestern Baptist Theological Seminary, a woman's training school for the Negro seminary, and several Baptist colleges favored by various state WMUs. All was agreed by the WMU Annual Meeting of 1919, to which thousands of women flocked in postwar euphoria for their first experience as messengers to the SBC.[31]

To that same meeting came representatives of the newly established Ministerial Relief and Annuity Board. They asked WMU to raise $1 million. Mallory and Sarah D. Stakely (Mrs. Charles A.) urged the women to undertake this project and with little discussion, they did.

Before this date, the total giving of WMU to all causes over 30 years had been only approximately $5 million. Suddenly the women took on goals amounting to $4 million. Furthermore, the two new causes were somewhat beyond the bounds of missions causes to which WMU members had previously restricted themselves. As new voters in the SBC, however, they were determined to act as auxiliary to the entire program of the Convention.

While WMU was taking on these major projects, the SBC, without coordination, heard President James B. Gambrell call the Convention to worldwide expansion. A committee was spontaneously formed and the Baptist $75 Million Campaign was launched. Observers were to say that this campaign sounded the death knell for small thinking and narrow vision. Actually that knell was sounded in the WMU meeting. The head of the Education Board (successor to the Commission) stated that if WMU had not endorsed the $15 million education campaign, the Convention would not have had courage to undertake the $75 million goal.[32]

A committee of men was appointed to design the campaign for $75 million with which to advance Baptist work on all fronts. This was the first time all SBC and state agencies had jointly planned and shared in a fund-raising drive. Kathleen Mallory was summoned to a private meeting in Richmond to gain cooperation of WMU, which she pledged.[33]

The all-male committee hurriedly called a meeting for June 4-5, 1919, in Atlanta, inviting the WMU officers by telegram. The president, Minnie Kennedy James (Mrs. W. C.), and Mallory already were booked elsewhere, but they sent Isa-Beall W. Neel (Mrs. W. J.), president of Georgia WMU. At the next meeting, July 2-3 in Nashville, state and national WMU leadership showed up in full force, complete with hats, brooches, gloves, and grim determination. This unprecedented meeting of WMU with Convention leadership foreshadowed big happenings.

Not until the Southern Baptist Convention of 1920 were James and Mallory officially named to the Committee on Future Program which carried out the campaign, the first time that women had been appointed to any Convention committee except the committee dealing with the WMU report. From beginning to end, WMU officers participated in every meeting about the $75 Million Campaign, and James was on its executive committee.[34]

The women agreed to raise $15 million. Their commitments to the Education and Relief and Annuity Boards were absorbed into their total campaign pledge. Later they were to admit that they carefully calculated past giving, had projected the trends, had exercised a conservative amount of faith, and had embraced a reasonable goal of one-fifth the total, rather than the usual one-third. They also gained consent to count the gifts of all women, whether WMU members or not, into the WMU quota.[35]

Following a high-pressure push for pledges during the fall, contributors had five years to pay off their pledges. There would be no other special appeals for money during this time. One pledge and one system of payment would cover the whole denomination.

WMU leaders adamantly insisted on one exception: the Lottie Moon Christmas Offering for Foreign Missions and the home missions offering. The amounts for these might be considered part of the pledge, but the offering plate would be passed as usual for these historic offerings which were really the only systematic part of Baptist giving already in place. As the campaign got underway, the women drew some criticism about breaking the unity of the campaign, but they stuck to their bargain.

Isa-Beall Neel, Georgia WMU president, was named WMU director for the campaign and Jane Cree Bose, secretary of Kentucky WMU, was borrowed for the task of WMU organizer. Neel, a brilliant administrator and powerful speaker, a woman of independent wealth, moved to Nashville for six months of volunteer work on the intensive pledge campaign. She wrote to her Georgia staff: "It seems to me there is no place to be but on my knees."[36] Bose took to the road speaking, as did the other officers. The campaign strategy called for both general and WMU organizers for each state, association, and church. WMU simply activated its existing organization, while the general campaign had to recruit workers in each association and church.

When the pledges were counted at the end of 1919, Southern Baptists had promised to give their denominational agencies more than $92,600,000. WMU had pledged $22,360,000. On the crest of these glorious promises, all agencies borrowed money to expand. The most graphic symbol of progress was the sailing of 84 missionaries and children for the Orient. This was claimed to be the largest party ever sent out by any mission board at one time.[37]

WMU declared 9:00 A.M. every Monday as an hour of prayer for the campaign. Throughout, WMU staff stopped their office work and housewives stopped their chores at this dedicated hour. It turned out that prayer was more desperately needed than they thought. After a vigorous start, the $75 Million Campaign turned to disaster. Baptist agencies did not like to share in cooperative giving. They found fault with each other's methods of calculating and processing this or that part of the money. The tight campaign organization which the agencies had hurriedly strapped together in 1919 disintegrated. Agencies tended to revert to old unilateral plans. But WMU's cooperative network stood strong. Fundamentalists unleashed charges of theological liberalism and heresy, undermining fund-raising efforts. Many Baptists soon tired of paying five-year pledges. They did not like the centralized authority implied by the campaign organization. As if these problems were not enough to sap the campaign's strength, a severe economic recession hit the nation in late 1920.[38]

WMU felt the impact of all these factors but was not seriously retarded by them. Minnie James calmly stated, "The fact remains that as depression came, the women advanced in their giving." She credited this phenomenon to WMU's meticulous record keeping and to the system of apportionment which made each segment of the organization responsible for producing a fixed sum.[39]

In local churches, women zealously kept count of their pledge progress, even though churches were also caught in the financial crunch.

At Woodlawn Baptist Church in Birmingham, the deacons decided to keep part of the WMU's campaign money to pay the salary of a new church staff member. The women rose up in righteous indignation at this misappropriation. "The men know nothing about missions, not having made a study of it," they noted. The men, duly chastened, forwarded the total amount to campaign headquarters.[40]

One of the WMU women faithfully tending her junction in the associational WMU network was Merrie Pender Sugg (Mrs. C. F.) of Richmond, Virginia. Like hundreds of other WMU leaders, she systematically wrote the church WMU leaders in her association and reminded them of their apportionment and pledge. They forwarded pledge cards and contribution reports to her. Couched among her firm reminders were sweet bits of family news, community gossip, and spiritual support. Sugg cheerfully passed information between the state WMU office and the local women.[41]

One of the state WMU organizers was Mrs. J. R. Fizer of South Carolina. She spoke in 29 of 36 associations in the state. She launched an emphasis on tithers, recruiting 3,280 by 1924. She then efficiently drew up a ledger showing contributions from each association and each church: WMS members, other women, YWA members, other young women, GA members, and so forth. For two years money generously rolled in, then more slowly, but the ledger filled up. At the end South Carolina WMU overpaid its quota by 34 percent.[42]

At the campaign midpoint WMU was not far behind on its payments, but leaders shared the panic of debts piling up on the mission boards. Kathleen Mallory urged "fidelity to the finish." Through the pages of *Royal Service* she collected signatures of 22,000 women who promised proper completion of the campaign. These she took to the Orient as a show of support to national women and missionaries abroad.

At the campaign's end in 1924, only 37.5 percent of Southern Baptists had made annual subscriptions to the campaign. Sixteen percent of the churches had paid absolutely nothing to the campaign (quite an improvement, however, over giving patterns of previous years). Of the 20,000 churches that did participate, 9,000 had not previously given to denominational causes.[43] This increase in participation constituted a turning point for Baptist unity.

The final tally showed that Southern Baptists gave more than $58 million—78 percent of the goal and 64 percent of the amount pledged.

But WMU gave $15,025,000—100 percent of its quota and 67 percent of its pledge. WMU would not have crossed the goal line without counting in $278,000 worth of boxes sent to home missionaries.

WMU exceeded its original target for education, giving $3,263,597. The goal for ministerial relief was not reached, as receipts credited to WMU for this cause were only $443,706.

The $75 Million Campaign is generally regarded as a turning point in Baptist history because it attracted more money in five years than had been given in the previous 74 years of the SBC. For Woman's Missionary Union, a new day of influence and recognition had dawned. The campaign was a prototype for the Cooperative Program, the unified church budget, and the Every Member Canvass for contributions, a trio that revolutionized Southern Baptist life. But the survival of the Cooperative Program would be in question for many years because of campaign hangover. Sadly, the agencies were left in a horrible mire of debt from which they would not escape for 20 years.

DISTASTEFUL, DEADENING, DISTURBING, DISCOURAGING, DISTRACTING DEBTS

WMU leaders habitually maintained opposition to denominational debt. ("Like all other women I hate the three D's—Debt, Dirt, and the Devil," said one leader.)[44] They never let their own affairs be touched by red ink. Yet SBC boards remained in debt throughout most of their first 100 years. The women knew they were not responsible for Home and Foreign Mission Board policies that had plunged them into debt. They had no vote in debt decisions. Even so, they felt the weight of the debts, believing that if they had only given more, indebtedness would not have been incurred.

In 1894 the Foreign Mission Board asked WMU to raise $5,000 toward the FMB debt of $30,000. Annie Armstrong immediately issued a promotional leaflet; the state WMUs divided up the goal, and WMU raised $5,397 "promptly."[45] Likewise in 1895 WMU attacked the HMB debt with what later became the Annie Armstrong Easter Offering for Home Missions.

Still the debts mounted. Fannie Heck in 1896 stated: "Debt is disgraceful. Write over every mission board's deficit sheet 'Robbed of God' and you write the truth." She also said, "Debt is extravagance," explaining the huge contributions wasted in the payment of interest on debts. Heck drove the point home: "Debt is unnecessary. If we can pay for our mission work in the end, we can pay for it in the beginning." She attributed the problem to lack of system in giving, and she urged the women to use their feminine powers to change the situation.[46]

Heck's hopes were not realized in her lifetime. Concern over the FMB debt contributed to the despair which took Lottie Moon's life in 1912, further alarming the women. R. J. Willingham suffered such anxiety over the FMB debt that he suffered a fatal breakdown in 1914.[47]

His successor, James Franklin Love, brought the matter of $180,000 in debt emotionally to both the SBC and the WMU Annual Meeting of 1916. He was later to call the WMU meeting "the holiest hour we ever saw." Love and George W. Truett stated the situation and told how the brethren of the SBC had pledged and given $80,000 the night before. Suddenly a woman rose and said she wanted to give $5,000 as a thank offering for her husband, who (she felt sure) would give the money. Mrs. J. S. Carroll of Alabama gave $1,000 to top off $30,000 she had given a few years earlier. Missionary Lottie Price of Shanghai gave the $200 she had saved for her burial. The beloved home missionary Marie Buhlmaier gave the money she had saved to enter a retirement home. A state WMU secretary gave the $100 she had saved to complete her college studies. A GA leader handed over her diamond brooch. A WMU Training School alumna promised two months' salary. Lila McIntyre of China gave her only $10 and a long string of amber beads. Evie Brown of Tennessee promptly "bought" them for $75 and gave the beads back to the missionary. A woman called out that she had her husband's consent to give her wedding ring. The total in the offering plate full of jewelry, cash, and pledges exceeded $17,000. J. F. Love commended WMU as a paragon of efficiency. "We have nothing like it in the Southern Baptist organization. No other commanders of the hosts of the Lord can so quickly mobilize and concentrate on a given task so large a company of trained veterans as can the officers of the WMU."[48]

The continuing debt situation led WMU to inaugurate the Emergency Women plan, paralleling the Laymen's Missionary Movement's Emergency Men. Those who agreed to be Emergency Women were committed to pay at least $5 in response to no more than one emergency appeal in a year.

The mission boards managed to pay off all debts as the United States came out of World War I. The Convention's momentary exhilaration led to the $75 Million Campaign, which left the mission boards in worse debt than ever. In the late 1920s, each mission board was struck by embezzlement which further increased the debt. Then the Great Depression of the 1930s put the boards into near bankruptcy. Stress over the debt killed J. F. Love.[49]

WMU leaders sounded a note of optimism throughout the depression. They were careful to have upbeat Annual Meetings. They chose "Joy to the World, the Lord Is Come" as the hymn of the year for 1931-32. Kathleen Mallory noted that if the letters d, e, i were removed from depression, the words press on would remain. Elizabeth C. Lowndes (Mrs. W. C.), treasurer of WMU, delivered her reports of declining contributions with a "serene and beautiful spirit," and said, "Now don't you think that is a beautiful report?"[50]

In 1932, with the mission boards sinking deeper and deeper into the depression, WMU promised it would "enter heartily into whatever plans the SBC may make" regarding debts. The mission boards reported that they would not survive the summer of 1932 without help. The SBC announced an emergency offering during June and July. It netted $203,909, of which WMU gave more than $52,000.[51] The boards survived 1932, but the Great Depression worsened. What would happen?

By 1933 debts on the two mission boards were nearly $3 million. Total denominational debts (including state causes) were estimated at almost $6 million. In Virginia, Blanche S. White, the indomitable WMU secretary, gave a compelling speech at Barton Heights Church of Richmond. The pastor, Wade S. Bryant, was so moved that he worked out a plan which Virginia WMU adopted in March 1933. The Wade Bryant Plan called for Foreign Mission Board debts to be paid by persons willing to give 25 cents a week beyond their regular contributions. Olive B. Martin (Mrs. George R.) of Virginia, the WMU, SBC, stewardship chairman, brought this idea and Wade Bryant to sell it to the May WMU, SBC, Annual Meeting. On motion of Annie N. Thompson (Mrs. Ben S.), who was also on the SBC Executive Committee, WMU endorsed the Wade Bryant Plan with its emphasis on the FMB.

Meanwhile, the SBC Executive Committee was in session to discuss a plan advanced by Frank Tripp of Missouri in which 100,000 persons would pledge to give $1 extra a month, with the proceeds going to all Baptist agency debts. After an intense debate, Annie Thompson reported to WMU that she was having trouble getting the Executive Committee to agree to free the FMB from debt ahead of the other agencies. She asked if the larger meeting would permit the WMU Executive Committee and officers to work matters out with the SBC.[52]

That night the SBC Executive Committee was to convene at 10:00 P.M. Louie Newton, editor of the *Christian Index*, boarded a taxi with Blanche White, and the two argued furiously while Juliette Mather, WMU's young people's secretary, cowered between them. All the way to the meeting, White insisted that WMU would support nothing but "foreign missions first," ignoring Mather who was trying to say that WMU had practically acquiesced to Frank Tripp's plan.

Kathleen Mallory was voiceless by that late hour. She could only sit in frustrated silence. Newton was appointed spokesman for the men. He informed Mallory that he understood her voice problem, that she need not say anything, just nod. Then he began his discourse with, "Now, Miss Kathleen. . . ." She shook her head violently.

At 2:00 A.M. Mallory made the men understand that WMU would go along with the Tripp plan which became known as the Hundred Thousand Club. Virginia WMU, however, stayed with its original Quarter a Week plan which favored the FMB. Olive Martin immediately resigned as Southwide stewardship chairman. She was returned to presidency of Virginia WMU and led the state to outgive other states in debt payment.[53]

Frank Tripp was made general director of the Hundred Thousand

Club. A small committee to work out details included his friend and neighbor Missourian, Laura M. Armstrong (Mrs. F. W.), president of WMU, who had undoubtedly favored Tripp's plan all along. The Hundred Thousand Club moved to first place in WMU's urgent promotion. From the start Tripp acknowledged that more than 60 percent of the Hundred Thousand Club members were women.[54] WMU publications were immediately full of the Hundred Thousand Club. Mallory wrote, "Denominational debts are distasteful, deadening, disturbing, discouraging, and distracting."

WMU added to its 50th anniversary celebration the recruitment of more Hundred Thousand Club members. As the 1940s dawned, Mallory printed on WMU's letterhead, For a Debtless Denomination by 1945. When the WMU Executive Committee met in May 1940, Blanche White proposed that WMU raise $1 million of the $3 million remaining on SBC debts. Alma W. Wright (Mrs. Carter) of Alabama, WMU's new stewardship chairman, said that if the goal were reached, it would be the most fantastic achievement in WMU history. She took the additional title, WMU Promoter for a Debtless Denomination. Mallory spoke "with more emotion and more power" than ever before heard as she pleaded for a debtless denomination. In unison the committee knelt for prayer. The Foreign Mission Board secretary announced, "We will have our debts paid by 1945. WMU has promised, and you can count on them."[55]

In 1942 the SBC Executive Committee made "especial mention and grateful appreciation to the WMU for their gracious, sustained, and increasingly substantial help. If our men will rally to this cause in a similar way we shall surely have a Debtless Denomination by 1945."

The women had such success that a new slogan was drafted, Debt-free in '43, Count on Me. Alma Wright had the women repeat at the 1942 Annual Meeting: "It depends on me." The $1 million goal was reached in 1943. On March 11, 1943, the FMB sent a cable to every mission that it was free of debt. In 1944, the WMU Promoter for a Debtless Denomination lay in a hospital bed from which she would never arise. Kathleen Mallory came to visit with the news that enabled Alma Wright to go to her grave with satisfaction: All the debts were paid.

When all the figures were tallied, WMU had given no less than 61.2 percent of all the debt payment money since the Hundred Thousand Club was launched in 1933. According to SBC figures, WMU gave 63.5 percent. James E. Dillard, director of the Hundred Thousand Club and the Cooperative Program at that time, said, "Women just hate debt."[56]

THE COOPERATIVE PROGRAM

By 1923, Baptist leaders knew that whether the $75 Million Campaign failed or succeeded, they would have to join financial hands to face the future. At the WMU Annual Meeting, Minnie James led an open discussion about how to develop a plan for systematic and proportional giving by individuals and by churches—the age-old dream of WMU. The SBC appointed a massive Committee on Future Program. This group included a WMU officer from every state, plus James and Mallory. The committee, one-third of whom were women, had the highest female representation ever achieved on an SBC-appointed committee or board, even to the present.

The product of this committee was the Cooperative Program, which was to become the lifeline of Southern Baptist work. WMU not only helped give birth to this program, but fed it, protected it, tolerated it, and finally shaped it into an instrument that the women loved.

The Cooperative Program actually was implemented in 1924. It got its name and policies in 1925 at the Southern Baptist Convention. Amid furor about theology at that SBC meeting, this new child scarcely drew attention. But WMU leaders had their eyes on it.

WMU agreed with the general principle of unified giving by all church members to a central budget. It agreed with the idea that each church should voluntarily forward a portion of its income to the state convention. It agreed that each state should forward a portion of its receipts to the SBC Executive Committee, and that these receipts should be divided among the various SBC agencies according to a predetermined scale. At the same time, WMU insisted that the right of designated giving be preserved; if a person wished to specify that his gift be restricted to a certain cause, the restriction would be honored.

At each dividing line, WMU believed that 50-50 should be the rule: 50 percent leaving the church, 50 percent leaving the state, and 50 percent leaving the homeland for foreign missions.

Through WMU's insistence, the guidelines adopted in 1925 stated that "the special thank offerings for state and home missions and the Christmas Offering for Foreign Missions ingathered during the Week of Prayer of the Woman's Missionary Union for these respective causes shall be recognized as gifts in addition to the regular contributions to the Cooperative Program and shall not be subject to expense deduction or percentage bases." Without this guarantee, WMU would never have promoted the Cooperative Program.

The program was hampered at the start because one-eighth of Southern Baptists were contributing seven-eighths of the money, and that was not enough money to cover the needs. Also, fewer than 28 percent of the churches had budgets or unified giving plans.[57] Next, the program was hampered because the 50-50 principle was not observed. Only six churches were known to have forwarded 50 percent of their funds in 1925. Four of these were Alabama churches highly influenced by WMU staff and board, including First Baptist of Montgomery, whose pastor was husband of a former WMU, SBC, president; and another was First Baptist of Richmond, in Foreign Mission Board territory.[58]

WMU Insists on Strong Support for Foreign Missions.—Most irritating to WMU was that the 50-50 standard was not willingly applied to allocations among SBC agencies. Leaders agreed with journalist E. C. Routh, who said, "Foreign Missions is the only enterprise which will float all the enterprises and lift them above the water line of danger. The appeal of Foreign Missions will more completely enlist . . . and elicit more resources for all the work of the churches than any other appeal which we can make."[59]

Yet during 1926 the FMB got only 25 percent of the undesignated dollars. WMU representatives felt so strongly about this that they withdrew the WMU Training School from the allocation list (it should have received 1 percent of the allocations, maintaining a pattern of allocations begun during the $75 Million Campaign), on condition that the money be yielded to the Foreign Mission Board.

Early in 1926 WMU announced in *Royal Service* that it would be officially asking the 1926 SBC to guarantee 50 percent of every undesignated dollar to the FMB. This advance publicity got the FMB its 50 percent in 1926-27, and the WMU Training School was restored to the list at the expense of the Relief and Annuity Board and the Education Board.[60]

When the Cooperative Program Commission met in January 1927 WMU was asked to solicit special large private gifts to the Cooperative Program. The WMU Executive Committee considered the proposal and refused, stating that spasmodic giving of this sort would defeat the purpose of systematic giving. "The Union is too loyal to the Cooperative Program to endorse anything that in the long run will tell against it." The women disapproved soliciting special gifts large or small through this channel of giving.[61]

WMU's Record Speaks.—Unquestionably, WMU strongly promoted the Cooperative Program, while not ceasing to critique it. Still, only one in three societies contributed through the CP in 1926. This fact is one explanation as to why the plan was not producing the money expected or needed by the agencies. But WMU cannot be disproportionately faulted for the problems. Although figures are hard to analyze, it would appear that WMU in 1926 contributed approximately 43 percent of all the money given to SBC causes. That was done when WMU had organizations in fewer than half the churches.

The treasurer of WMU and Frank Burkhalter, staff promotion director for the CP, reviewed unpublished figures and calculated WMU's portion from April 30, 1923, through April 30, 1928. WMU contributed 41 percent of the CP for that era.[62] In the 1931 report to the Southern Baptist

Convention WMU claimed contributions to the CP of 44 percent.

WMU treasurers in churches, associations, and states kept records of how much WMU gave to missions causes, even if contributed through the church budget. Despite attempts to stop the bothersome habit,[63] most WMU leaders felt it urgent to keep the statistics as a measure of effectiveness and as leverage to protect missions. Their case was proven. In April 1929 Kathleen Mallory circulated to the WMU Executive Committee a draft of the proposed SBC Business and Financial Plan. She warned WMUers to make a careful study and to take a stand "in order to safeguard the offerings of our three seasons of prayer as well as any other gifts which might be made with the longing to increase by such 'over and above' the maximum allotted to any object included in the SBC Cooperative Program."

WMU Tangles with the SBC.—Austin Crouch, executive secretary of the SBC Executive Committee, explained to the May meeting of the WMU Executive Committee that the SBC Executive Committee wanted to keep agencies from soliciting funds outside the CP. The SBC committee wanted to count the two missions offerings as Cooperative Program. WMU had clearly been in violation of the rules (which could not be forced on WMU as an auxiliary) by continuing to take collections for the Margaret Fund and the WMUTS. WMU felt that it had no alternative, since these matters, which were in their eyes essential to SBC life, were not being provided for through the CP.

Furthermore, Crouch seemed to be "after" WMU because the mission boards were using CP money to provide WMU's "recalls" for its operating budget. WMU had been discussing whether to forfeit these funds in order to leave the mission boards more spending money. Had WMU done this, its own operating funds would have had to be solicited directly from members. So, WMU continued to draw on the boards, following the 1888 gentlemen's agreement that if church WMUs sent their collections to the boards instead of sifting them through WMU's fingers, they were due whatever "refund" or "recall" for expenses they might require. After an unpleasant discussion with Crouch, WMU executives went on record as vehemently opposed to the idea that the Lottie Moon and Annie Armstrong offerings would be counted against the mission boards' allocations.

Despite WMU response, the SBC Executive Committee argued the Business and Financial Plan until 11:40 P.M.,[64] then passed it on for approval by the 1929 SBC. It restricted agencies from giving funds to other agencies of the SBC. Somehow this was never applied to WMU, presumably on the basis that WMU was an auxiliary, not an agency of the SBC.

Of more consequence was a small loophole which allowed designations for specific "extra budget items." Otherwise, if the LMCO and

AAO were turned in as general offerings as in the past, they would be charged against the agencies' allocation from the CP.

If the brethren thought that this strict statement would thwart WMU or limit the amount of the special offerings, they were soon to be reeducated. WMU simply drew up excruciatingly detailed lists of "extra budget items" for which the LMCO and AAO would be spent if given. WMU women loved raising money for specific missionaries' salaries, cars, refrigerators, church buildings, or whatever. They also enjoyed the intimacy they gained with mission board policy. The offerings began to grow dramatically, and just in time to save the mission boards from creditors. Because the women tightly controlled designations, creditors could not get the money for debt payments.

WMU had found a way around the CP rules, but they would not rest until what they regarded as an unbaptistic policy was overturned. WMU stated to the 1929 SBC: "WMU is radically opposed to any budget system which would preclude or discourage the offerings . . . which have been officially approved by the SBC. Certainly they have the seal of time's approval. Surely these offerings are no longer specials—really they are regulars."

WMU paid a price for their adamant stand. WMU representatives were struck from the Cooperative Program planning process. Right away the men set the Every Member Canvass for the church budget and Cooperative Program at the worst possible time for WMU, during the Week of Prayer for Foreign Missions. Yet M. E. Dodd, chairman of the canvass planning committee, came to the 1931 WMU meeting to request the women's help with the canvass.

WMU leaders privately protested and publicly instructed its members to cooperate fully with the canvass, especially trying to secure a contribution from every woman. The women decided to pray for the canvass along with praying for foreign missionaries. Very simply WMU stated in its report to the 1932 SBC: "Loyal support was unquestionably given to the Every Member Canvass . . . " but "the committee has been notified that for 44 years the Union has ingathered its Christmas Offering, naturally in December."

On the good side of the SBC Executive Committee's handling of the CP, it recommended in 1931 that the expenses of state WMUs be considered as a deductible promotional expense before state conventions divided funds with the SBC. Thus state WMUs were recognized as major promotional agencies for the CP and their funding was encouraged. And in 1932, WMU was restored to the Promotion Committee of the Convention, in the person of Kathleen Mallory.

In 1931 WMU again forfeited the allocation of 1 percent for the WMU Training School in order to provide more money for the mission boards. The WMUTS faculty simply cut their salaries and expenses, asked the

WMU women to send groceries to keep everybody fed, and weathered the storm without incurring debt.

The Cooperative Program Weathers the Great Depression.— These struggles did little to solve the real problem of the crumbling CP as the Great Depression dragged the mission boards under. To WMU's credit, the women never ceased to promote the Cooperative Program with intensity. Because of inconsistencies in fiscal years, exact figures are not possible but WMU in 1931 (according to 1932 reports) gave approximately 76 percent of all mission board receipts.

Nobody could question WMU's loyalty, so the women boldly said to the 1932 SBC: "Thousands of WMU members and organizations view with distress if not disheartened dismay the nonscriptural and therefore non-Baptist teaching and compulsion of those who would discourage freewill offerings at any time and in any way and for any purpose that a Christian heart feels led to give."[65]

But WMU was soundly criticized by the Relief and Annuity Board. The Board stated its case in WMU's Annual Report of 1932, saying, "If our good women and others are going to continue to designate a large part of their gifts, we feel that the needs of our aged ministers should be considered and 7 percent of such gifts should be sent to the Relief Board." Texas WMU began to sponsor an offering for that state's aged ministers and their widows. WMU, SBC, never did more than suggest that local women personally issue relief to needy ministers they knew, explaining that WMU's business was missions.[66]

Notable sages of the SBC went to the 1933 Convention with the intention of scrapping the Cooperative Program. Instead, the objectionable rule blocking designations was overturned. The Hundred Thousand Club was adopted, WMU redoubled its efforts to promote the Every Member Canvass, and *Royal Service* began to publish lists of churches in which every resident woman contributed to missions.[67]

By 1936 WMU made Cooperative Program giving a point in the Standard of Excellence and strongly stated, "Special offerings are important but must never take the place of week by week regular tithes and gifts to the Cooperative Program."[68]

WMU Again Fights for Missions and the Offerings.—But WMU still had a struggle about the Foreign Mission Board's 50 percent. Laura Armstrong and Frank Tripp organized a minority report to the SBC in 1944 and overturned an SBC Executive Committee recommendation that cut the FMB's allocation. A woman member of the FMB wrote to Kathleen Mallory about the proposed cut, and the women swung into action. Mallory wrote to Armstrong: "This [50 percent to the FMB] has a REAL appeal to Baptists whether men or women." She also said, "No discussions should be permitted to lay the blame on our School [WMUTS] for not keeping the Foreign Board at 50 percent."[69]

Armstrong, with her insider's view of the SBC Executive Committee, and Mallory, with her experience in wielding statistics, began in 1944 to publish WMU's contributions to the Cooperative Program so that the women's right to form policy would not be discounted.

Armstrong died in 1945, leaving no woman on the SBC Executive Committee. At the next year's Southern Baptist Convention a sheaf of SBC Executive Committee recommendations was approved as a block with little debate. Amid the proposals was the WMU-dreaded rule that the special offerings would be counted as part of the mission board's allocations from the Cooperative Program and not added to them.

In the same mood, an all-male committee on denominational coordination was appointed with the thinly veiled intent of altering WMU's relationship to the Convention. The SBC Executive Committee notified WMU that it must submit reports and budget requests for the WMU Training School, just as SBC agencies were required to do. WMUTS had never been required to do this since it began receiving cooperative funding in 1920, but it willingly complied.[70]

During the next year, the percentage of CP funds contributed by WMU declined. Designated giving (including the LMCO and AAO) increased a record 34 percent, while the Cooperative Program increased only 15 percent. WMU leaders entered into concerned correspondence with the mission board executives. They seemed less concerned about the blending of the WMU offerings into the allocations process than they were about a new capital funds section of the CP which eroded the FMB's 50 percent. M. Theron Rankin of the FMB took his objections to the denominational press.

The capital expenditure plan stayed, but the 1947 SBC amended the Business and Financial Plan. It effectively ended random fund-raising for mission boards outside the Cooperative Program, by forbidding the agencies from cooperating with any individual or group in special solicitations without approval of the SBC or the SBC Executive Committee. But the provision said that this did not apply to the Lottie Moon or Annie Armstrong offerings.[71]

In reporting CP receipts and disbursements, the SBC Executive Committee of the mid-1940s would not identify the Lottie Moon Christmas Offering and Annie Armstrong Offering by name. The SBC made every effort to downplay the offerings and to build up the Cooperative Program.

WMU did indeed support the Cooperative Program. WMU encouraged women to give their tithes undesignated to the church budget, which would in turn forward a percentage to the Cooperative Program. But when WMU could not assure women that the Foreign Mission Board would get 50 percent of the CP, and the HMB the next largest share, interest inevitably shifted to the LMCO and AAO.

Above their tithes, the women were encouraged to give to the special missions offerings. In some churches, the CP was not written into the church budget, so WMU people forwarded their CP money straight to the state WMU office. As late as 1950 WMU offices of Alabama and Kentucky regularly received significant amounts of Cooperative Program money, which they turned over to the state convention. Through this means the executive secretary of Alabama Baptists could say for a fact that WMU gave more than half the Cooperative Program money.[72]

WMU, SBC, financial reports, compared to the SBC reports on CP giving, reveal a startling picture of WMU's power in the CP. Fiscal years of WMU and the SBC did not coincide, making it impossible to compute exactly, but on the average between 1946 and 1951, WMU's reported contributions to the Cooperative Program (apparently including CP funds used in the states) equaled 83 percent of the SBC-level total.

WMU and the mission boards tried to keep the CP's focus on missions. During 1947 the FMB actually netted only 43 percent of the CP, and for 1948 the percentage dropped to 35 percent. At the 1948 Southern Baptist Convention the SBC Executive Committee issued a defensive and edgy report which seemed critical of the FMB's clamor for more of the Cooperative Program. But it promised to the FMB a cosmetic 50 percent of the 1949 CP (the 50 percent was calculated only after many preferred items were skimmed off the top). To WMU's disappointment, the HMB allocation was cut in order to supply foreign missions. And still the FMB received only 35 percent of the funds given.

The Home Mission Board openly told WMU: "The Southern Baptist Convention has cut our allocation from 23⅓ percent to a little over 14 percent in the past few years, which has reduced our income from the Cooperative Program over $400,000 a year on a five million dollar basis. . . . This means that we have to depend upon our women for a very large part of our mission program."[73]

A New Era Opens.—M. T. Rankin in 1948 issued a dramatic challenge for foreign missions Advance. Advance depended on a larger share of the CP and/or increased LMCO. WMU proceeded to finance the great growth era of missions with growing emphasis on the special offerings. In effect there came to be two more-or-less equal streams of support: the Cooperative Program and the special missions offerings of WMU. The former reflected the logic and the latter revealed the heart of Baptists. The special offerings from 1946 onward outstripped the CP in rate of growth. In 1961 the Cooperative Program slipped to second place, and the Lottie Moon Christmas Offering became the largest source of FMB funds. The HMB fared similarly.

In 1950 WMU decided to stop tracking its CP contributions, since they were bothersome to compute and irritating to some persons. State WMUs for the most part ceased to require their constituent associational and church WMUs to fill quotas to increase the CP. But WMU tightened its Standard of Excellence to require that 75 percent of its members give regularly through the Cooperative Program. By 1957, a local WMU had to report 100 percent of its members giving through the CP in order to get top ranking.

WMU continued to uphold the original CP standard of 50-50 division. The WMU Plan of Work suggested that WMU members exert influence in their churches to "lift the percentage of gifts through the Cooperative Program to a minimum of 50-50." To assist them with this lobbying task, WMU literature was filled with colorful stories about how the CP would benefit all programs of the SBC.

The Stewardship Commission of the SBC became operative in January 1961. The month before, its leaders, the state convention executive secretaries, and the officers of WMU, Marie Wiley Mathis (Mrs. R. L.) and Alma Hunt, met in Nashville to plan to strengthen the Cooperative Program. Mathis and Hunt were deeply moved by the men's request for more educational and prayer support from WMU. The women brought to the January 1961 Executive Board of WMU a proposal for a week of prayer for the Cooperative Program.

WMU leaders debated the proposal for two sessions that were so strenuous that Mathis repeatedly stopped the discussion for prayer. Hunt went to the 1961 Southern Baptist Convention with a strong promise to support the week of prayer for the CP in cooperation with other agencies. She acknowledged the criticism some pastors were voicing about the rapid growth of the special missions offerings, and suggested that a week of prayer and education for the CP might balance the growth.[74] The Convention discussed the proposal, but did not approve it.

WMU support for the Cooperative Program continued in a consistent way after this offer was turned down. WMU no longer felt the primary responsibility for the survival and success of the CP, but was willing to share promotion responsibility with others. Working closely with the Brotherhood Commission and the Stewardship Commission, WMU promoted Cooperative Program Day in April and Cooperative Program Month in October.

WMU staff occasionally reminded their friends in other agencies to be careful about their use of the word *missions* in relation to the CP. Some Southern Baptists referred to the CP and all its causes as missions. WMU insisted on a strict use of the word, pointing out that the FMB and the HMB were the only missions part of the CP at the SBC level. The other causes were legitimate Christian work, but they were not missions according to WMU.[75]

In 1974-75 WMU celebrated the 50th anniversary of the Cooperative Program with a resolution of support at the Annual Meeting, a resolution which again affirmed the 50-50 principle.[76]

In 1976 the SBC Executive Committee, the Stewardship Commission, and the Sunday School Board researched Cooperative Program knowledge and attitude among various groups of Baptists. The survey found that next to pastors, WMU directors scored highest in their knowledge about the Cooperative Program. Approximately 82 percent of those surveyed felt that the special missions offerings did not have a negative effect on the Cooperative Program.

In November 1983 WMU published the first leaflets targeted at the growing ethnic membership in the SBC. These were the first CP data published in the ethnic languages.

WMU never forgot that Minnie James had said at the end of her life that helping develop the Cooperative Program was the best thing she had done.

THE TITHE

In a 1936 study of 20 leading denominations, the United Stewardship Council reported that Southern Baptist per capita giving to missions, education, and benevolence was the lowest among denominations, at $1.87. Studied separately from other Southern Baptists, WMU per capita giving for the same period was $4.49.[77]

WMU's superior statistics grew out of WMU's emphasis on giving one-tenth of one's income for church work.

Long before the Southern Baptist Convention officially espoused tithing, women were sponsoring the idea. Nobody has explained why penniless women would have preceded moneyed men in interpreting the tithe as obligatory for Christians. But they did. As early as 1884 Margaretta D. Early (Mrs. M. D.), then of Arkansas, said that churches were in debt and lacking God's blessings because they failed to teach the tithe.[78] The first Baptist women's newspaper, the *Heathen Helper,* promoted tithing before WMU was organized. The *Heathen Helper* spawned a sister publication, the *Baptist Basket,* the first (and only) Baptist publication devoted to the subject of stewardship and tithing.

On the cover amid Scripture verses and couplets about stewardship, the *Basket* said, "Ho ye that would be wise, Oh, bring to Him His tithes!"[79]

Lottie Moon, pioneer missionary in China, was a tither. In the same letter which encouraged the formation of Woman's Missionary Union, she wrote that a woman should "lay aside sacredly not less than one-tenth of her income or her earnings as the Lord's money, which she would no more dare to touch for personal use than she would steal."[80]

At the 1888 Convention meeting when F. M. Ellis encouraged WMU and urged the SBC to implement systematic and proportionate giving, he made no mention of tithing, but only "giving as God may prosper."

But the women published a leaflet on tithing that year. They mentioned tithing in their 1890 Plan of Work. Finally in 1895, Ellis again was chairing an SBC money committee and got the Convention to endorse tithing for the first time.[81] That action convinced the *Baptist Basket* that it was no longer needed, and it appeared last in September 1895.

By that time the WMU had exchanged its gentle plea for the leftover penny to a demand for the tenth, sacredly laid aside as "first fruits," regularly given. Days of prayer for tithing sent women to their knees in 1909 and 1910.[82]

Launching WMU's 25th anniversary in 1913, Fannie Heck said she was convinced that even if tithing were not clearly taught in the Bible, it was the most practical way to support God's work. So, she nailed it to the mast of WMU. As an anniversary feature, WMU issued a tithing pledge and record card. Each woman was approached about signing it, giving a copy to her society president, and keeping a regular, public record of her obedience to God's command. WMU began to count the number of tithers and report them in the Annual Report. In 1913 there were 1,082 reported tithers in WMU, the next year, 3,124.[83]

Heck on her deathbed wrote to her best friend and successor as North Carolina WMU president: "Do not let the emphasis on the tenth be lowered."[84] She need not have worried; in 1918 WMU distributed 64,000 tithing cards, and the organization was in good form for victory in the $75 Million Campaign.

WMU publications began to be flooded with tithing tips. Women were taught they did indeed have access to money and they were responsible for tithing. Eggs and jars of jelly could be counted, one in ten set aside for sale and church.

If a husband refused to tithe the family income, the wife could earn an amount equal to a proper tithe by selling her own products, then give it to the church. If the family income had not been tithed, then the woman was at least responsible for tithing the household allowance that came under her management. In any case, a Christian wife held the key to whether the husband would agree to tithe. If she would adjust her spending to fit nine-tenths, surely the husband would permit one-tenth to go to the church.[85] From 1922 onward all WMU literature for all ages gave practical, specific guidance on how to tithe and why.

Perhaps the pinnacle of tithing promotion came in the 1926 Annual Meeting. Ethlene Boone Cox (Mrs. W. J.) had appointed Laura Armstrong chairman of a tithing committee. Armstrong's dynamic leadership in this committee was to carry her into the presidency of WMU. She designed a tither's pin, a new tithing record card, a tither enlistment ceremony, declamation contests, poster and storywriting contests for young people, and endless other inducements.

The most sparkling minds of WMU focused on the tithing topic for the 1926 meeting. Myrtle Robinson Creasman (Mrs. C. D.) of Tennessee, a popular writer and speaker, wrote such jingles as "When Baptists All Learn How to Tithe" (to tune of "Since Jesus Came into My Heart") and "Jesus Wants Me for a Tither" (tune of "Jesus Wants Me for a Sunbeam"). Alma Wright (Mrs. Carter) delivered a classic address which was later distributed via 60,000 tracts published by the Sunday School Board. Her topic was "The Tithe: God's Law, Our Test and Opportunity." Among her pungent sayings was this: "You can't take it with you, but you can send it on ahead."

To crown the tithing emphasis Willie Turner Dawson (Mrs. J. M.) gave a stirring address on the Cooperative Program. Then Ethlene Cox asked all in the audience who would endeavor to pay the tithe to stand. Almost the entire audience leaped to their feet.[86] The frenetic promotion of 1926 gained one-third more tithers for a total of 60,000. As the rest of the denomination began to count tithers, 1 person out of every 18 Baptists was found to tithe. But in WMU the count was 1 in 6.

Belief in tithing helped WMU stave off the effects of the Great Depression. As the economy worsened, WMU pushed the Prove Me plan, in which persons were asked to try tithing for a few months. Half the WMU members reported themselves as tithers in 1955; that number was almost half the total list of tithers among all Southern Baptists. (WMU membership at that time was 15 percent of the SBC membership.) WMU's tither total topped a half-million in 1960. The numbers became too enormous to compute; the 1960s generation did not like to keep detailed records of anything; and WMU stopped reportings its tithers. WMU officials never compromised their belief in the tithe as the minimum church contribution for the Christian, but structured promotion on the topic dropped out of WMU curriculum in the mid-1960s. By Southern Baptist Convention assignment, tithing promotion became the responsibility of the Stewardship Commission. WMU began to concentrate less on overall stewardship matters and more on specific missions finance.

But history is now repeating itself. Long-range plans of WMU, SBC, for 1988-95 call for renewed emphasis on tithing as the basic step in funding missions.

STEWARDSHIP ORGANIZED

Stewardship became a formal matter for education and administration just prior to the Great Depression. WMU made 1928-29, its 40th anniversary, a stewardship campaign. Alma Wright, anniversary chairman, began to write a steady stream of biblical and practical inspiration about stewardship. The anniversary was the ladder which helped WMU climb to a 26 percent increase in overall giving.

So important did the word *stewardship* become to WMU, a conventionwide stewardship chairman was appointed to continue the promotion. One of the brightest young faces in WMU, Olive Martin, gave up the presidency of Virginia WMU in order to take the post. Under her leadership WMU began to write letters of commendation to churches that reported 100 percent of women giving to missions. During 1933 the officers had to write only 89 letters. Most of the recognized churches were in Martin's own state.[87]

After Martin resigned as stewardship chairman in 1933, Alma Wright took the post and became inseparably identified with stewardship. During her ten-year term, the denomination straightened out its finances. Wright moved WMU beyond concern for stewardship of money to realization that the Christian was also responsible for stewardship of other resources. She stated in 1938 that a minimum of one-seventh of one's time should be devoted to Christian work.[88] She began to promote stewardship revivals, linking giving with evangelism and Christian maturity. She believed that "no revival is genuine that does not go deep enough to reach the pocketbook."[89] Under her leadership WMU per capita giving in 1943 reached $5.06 per year, whereas Northern Baptist women reported $4.54 per capita.[90]

Upon Wright's death the stewardship chairman was Amy Compere Hickerson (Mrs. Clyde V.) of Virginia. Myrtle Creasman took the post 1949-52. Creasman received a small stipend for her services, leading to stewardship promotion being made a staff responsibility.

The wolf was safely away from the mission boards' doors in the 1950s, so WMU stepped back for a more general study of stewardship. A series of stewardship study books for all ages was issued in 1954. State stewardship chairmen were invited to Birmingham for a meeting in May 1956. Alma Hunt explained to them that the emphasis on giving one-tenth for the church would not be lessened, but that the nine-tenths remaining must also be used in a Christian way. Moreover, WMU became concerned about Christian distinctives in acquisition of money. Stewardship conferences rippled across the country. In 1955 the WMU Executive Board adopted a definite stewardship policy for education of children.

The time-honored phrase *Tithes and Offerings* was replaced in the 1955-56 Plan of Work with the broader term *Stewardship of Possessions*. The purpose was to magnify WMU's position that stewardship was "a principle to be instilled, rather than a method to be installed."

WMU increasingly promoted the stewardship plans advanced by the SBC's Stewardship Commission and originated fewer of its own emphases. WMU supported the use of the envelope system, the Church Night of Stewardship, and the Forward Program of Church Finance—all generally popular ideas of the 1950s and 1960s. In January 1966 the

Executive Board dropped WMU's long-standing custom of distributing free leaflets about tithing and stewardship, since other agencies were claiming promotional responsibility.

Principles of stewardship moved again to center stage in 1979. For three years WMU's headline emphasis was Life-Changing Commitments. Leaders believed that the SBC's plan of Bold Mission Thrust (a goal of spreading the gospel throughout the world by the year 2000) would succeed only if persons radically changed their standards of living and giving for the support of missions.[91]

In 1980 the SBC Executive Committee appointed a Cooperative Program Study Team. Its task was to make and recommend a plan of action to increase the level of giving to the local church and through the local church to SBC cooperative ministries. Carolyn Weatherford and Christine Gregory (Mrs. A. Harrison) represented WMU on this committee which met until 1983. Among other items of discussion was a proposal that special missions offerings be factored into the Cooperative Program, with the goal set by the SBC on recommendation of WMU.

WMU was not willing to relinquish its final responsibility for the offerings, nor to admit them to being budgeted along with the Cooperative Program. Carolyn Weatherford told her staff, "I want the Cooperative Program to grow and to contribute a larger part of the mission boards' receipts than the offerings do. Ideally the offerings would be for 'extras' and not for 'basics.' "

The plan for expanding the Cooperative Program was developed by a writing team which reported to the Cooperative Program Study Team. Because of time, the plan was reported directly to the SBC Executive Committee without the study team or the agencies having a chance to evaluate it. The plan was called Planned Growth in Giving. WMU was given no special role to play in it. Weatherford wrote to state WMU officers April 15, 1985: "I am concerned that Woman's Missionary Union has not been included in a major way. In the past, when Southern Baptists made giant steps forward in mission support, WMU was assigned major responsibility. This happened with the $75 Million Campaign, the Hundred Thousand Club, and Cooperative Program. I believe we in WMU must guard carefully our tradition of lay leadership. I believe that Planned Growth in Giving puts too much responsibility on the pastor without utilizing the natural leaders in mission support. WMU members because of missions education already understand the need for growth in giving."

Giving is one way of living with all your might.

Ethlene Boone Cox
Following in His Train

The habit of victory

WMU has a habit of victory. Resolute, purposeful,
undiscourageable, they attend to their objectives.

Committee on WMU Report
Southern Baptist Convention,
1934

RUE TO ITS original purpose, Woman's Missionary Union has perfected expertise in collecting money for missions. Three times a year the women heap money on the missionary-sending agencies of Southern Baptist life and lead men and children to follow their example. Since the early 1930s WMU's habit of victory has steadily increased the special missions offerings ahead of the inflation rate. The offerings have become the largest source of funds for both home missions and foreign missions. In return the offerings have given WMU a highly visible rally point.

Management of the offerings through a century has revealed much about WMU's culture of commitment. WMU has tenderly nurtured, jealously guarded, vigorously promoted, and consistently cherished these projects. Each offering is floated on the breath of united prayer. In the giving, WMU's consistent plans of education, information, and organization come to bear fruit. During the past quarter-century, WMU ceased to maintain detailed records and reports of its other activities, but the special offerings continue to be tallied. Those reports stand alone to show that WMU is maintaining the habit of victory.

The special offering for foreign missions took flight in WMU's first year, 1888, establishing immediately the habit of victory. The home missions offering dates continuously from 1895. Offerings for missions of the various state WMU organizations began at the turn of the century and developed in a variety of formats. Each offering has at times saved its cause from destruction, has changed the course of missions history, has propped open the doors of advancement for the givers. The offerings have been the handles by which persons outside of WMU membership have taken a grip on missions involvement.

Each of the nationwide offerings is linked to a season of church celebration. Foreign missions spoke first for the Christmas season. More recently home missions claimed the Easter season. The offerings give a Christian, uniquely Baptistic outlet for holiday emotions.

The harvest of foreign missions money begins with the Week of Prayer for Foreign Missions, scheduled for the first week of December. Prayer and study that week overflow into the Lottie Moon Christmas Offering for Foreign Missions. WMU does not continue promotion of the offering beyond early January. When the second week of March rolls around, WMU is again leading the churches in prayer and promotion, this time for home missions. The monetary fruit of the Week of Prayer for Home Missions is the Annie Armstrong Easter Offering. September is the traditional month for state missions offerings.

In the early 1960s WMU, in cooperation with the SBC Committee on Denominational Calendar, adopted a permanent policy for setting the weeks of prayer dates. The foreign missions week is the first Sunday in December through the second Sunday, except when December 1 falls on Monday, Tuesday, or Wednesday. In such a case the week begins on the last Sunday of November. The home missions week is set for the first Sunday through the second Sunday of March.

In the case of both home and foreign offerings, funds flow efficiently through the same channels that contain the Cooperative Program: from church to state Baptist convention office, to Southern Baptist Convention headquarters in Nashville, to the Foreign Mission Board and to the Home Mission Board. The money does not go through WMU's hands at any point.

The Lottie Moon Christmas Offering has been described as one of the largest short-term financial projects in Christendom. The Annie Armstrong Easter Offering may be a runner-up. These victories no doubt result because Woman's Missionary Union is the largest Protestant organization for women. The recipients of the money—home and foreign missionaries—form the largest missionary corps of any evangelical or Protestant group, numbering more than 7,400 in 1986.

LOTTIE MOON CHRISTMAS OFFERING FOR FOREIGN MISSIONS

Lottie Moon was one of the best-known missionaries among Southern Baptists in 1888. When she had gone out as the first fully appointed woman missionary of the Foreign Mission Board in 1873, her example stimulated the development of women's missionary societies. Groups were formed in Georgia, Alabama, Virginia, and Kentucky especially for her support. Two of her college roommates were founders of state WMU organizations.[1] Her letters were widely published, and she was highly respected by both men and women.

Probably no other missionary had the imagination to propose or the magnetism to inspire what Lottie Moon brought to pass in 1888. She had been warning that Southern Baptists would continue existing on a hand-to-mouth basis unless the women were organized. When they did organize, they were aware that Moon was anxiously awaiting news in China, where she had worked without furlough, often alone, for 11 years.

At the WMU Executive Committee's first meeting, the Foreign Mission Board suggested that the women take seriously Moon's situation. She had proposed that the new Baptist women's organization take an offering at Christmastime in order to send new women missionaries to relieve her. She explained: "Need it be said why the week before Christmas is chosen? Is not the festive season, when families and friends exchange gifts in memory of The Gift laid on the altar of the world for the redemption of the human race, the most appropriate time to consecrate a portion from abounding riches and scant poverty to send forth the good tidings of great joy into all the earth?"[2]

With a daring investment of $72.82, Annie Armstrong printed envelopes and circulars for the societies to use in taking the offering. A goal of $2,000 was set so that two women could be sent to Lottie Moon's aid.

Martha McIntosh distributed 4,300 of those envelopes in South Carolina. Right off she faced a strategic question that was to perplex women in years ahead. She talked it over with her pastor, John Stout. Should women offer the offering envelopes to the men of the church, or reserve them only for the women? Stout said he saw no reason why men should be denied the privilege of giving.[3]

The final tally of the offering was $3,315.26, enough for three new women missionaries for China. McIntosh noted that South Carolina contributions amounted to one-third the total. Lottie Moon was overjoyed and urged that the new missionaries come without delay, as her health was in peril.[4] Only after they were duly trained would Moon come home, in 1892. Meanwhile, WMU kept repeating the Christmas offering's success. Moon's appearance at the 1892 WMU meeting created a sensation. She gave her approval to the idea that the Christmas offering be used for expansion of Baptist work in Japan. Annie Armstrong noted that "the loss of novelty has by no means diminished the charm" of the Christmas offering.[5] Another innovation of 1892 was a week of prayer observed in connection with the offering.[6]

In 1903 WMU began preparing promotional materials for young people to use in their own observance of the week of prayer and giving. The praying-and-giving emphasis quickly became a tradition. It was the earliest denominational activity of any kind, and certainly the first financial event, to become a standard fixture on the Southern Baptist calendar.

The Christmas Offering Grows.—In 1918 Annie Armstrong broke the silence of her retirement years to suggest that the offering be named for its originator. Still it was often referred to simply as "the Christmas Offering for China." When the mission boards fell into jeopardizing debts, WMU looked around for a rallying point. They found their most valuable weapon close at hand: the name and life story of Lottie Moon. The week of prayer for January 1925 for the first time dwelt upon the tragic circumstances of her death from malnutrition and despair on Christmas Eve 1912. The effect was electrifying. The next offering increased 629 percent (bolstered no doubt by an SBC-wide debt campaign at about the same time). By 1927 a full-length biography of Lottie Moon had been written by Una Roberts Lawrence (Mrs. Irvin), published by the Sunday School Board, and promoted by WMU. It stayed in print until *The New Lottie Moon Story* by Catherine B. Allen (Mrs. Lee N.) was released in 1980.

Until 1926 the praying and giving were done in early January, in the Christmas season's afterglow. Virginia WMU set the example of moving the observance to early December, and all WMU followed suit.[7] The result was that the popular offering began to provide an increasingly significant percentage of the Foreign Mission Board's receipts (see table, p. 482).

Two situations signaled a change in the LMCO in 1927. The Foreign Mission Board debt continued to grow and the treasurer was discovered to have embezzled $103,772. The FMB announced that it would soon have to call its missionaries home. This threat moved WMU to drastic action.

Kathleen Mallory led the way at the 1927 Annual Meeting. The women designated the first $48,000 of the next offering to pay for the return of 40 missionaries to their fields. More specifically, WMU's instructions called for 20 older missionaries and 20 younger ones. The 40 would be selected by a joint committee of the FMB and the WMU, and WMU would guarantee their salaries for the years ahead. Mallory said, "It is like a mother caring for her children when the husband has met with reverses." The funds rolled in, and true to its word, WMU in 1928 published the roster of the sponsored missionaries.

The 1928 offering coincided with WMU's big 40th anniversary emphasis on giving. WMU set a promotional theme, Christmas for Christ, and issued a theme poster for the first time. The women thought that debt retirement had lost its appeal to givers. They wanted a livelier object and proposed to the FMB that they restrict part of the 1928 offering for the sending of 20 new missionaries. WMU would aid in the selection, with priority given to graduates of the Woman's Missionary Union Training School. The Foreign Mission Board wanted the missionaries appointed, but was reluctant to act in face of the continuing indebtedness. After four months of negotiation, the Board agreed to WMU's proposition.[8]

The Foreign Mission Board told WMU after that offering: "The Lottie Moon Christmas Offering has been our salvation so many times that we have come to depend upon it. . . . The offering has certainly saved us this year." WMU told the SBC: "Certainly [the offerings] have the seal of time's approval."

The vitality of the offering began to pose a threat to the Cooperative Program, according to some. The SBC tried to clamp down on promotion of special appeals for the mission boards. WMU pumped up its gifts to the Cooperative Program, especially in 1928, but also took this action: "That WMU would at this time define its policy of designating its contributions to the Lottie Moon Christmas offering as an over and above gift that in no way is to be counted against the allocation or percentage designated to the Foreign Mission Board from the Cooperative Program."[9]

WMU Allocations Heyday.—The 1929 offering returned 60 foreign missionaries to their fields. WMU continued to ask that its training school graduates be given priority in new missionary appointments, but few new appointments could be made. Beginning in 1930 WMU appointed committees to work in detail on allocations for the special offerings. The 1930 offering again designated funds for 20 new missionaries, 15 of whom would be women. Offering goals were reached, missionaries were kept at work, and WMU permitted part of the offering to be used in debt retirement.

By 1931, with the dire burdens of the Great Depression ever on their minds, WMU members were responsible for guaranteeing the support of 100 missionaries through the Lottie Moon Christmas Offering. The women's involvement in designations brought criticism both to WMU and to the Foreign Mission Board. The WMU Executive Committee issued a lengthy statement of the history and intent of its policy, insisting that the offering was a love gift in response to special need, to supplement the basic program of the FMB. "The very strength and the appeal is lost if this primary purpose is not safeguarded." The statement explained that the designations were determined in cooperation with the FMB secretary. "The Executive Committee is convinced that the interests of foreign missions will be conserved by the inherent right of the Union to determine the objects of the Lottie Moon Offering," the report concluded. The FMB promptly answered that it recognized "cordially the inherent right of the Union to determine the objects . . . in conference satisfactory to WMU and the Board," and suggested that the current crisis rendered the support of missionaries the most practical aid that could be given.[10]

After the 1932 depression low point, the offering never again showed a decrease. The 1933 offering went substantially over the goal and WMU's first item of business in 1934 was to allocate the excess to send eight new missionaries and to bring some missionaries home for over-due furloughs. Among the appointees was Elizabeth Hale, who had waited two years for the FMB to have sufficient funds to send her to Shanghai. The new missionaries were brought to the platform of the 1934 WMU meeting at the sound of a cornet. Charles Maddry, FMB secretary, said, "The one thing that has saved our work from disaster and has enabled us to carry on at all has been the substantial and timely support given by the Woman's Missionary Union of the South." Maddry often said that the LMCO of 1933 stopped seven years of retreat on foreign fields, and that WMU had saved the FMB from utter collapse for ten years.[11]

The statistics bear Maddry out. The Lottie Moon Christmas Offering plus WMU gifts through the Cooperative Program and other sources provided the following portion of the FMB budget.

Year (reported in Annual of the following year)	Percentage of FMB revenue given by WMU
1928	59
1929	57
1930	63
1931	70
1932	57
1933	76
1934	65
1935	62

As late as 1934 WMU membership was only 13.3 percent of the total SBC membership, yet this minority was supporting the majority of the work.

This successful record firmly established WMU's involvement in the allocation of the offering. Some of the state WMUs began to determine allocation of their contributions. Virginia and Texas, with the largest offerings, were especially inclined to do this. The remainder was al-located under the watchful eye of Kathleen Mallory. WMU staff and Board became knowledgeable about field conditions. Missionaries wrote directly to Mallory or to their state WMU officers to request funds. WMU drew up the allocations list and sought approval by the FMB staff. The intended uses of the offering were formally adopted by WMU in annual session and were widely published. If occasion arose to alter the designations, Mallory conducted a referendum through the pages of *Royal Service* before she would grant WMU's permission to reallocate.[12]

WMU asked the FMB to open separate savings accounts for Lottie Moon funds that were awaiting allocation or expenditure. Beginning in 1934 these funds were handled so as to earn interest until the moment of expenditure. The LMCO funds on hand were shown as liability accounts on the FMB books. WMU sometimes budgeted the funds to accumulate several years in anticipation of a major building project abroad. The FMB fully cooperated with WMU in this system. Several women serving as FMB members filled the role of liaison with WMU officers. The FMB consistently invited the president and secretary of WMU, SBC, to attend their meetings. The officers seldom attended, and if they did, they made no public statements and took no part in debate. All the arrangements took place through letters and hall talk.[13]

WMU's leadership in the allocations had significant impact on field policy. The proportion of single women among the missionaries grew. WMU work abroad was given preferred funding through the Mrs. W. J. Cox Fund, a segment of the Christmas offering established in honor of the president of WMU. Through the Fannie E. S. Heck Fund, within the offering, WMU exercised a keen protective interest in women's training schools abroad. Like the WMUTS in the United States, these schools balanced the scale to give women an equitable chance with men to be trained for Christian leadership. Women missionaries specializing in the development of WMU work in foreign countries were favored. Thus strong women's work grew up in China, Brazil, Nigeria, Europe.[14]

As the LMCO grew in popularity, Mallory and the state WMU leaders tried to draw under its umbrella many independent designations habitually made by certain churches and individuals. Many of these had their roots in the Great Depression, when missionaries whom the FMB could not support induced friends to guarantee their salaries by designated gifts to the FMB. In an effort to bring things back into coordination, WMU absorbed most of these into the Lottie Moon Offering. For example, the WMS of Broadway Baptist Church in Knoxville provided the salary of William Wallace in Wuchow, China. In 1940 they did this by adding Bill Wallace's name to the Lottie Moon offering list and making their contribution through that channel.[15]

This system continued without much change until 1941. WMU then ceased to designate by name the 125 missionaries it had come to support, but let a general lump of the offering go into the FMB salary budget. By 1942 Mallory disclaimed any role in selection of missionaries. As the missionary force grew, new fields were added, an expanded FMB staff entered into the process. WMU was asked to discourage missionaries from making requests that had not been previously approved by the FMB and by the field group of missionaries.[16]

WMU Loosens Its Allocations Grip.—The dawn of widespread foreign travel and of big money in missions brought a change in the intimacy of WMU and the foreign missionaries. Texas and Virginia WMUs' allocations built buildings and bought vehicles all over the world. Both giver and receiver tended to publicize the donors. Meanwhile, most of the states were giving their money to be designated by WMU as a whole, and they got no spotlight. WMU, SBC, officers began cautioning the FMB not to overplay donor identities.[17]

WMU's grip on allocations might have loosened then if the SBC Executive Committee had not throttled the Foreign Mission Board's share of the Cooperative Program. The Board had a postwar vision of worldwide advance. Competition for the Cooperative Program dollar grew intense. M. T. Rankin informed WMU that without the Lottie Moon offering he saw no possibility for Advance plans.[18] Mallory wanted WMU to try to finance his Advance dreams, so she instructed him to rewrite his 1947 appeal for the LMCO in terms that would "touch the heart of the average WMS member" rather than describe the technical problems facing the Board.[19]

In order to keep the LMCO from being absorbed into the Cooperative Program, the FMB was careful to show WMU's LMCO designations as add-ons to the regular budget.[20] In response to the appeal of Advance, the LMCO grew dramatically in the late 1940s and early 1950s. The 1950 offering was a 20.8 percent increase and the 1951 offering increased 26.4 percent more, both significantly outstripping a modest inflation rate. Rankin said of the 1950 offering, "The offering of $2,110,019.07 has given renewed confidence to our fellow Baptists around the world who have put their hopes in the Advance program to provide help in their urgent needs."[21] In 1953 WMU designated $300,000 of the offering to appoint 100 new missionaries to advance the missionary roster toward Rankin's goal of 1,750 missionaries. This challenge increased the offering yet another 22.9 percent.

By 1952 the interest earned on LMCO funds awaiting expenditure on the fields had become a significant item in the FMB budget. With WMU approval, expenses for printing and promotion for the offering were paid from the interest account, and earnings were left over for field operations.[22]

The rapid growth and complexity of foreign missions and of WMU work prevented WMU officials from keeping current on field details of foreign missions. They admittedly were not well qualified to express opinions about the most advantageous use of the LMCO on the field. Alma Hunt told Rankin in 1952 that she could not in good conscience correspond with missionaries about the offering allocations and asked Rankin to assume this responsibility.[23]

A committee of the WMU Board made a long-term study of the

offerings and the weeks of prayer and suggested in 1953 that states limit to 10 percent the amount of their offerings that they designated. By this time, Virginia WMU was actually withholding some of its LMCO funds which it sent directly to the field, upon agreement of the FMB. The Virginia representative on the WMU board moved to strike out the recommendation to limit. But Marie Wiley Mathis (Mrs. R. L.), president of Texas WMU, offered a successful substitute, that "WMU discourage state designations." After 1953 Texas rapidly phased out its designations, leaving only Virginia, which at times spent their LMCO money on items definitely not favored by the FMB. The issue of LMCO allocations led to the selection of Mathis, a Texan, to succeed Olive Brinson Martin (Mrs. George R.), a Virginian, as president of WMU.[24]

WMU's control over allocations had served the purpose of protecting the special offerings as a valid channel of support in addition to the Cooperative Program. The system had helped the FMB survive the depression and the debt era, and it was smoothing the way for the Advance program. But now it was a nuisance for administrators and not necessary to a better-informed constituency.

By 1955 Baker James Cauthen, secretary of the FMB, told his Board that the Lottie Moon Christmas Offering ought to be considered as regular, dependable income. He saw no chance of decline.

> This offering is deep rooted in the hearts of Southern Baptists. It is preceded by weeks of prayer and mission study which make profound impressions upon the churches. It is becoming increasingly noticeable that where the Lottie Moon Christmas Offering is greatly emphasized and is widely supported there is a corresponding sharp increase in gifts to the Cooperative Program. The Lottie Moon Offering is to a church in its stewardship and spiritual life what a revival meeting is to its work of evangelism. We have by no means come to the maximum significance of this great offering in the life of Southern Baptists.[25]

Cauthen habitually described the Cooperative Program and the Lottie Moon Christmas Offering as twin tracks on which the train of foreign missions was equally propelled. The LMCO increasingly absorbed miscellaneous giving. In 1961 it passed the Cooperative Program to become the largest single source of foreign missions funds.

In the fall of 1956 Hunt went to the Foreign Mission Board meeting to make the first speech on record by a WMU officer to the Board. She announced that the LMCO allocations would henceforth be proposed by WMU, but with participation by the FMB staff, and that the FMB would have final approval over the allocations. She also announced that the entire Southern Baptist family (including males) would be invited to give to the offering. This news brought exclamations of delight from Cauthen and from his staff, one of whom told Hunt that she had added "dignity and beauty and brains" to the FMB meeting.[26]

A 13 percent LMCO increase in 1956 caused Cauthen to tell WMU, "This is the largest missionary offering ever brought at one time." In 1986, Cauthen's successor, Keith Parks, told the WMU Annual Meeting that recent international money-raising drives supported by leading entertainers with maximum media coverage had not begun to approach the results of the Lottie Moon Christmas Offering, quietly, inexpensively gleaned by WMU the preceding December, in the amount of $66,862,000.

The Lottie Moon Christmas Offering has become widely beloved as the Baptist way to celebrate Christmas. Helen Long Fling (Mrs. Robert) in her presidential address of 1967 challenged WMU members to give as much to the LMCO as they spent on all other Christmas activities combined. "I grant you it will make a difference in your family observance . . . it has in ours. It may make a difference in your clothes, in your furniture, in your home."[27]

ANNIE ARMSTRONG EASTER OFFERING FOR HOME MISSIONS

In 1895 the Home Mission Board was in debt and its secretary, Isaac Taylor Tichenor, faced the possibility of calling in the missionaries. But before taking that drastic action, he called on Woman's Missionary Union. Could the ladies raise $5,000 above their usual gifts? They agreed to take an offering in January during a week when they would practice self-denial and prayer. The result was more than $5,000 for that year and a cumulative total of more than $271 million by 1986. The Week of Self-Denial for Home Missions became an annual event. It went through several names as it grew. It was called a Week of Prayer and Self-Denial in 1903. By 1917 it was popularly known as a "thank offering," and the women tried to drop the self-denial name out of shame that so few were practicing the idea.

As an added incentive to give during the depths of the Great Depression in 1934, WMU renamed the offering week for Annie Armstrong, the first WMU corresponding secretary and earliest woman crusader for home missions. At the recommendation of the Home Mission Board, WMU further changed the name to Annie Armstrong Easter Offering for Home Missions effective in 1969, thus tying home missions to an important Christian season just as foreign missions had long been linked to Christmas.

In the early days, home missions was an unpopular topic among many Southern Baptists and WMU reaped criticism about the offering soon after it was begun. To spare the women bad publicity, the Home Mission Board did not ask WMU to promote the Week of Self-Denial in 1897. Fannie Heck protested that many of the WMU members would be disappointed if the week were omitted. So the WMU Executive Committee distributed a program for those societies who wished to participate.

The special home mission season worked itself into Baptist custom. Separate accounting records of the offering's total were kept beginning in 1907. Beginning in 1927 WMU selected promotional themes (such as The South for Christ) that deliberately enhanced the appeal of the offering. The Home Mission Board's financial plight became critical in 1928, when long-term embezzlements by the Board's treasurer came to light. Stumbling under a debt of $2 million, and muddied reputation, the Board faced extinction. WMU officials quickly briefed each other on the situation and without question loyally stood by the HMB. "It looks like the 'Prince of this World' has been let loose with all power, doesn't it," wrote one leader to another. "Oh, that this might strengthen our faith in God," she said.[28]

Alma Worrill Wright (Mrs. Carter) said that the treasurer may have robbed God after the money was put into the treasury, but that thousands of Baptists were routinely robbing God by failing to put their tithes into the treasury. "Shall we throw up our Home Board work? Had that been the right attitude, the 12 would have disbanded—one of them was a thief and arch traitor."[29]

One of the top staff members of the HMB, J. W. Beagle, came to Birmingham to ask the help of WMU. Sitting by Kathleen Mallory's little desk, he placed before her the plight of the home missionaries.[30]

The next month, January 1929, Mallory led the WMU Executive Committee to lodge a formal request that every penny of that year's home missions offering be spent on missionary support. WMU thus restricted the money from being used to pay off the nervous and clamoring creditors. This was a demonstration to people inside and out of the denomination that Baptists would stand by the Home Mission Board no matter what.

Mallory's plan was hailed as one of the most far-reaching, constructive, and statesmanlike achievements in WMU history.[31] Not only did it guarantee the HMB's survival of the theft, but also the Board's survival during the Great Depression. In 1933 the HMB could not pay even the interest in its debts. J. B. Lawrence, who had been brought into the HMB's top job in 1928 to straighten out affairs, negotiated an extension with the creditors. They accepted his proofs that the Church Building Loan Fund and the WMU home missions offering were designated gifts which could not be claimed for purposes (such as debt payment) for which they were not intended.

Lawrence deposited the offering each year in a separate bank account. Money was held for payment of missionaries in the year ahead. Thus the HMB proceeded on a cash basis, with the cash provided by

WMU and by individuals who gave for specific causes. The most prominent of these was Mrs. George Bottoms, who had participated in the
founding of WMU in 1888. Money from the Cooperative Program, the
Hundred Thousand Club, and other general SBC funds went exclusively
into debt repayment for several years.

With so much depending on the WMU offering, extraordinary gloom
fell on the first day of the week of prayer of 1933. The new president
of the United States closed the banks for a period of adjustment to
depression conditions. Women could not get their money, if their assets
had survived the crash of many banks. Nevertheless, the offering of
$68,197 slowly drifted in. Not only was the HMB again saved, but also
a few new missionaries were added.[32]

Thus WMU began in 1930 allocating the home missions offering for
very specific expenditures in home missions. The more specific the
designations, the more responsive the women were to the invitation
to give. WMU officers worked out allocations lists with Lawrence and
his staff. These lists were approved by WMU in executive session and
in annual session. They were printed in full in the WMU Annual Report.
For several years they were printed in the HMB minutes as well.

State WMUs began selecting certain pet causes to receive their offerings. For example, in 1930 Alabama WMU designated its contributions to Italian work in Birmingham. Kentucky designated its funds to
Indian work in New Mexico. By 1931 the home missions offering was
providing 30 missionaries their full salary and 77 partial assistance.

Lawrence said to the women, "The Home Mission Board has no better
friend than WMU. . . . Through all these years of stress the women
have, by their prayer and by their gifts, held up the hands of the Board."[33]
Lawrence stated that the offering of 1934 (the first one taken in Armstrong's name) checked the downward trend in home missions receipts
and put 36 new missionaries on the field.[34]

Throughout the crisis years WMU did not stop forwarding funds to
the HMB via the Cooperative Program and other designated gifts, as
well as through the home missions offering. WMU's combined contributions as a percentage of total HMB receipts are as follows:

Year (reported in Annual of the following year)	Percentage of HMB Receipts from WMU
1928	59
1929	61
1930	70
1931	91
1932	86
1933	79

1934	70
1935	70
1936	62

Well into the 1940s the HMB was supporting more than half the missionaries with "WMU money."[35] Another one-fourth of the missionaries were supported by the Bottoms Trust. In keeping with the spirit of WMU's designations, if home missionaries' needs changed, or if extra funds were available, the vote of WMU was required to reallocate the money.

Between 1942 and 1943, the HMB's debt was reduced sufficiently to change the Board's method of budgeting. The Cooperative Program began providing the majority of the operating budget. Both the HMB and WMU relaxed their rigidity about allocations.

But even after HMB debts were retired in 1944, Lawrence never forgot to acknowledge WMU's role in saving the Board. He welcomed Alma Hunt to office in 1948 by saying, "I don't know whether you realize the heritage of the organization you have come to serve or not, but I want you to know that there were years when the only home missionaries kept on the field were kept by gifts through the Annie Armstrong Offering. All the other funds that the Home Mission Board received from the denomination in those dark years had to go to pay off the debt of the Home Mission Board."[36]

The Annie Armstrong Offering tied the Home Mission Board to WMU more closely even than the Lottie Moon Christmas Offering linked the FMB and WMU. As they worked on allocations lists, the staffs of WMU and the HMB found many common causes. The offering came to be spent in part on matters close to the WMU heart such as salary for Una Roberts Lawrence, the HMB's publicist who served WMU voluntarily as mission study and personal service chairman. Also the offering supported several women field workers who were supervised by the Home Mission Board but who worked closely with WMU in the states. Then the AAO began to fund publications and missionaries to develop WMU work among ethnic groups. Using AAO funds, the HMB gradually took over WMU's Good Will Centers and built a program of Christian social ministries.

Inevitably, WMU became involved in determining mission board policy to an extent that some considered inappropriate. For example, Kathleen Mallory shared the platform with an Indian WMS president at a meeting in Arizona in 1939. The Indian pleaded, "My people are dying and they have never heard of Jesus. Won't you please send us a missionary?" At the conclusion of the meeting, Mallory fell into the Indian woman's arms and said, "God willing, you shall have your missionary if any more money comes in on the 'over the goal' offering for home missions." A few weeks later, the first full-time missionaries to the Pima Indians were appointed.[37]

Such situations probably did not usually run contrary to the HMB's desire. WMU's policy for the 1940s was stated clearly by Laura Malotte Armstrong (Mrs. F. W.): "We have always sought to guard with great care the principle that WMU recognizes that the mission boards are the administrators of SBC missions, that they employ the missionaries and the workers, and the Union's work is to stimulate interest and provide as much money as possible."[38]

Under Alma Hunt's leadership, WMU gradually took hands off the allocations. The HMB began pouring significant amounts of money into the development of WMU work in new state WMU organizations. Also the HMB funded staff to work under WMU's direction in the national WMU office. Courts Redford, successor to J. B. Lawrence, never let an Annie Armstrong Offering come into the treasury without dispatching a lavish letter of thanks to WMU.

The AAO was responsible to a large extent for the expansion of Southern Baptist influence into the North and West in the 1950s and 1960s. The AAO allocations were oriented toward the West and pioneer work. More recently challenges have been aimed at Bold Mission Thrust.

In 1961 the AAO for the first time provided more than 40 percent of HMB income. Soon afterwards it outstripped the Cooperative Program as the largest single source of funds.

Compared to the Lottie Moon Christmas Offering for Foreign Missions, the home missions offering showed statistical surprises in the last quarter-century. Since the depression low point of $68,197 in 1933, the offering declined slightly in only two years: 1958 and 1970. The 1970 decline was traced to the impact of bad weather during the Week of Prayer for Home Missions and possibly to adjustment to the insertion of *Easter* into the offering's name. The AAEO in some recent years showed increases of more than 16 percent, a peak the LMCO had not reached since the early 1950s.

Since 1960, the home missions offering has grown at an average rate of 10.56 percent per year, while the LMCO has grown on an average of 8.86 percent. The figures seem to indicate that support of home missions is gaining, and that the traditional gap between home and foreign support is closing. Both offerings have grown at a faster rate than the Cooperative Program.

Easter was added to the offering at the suggestion of the Home Mission Board staff. The WMU Executive Board in 1968 deliberated carefully before agreeing. Explaining the change to WMU members, Alma Hunt said, "We pray that the insertion of the word *Easter* will remind us that Christ arose victorious from the grave not only that we might be saved, but also that we might be saved for a purpose—a work to be done. This work we can do in part through the Annie Armstrong Easter Offering for Home Missions."[39]

STATE MISSIONS OFFERINGS

In 1906 WMU, SBC, recommended that each state observe a season of prayer and take an offering for state missions. The desire of WMU to work for state missions along with home and foreign missions emerged at the turn of the century. A Maryland women's society for state missions was begun in 1898. Louisiana WMU added state missions to its causes about the same time. Florida women had promoted state missions offerings prior to 1888.

Most state WMUs were interlaced with their state conventions, dependent to some extent upon the state for budget, office, and money handling. Naturally the women were willing to work for their own state's missions work. Tennessee began taking a state missions offering in 1901, Virginia in 1902, and other states soon afterwards. In some states, the WMU took an offering for its own operations and missions projects. This form of support still continues in Alabama and in South Carolina, although both allocate generous amounts of their offerings to causes espoused by the state mission board.

The Texas state missions offering found its roots in the work of Mary T. Corbell Gambrell (Mrs. J. B.). As the corresponding secretary of Texas WMU and as assistant to the secretary of the state mission board, Gambrell was irritated because WMU, SBC, did not give strong recognition or promotion to state missions work. Texas women (and other states) did the work anyway. Texas WMU named its state missions offering for its longtime president Mary Hill Davis (Mrs. F. S.). It had earlier given the financial start to such extensive undertakings as the River Ministry on the Rio Grande (begun in 1967).[40] In 1985 and in 1986 it underwrote a massive Mission Texas church extension drive and surpassed the $22 million mark.

Most of the early state WMU offerings, like that of Texas, were named for WMU pioneers. In several newer state conventions, the pattern was followed with the Viola Webb Offering in Kansas-Nebraska and the Nicy Murphy Offering in Colorado. In two young conventions the offering is named for couples. One state offering is named for a man. By common consent, the month of September is reserved for state missions emphases.

In 1985 the state WMUs raised $33,561,132 for state missions. (Historical figures are merged in the state column of the table on p. 482. The state offerings were never reported as a separate item in the WMU, SBC, records.)

THE CHURCHWIDE OFFERINGS

Martha McIntosh's efforts in 1888 and 1889 to involve the entire congregation in the Christmas offering did not immediately create a trend. WMU always encouraged local women's leaders to involve their pastors, and sometimes other men, and always boys, in the special missions offerings. But generally the offerings were given by women and girls within their own organizations.

The growing success and visibility of the offerings after World War II attracted male interest. The idea of churchwide appeal for the Lottie Moon offering had been proposed to a WMU committee in 1947 by M. T. Rankin, but the women turned him down.[41] As early as 1948 large churches in Texas, Louisiana, and North Carolina were making these events for the entire church.[42] The Week of Prayer for Foreign Missions and the offering were especially attractive because they gave a Christian alternative to increasing secularization of Christmas.

WMU began to formalize the churchwide movement in Texas. Marie Mathis, as president of Texas WMU, had harbored a fascination with the Lottie Moon offering. Early in her career as Texas WMU's youth secretary, she had boldly and successfully challenged Kathleen Mallory, Blanche White, and Juliette Mather as they considered dropping Lottie Moon's name from the offering.

From the beginning of Mathis's service as executive secretary of Texas WMU in 1945, Texas contributions to the LMCO skyrocketed. In 1944 Texas gave 31 percent of the entire offering, but Mathis did not think that was enough. She set out to lead Texas to give $1 million to the offering of 1951. To accomplish this feat, she sent massive promotional information to pastors of Texas churches and asked them to help the WMU officers make the offering appeal to every church member. Her effort made Texas give 37.5 percent of the entire 1951 offering, for an overall jump of 26.4 percent. Mathis was at the same time chairman of the southwide Lottie Moon Christmas Offering and Week of Prayer Committee. She naturally attempted to inject her successful Texas plans into the general plans. She was stiffly blocked by Virginians.[43]

Led by Blanche White and Olive Martin, Virginia took the position that only WMU members should give to the offering. They protested that phenomenal growth in the special offerings would undermine the Cooperative Program. Some thought they did not want to give up control of allocations, which they might lose if non-WMU people were giving the money.[44] White and Martin had triumphed in battles for mission board survival which had depended on WMU's absolute control over the offerings. They wanted to keep the policy unchanged. In the WMU Board's discussion, Mildred Green Herren (Mrs. Charles G.) of Birmingham said, "But Miss Blanche, where do you think we ladies get our money for the offerings? From our husbands!"[45]

In Mathis's first WMU Executive Board meeting as president of the Conventionwide organization, the issue hit the table. Hunt had surveyed the states and knew that 17 of them already promoted churchwide participation in the weeks of prayer and special offerings. WMU was in the process of transferring the Royal Ambassadors to custody of the Brotherhood Commission. If the boys could not give to the Lottie Moon Christmas Offering and the Annie Armstrong Offering, how could they live out their impressions gained from WMU? On this basis, WMU in 1956 "clarified" its position by "making it understood that the entire church is invited to participate in these Weeks of Prayer and to give through the offerings."[46]

WMU's desire to promote giving and praying among all Southern Baptists was formalized in 1964. The revision of WMU's task statements made clear the organization's intent to provide leadership for these and other special missions projects of the entire church.

By 1962 WMU ceased any serious involvement in control of the offering allocations. After 1963 they were no longer printed in the WMU Annual Report. The allocations lists became so voluminous that they could not reasonably be printed for mass distribution, but abbreviated lists were included in WMU magazines. As a matter of courtesy, the mission board executives annually brought full allocations lists to the WMU Board meeting for information and promotional purposes.

The success of the offerings brought gladness among the missionaries but criticism from some prominent leaders, on the basis that they were threatening the vitality of the Cooperative Program.[47] The Home Mission Board undertook a research project in 1971 to see whether the special offerings were indeed eroding the Cooperative Program. The findings indicated that churches that gave generously to the special offerings were likely to give to the Cooperative Program. The study showed that churches with higher per capita income were more likely to benefit the CP and the special offerings than churches with below-average income.

WMU had no apologies or regret about the growth of the offerings. But WMU responded directly to assaults on the methodology of the offerings.

When the offerings became churchwide a few churches began to include them in the church budget for a predetermined amount, rather than taking them as over-and-above spontaneous collections growing out of prayer, study, and seasonal emphasis. WMU vehemently objected to this movement, on the same grounds that WMU had resisted the absorption of the offerings into the Cooperative Program.

In 1951 WMU addressed this trend and opposed it "as a violation of the spirit and purpose of these offerings." M. T. Rankin stated his agreement with the WMU policy.[48]

In 1953 the WMU Board conferred with mission board staffs and again issued a statement to its constituents that the offerings must not be rolled into the church budget.[49] Baker James Cauthen stated that the LMCO must be preserved as a separate special offering—not absorbed in the church budget.[50]

Another challenge to WMU's philosophy of the offerings came from the SBC Executive Committee staff and from informal conferences with certain state Baptist convention executives. They wanted the mission boards to stop keeping separate records for the special offerings showing what each purchased. The idea was discussed by Porter W. Routh with Cauthen and Arthur B. Rutledge in a Nashville meeting to which WMU officials were not invited. Routh proposed that the funds be "comingled" so that no expenditure could be traced to either the Cooperative Program or to the special offering, but that all expenditures would be made from both funds. Rutledge agreed; Cauthen refused. When she learned of the discussion, Alma Hunt stoutly protested the idea of comingling. She cited to Rutledge examples of churches and associations who were experimenting with comingling, with the effect that money given for home missions never reached the Board. Rutledge quickly, but quietly, moderated his promise. Cauthen never agreed to change the FMB's bookkeeping, but both WMU and the FMB downplayed publicity which seemed to show the LMCO as more essential than the Cooperative Program.

As the 1970s dawned, another challenge to the special offerings emerged from Texas. Travis Avenue Baptist Church in Fort Worth adopted a plan of combining all the special missions offerings into one, taken at Christmastime. The plan was linked with a church schedule that eliminated WMU's missions education for children and youth. The staff of the church publicized the plan and an unknown number of churches adopted it. The plan supposedly gave higher visibility to missions in one annual week-long festival of missions information and attracted larger sums of money.

WMU officers took a hard line against the combined offering idea. They also avoided speaking at churches that were pushing a combined offering. Instead, they told their conference audiences that the combined offerings were just another way to reduce the consistent, repetitive appeal for missions. They objected on the basis of educational principles, on the basis that prayer would be cut, and on the basis that individuals would give more in two separate appeals than in one. Again, they had the backing of the Foreign Mission Board. Hunt brought the matter before the Foreign Mission Board in October 1971, sharing her "honest conviction that if the offerings are combined the weeks of prayer will ultimately be combined and we will lose one week of emphasis on missions now well established in the churches."[51] Cauthen said, "A combination of the three [foreign, home, state] offerings into one will mean serious loss both to the church and to the missions causes involved."[52]

The combined offering idea was still cropping up in the early 1980s. Speaking to 3,000 WMU leaders, Carolyn Weatherford criticized the combination. "We cannot achieve anything in a combined, once-a-year emphasis. Experience has taught us that when we combine emphases, we suddenly find that we don't have any emphasis at all."[53]

In order to extend the appeal of the offerings to the widest audience, WMU began to invite others to assist with planning. In the late 1960s the Brotherhood Commission was invited to planning sessions. They soon dropped out of the meetings, but they asked WMU to send promotional plans for inclusion in their publications.

In 1976 WMU and the Home Mission Board staff organized an informal coordination group to plan promotion of the Annie Armstrong Easter Offering. A similar group was formed with the Foreign Mission Board in 1981. Brotherhood was invited to have a representative on these bodies in 1985. Sunday School Board publications and programs traditionally granted publication space to advertise the weeks of prayer and the offering goals, and additionally included the observances in their curriculum materials. Baptist state papers beginning in 1966 were sent extensive press kits which were widely used in news releases about the weeks of prayer.

In 1986 Weatherford told her staff, "We now bear the responsibility of knowing that the special offerings are no longer the jelly of missions, but the bread. We have a tremendous duty to protect these offerings and to make them grow."

Though we must stay at home, our gifts may represent us on home fields and in faraway lands, extending our helping hands across the world.

Ethlene Boone Cox
Following in His Train

Come and go

The most important words in the Bible are come *and* go.

Mary T. Corbell Gambrell, 1898

MU spokeswomen have been attracted by two verbs that seem to gallop in opposite directions. Jesus says "Come unto me . . . and I will give you rest" and "Come . . . after me." He also says "Go ye into all the world, and preach the gospel."[1] Tying *come* and *go* together has been one of WMU's most consuming efforts.

As many women came into missions work by collecting coins, they found that a coin has two sides. One side was prayer, coming to Christ. The other side was action, going out with His word. One side pictured the woman who stayed home and supported. The other side pictured the woman who went out to win the world. In the program of WMU, both sides were welded together. A woman could have the best of both sides by joining forces with missions.

Unlike some organizations for Christian women, WMU has never said *come* without *go*. Spiritual deepening has constantly been encouraged and assumed among WMU participants, but only for the purpose of mightier service. Unlike secular organizations for women, WMU has never suggested service without spiritual preparation.

Prayerfulness was an important factor in the beginnings of other women's missions groups. One scholar observed that the early women's mission boards gained great strength from piety, prayer, and personal contact with missionaries. Then they laid these aside in favor of "the science of missions." By 1907 the earliest denominational women's mission boards stopped publishing a prayer calendar because demand had fallen so low.[2]

At that very time, WMU was also concentrating on structure, but it was structure for the purpose of prayer and kinship with the missionaries.

Missionaries from the beginning have been the centerpiece of WMU. The need for missionaries, the example of missionaries, the accomplishments of missionaries motivated WMU at every point.

In the view of WMU's first dominant leader, Annie Armstrong, every

Christian must be a missionary. If unable to go to a place that needed the gospel, she must send a substitute. Duty to God and obligation to the heathen required support of missionaries with prayer and friendship as much as with money. "Loyalty to the missionaries demands that we shall give support by prayer even as we in their places would wish to be supported," Armstrong said. "God does hear prayer, and our substitutes are tempted in all points like we are."[3]

In her writings and speaking Armstrong never failed to mention the missionaries with tender sympathy. She had studied their situations and knew the depressing surroundings. No matter what money might buy them, she believed that they needed prayer in order to feel the sympathy and comforts of comradeship. "Our duty to our risen Lord includes the imperative *go* as of equal importance with the persuasive *come*, may each one arise to the full measure of her responsibility and privilege."[4]

The connection between praying and the missionary job was never broken. In the current plans of WMU, the task of mission support is defined to mean not only money, but also prayer, the calling and preparation of missionaries, and personal ministries to missionaries. As late as 1977-78, WMU titled its annual emphasis To Be, to Do. It was the historic theme of come and go attached to Bold Mission Thrust. During that year WMU taught the need for missionaries around the world, outlined the multiple missionary roles that women might fill, and invited women to become missionaries themselves—but only in balance with prayer and personal obedience to Christ's commands.

PRAYER

Praying together in groups was the one religious activity that women of the nineteenth century could do with minimal opposition. Still, the history of every denomination's women's missions organization seems to contain the same apocryphal story. A man was reputed to rise in church meeting to complain, "You never could tell what those women might take to praying for if left alone."[5]

The 1888 constitution of WMU was polished by lawyers, preachers, and politicians before it was presented to the women for their vote. The women found a flaw in it and made amendment. They made it law that the Executive Committee meetings open and close with prayer.[6] This was the idea of Martha Loftin Wilson (Mrs. Stainback) of Georgia, whose organized prayer effort of 1884 was seeing its answers that day. From that day to this, where WMU is gathered, there is prayer.

The first women's missions literature, the topic card, was also a prayer card. The little leaflet listed missions matters requiring prayer each month.

Still, prayer did not come easily to many women. They had seldom heard other women pray. Woman's voice was not heard in public gatherings, not even at home if the father would lead. How could a woman learn to pray even silently if she had not first heard an example?

Desire to learn to pray was one of the magnets that drew women together. A woman who helped organize a missionary society in 1901 wrote, "One of the things for which we organized was for training in public prayer and speaking and the development of spiritual interests. It was understood that no members would refuse to lead in prayer and I can recall the struggle that many of the members made to comply."[7]

A 1909 Young Woman's Auxiliary member wrote, "Not one of us had ever led in prayer publicly and had heard very few ladies do so, but before we met we had each determined that we would begin with a devotional and not knowing which one to call on we decided to repeat the Lord's Prayer together." The girls learned to pray and then began to try money-making projects to help support missionaries. "Our study of tithing soon stopped that," she explained.[8]

One timid young woman who tried to lead in prayer broke down and cried. The other women cried with her. Bertha Hicks Turner (Mrs. J. Clyde), future president of North Carolina WMU, was in the group. "That prayer proved one of the most helpful we had," she reported.[9] Emma Byrns Harris (Mrs. R. L.), who would later be president of Tennessee WMU, belonged to the Ann Hasseltine Missionary Society at Judson College. Harris and the other students were afraid to lead in prayer. One member of the group was Willie Kelly, who would soon go to China as a missionary. If Willie was present, she did the praying. If not, the girls could only say the Lord's Prayer.[10]

WMU literature tried to give the women courage about praying together, for they often asked for help. "Remember that the Holy Spirit will give strength," they were told. Also they were reminded to speak in simple, sincere terms, loudly enough for the group to hear. Nerve-racking as it might have been, prayer was always prescribed in outlines of missions meetings.[11]

Calendar of Prayer.—By 1891 some WMU leaders were wanting a plan for guiding women in prayer for missions, something more than the topic-prayer card. Mary Emily Wright, an enterprising young author in Augusta, Georgia, decided to meet the need. She developed a calendar listing the names and stations of all the SBC missionaries. "Appropriate and stimulating Scripture texts" were appended. The calendar was published by the Woman's Mission Society of Augusta and copies were sent to the Mission Rooms in Baltimore for sale. Wright, who would become a recording secretary of WMU, SBC, put out the calendar in 1891 and again in 1892. At a selling price of 25 cents, the calendars could not produce enough income to reprint, so the Augusta ladies went out of the publishing business.[12]

Women asked at the Annual Meetings of 1905 and 1906 for the calendar to be resumed, and a careful study was made of calendars published by other denominations. Still, there was no action until the Fannie Heck administration of 1906. After several states guaranteed the purchase of 2,000 copies, the new WMU Literature Department agreed to publish a missionary calendar. The women gobbled up the whole supply and 2,000 more were needed.[13] It was continued as a special literature item through 1917. The 1916 edition was an object of beauty held together by a silken cord. Poetry, Scripture passages, and missionaries' names were charmingly arranged.[14] The women believed that the calendar gave the entire membership a bond of action—"the touch we together have secured on infinite things."[15]

Beginning in January 1918 the calendar was published in the pages of *Royal Service* rather than as a separate literature item. Whereas the separate calendar had seldom exceeded 5,000 in circulation, now the listing of missionaries was in the hands of more than 43,000. By issuing the calendar in monthly form, WMU could keep the information more current. As evidence of the sisterhood among WMU members and their "substitutes" on missions fields, WMU officers were listed along with the missionaries. Specific prayer requests, significant events, and matters related to the study topic for the month were included. Always Bible readings were suggested along with assignments to bow in prayer.

For more than 80 years the calendar of prayer has been read as if a ritual in WMU meetings. It has always been suggested as the guide to a woman's private devotions and prayers, but when the women gather, they use the calendar as a tool of group worship. Further, WMU has promoted the calendar as an aid to family prayers.

The daily Bible readings in *Royal Service* of 1927 were retitled the Family Altar page. Women were encouraged to think of themselves as worship leaders and religion teachers in their homes. Family prayer for missionaries has been a continuing theme among WMU members. Mothers and daughters heard suggestions in WMU to enhance home devotions with maps, table decorations, and items of news from missionaries. *Family Missions Guide* published in 1970 was WMU's first book-length guidance for training the family in missions, and use of the calendar of prayer was the anchor activity.

WMU gave the Sunday School Board permission in 1939 to begin publishing the missionary listing in its training magazines.[16] In exchange WMU began to use the Scripture readings suggested by the Sunday School Board. WMU at that time was maintaining the most up-to-date list of missionaries and their children. The WMU office had a great deal of direct communication with the missionaries concerning their financial needs and their children's education. The staff believed they were better informed about the location and needs of missionaries than were the mission boards who appointed them and issued their support checks.[17]

In the early 1940s, as the mission boards were able to employ additional staff members and as the roster of missionaries grew enormous, the boards took care of the record keeping. WMU as well as the Sunday School Board began using the missionary lists prepared by the mission boards.

The missionary list grew so large that a system was needed to avoid overlooking someone. In 1952 the calendar of prayer began to list each missionary on his or her birthday. Additionally, field of service and type of work were indicated. This universally popular approach enriched the feeling of personal touch with the missionary. Missionaries have reported receiving hundreds of birthday cards and miraculous assistance as a result of this custom. In 1978, at the request of WMU, the mission boards began listing married women missionaries with their given and maiden names indicated.

The length of the list caused WMU to list only a few representative names of missionaries in the prayer calendar provided for grade school girls in *Discovery* magazine. The list is printed in full in *Royal Service, Contempo,* and *Accent.* The calendar of prayer is for all ages. A readership survey taken in 1965 showed that the calendar of prayer was one of the most popular features in *Royal Service.*[18]

Weeks of Prayer.—For a century WMU has declared certain days, weeks, or other set seasons as concerted prayertimes. Most popular are the weeks of prayer for home and foreign missions. Prayer for foreign missions was inaugurated in connection with the Christmas offering suggested by Lottie Moon in 1888. A week of daily prayer was set in 1892. Originally observed after Christmas in January, the week was moved to December in 1926. WMU published, or had published, a study book for use during the week beginning in 1928. WMU authorities believed that praying could not be effective unless based on knowledge of needs. After a few years, however, study seemed to absorb too much of the praying time. The study was moved to a month preceding so that the designated week could be spent in prayer.

The Week of Prayer for Home Missions, a springtime observance, was first held in 1895.

A week of prayer historically has meant that WMU adults meet together for at least five weekdays. These meetings may happen in groups large or small; at breakfast, in the afternoon, at night; in homes, church, or office. In the 1980s some flexibility has been shown to accommodate daily prayer by women whose work schedules will not permit them to participate in a meeting every day.

Since 1956 WMU has officially encouraged churchwide participation in the weeks of prayer. This has been done in regular worship services and with the addition of churchwide banquets, dramas, early morning breakfast groups. Special prayer guidance literature has been issued to encourage eight days of prayer at home. Brotherhood has cooperated with WMU in promoting the weeks of prayer churchwide, as have pastors. WMU often furnishes the church with displays, posters, banners, exhibits, and other graphic reminders about prayer.

WMU has always taught that prayer results in action, and the action most associated with the special weeks of prayer is giving. WMU has tenaciously clung to the idea that the special missions offerings must not be promoted aside from prayer (see chap. 6.)

Other Prayer Projects.—The Intercessory League of Shut-ins was launched during the 1928 Ruby Anniversary celebration of WMU. Believing that "those who are physically weak are often spiritually strong," WMU enrolled shut-ins and assigned members to visit with them, take them literature, and guide them in prayer for missions.

In some ways this was a renewal of the Home Department of WMU, promoted between 1901 and 1904. The Sunday School Board began to promote the Home Department around 1896 at the suggestion of Annie Armstrong. WMU's involvement was to add a missions emphasis to the Sunday School's work with homebound persons. Shut-ins were enrolled as members and were asked to pray and give.[19] WMU occasionally has revived this idea through the years. In the 1980s the Missions Pray-ers Plan enrolled approximately 1,000 homebound women in assigned prayer for missionaries.

Intercessory prayer is a type of prayer emphasized especially in WMU. The idea is that women commit significant amounts of time to pray for specific persons and situations of need. To promote this idea, the Intercessory Prayer League was suggested for 1958, seeking to involve persons other than shut-ins.

During the Great Depression WMU's emphasis on prayer deepened. Prayer cards were issued, and women and girls were asked to sign a pledge that they would pray regularly about the missions crisis. In 1934 WMU recommended study of a book, *Prayer: The Golden Chain.*

The years between 1955 and 1964 might be considered the golden years of prayer in WMU's first century. This was the first administration of Marie Wiley Mathis (Mrs. R. L.) as president of WMU. Though usually remembered for her spectacular conventions and dramatic presentations of missions, she prompted development of WMU's spiritual emphasis.

Prayer had become such an automatic part of the WMU Plan of Work that it became commonplace. To spotlight prayer afresh, the 1955 WMU Year Book recommended that women elect a prayer chairman. With prayer as her exclusive duty, she could prepare prayer reminders, promotional skits, and posters. She could lead in more effective weeks of prayer. The WMU staff invited the statewide prayer leaders to a training conference at the national headquarters in 1957.

In Mathis's first executive meeting as WMU president, the weeks of prayer were declared churchwide events. Mathis was on the joint committee of Southern and American Baptists to plan the Baptist Jubilee Advance, 1958-64. She proclaimed this as an era of prayer in WMU, and the idea was approved by the WMU Board. It was also the anniversary era, with WMU celebrating its 75th, GA celebrating the 50th, Sunbeam Band the 75th. The Board designated July 18 through October 1, 1962, as a 75-day prayer period to open the anniversary year.

Prayer retreats were suggested as WMU activities for the first time. WMU, SBC, set the pace by having an executive prayer retreat in a San Francisco hotel in 1962. WMU officers from 28 states prayed not only about WMU's future, but also about the needs listed by SBC boards. The retreat lasted three days. One of the state presidents said, "It was a holy interval of silent meditation, spiritual conversation, and prayer . . . one of life's extras."[20] Alma Hunt, WMU's executive secretary, said that she believed that the prayer retreats held through the states and in most churches after the executive retreat would stand out as the best feature of the era.[21] Not to be overlooked is the fact that the prayer era brought WMU to its peak enrollment.

Further evidence of Marie Mathis's hands in prayer is found in several Executive Board minutes. Whenever debate grew tense, she stopped the discussion for prayer.

WMU agreed to pray in order to back up the Crusade of the Americas, a simultaneous evangelistic crusade in North, South, and Central American countries in 1968-69. At the suggestion of Mathis, WMU's prayer plan was called PACT, meaning Praying for the Americas Crusade Together. This was WMU's first venture into printing literature in multiple languages. Prayer registration cards and guidance folders were printed in Spanish and Portuguese as well as in English. More than 1 million pieces of literature were distributed through the hemisphere. More than 50,000 persons or groups from 49 states and 27 countries wrote to the WMU office to be matched with prayer partners. WMU employed a full-time secretary to keep records on the project.

Prayer retreats continued to be popular during the turbulent 1970s. In one of the new state WMUs, Michigan, more than 600 women registered each year for a spiritual renewal and prayer retreat. Although sponsored by WMU, the retreats were attended by many women outside the enrollment.

Missions prayer groups were instituted in 1968. These are an option in Baptist Women and Baptist Young Women organizations. A *Missions Prayer Guide* was published in 1973 and 43,125 copies were sold.

WMU sponsored several national prayer sessions in connection with Annual Meetings during the last decade. In the nation's bicentennial year, WMU happened to be in Annual Meeting on Flag Day. A noontime ceremony was held in concert with observances held in WMU organizations across the country. It was called a Day of Prayer, Humiliation, and Fasting.

One session of the 1977 WMU Annual Meeting in Kansas City was devoted to prayer for Bold Mission Thrust. More than 10,000 people were organized into prayer groups spread throughout the convention center complex.

National Prayer Conferences were held in connection with the WMU Annual Meetings of 1983 and 1984. Relatively small groups of between 200 and 400 persons participated in one-day prayer sessions. WMU officers and denominational leaders were the special invited participants. The prayer conferences were primarily directed toward the continuing Bold Mission Thrust. Prayer box suppers were held in 1985 and 1986 as part of the Annual Meeting. Participants bought a modest box supper, then gathered around tables in a hotel banquet room with missionaries and denominational agency officials for prayer. These events were directed not only toward missions needs, but also toward controversy disturbing harmony in the Southern Baptist Convention.

Bold Mission Thrust caused WMU to sponsor a churchwide Bold Missions Prayer Retreat for the entire congregation. This was suggested as an activity for April 1978, with an emphasis on identifying and encouraging persons to be career missionaries.

Looking toward 1990, WMU has led a team of missions agencies in launching the National Missions Prayer Plan. This plan supports a Convention-adopted Bold Mission Thrust goal to have every church involved in continuing intercessory prayer activities. WMU will launch the plan in churches with the 1987 Week of Prayer for Foreign Missions. It will continue at least through the 1989-90 church year. Persons will be asked to promise to pray daily using a marked prayer calendar. A state-by-state register will be kept on persons involved in the plan. All ages will be involved.

Prayer Leaders.—Through WMU, women not only learned to pray, and to pray in the earshot of others, but they also became committed to prayer as a way of life. The officers of WMU, some of them in prominent ways, have been models of praying women. An early survey of women leaders in prayer and personal devotion identified Fannie E. S. Heck as Southern Baptists' prime example.[22] Heck did advise WMU members to exercise themselves in prayer and meditation. She called them the "Marthas" of the heavenly household, always busy and productive, but too busy to partake of the spiritual food they prepared for others.[23]

Privately Heck tried to follow her own advice that women try to become more like Martha's sister Mary, who sat at the feet of Jesus to learn of Him. In 1895, when she resumed the presidency of WMU after a break due to illness, she wrote her mother, "Do you ever pray for me as though I were in very great need of help? You would if you knew my needs. Will you not? I am just now in great need of help that God alone can give."[24]

A written prayer in her notes showed her pleas for nearness to Jesus Christ, her desire for wisdom. "I would be more—far more—Christlike. I acknowledge my shortcomings and my sins of coldness of heart and indifference to thy concerns in the lives of those around me, my want of sensitiveness to thy interests; my selfishness and love of ease is [sic] continually before me."

She declared herself unfit for her task of leading WMU, so she asked God to achieve the goals of WMU. "May enlistment be real and vital, may the vice-presidents realize the great responsibility resting upon them in a larger mission, may the societies give $30,000 this year."[25]

As she prepared for death after a lingering illness, she wrote: "Looking back, I wish that I had led more prayerfully."[26]

A more recent president who was recognized as a spiritual leader is Helen Long Fling (Mrs. Robert). Her presidential addresses and writings have majored on prayer and attention to the leadership of the Holy Spirit in daily living. Spiritual Leadership was the theme of her addresses to a corps of women who led the National Enlargement Plan in 1980-83. A teacher of prayer, Fling wrote for girls how they might grow up as practitioners of prayer. "The best habit you can ever form is the habit of prayer. See if you can turn your first waking thought each morning into a prayer and let your last thought at night be of God."[27] Her own day, no matter how complex her travels and schedule, always has begun by rising early for prayer.

She asked a missionary what she needed in her field to make life more enjoyable. The missionary answered, "Helen, if you want to do something personal for me, spend more time in prayer."[28] Helen Fling tried to transmit to WMU members the power of meeting missionaries in prayer.

FOREIGN MISSIONARIES AND WMU

The prayers of WMU unstopped the ears of Southern Baptists so that God's call to women could be heard. God is known to have spoken to women, summoning them to special places of service on missions fields, before the forces of WMU began to combine. But without the organized backing of other women, few could follow their divine impressions.

Southern Baptists, like people of all walks, knew the story of Ann Hasseltine Judson, wed to Adoniram and commissioned with the first missionaries from America in 1812. While the men knelt for ordination, Ann and her friend Harriet Newell knelt quietly in the aisle, considering themselves missionaries whether anybody else did or not. The commissioning minister said directly to the women: "It will be your business, my dear children, to teach these women, to whom your husbands can have but little or no access. Go then, and do all in your power, to enlighten their minds, and bring them to the knowledge of truth."[29]

Several generations of Southern Baptist women read the biography of Ann Judson who has been called the "moral heroine of the nineteenth century."[30] Adoniram Judson visited among Southern Baptists in 1846-47. Perhaps he refreshed the memories of Ann Judson. Shortly there was a flurry of excitement at the young Foreign Mission Board about appointment of women missionaries. The Board made provision in its policies for appointment of "female missionaries" (not to be confused with wives of missionaries). Wives were entitled to the support of the FMB, and "in as far as domestic duties shall allow, will be expected to contribute their share of influence . . . giving attention to those of their own sex."[31]

The Board began to take notice of inquiries from unmarried women wishing appointment as missionaries. Of several applicants, the Board sent one, Harriet A. Baker of Virginia, to China in March 1849. All others were turned away until the "experiment" was evaluated. After perplexing difficulties with other missionaries and ill health, Baker resigned at the end of 1853, and the FMB closed the book on single women.[32]

The commotion stirred by Woman's Mission to Woman of Baltimore reopened the question in 1872. Behind every woman appointed (Edmonia Moon, Lula Whilden, Lottie Moon), there grew a network of women's mission societies prepared to furnish funds and encouragement. The efforts of J. W. M. Williams to secure endorsement of women missionaries at the SBC of 1872 met with grudging acceptance. Said one commentator:

> Our Foreign Mission Board has decided, very properly, to send unmarried women, in connection with our missionaries, to labor for their own sex in heathen lands. . . . We predict that, kept within her proper sphere, woman will be a most valuable auxiliary in the work of spreading the gospel. Why shouldn't she? Didn't she have much to do in bringing the curse upon race? And ought she not to do all she can to remove it?[33]

The door of opportunity for women in missions was barely cracked. Fannie Heck in North Carolina and Martha McIntosh in South Carolina, known to be excellent friends of the Foreign Mission Board, were politely discouraged when they tried to secure appointment of women who appealed to them for help.[34]

Women were appointed as auxiliary missionaries only when other women came bearing money. This was the case of Sallie Stein, appointed for China in 1880 only after the Woman's Missionary Society of Walnut Street Church in Louisville guaranteed her support.[35]

In 1882 and 1883, Caroline Thornton Moss (Mrs. O. P.), president of the women's society in Missouri, a woman of such force that she could not be ignored, created a surge of applications from single women. At least two were approved. The appointment of Emma Young for China was said to have started a missions revival fire in Missouri. At her farewell service in Missouri, Moss presided.[36]

Some missionaries became anxious about the threat of so many single women on the field; the Board set a policy that none would be appointed without consent of her future colleagues. In 1886 South Carolina women and children were guaranteeing the support of women missionaries in China and Mexico. Martha McIntosh was interested in Southern Baptists having a woman missionary doctor. The South Carolina women promised to support Ruth McCown throughout her medical school training in Philadelphia, then on the field in China. McIntosh even traveled to Philadelphia to make arrangements for McCown. After intense years of preparation, the young woman fell in love with a man she met on shipboard en route to China, painfully wrote asking to be relieved of her appointment, and married into another denomination.[37]

By the time WMU was organized, the close connection of missionary and mission supporter was assumed by the women and the FMB. Technically, WMU was contributing to the general fund and staying out of mission board policy. In fact, in 1892 they took responsibility for support of all 54 women missionaries. For 25 years WMU had the goal of providing funds for all the women missionaries. Annie Armstrong acknowledged that many missionaries were specifically supported by state WMUs, associations, and individuals.[38] After 1913 WMU considered that its support extended to male missionaries as well as female.

The Missionary Calling.—WMU began to formalize the idea that the organization was responsible for drawing out qualified missionaries from among the ranks. A leaflet was published about the need for female missionaries. North Carolina WMU set up a fund for the appointment of new missionaries; it was a memorial to the first North Carolina woman appointed by the SBC Foreign Mission Board, Eliza Moring Yates (Mrs. Matthew T.), who went out with her husband in 1846.

A central doctrinal thread in WMU thinking has concerned the call of God into mission service. WMU has believed that persons should become missionaries only upon God's invitation. WMU has believed, when others have not, that God does call women. WMU has also believed that God gives an equal calling to both spouses. WMU has lavishly honored the role of homemaking missionary but only on the assumption that she would be using her home as a base for definite witnessing.

Leaders of WMU's organizations for children have always had in mind that they were training future missionaries. Always the message was to consider whether God might be calling one of the youngsters to be a missionary. More pointedly, would God call one to be a missionary doctor, teacher, nurse, WMU developer, or evangelist. God's call to women to be missionaries has always been paramount in missions education.

WMU's significance as a developer of missionaries did not become apparent until the 1920s, however, when a disproportionate number of women hammered at the Foreign Mission Board's doors. In 1922 the FMB secretary, J. F. Love, estimated that twice as many women as men were volunteering for missionary service. He attributed this phenomenon to "the influence of mothers, female teachers, WMU Mission Study Courses, and is an answer to prayers which go up daily to Him."[39]

WMU began to be more deliberate in its encouragement of future missionaries after World War II. Both mission boards were out of debt and able to support large numbers of missionaries for the first time in 20 years. WMU decided to turn up the volume of God's call. The thousands of girls flocking to WMU summer camps were daily asked to consider whether God was calling them. In *Royal Service* in 1946 women missionaries wrote on Why I Am a Missionary. The theme of the 1946 Annual Meeting was the need for more missionaries. The women were serious about producing missionaries from their membership. At the WMU Training School in 1948, the president said, "This is not the place for a young woman who has not found herself. We are stewards of a great idea and a great deal of missionary money." The FMB told the training school to send it all the missions volunteers it could muster.[40]

But the FMB soon modified its appeal through WMU. The Board stated that it needed men, good strong men. The women were urged to "give of their sons to bear the message glorious." The FMB asked WMU to strengthen the missionary career appeal of Royal Ambassadors. WMU responded by the publication of *Ambassador Life* magazine and the continued sponsorship of the Young Men's Missions Conference in connection with the FMB's week at Ridgecrest. M. Theron Rankin, secretary of the FMB, stated what he considered a fact of questionable wisdom: There were 300 men missionaries, 300 wife missionaries, and 300 single women missionaries. "Why is it?" he asked. He took care not to criticize the "old maid" missionaries; in fact, he admitted that China's progress in Christianity was due to the single women. But he echoed the theme, "give of thy sons to bear the message."[41] Rankin's successor, Baker James Cauthen, gave strong emphasis to the missionary family as a unit.

The Foreign Mission Board's personnel secretary welcomed Alma Hunt to her first visit to the Board in 1949 by saying, "So many [missionary candidates] tell us that their first interest in missions came through the WMU auxiliary meetings."[42]

The Board reported a survey in 1957 about the ways recently appointed missionaries had been influenced to hear God's call. The most significant influence, responsible for 37 percent of the decisions, was WMU organizations. Among the 186 appointees surveyed, 23 percent were influenced by the Baptist Student Union, 9 by Sunday School, 13 by Training Union, and 33 percent by the contact of missionaries.[43]

WMU was willing to accept the FMB's request that it recruit men missionaries as well as women. Undoubtedly this was one of the pressures that moved WMU in the late 1950s and 1960s to think of itself as responsible not just to its women members, but for the entire congregation.

When WMU edited its statement of tasks in the mid-1970s, the responsibility for the missionary calling was set down on paper for the first time as follows: "Provide an environment in which persons can hear and respond to God's call to missionary service." Because the WMU environment was warmly productive, the organization produced two free leaflets as the 1980s dawned, "So You Feel Called to Missions" for teens, and "When a Youth Feels Called to Missions," for adult leaders of young people. These were to be made available through the Acteens organizations so that youthful willingness to answer God's call would not be blunted. Among 14,000 girls at the National Acteens Convention of 1984, 214 girls registered decisions to serve as career missionaries, while 490 others indicated tentative interest in special service.

The years 1977-81 were perhaps WMU's years of heaviest emphasis on the call to mission service. This was WMU's special contribution to the Bold Mission Thrust plans of the SBC.

Reflecting the low status of women missionaries in the early days of WMU, women were seldom required to give evidence of their beliefs or their competence as missionaries. They did not go to Richmond to stand examinations. If local Baptists (usually including the WMU leaders) vouched for an applicant, that was all that was required. Or, if a woman was married to a male appointee, no questions were asked. Men, by contrast, had to be interviewed by the Board, usually in Richmond. This policy changed in 1904. All unmarried female missionaries were required to stand the same examination that male missionaries did. Wives did not. Salaries of single women were set at slightly more than half the allotment for a married couple.[44]

This new rule for single women surfaced an underlying reason that they had not been more stringently interviewed previously: there was impropriety implied for a lone woman to sit before a panel of men. As late as 1903, when Lottie Moon furloughed, she did not go to the Foreign Mission Board office. This respected, mature, unquestioned woman went to Richmond, had dinner with the Board secretary's family, and permitted a committee of Board members to call upon her at her lodgings, but she did not sit down at the office conference table with them.[45]

WMU eased the social strains of the time by stepping forward to assist the women candidates. The WMU Executive Committee lodged a request with the FMB in 1912 that WMU be permitted to send official representatives to the FMB sessions when women were interviewed. Of course, the idea of women being elected to the Foreign Mission Board was unthinkable until after 1922. But in effect, WMU was serving on the Board. WMU reported "a signal victory" that the FMB had agreed that "our duly appointed representative" could meet with the Board when any unmarried woman was applying for appointment.[46]

WMU appointed a committee of local women to "meet with the Board." These included from time to time the secretary of Virginia WMU and the two presidents of WMU, SBC, who lived in Richmond, Abby Manly Gwathmey (Mrs. William Henry) and Minnie Kennedy James (Mrs. W. C.).[47] James's service in this capacity foreshadowed her demand in 1921 that women be placed on Southern Baptist Convention boards.[47]

The financial crisis which plagued the mission boards beginning around 1922 severely cut into the numbers of missionaries who could be appointed. WMU's heroic efforts to train missionaries at the WMU Training School were going to waste. In 1929, 1930, and following, WMU requested the Foreign Mission Board to give priority to WMUTS graduates. And, the women geared the Lottie Moon Christmas Offering allocations to protect this interest in the women candidates. Their action was not just to be sure that women were not pushed aside, but also "to keep the school safe from fear it cannot appeal to young women who feel definite missionary calling."[48]

In the last quarter-century, WMU has expressed two concerns informally to the Foreign Mission Board concerning women missionaries. One continuing concern has been the decline in the number of single women appointees. No official actions have passed between WMU and the FMB about this matter, but WMU has repeatedly raised the question around the conference table. In the 1940s, 119 single women were appointed. The next decade the number dropped slightly, then plunged to 75 in the 1960s. Ninety-four were appointed in the next ten years and the number has risen slightly in the 1980s.

The decline in the percentage of single women is a trend in most missionary-sending groups. Among all Protestants, the percentage declined from 36 in 1925, to 27 in 1948, to 13 in 1979. Among Southern Baptists, the percentage declined from 17 in 1948 to 7.8 in 1983, well under the overall average. Meanwhile, the percentage of women among seminary students has declined at a slower rate. More women are educationally prepared for missionary appointment, but seemingly fewer are choosing to become missionaries.

The other question concerns the continuing dilemma of the role of the missionary wife. At the beginning of her tenure as WMU executive director in 1974, Carolyn Weatherford, after discussion among the WMU Board, asked FMB officials to identify married women missionaries by their own names. She asked that they be permitted job classifications, if they wished, other than the *home and church* category to which wives were routinely assigned. Both these questions of wording came up daily in publication of the missionary birthday calendar of prayer. In 1978 Weatherford wrote her commendation to the executive staff of the FMB for "taking the giant step of classifying women's positions beyond home and church." She said, "I am a strong supporter of Christian homes, and I know of no more urgent need for married women missionaries to fulfill. Yet, they are filling many other roles. They, with women everywhere, will rise to call you blessed!"[49]

The spirit of sympathy between WMU and the missionaries has been deliberately fostered. Until 1968 WMU listed in its Annual Report the names of women missionaries who had died during the previous year. In the early 1890s WMU officers began to write personal annual letters to all the female missionaries. More recently men missionaries have been included in the mailing list, too. The number of missionaries became so large in the late 1940s that form letters were resorted to. Until the 1950s the WMU headquarters handled the mailing of occasional circular letters from the women missionaries to their friends. After the task of maintaining the many mailing lists became too large for the WMU central office, some local WMU groups assumed this service for their selected missionaries. Beginning in the spring of 1975 the new women missionaries who went through the FMB's orientation program then conducted at Pine Mountain, Georgia, were driven to Birmingham to have a day's orientation with the WMU staff. The WMU executive director has been invited to speak to every class of orientation since 1974. Since very early times, WMU has provided missionaries with complimentary copies of its publications.

HOME MISSIONARIES AND WMU

The story of women in home missions is similar to that of foreign missionaries, except that WMU and the appointees are more closely interwoven. In fact, they are often the self-same persons.

Because much Home Mission Board work has been conducted in league with a state convention, association, or church, consistent records listing missionary personnel are not available. In 1878 Fannie R. Griffin was appointed by the HMB to serve for six months for $125, working among women and children of the "wild tribes" of Indian Territory. Her co-worker was nearly murdered and the ministry closed. Apparently there were no other female home missionaries until 1882. Mrs. H. F. Buckner, recently widowed, was retained on missionary status when her husband died. They had been pioneer missionaries working with Indians. She had earlier been commended for her work, even though she had no formal appointment. Buckner was mentioned to the women's meeting in Waco in 1883 which was regarded as the first regular meeting of WMU. In that year, the HMB began giving a small stipend to Mrs. N. A. Bailey, WMU organizer in Florida.

Martha McIntosh negotiated with the Home Mission Board in 1884 to raise the pay of Maitie Cole of New Orleans, a city missionary supported by the women. If the women were willing to increase Cole's salary from $20 to $25 a month, the HMB was in favor.[50] A Miss Gardner was appointed the same year. Martha ("Mattie") J. Nelson in New Orleans was considered a home missionary by November 1884. Mississippi women and children's societies had built her a chapel. Nelson had been on the Mississippi Central Committee and would later be the first employed WMU worker for Mississippi.[51] For the next 20 years a half-dozen women would work in New Orleans. The city, with its culture so different from the rest of the South, was as near to a foreign missions climate as could be found in the nineteenth-century South. As on the foreign field, women in New Orleans could do things that would not be tolerated in polite Southern churches. The women operated "industrial schools." They led exercises in their chapel, taught simple job skills, and taught the Bible.

In 1886 the HMB list was showing several women in Cuba and at the Levering Manual Labor School in Indian Territory. The HMB reported to the SBC that women's societies were supporting a number of the board's appointees. Mary P. Jayne, later a WMU leader, had begun working for the HMB among Indians she had previously served as a Northern Baptist missionary. The Levering School had the support of Maryland women, and Cuba was an exciting attraction for all mission societies. Thus the days before WMU was organized saw natural support rising from women for women serving in the US and its territory.

After WMU was functioning, Annie Armstrong took an increasingly strong hand in gaining support for women home missionaries. In 1892 the Woman's Baptist Home Mission Society of Maryland, which was headed by Armstrong and was almost identical to the group of women

who formed the Executive Committee of WMU, SBC, decided to employ
a German woman missionary. Her work would be to assist WMU members with their meetings for mothers, and other ministries to
immigrants.

The woman ultimately selected by Armstrong was Marie Buhlmaier,
herself an immigrant who lived in New York. When Buhlmaier reached
Baltimore, she went to the Mission Rooms to receive her instructions
from Armstrong. Soon she was calling her Miss Strongarm.[52]

As Armstrong always worked her ideas through the Boards, it was a
mere matter of procedure that Buhlmaier became listed as a home
missionary with her salary and expenses paid through the HMB. In
reality the funds were raised by WMU and the WMU office supervised
her work. Buhlmaier was an effective missionary, a charming speaker,
an obviously pious woman. Enormously popular with WMU leaders all
over the country, she was the first home missionary to do what came
to be recognized as Christian social ministries and the first woman to
work with immigrants.

In 1893, Gertrude Joerg, a resident of Cuba who had helped open
the island to Southern Baptists, had come to the WMU Annual Meeting
to plead for missionaries. The HMB promptly sent a male missionary.
By 1899, two had gone to her aid. Florida WMU supported Mary Taylor
and Missouri WMU supported Adalee Branham who answered Joerg's
plea for Cuba.[53]

Filled with her success in launching these new models of work,
Armstrong and Lillie Easterby Barker (Mrs. J. A.), the WMU president,
next undertook two projects in 1901. These were so far-reaching that
the women traveled to Atlanta, cooled their heels in the corridor until
permitted to enter, then pleaded their case directly before the Home
Mission Board. The brethren told them that they would think over the
proposition. What the women wanted was female missionaries in the
mines of Oklahoma and black women to work with the newly organized
women of the National Baptist Convention. Only because the state
WMU organizations and individuals gave the money for each appointee
did the idea find approval. The women of Georgia supported Kate D.
Perry and Virginia supported Catherine Hansen as they worked among
Swedish miners. Mary T. Corbell Gambrell (Mrs. J. B.) and a committee
in Texas interviewed Perry upon request of the HMB and found her fit
for service.[54]

Armstrong's request for black women missionaries was granted in
1902 after she elicited the money from individuals (see chap. 10).[55]

Other women were added to work in the ports of Norfolk and Gal-
veston. Their numbers were few, their work scantily reported, their
names known only to the few women who guaranteed their lifelines.
Without WMU and its "Strongarm," there would have been none. Wher-

ever they worked, they also served as the officers of WMU.

Indeed, a thin line has separated WMU careers from home missions careers. In 1921 the Home Mission Board employed its first woman staff member, Emma Leachman. She was a pioneer at the WMU Training School. As a field worker for the HMB, she was salaried through the WMU home missions offering. The offering also provided salary for an assistant to Leachman in 1938. Both women worked primarily with WMU organizations and social work institutions supported jointly by WMU and the HMB. Ultimately a half-dozen women served in similar positions. This formed the pattern for HMB support of WMU officers in new areas of the SBC.

STATE MISSIONARIES

Without WMU support, those scattered women employed as missionaries by state conventions and associations would never have had a chance. Possibly the earliest state missionary was Mattie J. Nelson who was employed by Mississippi WMU as early as 1881. Her field was New Orleans.

Texas had its team of a half-dozen Bible women who worked among Hispanics. All were also WMU officers. Mina Everett, who served beginning 1888, was "one of the sweetest, gentlest, kindest, most winsome, most devoted Christians" known to Texas leaders. She was also one of the most controversial, because she spoke and took collections in audiences with men present. As the first Baptist missionary to Mexicans in Texas, she was jointly supported by the HMB, FMB, and Texas Board, and at the same time was the corresponding secretary of Texas WMU. Crushed by her critics, she left the state to serve as a Northern Baptist missionary in New Mexico, then California.[56]

South Carolina was also an early leader in the field of women state missionaries. Perhaps as early as 1888 Hassie Marshall of Greenville was serving as a state missionary. By 1891 Eliza Hyde was a state missionary in Charleston working at the Royal Bag Factory and the Cigar Factory with child laborers. By 1905 South Carolina women were supporting ten women missionaries in cotton-mill towns. A total of 37 were on the state WMU roster before 1916.[57]

The industrialized cities of St. Louis and Louisville gave opportunities for women missionaries. Emma Leachman became city missionary in Louisville in 1898. Minna Roesemann and Lydia Bonacker began their work in St. Louis in 1903.

During the 1920s WMU put much of its attention on the women employed by various state and associational WMUs to work in Good Will Centers. By the 1930s, approximately 13 percent of home missionaries were single women. Most of them were supported by specific designation in the Annie Armstrong Offering or by the trust fund controlled by Ida Blankenship Bottoms (Mrs. George).[58]

Women who might have been considered state or associational missionaries in the previous decade now were funded by the Home Mission Board. Most of them worked either in Christian social ministries closely identified with WMU or among ethnic groups. A number of women, married and single, also developed WMU work among ethnics.[59] Most work with Italians and Orientals was developed by women.

The majority of home missionaries in the last quarter-century have worked in church extension and pastoral roles. Few positions in these areas have been open to women. WMU has continued, however, to "call out the called," both men and women, to serve in home missions. A survey of recent home missions appointees showed that membership in WMU organizations for young people was the dominant factor in decisions of 44 percent of the women. The impact of the week of prayer had influenced 24 percent of the women and 20 percent of the men.[60]

As of 1984, 174 women were appointed as the "primary worker" in the home missionary personnel roster. Of more than 3,500 missionary personnel, 12 women were church starters, 4 were church planter apprentices, 32 were general language missionaries, 21 were student and resort workers, 14 worked in associational Christian social ministries, 42 were Baptist center workers, and 30 were endorsed chaplains.[61]

BAPTIST NURSING FELLOWSHIP

The Baptist Nursing Fellowship was organized in Oklahoma City, Oklahoma, in November 1983. Woman's Missionary Union agreed to provide advisory and administrative support for the BNF.

The stated purposes of the BNF are threefold: to provide nurses and nursing students opportunities for worship, witnessing, and ministering through professional association; to provide education and learning experiences through Bible study, theological training, ethical study and evaluation of denominational work and professional education; and to provide members opportunities for expanded Christian service and witness through personal involvement in home and foreign missions activities and through disaster relief projects.

The first president was Ellen Tabor, Winston-Salem, North Carolina, and the first executive director was June Whitlow, associate executive director of WMU, SBC.

The organization is closely tied to WMU. State WMUs provide advisory and administrative support for state chapters. In 1986 there were seven state fellowships: Arkansas, Oklahoma, North Carolina, South Carolina, Mississippi, Texas, and Georgia.

Special projects of the fellowship include these: prayer partners with missionaries, continuing education for furloughing missionaries, subscriptions to medical journals for missionaries, and health care projects both at home and overseas.

Membership dues are charged. Membership numbered 500 at the end of its second year. A newsletter is produced three times a year.

SUMMER MISSIONARIES

As World War II wore on, WMU women were eager to plan for the future. Confident of American victory and of need in other nations, they wanted to be prepared to seize the moment for missions. In 1942 and 1943 a few WMU Training School students had been employed as summertime home missionary workers at $100 each. Some thought this plan could be enlarged. A WMU committee chaired by Foy Johnson Farmer (Mrs. James S.), president of North Carolina WMU, conferred with the mission boards. They decided their idea would not work on foreign fields, but that student volunteers could assist with missions work in the USA. The WMU Board instructed the Week of Prayer for Home Missions committee for 1944 to allocate $3,000 from the Annie Armstrong Offering for this project. WMU would watch it for possible continuation.

WMU advertised in the *Window of YWA* magazine for "select" young women who could speak French and Spanish. They were asked to write Juliette Mather, young people's secretary of WMU, if they could assist the Home Mission Board during the summer. They were paid low salaries and expenses for a three-month assignment. These young women proved to be a part of a group of 71 men and women who went out as the first formal group of student summer missionaries.[62] By 1986 the number had grown to 2,600.

THE VOLUNTEER MISSIONARY

WMU first heard of women donating their time for missions projects in 1899. Mrs. Walter Clark of North Carolina, aided by Fannie Heck and Sallie Bailey Jones (Mrs. Wesley N.), organized a Teachers' Volunteer Corps. Pastors in areas with inadequate schools could request the help of these teachers, who worked for six weeks teaching Bible and elementary subjects. Their only compensation was travel expense.[63]

The plan reappeared in 1962 through the vision of a WMU Executive Board member. Susie Nabb Illingworth (Mrs. G. C.) of Birmingham, a widow with grown children, heard Wendell Belew of the Home Mission Board speak about pioneer missions during the Week of Prayer for Home Missions. After the service, she told Belew that she wished she could help in pioneer work. Three weeks later, Belew called to tell her about the need of Nicy Murphy in Colorado for help with summer WMU camps and leader training. Illingworth paid her own expenses to spend the summer in Colorado, North and South Dakota, Montana, and Wyoming.

This exciting experience brought the WMU Executive Board to ask that the Home Mission Board work out a definite plan for women to volunteer their services in home missions. Plans for the Christian Service Corps were agreed to in 1964, and at the January WMU Executive Board Meeting of 1965, Beverly Hammack of the Home Mission Board reported that she was screening applications.[64]

Thus began the phenomenon of volunteers in missions which has resulted in perhaps 100,000 people a year assisting the Home Mission Board and the Foreign Mission Board. One of the extensions of the movement was spawned by Jimmy Carter when President of the United States. He asked his fellow Southern Baptists to recruit volunteers who would serve a year at their own expense. Christine Burton Gregory (Mrs. A. Harrison), president of WMU, was invited along with other SBC leaders to the White House to hear Carter's idea. At the request of the group, Carter sent a videotaped message to the Southern Baptist Convention of 1977. Gregory, Carolyn Weatherford, and Bobbie Sorrill, associate executive director of WMU, SBC, served on teams to implement the resulting idea of the Mission Service Corps.

Evelyn Blount of the WMU staff served on a team of the missions agencies to coordinate the process of recruiting, training, and placing volunteers. One result of their work was Volunteers in Missions Day, observed on the fourth Sunday of February beginning in 1985.

MISSIONARIES' KIDS
AND THE MARGARET FUND

The tenderest spot in the WMU heart has been for the personal needs of the missionary, especially for the children of missionaries. At the 1918 Annual Meeting, the women spontaneously gave $1,629 for the education of the four Pinnock children, whose mother had died in Africa. Education for all missionaries' children became one of the favorite projects of WMU. It began with Annie Armstrong's trip to New York to secure money for the Negro missionaries the Home Mission Board had agreed to appoint.

Armstrong had written to a Bronxville woman asking for $100 and hoping for more. She was disappointed when the reply enclosed only $50 and an invitation to talk with the writer about an idea she had. But friends insisted that Armstrong go to New York to visit Kate Waller Chambers (Mrs. Frank).[65]

A belle of the Old South, Chambers had been born in Montgomery, Alabama, in 1855, the second child of businessman William Washington and Margaret Armstrong Stout Waller.[66] Margaret's father, Platt Stout, was a missionary among the slaves of central Alabama, and her brother, John Stout, was the South Carolina pastor who was instrumental in forming WMU. Kate and her mother were active in the first missionary society of First Baptist Church of Montgomery. Margaret Waller became first president, a position which she held for more than 30 years.

Kate Waller was Alabama editor of the *Heathen Helper*. She was asked in 1884 to become secretary of the Alabama Central Committee, of which her mother was second vice-president. She declined the high honor, reporting that she was soon to be married. On May 1, 1884, at a home ceremony performed by Uncle John Stout, she was married to Frank Chambers, a distant cousin who had recently been left a widower with two small children. Chambers worked for a men's and boy's clothier in New York, Rogers Peet and Company, which he eventually owned.

Kate Chambers had been married for 20 years and had two children when she summoned Armstrong for the mysterious visit. When the WMU leader left the lovely Chambers home in Bronxville, she held a promise of $10,000, an enormous gift for 1904, perhaps the largest single gift Southern Baptists had received. Kate Chambers wanted the money to be used for the purchase of a home in which children of missionaries, both foreign and home, might live while studying in America.[67]

WMU used the grant to purchase a large frame house and six acres of land in Greenville, South Carolina. It was named the Margaret Home in honor of three Margarets in Kate Chambers's family: her grandmother, mother, and daughter.

A local committee was established to govern the home for WMU. State WMUs undertook the furnishing and annual support of the home. Kate Chambers provided $500 more for adding electricity. Formally opened in 1905, it served as home for 40 boys and girls before it was closed eight years later. It was also a temporary resting place for 15 furloughed missionaries. By 1913 conditions were changing on missions fields, so that children could obtain an education there. When the last young woman resident entered college in North Carolina in January 1913,[68] WMU decided to close the home. There was no subsequent demand for its services, and with Chambers's permission the house was sold.[69]

The property had so appreciated in value that it brought almost $30,000. In accordance with the agreement made with Chambers, the proceeds became the nucleus of a fund to which additions were later made by many others. The income from the invested money was used to assist children of missionaries to attend a school, college, or graduate school of their choice. This was an item of support that the mission boards could not afford to provide. The fund was made a memorial to Kate Chambers's missions-minded mother, and became the Margaret Fund.

The first grants were made in 1916, when $1,350 was issued in scholarships to nine foreign missionary children. Elizabeth Chapman Lowndes (Mrs. W.C.) was the first treasurer of the fund. She established a tradition that was followed for many years of maintaining a close contact with recipients. She and her successor, Ethlene Boone Cox (Mrs. W. J.), who served 1934-54, were addressed by the students as "Mother."

The first named scholarship fund, the Elizabeth Lowndes Award, was begun upon Lowndes's retirement as treasurer in 1934.[70] It granted an additional $200 scholarship to the top-ranked Margaret Fund senior from the foreign missions field. Among recipients have been David Jester, later president of Wayland Baptist University, and Robert Bratcher, known for his translation of the Bible, *Good News for Modern Man*. Since 1973 annual awards have been made to children of both home and foreign missionaries.

The Burney Gifts Fund was created to honor Sarah Joe Hurst Burney (Mrs. Frank), chairman of the Margaret Fund committee from 1922 to 1938. Income was to be used to make occasional gifts to MKs (missionaries' kids) for their personal use. The increased number of MKs exhausted the fund, and after the 1971-72 year it was closed. State WMUs were urged to take up support of students whose parents were from that state.[71]

Mrs. Mattie J. C. Russell of Rossville, Georgia, donated a piece of property in California which was later sold for about $1,000. Her instruction was that the money was to be invested and the income from it was to aid home missionaries' children. At the time, Margaret Fund money was used only for children of foreign missionaries. Russell highlighted what appeared to be an inequity, and starting the following year (1937), the home MKs were given equal treatment. The Russell Scholarship Fund helps meet special needs of the children of home missionaries beyond the normal grants.[72]

Upon the death in 1949 of Mary B. Rhodes (Mrs. H. M.) of Memphis, whose late husband had been successful in the furniture business, the three daughters set up the Mary B. Rhodes Medical Scholarship Fund. Rhodes was chairman of the Margaret Fund committee 1938-42. MKs who were foreign medical missions volunteers were eligible for scholarships for medical school training.[73]

In 1953 a bequest by Anna C. (also known as Cynthia Ann) Pugh of Arkansas for a fund honoring her mother brought into existence the Julia C. Pugh Scholarship Fund. Deserving students who did not qualify for a regular Margaret Fund scholarship might be aided from this account.[74]

By 1961 approximately 164 students were receiving assistance. This was more than the WMU treasurer could administer, for she gave much personal counsel to the students. The WMU Board decided to turn over to the respective mission boards responsibility for keeping up with their own students. Since 1937 portions of the Lottie Moon Christmas Offering and Annie Armstrong Offering were allocated by WMU to provide all basic Margaret Fund grants. When the mission boards assumed responsibility for making the Margaret Fund scholarship payments, WMU retained all of the invested money and continued to make the special awards. The investments totalled $436,712 as of 1984.[75]

> In trying to interest the ladies in missions, the word to use is not go but come. The one who leads must show she is willing to do more than she asks of anyone else.
>
> Annie Armstrong to R. J.
Willingham, undated letter

8
First comes knowledge

After the study of God's Word comes study of the fields.
Then people pray, then they give.

Annie Armstrong's last message,
1938

EFORE WMU arrived on the Southern Baptist scene, people knew little about the subject of missions. No wonder the missionaries were few, the mission boards impoverished, the churches forlorn, many people opposed. Missions was a musty curio high on the shelf. Once a year a pastor (or once in a lifetime, a visiting missionary speaker) would take missions off the shelf and flail the congregation with it until a little money ran.

Women dusted off missions and set it on the dinner table as an object of daily pride. They polished the topic until every facet gleamed. They displayed it in packets, pews, and parlors. They sharpened the edge until it jabbed the corners of mind and heart. They turned a topic into a science, a leaflet into an encyclopedia, a short talk into a seminary course. They found skill to magnify missions at the same source that supplied their survival through the ages: "the born instinct of womanhood." Fannie E. S. Heck told the women: "The creation of sentiment is as womanly as powerful. It has been her chief power and protection through the ages."[1]

Southern Baptist women were not alone in their power to "create sentiment" for missions. Women's societies of all denominations taught the general mission boards the value of publicity, training conferences, classes, exhibits, flags, and costumes. Women of several denominations joined hands in 1900 to publish mission study literature, an enterprise in which they were highly successful. By 1915, each denominational women's organization had a roster of mission study books, magazines, conferences, and promotional schemes.[2] But whereas those denominations turned over mission study to other boards, Southern Baptist women grew as the primary source of missions information.

The women recognized in mission study a "therapeutic value, for the study acts as a beautifier as well as an elixir; it broadens the mind;

it warms the heart; develops the sympathies; deepens faith in God and in people; stimulates effort; helps us grasp the viewpoint of others, stiffens our imagination until we are able to put ourselves in other people's places and think ourselves into their lives."[3]

One WMU officer suggested that mission study was the "fount of mental youth" for women. She noticed two women of the same age. One had done nothing in church life but attend preaching services. The other had worked hard in missions work and mission study. "The woman who had done so much hard work looked ten years younger than the woman who had left out the study of missions,"[4] she decided.

The first woman to finish all the required mission study books in WMU's course, Mrs. W. S. Cordy of Rhine, Georgia, wrote: "I am 51 years old, have nine children, with many home duties, but I find time for mission study and get much joy out of it."[5]

In the awakening days of mission study, 1886-1906, women were attracted to mission study out of sympathy for other women. The Woman's Mission to Woman concept aroused their curiosity and turned it to concern. At the time, they had little else to do in church or community to relieve their hard lot as homemakers.

In the maturing days of mission study, 1907 until World War II, the thirst of women for education made them drink in books and intensive study classes. Some quenched their thirst in community study clubs. Although many Baptist women enjoyed these clubs, few gave them their utmost attention. They seemed to follow the deathbed plea of Fannie Heck. She was a founder of the Woman's Club of Raleigh, but she said to WMU women, "Bring all your powers into the best service of the best king."[6] Their desire to teach missions to children led them to form an age-graded ladder of organizations for teaching missions.

After World War II, mission study helped women adjust to a dangerous and shrinking world they had underestimated before. They studied missions in order to understand the daily newspaper headlines. They studied out of concern for world revolution, war, nationalism, and racism. Mission study grew to gigantic proportions in this era. Mission study might have been encouraged in the late 1950s and early 1960s by a general flocking of women into adult education classes. Some have suggested that boredom with boxed-in homemaker roles drove women to studies that led "nowhere or to insignificant do-goodism."[7]

The latest woman's movement, 1964 to the late 1970s, brought a reduction in WMU membership and in circulation of mission study publications. Then, as the pendulum swung to a more conservative, or perhaps balanced, stance on women's roles, women again seemed to seek direction for their own lives in the study of missions.

Although social movements and world events have definitely had their good and bad effects on mission study, two factors seem to remain constant. Women have studied and taught missions because the subject transcends the current moment. One WMU officer said:

> It helps us to grasp the meaning of the cross and to see more clearly into the plan of salvation. It throws light into the statement that God is not willing that any should perish but that all should come to redemption through Christ. Missions . . . helps us to enter into that interpenetrating relationship between ourselves, our fellowmen, and God. Mission study helps us to become world Christians and to follow the Lord Christ in sympathy, if not in actual effort.[8]

As a woman has tried to pray, she has been compelled to study missions. Martha McIntosh called prayer the flame, missions information the fuel.[9] The Christian compulsion has kept mission study warm.

Too, women have continued to lavish their best efforts on mission study because they have been successful. The women moved beyond the stage of investing information only for the purpose of reaping dollar dividends. In their children's organizations and in their careful curriculum planning, they began 75 years ago to reach for the long-term commitment of life in personal mission service. This accounts for the continued expansion of Southern Baptist missions activity. The Foreign Mission Board was prophetic when it said in 1918: "It is becoming commonplace to say that missionary intelligence and warm missionary sympathy are to be found among the women who compose the WMU organizations in a degree not found among any other class of our church membership. As the educational work of the Union is carried forward we may expect to see a larger liberality . . . and a growing missionary enthusiasm in all the local churches."[10]

THE MARYLAND BAPTIST MISSION ROOMS

"Next to the Word of God, there is no knowledge so essential to quicken zeal and arouse interest in missions as information about missions."[11] So said Annie Armstrong, who believed it so strongly that she managed two full-time volunteer jobs at once. When she was elected corresponding secretary of WMU in 1888, she was already the secretary of the Maryland Baptist Mission Rooms.

The Maryland Baptist Union Association, at its October 1886 meeting, took note of the dearth of missions literature in the Southern Baptist Convention. The men created a committee to begin missions literature ministry. And they provided a capital investment of $830. In an action almost unprecedented for the times, they invited representatives of the women's foreign missions organization and of the women's home mission society to join their committee. Those bold men were Amzi C. Dixon, a local pastor who would later travel the world as a leader in the fundamentalist movement; Frank M. Ellis, pastor of Eutaw Place Baptist Church who would later blast an opening in the 1888 Southern Baptist Convention so that women could safely organize; and A. J. Rowland, a pastor who would later head the powerful American Baptist Publication Society. Interestingly, all these men were as well known outside of the SBC as within. They were aided by another man of similar fame and freedom to move in all circles, Henry Marvin Wharton.

Wharton gave rooms over his bookstore, to be known as the Maryland Baptist Mission Rooms. The rooms could be reached only by a narrow ladder at the back of the store—a definite problem, because the men had put the long-skirted women in charge of the Mission Rooms.

Wharton volunteered to deliver a lecture to which the women might sell tickets. With the proceeds, they built an outside stairway. It was known as the "stairway of the women." It was just that, for up those steps the women climbed to success in missions education.[12]

Annie Armstrong traveled to Philadelphia to study the operations of Baptist and Presbyterian rooms. In characteristic fashion, she decided to make the Maryland Mission Rooms a much larger project than those. She planned to sell the best missions leaflets of all evangelical denominations.

She found there were no good leaflets about Southern Baptist missions. The Foreign Mission Board had published only five leaflets and its journal. The Home Mission Board published the Sunday School paper, *Kind Words,* but had funds for nothing else. So Annie Armstrong became an editor and her sister, Alice, a writer.

They tried to line up leading pastors to write for them, but none of the men knew enough about missions topics to assist. Of the 200 items listed in their first catalog, only 7 were written by or about Southern Baptists.

The Mission Rooms opened early in 1887. Nobody was paid for her work. Volunteers kept the rooms opened from 10:00 A.M. until 5:00 P.M. Curios and files and books could be consulted there as if in a library. The women's missions organizations held their meetings in the rooms, and they filled orders that began to arrive from all over SBC territory.

In July 1887 the Mission Rooms published the first missions education curriculum for Southern Baptists. It was a simple, small leaflet called "Programme for Monthly Missionary Meetings Home and Foreign." In outline form were three meeting plans for the quarter, requiring a song, prayer, roll call, business, collection, Bible reading, and presentation of leaflets. With the "topic card" leaflet were three small leaflets containing information about the three topics of the quarter. A person could place an annual subscription for 12 programs and 12 leaflets, mailed in quarterly packets, for 30 cents.

Despite the low prices charged, the Mission Rooms made enough profit (thanks to the women's free labor) to be a growing business. In the year WMU was organized, its sales doubled. Armstrong, reputed to be a sharp businesswoman, attributed her marketing success to "A Need Supplied." By 1905 the catalog contained 400 items and the year's sales included 168,500 leaflets; 232,000 collection envelopes; and 32,000 missions topic cards.

After 1888 there was really no difference between the literature business and Woman's Missionary Union except the matter of ownership. WMU published free literature and the Mission Rooms sold literature. In 1901 the Maryland Baptist Union Association turned over ownership of the business to the Home Mission Board and to the newly organized Sunday School Board of the SBC. From 1901 until 1906 the operation was known as the Mission Literature Department of the Southern Baptist Convention. This move was engineered by Armstrong. Thus the appearance of competition with the Sunday School Board's extensive publishing network was removed. In the person of Armstrong, who worked for everybody concerned, the bonds between WMU and the Convention were cemented without any cost to the Boards.

The publications of the Literature Department were by this time not the only sources of missions information. Wearing their WMU hats (and Annie did literally wear a hat while working at the office), the Armstrong sisters also produced leaflets for sale about WMU operations, bearing the imprint of WMU.

WMU's policy was not to compete with existing periodicals but to fill them with missions. From Baltimore and from state WMU offices a steady stream of missions information, some of it for teaching purposes, was sent into Baptist state newspapers. Annie Armstrong regularly wrote for the Sunday School Board's Sunday School and Baptist Young People's Union magazines. Alice Armstrong edited the children's missions page in *Kind Words,* which became the publication of the Sunday School Board. Others assisted with supplying regular columns to the *Foreign Mission Board Journal.*

OTHER PUBLICATIONS

Comprehensive current news about WMU was supplied by the *Heathen Helper* and the *Baptist Basket* of Louisville. Edited by competing sisters-in-law, Agnes Osborne and Charlotte Ray Osborne (Mrs. Thomas D.), both monthly newspapers were filled with pithy reports from missions fields and women's societies.

After Agnes Osborne had succeeded in her goal of getting WMU organized, the *Heathen Helper*, begun in 1882, ceased publication. The

Baptist Basket, with its broader goal of stewardship and tithing promotion, functioned from January 1888 through September 1895. Both
of these publications had exercised tremendous influence in bringing
the women together in 1888 and in publicizing their concerns through
the crucial early months.

Although they were not as widely influential as the Kentucky journals,
newspapers were published by WMU leaders in other states. Fannie
Heck in North Carolina published *Missionary Talk.* Missouri women
published the *Missionary Interchange.* Mississippians published the
Young Missionary for children. Georgia WMU had the *Missionary Helper*
and the *Missionary Messenger*, which had a long life from 1895 into the
1920s. Texas had the *Missionary Worker* and the *Texas Baptist Worker*,
edited by the states's first WMU president, Fannie Breedlove Davis
(Mrs. George Bowen) and her husband, 1889-97.

Besides this periodical roster, the state WMUs poured forth a goodly
supply of leaflets, information sheets, and even books.

THE DAWN OF MISSION STUDY

Information began to become education as the new century dawned.
The term *mission study*, meaning something definite and formal, had
been heard in the North in the Student Volunteer Movement beginning
in 1897. Jennie Lucena Spalding, secretary of Florida WMU, a northern-
educated young woman, was trying it in Florida. For some reason, the
Baltimore wing of WMU did not warm to the idea.[13] Instead, Annie
Armstrong planned to correlate the topic card series in cooperation
with the Baptist Young People's Union of America, headquartered in
Chicago. This approach seemed to please the Sunday School Board.[14]

At the Ecumenical Missionary Conference of 1900 in New York, a
number of Southern Baptists gathered, including Martha McIntosh Bell
(Mrs. T. P.) and Fannie Heck. Both were then out of office in WMU and
out of favor with Armstrong. Although the Baltimore staff and Executive
Committee were fully aware of the conference, they apparently decided
not to attend. Heck found the most "resultful" part of the meeting to
be a women's meeting on literature. There the women of several north-
ern-based women's missions boards agreed to form a confederation.
Through it, an interdenominational committee would prepare a uniform
course of mission study and publish the necessary books.

"When I heard all this, so much what I have felt the Union needed,
my heart grew heavy to think no member of that Union who could take
active steps that would help this, or any of the other great world
movements, was here; that not one single echo of this meeting will be
heard at Hot Springs in the woman's meeting [the upcoming WMU
Annual Meeting]," wrote Heck to her mother.[15]

As she predicted, the WMU Executive Committee declined to appoint representatives to the Central Committee on the United Study of Foreign Missions.[16] They also decided that the studies "could not be used officially." Whether the WMU Executive Committee feared connection with an interdenominational group or with northern women who did not mind making public speeches before men, or whether they feared that the United Study publications would be too competitive with Southern Baptist plans, records do not reveal. But unlike the other major women's missions groups, WMU did not cooperate with this significant movement.

Heck saw to it, however, that North Carolina WMU did, as did some other states. Eliza Broadus, president of Kentucky WMU, encouraged use of the United Study publications, even though some women complained that "the course is too difficult for the ordinary society." She further commented that "many feel that the tracts and leaflets that have so long furnished material for our meetings are inadequate as a source of information."[17]

Women came to the 1906 WMU Annual Meeting demanding more and better opportunity for study. Stopping short of promoting the United Study publications, the women did endorse the literature of the Young People's Missionary Movement, formed in 1902. The emphasis on mission study was all but buried under sorrow about Annie Armstrong's resignation. After three years of intense disagreement about the Woman's Missionary Union Training School, and perhaps about mission study, she withdrew, and with her the president, Lillie Easterby Barker (Mrs. J. A.). Barker's last presidential message to WMU was "Study, study, study."

OUR OWN MISSION STUDY

Annie Armstrong told the Sunday School Board and the Home Mission Board to return the assets of the Mission Literature Department to its founder, the Maryland Baptist Union Association. She refused any longer to serve as its secretary. She disposed of all the stock, wound up all the business, and dismantled the Mission Rooms.

Missions publishing could have come to an end right then. Or, the Sunday School Board, with its large resources, could have taken it over. Instead, with much chivalrous behind-the-scenes discussion, the capital of the Literature Department was conveyed to WMU. Under Fannie Heck's able pen, WMU became its own publisher. Southern Baptist women would develop their own body of literature, with their own writers, editors, buyers, and dollars.

Changes in WMU administration signaled a change at the Foreign Mission Board. T. Bronson Ray joined its staff in November 1906 as educational secretary. His job was to produce mission study literature and to foster study classes. He quickly found that he met with good response among WMU groups and little elsewhere.

The 1907 WMU Plan of Work heartily prescribed mission study using Ray's plans and the United Study Courses. Fannie Heck began attending the Young People's Missionary Movement Conference meetings. She stopped the plan of cooperating with the Baptist Young People's Union of America. In this she was backed by J. M. Frost of the Sunday School Board, who said, "I think it is best that we paddle our own canoe. Meaning by 'we' the Southern Baptist Convention and those who have its matters in hand."[18]

The phenomenally successful Central Committee on the United Study of Foreign Missions had many such competitors and began to lose money in 1916.[19] At this time, WMU designed its own course. In 1911 the Standard of Excellence required at least one mission study per year in a society. This meant the study of a book over an extended time, with a trained teacher, and with written examinations.

The drive toward independence became complete in the early 1920s, when the SBC backed away from all forms of interdenominational cooperation. In its place, WMU steadily promoted Southern Baptist missions literature, which could exclusively feature Southern Baptist fields and personalities.

IN ROYAL SERVICE

WMU marked its 25th anniversary by having the Foreign Mission Board publish Heck's monumental work, *In Royal Service*. This was the first book published specifically for WMU. Heck was an expert writer. She made the book both scholarly and entertaining. It was a history of Woman's Missionary Union, which Heck correctly recognized was the history of all Southern Baptist women in missions. It featured the biographies of all early women missionaries and the chronology of all women's mission societies that she could discover. Women across the SBC studied *In Royal Service* in jubilant classes for 20 years.

Clearly the appetite for mission study was growing. Beginning with the Heck book, mission study classes were held in connection with WMU Annual Meetings. The young people's secretary of Virginia WMU was among the leaders who stretched all abilities to get mission study established as a plan of work. Her goal was to have a class for every group of women and another for every group of young girls in the state. After telling a friend about all the letters she had written, Mrs. W. S. Leake said:

> This is a big undertaking and I'm far from well,
> so I feel burdened in it. Join me in prayer for

the success of this particular work. It seems to
me to be the best thing we can do in the present
stage of development in our work. Our women and
girls need to KNOW; and we can never have their
interest to the point of self-surrender and
sacrifice until we succeed in giving information.[20]

State WMU organizations began to select mission study chairmen or
superintendents to organize massive classes. The first of these seems
to have been Mrs. Joel T. Rice, elected by South Carolina WMU in 1912.
Mrs C. C. Longest became mission study chairman of Mississippi in
1914. Virginia took the cream of the crop in 1916 by employing Lillie
Barker, former president of WMU, SBC. She crisscrossed Virginia teaching mission study and WMU methods.[21] Barker's role shows WMU as
part of a broader craze for education among southern women. She was
on the board of the Southern Women's Educational Alliance, later
serving as its executive secretary. Based on northern philanthrophy,
the organization promoted opportunities for southern women to have
college and professional education.

Mission study became big business in WMU in 1918 when a prescribed course of study was issued, along with a reward system of
certificates and seals. The keystone of the mission study course was
the new *Manual of WMU Methods* by Kathleen Mallory. Along with it
went a study of the missions message of the Bible, *All the World in All
the Word* by WMU Training School Professor W. O. Carver. Missions
history was represented by *In Royal Service*. The course was balanced
with books on stewardship and contemporary SBC missions. In 1919,
2,115 people studied at least one book. Thirty-eight women and 2 men
finished the course of six books.

Between 1922 and 1926 the number of mission study classes tripled,
and in 1919 WMU instituted an advanced mission study course.

The Home Mission Board began to formalize its interest in mission
study by employing Una Roberts Lawrence (Mrs. Irvin) as mission study
editor in 1926. She became an authority on missions and a productive
writer. Though on the staff of the Home Mission Board, she lived in
Kansas City (after a career in the Arkansas WMU office). A WMU Training School graduate, Lawrence wrote no fewer than ten mission study
books. Beginning in 1931 she served also as WMU's volunteer mission
study chairman. Standing in the bow of a ship en route to South
America, Lawrence asked Kathleen Mallory what her duties as mission
study chairman would be. Mallory looked to the starry sky at the
Southern Cross and said, "Bring back the glow of mission study."[22]

In that same decade the Foreign Mission Board employed its first
woman professional staff member, Ina Belle Coleman, to work with
missions education.

Mission Study Expands.—The Southern Baptist Convention began to take note of the importance of mission study. In 1929 it formed a committee to plan a way to reach a wider audience with book studies. Kathleen Mallory served along with the heads of the Sunday School, Foreign and Home Mission Boards, plus the Brotherhood and a representative of the state mission boards. Their proposal in 1930 was the Church School of Missions. It was clearly an attempt to get men involved in mission study for the first time. WMU gave the movement full promotion, including approval of the idea that pastors should be encouraged to take a lead in mission study. By 1937 WMU was encouraging churches in an association to undertake simultaneous schools of missions.

WMU's mission study progress forged ahead while study declined in other denominations. The controversial interdenominational Laymen's Foreign Missions Inquiry in the early 1930s noted that the responsibility for missions education in most denominations had shifted from the women to the general education boards. Missions education was regarded as an essential part of the overall program of religious education. Although the intention was good, the effect was not. The volume of missions education and the immediacy of its appeal were lost. Less money was spent in producing missions literature in every denomination other than Southern Baptists. The inquiry concluded that the denominations were failing to produce literature cheaply enough and to distribute it widely enough.[23] WMU took no chances that Southern Baptists would follow this route or that they would agree with the Laymen's Inquiry that the day of foreign missions was over.

By 1933, with the aid of Mildred Dodson McMurry (Mrs. William), mission study chairman of Tennessee, the WMU course of mission study was a multilevel course involving the possibilities of study among 30 books ranging from ethnic religions to biography to soul-winning. Sales in mission study books were booming and women were wanting to shortcut their classes. Emma Leachman, Home Mission Board field worker who taught many mission studies, was asked if she could "cover a certain book in one hour." She replied, "I might with a blanket." Usually she taught a book in five classes of 50 minutes each, plus two or three inspirational addresses. As a traveling study teacher, she ate in different homes three meals a day, slept in somebody else's bed, and was expected to write a note of thanks to each hostess from her next stop. "These are more than bread and butter notes," she said. "They tie me up with the family and the family with the great home mission cause." One of her classes consisted of 1,037 YWA members.[24]

By 1946, WMU standards required that every woman read at least one missions book a year. The courses were so popular that WMU ceased to award diplomas and seals. The women made out their own awards. In 1948, 513 churches reported that every Woman's Missionary Society member had read at least one missions book from the approved list.[25]

This figure had been achieved in part by the popularity of a new approach to mission study. To replace the old advanced course, WMU launched the Missionary Round Table in 1945. The prescribed books were selected from a fairly intellectual list of choices proposed by Una Lawrence and the Baptist Book Stores, which provided a World in Books catalog for WMU readers. The books were to be the basis for individual reading and group discussion in circles of women who wished to devote special attention to mission study.

The Round Table was carried over into the 1970 reorganization of Woman's Missionary Society as Baptist Women. To aid in purchasing the recommended books, which were required by the thousands, WMU and the Baptist Book Store Division of the Sunday School Board organized the Round Table Book Club in August 1976. By membership in the club, a woman could automatically be mailed her standing order for books. More than 3,500 persons, some of them representing groups, were enrolled in the plan at the end of ten years.

Graded, Correlated Study.—Beginning in 1935, WMU asked that the two mission boards publish a cycle of graded, correlated mission study books.[26] These grew to consist of one series of foreign mission study books and another series of home mission study books each year, each series with a book for each age group. The Foreign Mission Board put out the first Graded Series in 1935; the Home Mission Board followed in 1943, after its financial crisis had passed. These books have continued to be produced annually to the present.

As popularity of the course increased, the planning process became more formal. The Missionary Education Council was formed by the concerned boards, including WMU, in 1946. The council broadened its concerns to include teacher's guides, supplementary publications, and overall missions education concerns, and took the name Mission Education and Promotion Conference in 1967. WMU and Brotherhood assumed publication of teaching guides. The group ceased to meet as such, but WMU, Brotherhood, and mission board staff members continued to consult annually on their planning for the mission study book series. The formal conference was revived and expanded greatly in 1976 as the Missions Education Council, a forum for all cooperative planning for education in missions by WMU, Brotherhood, Foreign Mission Board, Home Mission Board, and Sunday School Board.

When Mildred McMurry joined the national staff of WMU in 1951, mission study was given a new lease on life. She trained a team of promoters and trainers in each state, and class enrollment mushroomed throughout the decade. In Miami in 1955, what was billed as the world's largest mission study class enrolled 1,200 people.[27]

Enrollment in mission study classes and use of books as the basis of study still showed phenomenal success in the last years that records were published.[28] In 1961 more than 590,000 people read missions books and almost 125,000 book study classes were held. Children and youth and women of the video era were less willing, however, to spend long hours in class and to take written examinations.

Shift in Study Concept.—By this time the understanding of what constituted mission study and missions education had shifted. Although the study of a book was still regarded as a useful tool, WMU emphasized increasingly the week-by-week study that took place in meetings of the organization. The WMU magazines had reached circulation of almost 1 million. They provided an educationally sound, balanced approach to knowledge of missions. By 1965 leaders were stating that mission study meant not just teaching a book, but long-range participation in organized study. Under the leadership of Betty Jo Corum, who came to the national staff in 1965 as Editorial Department director, writers and editors emphasized principles of education, particularly the concept of study as a group experience rather than staged programs.

WMU slowly moved into being its own book publisher. In addition to its own full slate of age-level organizational methods manuals published from the 1950s, WMU published books on missions philosophy. Books in the "Aims Series," produced in the 1960s, concerning enlistment, soul-winning, stewardship, world awareness, and spiritual life development, were enormously popular.

In 1975 WMU began publishing at least one study book per year for adult women. The topics included women in Christian history, spiritual gifts, world hunger. A missionary biography series was launched in 1982.

In addition, the Sunday School Board has published at the request of WMU numerous books on missions topics. These range from two histories of WMU (1938 and 1963) to a children's missionary biography series (1980s).

COOPERATION IN MISSIONS EDUCATION

The 1960s brought WMU a new partner in teaching missions, the Brotherhood program for men and boys. Although the Brotherhood had accepted WMU's transfer of the Royal Ambassador organization with the commitment to continue it as a missions education program, the adult men in Brotherhood did not have an exclusively missions content to their activities. The siege of interagency programming agreements resulted in 1970 in identical missions education tasks for WMU and Brotherhood. This development was welcomed by WMU, and the two organizations explored the possibility of joint activities. Several plans were fielded, including some coeducational projects, but after 16 years the two organizations were basically pursuing two unique, though coordinated, approaches.

WMU and Brotherhood missions learning plans were closely kin at the root. In 1966 Hugo Culpepper, missions professor at Southern Baptist Theological Seminary, wrote for the WMU and Brotherhood staffs a comprehensive outline for mission study content. In 1984 WMU and Brotherhood approved a revised document by Luther Copeland, also a missions professor. These documents sketched in the scope of missions teaching from history to current strategy. They were not published, but were used internally by WMU and Brotherhood as guides to curriculum planning.

The Southern Baptist Convention appointed a Missions Challenge Committee in 1974. Its report in 1976 gave two recommendations involving WMU. Each of these asked for WMU to cooperate with the mission boards, the Sunday School Board, and Brotherhood to reach a wider audience with study of missions. The agencies jointly sponsored a Think Tank in February 1977 involving 50 denominational leaders and a cross section of church types. The Think Tank participants agreed that stronger WMUs were needed, that new ways of missions teaching must be used, that the pastor would be the key to success, and that stronger understanding of the missions message of the Bible was required.

CHURCHWIDE STUDY

WMU announced in 1965 that it would undertake to teach missions to the whole church. Among the new churchwide approaches tried were these:

Churchwide Study of Missions Book Series.—Beginning in 1977-78 these studies were placed on a specific date on the coordinated denominational calendar, foreign studies in November and home studies in February. Both WMU and Brotherhood suggested that the books be taught for the entire congregation.

Life and Work Curriculum.—In 1966 WMU joined with the Sunday School Board and Brotherhood in attempting a curriculum that would be coordinated across all programs. Whatever was being taught in Sunday Bible teaching would reinforce the missions topics taught by WMU and Brotherhood and vice versa. After a trial of three years, WMU dropped out of the planning process, which proved too cumbersome and not particularly beneficial to the students. The Sunday School continued one of its Bible teaching series under the name Life and Work Curriculum.

Missions Supper Theater—WMU used drama as a means of missions education beginning in 1913. For 50 years plays and pageants were a stock item for the literature department. In 1973-74 WMU suggested that women sponsor theatrical evenings to reach nonmembers with missions knowledge.

Missions Night Out.—Beginning in 1977 WMU produced books suggesting activities for one-day missions education experiences. These were aimed at couples, the entire church membership, families, and other groupings that might involve persons not previously reached with missions education. WMU leaders were responsible for staging the events.

Video.—In 1982 WMU began to "publish" through the medium of video. The first creations were for the purpose of leadership training. Jimmye Simmons Winter (Mrs. Charles), then the Mission Friends/GA consultant of WMU, worked with North Carolina WMU and the state's media department to produce a videotape *Working with Girls in Action.* This tape was distributed through the Video Tape Service (VTS) distribution system, a cooperative Southern Baptist plan developed to popularize the video medium among churches. Seeing the future importance of video communications, WMU added a staff member in the field in 1984. Stanley W. Hill's first creations were more WMU leader training tapes distributed through VTS.

The WMU national office building occupied in 1984 was engineered to be a telecommunications base. The site was licensed to transmit to satellite. The building included space and capability for a full-scale television studio, although it will be fully equipped at a later date.

In 1985 WMU began to sell videotapes along with its printed products. The titles began to include mission study aids. When VTS phases out of operation in 1987, direct sales will be WMU's main route of video distribution.

WMU cooperates with the missions agencies of the SBC in producing programming to be aired on BTN, the television network operated by the Sunday School Board. Budgetary limitations have kept WMU from expanding this outlet.

WMU has been the pacesetter among Southern Baptists in video conferences. Beginning with the 1984 Home Missions Teleconference, WMU worked with the mission boards and Brotherhood Commission to sponsor five national conferences by 1986. The largest was the 1986 Home Missions Teleconference, with more than 12,000 viewers in live audiences at 378 viewing sites. The second largest was the VISION 88 teleconference broadcast live from Ridgecrest Baptist Conference Center, when WMU was holding its conference there in 1986.

New Hope.—In 1985 WMU began testing a new line of missions education products under the publisher's name of New Hope. The name was taken from New Hope Mountain where the new WMU headquarters had been built. New Hope products were primarily books on content or techniques of teaching missions. Some of these were produced in cooperation with the Foreign Mission Board. The intent of New Hope was to provide missions literature to persons not necessarily enrolled in WMU. Some of the initial books were geared to the academic classroom student of missions, some to casual readers, one to newlyweds, one to new parents, and so on. The new venture tested methods of distribution not previously used by WMU, including direct-mail marketing and sales through bookstores serving the general public.

Teach Missions Emphasis.—The years 1976-79 were filled with teaching emphasis in WMU. The purpose was to involve more people in serious study of missions and to remind WMU leaders of the central importance of missions understanding. WMU enrollment showed declines during the first two years of emphasis but increases at the end.

Life-Changing Commitments Emphasis.—WMU's next major emphasis was on self-denial and life-style modification in order to give more support to missions activities of the church and denomination. All educational activities were focused on this aim. The result was growth in the organization.

One person who responded affirmatively was Olin T. Phillips. His wife was teaching a mission study during the Life-Changing Commitment emphasis and proved to be her own best student. Her husband wrote,"We were so touched. The Lord was speaking to us all the time." They became home missionary church extension workers in the West Virginia mountains.[29] Susan Stokeld, a WMU staff member, responded to the emphasis by going to the Philippines as an appointee of the Foreign Mission Board.

OUR OWN LITERATURE

With $1,402.17, the nest egg of cash from the Mission Literature Department of 1906,[30] Woman's Missionary Union built its literature sales to $8 million, 80 years later. Samples of the published materials, preserved in bound volumes and scrapbooks and boxes and file cabinets, fill a good-sized library. WMU distributed one-half billion pages of printed literature in 1986.

The WMU Literature Department started small, with the old leaflet and topic card mailings continued, so that women's societies might go on meeting for study without interruption. In 1906, WMU magazines began to roll off the press. Circulation grew astoundingly for the times and through the years multiplied into a family of magazines serving all ages. Nonperiodical literature and supplies grew to a catalog of more than 200 different items.

Publications soon became self-supporting (see chap. 2). Kathleen Mallory and her successors as WMU's chief executives have not hesitated to remind the women that their literature is their own literature, and they must buy it to keep it going. Literature sales revenue pays for most of the national WMU office activities and personnel.

Our Mission Fields.—This quarterly magazine was the first official periodical of WMU, begun July 1906 with Fannie E. S. Heck, WMU president, as editor. Circulation reached 9,000 by the time it was superseded by *Royal Service* in 1914. Individual copies were priced at 5 cents, with annual subscriptions for 15 cents; one copy was sent without charge to each missionary society until 1912.

Royal Service.—In October 1914 *Our Mission Fields* was discontinued and a monthly magazine named *Royal Service* took its place. No editor was specifically listed, but Elia Brower Nimmo (Mrs. William R.), secretary of the literature committee, appears to have performed the task. In 1916 the SBC proposed that the *Foreign Mission Journal, Home Fields,* and *Royal Service* be merged. WMU refused to merge *Royal Service*, although the other publications were combined into *Home and Foreign Fields*, published by the Sunday School Board. Ninety percent of the merged publications' subscribers were women. Still, *Royal Service* was larger.

In 1920 Kathleen Mallory reported 43,500 subscribers. By 1954 the number had risen to 260,000, and in 1986 was close to 325,000. In its earlier years *Royal Service* included material for the monthly meetings for all ages. *Royal Service* contained not only studies, but also news about overall missions, WMU, and denominational events. During 1984-85 *Royal Service* for the Blind was made available on tape on a cost-recovery basis.

World Comrades.—A quarterly magazine for young people, *World Comrades* began publication in October 1922. Serving Sunbeams, Royal Ambassadors, and Girls' Auxiliary members, it became so popular that it was made a monthly publication in only two years. The magazine was enlarged as young people's work expanded, and circulation increased to almost 100,000. *Ambassador Life* was created as a separate monthly magazine for boys in 1946. In 1953 *World Comrades* ceased publication and was succeeded by *Sunbeam Activities* and *Tell.* The slogan of *World Comrades* was To Girdle the World with Friendliness. Juliette Mather was the only editor during its 31 years.

Ambassador Life.—The monthly magazine for Royal Ambassadors, both Junior and Intermediate, was begun June 1946 at an annual subscription rate of $1.00. J. Ivyloy Bishop was the first editor, serving through December 1953. A spin-off from *World Comrades, Ambassador Life* inherited a subscription list of 11,000. Circulation increased to 67,000 by October 1, 1957, when the assets of the magazine were given to the Brotherhood Commission along with responsibility for RA. The last issue was published September 1970.

The Window of YWA.—Serving young women ages 16-24, the monthly magazine for YWA was familiarly called the *Window*. It began publication in September 1929 with Juliette Mather as first and longtime (to 1955) editor. She was succeeded by Ethalee Hamric. The last issue was dated September 1970.

Sunbeam Activities.—The quarterly magazine for leaders of Sunbeam Bands, *Sunbeam Activities* was introduced with the May-June 1953 issue, edited by Juliette Mather. The price was 25 cents per copy, $1.00 per year. The magazine was discontinued with the July-September 1970 issue.

Tell.—One of the last two successors of *World Comrades* was *Tell*, described as "A Missions Magazine for Girls." Begun in May 1953, with Juliette Mather as first editor, this was the monthly publication for Girls' Auxiliary, ages 9-16. The initial subscription list exceeded 70,000 and in its second year reached 94,000. It proved to have WMU's second largest circulation list before it was discontinued in September 1970.

Accent.—A monthly magazine begun in 1970 for leaders and members of Acteens, *Accent* is written for girls 12-17 (or school grades 7-12). Highlights is a special section in the leader edition. Oneta Gentry was the first editor. *Accent* circulation exceeds 98,000, with another 19,000 for the leader edition.

Aware.—A quarterly periodical begun in 1970, *Aware* provides curriculum material for leaders of Girls in Action, girls 6-11 (or school grades 1-6); Iva Jewel Tucker was the first editor. *Aware* circulation exceeds 38,000.

Contempo.—Published since 1970, *Contempo* is the monthly periodical for officers and members of Baptist Young Women, an organization for women 18-29 years of age (beginning in 1988, 18-34). Laurella Owens, formerly editor of the *Window of YWA*, was the first editor. Circulation exceeds 61,000.

Dimension.—A quarterly periodical for WMU general officers and church administration, *Dimension* has been published since 1970. Ethalee Hamric, formerly editor of the *Window of YWA* and *Royal Service*, designed and edited the magazine at first. Circulation is approximately 42,000.

Discovery.—Published since 1970, *Discovery* is the monthly magazine for members of Girls in Action (ages 6-11, grades 1-6). Iva Jewel Tucker was the first editor. Circulation is approximately 208,000.

Nuestra Tarea.—This monthly missions publication is prepared for Spanish-speaking people in the USA. The first issue was published in San Antonio, Texas, in 1955 with Esther B. Moye (Mrs. J. L.) as editor. In 1968 it was published in Atlanta at the Home Mission Board. Four years later (1972) it was moved to Birmingham with Doris Diaz as editor. Circulation approaches 5,000.

Our Missions World.—A magazine in simplified English was produced beginning in 1982. It is geared for the vocabulary of deaf persons or those learning English. Circulation is 1,000 copies per month.

Share.—*Share* is a quarterly packet of take-home pieces for Mission Friends members ages three, four, and five. It was begun in 1978 with Susan Stokeld as editor and has a circulation exceeding 14,000 reaching 140,000 preschoolers.

Start.—Published since 1970, *Start* is the quarterly publication for leaders in Mission Friends, the organization for boys and girls birth through age five. Helen Armstrong Allan was the first editor. Circulation is 31,000.

The opportunity to publish their own literature gave WMU women the opportunity to develop as writers. Most of the presidents and executive officers have been accomplished writers. Some, including Fannie Heck, Ethlene Boone Cox (Mrs. W. J.), Alma Hunt, Carolyn Weatherford, and Helen Long Fling (Mrs. Robert), produced significant books as well as a constant flow of periodical articles. Annie Armstrong and Kathleen Mallory were superb editors. Mallory's literary output, extending over 36 years of constant monthly deadlines, outweighed all others in volume. Unfortunately, her work load as editor of *Royal Service* in addition to other executive duties prevented her from writing the books on prayer and missions expansion that were requested of her.

Other tall figures in WMU literature would include two friends, Juliette Mather and Una Lawrence. Mather founded five WMU magazines. She traveled widely as WMU's young people's secretary 1921-48, always with proofs and manuscripts to spread out on trains and guest room beds. She was named the first editorial secretary of WMU in 1948 and developed a team of editors. She brought professional art and photography skills onto the staff, the first artist being Rachel Colvin.

Lawrence was on the Home Mission Board, rather than WMU, staff but she served in important voluntary chairmanships of WMU. Combining her roles, she did the first historical research on pioneer women missionaries.

The Publications Section of the modern-day WMU staff consists of 11 professional editors and managers, 7 artists, and other support personnel. Most staff members related to the church program write regularly. Otherwise, WMU employs no full-time writers. The editors conduct an annual conference for the writers of major portions of the magazines, usually approximately 60 people. Since the 1940s writers have been paid a small stipend based on the number of words published. Like the original WMU journalists, Agnes Osborne and Charlotte

Ray Osborne (Mrs. Thomas D.), WMU writers have been motivated by the cause of which they write.[31]

CAMPING

Camping has proved to be one of Woman's Missionary Union's most effective and enduring methods of missions education. As early as 1908 Virginia, and then other state conventions, sponsored summer encampments. Usually held at resorts, these attracted men, women, and children of all ages. Denominational activities were given slots on the program. Kathleen Mallory from 1912 until the 1940s spent most of her summers touring the state encampments. Like other encampment speakers, she would lead a conference on mission study or a conference on organizational methods. Perhaps she would have an opportunity to bring an inspirational speech at a general session of the camp.

As early as 1904 Annie Armstrong had represented WMU at Young Women's Christian Association meetings in North Carolina. Some Southern Baptist young women attended these conferences which emphasized missions. From 1912 until 1922 WMU encouraged attendance at summer conferences sponsored near Black Mountain, North Carolina, by the Young People's Missionary Movement (later the Missionary Education Movement). WMU officers covered these meetings in order to conduct sessions for the Southern Baptists who attended.[32]

Encampments gave rise to WMU's own camps for young people. The general encampments could not accommodate the many WMU youths who wanted to camp. Nor were WMU leaders satisfied with the experience Baptist girls had at interdenominational camps.

Valeria Lawrence Vines (Mrs. John F.), president of Virginia WMU, was looking for a way to heighten the interest of boys in Royal Ambassadors. When she had the inspiration to sponsor a camp, the idea frightened her. But she made the idea come true in 1917, in rented rooms over a drugstore in Virginia Beach. Girls wanted equal opportunity to camp, so a Girls' Auxiliary camp was added in 1919.[33] In that same year South Carolina WMU sponsored its first Young Woman's Auxiliary camp at Furman University.

The idea was reported and endorsed at the 1919 national WMU Annual Meeting and again in 1922. From that time on, the state WMUs carried on the camps with minimal assistance from the national office. The first camp property owned by a state WMU was the Girls' Auxiliary Camp at Virginia Beach, built in 1922. The Royal Ambassador Camp for Virginia was built the next year. From the beginning, Olive Brinson Martin (Mrs. George R.), a future president of WMU, SBC, was a director of the Virginia Beach camps. Those familiar with Martin's elegance could hardly believe that she camped. Actually, the early camps were proper occasions with dresses and neckties and studious conferences and services very similar to church, except for afternoon recreation periods. Katherine Test Davis (Mrs. George E.), pioneer camp leader in South Carolina, was reprimanded for "letting WMU down" when she wore bloomers and stockings to a marshmallow roast.[34] Still, camping meant much work for WMU women who hauled foods, bedding, and equipment; cooked; cleaned bathrooms; and petted homesick children.

The model camp for WMU was begun in 1924 for Young Woman's Auxiliary. It was the dream of Juliette Mather in her second year as WMU's young people's secretary.[35] It was the first regularly sponsored Southwide Baptist event at Ridgecrest Baptist Assembly near Black Mountain, North Carolina. It was held annually, except when prevented by wartime, drawing up to 1,200 young women a year. The YWA camp became a conference as Ridgecrest developed more comfortable accommodations. The conference continued through 1970, until YWA was discontinued in the reorganization of WMU.

By 1930 most state WMUs were sponsoring camps or house parties for GA, RA, and YWA members. Associational WMUs also sponsored camps. No more than 3,500 youngsters camped in 1935, but by 1940 the number had grown to 25,000. Almost half of these were in Texas, where camping had come under the persuasive touch of Marie Wiley Mathis (Mrs. R. L.), another future president of WMU, SBC. At that time she was the young people's secretary, and though hardly the camping type, she was willing to train leaders in each district and assist them with cooking for legions of boys and girls.

Campers steadily increased to 70,440 in 1955. After WMU transferred Royal Ambassadors to management of the Brotherhood, one-third of the campers were no longer counted in WMU camps. The 1958 WMU total was 53,000. Formal figures have not been maintained in recent years, but in 1984 approximately 20,000 young people were counted in state WMU camps.[36] This does not count camps sponsored by associations.

The role of the camps has been to reward and inspire participation in WMU age-level organizations. Juliette Mather warned against letting the camps be mere funtimes. She instructed state leaders in how to make them intensive times of training and life commitment.[37] Records of Oklahoma WMU's Camp Nunny Cha-ha from 1956 to 1986 indicated a total attendance of 28,653. More than 15 percent of these youth made public decisions about spiritual matters. Of these, 1,808 indicated a sense of calling to serve as missionaries or in another Christian vocation.

A little-known camp program of Woman's Missionary Union was a ten-year series of Young Men's Missions Conferences. Conducted by WMU, in conjunction with the Foreign Mission Board during the Foreign

Missions Conference at Ridgecrest, they grew from a concern of Charles Maddry, secretary of the Foreign Mission Board, that young men be cultivated to give their lives in missions after World War II. J. Ivyloy Bishop, WMU's secretary of RA work, managed the conferences. Bishop had tested this idea first at a small conference in Birmingham. Attendance was limited to a carefully selected group of young men in their late teens, technically beyond WMU's membership. One hundred fifty to 185 attended each summer between 1944 and 1954. From this group a large number of men did become missionaries.[38]

In 1939 Business Women's Circle members in Illinois staged their own camp. By 1943 adult women in New Mexico were asking for a camp. The popularity of missions camping and conferences resulted in BWC meetings at Ridgecrest in 1942, 1943, and 1944. These were relatively small events held in conjunction with the Foreign Missions Conference. They indicated, however, that women did want to gather for conferences and inspiration. The first full-scale WMU Conference was held at Ridgecrest in 1946. When Baptists opened the Glorieta, New Mexico, Conference Center, WMU held a duplicate conference there in 1953. Combined annual attendance at these events is approximately 5,000.

Kathleen Mallory, ever frugal, did not favor state WMUs spending money on camp properties. Her resistance deterred some of the state WMUs from obtaining their own camps. After her retirement, those states that did not have their own camps soon did.[39] Among the most recent to be built are Camp La Vida, owned by South Carolina WMU, opened in 1983 at a cost of $3,737,000. Virginia WMU's camp Little Cross Roads, opened in 1985 at a cost of $4 million, is nestled in a forest of 423 acres. Alabama WMU's GA camp, originally built in 1964, was given a $151,600 addition in 1984.

TRAINING FOR LEADERSHIP

To prepare women for public leadership, WMU instituted definite training courses. These ran along two tracks. The first to be laid was training for mission study. Beginning in 1908 WMU encouraged the state and associational officers to conduct institutes for training teachers of mission study. This idea borrowed from the interdenominational mission study movement spread rapidly among Southern Baptist women. Not only did women enjoy attending training conferences led by top officers of WMU, but they also wanted help for their own duties in teaching mission study books. Institutes enjoyed a revival of attractiveness in the 1930s when Mildred McMurry of Tennessee modeled mission study institutes based on more sophisticated study and modern educational methodology. In 1951, when McMurry joined the national staff of WMU as director of mission study, she conducted a conference for selected state mission study chairmen in Birmingham. They went home to lead 400 regional institutes.[40]

A general leadership training movement was paralleling the mission study training track. In 1917 WMU's first staff young people's leader, Mary Faison Dixon, developed training courses for adults leading children and youth. These were correspondence courses, sold to the women at a nominal fee. The students mailed their examinations to the national WMU office to be graded, and if they did well, they were awarded diplomas or cards or seals. The state WMU offices took over the leadership training course. In the 1950s, with a baby boom in WMU's young organizations, leadership training took another leap. The 1957-58 training course involved eight hours in class and a written examination. More than 7,200 women earned cards of accreditation for this course. They had to renew or validate their cards periodically with additional study.

In October 1961 courses in WMU principles and methods were added to the Church Study Course administered by the Sunday School Board.

One of the most massive training efforts in WMU history came in 1968 in preparation for the major changes in missionary society operations. WMU, SBC, staff and state WMU staffs covered the nation with a series of workshops. More than 8,000 persons were taught and 1.5 million pieces of literature were distributed.

During 1984-85 more than 85,000 women attended state and national conventions and training conferences conducted by WMU. Associational WMU meetings involved untold thousands more.

We ought not only to work, to pray, but to think.

Fannie E. S. Heck, 1898 Annual Address

Woman's soft hand

*. . . the soft voice and supple hands of women to lead
in God's praise, to bind the broken limb, to prepare the
tempting meal and meet the problems of women's lives in
woman's way . . .*

Jubilate program booklet, 1913

ROM THE beginning, Woman's Missionary Union's eyes
were lifted toward foreign and frontier lands. The tears
that fell in sympathy for those far away made a lens
through which women saw themselves able to introduce
redemption into their own communities. While most
Southern Baptists closed their eyes to society's ills,
WMU leaders rolled up their frilly sleeves for battle for right. In 1910
they designed a plan for personal missions and social action camou-
flaged with the innocent name of personal service.

Not until 1913 did the Southern Baptist Convention create a Social
Service Commission, and its concern was primarily with temperance.
It spoke of social action but proposed no specific plans. WMU's agenda,
by contrast, was to put the woman's hand directly on the throbbing
pulse of needy individuals and their social groups, and to do so in an
organized program.

That WMU should have organized Christian social work among Baptists is remarkable. Politically and economically women had little power
to do such a task. Within Baptist thinking they had to overcome intense
fears of the social gospel. They had to scale the barrier of Baptist
independence in order to unify their efforts, and they had to make
room in their original agenda of mission support. So why did the women
think that they should personally undertake reformation of southern
society?

Two answers are possible: either missionary belief or female characteristics. To a degree well beyond the typical Southern Baptist, WMU
members were attuned to the action mandate of Christianity. They
studied the Bible. They prayed. They knew that Christ was redeeming
lives and changing cultures. These perspectives enabled them to see
Christlike obligations that had escaped other believers.

As women, they were in the daily habit of caring and nurturing and serving. "Angel of mercy" was an acceptable role for women. Their status as ladies protected them as they stepped from the pedestal of their homes into the troughs of human need to do their motherly deeds on a community scale.

The standard works on Southern Baptists and social issues conclude that Baptists generally rejected the social gospel and reform movements other than temperance. One writer concluded: "One must speak of the Social Gospel among Southern Baptists with the understanding that the views of a small minority are being considered. The overwhelming majority of Southern Baptists repudiated anything resembling social Christianity; for them it represented a threat that had to be combated."[1]

Women were the majority of that "small minority" who practiced social Christianity. Christian benevolence had always been women's work among Southern Baptists. When blacks or whites were sick or hungry, when soldiers fought, women fed and nursed and sheltered the victims. Here and there, the work of Baptist women in relieving human suffering went beyond the family and the plantation. Mary Catherine Jeter (Mrs. Jeremiah Bell), the founding president of the Virginia Central Committee, also founded the Baptist Home for Aged Women in Richmond. Georgia Woman's Missionary Societies in 1890 established and operated the Georgia Baptist Children's Home. From the early 1880s Texas Baptist women were the mainstays of orphans and of aged ministers.

In the 1880s, when immigrants flooded into the ports, when families left their farms for factories and mills, when masses of poor people crowded into cities, women missionaries went to their aid. Those missionaries were sustained by Woman's Missionary Union, and they were joined in their work by WMU members. (See chap. 7 for the story of WMU's involvement with women home missionaries.)

Baltimore was the laboratory and Annie Armstrong was the inventor who first wired voluntary social work into the Home Mission Board. Baltimore women dotted their city with clubs and classes for the poor, the black, and foreign-speaking people. The same women sat on the Executive Committee of WMU, SBC. They organized it into subcommittees on work with the Chinese, with German immigrants, with blacks, with Italians, and with children. Armstrong convinced the Home Mission Board to allocate $10 to $12 for each center of activity.[2] Baltimore women publicized their efforts for other women's consideration, but suggested no organized methodology.[3] The Home Mission Board reported to the Southern Baptist Convention about the women's work: "Personal service of this character is not popular, but we trust the time is coming, when for Jesus' sake, many, many other Baptist women besides these now laboring in Baltimore and other sections will be willing to overcome all prejudice and minister to the lowliest in our midst."[4]

While WMU worked out a formal program of Christian social action, three tributaries flowed into its thinking.

Southern Sociological Congress.—WMU had already launched its own social movement before the first congress met in 1912, called by the governor of Tennessee. It attracted more than 700 leaders of education, religion, social work, and government, most of them the enlightened aristocracy of the New South. WMU was represented in the organization by Fannie E. S. Heck, who was elected second vice-president of the congress in 1914. Also Lulie K. Pollard Wharton (Mrs. H. M.), the first chairman of personal service; Maud Reynolds McLure (Mrs. T. E.) of the Woman's Missionary Union Training School; Mrs. T. R. Falvy, secretary of Louisiana WMU; and other WMU leaders took part in congress meetings. This involvement put WMU at the forefront of the southern social reform movement.[5] The Southern Sociological Congress challenged churches to work closely with social agencies and to develop social ministries in order to lift the quality of life in the region.

Social Gospel.—If WMU thinkers had somehow avoided awareness of the social gospel which had been raging among Protestants since the 1890s, they met it head-on in the Southern Sociological Congress. In 1913 Walter Rauschenbusch, a Northern Baptist who was one of the chief articulators of the social gospel, spoke to the congress.

The social gospel proposed that the church should seek the general improvement of society so that persons could be uplifted. Opponents feared that the emphasis on the social implications of the gospel would pull people away from the need for personal conversion. Individual conversion being a sacred tenet of Baptist doctrine, most Southern Baptists shied away from the social gospel, believing that social improvement would occur in due time if individuals first professed Christ as Saviour.

Rauschenbusch's thinking influenced the development of the Southern Sociological Congress social program, which called for prison and convict reform; improvement of juvenile courts and reformatories; proper care of physically and mentally handicapped; alleviation of alcoholism; uniform laws and high standards concerning marriage and divorce; abolition of child labor; compulsory education; suppression of prostitution; solving of the race problem; and "closest cooperation between the Church and all social agencies for securing of these results." These emphases definitely found their expression in WMU's personal service efforts.[6]

Social Work.—At the turn of the century, a new body of social science knowledge and new social work professions were becoming visible in the United States. Under the umbrella of social work, assistance was extended to individuals in crisis, attention was focused on broad social problems, and group relief efforts were organized. Settlement work, recreational programs, enlightened industrial management, and charitable work were organized on a communitywide cooperative basis.

A leading developer of social work was Jane Addams, who brought the settlement house movement to the United States from England. In 1889 she and Ellen Starr opened Hull House in the Chicago tenement district. From that base of operation she bent politics, labor, health, education, and sanitation to benefit the poor.

Social work provided a tool for Christian action which WMU adapted. The field was attractive to WMU because social work was viewed as a woman's profession prior to the 1940s. Also, most career women were engaged in work of a social nature. Social work became a certified profession in 1920.[7] By 1921 social work was a recognized method for Southern Baptist foreign missions.

Church social action and secular social action often ran in the same women's veins. Annie Armstrong's mother was a founder of the Union Protestant Infirmary of Baltimore. Annie Armstrong herself worked at the local orphanage and poorhouse, all the while fostering local Baptist ministries. Fannie E. S. Heck cut her social action teeth in WMU. By 1897 she had inaugurated a department of "neighborhood mission work" in North Carolina WMU.[8] Then she branched into secular benevolence. As the first president of the Woman's Club of Raleigh, she concentrated its program on community health and sanitation. She was a founder and president of the Associated Charities of Raleigh. Heck decided that charity without Christ was not enough. She thought that Jane Addams had "left religion far too much out of her plans." She wanted WMU to meet both physical needs and spiritual needs.[9]

PERSONAL SERVICE

In 1909 Heck appointed Lulie Wharton of Baltimore as chairman of personal service. Wharton had lived and breathed personal service all her life. Her father had organized the Chinese Sunday School of Eutaw Place Baptist Church. Her mother, the first recording secretary of WMU, SBC, died while playing "Higher Ground" on the organ at the Mother's Meeting for poor women. Her husband, Henry Marvin Wharton, was a broad-minded evangelist and orator, well-known in the US and in England.

Under the lead of Heck and Wharton, the WMU Executive Committee outlined its personal service plans. Instead of sending out two or three

dozen women missionaries, WMU would "convert itself into a vast
company of women who by their membership in it, feel called and
appointed each in her own community to do such work." Their work
would be "the Christian up-building of their own communities, acknowledging a spiritual duty to the poor, neglected, and outcast of
their own neighborhood." The WMU policy clearly warned against
putting "the ministry to the body before or apart from the ministry to
the soul."[10]

Not until 1935 did WMU actually use the term *social service* in connection with personal service, thus avoiding antagonizing opponents
of the social gospel. Not until the 1960s did WMU regularly use the
word *ministry* to describe personal missions, for that word had been
understood only in relation to work professionally done by males. A
1914 effort to describe personal service as *Christian ministration* was
not popular. In the 1940s WMU renamed personal service as *community
missions.* Then in the 1960s it became *mission action.* By whatever
name, it employed social work as a means of sharing the gospel.

Administratively, the women gave substance to the personal service
idea by asking each missionary society to appoint a personal service
committee. The committee would send detailed reports of its activities
through the WMU system. These were published from 1914 until 1962,
despite many objections to the labors of record keeping and to the
inappropriateness of bragging on good works.

By incorporating personal service into its program, WMU was able
to absorb the ladies aid-type benevolent groups of women which had
been in competition with the missionary societies from their beginning.[11] In 1912, personal service was written into the WMU Standard of
Excellence. No society, women's or children's, could make the grade
in WMU if it failed to do firsthand missions work. The standard made
plain that personal service was "definite, organized, and for the spiritual
uplift of your own community, conducted by the members of your
society, under its own oversight."[12] By 1911 the state WMUs were
forming personal service committees to spread the word.

Although personal service was closely akin to home missions, Heck
wrote that personal service must in no way overlap or interfere with
the work of the Home Mission Board or Foreign Mission Board. The
women were ever fearful of earning ill will of the boards by breaking
their promise to "disclaim all thought of independent action."

Heck recognized that the personal service plan was a revolutionary
idea and that it would take time "to grow up in the mind of the people."[13]
The statistics showed that the women were indeed slow to take up the
new idea. By 1927 fewer than 37 percent of the societies reported
participation.

WMU published a steady stream of literature to help the women proceed. Much of it was written to convince women of their obligation to meet human need as Christ did and to explain the intent of personal service. On one hand, the literature took a low-key note: "those gentle ministries to which women have always given themselves, such as clubs and centers." On the other hand, the writings had a militant tone: "A great engine of power to be attached to the nearest need."[14]

Personal service was defined as more than social service because it "had the gospel as its motive and conversion as its aim."[15] It was explained as "The Golden Rule at Work." Its chief aim was "to make Christ known in all his regenerating power." In other words, the knowledge of Christ would be the primary means of rebuilding the diseased social climate.[16]

The leading published resource was *A Manual of Personal Service*. This small book was the work of Heck, Wharton, and Emma Leachman, city missionary in Louisville who lived at the Woman's Missionary Union Training School and supervised the practical missions work of the students.

NEEDS FOR PERSONAL SERVICE

The personal needs of individuals rather than abstract societal problems brought out the good works of WMU. Persons in need were easy to find in WMU's native environment. After the Civil War, per capita income in the South was never more than half as great as in the North until after 1940. More households were headed by women, more children were employed in industry, more women worked, infants died at a higher rate, education was poorer, sanitation less healthy, and disease more rampant than in any other region.

WMU seldom responded to need by marching on the halls of government, although the power of the ballot was occasionally stressed. Most often WMU went to work alleviating distress in small groups. (Efforts that moved to the broader issue level are discussed in chap. 10.) On the personal level, WMU has consistently been concerned with the economically disadvantaged, especially women and children; with the sick; with the institutionalized; and with persons aided via charitable organizations. Persons consistently reached by WMU (other than blacks, who are discussed in chap. 10) during the period of personal service were these:

Immigrants.—The plight of the foreigner was one of the original compelling forces in personal service. Germans in Baltimore, Mexicans in Texas, Cubans in Florida drew out women's sympathies. From the first year of personal service WMU advised its members that leaflets in German, Italian, and Spanish could be obtained from the WMU office. Lulie Wharton was WMU's delegate at the Conference on Americanizing the Immigrant in Philadelphia in 1916, when 4 million immigrants were living in SBC territory. WMU had particular sympathy for the immigrant woman, homebound and least likely of the family to learn English. "Christian Americanization" was the goal. WMU was represented by its personal service chairman in the Neighbors League of America.[17]

In the 1950s WMU recognized a unique ministry due the temporary resident from abroad, the "international." Many state WMUs helped host conferences and house parties for international students at Thanksgiving and Christmas.[18] Efforts were made to place internationals in WMU members' homes for Christmas holidays.

WMU employed many methods to meet the needs of foreigners, but particularly good will centers and literacy lessons. Such efforts often resulted in permanent ethnic churches, such as First Mexican Baptist Church of Dallas. Other efforts aided the transition of Anglo churches into ethnically diversified church programs, such as at the Lee Street Memorial Church in Baltimore, where Susan Tyler Pollard (Mrs. James) was reaching 137 immigrant mothers and children by 1912.

Industrial Workers.—Persons affected by the development of mines, factories, and mills in the South were among the chief concerns of personal service. WMU publications regularly sensitized their readers to the changing southern economy. After just one year of personal service the chairman Lulie Wharton reported "great growth in sense of responsibility for social conditions in the community. In the large cities we lose our bearings and forget we are the keeper even of our unknown brother." She mentioned the horrors of child labor, of women overworked and underpaid, of men working long hours until too exhausted to hear the gospel.[19]

In 1917 WMU members were specifically advised to study state and federal laws relating to health and employment of women and children, reporting violations to proper authorities. In 1919 personal service workers were given a list of questions to ask employers: How many women at work? What kind of work? What wages? What hours? What conditions? How many children under 16 at work? In 1922, when the Supreme Court declared the Child Labor Act unconstitutional, *Royal Service* responded with alarm, stating that a child could be permitted to work ten hours a day in some states.[20] Members were urged to help working boys and girls through good will centers, teaching them through night schools. But they were also urged to see that "little citizens" were given the education rightfully theirs as Americans.

WMU recognized that many persons suffering from industrialization were from the same cultural group of typical Baptist churches. Many of them were Baptists displaced from rural churches. WMU used many techniques to aid their lot, but the likeliest was simply to provide Woman's Missionary Societies and Sunbeam Bands convenient to their

work place and schedule. These working women and children had
money to share for the missions cause. Often industry-related WMU
work grew into full-fledged churches.

Rural Residents.—WMU went into personal service recognizing
that the majority of southerners lived in a rural environment in need
of education, medical services, utilities, and recreation. Standard personal service techniques were suggested, except that good will centers
were not stressed for communities of fewer than 5,000 residents. When
Lulie Wharton heard protests that Daily Vacation Bible Schools, mothers clubs, and other activities could not be conducted in rural communities, she decided to prove the opposite. Her husband sent a driver
to collect the children around their summer camp site in Virginia, and
she organized a large Vacation Bible School.[21]

In 1937 Una Roberts Lawrence (Mrs. Irvin), then personal service
chairman, was named by Franklin D. Roosevelt to his Committee on
Farm Tenancy, which led to the Farm Security Administration. Sensitive
to the population shift to the city, personal service leaders suggested
aid to young people leaving home to work in the city. Farmers were
encouraged to share their products with charitable outlets in town.[22]

Similar projects were explored for southern mountain folk. In 1900
North Carolina women had paved the way with a call for volunteer
teachers to conduct summer schools. Fifty women went into the North
Carolina mountains to teach. Because the mountain schools of the
Home Mission Board were relatively isolated from most churches, WMU
aided them more through contributions than through personal service.
For many years the schools were assisted by boxes of food, clothing,
and household goods sent by WMU as part of the "box" program.[23]
Georgia WMU launched the Mary P. Willingham School for mountain
girls, while Virginia WMU funded the Buchanan School.[24]

Jews.—As early as 1925 WMU annually gave a small portion of its
earnings on literature sales for publication of literature directed toward
Jews. WMU regularly gave a platform to a home missionary, Jacob
Gartenhaus, who was a convert from Judaism. In 1935 WMU inaugurated
a personal service plan called Friends of Israel groups. These groups
were to distribute literature and establish personal contact with Jews.
For example, a Friends of Israel group in Kansas City sent literature to
6,000 Jewish families each quarter.[25] WMUs of Texas, Missouri, Illinois,
Kentucky, and occasionally other states employed their own missionaries to work with Jews.

TECHNIQUES FOR PERSONAL SERVICE

By 1920 WMU had fielded all the ministry and witness techniques
that were to distinguish personal service. Women's groups, girls'

groups, and young children's groups helped achieve WMU's ultimate objective of moving persons of special need into the mainstream of contributing Christians. For example, members of the Italian Mother's Club at the good will center conducted by Fannie H. Taylor in Tampa, Florida, became Christians. Then they became Baptists, and then they became a Woman's Missionary Society.[26]

An early Sunbeam Band for mill children in Charleston, South Carolina, grew into the Rutledge Avenue Baptist Church.[27] During the $75 Million Campaign a mill-town church, composed largely of women, decided to give $10,000. They arranged with the mill superintendent to work on their days off until the funds were raised.[28] In 1933, Omer Shermer Alford (Mrs. John I.), who would later become president of Georgia WMU, moved with her textile engineer husband to a mill village in Covington, Georgia. There was no Baptist church, so Alford organized a women's prayer group through which literacy was stressed, then a girls club which became a young woman's missionary society, and then a Woman's Missionary Society. By 1947 a full-fledged church dedicated its own building debt free.[29] This was not an unusual WMU approach.

Survey.—As personal service began, WMU issued a leaflet on how to conduct a personal service survey. Throughout 1914 *Royal Service* repeated the steps in amazing detail. WMU organizations were to take a map of their community, divide it in grid pattern, and learn the demographic characteristics of each section. Women were to go house to house, church to church, community agency after agency to learn the economic and employment picture, sanitation level, language and educational needs, and religious affiliation. Survey results were then to be studied and action planned accordingly. The survey was a worthy end in itself for it raised consciousness and led families to take corrective action as landowners, citizens, and employers.

The survey had been modeled in Baltimore in 1895. Julia Donnahaw, who was later to become a state missionary and good will center worker, made a survey of a neighborhood where Fulton Avenue Baptist Church wished to begin a new work. She was surprised to find a number of Germans who knew no English. The result was a sewing school for German girls which gained confidence of the families. Then a Bible school and weeknight services grew into West Baltimore Baptist Church.[30]

Clubs and Classes.—The earliest method of Christian social work was the industrial school. All that was required was a meeting place, a teacher, and supplies. The school was actually nothing more than a class which convened on a regular basis. Students might be children or adults. Usually simple skills such as sewing, cooking, woodwork, and child care were taught. The objective might be to help needy persons gain marketable skills; usually for women and girls the emphasis was on economical and healthful homemaking.[31]

In modern times, classes branched into arts and crafts. A popular format was the Mother's Club for women and the Cheer-All Club for girls. These often taught personal skills but had the added appeal of meeting social needs with teas and chats and lectures. Lectures often related to moral issues such as temperance, proper child rearing, and personal purity. In 1911 WMU published *The Homemaker*, a manual for mothers meetings and sewing schools.

Annie Armstrong herself was in charge of a mothers meeting as late as 1923. She was arranging Valentine dinners, sewing projects, and interesting programs for the women. The mothers functioned somewhat like a missionary society, collecting contributions for state, home, and foreign missions.[32] Sometimes WMU organized clubs such as Scouts, but usually preferred to form units of its own organizations on a club basis. Clubs not only put the advantaged women in touch with those needing assistance, but also helped the needy to organize themselves for mutual uplift. In some cases the clubs functioned as cooperatives to pool purchasing, to bring ordinary goods within convenient reach of persons, to share medical equipment, and to assist with child care. Child care was a lingering concern of WMU. Societies reporting conducting day nurseries and kindergartens ranged from 46 in 1919 to 1,372 in 1928, then stabilizing at around 500 in the 1930s.

Good Will Centers.—WMU's most sophisticated and far-reaching social work effort was the settlement house. The Woman's Home Mission Society of the Methodist Episcopal Church South led the way with settlements in major southern cities as early as 1901. A directory of settlement houses published in 1911 showed no Baptist ministries of that kind in the South.[33]

A settlement house was indeed a settlement. Privileged young women would take up residence in an underprivileged neighborhood, usually in a roomy house. They would furnish the house with the cultural appointments of their upbringing, then open their doors to be a center of improvement in the community. Religious influence was a feature added to some settlements. At the settlement house, clubs, classes, medicine, temporary refuge, legal intervention, pure water, bathrooms, and other practical aids to survival were available, in addition to refinements such as music, art, and recreation.

Settlement work was suggested to Baptists from the first mentions of personal service in 1909-10. The earliest Baptist settlements seem to have been led by women in Birmingham and in Norfolk in 1911. Following the 1912 WMU Annual Meeting, women from Macon to Dallas were discussing whether they could undertake a settlement. In 1913 WMU decided that a goal for the WMU 25th Anniversary celebration would be "some definite personal service left as a memorial of each

Jubilate meeting." This goal resulted in the formal establishment of settlement houses in Richmond, Meridian, Charlotte, Newport News, and Louisville.

In 1914 Lulie Wharton decided that the term *settlement house* needed to be replaced by something more appealing and uniquely Southern Baptist. She coined the name *good will center*, because the purpose was to demonstrate the good news of "peace on earth, good will to all men" (Luke 2:14). The name was commonly used for Southern Baptist social work institutions until the late 1960s.

The model Southern Baptist Good Will Center was operated by the Woman's Missionary Union Training School in Louisville. Its primary purpose was to give students a laboratory for missions experience. Secondarily, the WMUTS center was deliberately planned to set the pace for local WMUs. It was begun under the strict supervision of Maud McLure after a summer of study at the New York School of Philanthropy (later the School of Social Work). Emma Leachman moved her office to the center and became its unofficial director.

The WMUTS center was opened on October 25, 1912, in a rented building at 512 East Madison Street. A year later, WMU purchased a nearby residence at a cost of $5,000 for the settlement. Within two years, graduates of the WMUTS were directing settlements in Meridian, Norfolk, Atlanta, and Richmond. In 1925 WMU authorized the building of a model building for the WMUTS. It was sold to the Presbyterian Colored Mission in 1940 when the WMUTS moved to suburban Louisville. A new center was built at 1818 Portland Avenue in 1950. WMU retained this property until it was sold to West End Baptist Church in 1967.

The income from the sale of the good will center in Louisville was held until it was designated in 1986 to begin the Second Century Fund for WMU leadership development.

WMU leaders consciously borrowed methodology from Jane Addams. Leachman and McLure spent several days of January 1915 in Chicago at Hull House. McLure reported to Fannie Heck that Hull House showed that "without the love of Christ as the dynamic such work is a failure," merely cold mechanics. They determined to emphasize Christian witness, personal sympathy and enthusiasm, and a club-based program at the WMU settlement house.[34]

A glance at Leachman's report of personal service in the good will center for January 1913 indicates something of the typical activity of the center:

652 visits made
17 Bibles distributed
21 senior campfires
387 office calls

291 appeals for help
13 sick persons cared for
11 prescriptions endorsed
142 yards of cloth sold wholesale for the Friendly Circle
38 garments made
7 girls and women found jobs
2 cases in juvenile court
7 professed conversions.

Another Leachman opportunity came from the city morgue, which sent a hearse to bring her in any time parents were called on to examine bodies of dead children for identification.[35]

WMU expected that good will centers would be operated by volunteer help and be funded by the women themselves. But when the Woman's Missionary Union Training School began producing qualified professionals in the field of social work, WMU urged that they be hired. The professional directors would be given residence in the settlement house and a salary of $40 to $50 a month. The staff director would coordinate the work of the volunteers.

One of the most remarkable settlement-house workers was Agnes Osborne, editor of the *Heathen Helper* and secretary pro tem for the 1888 founding meeting of WMU. She followed the Jane Addams pattern, but added religious emphasis. Osborne was born in 1847 into a highly literate, Christian, progressive family. Once she had seen WMU into successful organization, she devoted her life to personal missions work. From 1905 she conducted an industrial school in connection with a mission in a needy section of Louisville. A doctor joined her in conducting a mother and child clinic in 1914. In 1916 she opened a settlement house and the doctor continued his clinic there. From 1916 until her death in 1930 she lived at the center. A board of women from local churches paid the rent and operating costs. She received no salary. When James P. Boyce, president of Southern Baptist Theological Seminary, died, a bequest from his estate made possible the purchase of a building. The center became known as the James P. Boyce Settlement. Because Osborne was a continuing member of the Central Committee of Kentucky WMU, the women were kept in close liaison with the center. Many WMUTS students worked with Osborne.

Another form of settlement was at the Sibley Mill in Augusta, Georgia. As in several other WMU settlements, the mill furnished the house and the Baptists of the city paid the salary of a 1915 graduate of the WMUTS, Carrie U. Littlejohn. The settlement furnished, among other services, a day nursery for the children of mothers who worked in the mill. In 1921 Littlejohn was called back to the WMUTS as director of the good will center. Ultimately she became the school's president.[36]

WMU stressed that good will centers be established in all cities with more than 10,000 population, but the figure was later lowered to population of 5,000. The number of societies involved with operating centers grew to a high of 993 in 1935. The number of institutions was not regularly reported. In 1925, 32 were known. These were owned and operated by state and associational WMU organizations, and in some cases by church WMUs.

WMU introduced a system of grading the centers. Only those with permanent property and a professional staff in residence were counted as Class A. The expense of maintaining a top-grade center was almost beyond the means of women's organizations, especially as the unified church budget and Cooperative Program gained acceptance in the late 1930s. WMU money flowed through the hands of the church treasurer, and churches as a whole were not as willing to budget for good will centers as women were. Some good will centers were funded in part by endowments or major gifts which built substantial buildings. One example was the Woody Barton Good Will Center built in Nashville in 1923 by Mrs. O. C. Barton in memory of her daughter. Another was the Stewart Center in Atlanta built by bequest of Mrs. Andrew P. Stewart, who had originally organized the center as a day nursery for mill workers.

In 1920, the Home Mission Board first provided a building for a good will center. In 1921 the HMB employed Emma Leachman as field worker and visiting consultant for the centers. Thus the Home Mission Board began to assume overall coordination of Christian social ministries.[37] Leachman's salary was provided through the home missions offering by WMU's decision.

By 1924 WMU reported total attendance at good will centers as 103,000. Minnie Kennedy James (Mrs. W. C.) in her annual address said, "Our personal service work particularly in the good will centers has assumed such proportions that like the brethren in the days of 1874-1888 some of the brethren of today are wondering what they are going to do with this rising power."[38]

What happened was that the centers continued to grow in number and in influence. They resulted in thousands of conversions and development of several new churches. They gave opportunities for professional ministry to dozens of dedicated women. To gain adequate funding for them, WMU sacrificed control and gave them over to the Home Mission Board. In the mid-1940s WMU allocated increasing amounts of the Annie Armstrong Offering for buildings and operating costs of the centers. Whereas the *Personal Service Guide* published by WMU in 1933 had been fat with instructions for good will center operations, the 1943 *Guide for Community Missions* and its 1959 revision spoke of the centers only briefly as magnets for voluntary aid.

In 1949 the state WMU executive secretaries informally discussed their concern about inequities in salary, pensions, and travel funds for good will center employees in comparison with others involved in home missions.[39] The remedy was to make the workers full home missionaries under the Home Mission Board. Jewel Beall (Mrs. Noble Y.), general field worker of the HMB, planned annual conferences for good will center employees, some years in connection with the WMU Conference at Ridgecrest and at other times in connection with the HMB Conference. As salaries and benefits improved, good will center management became an attractive field for males. The HMB employed a male good will center staff member, Clovis A. Brantley, in 1957 placing him over Beall, who had been the HMB's liaison with WMU. In 1967 the familiar term *good will center* was dropped in favor of the term *Baptist center*, describing a variety of church weekday community ministries.

One of the last good will centers to pass from WMU control was the House of Happiness in Richmond (several centers historically had used this name). This center was established in 1914 as the permanent memorial of the Jubilate by the city Woman's Missionary Societies in Richmond. A graduate of the WMUTS, Nannie West, was employed to take charge of the work. Over the years Richmond WMUs provided it a superior building and a country camp. During the 1940s, WMU began to share funding and control with men of the association. In the 1970s a male director was employed. Baptist center personnel in Richmond came under appointment of the Home Mission Board. Because of changing community and styles of ministry, the building was sold in 1980 and certain aspects of the House of Happiness ministry were continued in a new cooperative effort with the community.[40]

The only Baptist center remaining under WMU ownership as of 1986 was Stewart Center of Atlanta. It has continued under a board of directors of Atlanta WMU women. Its director is L'Nola Hall, who is appointed by the Home Mission Board.

Vacation Bible Schools.—The first Vacation Bible School was conducted in 1898 in New York City by a Baptist, Virginia Sinclair Hawes (Mrs. Walker Aylett). She was a native of Charlottesville, Virginia, and sister of the second Mrs. John A. Broadus of Lousiville. Therefore her success in teaching the Bible to street children was known not only to Robert G. Boville, who later founded the International Association of Daily Vacation Bible Schools, but also to Baptist women of Louisville. Maud McLure learned details of the VBS plan while visiting in Chautauqua, New York. She invited Boville to lecture about Vacation Bible Schools at the WMUTS, and in 1914 the students enrolled 102 children in the first Daily Vacation Bible School known to be conducted under Southern Baptist auspices.[41]

Already WMU had suggested that its young women members conduct Daily Vacation Bible Schools as a project of personal service.[42] From that point on, VBS was a standard component of personal service. The first recorded statistics indicate that 73 societies conducted VBS in 1918-19. Just three years before there had been only five times that many in the entire USA.

In 1924, ten years after WMU inaugurated VBS among Southern Baptists, the Sunday School Board of the SBC appointed its first staff promoter of VBS. In 1925 the Board issued VBS curriculum material. The Board promoted VBS as an activity for children within the church, whereas WMU conducted VBS as a missions outreach. In 1938 WMU was conducting approximately one-fourth the schools counted among Southern Baptists.

WMU continued promotion of missions VBS until the 1950s, then gradually began to leave such projects in the hands of the Sunday School. It had been an effective method for reaching immigrant, black, laboring, and underprivileged children. The schools were an important method of enlisting the efforts of young women for missions during their school vacations.

White Cross.—Involvement in personal service was bolstered by women's experiences in World War I and resulting ties to the Red Cross. WMU members gave 434,000 hours of nursing during four war years. Then personal service temporarily took on an international expression through White Cross work. In 1920 WMU recommended that women study the book, *A Crusade of Compassion,* offered by the Central Committee on the United Study of Missions. As follow-through WMUers were asked to prepare bandages, linens, and other supplies to be sent to Southern Baptist mission hospitals abroad. Through this project, WMU hoped to gain the involvement of women who enjoyed their wartime Red Cross work.[43] White Cross work was, at the beginning, a hybrid of personal service, box work, and mission study. In 1922 the reported value of White Cross contributions was $9,687. Each state WMU had a White Cross chairman and an assigned foreign hospital to aid. In 1926 White Cross efforts were extended to Baptist hospitals in the US. By the early 1930s, interest in White Cross had slackened, and fewer than half the state WMUs were participating. Rising wartime problems made delivery of White Cross goods difficult, and in consultation with the Foreign Mission Board, WMU, SBC, stopped emphasizing the program in 1936. Some state WMUs occasionally continued White Cross projects.

Evangelism.—From the beginning of personal service, WMU intended to win souls. Personal evangelism was an automatic aspect of all WMU activities. Many of the earliest personal service techniques were overt evangelistic activities: cottage prayer meetings (usually conducted in the home of a non-Christian, and cited as the best means of personal soul-winning); visits; and services in which women led singing and gave "Bible talks." These were routinely reported and counted, as were mission Sunday Schools.

In 1920 soul-winning was added to WMU's list of fundamental aims. WMU's mission study course required study of a book written by E. Y. Mullins at WMU's request, *Talks on Soul-Winning*. Then, in traditional Baptist fashion, the women began counting their converts. The numbers were so high (7,508 reported in 1923) that the personal service committee decided to narrow its report. Instead of asking for a report of "conversions witnessed," it asked for "conversions known to be a direct result of work done under supervision of a personal service committee." The number declined slightly, but hit 11,285 in 1927. By 1926 nearly 2,500 cottage prayer meetings were being held by WMU and 893 mission Sunday Schools.

During the $75 Million Campaign, Minnie James served on an SBC evangelism committee which proposed a summertime evangelistic campaign in every church. WMU suggested further study of the Mullins book on soul-winning and W. W. Hamilton's *Bible Evangelism*. In the first six months of 1939 WMU members bought 17,000 copies of a soul-winning book, *Helping Others Become Christians.* [44]

The SBC proposed to win 1 million converts in observance of the 1945 centennial of the Convention. WMU threw all its promotional forces into the drive, especially emphasizing cottage prayer meetings. The Texas evangelism secretary reported that in crusade activities he attended, women had comprised 90 percent of the attendance at morning revival meetings, 95 percent of attendance at prayer meetings, 95 percent of the personal evangelism workers, and 75 percent of the attendance at evening meetings.[45] The count of baptisms during the year was 256,699, or 39,879 more than the previous year. Kathleen Mallory said, "It is humbly believed that quite a few of the . . . baptisms were in part at least result . . . of community missions."[46]

So compelling was the soul-winning emphasis that the Illinois WMU secretary, Maude Hathaway (Mrs. John), resigned in 1942 to work as the state WMU's field missionary.[47]

With the change from *personal service* to the new term *community missions* in 1943, soul-winning moved into higher visibility, higher than alleviating human need. Between 1956 and 1967, *community missions* was usually replaced in WMU headlines with *Christian witnessing*. Women were reminded that the most effective soul-winners did not occupy pulpits, but were women at work with the multitudes.[48]

In 1959 WMU published its classic study book, *Christian Witnessing* by Floy Barnard, dean of women at Southwestern Baptist Theological Seminary. Through this book and voluminous writings in its magazines WMU developed a woman-oriented practical approach to sharing faith. WMU refined its approaches to adherents of the non-Christian world religions. This emphasis was to be strengthened in 1962 and 1963, when WMU gave major support to the Home Mission Board's effort to organize 30,000 new congregations.

Personal Nurturing.—Earliest elements of personal service were extensions of things women normally did anyway: sewing for the poor or teaching sewing; providing food for those in need or for the sick; nursing the sick; visiting the lonely or confined. When drawn into a structured plan of the missionary society, they became personal service. Many of the visits were for the purpose of explaining the gospel of salvation. In the 1914 personal service statistics, WMU reported 113,820 visits. The number grew to an astronomical 4 million in 1926.

Literacy.—In 1919 WMU invited the president of the Neighbors League of America to the Annual Meeting for the purpose of teaching a class on How to Teach English to Foreigners. This was WMU's first formal venture into teaching reading. By 1921 the organization turned its teaching skills toward the widespread problem of illiteracy in the South. Literacy missions appeared regularly in the Plan of Work from 1921 onward, with the added feature of Star Classes for uneducated adults. In 1922, 279 classes were reported.

Professional Christian Social Work.—By deliberate plan, Woman's Missionary Union Training School was closely tied to the development of personal service. Every WMUTS student took a course in personal work. Students learned to do professionally what WMU members did voluntarily in personal service. Many students found employment heading up institutional social work projects sponsored by local WMU organizations. Emma Leachman and Maud McLure were recognized as the professional authorities in personal service. They often taught and consulted with local WMUs.

When WMU sought a distinctive purpose and role for the WMUTS in 1952, no other Southern Baptist school had a full-fledged social work course, although Baylor University had projected social work studies. Still the primary promoter of social work in the SBC, and seeing social work properly linked with mission strategy, WMU decided to make its school a graduate-level institution for social work and missionary training. The school was renamed Carver School of Missions and Social Work, in honor of W. O. Carver. Carver had taught the first class in personal work and had been the school's most enduring guide.

PERSONAL SERVICE LIVES ON

The bedrock social work emphasis in WMU temporarily faded as the women lost control of Carver School of Missions and Social Work between 1957 and 1963. An independent school of social work could not gain accreditation, so WMU deeded the school's assets to Southern

Baptist Theological Seminary with the understanding that Carver School's emphasis would be carried on. The funds endowed the WMU Chair of Church Social Work (see chap. 11).

Personal service changed its name and its slant several times but it has never fallen from its central place in the recommended program of WMU. In order to give personal service a new lease on life, WMU renamed it in 1942 and put it in the portfolio of a national staff member. The new name was community missions.[49] Community missions was managed by Mary Christian, a former professor at the WMUTS, who gave primary attention to the race issue and to evangelism. The concentration on evangelism coincided with the intensive postwar Southern Baptist population explosion. Community missions was not as strongly oriented to social work as personal service had been. This shift may have reflected the disillusionment many Southerners felt in wartime.

Between 1943 and 1957 WMU grouped its community missions concerns around three stackpoles: Christian witnessing, Christian fellowship (a rather subdued form of social work or kindly deeds directed to those in need), and upholding moral standards. Christian citizenship received much attention as WMU encouraged women to exercise the ballot as a means of civic righteousness.

WMU employed its first full-time staff member to promote community missions in 1949. She was Edith Stokely of Tennessee, then campus minister at Southern Methodist University, who had been student body president at the WMUTS. During her term the evangelistic note continued in step with changing times. WMU believed that community charitable agencies would meet physical needs, so that WMU must concentrate on spiritual and moral needs.[50] Stokely led WMU into a more studious and scientific approach to the alcohol problem. A new prong of community missions was to provide recreation and entertainment for young people, both to prevent and to heal the rising plague of juvenile delinquency.[51]

Intensive training for state WMU community missions chairmen was offered at the WMU headquarters in Birmingham April 9-11, 1952. Although the impact of community missions on fundamental social issues was somewhat diluted during this period, involvement in the program deepened. Under Stokely's leadership, for the first time more than half the missionary societies reported community missions work in 1951. Still only 38 percent of the members were involved. By the time Stokely resigned in 1954, the number of organizations participating in community missions had risen to an all-time reported high of 64 percent.[52]

Instead of a staff promoter of community missions, WMU, beginning in 1955, employed staff experts to promote the age-level organizations. They, in turn, promoted community missions and Christian witnessing as part of each age's activities. Teaching children the precepts of Christian ministry and witness had been in WMU's mind from the beginning. As WMU organizations for children and youth rapidly grew in the 1950s, community missions became prominently fixed in their curriculum. For the youngest, community missions was simplified as Helping Others for Jesus' Sake. They studied books about community missions. Girls and teens had to be personally engaged in community missions in order to progress through the ranks of their organizations. As would have been expected in children's activities, the efforts were more effective as education for the doers than as social change for the recipients.

By 1961, the last year that WMU reported statistics of community missions participation, 63 percent of the organizations reported involvement.

RENEWED LITERACY EFFORTS

WMU began to revive its emphasis on literacy in 1946. Frank C. Laubach, who was to popularize literacy missions with his World Literacy Crusade, spoke that year at the WMU Annual Meeting. His wife spoke at the 1950 Annual Meeting. In the early 1950s Laubach and members of his staff visited the Carver School of Missions and Social Work (formerly Woman's Missionary Union Training School) to train students in literacy techniques. From this contact and others, Baylor University established a literacy center. Richard Cortright, a Laubach specialist, joined the Baylor staff and began teaching WMU groups how to teach reading. The techniques were used not only for people totally unable to read, but also for persons learning English as a second language. Cortright reminded WMUers that the WMU of Nigeria had taught 8,000 people to read in recent years and challenged the American WMU to equal the record.[53]

Lillian Isaacs (Mrs. John R.), wife of a professor at Clear Creek Baptist School in Kentucky, read in *Royal Service* about Baylor's literacy work and asked the WMU of First Baptist Church in Pineville to buy the correspondence course and begin teaching people to read. These women involved the Bell County Associational WMU, and Isaacs asked the Home Mission Board to assist with expenses in bringing Cortright for a full literacy teaching workshop. More than 200 people were trained, the largest group to that date. The workshop resulted in the Appalachian Literacy Council, headquartered at Clear Creek School.[54] Because of Lillian Isaacs and the Clear Creek experience, the Home Mission Board employed a literacy worker in 1960 as a two-year experiment. Then Mildred Blankenship of Birmingham joined the HMB staff in 1962. Working primarily among WMU persons, Blankenship trained a large corps of teachers and trainers. One of the early leaders in literacy was Agnes Jenkins Miller (Mrs. Ernest L.), president of Georgia WMU 1961-66. She attended a literacy training conference at Ridgecrest in 1960, began to organize Georgia WMU to do the work, and was asked to serve as consultant to the Atlanta Board of Education as it established an adult literacy program.[55]

In 1963-64 WMU made literacy work the community missions emphasis of the year, a rare concerted attack on a single social issue. In 1968 WMU published *Mission Action Group Guide: Nonreaders.* Literacy teacher training continued to be provided regularly at WMU conferences. WMU celebrated 25 years of Southern Baptist literacy missions at the WMU Annual Meeting of 1983.

THE MISSION ACTION ERA

When Helen Fling became president of WMU, she reactivated Christian social ministry as a means of personal missions work. After years of concentration on study of missions, she became convinced that study was worthless unless it resulted in action. She was concerned about the widening gulf between the haves and have-nots in American society. Fling asked the WMU staff to draft a plan whereby WMU might cope with the age of revolution. The result was mission action, which was introduced in 1965 to upgrade and revitalize community missions.

As American society grew more troubled and revolutionary, mission action made more sense to Baptists. WMU issued a precise definition of the program: "Organized effort of a church to minister and to witness to persons of special need or circumstance who are not immediate prospects for the church." It was more or less the old personal service definition with some modern improvements.

Through Southern Baptist interagency agreement, it was understood that mission action was the business of the whole church. This was the first time church program suggestions had officially said that social action should be on the recommended agenda for local churches. And by agreement, WMU was joined by Brotherhood in carrying out the mission action task of a church.

Like the old ideal of personal service, mission action was an ongoing, sustained, and well-organized effort focused toward one target of need. But like community missions, mission action might in some organizations be a series of short-term projects, especially if being done by children or by units of WMU that were primarily organized for another purpose.

To carry out the ongoing type of mission action, WMU and Brotherhood fielded a new organizational unit, the mission action group. WMU tested mission action groups in several churches before proposing them in 1967. The idea was for people dedicated to in-depth ministry to form a group.

Following standard procedure in WMU social ministry from the beginning of personal service, mission action was to start with a community survey. In consultation with the Home Mission Board and the Brotherhood Commission, WMU in 1967 published a *Mission Action Survey Guide.* A WMU (or Brotherhood or combined group) might select any mission action need it discovered in surveying. At the outset, WMU published guidebooks for work with internationals, the sick, juvenile rehabilitation, language groups, and economically disadvantaged. In less than six months more than 60,000 copies of the guides had been sold. In subsequent years WMU added other guidebooks and promoted several guides, such as one to work with prisoners, which were published by the Brotherhood Commission. Other possible target groups include the following: military personnel, alcoholics, drug abusers, migrants, travelers and tourists, nonreaders, aging, unwed parents, the institutionalized, and minority groups.[56]

To kick off mission action groups the 1967 WMU Annual Meeting was based on the need for Christian social work. Helen Fling deliberately framed the meeting around Bible passages which stressed Jesus' commands to minister to human need. Dramas and addresses alluded to Isaiah 61:1 and Luke 4:18. Denominationwide emphases on social ministry and witness in 1967 and 1972 strengthened mission action.

When WMU's organizational plans were overhauled in 1968 and again in 1970, mission action and mission action groups were carried forward and continued as an integral part of the contemporary WMU slate of concerns. In 1972 WMU and the Home Mission Board conducted 15 workshops across the nation to train persons for mission action.

Mission action was an instant hit among Southern Baptists, and people began to use the term loosely to apply to a variety of good deeds. WMU vociferously objected, desiring to restrict the term to WMU and Brotherhood-run genuine social ministry and witness beyond the usual good deeds among insiders of the church family.[57]

The Home Mission Board and Mission Action.—By 1966 the Home Mission Board had developed a full-fledged department of Christian Social Ministries. The philosophy of the department was to de-institutionalize social work (which ended many of the centers which had originated with WMU). Instead, the HMB urged every church to use its facilities throughout the week for Christian social ministries. The HMB's weekday ministries program and WMU's mission action work had the potential of overlap. Agreements reached in 1983 cast WMU and Brotherhood in the role of being the HMB's agent in the local church for organizing and training and involving laypersons in Christian social ministries. If a church launches a ministry which WMU and

Brotherhood cannot handle, such as a program employing professional staff, a church missions development program is suggested as the coordinating body, using HMB guidance materials. In such cases, WMU would aid the work through voluntary mission action.

Three Ways to Do Mission Action.—Among contemporary ways of doing mission action are migrant ministries, Big A Clubs, and prison ministries. The Home Mission Board began in 1948 a limited program to aid agricultural migrants. By 1954 more than 750,000 migrants were living in SBC territory. The Board had no staff director of migrant missions until 1960, but by that time, WMU was heavily involved. For example, Mrs. Willard Chandler, superintendent of WMU in Accomac Association, Virginia, began holding services for Mexican and Puerto Rican migrants in 1956. Virginia WMU's missions offering in 1958 began to fund involvement of missionaries. In 1985 Bob Gross, director of the Migrant Mission Center in Hope, Arkansas, said that without the personal help of WMU members over ten years his task would have been impossible.[58]

In 1977 WMU introduced plans and literature for Big A Clubs. The club is a plan for teaching simple Bible truths to children who have no church background, often children who are victimized by poverty or educational limitations. No statistics have been collected on the numbers reached through Big A Clubs though thousands of teachers books have been sold. Home missionaries, foreign missionaries, individuals, and adult and youth groups in WMU have organized Big A Clubs. More than 20,000 copies of the beginning teacher's book have been purchased.

In some states WMU gives special coordinated focus to particular target groups or issues. North Carolina WMU, for example, has stressed work with prisoners. A Baptist Young Women organization was established at the North Carolina Correctional Center for Women—the first known WMU group within a prison. North Carolina WMU was named the volunteer group of the year in the state as a result of its prison ministries.

Evangelism in the 1970s and 1980s.—The definition of mission action has always carefully included both ministry and witness. In the early 1970s WMU promoted the Home Mission Board's lay evangelism schools. WMU published "Faith Sharing in Mission Action," a booklet to reinforce witnessing technique with persons of special need. In 1972 WMU published "Leading Coffee Dialogues," a guidebook for neighborhood Bible studies of the Gospel of Mark, designed to present the gospel by discussion method. This approach was revived in 1986 when WMU published *Mark My Word* under the New Hope label. Believing that female approaches to witnessing were not being proposed by others in the denomination, WMU published a complete teaching kit for group training, *Witnessing Women*, in 1981. By 1986, 6,700 copies of the complete kit had been sold, along with 2,500 additional copies of the learner's book.

In 1982 WMU joined the Home Mission Board in sponsoring the first national evangelistic conference for women. Under the title of Day-spring, the conferences were attended by 2,800 women at Ridgecrest, September 30-October 2, 1983, and by 2,600 women, April 12-14, 1984, at Fort Worth. The conferences were led by Laura Fry Allen (Mrs. Bruce), consultant for women in evangelism at the Home Mission Board. She was assisted by the HMB's National Council of Advisors for Women in Evangelism, a group of 29 women, 4 of whom were state WMU presidents. Eight WMU staff members served on the faculty for the meeting.

WMU has again revised its statement of purposes to emphasize direct personal witnessing equally with witnessing done as part of ministry in mission action. In 1986 WMU voted to add a new element to its organizational chart, personal witnessing groups for women. These are slated to be implemented beginning in 1988.

According to the latest WMU program design, mission action is defined as follows: "ministering and witnessing to persons of special need or circumstance who are not members of the church or its programs; mission action is also combating social and moral problems" (see chap. 10). Personal witnessing is defined as "a Christian's sharing the gospel of Jesus Christ with another person and giving that person an opportunity to confess Jesus Christ as Saviour and Lord."

Looking ahead to its second century, WMU set a priority of continuing its local missions work on the front of social needs. The organization continues to publish books to aid in the training and inspiration of mission action workers.

In 1986 WMU asked the new Carver School of Church Social Work of Southern Baptist Theological Seminary (descendant of WMU's school) to undertake a formal research project to determine mission action motivations and methods.

> . . . *society needs woman's interpretation of life in every department of it. The world needs the contribution woman can make to its welfare and this contribution can never be given in full measure so long as the notion prevails that her thoughts, her feelings and her actions are a real worth only when they have been strained through a masculine percolator. Just where you stand in that conflict is your place and there may begin personal service.*
>
> Lulie P. Wharton (Mrs. H. M.)
> *Royal Service,* September 1925

10

In sympathy with all righteousness

*We declare ourselves in sympathy with all the forces of
righteousness: international and interracial justice;
world peace; patriotism, national prohibition;
Christian Americanization;
universal education; Sabbath observance;
sacredness of the home; the family altar; high standards
for womanly speech, dress and conduct; improved industrial
conditions; child welfare; public health.*

WMU Plan of Work
1914-1960

HE CROSSROADS between women and missions created
a wide but well-fenced arena in which WMU grappled
with social issues. Issues strictly of concern to women,
but not to missions, fell on the fence and received only
casual nods from WMU. Woman suffrage, for example,
was not identified as either friend or foe of missions,
and accordingly received no official attention.

By contrast, WMU saw liquor clearly as an enemy. Strong drink was
often a contributing factor to the plight of women and children.

The fact that missions and women intersected in the South automatically confronted WMU with the race issue. WMU's leaders willingly
stepped forward to tangle with the web of a two-culture society in
which Negro Americans were so near yet so far away from the missions
effort. For no other American social cause did WMU do as much.

Early progressives in WMU were well informed about shifting sands
of social change on which they stood, and they firmly posted their
position. They were "on the side of all the forces of righteousness,"
and said so in each year's official Plan of Work from 1914 until 1960.
They undoubtedly drew their first "declaration of sympathy" straight
from the agenda of the Southern Sociological Congress of which Fannie
E. S. Heck was then vice-president.

Having advertised their sympathies, WMU leaders addressed them through two avenues: education and action. Educationally, they gently, slowly probed attitudes and equipped individual members to grapple with the issues where they personally found them. The voluminous pages of WMU literature and the wide platforms of WMU conventions were the channels of education.

For action, WMU fielded a generic strategy known originally as personal service and currently as mission action. The organization form was left flexible so local groups could choose their targets. Being in sympathy with a cause did not necessarily mean that WMU would take up arms for it. The national organization identified possible targets, but rarely rolled out a corporate attack. Some issues listed in the declaration of sympathy were potentially distractive from WMU's central purposes and therefore were left to others.

The contemporary WMU program beginning in 1968 recognized that in mission action women might address target issues, as well as target groups. Among the issues listed for potential action are family problems, gambling, pornography, obscenity, substance abuse, racial tensions, economic problems. These problems have been reflected in manuals for WMU organizations, as women are encouraged to confront them.

WOMAN SUFFRAGE AND CITIZENSHIP

Commitment to missions may have kept some WMU women from involvement in the campaign for women to vote as citizens.

The topic of women voting was controversial among Baptists. WMU members may have hesitated to risk embarrassment for missions by taking a stand in favor of the vote. Only concern for alcoholic beverage control moved a few WMUers to advocate the vote. A popular belief at the turn of the century was that if women could vote, alcohol would be controlled.[1] It was true also for other reforms (such as abolition of child labor) that many entered the suffrage ranks as the surest route to the desired reform. Because members of WMU were so strong in their advocacy of Prohibition, it is surprising to discover that few Baptist women openly advocated woman suffrage and that WMU itself never directly urged votes for women.[2]

A few men of the denomination were outspoken advocates of woman suffrage.[3] Among them were James B. Gambrell, editor of the Texas *Baptist Standard*, and Leslie L. Gwaltney, longtime editor of the *Alabama Baptist*. Neither man's wife, however, became an open advocate of woman suffrage within WMU circles. Mary T. Corbell Gambrell, a WMU officer in three states, was an example of a working woman in a responsible position of influence. J. B. Gambrell was president of the

Southern Baptist Convention when women were admitted as voting messengers in 1918.

James P. Eagle was another prominent denominational leader whose outspoken advocacy of woman suffrage was well known. He was elected governor of Arkansas in 1888 and served two terms. Susan B. Anthony, the national leader of the suffragists, visited Arkansas in February 1889 and was introduced to a large Little Rock audience by Governor Eagle. For 25 years Eagle was president of the Arkansas Baptist Convention. In 1902 he was elected president of the Southern Baptist Convention and served three terms.

Mary K. Oldham Eagle (Mrs. James P.) was a determined woman. She might have played a more prominent role in the denomination had she not been so forthright and aggressive in her views. Always a staunch and loyal supporter of missions, she helped organize the Central Committee of Arkansas in 1883. Two years later she was one of two women refused seats at the Southern Baptist Convention.[4] During the next few years, as her husband rose through the political ranks, she became an authority on parliamentary procedure and was noted for her skill in leading denominational meetings. Admirers spoke of her stately beauty, intellectuality, and deep spiritual tone. Those who disagreed with her found her use of parliamentary tactics to be tedious and trying. In 1899 she was a leading candidate to succeed Fannie Heck as president of WMU. Annie Armstrong could not bear her and on one occasion later exclaimed in a letter to R. J. Willingham, secretary of the Foreign Mission Board, "Isn't she a horror!"[5]

Throughout the South, most people opposed, or at best were indifferent toward, woman suffrage. No Deep South state granted any form of woman suffrage prior to the Nineteenth Amendment to the Constitution. Around the fringes, partial suffrage was granted, as, for example, Arkansas, which admitted women to vote in primary elections in 1917. Of states which were early parts of WMU, Oklahoma alone adopted statewide woman suffrage prior to ratification of the Nineteenth Amendment in August 1920. Only five southern states ratified the so-called Susan B. Anthony amendment. The other states rejected it (as did Alabama) or failed to take action prior to final ratification.

Arguments used against woman suffrage sound unreal to a modern ear. The strongest argument used by antisuffragists was that woman suffrage would reopen the question of Negro voting which had been buried in the South with qualifying tests and poll taxes. Others contended that woman suffrage was "unwomanly" or that they were saving women from the "mire of politics." Advocates of states' rights strongly opposed the federal amendment as a violation of the historic division of powers. For most, the cry of state's rights was no more than a cover-up for antifeminism. Some seized on the militancy of the fanatical fringe group and pointed to them as horrible examples of what votes for women would lead to. All of these arguments were heard in Baptist churches where preachers were opposed to woman suffrage, and they appeared in Baptist state papers whose editors were in opposition.[6]

WMU took no public note of the movement. Fannie Heck, while president of WMU, was frequently approached as a spokesperson of Southern Baptist women. When asked her views on woman suffrage (or any other current topic), invariably she would respond that her only interest was in missions. The reporters, she wrote, would "go away thinking them very poor copy."[7] This position is typical of the silence of the organization and its leaders on one of the most significant issues of the day. Many members of WMU were known to be opposed to woman suffrage. WMU habitually avoided behaviors that would unnecessarily antagonize the males of the Convention or divide the ranks of women. WMU's purposes could be as well achieved without woman suffrage as with it. Nothing was to be gained by fragmenting the organization simply to be on a crusading bandwagon. So ingrained was this ethic that no national WMU officer is known ever to have expressed an opinion, much less campaigned in public, for suffrage. But Mary Hill Davis (Mrs. F. S.), president of Texas WMU, admitted that Baptist women might have been "quiescent factors" in the suffrage struggles.[8]

Once women had been granted the right to vote, however, the position of WMU changed. Leaders were no longer silent. The vote brought WMU leaders a feeling of responsibility, a feeling of need to adjust to "increasing responsibilities being thrust upon women in these stirring times."[9] Minnie Kennedy James (Mrs. W. C.), president of WMU, SBC, said of the American woman, "Whether she wanted the vote or not the responsibility has been placed upon her and she must use this privilege in such a way that she will influence the life of the nation for good."[10] Repeated references in *Royal Service* were made to the importance of registering to vote.[11] With ballot in hand, women were encouraged to face the great moral problems of the day. Mary Hill Davis told the Texas WMU in 1922: " 'What is in thine hand?' . . . power, influence, and the ballot. . . . Then use them, my sisters for the glory of God and the betterment of the world."[12]

A few leaders, like Blanche Sydnor White of Virginia, never registered to vote, but most leaders became active participants in the electoral process. A study following the 1964 elections revealed that nationally about 67 percent of women voted, but 83 percent of *Royal Service* readers cast ballots that year.[13] Once opposed or indifferent to the right to vote, WMU members became model citizens by exercising the franchise once it was extended to them.

TEMPERANCE

Ella A. Boole of Brooklyn, New York, president of Woman's Christian Temperance Union, was one of the principal speakers at the WMU Annual Meeting of 1928. Knowing in advance that she was to be on the program, women who were members of WCTU wore their distinctive white ribbons. After she was introduced, all WCTU members were asked to stand; so many rose that Boole remarked that she felt that she was at a WCTU rally.[14] In one sense she was, for WMU was keenly allied with the temperance cause.

The WMU organization was only three years old when it adopted its first resolution on alcohol.[15] Thereafter, there was seldom a year in which the topic was not discussed or studied somewhere in the organization. This aggressiveness was amazing, for Southern Baptists of the nineteenth century were not uniformly in favor of the temperance movement. In the very year of WMU's organization, 1888, the president of the Southern Baptist Convention ruled a temperance resolution out of order on the grounds it was not relevant to missions.

Nor did the SBC endorse the Woman's Christian Temperance Union until 1912. The WCTU was not organized in the South until just prior to WMU. Its members were condemned for public speaking, political action, and such "unwomanly" behaviors. However, Frances Willard, founder of the WCTU, had been accompanied on her travels by Elizabeth J. Scovel, the first secretary of Tennessee WMU.[16]

Members of the WCTU addressed national and state WMU meetings; the work of both WCTU and the Woman's National Committee for Law Enforcement were commended; pamphlets from these and similar organizations were recommended, reproduced, or distributed by WMU; the subject was included in the Plan of Work between 1914 and 1960; and articles were found on the pages of *Royal Service* and became the basis of many local studies.

From its earliest years, WMU opposed both the personal consumption of and the manufacture and sale of alcoholic beverages. The call after a few years was invariably to total abstinence from all alcohol. Temperance in the sense of moderation was never considered.[17] Alma Worrill Wright (Mrs. Carter), president of Alabama WMU and national stewardship chairman, was often quoted on the topic. "It would be contrary to all scripture, to the nature of God Himself," she said, "to say that 'moderation' in the practice of any evil is permissible."[18]

Wartime Prohibition, instituted in 1917, made necessary by the use of alcohol in the manufacture of munitions, was applauded by the women.[19] Before peacetime manufacture of whiskey could be resumed, the Eighteenth Amendment to the Constitution and its companion Volstead Act introduced "permanent" Prohibition to the United States.

Ratified January 1919, it took effect January 1920.[20] WMU began to give more attention to temperance after it became apparent that the government was not able to enforce Prohibition. The Executive Committee of WMU adopted a resolution in 1926 introduced by Harriett Ellis Levering (Mrs. Eugene) calling for prayers for and cooperation with the Woman's National Committee on Law Enforcement. The committee agreed further: "We heartily endorse the suggestion made by the Woman's National Committee for the enforcement of the Eighteenth Amendment without any modifications and that we cooperate in every way possible."[21]

Repeal of the Prohibition amendment was an issue of the US presidential elections of 1928 and 1932. WMU took a position in favor of the Republicans, who favored continuation of Prohibition. Some issues of *Royal Service* mentioned the issue and resolutions were adopted at Annual Meetings. When Prohibition was repealed in 1933 and states had the right to decide about selling alcohol, WMU joined forces with many other groups in an attempt to keep the states "dry." In Alabama, for example, all of the Prohibition organizations founded the Alabama Temperance Alliance in 1934 and kept Alabama in the dry ranks. WMU organizations amd members were active in this campaign.[22]

As Prohibition forces increasingly lost ground in most states, WMU was concerned about educating women and children on how to abstain from drinking in a world in which alcohol flowed freely. Throughout the 1940s and 1950s total abstinence was given as one of the moral standards to be espoused in WMU's community missions fundamentals. When Edith Stokely joined the WMU headquarters staff as community missions director in 1949, she slanted the emphasis toward alcohol education. She prepared for her task by studying at Yale School of Alcohol Studies.[23]

The Christian and the Alcohol Problem was the emphasis for the WMU year 1956-57. The 1956 Annual Meeting adopted a resolution without debate calling on members to urge passage of pending federal legislation to prohibit interstate advertising of alcoholic beverages. To the familiar call for total personal abstinence from use of alcohol, WMU added narcotics in the mid-1950s. In the early 1970s WMU promoted mission action dealing with alcoholics and drug users.

The relationship between Woman's Missionary Union and Woman's Christian Temperance Union makes an interesting study. The WCTU slogan was For God and Home and Native Land. Without credit or apology, WMU borrowed and modified it to read For God and Home and Every Land, and printed the motto on its publications for many years.

Most of the members of WCTU were active Protestant church members.[24] Those who were Southern Baptists were also generally members of WMU. Woodlawn Baptist Church of Birmingham, Alabama, may have been typical. Meetings of the WCTU were advertised at WMU meetings; they often were held in the same room of the church; members for WCTU were enlisted at the missionary meetings; the church calendar listed the meeting as one of the announced opportunities of the week. However, women seldom held major offices in two organizations at one time.

Many Baptist women preferred missions work, but others alternated organizations. Jennie Dixon, editor and publisher of the *Texas White Ribbon,* explained her involvement in Prohibition work at the expense of WMU work: "Temperance work came right to me, and demanded my time, and you know that one person cannot give to different subjects the same amount of thought, although they may think they are equally interested."[25] Few Southern Baptist women achieved high office in WCTU, but many were active at lower levels.

Ruth Provence, reviewing the relationship of Baptists of South Carolina to WCTU work, discovered that many who were leaders in their church or association also assumed leadership in WCTU. Mrs. J. L. Mims of Edgefield, South Carolina, state president of WCTU 1928-45 and editor of the state organ, *Palmetto White Ribbon,* for almost a half century, was also associational WMU superintendent, 1906-29. The daughter of a devoted WMU member, Mims said that her experience in WMU led her to accept the challenge of WCTU. She believed that the moral, ethical, and social values that she learned in her home and in church could best be achieved in a more activist organization. She chose to devote her greater energies to WCTU without abandoning the soil from which she was nurtured. Provence's detailed analysis reveals that this story was repeated many times in South Carolina, and a perusal of local church histories elsewhere bears out the close affinity of the two organizations.[26]

The WMU-WCTU relationship was endorsed by Kathleen Mallory through the columns of *Royal Service.* [27] Mary Gambrell, when her husband was a pastor in Mississippi, was a founder of Mississippi WMU in 1878, and was one of the founders of the WCTU in Corinth in 1883. Twenty-five years later she was secretary of Texas WMU and was a staunch supporter of Prohibition there.[28] Olivia Davis, treasurer of Texas WMU, edited the WCTU journal for the state and in 1930 represented Texas WMU at the national WCTU meeting.[29]

The WCTU was an activist political action outlet for WMU's more spiritualized and educational flavor. As a religious organization, WMU would not consider public demonstrations and marches on the legislature. On the other hand, WCTU was never limited in its arsenal of weapons. Women who felt the need for more direct action than WMU was ready to advocate found a ready outlet in WCTU. As a member of

WCTU a woman could pursue any course of action without giving up membership in WMU, which might possibly have been the wellspring of her original concern about alcohol. As the WCTU lost prestige and power, WMU grew.

"OUR SISTERS IN BLACK"

The founders of Woman's Missionary Union carried into the organization a responsibility for the conditions of black persons. While WMU was developing organizational wings, blacks formed the National Baptist Convention in 1886. For a century WMU would neither lay down its burden of the race issue nor find a stage for action that was not also occupied by women of the National Baptist Convention. By relating closely to the National Baptist Convention, WMU was potentially in touch with three-fourths of all southern blacks.

When Ann Graves organized Woman's Mission to Woman, she automatically gave mite boxes to the colored churches of Baltimore. Like many Southern Baptists, she assumed that black Americans would bear the gospel to Africa.[30]

WMU's official action on the race issue was influenced by the fact that early officers were from the border states of Maryland, Missouri, and Kentucky. Many of the Deep South founders of WMU had been reared in slaveholding households. They delicately referred to blacks as "servants." When a German speaking to an early WMU meeting got her tongue twisted and spoke of whites and blacks being kinspeople, the women laughed good-naturedly. Mary Gambrell explained, "You are right. We all had black mammies."[31] Those black surrogate mothers had left their white children with warm feelings.[32] Nor were all the familylike relationships with mammies. Kate Waller Chambers, donor of the Margaret Fund's original money, was a lonely child, so her father bought her a playmate and maid.[33]

Some of the early WMU officers had cut their missions teeth on the religious instruction of blacks. Abby Manly Gwathmey spent her childhood afternoons at the University of Alabama teaching Bible verses to young black girls, while her mother broke the law to teach them to read the Bible, and her distinguished brothers practiced their preaching on the colored members of their church. The founders of WMU liked to congratulate themselves on having brought Negroes to their day of freedom as a Christianized people.[34]

Yet WMU women sensed that their guilt for the past and their survival in the future could only be lifted as they lifted blacks. Fannie E. S. Heck put it plainly: "A race side by side with our own, yet still and forever apart, to whom we must lend an uplifting hand in Christ's name or be grappled and drawn downward by their dark fingers."[35]

Not all WMUers found it easy to work with free blacks on a respectful basis, but those from Maryland seem to have done so. Annie Armstrong and the Maryland Woman's Baptist Home Mission Society helped local black Baptists to organize an orphanage. They taught in "industrial schools" for black children and in mothers' meetings. They involved Negro churches in their projects on behalf of Indians (some of whom intermarried with blacks) in Oklahoma.

"With and For."—From this laboratory, Armstrong elevated work with Negroes into the WMU Plan of Work approved in 1892. "With and for" was the phrase to describe WMU's approach to colored people. The Home Mission Board endorsed WMU's plans as being part of its strategy, and the Board allotted the Baltimore women a few dollars for conducting their industrial schools and mothers' meetings. WMU organizations across the South were encouraged to follow Baltimore's example. WMU had its first black Annual Meeting speaker in 1895, a woman with whom Armstrong had worked closely for many years. The speaker declared that "nothing so good as the mothers' meetings had come to [the Negroes] since the emancipation."[36]

Annie Armstrong unleashed a sheaf of tracts which urged Southern Baptist women to organize their efforts for colored women. Among her guest authors were Mrs. V. W. Broughton, a leading black Baptist woman, and Booker T. Washington. When a prominent pastor submitted a manuscript saying that blacks were too degraded to be helped, she refused to print it.[37]

Armstrong viewed the race question as a strategic matter. She believed that blacks were the personal responsibility of Southern Christian white women. She resented the presence of Northern Baptist missionaries in the South and knew that they could not be vanquished until Southern Baptists took over their work with blacks. She feared that Roman Catholics would win blacks and then the whole South if Protestants did not meet the needs of blacks. And finally, her urgent concern for Africa made her view American blacks as potential missionaries. Armstrong was regarded as an authority on blacks. She delivered an address to the Atlanta Woman's Congress in 1895 on Woman's Work in the Evangelization of the Homes of the Colored People.[38]

The more typical WMU member might share Armstrong's lofty thinking at points, but she would also have more self-seeking motives. Most WMU leaders had black servants, described in WMU literature as "the white woman's burden." While acknowledging black servants as an open door of missions opportunity, they also had to deal with their lack of training. Small wonder that the mothers' clubs and industrial schools taught household skills and hygiene useful to the employer as well as to the employee.[39]

Armstrong had her share of servant problems, but these did not dominate her thinking. She believed that white women must recognize the emerging leadership potential among blacks. Acting on that belief, she was an insider in the development of the National Baptist Convention of black Baptists. In November 1896 the Sunday School Board began assisting the National Baptist Publishing Board in Nashville. As right hand to J. M. Frost of the Sunday School Board, Armstrong placed herself in the midst of the new black-white liaison.

The Great Nannie Burroughs.—In December 1896, L. G. Jordan, corresponding secretary of the National Baptist Foreign Mission Board, called on Armstrong. He undoubtedly saw her as the key to Southern Baptist sympathy and money; she saw him as the key to developing a WMU counterpart organization among the black women. The next month, Jordan brought a young black woman, his assistant, to call on Armstrong. She was Nannie Helen Burroughs. The three mapped out a National Baptist woman's auxiliary like WMU. Armstrong and Burroughs began visiting black churches to organize women's societies. Armstrong began writing the women's pages in Jordan's *Afro-American Herald*. She guided the blacks to inaugurate Missionary Day in Sunday School just as she had done for Southern Baptists. She wrote children's curriculum and other regular features for the National Baptist Publishing Board's *Teacher* magazine, just as faithfully as she did for the Southern Baptist *Teacher*.

She liked the black leaders and the local black pastors and women she worked with. She spoke of them with respectful titles and tones. She referred to them as "brunettes," and as "brethren in black," in her usual breezy and blunt style, without any intent of insult. She saw that she was to "have a large part in the mission work of the colored people."[40] Because she was in regular touch with Mary Burdette, the Woman's American Baptist Home Mission Society secretary, and with officers of the American Baptist Publication Society, she enabled Southern Baptists to beat the North in winning blacks' allegiance.

Armstrong felt a personal victory when the Woman's Convention, Auxiliary to the National Baptist Convention, was organized in Richmond, October 1900. Burroughs and Jordan continued to seek Armstrong's guidance. In 1901 and 1905 Armstrong attended the black women's convention, and after some difficulty in clearing the hall of men, spoke to the women. She placed her hand on Burroughs's shoulder and gave her encouragement that Burroughs still remembered 60 years later. The black women duly noted in their minutes that Armstrong "showed them God's hand in bringing them to America to Christianize and save them from degradation of their race in Africa." They noted that she said they should work to improve the purity of life among their people. They set up their printed annual minutes exactly as Armstrong set up WMU's.[41]

Armstrong arranged for the Home Mission Board, SBC, to employ black women field workers for the Woman's Convention. To bring this to pass, Armstrong and the president of WMU, Lillie Easterby Barker (Mrs. J. A.), made one of their rare appearances at the HMB meeting in Atlanta. After getting the men's agreement, Armstrong secured the money from a Mrs. Height of Maryland and Mrs. W. H. Wiggs of Georgia, routing it through the Home Mission Board to the black appointees. These included Mrs. L. C. L. Murchison; Mrs. L. S. Edwards of Greenville, Mississippi; Mrs. Lillian Mebane of North Carolina; and Mrs. E. E. Whitfield, whose service continued for many years.[42]

The 1904 WMU Annual Meeting was an emotional high point for women of both races. Shirley Willie Layten of Philadelphia, president of the National Baptist women, spoke. Then Armstrong invited the delegates to attend an assembly of black women in a local black church. The black women discussed their needs; the white women encouraged them to develop their organization and keep it free of men's control. "Tears flowed freely from the eyes of many white and colored women and many hearty amens were heard."[43]

That the women indulged in such fraternization is amazing in light of the actions surrounding the Southern Baptist Convention that year. The Home Mission Board was criticized for its work with Negroes. Some of the strongest leaders thought the SBC had no business doing anything about the Negro except to evangelize him, fearing that any form of social acceptance or education would lead to amalgamation of the races.[44]

Nannie Helen Burroughs, one of the most remarkable blacks in American history, was to dominate Southern Baptist women's official contacts with blacks from 1897 until 1961. This young woman, who electrified the Baptist World Alliance Congress in London in 1904, was a clever, commanding speaker. She served as corresponding secretary of the Woman's Convention from 1900 until 1948, when she at last succeeded Shirley Layten, her confirmed opponent, as president. Her troubles with Layten and with the men of the National Baptist Convention involved WMU in sticky politics with the NBC and the SBC. WMU stood behind Burroughs with scarcely a question. The compelling cause of her life was a school for girls in Washington, D.C., which became known as the Nannie Helen Burroughs School. The school was run by Burroughs's "three B's—the Bible, the Bath, and the Broom."

She was an articulate spokesman for several black causes, becoming the first black woman to speak on a nationwide radio network. One of her first and most enduring causes was to fight the Jim Crow laws which restricted blacks to separate, usually inferior, public accommodations. In 1902 she called on white Christian women of the South to speak out against such laws. Surely she was asking, in an indirect but pleading way, for the help of the white women she knew best, Woman's Missionary Union. She got no answer. In fact, the next year's response from WMU was almost dead silence.

Still Burroughs believed "the southern white woman is the molder, shaper, and changer of attitudes, sentiment, and actions of whites. . . . She holds the key to the solution of the race problem in Dixie. Her word is law and gospel to southern white men."[45]

A Quiet Period in Race Relations.—After Armstrong's exodus in 1906, the race issue hibernated in the state WMU organizations for almost ten years. Missouri and Kentucky WMUs began to pay the salaries of black women who developed women's work in black churches. The most progressive work done among Negro women, however, was in the hands of Northern Baptist women missionaries. Women missionaries of the Woman's American Baptist Home Mission Society worked in most major southern cities.

Despite the fact that men leaders, North and South, solemnly agreed in 1894 that the North would not send missionaries South except as jointly sponsored by Northern, Southern, and National Baptists, the Northern women quietly continued to send missionaries to southern Negroes well into the 1930s. This was the task the Woman's American Baptist Home Mission Society (Northern) had organized to do in 1873, and Southern Baptist women did not object. In major southern cities, the northern missionaries and southern WMU women made their own terms of peace. In Birmingham, for example, Ella Knapp and Annie Boorman quietly represented the Woman's American Baptist Home Mission Society from 1894 until 1927. They joined and were well accepted in a leading Southern Baptist church. They organized 30 centers of Bible teaching enrolling 500 Birmingham black children in 1916. These northern missionaries were routinely welcomed and heard at Birmingham associational WMU meetings as "our missionaries." The black women they trained and employed as assistants later transferred to the sponsorship of Birmingham WMU and Alabama WMU.[46]

In Nashville, the famed Joanna P. Moore, the original missionary of the northern women's society, established her model Fireside School and began publishing *Hope*, a paper for Negro families. She and her assistants often spoke to the Nashville associational WMU. When the northerners withdrew in the 1930s, local WMUers continued the Fireside School, ultimately making it an adult education program in connection with the YWCA, then ceasing connection in the 1960s.[47]

Meanwhile, tensions grew within the National Baptist Convention, resulting in a 1915 split. The original convention became known as the National Baptist Convention, USA, Inc. (often called simply the "Incorporated" convention), and the other as the National Baptist Convention of America (the "Unincorporated"). Just before the split, the woman who would head the National Baptist Convention of America's Woman's Auxiliary appeared at the 1915 WMU Annual Meeting. She was M. A. B. Fuller of Texas, a successful mortician, and she entered into WMU's discussion on personal service among Negroes. A collection was taken on the spot, with $43.30 turned over to Fuller for a Negro Training School at Seguin, Texas. She would continue to appear at Annual Meetings in 1926, 1927, and 1942. WMU never seemed to comprehend until the 1950s that M. A. B. Fuller and Nannie Helen Burroughs represented two differing branches of the Negro Baptist world.

When the program of personal service was introduced into WMU in 1910, the racial issue was consistently mentioned as a central concern. But a 1917 survey showed WMU to be lagging behind Methodists and Presbyterians in work for and with blacks. The findings were reported to WMU, along with a reminder that privileged women (such as in WMU) set the moral tone of the community.[48]

The Woman's Committee.—Action came in 1921 in the form of one of WMU's rare entries into an interdenominational group. This was the Woman's Committee of the Commission on Interracial Cooperation, headquartered in Atlanta. The mood of the South was growing violent in 1920. The Interracial Commission invited key women to an unpublicized meeting in Memphis, October 6-7, 1920, to see if women of clubs and churches could alleviate the crisis. Some leaders declined to attend. Only 3 Baptists responded, while 69 Methodists and 9 Presbyterians were in attendance. The Baptists were Mrs. J. G. Jackson of Arkansas, Ella Broadus Robertson (Mrs. A. T.) of Kentucky, and Mrs. Ashby Jones of Atlanta, whose husband was prominent in the commission.[49]

Four black women spoke to the interracial audience of about 100 women. The emotional response to these women's tales of disgraceful treatment by whites convinced the women to form a permanent Woman's Committee.

Jackson told the WMU Executive Committee about the new group in January 1921. She explained the crucial points of cooperation: domestic service, child welfare, travel facilities, education, lynching, public press, and the ballot. Both black and white women would work as equals in the group. WMU voted to participate.

By the time of the Woman's Committee's first meeting in Atlanta, October 7, 1921, several Baptists had joined the group. Among the major speakers was Minnie James, president of Woman's Missionary Union. After the glowing report of Presbyterian women's outstanding social work for blacks, James's report sounded anemic. She explained that through the personal service program, Baptist women would sympathetically work with the Interracial Commission. James consistently used the word *Negro* in speaking of blacks, while the other speakers, including blacks, used the word *colored,* which was then the common form of reference to blacks.

WMU named the personal service chairman as its official representative on the Woman's Committee. Annie Barksdale Eubank (Mrs. Peyton A.) of Birmingham, Una Roberts Lawrence (Mrs. Irvin), and Frances Acree Lowrance (Mrs. P. B.) in turn met with the committee. The Interracial Commission was endorsed in the Plan of Work and personal service methods from 1921 onward.[50]

James had to take a strong hand to preserve WMU's ties to the Interracial Commission. The organization had a kinship with the Federal Council of Churches, and Southern Baptists were taking scissors to any affiliations that led in that direction.[51]

From this era until the Interracial Commission dissolved in 1943, WMU significantly raised the visibility of work with blacks in its publications and programs. Long before the Southern Baptist Convention took notice, most state WMUs officially endorsed the commission and participated in forming state affiliates of the Woman's Committee. As suggested, they began taking statewide surveys of the conditions of Negroes.[52]

At the commission's request, in the 1927 Week of Prayer for Home Missions, WMU included prayer about the disgrace of lynching.[53] In the same year WMU published a leaflet, "Racial Revelations" by T. B. Maston, on the race issue. Maston became the dean of Southern Baptist scholars in Christian ethics.[54]

At least four Southern Baptists were among 23 women who spawned the Association of Southern Women for the Prevention of Lynching in 1930. They were Una Lawrence; Margaret McRae Lackey, secretary of Mississippi WMU; Emma Byrns Harris (Mrs. R. L.), president of Tennessee WMU; and Mrs. W. T. Martin, personal service chairman of Georgia WMU. WMU officers in almost every state were among those endorsing the call to prevent lynching.[55] The director of the Interracial Commission's women's work, Jessie Daniel Ames, made a bold impression at WMU meetings and in WMU publications. After she spoke at the 1932 WMU Annual Meeting a resolution was passed condemning lynching.

The antilynching association was a loosely linked group of 40,000 women who promised to bring pressure to prevent lynchings. They believed that if white women would not encourage white men to avenge their honor outside the law, black men accused of assaults would not be lynched. In case a black person was accused of crime, the ASWPL women were pledged to demand security and a fair trial for the accused. Katherine Test Davis (Mrs. George), longtime young people's leader for South Carolina WMU, was one whose home was a communications point in times of racial troubles in Spartanburg, South Carolina. If violence was building, black opinion leaders furtively met at her house

to plan their actions.[56] Under such informal effort, the number of documented lynchings in the South declined from about 20 a year to 5 a
year in the 1930s.

A More Aggressive Posture.—From the moment Una Lawrence
took office as personal service chairman in 1929, WMU's posture on
the race issue dramatically grew more aggressive. In that year a scant
255 missionary societies reported doing work for Negroes. By 1936 the
number had grown to 2,437. That was only 7 percent of all missions
organizations. Lawrence pushed books by and about Negroes into the
pages of *Royal Service*. The mission study course took in books on the
racial issue. Minnie James joined her in pointing out the deteriorating
communications among the new generation of blacks and whites who
had not known each other in the intimate days of the nineteenth
century. Lawrence and James told WMUers that they did not know the
rising class of educated, cultured blacks. WMU published a new leaflet,
"Experiences with a 'New Woman,'" explaining that the new woman
of the 1920s was "our sister in black . . . worthy to be called 'Mrs.,'"
deserving of protection from rape and abuse. WMU publications began
to capitalize the word *Negro* in its magazines.[57]

Lawrence renewed WMU's communication with Nannie Helen Bur-
roughs, whom she knew through the Interracial Commission, but whom
Kathleen Mallory had never met. In 1932 the WMU president appointed
a committee to advise on relationships with National Baptist women.
This committee functioned until 1939 with membership unchanged:
Una Lawrence; Blanche White of Virginia; Harriett Levering of Maryland;
Carrie U. Littlejohn of the WMU Training School; and Juliette Mather
of the WMU staff. This committee was introduced in the 1932 Annual
Meeting, then quietly but vigorously functioned as a subcommittee of
the Personal Service Committee. Lawrence was appointed official representative to the Woman's Convention (National Baptist) of 1932, and
thereafter for nearly 20 years a WMU representative was invited to the
meeting.

With Burroughs as editor and Lawrence as "special contributor," the
black women began publishing the *Worker* in January 1934. Every issue
of this quarterly magazine until 1961 carried credits to WMU for its
support. Lawrence, White, and other SBC women assisted with writing
and editing.

In 1936 WMU celebrated the 50th anniversary of its own literature
department by handing Nannie Helen Burroughs $250 to start a litera-
ture publishing department. With the money went permission, even
encouragement, to modify and reprint WMU literature. Lawrence and
Blanche White again aided Burroughs as she adapted WMU's *Personal
Service Guide* and *The How and Why of Missionary Education*. The
$250 gift flowed annually into the 1950s, except for 1939 when it was

omitted, and except for 1941 (and perhaps other years) when it was boosted to $700.

Burroughs spoke at the 1936 WMU Annual Meeting and afterward at four- to six-year intervals, proving to be a popular platform personality. In 1939, at the invitation of Blanche White and Olive Martin, she became the first woman to speak to the Baptist General Association of Virginia on any topic other than WMU reports.

Burroughs did not stand alone among blacks on the WMU official platform. Blacks have spoken in more than 25 percent of WMU's Annual Meetings. This was done in Birmingham in 1931 and 1941, with blacks sitting in carefully segregated and well-marked seats, when interracial meetings were against city ordinance.

The intense friendship that developed among Burroughs, White, and Lawrence was remarkable for the times.[58] To each other they revealed the complexities of the changing racial situation in the South. Their immediate challenge was to win the Old South heart of Kathleen Mallory. Only the direct request of the president, Laura Malotte Armstrong (Mrs. F. W.), persuaded Mallory to represent WMU at the Woman's Convention of 1935 in Jacksonville, Florida. Trembling all the way, Mallory prayed and read the latest books on the racial issue. Later she spoke of feeling God's presence throughout, and she greatly enjoyed herself. She found that Florida WMU women were serving as hospitable local hostesses for the meeting. She noted with great appreciation the poise and competence of the black leaders.

Burroughs had heaped praise upon Mallory for her kindly presence, considering it as significant as Annie Armstrong's role in the 1901 Woman's Convention. In Mallory's routine written report to the WMU Executive Committee, she commented incidentally on the color variations of the NBC officers ("exceptionally gifted mulatto," and "the dusky Miss Burroughs"). The confidential report found its way into public print. When Una Lawrence saw the potentially offensive report she rushed a copy to Burroughs with apologies. Burroughs answered, "This shows how badly we need contact. Poor Miss Mallory doesn't know. . . . I'm glad you told me. We can help the dear soul and she will never know it."[59] The experience proved to be decisive for Mallory. She quickly learned the diplomacy of race relations, and Burroughs came to adore her. She later said, "Miss Mallory is God's gift to us in this program of Christian service. Her soul is enlisted. She is genuinely sincere and far ahead in her thinking and desire."[60]

Problems.—Mallory's desire to work more closely with black women quickly educated her into the practical barriers to communication. Her simple invitation to Burroughs to meet with the WMU Executive Committee and to attend the WMU Annual Meeting of 1934 in Baltimore (at which Burroughs was to speak) took weeks of delicate planning. To get Burroughs into the hotel meeting room where the Executive Committee awaited her, Mallory nervously exacted the hotel manager's promise that there would be no embarrassing scene of throwing out the honored guest. Burroughs was meticulously instructed to call for the manager at the door and to await his personal escort to the room. Similarly, Mallory had to issue Burroughs a card of admission, and had to carefully alert ushers in order to get her into the public building where the Annual Meeting convened.

Almost without fail, WMU's approach to racial matters was to assist black Baptist women with their WMU-type organizations. One exception was WMU's decision in 1934 to promote Open Door projects, a community center approach to reaching needy black youths and adults. Although often mentioned, the plan did not seem to enjoy the success of woman-to-woman plans. State WMUs in the 1930s blossomed with projects to assist blacks. Virginia WMU blazed a trail in 1934 by employing a trained black woman, Fletcher Howell, to work full time in strengthening black women's work. She was given an office next door to Blanche White in the WMU offices, the first black treated to equal staff status in all of Southern Baptist life. (Although the Home Mission Board employed a black staff member in 1941, he was not given an office.)

By the mid-1940s almost every state WMU had a black staff member, sponsored camps for black children, and published literature for black churches. Some forged strong ties with black Baptist colleges.

Among WMU's 50th anniversary projects was raising a $10,000 fund for development of work with Negro women and children. WMU planned to administer the fund jointly with the Woman's Convention, National Baptist Convention, Inc. The announcement ignited a feud among NBC leaders, each of whom hoped to control the money. Smoke came to hover over WMU's relations not only with the NBC, but also with the HMB whose staff sided with the NBC men. In 1937 the NBC repudiated its ties with the Burroughs school, and did not resume its endorsement until 1948. But WMU loyally stood behind Burroughs. The women insisted that WMU was not doing "Negro mission work," which the HMB defended as its business, but merely doing "woman's work with women, in the time-honored way."[61]

At the gala anniversary meeting in Richmond, WMU readily raised the $10,000, while Negro ministers refused to attend the Southern Baptist Convention because the Convention first ignored them, then required segregated seating. And, the Convention turned down progressive recommendations for black theological education that came from a committee staffed by persons active in the Interracial Commission.[62]

In trying to secure a representative committee of NBC women to administer the Golden Jubilee Fund, WMU ran afoul of the black women's president. Shirley Layten refused to appoint the black women WMU thought best qualified to serve on the committee. In fact, Layten herself did not show up for the planning meeting held during the Baptist World Alliance in Atlanta in 1939. In the alarming tension with Layten, the officers clung ever more closely to Burroughs, "the one person whom our group completely trusts, and with whom we have worked enough to understand."[63]

Interracial Institutes.—WMU's chosen black women and a new committee from WMU ranks planned to use the Golden Jubilee Fund for a series of interracial institutes. The purpose was to train black women as leaders of missionary societies in their own churches. The plan had been tested on a large scale in Virginia, Oklahoma, and other states. The methodology taught was that of the Woman's Convention, which was based on familiar WMU plans. WMU footed the bill for mimeographed literature and increased Burroughs's allotment for publications.

Kathleen Mallory took the lead in coordinating the institutes, canceling many of her traditional responsibilities in order to have the time. The first series of three was held in Mississippi, Alabama, and Georgia in the summer of 1940. Burroughs, ill from cancer surgery in New York, struggled from her bed to advise Mallory. They agreed on an impressive traveling faculty of prominent blacks and whites. Among them was M'bola Ayorinde (Mrs. J. T.) of Nigeria, WMU's pride and joy, the first world-class Baptist woman leader from Africa.

And then Mallory ran into the stone wall of Jim Crow travel restrictions. Burroughs raised again her 1902 plea for white women's help. Mallory could well sympathize with the impossibility of her counterpart's situation. Burroughs and Ayorinde could not get sleeping accommodations on a train or at a decent hotel.

Mallory or another WMU official at each leg of the journey had to go personally to the train ticket agent, pull strings, beg, and pay a premium in order to assure comfort on the train for the black travelers. Each reservation meant pages of letters from Mallory, many of them written by hand, perhaps to avoid the criticism of her own office workers. The fact that both of the veteran corresponding secretaries carried through their duties in the face of such logistics showed extraordinary commitment to each other and to the dream of interracial cooperation.

The heroism of Nannie Burroughs in relating to white women can hardly be overstated. She had told Una Lawrence why: "I love your race a great deal more than they love mine."[64] She had the greatness to overlook slights if intentions were good. But she commanded respect, keeping her white friends on a *Miss* and *Mrs.* name basis.[65] Blanche

White invited Burroughs to attend a meeting with WMU women responsible for promoting racial cooperation in Virginia. When Burroughs
arrived, a blanket of awkwardness fell over the white party. One woman
had agreed to sit beside the guest, along with White, but others fled
the table. Burroughs instantly mentioned that she had a headache.
White as if on cue asked if she would like to rest until time for her
speech. Hostesses found her a private room and took in a tray. Afterward Burroughs emerged to give a winning speech on the race issue.
At least some of the WMU women present had the grace to appreciate
both leaders' magnanimity.[66]

Such escapades got White called on the carpet by some of her
constituents who felt she was pushing race mixing inappropriately.
Two national WMU presidents were called in to arbitrate the tense
showdown. They took a progressive stance and got White off the hook.
But White thereafter knew her limits. No matter that she ardently
believed it a sin to segregate seating at religious meetings. She knew
that her women would not back her, and she did not push it again.[67]

While the institutes were for the benefit of black women, local white
women were to assist not only with the teaching but with arrangements,
food, and attendance. Kathleen Mallory after the introductory institute
of 1940 reported that local WMU leaders "cooperated 100 percent in
preparations though some were prevented from attending."[68] Most local
whites were willing to give money, but not to sit in a meeting shoulder
to shoulder with blacks. Still the WMU officers conducted their institutes in the face of husbands' objections and opposition from male
SBC leaders. When Sarah Joe Hurst Burney (Mrs. Frank), president of
Georgia WMU and an enthusiastic leader in racial communication,
attended an institute, her lawyer husband accompanied her "so people
wouldn't talk."[69]

Despite difficulties looming, the three 1940 institutes were attended
by almost 900 women, and WMU decided to continue them. WMU
resolved the dispute over control of the Golden Jubilee Fund by paying
all the bills directly. Mallory and Burroughs remained personally involved in institute planning for four years. Although attendance records
were not complete, a year's attendance had grown to approximately
5,500 women in eight southern cities in the summer of 1943. Then
grants from the Golden Jubilee Fund were awarded to state WMUs who
conducted localized institutes. WMU allocated Annie Armstrong Offering funds to perpetuate them. Finally the last Golden Jubilee institute
was held in 1951. The 1932 planning of Burroughs, Lawrence, White,
and others, had been fully realized, and the era of tangible accomplishments with and for black women had ended.

National Baptist women's work began to grow wherever the institutes
were held.[70] In the interracial institutes WMU gained more insight into

the complexities of Baptist work within the black community and came to recognize the standing of M. A. B. Fuller, president of the women of the NBC of America. After her Annual Meeting speech of 1942, *Royal Service* printed her suggestions for improved relations between the races. Fuller succinctly pinpointed WMU's unique responsibility:

> You can do these things because you have more time, intelligence, and influence. When white Christian women stand for justice between the races, they meet less opposition; they are less likely to be attacked and condemned. You can visit the mayors, city councils, county commissioners, school superintendents, and police departments and intercede in our behalf. They are your husbands.[71]

Postwar Tensions.—World War II changed the old order. In 1942, 1943, and 1944 WMU asked the Home Mission Board to allocate substantial amounts of the Annie Armstrong Offering to support of Negro Baptist colleges. In 1942 a group of southern blacks, encouraged by Jessie Daniel Ames, met in Durham, North Carolina, and issued a demand for the end of racial discrimination in the South. Their move was social dynamite. In April 1943, 113 southern white leaders met in Atlanta to frame a response. Kathleen Mallory was among them, and she willingly signed the statement drafted by Ralph McGill, editor of the *Atlanta Constitution*, showing a willingness to make changes. Blanche White represented Mallory at the subsequent biracial meeting in Richmond. White feared that whites would not yield. She believed a better approach would be for women, black and white, to keep on working with each other until life became mutually agreeable. She believed women would resolve the issue before men would.[72]

The lines were drawn for a tense new phase of the racial issue in WMU. WMU's educational materials had increasingly grown frank in saying that white women must recognize Negroes with brotherly respect, not as servants, but had assured women that Christian courtesy would not lead to "social equality." Yet, beginning in 1943, *Royal Service* pointedly defended the "separate but equal" idea. The magazine's strongest defense of segregation came in 1946, calling the demands of the Negro "frightening, difficult, dangerous, revolutionary, and unreasonable."[73]

The statements of 1946 apparently rang too loudly for the leading WMUers, for segregation was never again defended in WMU publications. In June 1947 Nannie Burroughs was featured on the cover, the first black American pictured in WMU literature except as the recipient of ministry. In 1949-50 *Royal Service* boldly condemned the Ku Klux Klan. The magazine directly identified and defused the "two questions we most fear," social equality and intermarriage.[74]

The rising generation of young WMU leaders wanted to integrate

WMU conferences. They quietly did so at the Young Men's Mission Conference sponsored by WMU at Ridgecrest in 1949. An effort to integrate the Young Woman's Auxiliary Conference was tabled in 1954, but gained approval in 1958, provided the blacks were a legitimate part of WMU's organized work.[75] WMU integrated its Louisville training school in 1952, at the same time admitting males.

The Civil Rights Movement.—The 1954 Supreme Court decision banning school segregation was approved by WMU leaders. The 1957-58 WMU Year Book and the 1959 revision of *Guide for Community Missions* urged women to support enforcement of the laws opening public facilities to all races, while maintaining friendly contacts with blacks.

WMU's forward-looking stance was directed by Mildred Dodson McMurry (Mrs. William), who had joined the WMU staff in 1951. McMurry had first sounded the note of racial justice at the 1930 WMU Annual Meeting.[76] After living outside the Deep South for a few years, she returned to the Southern Baptist scene as a pacesetter in race relations. Her stirring speech at the 1953 WMU Conference, "Probing Our Prejudices," was a revelation in the thinking of several women.

McMurry gave WMU readers a big buildup for the 1958 home mission study book on Negro work of the Home Mission Board. Forewarning the women that the subject could be controversial, she advised them to start their study with a review of Bible teachings on race. The book, *The Long Bridge*, was already in the hands of many WMU leaders when several state convention leaders pressured the Home Mission Board to recall the books. There was nothing at all controversial in the book itself, for it only described long-standing programs of the HMB concerning Negroes. But many southerners were too inflamed to tolerate the mention of Negroes. In order to avoid open controversy, WMU agreed to the withdrawal and suggested an alternate study. *The Long Bridge* study proceeded in many places. As predicted by some, the Annie Armstrong Offering taken following the designated study time declined from the previous year's.[77]

The racial controversy became so heated from then until the 1970s that Executive Secretary Alma Hunt felt her job was to "keep the cars from being uncoupled from the train." Some WMU officers were lunging far ahead of the majority of their constituents on the race issue. Race was continually mentioned in WMU magazines, and each mention brought a barrage of hate mail and cancellations.

A survey of Southern Baptist periodical indexes for the 1960s show WMU magazines giving more attention to the race issue than any other publications. The thematic statement of September 1964 in the *Window* (which especially elicited cancellations and criticism) urged Southern Baptist young people to "involve themselves positively—under God's leadership" in the racial revolution. T. B. Maston in a survey of Baptist literature of the period noted that "Woman's Missionary Union has generally made and continues to make the most directly challenging approach to the whole area of race."[78]

If leaders would have liked to sweep the issue aside until a cooler time, they could not. Foreign missionaries and Baker James Cauthen of the Foreign Mission Board constantly reminded WMU that news of racial violence in Southern Baptist territory was destroying their efforts abroad.[79] Here as in other issues, the "reflex influence" of foreign missions brought social awareness in the homeland. WMU took a progressive stand through its speakers at every Annual Meeting throughout the 1960s. WMU instituted a letters-to-the-editor feature in *Royal Service* in which women vented their feelings on the times, both favoring and condemning integration.

Pressures were so intense that several state WMUs had to curtail their long-standing projects with blacks. White women in Alabama were no longer able to go safely to the camp for black children which they had operated for years, because threatening white men spied on their comings and goings. The interracial committee of Virginia Baptist women after a triumphant meeting in 1964 found it "inconvenient" to continue their meetings.[80]

But state WMU leaders doggedly found quiet ways around troubles. They put money, property, and encouragement in the hands of black women to continue projects that were needed. Maryland WMU joined in an interracial Baptist women's organization in 1964. Florida WMU worked with black women's conventions to sponsor a statewide series of interracial prayer retreats in 1963. Missouri kept support flowing into its interracial women's council begun in 1950. Mississippi WMU with Negro Baptist women visited homes of blacks to distribute 30,000 Bibles.[81]

The WMU national office was in Birmingham, a stone's throw from bombs, fire hoses, and jails infamous in the civil rights movement. National WMU leaders found themselves under attack by northern white Baptists because they were not out marching for black rights. WMU officers never participated in the Birmingham demonstrations, though Mildred McMurry was on the Birmingham mayor's committee concerning school desegregation. She was a target for intimidation and harassment by radical whites while she was writing her classic book, *Spiritual Life Development.*[82]

In an era when most southern blacks and whites had ceased to communicate, Baptist women leaders maintained their contact through the North American Baptist Women's Union of the Baptist World Alliance Women's Department. In 1962 the NABWU elected two officers who scarcely knew each other, even though they both lived in Birmingham. Mildred McMurry, white, was the president and Margery B. Gaillard (Mrs. L. S.), black, was the secretary. Returning to Birmingham, these two women quietly established an interracial group that prayed their way through the Birmingham racial crisis.[83]

After McMurry's death in 1964, Alma Hunt assumed her NABWU term and invited Gaillard to her home for dinner, along with Marie Mathis (Mrs. R. L.), president of WMU. Since blacks did not often visit socially in Birmingham's white neighborhoods, the hostess was apprehensive about the evening. Gaillard lost no time surfacing her feelings. "Why is it," she said, "that you call all the white officers by their first names, but you always call me *Mrs.*?" Hunt had to admit that she was taking extreme care to show her the full respect she was due. Gaillard said, "I wish you would call me Margery."[84]

Helen Long Fling (Mrs. Robert), president of WMU, took up McMurry's mantle as WMU's leader on the race question, though she came to dread opening her mailbox with its venomous messages.[85] In 1967 the Foreign Mission Board appointed its first black missionary since the 1880s and WMU showcased her at the Annual Meeting. That same year Fling rejoiced over the fact that WMU's new program of mission action had brought blacks into some Southern Baptist church buildings for the first time.[86]

Hunt joined other SBC leaders in signing the Statement Concerning the Crisis in Our Nation, which was then adopted by the Southern Baptist Convention in 1968. WMU leaders believed they had paved the way for its acceptance with their strong Annual Meeting featuring a prominent black woman speaker. Hunt considered 1968 the turning point in Southern Baptist attitudes toward blacks.[87] The 1969 Annual Meeting was built around the crisis statement with the theme, The Future Is Happening. Representatives of black Baptist women's groups were guests of WMU at the 1969 summer conferences.

Blacks in the SBC.—WMU members in the South became aware that Southern Baptist churches in the West and North had black members, and that those blacks were solid, contributing members of WMU. Helen Fling moved to New York and an integrated church. Blacks as Southern Baptists were a minority, but welcomed and visible in WMU by 1965. WMU national officers, aware of the protectiveness of leaders in the black conventions, reminded state leaders not to push WMU organizational plans into black churches of the National Baptist Conventions.

In the mid-1970s Carolyn Weatherford was sitting in the St. Louis airport talking to Emmanuel McCall, director of Black Church Relations for the Home Mission Board. They decided that WMU, SBC, needed a black member on the professional staff to further the Home Mission Board's work and WMU's work with black churches. With HMB funding,

Margaret Thomas Perkins (Mrs. William) joined the national staff of WMU in Birmingham in January 1978. McCall had observed that WMU groups had been the most effective innovators and practitioners of cooperative ministries with black churches. "In most instances WMUs have prodded men in other denominational structures to take seriously racial reconciliation and interracial ministry," said McCall, the first black to head a department in an SBC agency. He hoped to tap WMU's creativity by sharing a staff member with WMU.[88]

The HMB's Department of Black Church Relations advised churches, "Start a WMU at the same time you start Sunday School." McCall said that he saw WMU as a strategy for developing healthy churches committed to missions purposes.

By 1986 the number of black churches in the SBC had grown to around 1,000. At least 50,000 blacks at that time were members of predominantly white churches. In 1986 a home missions leader stated that the SBC is "now the most ethnically diverse Protestant-Evangelical denomination in the United States."[89]

Perkins and the WMU staff invited key black WMU leaders and pastors to Birmingham in 1980 to consult about the expansion of WMU in black churches. After that time blacks multiplied at WMU conferences. Possibly the first black to be elected to a statewide WMU office was Thelma Kennedy (Mrs. James), assistant recording secretary of Michigan WMU in 1981-85.

The racial character of WMU was clearly changing by 1980, but some of the veterans of WMU and National Baptist bravery in the 1940s longed for the old hard-won sisterly friendships black with white. They sensed a reduction in interracial participation in the Deep South.[90]

HUNGER

Because early WMU members generally reigned in the kitchens and vegetable gardens of the South, they had the means to feed the hungry at their door. Early personal service efforts tended to revolve around the sharing of food with the poor. Nutrition and cooking classes were often recommended as local missions projects.

WMU first confronted hunger on a global level in response to relief efforts initiated by missionaries in World War I. Beginning in the 1920s WMU promoted the sending of food parcels and clothing to Russia, then Eastern European countries. Food for China was a concern of the 1930s. Each major war involved WMU in relief efforts coordinated by the Foreign Mission Board.

Hunger awareness became an issue throughout American life in the 1980s. Public news media made WMU members aware of the worldwide food shortage. WMU began calling attention to this situation in its study materials. Spontaneously in 1974 and 1975 the Foreign Mission Board began to receive contributions designated for hunger and relief.

WMU took a cue from deep within its constituency. At the 1976 Annual Meeting a noonday prayertime was held on behalf of the hungry. *Royal Service* and *Contempo* featured the hunger crisis on covers of the June 1976 issues. The magazines gave their entire issues of July 1978 to the topic. The Brotherhood Commission invited WMU and SBC agencies to form an ad hoc committee to deal with hunger. They agreed that the Christian Life Commission would take the lead in coordinating the efforts of all the agencies and WMU concerning hunger. WMU and various agencies contributed for several years to pay for the educational materials the CLC produced.[91]

The first World Hunger Day was observed in 1978. In November 1978 WMU joined with the Foreign Mission Board, Home Mission Board, Brotherhood, Sunday School Board, Baptist Joint Committee on Public Affairs, Baptist World Alliance, and Christian Life Commission to sponsor a Convocation on World Hunger. Eljee Young Bentley (Mrs. Arthur L.) represented WMU on the planning committee for the event.

State WMU offices assisted in distributing promotional material for World Hunger Day, which became a fixed event on the denominational calendar, set for the second Sunday in October. From the beginning, World Hunger Day was an educational, not a money-raising event. But the agencies, with endorsement of the SBC Executive Committee, agreed to state that if a person wished to make a financial contribution towards feeding the hungry, the money might be sent through the local church to the Foreign Mission Board or Home Mission Board. WMU adopted the policy of stating this information regularly in its publications. In 1974 the hunger and relief money sent spontaneously to the Foreign Mission Board was $299,000. In 1985 the hunger and disaster contributions grew to $11 million, plus another $1,150,000 given through the Home Mission Board.

WMU's biggest push on the hunger issue came during the 1979-82 WMU emphasis on Life-Changing Commitments. Women were encouraged to live more simply so that others might eat. In April 1980 adults in WMU studied a book and cassette published by WMU, *The Woman I Am in a Hungry World.*

WAR AND PEACE

WMU's attitude about war was silently symbolized at the 50th anniversary meeting. A guest, Moonbeam Tong, representing WMU of China, told of the atrocities her people had suffered at the hands of Japan during wartime. As she spoke, the Japanese representative, Kyoko Shimose, sat on the platform, head bowed, eyes downcast. While the women prayed at the end of Tong's stirring message, Kathleen Mallory quietly walked across the stage and put her arm around Shimose.[92]

WMU never took an official position on the subjects of war and peace. Except for a generalized feeling that peace is desirable and war a tragedy, WMU's records betray little interest in war and peace as issues. Because the WMU family network of missionaries and nationals was worldwide, WMU could hardly boast of American superiority. Because WMU was well informed about the national sinfulness of the United States, which conditions made necessary programs of home missions and personal service, WMU shied away from claiming divine status for its own land.

Still, WMU declared itself on the side of righteous patriotism. Patriotism for WMU meant effort to see that citizens were Christians, to see that religious liberty was preserved, to see that just and moral laws were enacted and enforced fairly for all. The Annie Armstrong Offering for Home Missions was often promoted with a patriotic theme.

Once declared, war profoundly affected WMU, and the women expressed their loyalty to the USA in nonmilitaristic ways. When the USA entered World War I, the WMU Annual Meeting of 1917 sent a telegram of loyalty and sympathy to US President Woodrow Wilson. They pledged daily prayer for those in authority, for soldiers and sailors, and for peace. WMU of Texas expressed concern for "war mothers everywhere," even those of the enemy.

WMU's personal service chairman, Lulie K. Pollard Wharton (Mrs. H. M.), went to the national Red Cross headquarters to offer WMU's assistance in 1917. Wharton put local WMUs in touch with their local Red Cross chapters and the women began to knit. Kathleen Mallory knitted everywhere she traveled until the needles became second nature to her. By mid-1918 WMU women reported making 106,457 war relief articles. Through *Royal Service* and *Home and Foreign Fields* WMU leaders urged women to conserve food. The Home Mission Board's representative in US military camps asked WMU to place a service flag in each church to keep the members mindful of its representatives on the battlefront. These flags were to hang on the pulpit stand.[93]

WMU lost two of its top officials to the war effort. Mary Faison Dixon, young people's secretary, went to work with the YWCA in France and remained a resident of that country. Maud Reynolds McLure (Mrs. T. E.), principal of the WMU Training School, took a leave of absence to coordinate YMCA workers in military camps in the Southeast.[94]

At the 1918 WMU Annual Meeting, soldiers from a nearby military camp marched in to sing for the ladies. The motherly audience was so moved that they took up $100 to buy the men a fine hotel dinner and asked the camp to extend their leave for more visiting.

At first, the war had a deadening effect on WMU. Associational leaders felt that their best talent and money were siphoned off by the Red Cross and war efforts. Seeing their husbands and sons march away psychologically paralyzed the women, as they had to give their strength to keep the home fires burning. But at the end, women applied their new-found powers in WMU. They won the right to seats in the Southern Baptist Convention, and the organization grew in every way.[95]

The most lasting effect of World War I was its lesson about the need for the Christian message all over the world. Awareness of the world-wide significance of the gospel and the capability of American Christians gave rise to the $75 Million Campaign.

A similar set of reactions occurred during World War II. Because of its prolonged nature and because more women were pulled into the public work place, it had a deeper impact on WMU's organizational workings. Kathleen Mallory remarked that the war showed the value of having a smooth-running organization that could withstand the blows of missed meetings, curtailed travel, and abbreviated publications.[96]

The 1940 Annual Meeting was conducted in the looming shadow of war in Europe and Asia. Charles A. Wells, a pacifist-oriented cartoonist who was a favorite at WMU meetings, warned the women that their sons might be at the battlefront in a few months. Despite the advisability of international communication that such a mood might have indicated, the SBC of 1940 declined to enter into the World Council of Churches. The SBC did reach out to Baptists around the world by appointing a Baptist World Emergency Committee which included Laura Armstrong, Kathleen Mallory, and Blanche White.

Among the special financial appeals WMU responded to were China Relief, emergency funds for British Baptist missionaries, funds to bring missionaries home from the Orient, and the Home Mission Board's work among US military camps.

Charles Maddry, executive secretary of the Foreign Mission Board, happened to be in Honolulu on Pearl Harbor Day. WMU leaders happened to be the ones who collected him and his luggage and moved him to safety.[97] This circumstance made the dangers of war to the missions cause seem even closer.

The war left several women missionaries with nothing to do. A number of these went to work for state WMUs as field workers for the duration of the war.

WMU felt keenly the separation from Baptist sisters in Japan, Italy, Palestine, and Eastern Europe. The women went ahead with their usual allocations of the Lottie Moon Christmas Offering for enemy lands, asking the FMB to reserve the money until war's end. The plan was a wise one, for the reserve fund gave the FMB a running start on its postwar advance and rehabilitation efforts.

WMU expressed no official opinion about the internment of Japanese Americans in the United States, but it took immediate action to see that a Baptist ministry was provided for the camps. WMU leaders swarmed over Home Mission Board authorities at the 1942 SBC meeting, with the result that a woman representative was placed at the internment camp near Phoenix, Arizona. Oklahoma WMU gave a college scholarship to an interned young woman, and she later became a home missionary. The HMB's Japanese American woman representative at the camp in McGehee, Arkansas, appeared on the program at the 1943 Young Woman's Auxiliary Camp, "quite winsomely disarming lurking anti-Japanese hatreds."[98]

WMU enrollment declined, although contributions rose, at the outset of World War II. WMU countered this, and complied with restrictions on gasoline consumption, by altering its recommended meeting schedule. Because families were disrupted, WMU suggested for the first time that nurseries be provided while mothers were in meetings.

In the Birmingham office of WMU, the staff battled for paper supplies for printing of magazines. State offices interceded to keep WMU meetings from being declared unsuitable for use of rationed gasoline. Kathleen Mallory asked two family friends in the US Congress to intercede to get paper to print *Royal Service.*[99]

Because of war conditions, no city could accommodate both the SBC and WMU meetings at the same time. So the 1944 Annual Meeting was held separately from the SBC. In 1945 war travel restrictions caused WMU to cancel both the Annual Meeting and its planned make-up meeting. When the YWA camp also fell to the 1945 travel curtailment, WMU promoted localized "camps that stayed at home." Their theme was world understanding and prayer for peace.[100]

As in World War I, the conflict brought out the ministering instincts of women. Their concerns were applied to military camps. As the population shifted toward military installations, WMUers helped to establish new WMU groupings and to start churches. Virginia WMU, through its state offering, placed two WMU Training School graduates in the Portsmouth and Norfolk area to assist local women in establishing WMS and Sunday School for those in temporary war housing. The result was two new churches.[101]

As soon as Italy surrendered in 1943, WMU started sending food and clothing parcels to Italian Baptists via their WMU contacts. The same spirit extended to Japan through returning missionaries, then to northern Europe via Baptist World Alliance contacts.

Relief was the cry of 1946 and 1947. Young women at the 1946 YWA camp gave a record $4,207 for relief. When the Annual Meeting that year took an offering for relief, missionaries came forward to describe the needs of their fields, and Kathleen Mallory knelt on the stage to pray. By 1947 the WMU report showed more than 1 million WMU dollars given for relief, or approximately 26 percent of the SBC total.

The wartime slowdown in WMU, with the march of women into employment, was only a temporary liability. WMU closed the war era with phenomenal growth.

Peace WMU-style was made in the fellowship of the Baptist World Alliance, where WMU's president and funds brought Baptist women of Europe together regardless of their recent status as enemies for unity in organization and prayer. A scene never to be forgotten by WMU officers took place at the 1950 Baptist World Congress in Cleveland, Ohio. Ayako Hino, who would later be secretary of the BWA Women's Department, came to carry the flag of Japan in the Roll Call of Nations. Her body and spirit shook with fear of carrying that flag in the United States. WMU leaders were apprehensive about audience reaction when Hino and the flag of Japan appeared. Then the BWA president, C. Oscar Johnson, called out to the audience, "We'll all rise for Japan."[102]

The antinuclear and peace movements of the 1970s and 1980s received scant attention from WMU. An ad hoc peace group within the SBC circle caught the support of Carolyn Weatherford. In 1982 she spoke to a peace convocation of Southern Baptists. She made the point, predictably, that war prevents missionary expansion and effectiveness, while peace enhances missions.[103]

She [WMU] has heard the gospel and is behaving it.

Lulie P. Wharton (Mrs. H. M.)
1924

Our daughters as cornerstones

That our daughters may be as corner stones, hewn after the fashion of a palace (Psalm 144:12).

Chiseled on the cornerstone
of Woman's Missionary Union
Training School, 1917

S THE twentieth century arrived most Southern Baptists were willing to grant women places of service on missions fields. But they would not grant women diplomas for professional education for their task.

Theological education for women was left to Woman's Missionary Union, which opened its own training school in 1907. The school was considered by some to be WMU's greatest achievement.[1]

As early as 1883 Southern Baptist Theological Seminary was admitting unmarried women to classrooms without the privilege of grades or degrees. Married women had been attending classes with their husbands even before that time.[2] Women who wanted diplomas or more thorough training went north to the missionary training schools operated by Northern Baptist women in Chicago and Philadelphia.

Those schools seemed too far away from Texas, where women thought that Southern Baptists should have their own school for women. When the WMU officers polled the states for items to place on the agenda of the 1895 Annual Meeting in Louisville, the Texans proposed that the women make plans for a missionary training school. Mina Everett, secretary of the Texas women and a returned foreign missionary, had discussed this possibility with E. Z. Simmons, a missionary to China, in 1889.

The Texans prepared a paper to read at the meeting, but they were blocked from the agenda. Annie Armstrong wrote them, "It is not time yet to discuss the subject."[3] A prominent Louisville woman did not want such a controversial topic spread in her town. She was Eliza Broadus, daughter of a founder of Southern Seminary well known at that point for his earlier statements that women must keep silent in the church. Eliza Broadus sent Mina Everett a kindly worded, but severely critical, letter saying, "Are you wanting to make preachers of our southern girls?"[4]

Instead, at the Louisville meeting, the president of the Baptist Women's Missionary Training School of Philadelphia invited WMU to use this school until WMU "shall have a Training School of their own."[5]

Undaunted, the Texas women aired their proposal at their own state meeting, then sent it to the WMU, SBC, Executive Committee November 12, 1895. They asked that a school for young women be centrally located in SBC territory. On Armstrong's motion, the Executive Committee told the Texans, "For the present we deem it wise not to undertake new work. We would recommend the Chicago and Philadelphia Training Schools."[6]

Soon Everett and the Texas women got their comeuppance. Everett's salary funds were cut off by the mission boards and B. H. Carroll, a pastor and Baylor religion professor, proposed that the Texas Baptist Women Mission Workers (WMU) organization be disbanded.[7] There the matter lay until E. Z. Simmons again furloughed from China in 1899-1900. This was his testimony about women missionaries: "When they come to China, they readily learn the language but they do not know how to teach the Bible for they do not know it themselves. There should be a school for training women."[8] He stressed that social conditions in China made women missionaries a necessity. He also pointed out that the training available in the North was not acceptable for southern ladies: "visiting the slums and other bad places without men as escorts . . . loose doctrinal views."[9]

Simmons campaigned all over the country for a women's training school. His idea was that Southern Seminary in Louisville would provide the academic teaching by admitting women to classes with credit privileges. He wanted WMU to provide and staff a home for the single women and to offer additional classes suitable for females' concerns. Louisville ladies, primarily wives of seminary faculty, said they would help. J. M. Frost of the Sunday School Board readily saw this school as a way to strengthen his Bible teaching program, for most Sunday School teachers were women. R. J. Willingham of the Foreign Mission Board willingly supported the idea of training missionaries. E. Y. Mullins, president of Southern Seminary, saw this approach as a solution to the awkwardness women students caused the Seminary.

Simmons had his school fully planned and duly endorsed before he consulted Woman's Missionary Union just weeks before the 1900 Annual Meeting. At first Annie Armstrong was approachable about the idea and dutifully wrote the agency heads for their opinions. Then she found that all the men had presumed upon the willingness of WMU to be forced into the project.[10]

She was furious that she had not been consulted and that WMU's approval was taken for granted, and she said so. Having walked a straight and narrow path in order to protect Woman's Missionary Union from criticism, and knowing of strong opposition in the past, she did not want WMU to have to handle this hot issue. Yet she was trapped in public disagreement with the Sunday School Board and the Foreign Mission Board executives—her cardinal allies. Before she could catch her breath some women were writing her of their opposition, as did B. H. Carroll.[11]

The press took up the campaign, generally favoring the school, but on a basis that offended many of the women. They joked that a women's school in Louisville would help the male seminary students get partners with whom to go "two by two" to the missions field.

With no intention of running a matrimonial bureau, the WMU Executive Committee squelched the idea April 10, 1900, stating that "If there is to be a training school, Louisville is not the place."[12] No one dared bring the issue into the light of the Annual Meeting.

But this was an idea whose time had come and would not wait even for Annie Armstrong. Again Texas women pushed for a school. In July 1902 the Texas Baptist Women Mission Workers officers in Dallas recruited a brilliant young women's missionary society president to prepare to open a school. She was Annie Jenkins, from a prominent family of Baptists connected with Baylor University in Waco. After consulting with the Dallas ladies, she got her father's long-delayed permission to enroll in the Chicago training school. The plan was for her to return to Waco and to operate a missionary training school for women in connection with Baylor.[13]

Jenkins prepared a paper about training schools. Her sister, Josephine Jenkins Truett (Mrs. George W.), read it to the WMU Annual Meeting of 1903. The result was that Lillie Easterby Barker (Mrs. John A.), WMU president, appointed a committee of women to work jointly with a committee of the SBC to study the matter. Armstrong spent the year traveling to training schools in New York, Philadelphia, Kansas City, and Washington. There was no hint of her having any intentions other than to learn how to operate a women's school.[14] In fact she was unalterably opposed to the idea.

Anticipating WMU's provision for women students, the Seminary in 1903 gave women official seats in the classrooms and permitted them to take examinations. The first woman to stand for the exam in comparative religions and missions made the highest grade in the class.[15]

Baptists in other areas were not content to let Louisville have the women's training school without competition. Convention gossips reported that Baltimore wanted to host the school. New Orleans claimed that it was the place.[16] The *Baptist Argus* strongly campaigned for Louisville as the site. In so doing, it gave Armstrong the ammunition

she needed to resist. The *Argus* stated that a women's school was
already in successful operation at the Seminary. So, the report approved by the SBC and by WMU in 1904 simply recommended that
"the subject be left with the Seminary for the present."[17] But to show
his real feelings, J. M. Frost rose to make a motion that put the Convention on record as endorsing the school and pleading for its future
support. From that day Armstrong gave Frost a cold shoulder.

Armstrong's effort to stamp out the school flame spread it like wild-
fire. Dallas representatives went home and started their own school
October 3, 1904. It arose in the meeting of the Dallas Baptist Ministers
Association when R. C. Buckner, beloved head of the Buckner Orphans
Home, announced that it would be a reality. The women's school
operated out of the orphans home. The part-time teachers included
J. B. and Mary T. Corbell Gambrell, George W. Truett, George W.
McDaniel (the men were all later presidents of the Southern Baptist
Convention). Six students enrolled immediately. "While others hesitated and doubted whether the time was ripe . . . he heard the plea of
noble young women . . . and gave shelter and the prestige of his name
and fame for benevolence to this new enterprise," Texas women said
of Buckner. Who owned the school, if anybody, is not clear. It had a
board of women closely paralleling the officers of the BWMW of Texas,
which included the school in their annual plan of work. An outstanding
home missionary and WMU pioneer, Martha ("Mattie") J. Nelson, was
employed as preceptress of the school.[18]

Meanwhile, the Maryland Baptist Union Association resolved on October 31, 1904, to organize a women's training school in Baltimore. It
formally opened on March 20, 1905, with Belle Randolph, city missionary, as preceptress. Nine students were accepted. They received free
tuition and expenses, plus a salary. In return they worked four hours
a day in city missions work, along with their schooling conducted by
pastors and by Randolph.[19] What connection did Annie Armstrong have
with this movement? She claimed to oppose it.

WOMEN STUDENTS FLOCK TO LOUISVILLE

Despite Dallas and Baltimore, most Southern Baptists were convinced that women could best get their needed training in the proven
classrooms of Southern Seminary. At the expense of a Louisville woman,
Southern's professor W. O. Carver went to Chicago to study classes in
missionary methodology at Moody Bible Institute. He opened a methodology class for ladies with 25 enrolled.[20] To Southern Seminary the
women flocked. In the 1903-04 term 48 women were enrolled in Southern Seminary classes. They needed a base of operation; single women
needed accommodations and proper chaperonage.

So Kentucky women, headed by Eliza Broadus (who had apparently had a major change of mind following her father's death in 1895), decided to take action. In the summer of 1904 they voted to sponsor a home for single women. Broadus arranged a meeting in Louisville in September 1904. She put Emma McIver Woody (Mrs. S. E.) in the presiding chair. Woody was a young, beautiful, rich newcomer from Texas. The women chose her as the chairman of a board of managers; Anna C. Eager (Mrs. George B.), wife of a new seminary faculty member from Alabama and a known progressive, was chosen vice-chairman. Fannie Moses was recording secretary and Mrs. W. J. McGlothlin, another faculty wife, was treasurer.

Among the students arriving in Louisville that month were four single women, all foreign missions volunteers. These courageous young women found each other and secured an attic room. Two shared one single bed. They were eating bread and milk for breakfast, canned beans for lunch, and cold sandwiches for supper. Two seminary faculty wives came to investigate and were appalled. They invited the young women to Sunday dinner. "Think of it—we will sit at a home table and eat a home dinner," the young women exclaimed.[21]

They quickly prompted the board of managers to rent a two-story house on South Fourth Street near the Seminary. Ann Weigal, a widow and local Baptist church member, and her two young daughters moved in with their furniture. Thus a proper home was established for the single women. But they declined to move in; they could not afford the charges.

The board of managers sent W. O. Carver to speak with the students. He knew them best and had orchestrated the entire plan for their home. Carver convinced the women that they must cooperate with the home in order to strengthen it for others who would come later. And, to help at least one of the students meet expenses, he personally advanced a loan. On November 26, 1904, the four moved in with "Mother" Weigal, and the home was established.

The four original students were Clemmie Ford of Tennessee, who became Mrs. G. E. Henderson and remained in the USA as an active church worker; Alice Huey of Alabama who went to China as a missionary; Ella Jeter of Oklahoma who also went to China; and Rena Groover of Georgia, who married W. O. Carver's brother-in-law and went to Brazil as Mrs. J. W. Shepard.[22]

Soon they were joined by a local city missionary who served as teacher and chaperone, Emma Leachman, and by more students. By February the house was full. Emma Woody had personally guaranteed the rent and utilities for the home; now they needed a larger house and more money. The founders mounted a publicity campaign to get the support of WMU, SBC. Knowing that the president and secretary of WMU were united in opposition to the Louisville program, they wrote directly to the vice presidents in the states. And they asked the mission boards and the Sunday School Board to make official recommendations to WMU that the home be supported.

The vice-presidents of Alabama, Florida, Virginia, Maryland, and Kentucky applied pressure to Armstrong and Barker. The resulting explosion in Baltimore made Olive May Board Eager (Mrs. John H.), sister-in-law of Anna Eager, and presiding officer of the WMU headquarters Executive Committee, resign on April 11, 1905.[23] Barker told the vice-presidents that if they wanted the matter discussed at the Annual Meeting, they could bring it up from the floor in a resolution without help from her, which they did.

The Louisville women's case was so strong that the competing training schools in Dallas and in Baltimore made no appeal for support of the conventionwide WMU. Texas women were willing and able to support both their own school and the Louisville school. The Dallas school won an endorsement from the 1905 Southern Baptist Convention. Nothing was heard from the Baltimore school.

The 1905 Annual Meeting was marked with uncharacteristically tense debate. Armstrong became so angry that she refused to speak of E. Y. Mullins (whose wife had formerly been on the Executive Committee in Baltimore) as *Dr.* or as *Mullins*. Instead she called him *Mr. Mullin.*[24] Armstrong's opposition caused the women to vote against adopting the home by a slim vote of 25 to 22. But Barker and Armstrong knew they were losing their defensive battle. They announced that they would not consent to reelection in 1906.

A subsequent resolution called for the individual states to lend support to the school if they wished, and this is what happened. Brochures about the "Baptist Women's Missionary Training School and Home" were sent to the state WMU officers along with an appeal for support, which was forthcoming.[25] The Louisville board of managers leased a large old mansion and cut rags for rugs to prepare for the avalanche of unmarried women students. At their monthly meetings often they tallied more expenses than cash in the treasury. Anna Eager would say, "Dear women, let us get on our knees and pray." The next morning's mail never failed to bring the needed check.[26]

Annie Armstrong was not a graceful loser. She persisted in trying to discredit the training school. She argued that if the Seminary permitted women in its homiletics class, it was unscripturally teaching the women to be preachers. By the time of the 1906 Annual Meeting she had been publicly humiliated. She lost the support of her most loyal friends in Baltimore and of the men friends of WMU.[27]

The Louisville ladies went to the 1906 meeting expecting to have their school adopted by WMU, SBC. Instead, Lillie Barker fired one

parting shot, ruling the plan out of order on a constitutional techni-
cality. In 1907, after a new slate of WMU officers had taken hold, the
longed-for approval was given and the Woman's Missionary Union
Training School came into existence.

A SCHOOL OF WMU'S OWN

The 1907 WMU Annual Meeting was full of bold advances. Presiding
over all was Fannie E. S. Heck, ardent advocate of the Training School.
She wore a lavender lace dress with high neck, large sleeves, fitted
waist, full-gored long skirt. The hand that wielded the gavel was gloved
in white. On her stunning white hair was a lavender hat with plumes
that nodded as she called for the vote that made WMU owner of an
academic institution.

Heck stood aside as Olive Eager, now back in office as vice-president
from Maryland, made her plea for the project so dear to her sister-in-
law's heart. Eager stated that she and her children were not wearing
lace trim on their underwear, and were giving the money saved to
missions. Somehow this and other admonitions moved the women to
pledge more than $10,000 for their new school.[28]

Anna Eager, with characteristic graciousness and sagacity, rose to
suggest that a message of love be sent to the absent Annie Armstrong,
who remained in self-imposed exile in Baltimore.[29]

The trustees of Southern Seminary surrendered to WMU the entire
management and control of the women students with all the advantages
of the Seminary's classrooms. The local lady board of managers turned
over the furnishings and other scant assets of their home.

On May 18, the Southern Baptist Convention welcomed WMU delegates to the official floor of the Convention—for the first time—in order
to hear the men discuss the Training School. The Convention approved
all plans, then spontaneously raised pledges and cash of approximately
$4,700 for the school.[30]

WMU set up a board of managers representing each state, plus a
local board of managers in Louisville. (The two boards were merged
in 1937.) Also, an advisory board of men was established to gain cooperation of the Seminary, the three SBC boards to which WMU was
closely tied, and local laymen. WMU's own board of managers would
control the property and endowments. Money for the school would be
raised by apportionment to each state, and their school would open
in the fall of 1907.[31]

TRADITION!

On a hot July afternoon, the ladies, joined by James M. Frost of the

Sunday School Board, perspired through a long tour of Louisville. They found an apartment building located at 334 East Broadway, which could accommodate 50 students, at the alarming price of $23,000. The owner reduced the price to $20,500 and the committee made a down payment.

Opening ceremonies for the Training School were conducted by the brethren of the SBC agencies and of Louisville. Fannie Heck, the other founding women,[32] and the WMU Executive Committee sat decorously in the audience. But Heck stood up when Frost delivered to her a check for $20,583.47—the total purchase cost to the penny of the first building.

Even more crucial than the need for an appropriate building had been the search for a principal. To Anna Eager fell the task of finding the right person. Eager's mind turned to her Alabama connections. She arranged an interview between Heck and Maud Reynolds McLure (Mrs. T. E.).

McLure had been born in 1863 at a 14-room antebellum showplace, Mount Ida, near Talladega, Alabama. Maud Reynolds received every advantage, including schooling at Judson College and at a finishing school in Baltimore. Her wedding to Thomas Edward McLure of Chester, South Carolina, in 1886 was a fabled celebration. Her son, Tom, was just a year old when her husband suddenly died.[33]

McLure was a musician with a rich, well-trained voice. After living a few years with a sister in Jacksonville, Alabama, she put Tom in boarding school and pursued a career as a touring singer. In 1904 she joined the music faculty of Cox College in College Park, Georgia, where Tom attended a military academy. It was there that Eager found her.

Heck soon agreed with Eager's assessment that this woman possessed unusual powers. She was beautiful, regal, firm, cultured, competent. Her relatives were all leaders in Southern Baptist life. A young cousin, Kathleen Mallory, was destined to become the secretary of Woman's Missionary Union. McLure had given generously to the Home Mission Board, headed by her brother-in-law. Heck and McLure chatted on a massive sofa at the Margaret Home in South Carolina until McLure agreed to become principal for the salary of $75 per month plus room and board.[34] She served as principal until 1923. W. O. Carver called her the "soul of the school."

McLure's ancestral family slogan was Noblesse Oblige—the obligation of the privileged to lift those less fortunate. In the South, noblesse oblige was said to be the equivalent of northern humanitarianism. Others identified noblesse oblige with the Christian gospel which attempted to redeem southern life.[35] All these definitions seemed to fit the atmosphere which Maud Reynolds McLure created in the WMU Training School.

She spent a month observing the Chicago Missionary Training School, then arrived in Louisville just in time to join in scrubbing the new building. On the night before the October 2, 1907, opening, she and Heck lay down to sleep in a Louisville guest room. For her lullabye McLure heard Heck describe her high dreams for the school. McLure turned her face to the wall, and prayed to die before morning, knowing that she would have to implement those impossible dreams. The Lord did not answer that prayer, so McLure set out to create a school.

Wives of seminary students were permitted to enroll in classes by day. But unmarried women were required to live along with the faculty in the WMUTS building. The building was not referred to as a school or dormitory, but as a home. Students were advised to bring aprons and work dresses along with simple school clothes, for they would be doing household duties three times a day. They brought napkin rings, for mealtimes were formally served with prescribed rituals and courtesies.

Thus the WMUTS proved to be more than an intellectual exercise. It provided cultural and spiritual conditioning.[36] The day began with a processional to group devotionals before breakfast. Prayer partnerships were established. Students were taught to lead elaborate worship services, usually wearing white and carrying candles. They became a closely knit group that celebrated self-sacrifice as a sign of devotion and hardship as a sign of God's favor.

Until the 1920s no woman aspiring to a place of Christian leadership cut her hair or allowed cosmetics to show. Students were expected to have serious intentions about Christian service. They were graded as much on spirituality as on academics. Those who did not measure up were stripped of their training school pin.

The school's high-toned atmosphere was more often cited than class content. The women showed their ability, however, to compete in seminary classes. In the 1908 Old Testament class, all 14 women made grades of 90 or more, and 3 made 100. Out of 108 men, only 1 made 100.[37]

A WMU staff member who had not attended the school dreaded her field assignment there, expecting that the students were perpetually in prayer meetings. Especially she dreaded Maud Reynolds McLure, who she imagined "spent most of her time on the pedestal, descending every now and then to take the starch out of any Scribes and Pharisees who might have wandered into the student body." She said, "Nobody could be as perfect as she is pictured and I'm not going to like her."

Students formed an honor guard along the corridor as McLure escorted the visitor into the lovely dining room. The visitor thought, "I can't stand it." Then McLure began to introduce the guest to speak to the students. "I knew I couldn't say a word," she later reported. "But then I felt under the table a hand on my clenched hand, and through that hand flowed into my spirit a calm, a poise, an assurance, a forgetfulness of my miserable self. And that night before retiring I wrote, 'I came, she conquered, I am worse than the worst of you.' "[38]

Maud McLure established most of the school's heavy roster of traditions: a chant from Psalm 91; Tuesday afternoon prayer meetings; Christmas caroling in faculty members' homes; sunrise singing by seniors on Easter; the "Take the Light" processional from the *Pageant of Darkness and Light*; the vigil dedication service for seniors at graduation time; monthly praise services; massive daisy chains carried on the shoulders of seniors (later replaced by palm branches).

This unique community helped women define themselves in new roles. Annie Armstrong's worst fears were realized: the school did become a matrimonial bureau for some. Many women took pride that the engagement and wedding business was good, perhaps the best work that the school did.[39] Students could entertain seminary men under strict conditions, and the men contributed a hat tree for the parlors. Many students married pastors, and their education gave them credentials for a professional's share in their husbands' ministry. But the school also accorded a place of honor to the single woman, especially if she were rejecting marriage in favor of God's call to Christian service.

THE FOUNDERS' FOLLOWERS: PRINCIPALS AND TRUSTEES

The school traditions begun by Maud McLure were maintained by Jane Agnes Walker Cree Bose, the second principal. A native of England, she was a widow with one son. She served Kentucky WMU as office secretary 1913-16, then as corresponding secretary 1916-25. Because she was a gifted speaker, she was asked to be WMU's chief conventionwide organizer for the $75 Million Campaign. When Maud McLure resigned, the WMUTS asked the Good Will Center director, Carrie U. Littlejohn, to be acting principal until they could agree on Bose as principal. Although Bose had some difficulty following the lingering charisma of McLure, she won the students' affection, and they were distressed when she unexpectedly resigned in 1930 to marry. Her new husband was a wealthy, influential layman of Knoxville, James Hughes Anderson, whose wife had been a school trustee. He continued to be a benefactor of the school.

The next principal had the longest tenure, serving until 1951. She was Carrie Littlejohn, born in Spartanburg, South Carolina, in 1890. She earned degrees from Converse College, WMUTS, Hartford School of Religious Education, and Northwestern University. After a career in settlement-house work at Georgia textile mills, she joined the WMUTS faculty in 1921. Littlejohn maintained the strong pietistic flavor of the school and nurtured it through the depression, war, move to new campus, enlargement. She was unprepared for the more aggressive, less self-sacrificing attitudes of postwar women. Upon retiring in 1951 to make way for changes in the nature of the school, she served as dean of women at Limestone College in South Carolina.

Her successor did not bow to Training School tradition. She was Emily Kilpatrick Lansdell, born in Hephzibah, Georgia, 1913. Although her mother was the first woman to stand the Southern Seminary exam in comparative religions and missions, Lansdell did not attend the WMUTS. After graduating from Coker College, she earned the MA at both Duke University and Yale University, and she studied Chinese language and literature at the University of California. She was appointed by the Foreign Mission Board in 1943 to teach at the University of Shanghai. She left Shanghai in 1949 and served briefly on the FMB staff before her election in 1951 as president of the WMUTS. She presided over the school's name change and ownership change. Then she resigned. She became professor of missions at Southeastern Baptist Theological Seminary, where she married J. B. Weatherspoon in 1962; then she taught at Georgia Southwestern College.

Throughout its history the WMUTS was the child of Woman's Missionary Union like no other cause. The president of WMU was the president of the WMUTS trustees. The secretary of WMU was the secretary of the WMUTS trustees. The treasurer of WMU was the treasurer of the WMUTS, disbursing most funds and handling its investments from her office in a distant city. The principal of the school was a member of the WMU Executive Committee from 1930 to 1954 and frequently represented WMU as a speaker and writer. The school was featured in every WMU publication.

While the Southern Seminary faculty controlled the seminary curriculum, WMU constitutents controlled the curriculum of the training school.[40] WMU called its academic head a principal until 1948, only reluctantly according her the normal title of president. She operated in a narrow scope of authority hemmed in by intensely possessive WMU women on one side and the imperiousness of seminary academicians on the other. No wonder Carrie Littlejohn considered W. O. Carver her father figure and needed his guidance.

The president's chief duty was "to keep the school in the sympathy of WMU." Students were expected to graduate with intense loyalty to WMU and ability to operate in church, state, or national roles of WMU leadership. The school was expected to be a distillation of WMU values. Worship, prayer, mission study, social action, sacrificial giving, commitment to mission service—all these features were stressed.

WMUTS trustees reported to the WMU Annual Meeting and to the WMU, SBC, Executive Committee. The women knowingly paid themselves lower salaries than they paid the male faculty of the seminary, thus demonstrating their idealism and willingness to suffer for the cause.

The trustees, representing the state WMU organizations, had a two-fold task: first, to recruit, screen, encourage, motivate, and find employment for students; and second to enlist financial support for the school. Not only did they elicit contributions in excess of $1,651,000 (see table, p. 482), but they also kept a steady stream of supplies flowing. To the WMUTS kitchen went barrels of apples from Virginia, hams from Tennessee, home-canned produce, cakes, peaches, turkeys, pecans, peanuts, candies, even holly boughs. To the linen closets went sheets, quilts, hemstitched napkins, lace-edge pillowcases. To the parlors went music boxes, grandfather clock, cloisonne urns, fine carpets, portraits, Victrolas. To the familylike dining tables went crocheted placemats which were meticulously starched and blocked on custom-made stretcher frames. The WMUTS must always look elegant, but cost little.[41]

This approach to financial support enabled the school to keep adequate, attractive roofs over the heads of a growing student body. The quaint care-taking culture wore thin after World War II. But to an extent not matched in the freewheeling 1950s and later, WMUTS graduated women who could find a niche for successful ministry among Southern Baptists.

DEBT-FREE EXPANSION

The training school's first building had to be expanded in 1908. Within seven years the need for a completely new building was obvious. In 1915 plans were launched for the magnificient stone building on Broadway that was to be fabled House Beautiful.

J. M. Frost wrote to assure Fannie Heck that the Sunday School Board would again aid WMU, promising $10,000.[42] Before the building was completed in 1917 another $10,000 came. Into the cornerstone went a WMU prayer calendar, copies of WMU publications, Heck's history of WMU, and her biographical sketch. On the outside was chiseled a portion of Psalm 144:12 that speaks of the people's aspirations that their daughters might be cornerstones of God's kingdom.

Students and visitors could walk up the grand marble Frost staircase to the handsome Heck Chapel and find women in charge. Prior to the time when the WMUTS had its own chapel, only men could speak at its important services. Now, the school could have women speakers. The first was WMU president Minnie Kennedy James (Mrs. W. C.), speaking at graduation in 1918.

House Beautiful was expanded to its limits. After recovery from a depression slump in enrollment, when the mission boards could not afford to send out missionaries, it was time to build again. Southern Seminary lured WMU to Lexington Road, where the seminary had moved earlier. There, under the leadership of Laura Dell Malotte Armstrong (Mrs. F. W.), during 1941-42 WMU invested nearly $300,000 to erect a graceful Georgian building in harmony with the nearby seminary campus. Again, the move was made without debt.

Except for student fees for room and board and Sunday School Board contributions, the school had no source of support but WMU contributions, until 1919. Then WMU wholeheartedly entered into the promotion of the $75 Million Campaign. There was a payoff—allocations from campaign contributions to the WMU Training School. While other agencies plunged into debt in expectation of enormous receipts from the campaign, the women held the school's purse strings with characteristic conservatism. Later when receipts slackened during the depression, salaries were cut, and WMU held its head high above debt.

Success with its $75 Million Campaign quota put WMU at the head of the line when allocations were made from the first Cooperative Program budget in 1925. From the beginning the WMUTS received a small amount—usually ½ to 1 percent. The Cooperative Program money was remitted directly to the school office in Louisville and did not go through the WMU treasurer's hands as other WMUTS funds did.[43]

In addition to funding its own school, in 1943 WMU began paying $15,000 a year into the seminary budget. That additional support enabled the seminary to launch a school of music. WMUTS phased out its music classes and music students were the first women to be admitted to the seminary.[44] In 1943 W. O. Carver retired, leaving WMU without its strongest advocate within the seminary.

In 1945 WMU was asked to strip its treasury to give the seminary $50,000 with which to build additional classrooms.[45] The money was paid over the strong (private) protests of key WMU leaders, who could not understand why the Cooperative Program could not take care of the seminary.

After the SBC struggled out of its indebtedness in 1943, the Executive Committee of the Convention began to tighten controls on Cooperative Program allocations. As long as Laura Armstrong was strongly present in the SBC Executive Committee, nobody raised a hand against the training school. But immediately after her death in 1945, the training school allocation was slashed. The new WMU president, Olive Brinson Martin (Mrs. George R.), and Kathleen Mallory complacently ignored the action, but Ethlene Boone Cox (Mrs. W. J.), treasurer, with her eye on every cent, resisted.[46]

When the WMUTS was restored to the allocations list, it was with the proviso that the school adhere to the Business and Financial Plan for SBC agencies. This meant that the school would have to send a copy of the budget to the SBC Executive Committee and render an annual report to the Southern Baptist Convention, just as if it were owned by the Convention.[47]

Again in 1949 the SBC Executive Committee approached WMU about reducing the training school allocation. WMU coolly reminded the brethren that if the Cooperative Program did not supply the needed funds, they would have to redouble their solicitations from women in the churches—a method they had been soft-pedaling in favor of building the Cooperative Program.[48]

When the SBC assumed the major funding of the school in 1957, WMU had to relinquish control. The distinguishing identity and function of the school were lost.

SISTER-BROTHER SCHOOLS

The Woman's Missionary Union Training School in effect was the second seminary of Southern Baptists. It was wholly owned by Woman's Missionary Union, but it always worked in rhythm with Southern Baptist Theological Seminary, which was the ward of the SBC.

The two institutions were most closely linked through the classroom. As promised in 1907, the seminary welcomed WMUTS students to its classrooms. Examinations were taken there; credit was given toward diplomas granted by the training school. The faculty of the seminary signed the diplomas along with WMU and training school officials.

The WMUTS first established the bachelor of missionary training (BMT) degree; later the master of missionary training. To supplement the seminary courses, women faculty were hired to teach such subjects as medicine, public speaking, music, missions education, domestic science. The backbone of the WMUTS intellect was W. O. Carver, with his pioneering courses in missions.

Aside from its enablement of women in ministry, the school's main contribution to Baptist life emerged from Maud McLure's noblesse oblige philosophy. The industrialization of the South created many social problems, and Baptists had no organized response. The settlement house was the state-of- the-art approach to social problems. In keeping with WMU's new program of personal service, and in keeping with the rise of social work as a profession, McLure led the school to open a settlement-house program in 1912. The house was renamed Good Will Center in 1914. All training school students were required to practice their personal witness and ministry skills in the Good Will Center (see chap. 9).

What the training school did was to build principles and to develop role models for the social work profession. More than any other entity in Southern Baptist life, WMUTS graduates were willing and able to apply the controversial social gospel.

In 1920 Gaines S. Dobbins joined the seminary faculty and began to teach religious education. He found his most eager students at the WMUTS, where the women seemed to appreciate what he was trying to accomplish in developing a body of knowledge for church administration.[49] Dobbins's classes, plus others unique to the training school, eventually shaped its curriculum away from missions and into religious education. In 1927 the school addressed a growing opportunity for women by adding courses for church secretaries.

In 1931 the training school degrees were changed from bachelor of missionary training and master of missionary training to bachelor and master of religious education, degrees which were already being offered women at Southwestern Baptist Theological Seminary. The religious education slant was encouraged by the Sunday School Board, which granted enough funds to WMU to cover Dobbins's salary.[50]

The BRE degree had come to be the standard which qualified women for missionary appointment and other church-related posts. Male missionary candidates (who were expected to be ordained) were usually equipped with divinity degrees.[51] Religious education was essentially a female domain.

But the situation was shifting. In 1934 the seminary catalog defined the title *minister* to include persons committed to the calling of Christian education, although not purposing ordination to the pastoral ministry. After World War II, with men and women receiving virtually identical classwork in many subjects, they began to eye each other's job markets. The possibility for women to capture theology-related jobs associated with ordination was out of reach. But men easily moved into positions previously available to women—educational directors, music directors, student work directors. Men who took these jobs were often called minister instead of director, and they gradually popularized ordination for these tasks.

By 1948 the seminary was granting men bachelor of divinity degrees in religious education. The seminary let WMU know that changes were ahead and put pressure on WMUTS to grant a religious education degree to men.[52] Increasingly the denomination regarded the training school as another of the official seminaries. But when the SBTS mentioned the possibility of merging their commencement ceremonies, WMU answered with icy silence.[53]

The training school's social work orientation colored its approach to the maturing field of religious education. While other Southern Baptist seminaries' religious education classes concentrated on preparing for educational leadership in churches, the training school applied its educational principles in "group work," or institutional education situations.

This difference in perspective came into sharp focus when Southern Seminary invited WMU to discuss the future of religious education. In 1952 the seminary offered WMU the option of serving as its religious education school for both men and women. The women already took more than two-thirds of their classes at the seminary. Would that be the best fulfillment of the training school's purposes?

CARVER SCHOOL OF MISSIONS AND SOCIAL WORK

As usual, the women turned to their mentor, W. O. Carver. From the time of Carver's class in missions methodology which made him the first professor of the WMUTS, until his death in 1954, he lectured almost every WMUTS student.

Aside from his paternity of the WMUTS, Carver made history by establishing the first formal department of missions and comparative religions in higher education. This he did at Southern Seminary in 1899. The Southern Baptist man most knowledgeable about missions was also the one who did the most to lift and encourage women.

Stemming from a deep respect for women beginning with his mother (to whom he dedicated one of his books, *Missions in the Plan of the Ages*), and extending through careful analysis of the Scriptures, he believed that Christianity placed responsibility and opportunity equally upon women and men.[54]

Carver as a student at the University of Richmond was an eyewitness to the 1888 founding of WMU. He demonstrated his advocacy of WMU's independence. The women found him easy to trust and follow on all matters. Even after he retired in 1943, he remained on the male advisory board of the WMUTS.

At the big turning point in 1952, WMUTS followed Carver and chose a missions and social work specialty over local church religious education. WMU decided to magnify the school's original specialties of missions and social work. They voted to drop the antiquated name training school, and to admit students regardless of sex or race.[55] So the seminary announced that it would open a school of religious education in the fall of 1953 and open its doors to women.

Carver was asked to address the WMUTS trustees at their May 1953 meeting about the implementation of the plans. His stunning address, "If I Were Under Thirty," sketched out a curriculum for a school of world Christianity. Carver's broad sweep of content area included religious education as it applied to social work groups and institutions. The school would give top professional training to missionaries prior to their appointment and would provide them research and retooling throughout their careers.

As usual, once he had helped the women catch a vision, Carver went home to let them work out details in their own way. Unanimously they agreed to rename the school Carver School of Missions and Social Work. The choice was acclaimed by SBC missions leaders.[56]

Realizing that they would need increased funding, WMU in 1952 had asked the SBC Executive Committee for 1½ percent of the Cooperative Program instead of the usual 1 percent. The request was denied because the school was not controlled by the SBC—a point which had never been raised in the 27 years of the Cooperative Program.

Even more controversial was the request by WMU for $320,000 in capital funds to build a new building. Never had the SBC invested capital funds in the WMUTS. In keeping with the times, and with the SBC Business and Financial Plan to which it had voluntarily adhered, the school decided not to solicit funds directly from the women. Instead, it asked for Cooperative Program funds.

The women would not have gotten a penny except for the intervention of the mission boards. During a coffee break at the SBC Executive Committee meeting, some of the agency executives caucused in the men's room. One said to M. Theron Rankin of the Foreign Mission Board, "If the women get this money it will mostly have to come out of your allocation." Rankin said, "Let them have it."[57] He was on the Carver School advisory board and was fully sympathetic with the possibilities of training missionaries. Yet this was a significant sacrifice of the very funds he had begged for the Foreign Mission Board Advance Program.

Carver School had proceeded to launch its new studies. Frank Laubach, developer of an approach to literacy training in conjunction with missions, was brought in to introduce literacy missions to the SBC. Summer school was introduced. Seminars in missionary problems were developed, with documents preserved for future researchers.[58] Faculty members were added to CSMSW and students were required to take more than half their course work there instead of at the seminary. Courses were added in phonetics, linguistics, cultural anthropology, world revolution, child welfare, law, social pathology, social casework, and similar specialized topics.

The first black student was enrolled in 1952; the first male graduated in 1955, with a master of science in religious education (the social work degree); the first master of science in missions was awarded in 1955. That year 22 Carver School graduates were appointed by the Foreign Mission Board and 11 others went into professional social work. The school's president pointed out that no other Protestant group had a two-year graduate program of social work.[59]

More changes were in the wind. New executives took office at the Sunday School Board, Foreign Mission Board, and Home Mission Board.

They lacked the WMU Training School heritage and the Carver School of Missions and Social Work dream. Olive Martin was going out of office as president of the board of trustees. The new president of Carver, Emily K. Lansdell, was frank to say that she was not interested in preserving the school unless it could meet a distinct need.[60]

With funds received in 1953 and 1954, Carver School built a classroom building and named it for M. Theron Rankin. The school got bad press, however, for sapping the funds of the Foreign Mission Board and the Home Mission Board. The SBC saw little connection between the school's proposed program and the future of missions.

THE SBC TAKES OVER

The pressure for Cooperative Program funds triggered appointment of a committee to study the needs for theological education. This committee, headed by Douglas Hudgins of Mississippi, was soon joined in the study by the SBC's controversial Committee to Study the Total Southern Baptist Program, chaired by Douglas Branch of North Carolina. On this committee were two women: a CSMSW trustee and a state WMU president. There were also powerful laymen with definite convictions that Carver School was not worth its cost. A subcommittee headed by Herschel Hobbs of the SBC Executive Committee worked out a compromise solution. Carver School would be transferred to Southern Baptist Convention ownership. But unlike any other SBC agency, half the Carver School trustees would be named by Woman's Missionary Union. Both WMU and the SBC agreed to this arrangement in 1956. In 1957 WMU transferred to the newly reincorporated Carver School land, buildings, equipment, and funds valued at more than $1,146,000.[61] In 1959, the Committee on Total Program recommended that CSMSW be retained on this basis, but with annual review over a five-year period, during which it must gain accreditation.[62]

When the SBC assumed ownership of Carver School of Missions and Social Work in 1957, Lansdell submitted the resignation she had been holding for more than a year. She believed that the school must be headed by a man if it was to succeed.[63]

The trustees employed Booz-Allen and Hamilton, a firm of Chicago management consultants, to study the school. Their report in 1957 was that the objectives set in 1952-53 were not being achieved. Enrollment was dropping. The school was still viewed only as a school for women, and women's schools in general were declining. Lack of accreditation turned potential students away. Although the school had declared itself a professional school, the student body still reflected a dominance of women who served in lay positions, primarily as pastors' wives.[64]

Ultimately four factors sapped the strength of Carver School. It was cut off from the strong psychological roots which had made Woman's Missionary Union nurture it through thick and thin. Its academic focus was too narrow and too far in advance of its times to obtain accreditation. The new owners were not committed to the school's purposes. Women who wanted theological training could get it at any of six Southern Baptist seminaries.

Between 1961 and 1963 the trustees negotiated a merger of the school into Southern Seminary. In 1962 WMU made the seminary beneficiary of a trust of the remaining assets of Carver School, $355,547 of endowment funds, administered by the Southern Baptist Foundation. These were conveyed with the proviso that the seminary use the funds in perpetuating the purposes of Carver School. The foundation and seminary were required to render to WMU annual reports of the fund earnings and use.

One action of the seminary was to establish the WMU Chair of Social Work. In 1984, after lying dormant for 20 years, the dreams of WMU found a stage on which to act. The seminary created the Carver School of Church Social Work with C. Anne Davis, a graduate of the WMU Training School, as dean. The seminary granted the first master of social work degrees in 1986, and accreditation soon followed.

LOST BUT LINGERING MEANING

Meeting with the WMU staff in 1979, Duke K. McCall, then president of Southern Seminary, lamented the absence of Woman's Missionary Union Training School values from the denomination. The years since the school's demise had been filled with turmoil concerning the role of women in the Southern Baptist Convention. WMU enrollment had declined. The percentage of single women missionaries had dropped. A rising generation of women students was seeking theology degrees, with which they would have difficulty finding employment. Wives of some male pastors brought no religious training or ministry commitment into their marriages.

In all SBC seminaries, enrollment of women declined from 17.1 percent in 1950 to 10.6 percent in 1970, contrary to national trend. Seminaries were called "a masculine subculture."[65]

The discussion caused WMU officers to dust off statistics about the WMUTS. They found that in 1949 the school had enrolled only 7 percent of all seminary students then studying with Southern Baptists. But 29 percent of all missionaries then under appointment by the Foreign Mission Board were WMUTS alumnae.

In the years 1944-49, 11.5 percent of 295 graduates had become foreign missionaries; 35 percent were serving on church staffs; 16 percent had missionary appointments in the US; 12 percent were student work directors; 7 percent were in professional WMU work. Of the graduates, 57 percent had married seminary students, and most of these were steadily leading and teaching within the church as if they were professionals.[66]

In a 1957 survey of 2,959 graduates, the statistics had not significantly shifted except to show a larger percentage of social workers.

Although the school never enrolled more than 233 students at one time, its 50 years and 4,000 students had indelibly, though intangibly, marked the denomination.

WOMAN'S PLACE AT OTHER SEMINARIES

WMU had expressed its concern about theological education for women mainly through the school it owned. But that concern popped out on other fronts as well.

Texas women never gave up their desire for a conveniently located women's training school. While the WMUTS was getting off the Louisville ground, Texas women were making sure that women were included in the theological school taking form at Baylor University. When the school became Southwestern Baptist Theological Seminary in Fort Worth in 1910, 15 percent of the students were counted in the Woman's Missionary Training School. The new school had taken over R. H. Buckner's 1904 school. Texas women's missionary societies promised to erect and equip a special building for the school. To the delight of the women, their former foe, B. H. Carroll, heartily endorsed the school as scripturally appropriate.[67]

The leading feminine mind behind the matter was Lou Beckley Williams (Mrs. W. L.), president of Texas WMU (then known as Baptist Women Mission Workers). Williams had been present in 1888 for the founding of WMU, SBC. Under her inspiration, another WMU leader, Mrs. R. F. Stokes, traveled the state to raise more than $120,000. The Sunday School Board contributed $10,000, subject to stricter controls than those placed on the WMUTS. L. R. Scarborough, president of the school, pointedly said that the women were offered all courses on the same basis as male students "without in any way recognizing women as preachers."[68]

The early publicity sheets of the training school took the same slogan WMU women used for the WMUTS in Louisville: "That our daughters may be as corner stones. . . ." The first principal of the school was Mary C. Tupper, daughter of the secretary of the Foreign Mission Board, former missionary in Mexico, and former officer of Virginia WMU. Following the Louisville example, the Fort Worth Training School opened a good will center. It emphasized religious education and stressed missionary service as the ideal for women.

By 1917 the Fort Worth Training School had one-third more students than the Louisville school. Texas WMU had an advisory board which knitted the women to Southwestern Baptist Theological Seminary. Each WMU district was expected to sponsor a "scholarship girl" at the school. That meant not only money for fees, but also regular correspondence, encouragement, gifts, visits, and help with employment.[69]

When Southwestern Seminary came under control of the Southern Baptist Convention in 1923, WMU, SBC, was immediately asked to assume a fostering role with its training school. In 1924 WMU appointed an advisory board "to cooperate with the Trustees of SWBTS in administration of the training school."[70] That began 30 years of close kinship between the Woman's Missionary Training School in Fort Worth and the women of the South. The advisory board had no control. It served only promotional purposes. A representative of the school reported at every annual session of WMU, SBC, until 1948. Then state WMUs were invited to name representatives to the advisory board rather than WMU, SBC, naming them. Annual reports from the WMTS were printed in WMU's minutes until 1953.

Under the management of Ray Osborne McGarity (Mrs. William B.), daughter of the founder of the *Baptist Basket*, life in the WMTS in Fort Worth of the 1920s and 1930s closely paralleled that of the WMUTS in Louisville, with strict schedules, discipline, prayer, and plain living. Curriculum was basically religious education courses under J. M. Price. Domestic science, good will center, nursery, typewriting, shorthand, and home nursing courses were taught by women teachers.[71] Like the Louisville school, the Fort Worth school had a "Mother" living in, Lou Williams, who retired to the building she had helped fund, and spent her last days planting roses on the campus.

Similarly, a women's training school was central in the establishing of New Orleans Baptist Theological Seminary. At its founding by the SBC in 1917, the seminary was called Baptist Bible Institute. Women were admitted as students and were housed in their own dormitory. By 1923 almost half the students were women.[72] Woman's Missionary Union took no particular note of the school until 1920, when an advisory board appointed by WMU met at the BBI campus. The advisory committee addressed the overall needs of the school, for males and females, in its annual reports for several years.

The amenities and visibility for a distinct women's program were missing from New Orleans Seminary. The men of the seminary took their meals in the women's dormitory and therefore had the initiative in conducting morning worship.[73] From 1924 on, WMU, SBC, or the state WMUs appointed the advisory board. WMU, SBC, printed annual reports and included the school in its plan of work. In May 1930, as the Great Depression struck, WMU, SBC, campaigned to raise $5,692 to establish a chair of missions at the Seminary.[74]

When WMU, SBC, observed its 50th anniversary in 1938, the celebration thank offering was spent in part on the WMUTS in Louisville.
This action, though logical in light of WMU's ownership of the school,
stirred the jealousies of those closer to New Orleans and Fort Worth.
Crickett Keys Copass (Mrs. B. A.), president of Texas WMU, protested
that Texas was having to bear the load of the SWBTS Training School
alone. She threatened to curtail Texas's support of other causes if help
were not forthcoming for the Fort Worth school.[75]

After WMU contributed $50,000 to Southern Seminary in 1945, Copass
again rose up,[76] as did other states who were raising special gifts for
the three different seminaries. The result was a WMU committee appointed to study WMU's relations with the two training schools not
under its management. The 1947 decision was that WMU's strongest
tie must be with its own school, but that the other schools were helping
to meet the needs of women and should also be supported. From that
time state WMUs were to assume the appointment of representatives
to the New Orleans and Southwestern training schools. The states were
encouraged to award women scholarships to these schools and to
recommend suitable students. Between 1946 and 1948 WMU, SBC, gave
$25,000 each for the Fort Worth and New Orleans schools.

When Golden Gate Theological Seminary and Southeastern Baptist
Theological Seminary entered the SBC arena in 1950, WMU simply
added these institutions to its literature which advertised possible
schools for women. Although WMU leaders had spoken privately of the
possibility of fostering a training school at Southeastern, the idea
seemed superfluous by 1952.[77] Also, in 1952-53 WMU recognized the
Mather School of Nursing of Southern Baptist Hospital in New Orleans.
This school had been founded by and named for the sister of WMU's
young people's secretary.

WMU AND THE COLLEGES

The interest of Woman's Missionary Union in higher education was
a natural outgrowth of what education had done for women. The founders of Texas WMU were an alumna and teacher of Baylor College
(now Mary Hardin-Baylor University), Fannie Breedlove Davis (Mrs.
G. B.), along with the college president's daughter, Anne Luther Bagby
(Mrs. W. B.). Even before Davis organized Texas WMU in 1880, she was
one of eight women seated at the 1872 meeting of the Texas Baptist
Education Society. Another product of Baylor College was Emma McIver
Woody, who was to be one of the five founders of the Woman's Missionary Union Training School.[78]

Albemarle Female Institute, organized by Baptists as a female alternative to the University of Virginia, provided two WMU founders. It awarded the first master's degrees to women in the South. Three of the five recipients were Lottie Moon; Jennie Snead Hatcher (Mrs. W. E.), who was to head Virginia WMU and host the 1888 founding of WMU, SBC; and Julia Toy Johnson (Mrs. J. L.), the first president of Mississippi WMU.

The president of Mississippi WMU who secured approval to affiliate with WMU, SBC, was Adelia M. Hillman (Mrs. Walter). With her husband she operated Hillman College; she succeeded him as president. Hillman later became part of Mississippi College, which was led by the husband of another state WMU president, Mary Bailey Aven (Mrs. A. J.).

When J. B. Gambrell was president of Mercer University, his wife was corresponding secretary of Georgia WMU. Mary Gambrell attempted to lead WMU, SBC, to make Baptist colleges a focus of its plan of work. She believed that women's missionary societies should raise money for colleges as well as for missions work. Alice Armstrong, sister of Annie, successfully blocked Mary Gambrell's proposal.[79] The conventionwide WMU undertook no official projects for Baptist colleges until 1919. When Minnie Kennedy James (Mrs. W. C.) was president of WMU and her husband was heading the Education Board of the SBC, WMU articulated the idea that Baptist schools were a means of training missionaries and bringing in God's kingdom. For the next 30 years WMU made record of the women's financial support of Christian higher education. Amounts reported exceeded $15 million (see table, p. 482).

During the first quarter of the century, enrollment of women in Baptist schools increased seven times, while enrollment of males only doubled. Naturally WMU's concern followed this trend.[80] Interest in higher education was strongest where women were linked with a local Baptist college. At the founding of Meredith College Fannie Heck campaigned to raise its funds. Georgia WMU raised $70,000 for the endowment of Bessie Tift College. Arkansas WMU bought and equipped buildings for Ouachita Baptist University. Oklahoma WMU built a massive WMU dormitory at Oklahoma Baptist University, breaking ground on the eve of the depression and paying for it in 1937. Virginia WMU built the library for the University of Richmond.

District 17 in Texas WMU lovingly supported Hardin-Simmons University with fund-raising projects and sponsorship of women students. The women of District 9 built a $150,000 building for Wayland Baptist University in 1952, having begun contributions to the endowment and operating budget during the depression. Memorial Dormitory of Baylor University was funded with $350,000 raised by Willie Turner Dawson (Mrs. J. M.) in the depths of the depression. Texas WMU in

1944 raised $991,049 for the endowment of the state's Baptist colleges and hospitals.

The buildings they built and the amenities they provided served the women well. Most state WMU groups traditionally held conventions, camps, and house parties in college properties. Alabama WMU young women were holding a houseparty at Judson College in 1949 when lightning struck and burned the dormitory to the ground. The women promptly raised $100,000 to rebuild it.

Alabama WMU built a nursery at Howard College (now Samford University) for the care of children of ministerial students whose wives wished to be students. Oklahoma WMU endowed a chair of sociology, thus anchoring WMU's traditional interest in social work to the curriculum of Oklahoma Baptist University.[81]

WMU's sisterly interest in colleges and seminaries also extended to the secondary level when high schools were needed for missions outreach. Virginia WMU built a mountain mission school in Virginia, in Buchanan County, in 1908 and provided the salary of the missionary who operated it. Georgia WMU built, owned, and operated (1916-31) the Mary P. Willingham School (named for a state WMU president) for girls in the north Georgia mountains. Louisiana WMU funded the Acadia Academy, targeted to French-speaking persons.

By the 1950s, Southern Baptist fund-raising had been efficiently and evenly centralized in the Cooperative Program. In support of this common cause, WMU tapered off its project approach to fund-raising. The era of WMU buildings on campuses was over.

WMU SCHOLARSHIPS

WMU sympathy for women students has persisted. Most older state Woman's Missionary Unions have maintained scholarship funds to assist young women, especially those preparing for church vocations and missions. In 1985, state WMUs issued scholarships valued at more than $140,000. Most of these funds were rooted in sponsorship of girls attending the Louisville Training School and the Southwestern Training School. Missouri, for example, began awarding scholarships to WMUTS girls in 1917, setting aside egg money on certain days for the purpose.[82]

Alabama WMU's scholarship fund was frankly established to give women an equal chance. The Alabama Baptist State Convention provided tuition to male ministerial students but nothing to unordained females. Alabama WMU scholarships provided a touch of justice.[83]

The largest scholarship fund is Louisiana WMU's which granted $55,000 in scholarships in 1985. Kentucky WMU's scholarship fund was boosted in celebration of the state WMU's 50th anniversary. Arkansas's scholarships memorialized Nancy Cooper, the longtime state WMU secretary.[84] Some of the states, including Virginia and Georgia, earmarked funds for education of persons assisted by missionaries, such as Indians and international students. Several states award assistance to men as well as to women.

In return, most Baptist colleges usually award scholarships or tuition discounts to girls who have actively participated in WMU's Acteens program. Most Baptist colleges have awarded one or more honorary doctorates to WMU officers. WMU cooperates with college administrators to foster Baptist Young Women organizations on campuses (see chap. 4).

Beginning in the 1970s several state WMUs and WMU, SBC, employed seminary students as intern staff members. After 1974 WMU, SBC, staff members regularly were invited to lecture in seminary classes on church administration, missions, religious education, and social work.

INTO THE FUTURE

Looking backward at its achievements for education of women, especially in theological fields, Woman's Missionary Union established the Second Century Fund to mark the Centennial of the organization. Launched in January 1985, the fund will be an endowment, the earnings of which will help to foster WMU leadership development in the future. One of the areas of expenditure will be for women's programs at Baptist theological seminaries—"that our daughters may be corner stones."

> *Now you have gone, but you have left to me*
> *A priceless beauty in your legacy:*
> *The clear clean vision of the dreams you knew,*
> *The splendid courage that was a part of you,*
> *The fearless wisdom and the tender heart,*
> *The high white faith that marked you one apart,*
> *The soul that drew the world into its ken*
> *With sympathy for all its fellow men,*
> *The bigness of yourself, your soul, your mind—*
> *These are the things you left behind,*
> *And I would not change with king or sage.*
> *God, make me worthy of my heritage![85]*

Read by Kathleen Mallory
at memorial service for Maud
Reynolds McLure, 1938

In union there is strength

In union there is strength, and the more "union" we can get the more strength we will have.[1]

Annie Armstrong, 1899

OMAN'S Missionary Union was the Southern Baptists' fourth child to survive infancy. The Home Mission Board and the Foreign Mission Board were the first offspring, twins created at the 1845 founding of the Convention. Next came a stepchild, Southern Baptist Theological Seminary, formed in 1859 and later fully adopted into the family. Baptists were wary about their independence. They rejected any new arrivals that seemed to centralize interests, run up expenses, and create "machinery."

The climate was not favorable to another family member, especially a daughter. Yet she came in 1888, tolerated because she paid her own birthright, treated somewhat as a foster child. This daughter was Woman's Missionary Union. The family found a word to explain her status: *auxiliary.*

She was happy to be permitted any role, even on the outskirts of the Convention. When others joined the family as normal descendants—the Sunday School Board, other seminaries, and agencies to deal with education, annuities, and other matters—she cheerfully helped to tend them. WMU did the housework, indeed helped build the house, that became the magnetic, strong Southern Baptist Convention.

Annie Armstrong, as WMU's first executive leader, believed that division of labor among the SBC agencies was necessary for efficiency, but that the parts, including WMU, must work as part of the whole. "One of the greatest hindrances to the efficiency of the work of Southern Baptists is the lack of genuine and thorough cooperation," she declared. "I thoroughly believe 'in union there is strength.' "[2]

AUXILIARY TO SOUTHERN BAPTIST CONVENTION

Since 1872 the women had been trying to get under the Southern

Baptist roof, but only their purses and their prayers had been accepted. Their minds and their hands were still outside, knocking ever more persistently from 1883, slapped rudely in 1885 (see chap. 1). They could have fractured the Convention in 1888 with a rival board of missions. Instead, because of the kind guidance and wisdom of many men, they chose to call themselves "Auxiliary to Southern Baptist Convention." They wanted to cooperate. Auxiliary was as close as they could get to the Convention without an invitation to be fully participating members. When the 1888 SBC did not reject the women's claim to being auxiliary, the women took silence for consent.

Susan Tyler Pollard (Mrs. James) of Baltimore, whose husband had paved the way for WMU at the 1887 Convention, reported that the brethren breathed easier after they learned that the sisters had not organized a rival convention, but only an auxiliary.[3]

Although the SBC as a whole took no note of the new conventionwide organization, the two mission boards did. WMU appointed Martha McIntosh and Annie Armstrong to confer with the mission boards, which readily agreed to pay the expenses of WMU in return for receiving their contributions. WMU rendered annual reports to the two mission boards, who in turn reported to the SBC.

WMU was actually auxiliary to the boards of the Convention. The meaning of this relationship would be determined most of all by Annie Armstrong and her brother secretaries. In 1895 she reported:

> Truly this child is no weakling! Nor has it grown at the expense of the family, despoiling the older brothers and sisters; the general receipts of the Boards have increased also. And more: by its amiable and proper conduct, we believe this child is now entirely welcome in the family circle, where at first some of the members looked askance and shook solemn heads in warning at the awful things which this youngster was going to perpetrate—disintegrating church and other seismic performance. We are a part of the church, at work for and in the church and we believe that it is coming to be so understood.[4]

A few years later she commended WMU's good relations with the boards and claimed for WMU the role of unifier.[5]

The WMU Plan of Work reminded women to keep prominent the dependence and subordination of the Woman's Missionary Society on and to the local church, for it was God's ordained agency for saving the world.[6]

Armstrong's technique for being the great unifier was first to set up lines of communication among the SBC boards. When the Sunday School Board joined the family in 1891, she welcomed it heartily. She believed that WMU should be auxiliary to the whole Convention and all its boards. Not all the officers agreed with her, but by 1895 she succeeded in putting the Sunday School Board on a par with the Foreign Mission Board and Home Mission Board.[7] In the absence of any forum for interagency cooperation, Armstrong took the role. She dispatched masses of letters to each board's secretary, sent them copies of each other's letters, shared their family news, and laid on the table their internal problems with ruthless honesty. She bought WMU's intimacy with the administrators at the price of her hard work and no pay. For example, she found that each of the three boards wished to send a communication to pastors. She pulled all the literature together, assembled it, and mailed it from Baltimore. "It proves conclusively . . . that in union there is economy as well as strength," she said. She also noted that the women had hauled the 6,363 packages of literature to the post office in their own hands rather than pay a porter.[8]

Annie Armstrong's strategy gained not only strength for the Convention, but also safety for WMU. James M. Frost of the Sunday School Board believed Armstrong to be indispensable to the Convention. Gentlemen of three boards could be counted on to champion WMU. And they could be counted on for advice, arbitration, and funds.

So close was the union of WMU and the boards that the women hesitated to incorporate in 1904, when given a home for missionaries' children. The Foreign Mission Board held title to the Margaret Home until WMU was incorporated in 1906. The Margaret Home led WMU to amend its constitution to allow the organization to receive and disburse funds. This passed only when another resolution affirmed that in the future, as in the past, WMU would "maintain the closest possible connection with the Boards of the Convention."[9] WMU continued for 30 years to report to the SBC through the three boards. For those same years, the women annually framed their program only on the specific recommendations brought from the boards (which had been thoroughly approved, even suggested in advance by the WMU officers) to the Annual Meeting.

When Auxiliary Meant Independent.—The word *auxiliary* took on a new shade of meaning during the next quarter-century. The Education Board and the Relief and Annuity Board were formed. WMU at first followed its custom of declaring itself duty-bound to both. In the $75 Million Campaign the women enthusiastically raised money for every cause, and in return received operating funds from all five SBC boards. Women were admitted to the SBC as messengers. This acceptance of women perhaps should have led to the end of the auxiliary status, with WMU in some way voted fully into the SBC on the same terms as the boards. Instead, WMU began to keep an arm's length away from the SBC. Auxiliary came to mean independent.

Why would the women not have welcomed complete absorption into the SBC? Laura Malotte Armstrong (Mrs. F. W.) noted in her presidential address of 1933 that amid the frequent reinterpretation of the word *auxiliary*, WMU was now confining its efforts only to the field of missions. She stressed singleness of purpose, whereas 14 years earlier WMU was working equally for the whole. Part of her thinking was undoubtedly the deep debts of the SBC. Kathleen Mallory had been sufficiently alarmed to consult lawyers about the meaning of auxiliary status. They assured her that WMU assets could not be seized to pay debts of the Convention "since we are merely its auxiliary."[10]

The pitiful condition of the mission boards and the cutbacks in missionary forces appealed to the women's original sense of missions. Had WMU been a Convention board, the women would have competed with the other causes. As an auxiliary they could defend the mission boards. In their anxiety to save the boards, they were glad to stand slightly outside the control of the SBC, for they could argue as a block for preferred treatment of the mission boards. They could state categorically that they would continue to collect the special missions offerings and designate them for current missions work. They could plead forcefully about the allocation of the Cooperative Program (see chaps. 5, 6, and 11).

Some WMU leaders moved to a more extreme advocacy of auxiliary status in the 1930s. They stood on the outskirts of a dispute over control of the women's training school operated by the National Baptist Convention women (see chap. 10). Blanche Sydnor White of Virginia wrote to Nannie Burroughs of the NBC about "whether or not the Woman's Auxiliary is to be a puppet or a power. If the SBC had control of our union, we might have faced what the Auxiliary is facing. Don't surrender without a battle."[11] Indeed, the WMU Training School at that time was operating with a subsidy from the SBC and no control by the SBC because of WMU's auxiliary status.

White wanted to extend the auxiliary relationship of WMU, SBC, into the local congregations. WMU, SBC, had never advocated that the local missionary society operate outside the bounds of its church. The proposal came in 1944 for missionary society officers to be elected by the entire congregation, rather than by the women members of the society alone. A WMU, SBC, committee devised the compromise plan of having the society nominate its officers for election by the church. This White opposed. "Now I have as nice brethren as we have in the South. They are perfectly lovely to me. Yet I believe we do better work as an auxiliary, independent body than as a department."[12]

The auxiliary topic was apparently becoming heated at this time, for WMU brought out its prime mentor, W. O. Carver, to comment. Carver was retired with the status of denominational sage after a career as the SBC's leading professor of missions. Carver declared the idea of auxiliary status to be nothing less than the inspiration of the Holy

Spirit. "Only by freedom to think and devise means for their own deepening and expanding desire to promote the interests of the Master's kingdom could the women make progress." Noting the WMU founders' conservatism and modesty, he stated that as an auxiliary was the best way for them to work. Further he said:

> It would be a great misfortune and a serious check on progress if WMU should anywhere lose its consciousness of direct calling for a peculiar responsibility for efficient implementation of its own peculiar spirit in autonomous organization. WMU could not become merely one department of state or local organization, like Sunday School work, Training Union, etc., without most serious loss to our larger visions and our increasing undertakings. . . . The women have never had and do not desire any but an auxiliary status.[13]

Carver supported WMU as auxiliary not because it was inherently right, but because it was a workable way to get the best support for missions.

Auxiliary Means "Helper."—When Alma Hunt took office as WMU's executive secretary in 1948, she was frequently quizzed about her attitude on auxiliary status of WMU, SBC. One prominent minister said, "I know what Mrs. George R. Martin means when she says auxiliary, but what do you mean?"

Olive Martin shared the strict views of her fellow Virginian Blanche White, believing that auxiliary status gave WMU freedom to dictate policy to the mission boards and the moral right to control use of contributions made by the women. The independence of WMU in the 1940s was probably the result of personality. Kathleen Mallory's monumental term of 36 years as executive secretary, during which WMU statistics outstripped all others, was unequaled. She was virtually beyond reach of negotiation. Martin was a formidable person. Men officers of the SBC viewed her as commanding, aggressive, powerful.[14] When Martin went out of office White was certain that the tides would soon dissolve WMU as an auxiliary.[15]

Alma Hunt had other advisers about the status of WMU, SBC. Ethlene Boone Cox (Mrs. W. J.) thought the time might come for change, but not "without an assurance of equal representation on the Boards of our state and southwide conventions. When women are accepted by Baptists then we will have accomplished that which we were denied in 1888."[16]

Hunt led WMU, SBC, to return to the original definition of auxiliary. Upon her arrival WMU was invited to help form the SBC Inter-Agency Council. She served as its president 1955-57. She gradually withdrew WMU from control of expenditure of the special missions offerings. During her administration WMU seized every opportunity to cooperate with the Convention. Carver School of Missions and Social Work (formerly WMU Training School) was placed under dual sponsorship of WMU and the SBC, then peacefully merged into Southern Baptist Theological Seminary. At Hunt's retirement she was commended by Porter W. Routh, executive secretary-treasurer of the SBC Executive Committee, as one who defined auxiliary as "augmenting a basic power ... not to control policy for the mission boards, but to be a source of help."[17] Routh himself had been influential in maintaining WMU's special relationship with the SBC. At his suggestion, in 1953 the president of WMU was made a member of the SBC Executive Committee by virtue of office.

Not until 1959 did WMU find a place in the Southern Baptist Convention's constitution and bylaws. After the bylaw listing the agencies of the Convention, a new section was added: "Auxiliary: The Woman's Missionary Union, Birmingham, Alabama, is an auxiliary of the convention." This amendment was adopted on recommendation of Marie Wiley Mathis (Mrs. R. L.), president of WMU, SBC.

Though quietly discussed in some denominational committees of the 1950s, change of auxiliary status was viewed as not necessary or desirable, even if possible.[18] The Committee to Study the Total Southern Baptist Program recommended that WMU be continued as auxiliary to the SBC. (Really, the SBC had no power to change WMU's status or terms of existence, but only to recommend or invite change.) The committee further stated that the SBC and WMU should continue to be two independent organizations cooperating on the basis of mutual concerns and a common purpose. "The present relationship between the Convention and Woman's Missionary Union has proved satisfactory for both groups over the years . . . no significant benefits would be achieved from a change."[19]

When Mathis succeeded Martin as president of WMU, Hunt had a strong ally in leading WMU to closer harmony with the SBC. Again WMU played the unifier as these women sat in interagency committees.

When WMU suffered membership and financial losses, again its relationship to the Convention was informally discussed. This time some thought WMU might need to come under the SBC's protection because of finances. The Committee of Fifteen appointed by the SBC Executive Committee in 1970 included WMU in its studies of agency coordination and effectiveness. The committee did not make any recommendation about WMU's standing with the Convention, but did express the hope that membership and finances would stabilize. WMU officers simply cut expenses, dipped into reserves slightly, and regained the organization's composure. In no way did they favor changing auxiliary status.[20]

During the last quarter-century WMU, SBC, as an auxiliary has differed from the SBC's own agencies at three significant points: WMU holds its own Annual Meeting; WMU has an Executive Board elected by state WMUs and it does not answer to the SBC; WMU receives funds indirectly from the Convention through the mission boards.

STATE CONVENTION RELATIONS

Relationships between state WMU organizations and their state Baptist conventions have evolved differently. The last 30 years have brought major changes in the customary pattern of auxiliary status. Until 1955 every one of the 24 state WMUs functioned as an auxiliary. All but two of them had been founded as auxiliaries; Missouri and Florida had begun as departments of the state convention, but had later adopted the auxiliary form of other states. Each state had its own understanding of what *auxiliary* meant. Some WMUs received all or part of their operating funds from the state convention's Cooperative Program budget. Yet they retained the privilege of electing their own officers, selecting their own staff, and determining their own programs. Most had other sources of funds, ranging from assessments of women in the churches to special statewide missions offerings.

Geographic expansion of the SBC in the 1950s introduced an alternate form of state WMU, the department status. The older state WMUs had grown gradually, and they drew from large constituencies in well-established churches with deep pockets. But in the new areas, a sparcity of leaders and small, scattered churches struggling for financial survival could hardly afford to leap full grown into WMU structures. In some states the leaders wanted to take a shortcut by having one woman serve both as president and as executive director. This pattern was tried briefly in Ohio, Utah-Idaho, and Nevada. WMU, SBC, leaders advised against this. They saw wisdom in retaining WMU's historic two-headed organization. The president was needed as an elected officer to represent the states on the WMU, SBC, Board. She was to represent the viewpoint of the broad volunteer WMU constituency. The paid executive was to represent WMU among the professionals of the other church program organizations and do the office tasks they normally did.[21]

A major obstacle to traditional organization in the new state WMUs was money. At the request of WMU, SBC, the Home Mission Board came to the rescue. In 1952 WMU allocated, with HMB agreement, $5,000 of the Annie Armstrong Offering for Home Missions to "WMU promotion of missionary education in weak states."[22] By 1955 the amount had grown to $10,000, designated for Oregon-Washington, Kansas, and Arizona, plus $10,000 more for summer field workers assigned to help in WMUs of the new areas. The amount grew annually until the 1960s when it reached $60,000. By this time WMU was no longer controlling the Annie Armstrong Offering allocations directly.[23] Still the Home Mission Board through its state-by-state agreements continued to provide salaries and operating budgets for some state WMU offices. By 1986, 22 state WMUs received part of their funding from the Home Mission Board, and 20 state WMU directors were salaried at least in part by the HMB.

Because the Home Mission Board had funding agreements with the state conventions, the money earmarked for WMU was subject to some control by the state (always male) convention staffs. And, the money arrived too little and too late to halt a change in philosophy in the newer states. Just as WMU was being organized in Ohio (1954) and Colorado (1955), one of the old states, Missouri, suddenly switched its auxiliary status for departmental relationship to the state convention. The change was made with some reluctance and hard feelings on the part of the women. They were concerned about preserving their body of constituents and their representation in WMU, SBC. The WMU had been funded by the state convention, and that factor brought about the departmental organization.[24]

The Case of Ohio.—Missouri's change coincided with tensions about WMU in new states. Ohio WMU had been guided in organization by Kentucky WMU according to traditional plans. The Ohio president, Virginia Cross Ford (Mrs. Gerald), was also designated as acting executive secretary. With $600 from the Home Mission Board (directed to her at WMU, SBC's, request), she set up an office in the church where her husband was pastor. Women of the state were asked to contribute the operating expenses. When the first year's income was not sufficient, Ford appealed to the Ohio convention's secretary, Ray E. Roberts, for financial assistance. He, and then the state convention executive board, refused to grant the money without controls by the convention, including a budget approved by the state executive board. Roberts wanted the employed executive secretary of Ohio WMU to be responsible to him.

Ohio WMU held its convention in October 1955 and heard a request from the state convention to place their program under Roberts's management and not to "work in opposition to the state convention."[25] Alma Hunt was present at the meeting. She advised the women to hold on to their auxiliary plan and they agreed after heated discussion. Ohio WMU proceeded to employ a staff member. Despite financial aid from the Home Mission Board, lack of funds forced the women to move their headquarters into the state convention office. The convention began to allocate funds to WMU. In 1958 WMU reported that it was trying to "conform to convention guidelines." Women began to believe that the state convention was not trying to do away with their organization. In 1961 representatives of WMU and the state convention executive board concurred in the employment of Becie Shewmake Kirkwood (Mrs.

A. L.) as executive secretary. Shortly afterward, in 1962, Ohio WMU voted to relinquish auxiliary status, provided the women would be permitted to cooperate with the program of WMU, SBC. Only two women voted against the move. The process of departmentalization had cost six years and much misunderstanding.[26]

The Ohio case proved to be pivotal in the development of new state WMUs as departments rather than in traditional forms. Colorado forsook its auxiliary form after one year. When Michigan WMU was formed in 1957 and Indiana WMU in 1959, they agreed to the departmental status at the outset. Hunt was present when Michigan WMU took shape. She learned that the state convention executive secretary had visited Ray Roberts in Ohio and had decided to follow his plan. When Hunt read the proposed Michigan constitution and bylaws, she called Courts Redford, executive secretary of the Home Mission Board. "They haven't given the women a chance. WMU has no room even to exist," she exclaimed. Redford arranged an impromptu conference and negotiated a compromise that permitted Michigan WMU to be a department with some initiative.[27]

A Trend to Departments.—In 1958 another old state, Illinois, changed its WMU to department status. WMU, SBC, leaders and those in the old auxiliary states expressed alarm at the trend. It was discussed at the May 1962 WMU, SBC, Board meeting. Marie Mathis told the group: "I don't believe Woman's Missionary Union will amount to a hill of beans in 50 years if most of the states become a department." She and Alma Hunt believed that if WMU were treated as just another church program, the lay leadership that had powered WMU would be lost. They believed that the male-dominated staffs of the state conventions would not tolerate the strong initiatives customarily taken by WMU leaders. Mathis thought that the departmental plan would do away with WMU's democracy, leaving no role for the president and, therefore, no valid representation of the women on the national WMU board.[28]

Hunt pointed out that the employed WMU secretary would have allegiance torn between the state convention secretary and the women. She was suspicious of the plans which put WMU's destinies in the hands of people not elected by the members.[29]

The strong opposition of the national WMU office did not stop the departmental trend. Becie Kirkwood of Ohio, Nicy Murphy of Colorado, and Louise Berge (later Mrs. Otha Winningham) of Indiana took the departmental approach with them as they established WMU in other states. They saw advantages in department operations. Kirkwood saw to it that women were elected to the state convention executive board. She forged closer ties with pastors by having them named to the WMU committee of the state board. She felt that funds allocated to WMU by the convention were fair and adequate. The employed WMU staff members were paid on a par with men. Essential to the plan was a commitment that WMU members would retain some autonomy and participation in planning, and that WMU, SBC, plans would be followed.[30] Murphy found that the new state conventions were more open to women's leadership than were the traditional states.[31]

WMU, SBC, had its own representative in the new area in late 1961 (see chap. 3), and part of her job was to advise in setting up state WMUs. Bernice Elliott found that instead of bylaws and constitutions, the new state WMUs could work with guidelines. The guidelines of WMU of New England, adopted in 1983, would be representative. The statement characterized New England WMU as a department working with other departments to advance the total work of Baptists in New England. It was to cooperate with WMU, SBC. A WMU council made up of directors of associational WMUs and other officers was to advise in planning and in selection of professional WMU staff, though employees are subject to policies of the state convention. The WMU was to have an annual session for election of officers.

In some cases the guidelines of departments seem not radically different from auxiliary plans. Mathis had predicted that gentlemen's agreements and good relationships would be highly dependent on personalities. After a change in personnel, WMU might be in peril.

By 1968, ten state WMUs were departments rather than auxiliaries. Each was fully funded by the Cooperative Program. All but one had a WMU council or executive committee with some power of selection over its staff and ability to recommend budget. Some of the state conventions pigeonholed WMU as an educational department while others classified WMU as a missions outreach arm. Others placed WMU in an adjunct position to the state convention executive director.

Florida was among the old state WMUs that dropped auxiliary form for department. This move was strongly supported by its executive director, Carolyn Weatherford. When she broke the news to Mathis and Hunt, they showed little reaction. She was relieved, as was the state convention director, Harold Bennett, who had heard of their objections.[32] She asked for their guidance in avoiding pitfalls experienced by other states. They said nothing. Later, when Weatherford was under consideration as Hunt's successor, the selection committee grilled her about her thinking on department versus auxiliary organizations. She assured the committee that she favored only auxiliary status for WMU, SBC. When her former boss in Florida, Harold Bennett, became head of the SBC Executive Committee in 1979, speculation rose that Bennett and Weatherford might transplant Florida's experiences to the national level. Instead, Weatherford took a stand for auxiliary status nationally and in states. She expressed the hope that some departmental states would eventually reorganize as auxiliaries or with more autonomy.[33]

As of 1986, 26 out of 37 state WMUs were working as departments. The latest to adopt the plan were Louisiana and Oklahoma in 1981. Seventy-five percent of WMU membership, however, was states with auxiliary WMUs.

Reflections on the Department Trend.—The effect of the department trend on WMU standing in the Southern Baptist family is not yet clear. There has been little direct effect on the government and operation of the national organization. State WMUs with department status do not own camp property, do not have as large staffs as they once did, and as a rule do not have projects involving raising or spending money outside of routine or convention-approved plans. Whether these states' WMUs will enjoy the growth, involvement, and stability of other states remains to be seen.[34]

The department trend on the state level may be the Southern Baptist application of what happened in several other denominations 60 years ago and in the American Baptist Convention 30 years ago. The women's missions organizations merged into the male-dominated boards and women soon had little voice in them. Lucy Waterbury Peabody, a widely respected Northern Baptist authority on women's organizations in the 1920s, commented that mergers would not likely train women for their highest effectiveness. "No great plan of men which weakens or lessens this work of women or removes from them responsibility and initiative really marks a gain. Unless the church has large tasks to assign to its women with the same freedom and representation given to men they would better leave the women to their own methods. It does not matter so much about the older women who love the work enough to do it under almost any form of organization." She feared that the few women permitted places on boards of the merged organizations would not be able to hold their own against a male majority.[35] Earlier her colleague, Helen Barrett Montgomery, Bible translator and the first woman president of Northern Baptists, questioned whether men would be able to free themselves of "the caste of sex" in order to accept women's leadership in missions.[36]

Both Peabody and Montgomery seemed to write out of concern that women have a large enough place of service to protect missions. They were especially concerned about maintaining sufficient missions outreach to women in foreign cultures—the old idea of "woman's mission to woman." Their influence undoubtedly delayed the merger of the American Baptist women's mission boards into the American Baptist mission societies until 1955. Although women were guaranteed a significant number of places on the merged board at first, they were replaced by men over time.[37]

The result of mergers on missions was disastrous. R. Pierce Beaver pointed out that missionary appointments and contributions declined in denominations that no longer had an autonomous women's missions organization.[38]

Beaver's study had enormous impact on WMU leaders. Working in relative isolation from women's groups of other denominations, they had not realized that most of them had lost their autonomy at the national level and their exclusive missions focus at the local level. They were aware, however, that Southern Baptist missions efforts were continuing to grow while those of other denominations were slipping. Once WMU leaders had made the connection, they were fired with new determination to maintain their distinctiveness. Carolyn Weatherford launched her administration in 1974 with lengthy staff conferences about WMU's role in the denomination. Three commitments emerged: missions, women, auxiliary.[39]

INTERPRET AND UNDERGIRD THE WORK OF THE CHURCH AND THE DENOMINATION

James L. Sullivan, executive secretary of the Sunday School Board, 1953-75, analyzed WMU's standing as: "auxiliary to the Convention, but not to the denomination." In other words, WMU was an integral partner in Baptist life regardless of the particular organic plan being followed. In this vein WMU named as one of its four church program tasks, "provide and interpret information regarding the work of the church and the denomination." A statement to this effect has been listed fourth in WMU's tasks since 1965. It had been assumed from the beginning. From 1950 WMU suggested that the woman heading WMU in the church meet with the church council as a partner in planning a correlated church program. From the 1960s WMU recommended that its age-level organization leaders participate in cooperative planning with their peers in Sunday School, Church Music, Church Training, and Brotherhood.

These actions helped to remove the suspicion that local church WMU organizations would operate as auxiliaries, an idea that WMU, SBC, had never promoted. Some pastors and religious education specialists, however, have not considered WMU as a partner in their churches. Ryland Knight of Second Ponce de Leon Baptist Church in Atlanta told the SBC Pastors Conference in 1941 why some pastors were hostile to WMU. "Certainly one reason is because the average Woman's Missionary Society is more denominationally minded than the average pastor. Too often the pastor lets the local work retard his active interest in the great denominational enterprise. But the WMS in season and out of season carries forward unfalteringly its great missionary undertaking."[40]

Beginning in 1974, WMU, SBC, made deliberate efforts to communicate directly with pastors. WMU regularly inserted printed information in the *Baptist Program*, a magazine mailed to every pastor by the SBC Executive Committee. WMU, SBC, and several state WMUs began holding conferences and consultations for pastors, ministers of education, and ministers' wives. Beginning in 1979 WMU, SBC, assisted the SBC Ministers' Wives Conference with funds and staff services as the officers requested. Carolyn Weatherford invited key pastors to the national WMU office for a consultation in 1981.

THE ASSOCIATIONAL ORGANIZATION

Just as Woman's Missionary Union built an organization just outside the established walls of Southern Baptist life nationally and in the early state organizations, so WMU formed associational organizations along the same borders. There the women labored together in a way that showed their executive ability and strengthened their work.

Use of the associational grouping to promote women in missions was an automatic step. As early as 1882, Caroline Thornton Moss (Mrs. O. P.) was encouraging associational organization in Missouri. In 1883, Florida women had at least two "ladies associational unions."[41] The South Carolina Central Committee had a system of associational vice-presidents by 1885. The *Heathen Helper* in March 1885 published a suggestion from the Foreign Mission Board that each state central committee appoint a woman in each association to serve as its vice-president. That very month Mississippi and Virginia Central Committees began appointing vice-presidents in every association. These women had the assignment of distributing literature and organizing societies in churches that had none.

Inevitably women interested in this common cause wanted to meet with each other. The natural opportunity was at the associational meeting where their pastors, husbands, and fathers were meeting. In some associations, particularly in the West, women were seated as messengers or delegates to the association. But usually in the East, their presence was considered a mixed blessing. According to custom and the absence of other alternatives, the host church for associational meetings provided free lodging and meals in private homes. As one man was sensitive enough to observe, "The burden of entertaining our public meetings falls largely on the ladies." He thought it a pity their hospitality was not returned by their being invited to travel along to the associational meeting next year. "The most serious obstacle to the entertainment of ladies at our large meetings is found among the ladies themselves. . . . They are unwilling to entertain their own sex at public meetings . . . from the simple fact that women require more attentions than men and cannot be so easily left to take care of themselves."[42]

Such difficulties, real or imagined, fell by the wayside at the turn of the century. Women wanted to go to associational meetings and they did. But how could they have a meeting when the men tied up the church building? Sometimes they were able to borrow the church of another denomination. A popular alternative was for the women to gather under the trees or under a brush arbor, where they conducted their business amid dust and bugs. Some chivalrous men swapped locations with the women during the hot afternoons. Or the men hovered in the vestibule and under the windows to watch the women at work.

At the first Annual Meeting of WMU, SBC, the Plan of Work called for attention to the association, and this method was consistently encouraged. In the 1904 Annual Meeting Mary T. Corbell Gambrell (Mrs. J. B.) gave a ten-minute talk about improvement of associational meetings. She declared that she did not allow men to drop in and break up her meetings. She had found that women's meetings were well planned and the women speakers well prepared and well informed. By contrast, she noted that in many ministerial meetings the only features were reading of reports as follows: "Baptized, one; excluded none; gave nothing to foreign missions, gave nothing to home missions, gave nothing to aged ministers. Pray for us brethren, that we may continue faithful to the end." She did not advocate prayer to keep preachers faithful doing nothing.[43]

Whether to hold associational WMU meetings during, before, or at a different time altogether from the overall association was a continuing dilemma. If the men were on hand, the women had to "spread the proverbial 'dinner on the grounds,' . . . 'cumbered with much serving,' " so that even an hour's meeting was impossible.[44] When opportunity came at the turn of the century in most associations for women to serve as delegates, they did not wish to be absent from the general meeting. So WMUs began to meet at a separate time.

Before the 1920s, most associational WMUs were highly organized, efficient, independent bodies that met separately from the main association. In some metropolitan areas, the officers had expense accounts, honoraria,[45] and paid staff.

The corresponding secretary of South Carolina WMU in 1906 called the associational WMU superintendents (or vice-presidents) "the backbone of the Union, the muscle and sinew of their respective associations." Here is an example of why the statement is true: In 1908 a Mrs. Winters was sent from her church in Texas as a messenger to the associational meeting. At that meeting, a young woman from Baylor College was going to organize an associational WMU. Winters had to travel 30 miles in an open buggy over dirt roads. She was late getting started because her baby had been sick with croup all night. Halfway to the meeting a rainstorm came up, and she and her children had to take shelter in a farmhouse. She arrived late. Three gentlemen informed her that she had been elected president of the associational WMU. There was nothing to do but write the state WMU office to learn her duties. The other elected officers moved away. She made little progress that year, but she did want her report included in the associational minutes. Some men objected, but after debate permission was given. She and two other women were sent to write the report. Only two churches reported women's societies. But the next year, she traveled to the country churches, convinced the pastors to let her speak to the women, and organized seven new societies.[46]

Many associational WMU organizations, especially in the cities, have owned social work institutions and camps. They have had major projects such as packing boxcars with goods for orphanages, sponsoring major training conferences, and bringing guest missionaries into the area as speakers. Most early associations obtained their finances by contribution from the women's societies in the churches. As in the case of Birmingham WMU, they paid rent to the general association for office space, hired their own secretary, in some cases employed missionaries, and maintained a great deal of independence.

As WMU grew in complexity, the national officers divided the labor by taking hands off the associational organization. Each state directed its associations. Just as the state presidents were vice-presidents of the national organization, associational presidents were usually vice-presidents or board members of the state WMU. This pyramid of leadership fairly and clearly represented the members, and it was totally different from the Southern Baptist Convention's structure.

In the 1950s, the national WMU office began to share in communication with the associational WMU. The 1958 Year Book carried suggested operating plans. In 1962 the national office began publishing a bulletin for associational presidents.

Most older associations were organized as auxiliaries to the parent association. In newer state conventions, they were organized as entities of the association. WMU, SBC, ceased to recommend the auxiliary form of operation for associations, although many continue to use it successfully. WMU officers are selected by the women but elected by the association as a whole, just as in the local WMU. The pattern of meetings has continued to vary. In the 1960s some associational WMU meetings were being combined with overall associational meetings. Whereas WMU leaders had been accustomed to meeting all day for inspiration and business, now they might have ten minutes before a group not totally sympathetic with their work.

Marie Mathis and Alma Hunt wrote every associational director of missions to advise against this trend. They pointed out that WMU leaders were usually leaders in several organizations and could not

attend conferences for all at the same time. They protested the way in
which women were losing their opportunities for leadership:

> The associational officers are, in the main, men. Only in WMU
> do women have the opportunities to use leadership abilities on
> the associational, state and conventionwide levels. . . . Through
> WMU women find satisfaction in choosing their officers, having
> their executive board meetings, planning and conducting their
> meetings. In these and other ways WMU can hold the interest of
> the ablest women in the churches and can harness the woman
> power in our churches for missions. If they do not find satisfaction
> in WMU, they are going to use their leadership abilities in . . .
> secular organizations.[47]

In 1985, 95 percent of the 1,215 associations in the SBC reported
organized WMU work. Thirty-eight percent of them were performing
at honorable levels of activity. In addition to these total WMU organizations, more than three-fourths reported age-level organizations.

STANDING SIDE BY SIDE

No matter what *Auxiliary to Southern Baptist Convention* may have
meant to men and women through the years, both WMU and the SBC
have stood on the same rock. If the ground shifted, the two organizations swayed together and held each other up. Such has been their
unity.

When WMU was three years old the two bodies began adjusting their
meetings so women could participate in both. "Our best friends among
our brethren earnestly desire our presence, saying they need our inspiration," the women said in 1891, on motion of Margaretta Dudgeon
Early (Mrs. M. D.), who had been denied entrance to the 1885 Convention. So WMU curtailed sessions, and the brethren ordered their agenda
so the women could be present when the SBC considered mission
board business.[48]

Some of the women were disgruntled that they were confined to the
visitors gallery, subject to jibes about distractive hats and whispering
and crowding. One woman attempted to enter the main floor of the
1899 Convention and was pointed to a placard on a post which said
"Delegates Only." The usher said, "That shows that you cannot enter
the Convention." She replied, "I thought it meant that delegates only
were to climb the post." Another woman said, "I think that since the
100 or less lady delegates to the Woman's Convention report over
$60,000 of contributions to the Convention's boards, that they ought
to be allowed seats on the floor."[49]

In 1900 the SBC spoke directly to WMU and asked help with the New
Century Movement. This was the first official request from the Con-

vention to WMU, and not surprisingly, it was for money. The women were nervously aware of the admiration and potential reflected by this opportunity. According to the men, Annie Armstrong must join in conference with a SBC committee for the first time.

This idea frightened Armstrong into a barrage of protest letters to her men friends on the mission board staffs. She had never openly negotiated and discussed a project with men and was much more comfortable working behind the scenes. The mission board secretaries convinced her and Sarah Davis Stakely (Mrs. Charles A.), WMU president, to attend a meeting of the New Century Committee in August 1900. The men got into serious disagreement because some wanted to employ a coordinator for the movement. Instead, Armstrong played part of that role and WMU did massive amounts of clerical work.[50]

WMU's heroic response (see chap. 5) earned the women messengers' badges and seats on the main floor of the Convention of 1901.[51] Again in 1903 and in 1907 delegates to the WMU meeting were admitted to the floor of the Convention. These times, their presence was, in effect, for joint consideration of WMU's sponsorship of a woman's seminary (see chap. 11). No woman said a word, but they observed the men's positive reaction to their plans.[52]

The women were admitted again "on their badges" for the 1913 SBC, when the women presented their report directly to the Convention for the first time. This was a significant shift in WMU's role in the SBC. A year in advance Fannie E. S. Heck had gained permission of the mission boards to send WMU's report directly to the SBC, by the women's chosen man. Heck prepared the report and gave it to W. O. Carver. As procedure required, it was turned over to a committee on women's work consisting of John E. White and Carver. Like Carver, White was a friend of WMU, a close associate of Heck in the Southern Sociological Congress. They noted, and the Convention agreed:

> Whatever fears or forebodings may have existed at the beginning of the Union have long ago been overcome by the loyal wisdom which has guided it and by the undeniable tokens of Divine favor upon it. Therefore today this Convention with absolute assurance entrusts to the WMU the good task of continuance of the work of eliciting, combining, and directing the energies of the Baptist women of the South in the sacred cause . . . and makes grateful record of the fact that one-third of our increase for missionary work as a Convention has been through the treasuries of its consecrated womanhood.[53]

It was an exciting year for women. Someone proposed that the Convention hear an address by Mrs. F. H. Ingalls of St. Louis, representing the Woman's Christian Temperance Union. Some objected, but she was introduced for a brief talk in eulogy of the WCTU. This intrusion was not recorded in the Convention minutes.[54]

More significantly, Robert H. Coleman, business manager of the *Baptist Standard,* filed notice that next year he would seek a constitutional amendment admitting women as delegates on the same terms as men.[55] But Coleman was not heard from again until the mood of the Convention improved in 1917.

WMU tried to maintain its toehold in the Convention's center stage in 1914 and 1915, but to no avail. Reports were handled in the old routine. In 1916 the report was submitted by W. C. James, whose wife was being elected president of WMU. For the first time WMU's officers were listed in the SBC Annual, just as if they were officers of the SBC.

Tradition quaked again in 1916 when two officers of WMU arose and spoke. Women missionaries had been seen and perhaps heard before this time. For example, in 1900 the Foreign Mission Board introduced a missionary, Claudia White, who appeared in her Chinese dress. The Convention arose to greet her and sang "Jesus, I My Cross Have Taken." There was reportedly scarcely a dry eye in the house when SBC president W. J. Northen (whose wife was a prominent WMUer in Georgia) placed his hand on White's head and said, "My sister, in behalf of this Convention, I ask God's blessings upon you."[56]

In 1904 the Convention gave unanimous consent to a break in rules to "hear" a woman. She was Myrtle Morris, a deaf mute who was going to Cuba to open a school for deaf mutes. She stood on the stage while a man took his stand on the floor. He sang "Nearer My God to Thee," while she read his lips and interpreted. The admiring congregation rose and waved at Morris, who waved back.[57]

The next year, without plan or permission, Minnie Elliott of Phoenix, Arizona, seized the attention of the male delegates to urge that men give up tobacco and that women give up their trains and their hats that looked like inverted umbrellas, so that they might contribute more to missions. The Convention secretary was apparently so shocked that he forgot to write down her participation.[58]

In 1911 several missionaries of the Foreign Mission Board were presented, including Eugene and Annie Jenkins Sallee of China. The secretary did not report it, but Annie Sallee wrote in her diary that she spoke for about two minutes. "It was not hard. They all spoke in highest terms of my little talk." By contrast, she was given 20 minutes at the WMU meeting and a major slot before 3,000 people at the Texas general convention.[59]

These hidden intrusions of women's voices into the bass and tenor harmony of the SBC were as nothing compared to what happened in 1916. The evening session of the Convention opened in a routine way and B. D. Gray, secretary of the Home Mission Board, was presented for his report. He announced that he was giving the first 30 minutes

of his time to WMU, and he introduced Kathleen Mallory. A news report
of the meeting said,

> As Miss Mallory stood before that great congregation in her dainty
> gown of white, I wondered if it occurred to her, that dainty woman
> though she was, she was smashing a custom that was sixty-five
> years old and maybe more. I wondered, as she made her graceful
> speech if it occurred to her that she was the first woman to speak
> to the Southern Baptist Convention.[60]

The performance of Mallory and Maud Reynolds McLure that evening
in raising money for the WMU Training School ignited a tremendous
blaze of debate about women's rights in the SBC. Sparks flew between
the *Western Recorder*, still as opposed to women speaking and organizing in 1916 as it had been in 1888, and the *Baptist Standard*, edited
in Texas by James B. Gambrell.

Gambrell had spoken up for WMU many times. As a young man
presenting the women's work report in 1892, he said that he feared the
SBC did not realize a woman was a person. "We say husband and wife
are one and the husband is that one." However, he "drew the line where
the New Testament did, at the pulpit."[61] His wife, Mary, had rebutted
the *Western Recorder* in 1891 for trying to guard "the pulpit against
the sacrilegious tread of feminine feet." She assured readers that she
did not think women's work in missions would lead to violation of the
Scriptures.[62]

Mary Gambrell had made a career as notable as her husband's as
they worked together. They reared nine children, sharing the household
chores. She sometimes supported the family by teaching. Husband and
wife coedited the Mississippi *Baptist Record*. A sparkling and witty
speaker, she had been her husband's assistant when he headed the
Texas state mission board. She had helped to establish WMU in Mississippi and then in Georgia while he was president of Mercer University. Then she was secretary of Texas WMU, pulling in women's support
for missions among the Mexicans. Now she was dead, and James Gambrell could not stop grieving for her, giving instructions that at his
death his grave should be dug into hers.[63]

Perhaps the memory of Mary drove James Gambrell to make the
defense of WMU in particular and women in general one of the chief
causes of his golden years. He praised the Mallory-McLure speech as
the most thrilling moment of the 1916 Convention, and he would not
let up on his defense of women's rights to speak.

No wonder WMU selected him to present the WMU report to the
1917 Convention.[64] When Gambrell got to the Convention, he was
elected president, and he used his position to help the women. Robert
H. Coleman, his close associate, famous as a music publisher who had
sold 2 million copies of his hymnal, proposed that the SBC constitution

be restored to its original wording of "messenger" instead of the 1885 wording of "brethren," thereby opening the door for women. The motion precipitated one of the "most acrimonious debates and difficult parliamentary tangles of the Convention." Applause erupted from women in the gallery as Coleman read his motion. Gambrell ruled, amid the near hysteria of the moment, that two-thirds of the registered delegates must approve, and the motion failed. Gambrell saw that the time was not right to change, so he deferred action. He appointed a committee "On Woman's Relation to the Convention," chaired by Coleman, to report in 1918.[65]

Coleman's bold proposal to admit women as messengers to the Convention alarmed WMU. Mallory wrote Gambrell:

> Personally Mrs. James and I feel that the usefulness of our Union will be lessened rather than increased by the adoption of the amendment. The unwieldy personnel of the Convention is well known to you and we do not believe that our women would ever feel free to take part in discussions on the floor. On the other hand, we believe if membership was granted to the women that many of them would divide their time between the sessions of the Convention and the Union and not be adequately identified with the plans of either.

Speaking freely and confidentially to Gambrell, she stated that WMU's real desire was to have official representation on the mission boards.[66]

Gambrell replied that the Convention must be open to women.

> Logically women ought to be in the Convention, a body which presumes to represent all the work we are doing. The union of the forces would add strength to all the work. Women would do their best work on committees where the woman's view is often badly needed. It is to me, incongruous, that the men of our churches should control all the work, when so large a part of it is done by the women. Just as I do not want man churches, so I do not wish man conventions. The opening of the SBC to women is inevitable, just as woman's suffrage is inevitable. I favor both.
> . . . Your meeting will not be disturbed.[67]

Gambrell predicted that the number of women delegates to the Convention would not be large at first, allowing a period of mutual adjustment.

I. J. Van Ness of the Sunday School Board advised WMU to let the men fight the question to conclusion. He pointed out that the movement's supporters were friends of WMU, while its opposers were WMU's enemies.[68]

So, WMU stayed quiet about the constitutional amendment which came from Robert Coleman in 1918. When the favorable vote was tallied, approximately 80 women promptly registered as messengers amid

1,500 men. Among them were Mrs. Robert Coleman and the WMU officers of Texas, Illinois, and Tennessee.[69] After discussion, the WMU Annual Meeting voted to thank the brethren for their courtesy in granting the privilege of being messengers.[70]

Gambrell began his presidential address to the 1919 Convention by saying pointedly, "Brethren and Sisters of the Convention!" Then he proceeded to launch the $75 Million Campaign, the first truly cooperative effort of Southern Baptists, in which WMU showed its gratitude. Women flocked not only to the Convention, but also to the WMU meetings, lightened with an entirely fresh attitude about their significance.[71]

The women owed J. B. Gambrell much, and gave him an unprecedented two-page obituary notice in *Royal Service* when he died in 1921.[72] In their adoration of this man, widely beloved as the "Baptist Commoner," even WMU forgot to mention his remarkable Mary.

WORKING TOGETHER

Changing a word in the constitution did not bring women fully under the Convention roof. WMU rearranged its Annual Meeting schedule so that activities were completed before the SBC convened, and women were free to participate fully in both. By 1946 Kathleen Mallory would say, "WMU is auxiliary to the SBC and I cannot conceive of our meeting in conflict with the Convention."[73]

Whereas WMU had not argued for messenger (delegate) status, its officers did demand the right to be represented on the Convention boards, which right they had desired since 1912. WMU believed that board participation would strengthen WMU, would improve missions work with women and children, and give the givers a fair representation. "When women were admitted as messengers to the Convention they waited quietly and hopefully for some recognition, such as being asked to serve on boards and on the Executive Committee and on other such committees of the Convention," said the officers.[74]

The $75 Million Campaign gave women their first slots on Convention boards, in 1920. They had one or two representatives on the Committee on WMU Work, which continued to handle the WMU report, and Kathleen Mallory was on the Inter-Board Commission for Student Activities. WMU wanted more representation, so its Annual Meeting petitioned the SBC in 1921. Their memorial was presented to the Convention, at WMU's request, by L. R. Scarborough, president of Southwestern Baptist Theological Seminary and general chairman of the $75 Million Campaign. "Our sole aim is the progress of the cause of our Lord and Master and for this reason alone we desire to see the Woman's Missionary Union grow along with the Convention in usefulness, in power, in vision."[75] The request was for WMU to nominate 9 representatives on the SBC Executive Committee and 12 on each of the five boards of the Convention. This was WMU's most direct demand of the Convention in a century.

The resolution touched off intense debate and was initially approved, then rescinded, with instructions for a committee to bring a further report in 1922. Only one woman was named to a Convention board in 1921. The Education Board, headed by the husband of WMU president, Minnie Kennedy James (Mrs. W. C.), gained a local board member, Alberta Williams Bush (Mrs. T. G.) of Birmingham. The women waited quietly.

In 1922 the SBC began by saying that representation would be decided according to "personal fitness including women as well as men." Further attempts to get a guaranteed quota of women on each board, led by W. J. McGlothlin, president of Furman University, failed. When nominations to committees and the boards were reported, only 23 women were named. Instead of one-fourth to one-sixth of each entity being women, women composed one-eighteenth to one-ninth of the boards and none of the Executive Committee. Clearly WMU was upset and so reported to its members.[76]

All the women members of the major boards were local members. That status meant they were more involved in daily operations, but less prominent as true representatives of the broad constituency. By 1933 five local WMU leaders were on the Foreign Mission Board, and each had long years of service. Not until 1935 did the Foreign Mission Board have an out-of-state member, Mrs. W. C. Henderson of Arizona. Later Cora Cowgill McWilliams (Mrs. George) of Missouri was elected in 1941; Foy Johnson Farmer (Mrs. James S.) of North Carolina in 1954, and Marie Mathis of Texas in 1954. Amy Compere Hickerson (Mrs. Clyde V.) of Virginia was the first woman to chair a FMB committee, in 1955. Not until 1942 did the Home Mission Board have a state representative, Mrs. Raymond H. Morrman of Virginia. Willie Turner Dawson (Mrs. J. M.) of Texas pioneered as the first woman on the Relief and Annuity Board, a position she retained for many years. Myrtle Robinson Creasman (Mrs. C. D.), one of WMU's most popular personalities, found her service on the Sunday School Board to be bittersweet. For years her husband, a Nashville pastor, had longed to be on the Sunday School Board. When the call came, it was for her, not him, a turn of events she found painful. Without exception, all women board members until the 1980s were WMU leaders, usually state WMU presidents.

The first women on the SBC Executive Committee were state WMU presidents: Laura Armstrong of Missouri and Annie Newton Thompson (Mrs. Ben S.) of Georgia, named in 1927. They were voted into office at an 11th-hour session of the Convention. In 1929 Harriett Ellis Levering

(Mrs. Eugene) of Maryland took over the unexpired term of her husband. Armstrong, who was one of the chartering members of the revised Executive Committee in 1928, became president of WMU, SBC, in 1933. She naturally welded WMU to the SBC through that medium. When she suddenly died in office in 1945, WMU keenly felt the lack of represen- tation on the committee. In the next year, the new president of WMU, Olive Martin, and Sarah Joe Hurst Burney (Mrs. Frank) of Georgia were added to the committee. Not until 1953, on action of Porter Routh, executive secretary-treasurer of the Executive Committee, was the WMU president made an ex officio member of the Executive Committee. Three of the four women on the SBC Executive Committee in 1976 were former state WMU presidents.

WMU was not content with the unevenness of women's represen- tation on boards. In 1941 Laura Armstrong agitated privately for more women to serve on the mission boards, not as WMU's representatives, but as women. She was prompted to do this because someone had questioned the constitutionality of a woman serving as a state member of a board, when her best friend, Cora McWilliams, was being consid- ered for appointment from Missouri.[77] McWilliams then served on a Foreign Mission Board subcommittee that decided not to amend FMB bylaws to mandate further women's representation.[78] Apparently, Arm- strong had decided not to press her point.

The first woman to chair a SBC committee was Bertha Hicks Turner (Mrs. J. Clyde), president of North Carolina WMU, who chaired the committee handling WMU's report in 1938. Afterward the officers of WMU composed this committee. Blanche White was the first woman on the SBC Order of Business Committee, 1946 and 1948. Janice Sin- gleton, WMU executive secretary of Georgia, served on the committee in 1947. Since 1950 WMU officers have been ex officio representatives to the Baptist Joint Committee on Public Affairs. Carolyn Weatherford served two years as vice-chairman of the BJCPA.

The number of women did not improve until after 1958, when SBC bylaws were changed to require laypeople on SBC boards. This change was facilitated by Porter Routh, a layman himself. In 1938, only 2.4 percent of board and committee members were women. By 1943 the percentage had risen to 4, perhaps because of Laura Armstrong's quiet campaign. The number fell to 2.2 percent in 1958, then slowly rose to 3.5 percent in 1968; 5 percent in 1973; 8.4 percent in 1978; and 10 percent in 1983.[79] The 1921 standard of women's representation re- quested by WMU has not yet been met.

During the 1980s the process of naming boards and committees became politicized amid controversy rocking the SBC. Porter Routh, retired and a recognized expert on SBC operations, suggested to Charles Stanley, president of the SBC in 1985, that he name the presidents of the state conventions and of the state WMUs to be the Committee on Committees, thus bringing guaranteed democracy and fairness to the committee's makeup. He had previously made that proposal to Bailey Smith when he was president of the Convention. Neither president took his suggestion.[80] In 1985 an attempt was made on the floor of the Convention to replace nominations for the Committee on Boards with the state WMU presidents and state convention presidents. The procedure was ruled out of order by Stanley.[81]

Nominees and Officers of the SBC.—The matter of women officers of the Southern Baptist Convention was never directly pressed by WMU, but the few prime women candidates for office have emerged from WMU. The first woman ever nominated for SBC office was Willie Turner Dawson, proposed for vice-president in 1923. Sixteen persons were nominated and the top four vote getters were declared vice-presidents. Dawson was not elected.

No other woman's name was mentioned until 1963, when Marie Mathis was completing her first term as president of WMU and the organization was celebrating its 75th anniversary. Porter Routh, sitting on the SBC stage, prompted Leonard Sanderson of Texas to nominate Mathis for second vice-president. She readily won, and simply said the victory was recognition of WMU.[82] A subsequent motion to limit Convention offices to men was ruled out of order.

The former president of WMU, Helen Long Fling (Mrs. Robert), was nominated for second vice-president in 1973 and for first vice-president in 1974. These were years of controversial resolutions and debate concerning women's role in the church, and Fling was nominated as a means of affirming women. She was defeated in the runoff election both times, although she had been elected second vice-president of Texas Baptists in 1967.

Marie Mathis was nominated for president of the SBC in 1972 by Russell Dilday, an Atlanta pastor who was to be president of Southwestern Seminary. She did not make the runoff.

Myra Gray Bates (Mrs. Carl) of North Carolina in 1975 became the first woman to make a nominating speech in the Convention. She herself was elected second vice-president in 1976. WMU considered her a sympathizer although she was not nationally known as a WMU leader. Anita Bryant of Florida, a well-known entertainer not affiliated with WMU, was defeated in a bid for first vice-president in 1978.

When Christine Burton Gregory (Mrs. A. Harrison) went out of office as president of WMU in 1981, she was elected first vice-president of the SBC. In 1983 Dorothy Elliott Sample (Mrs. Richard), then in office as WMU president, was defeated in a nomination for second vice-president.

The first woman ever to preside over a meeting of the Southern

Baptist Convention was Laura Armstrong. Southern and Northern Baptists planned joint sessions in St. Louis in 1936 to celebrate the centennial of Baptist missions in China. The program planners put Armstrong in the chair for one of five sessions.

Balanced participation of women in Southern Baptist Convention business, especially on the floor of the Convention, still has not come. In the 1940s the custom of having a committee on women's work (or on WMU) to bring the WMU report was dispensed with. Since then WMU officers have routinely brought their own report in a small ten-minute slot. On two or three occasions the SBC and WMU held joint sessions. In 1926 WMU published a leaflet, "On Being a Delegate," to tell women how to flex their powers in the Convention. This step was synchronized with WMU's published plan to win 50 percent of the Cooperative Program for the Foreign Mission Board.

Again in 1986 WMU issued information for potential messengers. This was an extensive training kit complete with teaching aids for group study about the workings of the SBC. Entitled *Missions and the SBC*, it was introduced to help persons know how to protect the SBC's missions work amid controversies about other matters.

Perhaps the high point of women's participation, at least a moral victory, came in 1929. The 1928 Committee on WMU Work recommended that Ethlene Cox, president of WMU, be officially invited to address the Convention in conclusion of WMU's 40th anniversary year. Scarcely a word had been heard from female lips since 1916, and Cox had a wide following as a speaker. When the 1929 Convention opened in Memphis, J. W. Porter brought a resolution from the Kentucky Baptist General Association protesting any woman addressing the SBC, on grounds that it would be unscriptural. Porter said, "Eve tempted Adam. Now the SBC is tempting women. The women would do all right if the petticoated preachers would leave them alone." M. E. Dodd, pastor of First Baptist Church of Shreveport, replied, "In Christ Jesus there is neither male or female. We are one in Christ." Applause greeted Dodd and a "thunderous avalanche" of "noes" greeted Porter's resolution. He picked up his hat and left.

George W. Truett was presiding. Quite a crowd assembled in the Memphis Municipal Auditorium. Cox, tall and beautiful, musical of voice, said, "No woman went to sleep in the garden. No woman denied Him. No woman betrayed Him. It was the women who followed Him to Calvary and wept for Him. It was the women who were at the tomb."[83]

In the 1956, 1957, and 1958 Conventions, many women, all WMUers, led in prayer and spoke. For the next 20 years few women went to the podium except WMU officers bringing their reports or routine business, with the exception of Virginia Robinson Chandler, who chaired the denominational calendar committee in 1975 and 1976. The first woman

to chair an SBC agency was Margaret Fraser Bryan of Tennessee, chairman of the Southern Baptist Commission on the American Baptist
Theological Seminary in 1980.

From 1976 until 1981, women served on the Convention Order of
Business Committee. Included among them was Betty Collins Gilreath
(Mrs. J. Frank), president of North Carolina WMU and recording secretary of WMU, SBC. Others were Gladys Sherman Lewis (Mrs. Wilbur
C.), a WMU leader from Oklahoma, and Marian Grant (Mrs. Marse),
journalist from North Carolina, who served as chairman. While they
served, several women were given spots of prominence on programs.
The percentage of women serving as messengers of the SBC varied
from 33.5 percent in 1968 to 42.1 percent in 1978.[84]

WMU has always adjusted its activities to fit the schedules of the
Convention. The Convention in turn has since 1925 chosen its Convention sites to meet the requirements of both meetings. Since 1950
the SBC has paid rent for WMU's meeting place and has generally made
provisions for WMU's accommodation along with its own arrangements.

SBC COORDINATION

Approximately once a decade for 80 years the SBC has had crazes
to coordinate, and WMU has been affected by these.

WMU, SBC, has never initiated a coordination move or tried to take
over work already being handled by another agency. WMU has taken
the posture of filling unmet needs relating to missions, especially with
regard to what women and children might do. If others entered the
field later, WMU has not usually resisted giving up its own workable
programs. Not until the 1960s did WMU become a strong campaigner
for coordination.

The first coordination move came in 1917 after several years of
growing competition between WMU and the Baptist Young People's
Union organizations for children. From the earliest days of the nationwide Baptist Young People's Union of America, Annie Armstrong had
been skeptical about the organization. She did not like its coeducational
classes in which girls were encouraged to make speeches to boys. Yet
she corresponded regularly with the BYPUA offers in Chicago and
coordinated WMU study topics with the mission study course of that
group.

When Southern Baptists broke away to form their own BYPU, WMU
voted this rule: "As the baby reaches out to mother for help and
guidance, let the WMS take hold of the BYPU, the latest admitted
organization, and guide it to right channels."[85] Armstrong saw that the
BYPU could destroy Sunbeam Band and urged that the two groups be
kept separate.

The BYPU came under management of the Sunday School Board and began to emphasize age-level groupings. By 1916 the BYPU field worker and the WMU secretary in Georgia had decided to merge the junior organizations of each. This move caught the unfavorable attention of both the Sunday School Board and WMU general officers. I. J. Van Ness, Kathleen Mallory, and Minnie James carried on amiable, scant correspondence about the matter, each desiring to reach the best solution for common good. But the age-level workers were more intense. WMU's youth secretary, Mary Faison Dixon, stated, "There is entirely too much and too vigorous life in our organization for a funeral to be in order now."[86]

Field workers of both organizations reached agreement which WMU freely publicized. WMU offered to conduct the junior BYPU organizations, to combine with them, or to promote GA and RA separate from BYPU, according to local church needs. "There is no danger in teaching too much missions," Kathleen Mallory wrote.[87]

When Oklahoma WMU consented to a merger, however, WMU officers again got involved in discussions. They no longer wanted to "mother" BYPU, as suggested by Oklahoma's WMU secretary. They wanted distinctive girls and boys missions organizations. The merger movement was canceled and the two organizations worked out distinctions. The BYPU was to meet on Sundays, give overall inspirational attention to missions, support stewardship in general, and be a coeducational organization. WMU's programs for girls and for boys were to meet on weekdays, conduct serious study of missions, raise money for special missions offerings, and remain segregated by sex.[88]

Calls for Coordination, 1923, 1937, 1946.—The next siege of coordination was instigated by the 1923 Southern Baptist Convention when a committee was appointed to correlate and define work of the various Convention activities.

The Coordination Committee decided to "recognize the great and valuable work of the WMU, yet realize that there are some points where a closer cooperation and understanding are needed." When the report was brought to the SBC, a minority report was presented by S. E. Tull of Arkansas, long a critic of WMU. He suggested that a massive Education Board be formed, absorbing WMU and other church programs. His motion failed, and WMU seemed to take little note of this controversy. A committee was formed to coordinate WMU and the rest of the Convention programs, but it was never powerful.[89]

At the 1937 SBC, again came the call for coordination. WMU had anticipated this one. A study committee was appointed, chaired by M. E. Dodd. Laura Armstrong represented WMU, along with representatives of the Sunday School Board, Brotherhood, pastors, and the two foremost religious education experts: Gaines S. Dobbins of Southern

Seminary and the WMU Training School, and J. M. Price of Southwestern Seminary.

WMU leaders sensed that there might be a takeover attempt on their girls and boys organizations. When the study committee made a survey of changes Baptists wanted, WMU called in the faithful to respond. *Royal Service* told the women that "to ignore this appeal is to dodge your duty." They were asked to get their pastors to write the committee why they believed WMU organizations were needed for young people.[90] The net result of the committee's work over three years and more was that WMU made few changes. It joined other agencies in recommending a church council to coordinate church activities. WMU called on W. O. Carver to be prepared to speak its defense at the 1939 Convention, but this was not necessary.[91]

The 1946 SBC again demanded a solution to "too much organization" and "too complex plans." Dobbins was carried over from the 1937 committee as chairman of a coordination study group. Price also was appointed. Not surprisingly, with two religious education professors on the team, the committee decided to use religious education principles to coordinate and revise the church program. WMU, with a reputation of being too rigid to negotiate, had a pipeline into the committee via Carrie Littlejohn of the WMU Training School, who conversed regularly with Carver and Dobbins. Carver, as usual, tried to keep peace.

Kathleen Mallory and Ethlene Cox met briefly with the committee before Mallory's retirement, and the leading women thought they were treated unpardonably. Olive Martin tried to get Dobbins to say exactly what he wanted WMU to do. She claimed she was keeping an open mind, unlike the old WMU regime, but she also considered Dobbins to be naive. Dobbins already had drafted a plan for a simplified church program which eliminated WMU's young people's organizations and proposed that the women meet on their own outside the church building, so they would not disturb the church's efficiency.

A massive research project revealed that few pastors desired to change or eliminate any church organization. But a 1947 report made a point of saying that "here and there" a few favored combining WMU's youth organizations with Training Union's.

Martin called in defenders from the Foreign Mission Board and the Home Mission Board. Women inside WMU considered that Martin saved the WMU youth and children's work by standing "like a stone wall during this agitation of Dr. Dobbins's committee."[92]

The net result of this era of coordination was the establishment of an effective Inter-Agency Council in 1948. Martin and Alma Hunt served on it from the beginning. WMU and the agencies cooperated in compiling a *Guidebook* for pastors which summarized the plans, standards, and literature for all organizations. The correlated Church Study Course was established, but without WMU's full support until 1961. The church council was strongly promoted. Many of the original proposals of the Dobbins committee were shelved. Certainly no public suggestion was ever made that WMU relinquish its age-level organizations. Instead, WMU drew closer to a fully functioning in-church program.[93]

Hunt, new on the scene of denominational coordination, believed that WMU was not the center of the problem as much as were the three competing church programs administered by the Sunday School Board. Nevertheless, WMU leaders became defensive against attacks on their children's organizations. In reality, the critics of WMU must not have been numerous, for no changes were ever enforced on the organization. Perhaps there would have been, had Hunt not opened her door to dialogue with different groups in the denomination.

Committee on Total Program.—In 1955 a Texas layman, Carr P. Collins, proposed that the SBC appoint a committee to study the total program of the Convention. Collins was named to the committee and lost no time in stating his agenda. Among many other major changes, he wanted to redefine the status and work of WMU, which he viewed as too independent. Later his sights settled on abolishing Carver School of Missions and Social Work.[94]

When the Committee to Study the Total Southern Baptist Program settled down to work, it had two women members, both active in WMU. Omer Shermer Alford (Mrs. John I.), president of WMU of Georgia, served as secretary of the committee. At its first meeting, at Carr P. Collins's ranch, a member of the committee proposed to Alford that Sunday School classes instead of WMU teach missions once a month. J. M. Price, who had served on previous correlation committees, met with the new group to express his concern that church programs were growing more cumbersome. Some committee members pointed out that Southern Baptists were growing more successful. Although some WMU members feared that the committee might recommend a drastic program change such as was mentioned to Alford, it never came. "Conflicting opinion can be resolved with patience, love, and persistence," she wrote later. James L. Sullivan believed that the Sunday School Board, not WMU, was the target of those who set up the committee.[95]

The Committee on Total Program suggested that WMU continue as an auxiliary, continue to perform the same functions, and continue coordinating its activities through the SBC Inter-Agency Council. The committee suggested that the agencies take care not to duplicate the missions education programs. The Committee on Total Program also set in motion the process which caused Carver School to be merged into Southern Seminary.[96]

Moving Toward Unity.—While the Committee on Total Program was working, WMU was discovering its own way into greater unity with the SBC agencies. President Marie Mathis was named to an interagency committee to plan with Southern Baptists and other Baptist groups in the US. Called the Baptist Jubilee Advance, the cooperative effort for six years led up to the 150th anniversary of the first Baptist convention. This was the Southern Baptist Convention's first attempt at long-range planning, and WMU was in the thick of it. In 1958 WMU adopted themes and goals for the years 1958-64.[97] Each year's theme was tightly tied to the Baptist Jubilee Advance. Never had WMU planned so comprehensively, so far in advance, or so intelligently with kindred groups.[98]

When the Baptist Jubilee Advance culminated in 1964, Mathis was at the heart of creating and staging fabulous dramatic presentations of Baptist cooperation. These were presented at the WMU Annual Meeting and the Southern Baptist Convention, which met jointly with the American Baptist Convention. She tried to show on stage the excitement she personally felt about the power of Baptists when they cooperate around the cause of missions.

Genuine coordination of church programs, and major changes for WMU, came because of a remarkable group of leaders. Marie Mathis as president and Alma Hunt as executive secretary of WMU were at the forefront. They feared neither cooperation or coordination. They trusted the men heading the other involved agencies and genuinely enjoyed working with them. Among the circle of leaders who accomplished what had been impossible for 50 previous years were Porter Routh and Albert McClellan of the Executive Committee; James Sullivan, W. L. Howse, and W. O. Thomason of the Sunday School Board; and George Schroeder of the Brotherhood Commission. Marie Mathis was considered highly influential among this group, serving as a unifying agent between the theoretical ideas of the committee room and the practical needs of ordinary WMU members.[99]

The SBC mandated coordination in 1959. W. L. Howse was architect of the process from the church program point of view. He and his assistant W. O. Thomason wrote a document called "The Educational Task of a Church." This was the origin of "tasks" later described in a pivotal book, *A Church Organized and Functioning*, published in 1963. Howse and Thomason identified five church programs: Sunday School, Training Union, Church Music, WMU, and Brotherhood. Each was assigned a set of unique tasks to perform for the church. The sum of the tasks gave a balanced content for a church program.

Unlike earlier attempts at coordination, this plan did not hint at elimination of WMU. Instead, Howse and Thomason acknowledged WMU, hailed its strengths, and eliminated features of other programs which duplicated it. Although the Sunday School Board staff planned to concentrate on the design of programs around the tasks of Sunday School, Training Union, and Music, they wanted WMU's program to be considered in order to avoid overlap. From the beginning they asked WMU officers to evaluate their manuscripts and made adjustments to suit the women.[100]

The SBC vote of 1959 required that a Convention organization manual be prepared. The SBC Executive Committee coordinated the work of having each agency write a program statement, having the statements reviewed and duplication or conflict removed by the agencies, and then getting Convention approval. McClellan asked if WMU would like to be included in this process. The WMU Executive Board voted in 1963 "that WMU invite the Executive Committee, SBC, to study its background, programs of operation, relationships with the other agencies, and to formalize for WMU's consideration a program statement similar to that being prepared for the other agencies."[101]

"The Church Is Central."—With this statement WMU was seeing itself as one of the family, even an agency of the SBC. WMU began the process of programming at the January 1964 Board Meeting with addresses by Howse and McClellan. In typical WMU fashion, the entire elected Board, the state WMU staffs, and the WMU, SBC, staff shared in training for the coordinated church programming of the future.

Already WMU staff had accepted the SBC's invitation to be involved in planning the cooperative denominational emphases for 1965-68. These grew out of the Sunday School Board staff's work in defining the functions of a church. A different function was examined each year: worship, proclamation, education, ministry. At the Home Mission Board's insistence and with WMU's support, a fifth year's emphasis on missions and evangelism was added for 1969.[102]

WMU officers later admitted that they had not understood all the concepts proposed when they took each step of cooperative planning with the other agencies. But Alma Hunt was sure of one thing: WMU would not be ignored or left behind. In October 1964 WMU's top staff decided to hold monthly meetings with the staffs of Sunday School Board and Brotherhood. Eventually WMU was taking its entire professional staff to Nashville each month, and the chief managers were meeting 16 times a year. W. L. Howse was to call the six years of intensive work together the most productive period in the agencies' history.[103]

The willing cooperation of WMU, without any pressure from the SBC, was a powerful influence on the Sunday School Board and Brotherhood. The SSB and Brotherhood had been ordered to coordinate. The departments within the Sunday School Board were strongly competitive internally. Seeing WMU's officers voluntarily sitting at the conference table motivated the other program leaders to compromise. WMU had shed its splendid isolation, buried all shreds of auxiliary reputation in the churches, and voted to do what was best for the whole.[104]

WMU consciously made room for Brotherhood to step into equal partnership in the missions task, a role WMU had been urging on the men for at least 40 years.[105] In October 1954 Hunt had said, "I dream of the day when the Brotherhood becomes the missionary organization for men in the church, giving to men the same opportunities women and young people have in WMU." Twelve years to the month later, Brotherhood introduced its first full-fledged missions magazines. Hunt told the women to "welcome the Brotherhood organizations in the churches as partners in missionary education."[106]

The changes WMU made between 1964 and 1974 were perhaps the most drastic and significant of the century. WMU had always developed its plans by pulling together two different poles: the worldwide cause of missions on one hand and the practical abilities of an individual woman or child on the other hand. It was a major shift when Hunt said, "Woman's Missionary Union is committed to the belief that the church is central in all planning."[107]

The commitment of WMU to union with the SBC agencies was never clearer than during this decade of change. Elaine Dickson, as assistant to Marie Mathis, was responsible not only for formalizing WMU's process of change, but also for much of the interagency coordinated planning. For example, she wrote a study paper, "Basic Understandings of Program Design," which was adopted by the Inter-Agency Council in 1967. This paper has continued to be the foundation of church program development by all SBC agencies. Dickson then wrote WMU's first formal program design documents.

In 1966 WMU and the SBC adopted WMU's program statement. The statement assigned to WMU the objective of promoting Christian missions. Because every agency of the SBC had a program statement and the agencies were all coordinated to eliminate overlapping, WMU had clear sailing as a specialist in missions.[108]

Distinctive Tasks and Organization Changes.—Cooperative planning led to significant changes for WMU. In 1964-65 WMU introduced the task statements to its members. Leaders of the five church programs had agreed to these statements. In 1966 WMU published the first results of cooperative curriculum planning (see chap. 8). In 1965 WMU pushed social ministries to a new level by introducing mission action. In 1968 WMU unveiled a new organization plan for its adult organization. Overall plans and terminology matched those of other church programs. In 1970 came the most sweeping change of all: new organization names, age groupings, and publications, all altered to conform to a uniform age-grading plan used by each program.

Then the officers drew the line. They were willing to change anything but the distinctive work and purpose of Woman's Missionary Union. Alma Hunt in 1971 issued a forceful memo to 35 men and 1 woman who made up the interagency program coordination staff group. She stated that "unified" did not mean the end of distinctive tasks. WMU refused to approve a proposed design for a small church that did not encourage WMU age-level organizations. WMU refused to approve a proposed design for an association, and another proposed for a state convention, because they did not include WMU as a beginning point. Likewise WMU refused to go along with statements of curriculum content that did not treat missions as a unique arm of education.

> We cannot deny the right of any agency or department to promote the idea that its own organizaton be reduced or done away with. We do, however, strongly deny the right of any agency or department to promote or encourage directly or indirectly the weakening or destruction of another agency. WMU has not agreed to reduce organization beyond the reductions made in 1968, when new organization patterns were adopted. WMU has not agreed to reduce involvement of persons in carrying out its purposes in churches or associations, or on the state level.[109]

Meanwhile, the changes had cost WMU significant numbers of members and dollars. But the result was a coordinated, doctrinally and educationally sound church program that gave missions and WMU a spotlight. A loyal core of 1 million members stood by WMU, and WMU stood by its agreements to keep its actions coordinated. After W. L. Howse retired, the Sunday School Board bowed to pressure from some state convention officials and revealed a plan to take over part of WMU's work. Hunt said, "I felt I had seen the best years of my life go down the drain along with WMU's resources in personnel, budget, and time. We have given our utmost since 1959 to the programming process and cooperative efforts within the Convention framework."[110] She successfully blocked the announced change of plans.

The statistical result of ten years of change was dismal: Enrollment was down in every church organization, with WMU and Brotherhood hardest hit. The percentage of Cooperative Program funds leaving the state conventions for SBC-level work, including the mission boards, was down. The Committee of Fifteen was named by the SBC Executive Committee in 1970 to study the SBC structure against the goals of the old Committee on Total Program.

Marie Mathis was named to the Committee of Fifteen, but she resigned in order to give the committee freedom to examine WMU's program objectively. When the committee published a draft of its report in 1973, it claimed that Baptists had less missions information than in the past. It recognized WMU's enrollment drop and attributed this to an overemphasis on mission action rather than missions education. It expressed concern about WMU's financial losses.

WMU issued a rebuttal. Pointing out that there were few gauges for measuring the level of missions awareness among constituents, WMU claimed that awareness was increased, not decreased. The major increases in special missions offerings were pointed to as evidence. WMU reminded the committee that only four years had elapsed since task assignments were fully implemented and suggested that any alterations would be premature and demoralizing.[111]

The Committee of Fifteen reported to the SBC in 1974 and recommended that WMU and the other church organizations reevaluate task agreements. Also WMU was asked to work with the mission boards and Brotherhood to develop a strategy for using all channels of all agencies for missions education.

WMU's response was to hold steady. The WMU Board was convinced that the women in the churches would tolerate no more change. As WMU had told the Committee of Fifteen, "time will heal the changes," and WMU wanted time for the decade of cooperation and change to bear fruit.

WMU officers were more concerned about the Committee of Fifteen's impact on the mission boards than on WMU. Baker J. Cauthen of the Foreign Mission Board was particularly disturbed. Porter Routh negotiated a compromise that called for another committee, which became known as the Missions Challenge Committee.[112] Helen Fling, former president of WMU, was one of its members. Suddenly, for the first time in WMU's life, the entire Southern Baptist Convention was serious about doing missions and teaching missions.

While the committee worked, WMU continued its cooperation in planning unified promotional emphases and long-range planning. Sitting with a group planning the end of the 1970s decade, Marie Mathis insisted that the SBC must end the decade with missions, bold missions. She coined the phrase which became the slogan not only of the 1977-79 denominational emphasis, but for the remainder of the century: Bold Mission Thrust.[113] This emphasis came onto the horizon just as the Missions Challenge Committee reported in 1976. WMU was in a three-year emphasis on teaching missions. The Missions Challenge Committee affirmed the continuation of Bold Mission Thrust and recommended that WMU, Brotherhood, the Sunday School Board, and the two mission boards develop broader plans for missions education.

Carolyn Weatherford, the new executive head of WMU, considered that a wholesome respect permeated relations among Convention leaders. She found that WMU staff were participating in more than 20 major interagency committees and teams.[114] WMU went into the 1980s in unity with a Convention where missions was mushrooming in volunteerism, increased giving, and thrilling strategies for taking in more territory around the world. Membership and finances in WMU stabilized, as predicted. The correlation and combination efforts of the 1970s cooled into the coordination and cooperation of the 1980s.[115]

A CORD OF THREE STRANDS IS NOT QUICKLY BROKEN (Eccl. 4:12)

In the beginning there were just three: Foreign Mission Board, Home Mission Board, and Woman's Missionary Union. Nothing ever separated them. For 25 years WMU undertook no plan without recommendation of the boards. When the Sunday School Board was added in 1891, and when the Layman's Missionary Movement (later Brotherhood Commission) appeared in 1907, the union became even stronger.

The five-strand cord was visibly demonstrated in 1977 after the SBC's Missions Challenge Committee asked the five organizations to make a plan using all the resources of all the churches for promotion of missions. Carolyn Weatherford stood with the men who headed the SBC agencies and pledged to do that. The same five agencies reaffirmed that pledge in 1986. Their daily contacts and coordination are fulfillment of WMU's original philosophy that "in union there is strength."

Annie Armstrong gave the model for interagency relationship when the Sunday School Board first tried its wings. She furnished the Board with a mailing list. She gave James M. Frost names of key frontier missionaries. She interceded with the missionaries, whom she knew well from having arranged their boxes of supplies, to accept and promote the Sunday School Board.[116] She led WMU to send boxes to the missionaries (field workers) of the Sunday School Board. She and her sister wrote for the Board publications. She could easily promote the use of the Board's publications because their content was in reality WMU's story. She led the Board to establish, and the women to contribute to, a Bible Fund, which in turn she helped various missionaries to tap for free Bibles. Armstrong said, "It is getting to be appreciated that the Woman's Mission Societies can do a large work not only in raising money, but in creating public sentiment."[117]

One of Armstrong's chief contributions to the SSB was to help it gain the upper hand on its chief rival, the American Baptist Publication Society. This publisher, controlled by Northern Baptists, had sold its products without competition in SBC territory. Such persons as J. B. Gambrell withheld warm support from the SSB because it competed with a publisher that was reinvesting money in state missions projects. In fact, this opposition deterred WMU from giving approval to the SSB for a few months. Armstrong was in a position to strengthen the SSB, because the main officers of the ABPS were former Baltimoreans, friends of hers. Her own church used their literature. But she believed in exclusive Southern Baptist unity. Pressured by the ABPS to let them use her name, she said, "The secretary of the Woman's Missionary Union is not for sale." She refused to let Publication Society representatives speak to WMU audiences.[118]

Armstrong arranged for Missionary Days in the Sunday School, serving as liaison among the three boards to prepare the curriculum material. This special day, begun in 1895 and later divided into separate observances for home missions and for foreign missions, raised money for missions. In 1958 Missionary Day was moved into relationship with the weeks of prayer for the respective mission boards, being observed on the last Sunday of the week. To benefit the SSB Bible Fund, Armstrong devised Children's Day and prepared literature for it.

Quickly the SSB proved a success. Even though personal relations between Armstrong and Frost became strained in 1905-06 because he favored the WMU Training School and she opposed it, Frost never failed to heap praise on her. "She was largely the inspiration and guiding genius of [the Bible Fund] and in many ways helped to give the Sunday School Board its proper rank among the forces which make for denominational life. . . . Woman's Missionary Union and the Sunday School Board have from the first given themselves to each other's work in many ways, and will go down in history as agencies working together for the building of the kingdom."[119]

The SSB contributed generously to WMU's operating expenses. Whenever WMU had a special fund-raising project, such as the Tichenor Memorial Church Building Loan Fund, the SSB made a handsome gift. Each building built by WMU, at the Training School in Louisville or at the national office in Birmingham, elicited a significant contribution from the SSB and the Board contributed to WMU's rent from 1921 until 1949. The SSB contributed funds to the WMUTS to assist with the teaching of religious education.

WMU owes its publishing ministry and resulting revenues to the SSB, which was in a position to take these over in 1906. Instead, Frost and his successor, I. J. Van Ness, did all in their power to help WMU succeed as a publisher. Beginning in 1964 WMU sold nonperiodical literature through Baptist Book Stores, operated by the SSB. The SSB and WMU agreed on sympathetic rates for wholesaling. Next to Broadman Press, WMU publication sales became the largest sold through the stores.

When WMU moved to its new national office building in 1984, the Sunday School Board sent a handsome Holman pulpit Bible which every employee signed on the first day of work at the new site. Then at noon, lunch arrived for all 150 workers on hand. Later, the Board delivered a beautiful set of pulpit furniture.

In 1915, as Fannie Heck, president of WMU, lay dying, she told the young WMU secretary, Kathleen Mallory, to arrange the support of a few trusted friends. Mallory wrote J. M. Frost asking if he would be her confidential adviser. He readily consented. One of his words of advice to her was this: "You will never lose anything in all your perplexing problems by staying close to our denominational policies."[120]

CLOSER THAN BROTHERS

The three-strand cord of WMU, Foreign Mission Board, and Home Mission Board has stood the test of time. Anything that can be said about developments in the mission boards has a footnote in WMU history. Alma Hunt frequently said, "WMU has no program of its own. Our program is that of the Foreign Mission Board and the Home Mission Board."

By 1948 M. Theron Rankin of the Foreign Mission Board was stating the relationship in contemporary terms, calling WMU the FMB's "channel to the churches."[121] This became clearer in the 1960s when inter-agency programming defined WMU in just that way. Neither the Home Mission Board nor the Foreign Mission Board offers programs for churches (although they offer resources and information to churches). Activities in local churches necessary to the accomplishment of work on missions fields are conducted by WMU or Brotherhood.

In many ways, the Home Mission Board stands even closer to WMU than the other brother agencies. In its strategies in church planning and development, in Christian social missions, in black church relations, in interfaith witness, in establishing new state conventions, and in fostering associational work, the HMB views WMU as ally and partner. The Board's funding of a department of work at the WMU national office and its support of state WMUs gives evidence of this close unity.

Not purpose alone, but also relationship have found the three organizations together. The accumulated correspondence of WMU executives with their peers at the mission boards shows remarkable tenderness, sharing of mutual woes, "in honor preferring one another."

In much counsel there is wisdom.

Laura M. Armstrong (Mrs. F. W.),
1939 Executive Committee
meeting

Louder, please

Grateful for the social and intellectual elevation of women,
the result of Christianity, and above all for the hope of
salvation it inspires; impressed with the importance of carrying
to the homes and hearts of our oppressed and degraded
sister in other lands the Gospel which has done so much for
us, we . . . have associated ourselves together.

Constitution (1872), Woman's
Missionary Society of Richmond

OMAN'S Missionary Union members have seldom uttered complaint about their own status in church or society. In the formative days of WMU a glance at their non-Christian sisters in the neighborhood, or a glimpse of the status of women in heathen lands convinced them to be grateful for the liberation they already enjoyed. The hope of early women's missions organizations was to pass their liberation on to women of other lands. The president of the Foreign Mission Board told the women at the first annual session of WMU that their privilege was "to tell these low ones of the gospel which makes all equal; to teach that Jesus is the truth; to lift up these women. . . . This work is purely unselfish. When we work for home it is selfish, it betters us. It takes faith to go to heathen lands."[1]

The more WMU members worked to lift women abroad, the more they lifted themselves and the women of their communities. While rejecting all visible affiliation with the woman's rights movements, they campaigned for the liberation of women from the shackles of men who were "heathens, infidels, alcoholics, and slaveholders." WMU leaders disclaimed any concern for their own rights, but they prayed and gave money in order that other women might experience liberation through Christ. The efforts for women abroad changed the roles of the women at home. Their spheres of influence enlarged, their unused abilities were in demand, and their outlook broadened. This link between woman's rights at home and abroad became known among other evangelical women as the "reflexive influence of missions."[2]

Some historians now recognize that heroic women missionaries of the nineteenth century, such as Ann Hasseltine Judson (Mrs. Adoniram) and Lottie Moon, were powerful role models for American women. They were activists while angels, skilled while submissive, daring while demure. Few could fault women for teaching their daughters to aspire to be missionaries.

In Southern Baptist life, the most progressive woman after the missionary was the Woman's Missionary Union leader. While every pressure in the culture of the South and in the custom of Baptist churches wanted to confine her to the home, the WMU activist lengthened her tent cords. Her sphere became the world. She traveled, she was knowledgeable, she managed, she led, she spoke. She was attractive and well groomed, she had exciting friends, she received mail from abroad, she knew the meaning of world news. She could pray, she could talk about her faith, she had the strength to help others find Christ. The WMU leader became a role model for her sisters and daughters.

Not one national officer of Woman's Missionary Union in a century has campaigned for woman's rights in the political or secular sense. Some privately favored these. Others were opposed. Each was willing to wait for history to deliver changes to her or to the next generation. These leaders had more important things to do, things of eternal significance. Within a century, their work for others reflected on themselves, and change slowly came in the roles of all Southern Baptist women, as an indirect result of WMU.

"LET THE WOMEN KEEP SILENT" (1 Cor. 14:34).

When Helen Long Fling (Mrs. Robert) was a little girl, she wanted to grow up to be beautiful, charming, and graceful like Mrs. J. E. Leigh, secretary of Texas WMU.[3] But she also wanted to be able to make speeches like Willie Turner Dawson (Mrs. J. M.), a state WMU officer who was reputed to be a better speaker than any man except one.[4]

Helen grew up to be president of Woman's Missionary Union and her voice was heard around the world. She was one of many women who learned to talk in a mission society and found themselves public spokespersons for the gospel.

Fear of women speaking publicly choked the development of Woman's Missionary Union for 15 or more years before 1888. The women organized in a secret whisper. They discovered their voices in prayer, rehearsed quietly before women only, and when invitation came, opened their mouths to pour out words that changed the course of history. Without WMU, women might never have reached the stage of Southern Baptist leadership.

No sooner had the SBC begun to permit formation of women's mission societies than the brethren began to get nervous about women speaking. John A. Broadus told the Southern Baptist Convention of 1881 that the missionary movement required caution against "the idea of women speaking before promiscuous assemblies."[5] Broadus was a professor at Southern Baptist Theological Seminary and widely acclaimed for his book *A Treatise on the Preparation and Delivery of Sermons.* He believed that women might speak in ladies parlor meetings, but never in the presence of men.

Courageous women trying to organize mission societies quickly took their cue. Caroline Thornton Moss (Mrs. O. P.), certainly a fearless character, told the statewide organization of Missouri women whom she headed: "The Southern Baptist Convention has spoken! With absolute unanimity they have pronounced against the sisterhood going beyond, and above what God says." Moss urged the women in their official capacities as representatives of the cause of the Foreign Mission Board not to speak in public mixed assemblies with men. "It breaks the 'ban' which enforces 'silence,' " she said.[6]

As the battle for organization raged on, women like Alice Armstrong of Baltimore were glad to agree to restrict their speaking to meetings of women only, if they could be granted that much privilege.[7]

The month before WMU met to organize, Broadus warned the women again about speaking. He tied this outrage directly to the woman suffrage movement. He gave his blessings to women speaking in female prayer meetings and mission societies, provided men were kept out. He warned, "Beware of some 'entering wedge' in the shape of an editor or a masculine reporter." He believed that Southern Baptist women would not mind obeying the Apostle Paul's order to Corinthian women to keep silence, because they so readily obeyed his order to keep heads covered by wearing hats to church.[8] Broadus's writing may have been deliberately generated by the editor of the *Western Recorder*, who was frantically trying to fend off the organization of WMU.

The first generation of WMU officers firmly believed in keeping silence before men. Many sincerely believed this rule was required by the Scriptures; others adopted the custom as politically expedient. Martha McIntosh did not like to speak in a mixed audience, because the opponents of WMU organization believed that women who did so would lose their modesty in speaking.[9] Lottie Moon hesitated to speak or to lead worship before men, even unconverted Chinese. On her furloughs in the United States the male leaders of the Foreign Mission Board had a hard time getting to hear this famed missionary.[10] One of WMU's earliest guidance manuals for women's societies stated that public meetings might be held, especially on the annual anniversary, perhaps on a Sunday evening at church. But reports must be read by the pastor or some other gentleman friend.[11]

WMU operated its own Annual Meetings under the strictest rules. Its first annual session, 1889, began with singing. A. J. Diaz, missionary in Cuba, was introduced to speak. Fannie Breedlove Davis (Mrs. George B.), president of WMU in Texas, where women's voices were sometimes heard aloud, noticed gentlemen crowded around the door. She made a motion that they be seated. The motion was all but carried when Annie Armstrong objected. This was a women's meeting and must be kept as such, she said, and demanded a standing vote. The men were sent away. One woman was heard to remark, "I don't think they ought to be selfish over a good thing." A neighbor replied, "The men are as bad as we. They won't allow women at the Convention. I am real glad they won't let them in."[12] The men were excluded from WMU Annual Meetings for 20 years, entering only when invited to speak and leaving immediately. The women took that long to gain confidence that they could speak up without endangering their standing before God or man.

But behind closed doors, they were not silent. They were learning to speak. Eliza Broadus, privileged eldest daughter of the forbidding Professor John, was one who learned. She was a vice-president of WMU, SBC, representing Kentucky. The 1889 meeting was her first experience speaking in a big church full of women. "I did not know how to speak louder when a call came, 'Louder, please.' But I determined to learn: I practiced in churches at home and my father helped me to articulate each syllable." Telling this experience in later years she said, "I mention this because so many women do not seem to know they can improve their delivery."[13]

Early Annual Meetings often included discussion of the problem of women speaking. "How can our women be trained to lead in prayer in their own meetings?"[14] The problem was real. The women addressed it head-on. One writer stated:

> A dozen ladies in a parlor together always find something to say, and a way to say it, and 'tis said they often all talk at once; but take the same dozen ladies, put their bonnets on them, seat them in straight rows in the pews of a church and call them a missionary society, and what a change comes over them! They are actually afraid of their own voices, and sometimes are too faint-hearted to make a motion or even second one.

The writer suggested that if pews prohibited, the women should arrange chairs in a circle. If their Deep South custom forbade speaking in the house of God, they should meet in a home.[15] When Willie Kelly was leaving for China in 1894, Alabama WMU had a farewell service for her. "They were so timid they spoke in whispers lest the men hear them," she recalled. Kelly was amazed when she returned to the US in 1940 and found that WMU, SBC, was said to be the largest deliberative body of women in the world.[16]

The limits enforced by WMU, SBC, catered to the middle of the road. On one hand were extremists who doubted that women should speak even to women. On the other hand were women like Mary K. Oldham Eagle (Mrs. J. P.), who had been ousted by the Southern Baptist Convention in 1885. She was one of the first women to speak in an Arkansas state convention, in 1896. The bar fell in Alabama in 1909, when Grace Hiden Wilkinson, a state WMU officer, spoke about the relief needs of aged ministers. Mary Northington, state WMU secretary, spoke for the WMU report to the Tennessee Baptist Convention in 1925. The last state convention to allow a woman to speak was Kentucky in 1961.

As ears unstopped to hear women, opponents resorted to ridicule. Women were informed that their speaking out was keeping men away from church. "Many a church is dying in the borders of the North because the women insist on doing so much of the talking in all kinds of meetings." Not only did women have to bear guilt because they outnumbered male church members two to one, but they were also pronounced unfit for public address because of delicate nerves. Speaking was said to make them unwomanly, hardened, uninviting. "Can any woman afford to do this, on slight grounds? ... The outlook for marriage in the case of multitudes of noble women is exceedingly unpromising."[17]

John A. Broadus may have been training his daughters to make speeches, but he could not recapture his words of 1888. By 1890 his writings were circulating in a leaflet, "Should Women Speak in Mixed Public Assemblies." Some women were outraged and arranged for rebuttals to be published in denominational papers.[18]

Mina Everett, who was the first missionary among Hispanics in the US, also served as the paid WMU organizer for Texas. After hearing her speak to a group of women, a man said, "Sister Mina ought to be heard in every Baptist church in the state." The Home Mission Board, Foreign Mission Board, and Texas board joined in her paltry support. Riding on buckboards and freight wagons, suffering from sunstroke and dehydration, she spoke her way across Texas. R. C. Buckner said, "Sister Mina, every time I hear you talk, I want to give." Everywhere she spoke, the funds for missions rolled in at a phenomenal rate. Men began to insist on hearing her. She was reluctant. "I wanted to do right. . . . I prayed. . . . I was awake much of the night. . . . The restful calm which came about noon on Sunday, I perceived as an answer to my prayer. . . . I said, 'Yes.'" In 1895 she was severely criticized and the mission boards cut her pay because she had crossed the bounds of propriety. The women gladly took up her support, but in 1896 she resigned: "I wished not to be a hindrance to even one."[19]

On the East Coast few women would have shown Everett's audacity. One woman appealed for a halt to criticism of WMU women:

Should we be termed woman's rights because in a little company

of women only we tell of the needs of the heathen and lift voices
in prayer and praise determined in a humble way to brighten
the world because the risen Lord tells us to go? Must we bear
stigma because we speak a word for the master. . . . The idea of
calling us woman's rights! Why our cheeks are made to tingle
with blushes. . . . Let us say to those who antagonize our Woman's
Missionary Societies that never with God's help will the women
of South Carolina ascend the rostrum or let our voices be heard
save in our own retreats.[20]

Caught in these crosswinds, Annie Armstrong and the WMU, SBC,
Executive Committee took their stand. Texas WMU wrote to Baltimore
for advice about Everett's case.[21] Armstrong replied: Let the women
keep silence if men are in the house. T. P. Bell of the Sunday School
Board and Isaac Taylor Tichenor of the Home Mission Board advised
her that southern women would ruin their reputations if they spoke to
mixed audiences. Armstrong was not collecting their opinions out of
idle curiosity. She wanted the WMU Executive Committee to form a
definite opinion about the Baptist Young People's Union, which encouraged boys and girls to meet, study, and speak together. The opinion
was unanimous: silence for women; opposition to the BYPU.[22]

Armstrong understood Paul's biblical writings in the most literal
sense. She agreed with Broadus's writings, and despite his daughters'
more moderate opinions noted, "Dr. Broadus is in his grave and can
no longer exercise his authority in the matter."[23] Arriving in Oklahoma
City and finding that she was expected to "take care of the services"
at First Baptist Church on Sunday morning, she refused. After she
refused a string of speaking engagements, a preacher said, "Miss Annie,
do you not know there are women preachers in Kansas?" She replied,
"I am not one of them."[24] If a man wanted to hear Annie Armstrong
speak, he had to lurk outside the door or lie down in a church pew
out of her sight.[25]

Armstrong sacrificed herself on the horns of an outdated custom
when she tried to hold back the tide of women preparing to proclaim
the gospel professionally. When she walked out of the halls of WMU
in 1906, she left the doors open for men to come in to hear the women
speak.

Outstanding women orators sprang forth from the next generation
of WMU officials. Charles A. Stakely, husband of the former president
of WMU, SBC, told Southern Baptist Theological Seminary students in
1912 that God did not exempt women from the call to proclaim the
gospel. He further told the men students that "these women are not
going to sit under an ignoramus for a preacher."[26]

E. Y. Mullins, president of Southern Seminary, admitted that his views
on the subject of women had changed. "The practical impossibility of

interpreting literally the passages which some of the brethren are insisting upon about women keeping silence in the churches has convinced me that that interpretation was wrong. . . . I have no compunctions about changing my view on a question of this kind.[27]

Mullins commended James B. Gambrell for agitating the "woman question" in the *Baptist Standard* of Texas during 1916.[28] This was Gambrell's way of preparing for a major change in the constitution of the Southern Baptist Convention—admitting women as messengers.

THE WOMEN POLISH THEIR SKILLS

If the women were going to have opportunity to speak, they must polish their skills. "Louder, please" became a standard phrase of WMU meetings. When a young woman prepared to read a report at the 1907 Annual Meeting, Fannie E. S. Heck whispered, "Speak loudly." By 1903 the women felt at home meeting in a church auditorium and speaking from the podium, whereas they had been confined to Sunday School lecture rooms in earlier years. The officers could not be heard from the podium, however, so they "descended from their high estate" to desks at pew level.[29] Until the later 1920s women spoke at WMU Annual Meetings without benefit of amplification equipment. The body grew to more than 1,000 delegates who actively debated. Ability to speak loudly was a necessity. Women with placards or electric light signs were stationed at the back of the room to remind speakers to give more volume.

In 1924 Kathleen Mallory reported that the huge WMU Annual Meeting was handled with superb parliamentary skill and that many women speakers could easily be heard in a big church building. "It was marvelous also, to see how patiently the women sat through the long sessions and how little whispering was indulged in."[30]

For many years WMU's how-to publications advised women about how to make a speech: "Try to make any remarks in a simple manner, and directly to the point. Do not try to go on after you have finished what you have to say. In reading, or speaking, or leading in prayer, do it in a way that your voice may be heard."[31] Even in the 1950s the WMU Year Book regularly gave help to the women speakers: "Remember the audience is watching every move. Acquire platform poise. Keep head and shoulders erect and both feet planted firmly on the floor." Much guidance was given to the presiding officer: "Don't stand while a report is being read or while the secretary is reading minutes. Do not sit down until the speaker has risen. Do not leave the speaker on the platform alone. Do not comment on the speaker's message. The presiding officer is the link between the speaker and the audience."

When WMU officers began to receive invitations to speak at Sunday church services and to speak at male-dominated state conventions, they reached beyond mechanics of platform behavior for help with content. *Royal Service* carried instructions on how to make "a Bible talk." A leading authority on the subject was Ella Broadus Robertson (Mrs. A. T.), another daughter of John A. Broadus. She drew from the principles her father taught seminary students about Bible exposition: use of study tools, selection of a topic, making an outline. She advised a slow delivery, with low-pitched voioce, loud enough, practiced, calm. After writing her short course copied from male standards of speaking, she made "a very feminine suggestion":

> When a woman speaks or presides she ought to look as if she had just stepped out of a bandbox, and she doesn't have to be expensively dressed to look that way. Think in advance, leave early.... The family and telephone can be depended on to furnish all the complications one can stand at the last minute.... Forget yourself, think of those you wish to help and lift your heart to the Lord for whom you are to speak.[32]

A decade later Ella Robertson wrote a Bible study on Moses, noting that his education had not included public speaking. "All boys should be taught that nowadays; girls too, for many are the club-meetings and missionary meetings for women."[33]

WMU was aware that it was rearing a new generation of speakers through the missions organizations for girls. Parliamentary law was taught and girls were enrolled in declamation contests. Young women's camp programs in the 1940s included daily conferences on public speaking.

Public speaking was not neglected at the Woman's Missionary Union Training School. Elocution was in the earliest curriculum. By the 1920s the students had special coaching in storytelling by Annie Williams of Birmingham, a WMU member who was the first woman field worker of the Sunday School Board. WMU officers routinely visited the school to demonstrate the state of the art in female speech making. By 1930 a full public speaking course was offered. Explaining to WMU members why this was necessary, a school representative wrote: "Our aim is to present the application of fundamental principles to the interpretation of simple storytelling, of masterpieces of literature, the Bible and hymn reading."

The school's faculty was concerned because "self-consciousness and timidity are 'bushels' under which so many of our splendid women are hiding their lights while countless multitudes grope in darkness." The speech course became a department in 1942 and every student was required to enroll. Half of the students were ministerial students' wives who were studying diction, oral Bible reading, and public speaking. The principal of the school stated, however, that since there were no women preachers in the SBC, the school had no women studying for this field of work. "Southern women don't seem to take to preaching. They recognize that there are so many other important fields where they are needed," said Carrie U. Littlejohn. Another WMU leader commented, "It is right that women do everything in the church—everything but preach."[34]

Likewise, the Woman's Training School at Southwestern Seminary stressed speech making. Under the management of Ray Osborne McGarity (Mrs. William B.), daughter of the founder of the *Baptist Basket*, all the women students studied with Jeff Ray. He was listed as teacher of public speaking in the training school (for women), but as professor of homiletics in the school of theology for men.

After years of practice in public speaking, most WMU officers had come to peace with the Apostle Paul's prohibitions on women speaking in church. One woman sardonically wrote: "Paul could not have had missions in his mind when he gave the injunction that if the women of the church of Corinth wished to 'learn anything let them ask their husbands at home.' We wonder how many husbands could tell us very much about missions and mission work and missionaries. A good way for the women to keep silent in the church would be to get some intelligent layman (spare the hard-worked pastor) to conduct the adult classes [mission study]."

Royal Service urged women as a matter of "church courtesy" to bear two-thirds of the responsibility for winning souls, since women made up two-thirds of the congregation. "We are not seeking the rostrum but great duties devolve upon us. Only once have we ever wished to see a woman in the pulpit and that was on 'Mothers' Day' when a dear young bachelor pastor told the mothers in Israel how to raise their families . . . That was but a passing vision. Woman can best bear her share in the Kingdom service in other ways, such as missionary intelligence, Sunday School teaching, relief work, and above all in praying."[35]

WOMEN SPEAKERS IN THE LIMELIGHT

In the 70 years that women's voices have been heard as speakers in Southern Baptist realms, many have gained notable reputations, but none outside the nurture of WMU. The $75 Million Campaign put women in the Baptist speakers' limelight. Kathleen Mallory was the first woman, apparently, to deliver a major address at a Baptist state convention. She spoke in 1919 to the Missouri convention. Observers reported that she was delightful, her address "chaste, informing, and inspiring."[36] That same year WMU put one of its best speakers on the road to organize for the $75 Million Campaign. She was Janie Cree Bose, later to be principal of the WMU Training School. But she was already known

as "an unusually interesting and forceful speaker." On her tour of
Florida she and Charlotte Rinckenberger Peelman (Mrs. H. C.), secretary
of Florida WMU, spoke during church services.[37]

By 1926 Alma Worrill Wright (Mrs. Carter), a sparkling orator who
had taught elocution in a college, was a favorite speaker on tithing and
stewardship. As WMU's southwide stewardship chairman she made
between 156 and 223 talks per year.[38]

Perhaps the most awesome woman speaker was Ethlene Boone Cox
(Mrs. W. J.), president of WMU 1925-33. A news reporter covering a
speech wrote:

> She has a clear musical voice that easily carries to the utmost
> limits of any ordinary auditorium. Her dignified, yet easy, manner,
> her scintillating mind, her deeply pious spirit, thoroughly cap-
> tivated her audience. . . . Mrs. Cox cannot be adequately reported
> by this scribe. The fact is, he was so spell-bound that he found
> when she had finished her matchless address that he had only
> the meagerest notes. . . . You must hear her to appreciate her
> fully.[39]

Juliette Mather, who served on the WMU staff from 1921 until 1957,
had powers to move audiences. On her first week's assignment she
spoke in Arkansas, and 28 persons made decisions about Christian
commitment.[40] Petite, energetic, feisty, inspiring, she was at her best
speaking to young people. At age 79 and again at age 84 she captivated
crowds of more than 10,000 girls at National Acteens Conventions
speaking on the potentially boring subject of current events and their
impact on missions.

Blanche Sydnor White served as a WMU, SBC, field worker, 1922-24,
before returning to Virginia as WMU secretary for the state. A compelling missionary speaker, she attributed her skills to the instruction
of Minnie Kennedy James (Mrs. W. C.), president of WMU when White
began her career. James told her to read the minutes of WMU through
from 1888 before stepping out in public. And she said, "Blanche, be
sure to curl your hair when you go on the platform. The women are
faithful and they have to look at you, so make it as painless as possible.[41]

Emma Leachman was reared to be quiet in church, not even to vote.
Her pastor and her mother were both strict on these points, so she
was greatly frustrated when she realized that God was calling her to
missionary service. She prayed in the orchard and cornfields until sure.
When she walked forward in a protracted meeting to inform her pastor
that she was willing to serve as a missionary, he took her hands and
said, "Emma, I have felt for a long time that God was calling you. God
bless you."

She later wrote: "How far from either thought or imagination that I
would ever be called upon to stand before a Baptist audience of five

to seven thousand people to plead with them to love the Lord more
and to serve him better."[42] Though famed as a speaker, she found it
difficult to communicate effectively in church services.

> In the first place, the majority of men object to a woman speaker
> at the preaching hour. They don't know why they do, but they do.
> It takes the first fifteen minutes to convince them that I am telling
> them something they ought to know. The second fifteen minutes
> they become deeply interested and concerned. . . . Fifteen minutes
> is a heavy dose of missions for some folks.

Willie Turner Dawson rose through WMU ranks to be one of the
most acclaimed speakers of three decades. She was married to J. M.
Dawson, pastor of First Baptist Church of Waco and later head of the
Baptist Joint Committee on Public Affairs in Washington. J. M. Dawson
was renowned as a speaker, but he was proud that his wife was said
to be better than he.[43] She used her gift of speaking to spark an enormous growth spurt in the Lottie Moon Christmas Offering during the
depression. She raised money for a dormitory at Baylor University in
the same period. She leaped from her success as a speaker for Young
Woman's Auxiliary work into the circuit of college campuses, Baptist
conventions, and churches. One of her engagements was a week of
mission study and evangelistic meetings in connection with Young
Woman's Auxiliary in Atlanta, resulting in many conversions and re-
consecrations.[44] She was closely associated with George W. Truett,
sometimes regarded as the greatest preacher of the century. A member
of his family claimed, "She was the greatest woman speaker that we
had and she could beat any of the men but Brother George."[45]

No wonder Alma Hunt was advised by her college president in 1948
that the WMU executive secretary's job, in the final analysis, would be
a speechmaking job. He later evaluated her performance speaking before the Southern Baptist Convention: "Your voice was pleasing. Do
not change it. Do not cultivate that 'sweety' voice that has sometimes
been heard in WMU. You were perfect."[46]

As WMU's leading model speaker for 25 years, Hunt ruled on many
points that became standard female platform etiquette: never cross
legs on the platform; carry a white handkerchief; while seated on the
stage keep eyes fastened on the one speaking; do not touch your clothes
or straighten your skirt. By 1964 she had dispensed with the gloves
previously required to be held, but not worn, on stage.

Hunt was occasionally invited to speak in male domains during the
1950s. But as the 1970s arrived she and other women speakers were
in constant demand for conventions and Sunday church engagements.
Her successor, Carolyn Weatherford, from 1974 onward rarely missed
a Sunday speaking in morning or evening worship services.

A FORCE FOREORDAINED

The history of WMU women as speakers is only one example of WMU's impact on roles of women as public leaders in Baptist life. Opposition to women speaking was a surface indicator to more basic issues.

Annie Armstrong wrote at the turn of the century: "The Savior's precious words of commendation of a woman's service have been ringing down the ages. . . . But not until the 19th century was 'the fullness of time' in which she heard and heeded the Master's voice which summoned her to untried, enlarged and systematic endeavor." She considered WMU to be "a force fore-ordained of God." She considered that force suitable only for the advancement of missions.[47] On the subject of women's roles, she talked as conservatively as anybody, but the force of her actions was to lead women to do things they had never considered doing before.

Like Armstrong, many of the WMU founders saw themselves initially in a limited sphere of home and heart. Fannie Coker Stout (Mrs. John), one of the two major speakers at the 1888 meeting, a women whose husband was one of the strongest advocates of women's organization, quoted critics of organization. Critics feared that women would become unwomanly, that they would leave the sphere that God had ordained for them, that they would assume a role for which they were not intended, that they would succumb to the desire for fame, that they would seek place and power. Stout thanked those who had alerted the women to these dangers, but said that if the women waited until such dangers no longer existed, they would be "safe in the heavenly home" before they could organize.

> The brethren are our guardians, and if they have feared for us, and tried to hedge us around, it is a proof of their concern, and when they realize what we want to do, that we do not wish to wander in any dangerous ways, but are only trying to follow them as our leaders and trying to carry into practice what they have taught us from pulpit and press, their anxieties will cease.[48]

Armstrong's own horizons began to enlarge, and she spoke of "growing ability, and of decreasing impediments to progress, which inevitably lead to a fuller understanding and acknowledgement of our position as factors of usefulness in the world's advance and evangelization. We thereby lose not an iota of womanliness."[49]

Women's work in the church still had its bitter opponents. A pastor speaking to the WMU report at the Southern Baptist Convention in 1894 compared WMU with a yoke of contrary oxen that so exhausted the patience of the farmer that he knocked them in the head. His advice, readily understood by the WMU officers, was, "Knock the women's work in the head."[50]

When such an inflammatory statement was made, one of WMU's many defenders would either make public rebuttal or comfort the women privately. One of the kindest in this regard was Henry Allen Tupper, secretary of the Foreign Mission Board, 1872-93. According to his daughter, the first president of WMU in Alabama, where opposition was particularly bitter: "He warned against being discouraged by opposition . . . that no good thing had ever failed to arouse opposition but that the great lever for overcoming it was kindness. He advised the Central Committee to make no resistance . . . by gentleness and kindness to disarm criticism." Even John A. Broadus told Eliza when she was discouraged, "Just keep on daughter. The stars in their courses will fight for you."[51]

After 20 years the WMU officers began to see that they had been incidentally part of a major shift in culture. WMU published this statement:

> The "Woman Question" still claims consideration. The old idea was that the place and work of woman was in the home . . . unostentatious service in the church and private charities . . . The new view . . . would grant woman all civil rights except the ballot and all religious privileges except the pastorate of a church. . . . There is sex in souls and woman's moral nature is thinner, more delicate, deeper, more intuitive than man's, always refining, instructing and ennobling his. . . . Yet you do not want merely the passive virtues.

The leaflet continued with the idea that a women's missionary society develops activistic Christian qualities in a woman: conscientiousness, courage, sympathy, and self-devotion.[52]

Just as women believed their work to be divinely mandated, so did men come to recognize it. W. J. Elliott told the Ministers Meeting in Montgomery, Alabama, in 1900:

> This remarkable movement of the Christian women, embracing all classes of women . . . is evidently of the Lord. This onward movement has not been without obstructions and barriers; but one by one they have disappeared, and now it is too late to set limits to the achievement and aggressions of 'Eve's daughters.' It is gratifying to know that our Southern women are not seeking to rule in the church and state. All they want is to cooperate with men in trying to save souls and build up the cause of our Master.[53]

B. H. Carroll of Southwestern Baptist Theological Seminary once visited the WMU Executive Board of Texas and urged them to disband. He explained that he had organized the women of his church as he wanted them to be and directed each group to handle certain duties. Mina Everett spoke through Carroll's ear trumpet, "Will you tell us, Dr. Carroll, by what scriptural authority you direct your women's work?" Looking at her in quiet dignity, he laid aside his ear trumpet and ended the discussion. The WMU did not disband. Fourteen years later he came back with praises and endorsements, and the women turned over their training school in Dallas to his seminary. This story was cited by a later generation of WMU leaders with this moral: "If it required such a colossal intellect 14 years to reverse his opinion, why grow impatient with lesser lights who are obdurate?"[54]

WOMEN ACCEPT THE HIGH CALLING

Only after women had won the right to vote, and after WMU had proven its indispensable powers in the $75 Million Campaign, did WMU leaders speak of the woman's movement. Minnie Kennedy James (Mrs. W. C.) quoted another officer as saying: " 'The women movement' has moved with amazing momentum and irresistible power and the time has come when we must widen yet further the widening work of our WMU." In this context James led WMU to demand a quota of representation on Southern Baptist Convention boards.[55]

By 1928 WMU occasionally provided studies of the history of women in various cultures, in the church, in the Bible, and in missions. Such studies usually began with the belief that women's first obligation was to make their own homes and children Christian. The studies pointed beyond this sphere to a woman's responsibility for making her community Christian. "We can help the Christian women of other lands put Christ into the 'woman's movement' of the world," said James.[56]

The leaders of WMU for the most part have believed that women are innately qualified for the work of missions and personal ministries. Martha McIntosh believed: "Man deals with the great things of life; woman with its details. Man makes governments, orders politics, controls taxes, forms great financial combinations, carries in his mind and heart the care of wife and children. . . . But woman, made to be man's helpmeet, not his rival, transfers this feature of her character into every department of life." McIntosh was willing to leave to men the big appeals for missions, while women worked with individuals.[57]

WMU publications occasionally referred to WMU as "The Great Mother Heart of the South," and men missions leaders also believed that the maternal instinct motivated the women to serve in missions.[58]

Acknowledging that a woman was mentally, morally, and spiritually fitted for any vocation and any Christian service, Lillie Easterby Barker (Mrs. J. A.), president of WMU, believed that a woman's best powers were called into action in the home. "That is pre-eminently her sphere.

There her influence for missions can be strongest." Though childless herself, Barker believed that a mother's hands in the clay of her child's unformed character was the greatest missions accomplishment.[59]

Between 1907 and 1963, ideals of women's role in Southern Baptist life were highly influenced by the WMU Training School. Approximately 4,000 young women who would become leaders in Southern Baptist life studied there under W. O. Carver. One of the earliest missiologists, and one of the top scholars ever produced by Baptists, he had a reverent appreciation for women and missions and Woman's Missionary Union. Carver said to WMUTS graduates in 1941:

> A too masculine cast has been given to interpretations and ex-positions [of the Scriptures]. Jesus Christ has not been thoroughly understood nor has his mind found full expression in the polity and procedures of his churches. . . . Now the time has come when women in their freedom must accept the challenge of the high calling, and demand of men a reevaluation of themselves and a readjustment of social responsibility. The hope of the hour and of the future lies with Christian womanhood emancipated from masculine subordination by the freedom of truth in Jesus Christ; and in Christian men and women accepting the high calling of God in Jesus Christ to work together for the saving of mankind to the glory of God.[60]

Yet Carver's students did not demand or revolutionize. Carver also stressed mutual subordination of men and women as a Christian tenet. He stressed self-sacrifice. "The oppressed and suppressed elements of society were not taught or encouraged to go forth crusading for rights. Christianity calls upon its followers to serve, not to assert themselves." His students and his readers in WMU publications found fulfillment in both professional ministry careers and in WMU leadership, assured of their worth to God's cause.[61] A survey of WMUTS students conducted in 1985, including persons who studied in the school over a 54-year period, indicated that the women were well satisfied in their life roles.[62]

WMU AND THE WOMAN'S LIBERATION MOVEMENT

At the dawn of the modern woman's liberation movement, WMU presidents still believed in women's unique powers in missions. Helen Fling told the Southern Baptist Convention in 1964:

> God has endowed woman with certain feminine qualities of com-passion needed in a world of sin . . . Has thrust upon her awesome responsibility but has offered spiritual resources commensurate with that responsibility. Woman's role in the kingdom is not competitive to man's, it is complementary. . . . Woman's function

is that of a supporting helper, her position is auxiliary, and her service is essential. . . . We believe that woman's greatest power lies not in her bank balance, not in her stocks and bonds, nor even in her ballot, but in her power to mold human lives and influence society.[63]

WMU failed to herald the modern woman's liberation movement. WMU publications took no note of it until 1970 and the possibility of changed roles for women in church was scarcely mentioned before that year. During the 1970s, the escalation of involvement and influence of Southern Baptist women was predicted.[64]

Marie Wiley Mathis (Mrs. R. L.) wrote in a major position statement for WMU: "By nature women are sensitive to human need. This innate sensitivity, endowed by God, has caused women to respond in self-giving ministries to meet the needs of persons in Jesus' name. By nature women are creative. A woman's function in society requires that she cultivate her creative instincts. . . . By nature women are helpers. In the design of God this role is natural and right."[65]

As the woman's liberation movement accelerated in the 1970s, WMU officers were constantly quizzed by news reporters. Mathis and Alma Hunt acknowledged that the movement would have its effect on WMU and on Southern Baptist women. One reporter concluded that while militant churchwomen in some denominations were "storming the pulpits . . . other soft-spoken women are following a circuitous route to high church positions." Mathis said, "Don't think we're not progressive." Hunt added, "We're just not militant."[66]

The 1973 WMU Annual Meeting acknowledged the woman's movement, featuring a young woman, Saralyn Monroe Collins (Mrs. Marshall T.), doing monologues about a woman contemplating changes in her role. "Through Christ, we have achieved the greatest freedom and liberation possible. WMU can help women find their rightful place and make this place one of service."[67] Kenneth Chafin, speaking in WMU's opening session in 1973, urged WMU to be true to its historic purposes and femininity. The woman's liberation movement, he said, would influence WMU. "I'm convinced that WMU ought to become the largest and most influential women's organization in the world," he said.

These comments about the woman's liberation movement and WMU caused one member in the audience, Jessie Tillison Sappington (Mrs. Richard Lee) of Texas, to bring a resolution to the Southern Baptist Convention later in the week on the "Christian woman vs. woman's lib."[68] Helen Fling was on the resolutions committee which processed the resolution, and the committee sent to the Convention quite a different statement, one that "gave recognition to women in leadership roles in church and denominational life." Sappington succeeded in replacing the committee's resolution with one which affirmed "that

God's Word teaches that woman was made for man, is the glory of man, and that they are dependent one upon the other."[69] In intense debate, messengers understood that Sappington was opposing liberation of women and was desiring that women be subject to men.

The national officers of WMU sensed a criticism of WMU in this action. Marie Mathis, giving the WMU report later in the Convention, attempted an indirect rebuttal. She re-emphasized WMU's auxiliary, helper role in the Convention; at the same time she cited examples from the Bible of the courage of women in following Jesus. To the WMU Executive Board, she wrote: "I am disappointed [in the Sappington resolution] and I do believe . . . that this may turn in our favor rather than against us."[70]

In the 1974 Annual Meeting, Alma Hunt said in her retirement address: I believe Woman's Missionary Union lifts a woman's perspective above the kitchen sink, or above the desk, or above the industry where she works to see a world in need and to see that she herself can have a part in it. I believe that WMU enables women to be molders of circumstances rather than victims of circumstances.[71]

In the SBC that year and the next, the matter of women's roles was hotly debated at the SBC. Jessie Sappington continued to be a prominent figure in these discussions that resulted in very conservative statements about women's status. Later Sappington published a memoir in which she identified her root concern as being the ordination of women, and she considered WMU as one of the encouragers of ordination.[72]

Carolyn Weatherford decided that WMU officials must give serious attention to the woman's movement, since it was becoming increasingly controversial and affecting its members. At WMU's invitation the Christian Life Commission conducted a seminar on Freedom for Christian Women at the 1975 Executive Board meeting. This was a study of biblical and current views of women. A self-consciousness about women's roles, seldom before revealed in WMU, was displayed through publications.

WOMEN AND GOD'S CALL TO SERVICE

In the 1970s WMU leaders were concerned with the declining percentage of women going into mission service. Also they were concerned that the proportion of women among employees of SBC agencies was declining while the proportion of women in the national labor force was increasing. These trends, linked with the decline in WMU enrollment, made WMU officers feel a responsibility to open more opportunities for women and girls to serve, and to encourage them in answering God's call. Carolyn Weatherford stated in several public

addresses that the central issue for Christians in the woman's movement was "Does God call women?"[73] WMU magazines began to deal
with the call of God to women, with the realities of types of mission
service open to women, and with the appointment processes for women
missionaries.[74]

In 1978 WMU and ten SBC agencies cosponsored a Consultation on
Women in Church-Related Vocations. The need for this meeting
emerged from the Missions Coordination Subcommittee of the Inter-
Agency Council, which was concerned about the slowdown of women
going into missions. The consultation sponsored two research projects
and produced a body of findings for the use of the agencies in employment, policy making, education, and vocational guidance. More
than 300 persons paid registration fees, including SBC and state convention executives, pastors, college and seminary faculty, students,
WMU leaders, and missionaries. Catherine B. Allen (Mrs. Lee N.) chaired
a steering committee of the sponsoring agencies. Other WMU staff
members chairing subcommittees were Bobbie Sorrill, program; and
LaVenia Neal, finance.[75]

The consultation convinced WMU to issue a plan of action to encourage women in church-related vocations. The issue received increased attention in publications. WMU sponsored dinners for women
in church-related vocations in connection with Annual Meetings in
1979, 1982, and 1986. After the 1982 dinner, some of the participants
lingered and planned to form a permanent Women in Ministry organization. WMU assisted this group each year in arranging a meeting
place prior to the WMU Annual Meeting and in clerical work. Carolyn
Weatherford has served on the steering committee of the group. WMU
allocated up to $500 a year for several years to assist the group with
its promotion.

In 1984 this allocation brought several letters of criticism to WMU.
In that year the Southern Baptist Convention passed a resolution encouraging service of women in all aspects of Christian work "other
than pastoral functions involving ordination."[76]

Explaining WMU's encouragement of Women in Ministry, Weatherford wrote that the term *women in ministry* was a modern phrase for
what had been known as *women in church-related vocations.* "The
word *minister* doesn't necessarily mean ordination. Each church de-
cides for itself whether or not to ordain specific staff members. WMU
always used the word *minister* even for laypersons," she wrote. "WMU's
biggest concern is that women not forget missions careers, no matter
how many secular and church jobs might open to them. . . . One of
WMU's important jobs is 'to create an environment through which
persons can hear and respond to God's call into missions.' If WMU is
to be honest with girls about listening to God's call, we must be in-

formed and concerned about the problems they encounter."[77]

WMU AND CONTROVERSY

As the foregoing study indicates, WMU has been the target of continuing controversy, yet has been sustained by its friends and its purposes. Controversy also splashed on WMU as it stood beside a Convention which suffered intermittent feuds, and WMU helped the Convention to survive these. WMU has had a few controversies within. These were dispatched with a style unique to the organization.

Only those SBC controversies that affected missions are discussed here. Others, such as the Whitsitt controversy of 1899 and the fundamentalist movement of the 1920s, left WMU unscathed.

Landmark Controversy.—The open flame of this long disagreement had died out before WMU's time, else WMU probably would not have organized as early as it did. Basically the Landmark advocates did not believe in cooperation through mission boards and other denominational organizations. They would not permit cooperation or even courteous relations with other denominations.

The daughter of J. M. Pendleton, one of the patriarchs of the Landmark movement, was a strong supporter of mission boards. She was Lula Pendleton Proctor (Mrs. B. F.), of Bowling Green, president of Kentucky WMU 1903-1909. The most visible eruption of Landmarkism came in Arkansas at the turn of the century, resulting in a split in the state convention in 1902. The defender of the Arkansas Baptist State Convention was J. P. Eagle, whose wife was president of Arkansas WMU. Returning from a convention on a train, Mary O. Eagle became involved in a discussion with Ben L. Bogard, leader of the Landmark faction. She gave him a stern lecture before a group, then turned and left. Bogard commented, "If she had been a man, I would have knocked her down." Mary Eagle's many admirers were furious and Bogard lost some of his following.[78] The state convention split took away a few WMU members, but not many, for cooperation with the mission boards was the essence of their work.

Gospel Mission Movement.—For WMU this was potentially the most damaging of the nineteenth-century SBC controversies. Almost all the missionaries in North China resigned or were dismissed from the Foreign Mission Board in the early 1890s because they preferred to receive their support directly from churches and associations. Their leader, T. P. Crawford, had a long history of argument with the Foreign Mission Board, refusing to abide by many of its policies. Although Martha Foster Crawford, his wife, was retained as a missionary of the FMB after her husband was severed from it, she inevitably had to submit her resignation, which was accepted with regret.[79] She was closely tied to the organization of WMU and was widely beloved. WMU leaders felt the split keenly.

One of the handful of missionaries remaining loyal to the FMB was Lottie Moon. Henry Allen Tupper, secretary of the FMB, was the main kick post of the Gospel Mission adherents. Love for Moon and friendship for Tupper kept all but a handful of WMU members in the fold.

WMU lost two important founders in this split: Sallie Rochester Ford (Mrs. S. H.) and Martha Loftin Wilson (Mrs. Stainback). Both were close personal friends of Martha Crawford from the 1883 meeting of women at the SBC. Sallie Ford attempted neutrality, pledging to the readers of Ford's *Christian Repository* that she would criticize neither the split-off faction nor the supporters of the FMB. WMU was not willing to put up with this compromise, and Ford quietly faded out of WMU's inner circle (see chap. 1).

The case of Martha Wilson was more complicated, because it led to a temporary split among officers in Georgia WMU. She and her sister, Mrs. M. E. Kerr, openly supported the Gospel Mission Movement in the pages of the Georgia WMU paper, the *Missionary Helper*, printed by Kerr. Since Wilson was the salaried corresponding secretary of the Georgia women, the central committee was able to force her resignation. Using the *Missionary Helper*, she and Kerr and a few other officers tried to function as rivals to the state women's organization. They planned to recognize contributions either to the Gospel Mission or to the FMB. Meanwhile, Georgia leaders such as Mary Emily Wright and Mary Tichenor Barnes put Mary T. Corbell Gambrell (Mrs. J. B.) in office to succeed Wilson.

Both sets of officers wrote to Baltimore for recognition, expected to receive mailings from Annie Armstrong, and planned to submit reports to the 1895 Annual Meeting. Armstrong kept in constant communication with the Convention boards about the matter. The WMU Executive Committee would not recognize Martha Wilson.

The American Baptist Publication Society began giving publicity and encouragement to the Gospel Mission missionaries and to Kerr, taking out paid advertisements in the *Missionary Helper*. The Sunday School Board dropped its ads in the *Helper*. Annie Armstrong wrote strong objections to the Publication Society.

The general officers of WMU handled the matter very discreetly, although it was thoroughly aired in Georgia. By 1899 Gospel Mission matters faded from WMU, SBC, concerns. Martha Wilson eventually returned to the good graces of her state WMU, and most of the Gospel Mission missionaries returned to the FMB because their support dried up.[80]

The Gospel Mission Movement had some of its strongest home bases in North Carolina. Some WMUs apparently routed funds to Gospel

Mission missionaries, thereby reducing the amount which had been sent to the Foreign Mission Board.[81] The presence of Fannie E. S. Heck undoubtedly kept the majority of the women pledged to the FMB so that the impact on WMU was less than the effect on the state at large.

Ecumenical Issues—Southern Baptists generally have shied away from serious involvement with other denominations. The independence of each church, a strong preference for conservatism, and a hangover from Landmark influence are factors in this aloofness. For a period, WMU was more loyal to interdenominational groups than the SBC was.

During Annie Armstrong's administration, WMU, SBC, had little contact with interdenominational women's activities because of the issue of women speakers.[82] Interdenominational women's activities were dominated by northern groups whose leaders thought nothing of making speeches to open meetings including men. Nevertheless, WMU women were heavily involved in one of the earliest major events for women of all denominations, the Woman's Congress of Missions at the World's Columbian Exposition in Chicago. Mary O. Eagle, president of Arkansas WMU, was on the Board of Lady Managers of the exposition and served as chairman of Woman's Congresses. She presided over several significant women's meetings including the Congress of Missions held in October 1893. Among other Southern Baptist women who attended this meeting was Lottie Moon. Mary Eagle pulled together the papers of the congress for publication and it became one of the most comprehensive surveys of women in missions in the nineteenth century. (It claimed an organization date for WMU, SBC, of 1884.)[83]

Annie Armstrong declined to participate in the Ecumenical Missionary Conference in New York in 1900, but she was pressured to provide accreditation to several Southern Baptist women who wished to attend. Among them was Mary Belle Wheeler (Mrs. A. J.), president of Tennessee WMU, who read a paper on the relation of young people to missions. The leaders of the resulting Committee on the United Study of Foreign Missions knew Armstrong, but she did not permit WMU as an organization to relate to this significant ecumenical effort.[84]

On the eve of her resignation Armstrong represented WMU, SBC, at an interdenominational conference. The southern conference of the YWCA was drawing Southern Baptist young women, so she went to meet with them. Until the early 1930s WMU continued to have close contact with YWCA leaders.

Edith Campbell Crane came from a YWCA career to succeed Armstrong, and with her brought a keen sensitivity to interdenominational thinking. Several WMU members contributed to her expenses to attend the Edinburgh Conference of 1910, which proved to be a decisive step toward the interchurch movement. Aboard ship Crane traveled with representatives of other women's missions organizations and learned of their businesslike approach to their work. She was deeply impressed with the spiritual tone of the meeting and seemed in favor of the decision to form a Continuation Committee in order to centralize the worldwide missions effort.[85]

Already WMU had begun to cooperate with the Central Committee of the United Study of Missions. When the women of this interdenominational group decided to celebrate the 50th anniversary of the founding of the Woman's Union Missionary Society, WMU agreed to cooperate with the Woman's Jubilee of Missions. At the same time WMU declined to attend meetings of the interdenominational Home Mission Council, because the SBC Home Mission Board had refused to affiliate with it in 1909.[86]

Edith Crane belatedly assisted with the spectacular interdenominational Woman's Jubilee rallies and conferences held in major northern cities coast to coast in October 1910 to March 1911. A team of women's leaders, headed by Helen Barrett Montgomery, who had written *Western Women in Eastern Lands* for the occasion, appeared at each meeting. Crane led in forming a Southern Committee for the Extension of the Jubilee in the autumn of 1911. That fall Jubilee meetings were scheduled for Norfolk, Greensboro, Charleston, Jacksonville, Atlanta, Birmingham, Mobile, New Orleans, Memphis, Little Rock, Oklahoma City, Dallas, Houston, and San Antonio.

Edith Crane distributed publicity for these events, but Southern Baptist participation was apparently not strong. Crane became ill in the fall and was not able to attend the meetings. WMU was represented in the touring party of speakers by Annie Jenkins Sallee (Mrs. Eugene), furloughing missionary from China and a former officer of Texas WMU. Fannie Heck used the Jubilee to stress WMU's sympathy with women's societies of other denominations, pointing to communitywide enthusiasm for women in missions as an enlistment tool.

Nationally, the Woman's Jubilee of Missions raised almost $1 million for women's colleges on foreign missions fields. Apparently WMU contributed approximately $20,000 beyond regular contributions. This money was designated to FMB women's schools in Mexico and China, including Annie Sallee's school.[87]

By this time the WMU Executive Committee's policy required the president and others to represent WMU at interdenominational meetings at which WMU wished representation. The Woman's Jubilee led to formation of a permanent interdenominational Federation of Woman's Boards of Foreign Missions. WMU was involved in its meeting in 1912, then named Mary Belle Wheeler to a Southern Commission of the Federation, which was headquartered in Nashville.

Not only did WMU officials faithfully attend meetings of the federation, but they also were active in this decade in the Young People's

Missionary Movement, in the United Mission Study plans, the YWCA, and various interdenominational conferences concerning students. In 1915 WMU proposed observance of the interdenominational women's day of prayer.[88] Study materials in *Royal Service* fully informed the WMU constituency about its liaisons with other denominations.[89]

For WMU to pursue this much open cooperation with other denominations was contrary to the mood of the Southern Baptist Convention. In 1914 the SBC had strongly advised its entities against "entangling alliance with other bodies holding to different standards of doctrine." The actions of the SBC practically ordered women's and young people's societies to avoid interdenominational liaisons. The Foreign Mission Board pulled out of the Foreign Missionary Conference of North America (with which the women's federation was affiliated) and required its missionaries to sign pledges not to engage in interdenominational unifications abroad.[90]

In 1915 James Frost informed Kathleen Mallory that he was having to defend WMU from critics about her continued interdenominational activities. She replied that the sole purpose was to "promote greater unity of action in methods . . . share missionary speakers, stimulate united prayer and study, develop simultaneous effort when possible or desirable, organize summer schools, and gain acquaintance with each other's literature, leaders, and methods. . . . You need not worry in the slightest."[91] WMU later dropped out of the federation on the grounds that membership dues were raised beyond their budget.[92]

Not deterred, Minnie James attended meetings of the federation, the Foreign Missionary Conference of North America, and the Woman's Council of Home Missions in 1919, and reported her action to the constituency. At the Southern Baptist Convention in May, J. B. Gambrell issued a scathing denunciation of interdenominational movements, and a Texas woman arose in the WMU Annual Meeting to present a strong resolution against church union. A contemporary WMU historian noted that this resolution was "speedily adopted; and thus did the Woman's Missionary Union cut the 'Gordian Knot' of the 'Inter-Church World Movement' in so far as her own organization was concerned."[93]

Nancy Lee Swann, the assistant corresponding secretary of WMU in 1912, came out of a YWCA background and soon left WMU to serve as a missionary of the FMB. She was offended at the FMB's isolationist stance and resigned her appointment. Later the FMB resumed its membership in the Foreign Missionary Conference of North America, but WMU never resumed its contacts with the women's groups, for they had become connected with the Federal Council of Churches.

Some individual officers, however, have privately had contact with Church Women United, now affiliated with the National Council of Churches. Olive Brinson Martin (Mrs. George R.) participated in CWU meetings. Laura Malotte Armstrong (Mrs. F. W.) was in contact with the group and may have attended meetings. Marie Mathis was invited to serve on the board of Church Women United but declined. Carolyn Weatherford was invited to participate with a group of executives of other religious women's groups but declined in order to have time to meet with executives of Baptist women's groups who informally began meeting in the late 1970s.

On the local level, in random associations and churches, WMU women have participated in interdenominational projects, though such activity has not been promoted or recognized by WMU, SBC. A member of the WMU, SBC, Executive Committee, Louise McEniry (Mrs. William Hugh), was elected in the early 1950s by the women as president of Bessemer (Alabama) Baptist Associational WMU, but rejected by the Bessemer Baptist Association. In her letter recorded in the associational WMU minutes, she said,

> I am not ashamed of the connection I have had with the United Church Women of Bessemer. I look upon this organization as a band of Christian women gathering together as God's children should in community interest, more or less in the same fashion our pastors meet with pastors of all denominations. Since we are commanded by Paul, "in as much as lieth within you live peaceably with all *MEN*," I hereby tender my resignation as president.[94]

Despite its experiences in interdenominationalism, WMU remained loyal to the SBC. In the years they had spent struggling out of debt and depression, the women several times took positions contrary to those of the SBC Executive Committee and of the Southern Baptist Convention (see chap. 5). These disagreements were not full-scale controversies, but they showed the willingness of WMU leaders to differ with their friends if necessary to protect the missions cause as they saw it.

FOR THE GOOD OF THE CAUSE

Compared to the Southern Baptist Convention, which has known wrenching interpersonal disputes and public name-calling in almost every generation, WMU has been a bed of roses. Only in one era did differences of opinion rock WMU. Each episode was traced to two women: Annie Armstrong and Fannie Heck.

During Heck's first term as president, 1892-94, she and Armstrong worked smoothly together. Heck and her family were ill part of that time and she remained in relative isolation in Raleigh. Armstrong favored her return to the presidency in 1895.

During 1896 the Sunday School Board established a Bible fund and Armstrong led WMU in promoting it, even though WMU had not formally voted to do so. The Sunday School Board, at her invitation, mentioned this cause in its recommendations for WMU's work at the 1897 Annual Meeting. Heck objected in public and private, believing the Bible Fund would sap support for the two mission boards. The women left the 1897 meeting with differing interpretations of what had been approved. When Heck consented to reelection in 1898 she was determined to set some limits on Armstrong's promotion of the Sunday School Board, or perhaps simply on Armstrong herself.[95]

Heck demanded to participate in the Baltimore Executive Committee's deliberations by mail. Armstrong refused to send her the agenda in advance or to facilitate her influence, on the grounds that the president's powers were limited to presiding over the Annual Meeting. Heck appealed to the Executive Committee, and both women appealed to the board secretaries.

Heck courted the support of R. J. Willingham of the Foreign Mission Board, reminding him that Armstrong's advocacy of the Sunday School Board would pull support from foreign missions. Armstrong was indeed devoted to the Sunday School Board and to the Home Mission Board, and she appealed to J. M. Frost and I. T. Tichenor. The board secretaries took the matter seriously, for their support and the peace of the Convention were at stake; they did not regard it as a spectator duel. T. P. Bell, however, formerly on the staffs of both the FMB and the SSB and now editor of the *Christian Index*, maintained a confidential and bemused view of matters. He thought that at last Annie Armstrong's powers had met their match.[96]

Armstrong appealed privately to Jonathan Haralson, president of the Southern Baptist Convention and a justice of the Alabama Supreme Court, to decide which woman was doing the will of WMU. Haralson initially supported Armstrong, after receiving the viewpoint of J. M. Frost, who was his former pastor. But Haralson gently told Armstrong that the dispute was beyond the letter of the law, that peace was needed.

Willingham called Tichenor and Frost to Montgomery, where they could meet with Haralson, in July 1898. The men considered the gravity of the situation and agreed to bring the two women to the conference table. After several weeks of jockeying about time and place, each woman claiming that her personal situation demanded the meeting at her convenience, all parties gathered in August in Norfolk.

Armstrong was tense, emotional, bitter. Heck was cool, calculating, and focused on one issue: the rightful powers of the two offices. Alice Armstrong (sister of Annie) spoke of Heck's "insufferable vanity." Heck referred to "those who in all future times shall hold the office I am now so unfortunate to occupy." The men wrote in pencil on Home Mission Board stationery:

After having patiently considered the existing conditions, while

we feel that under all the circumstances the sisters will not find
it altogether congenial for them to work together in the prose-
cution of the great interests which they have in hand, yet we
recommend that they hold their respective positions at least
until the end of the present Convention year and so far as possible
forget past personal differences for the good of the cause and
the glory of the Master.

On the next page the familiar signatures of Fannie E. S. Heck and Annie
W. Armstrong were affixed to this statement:

We hereby accept this paper with its recommendation as a settlement of the differences between us and enter into an agreement that we will keep these matters private—not giving them
out to the public nor to friends.[97]

The two great leaders went about their duties without further contact
until the 1899 Annual Meeting. Heck had apparently promised not to
stand for reelection. With a touch of petulance, she arrived late, then
she permitted herself to be reelected "by an overwhelming majority"
before declining the office.[98] She quietly returned to North Carolina,
led the state magnificently, but kept it out of Armstrong's influences.
When she resumed the presidency after Armstrong's resignation, she
wholeheartedly supported the Sunday School Board.

This private dispute explains much about the succeeding character
of WMU. The SBC boards could have easily let WMU dissolve in the
heat of two women's disagreements, but they took pains to save WMU.
Heck and Armstrong could have divided WMU into two camps, for each
had great popularity and persuasiveness, but they took pains to confine
their dispute to the committee room. Likewise, the small circle of
leaders who were aware of the problems could have seized the opportunity to make inroads, but they maintained strict confidentiality;
even members of the press were quiet. The dual powers of the presidency and of the executive officer were firmly established.

Only one internal WMU controversy became public property, and
that was the case of the WMU Training School (see chap. 11). Although
personality definitely entered into that turn of history, major issues of
importance to other institutions were involved. It was already a public
matter before WMU officers were asked their opinion, and it was a
matter of business in the SBC in 1903, 1904, and 1907. It could not be
contained. The resulting humiliation for Armstrong, half the Baltimore
Executive Committee, and Lillie Barker resulted in a painful dismem-
berment of WMU.

The question then became, Can WMU, at 18 years of age, survive the
loss of its founder and enduring leader? The answer was found again
in the willingness of women to compromise for the good of the cause.
Again the Convention boards provided a safety net. And again Fannie

Heck took office. In reality, the continuity of WMU leadership was hardly ruffled.

Not another ruffle or wrinkle occurred in WMU even internally until 1944. Like the WMU Training School dispute, this one jutted out of the clash between changing times and unchanging leadership. In February 1944 Laura Armstrong appointed a survey committee to plan for the postwar and post-SBC centennial era. The committee had been proposed, according to Armstrong, by Kathleen Mallory two years earlier.

Laura Armstrong appointed her best friend, Cora Cowgill McWilliams (Mrs. George A.), former president of Missouri WMU, as chairman of the Survey Committee. When the committee reported to the WMU Executive Committee in January 1945, after a year of serious research, the members knew they would encounter heated discussion. McWilliams found herself standing against the combined opposition of Armstrong and Mallory.

So controversial was the report, Mallory sealed it in the vault with orders that it not be seen without permission of the WMU president.[99] These were the points of intense debate:

The committee suggested that the time had come for WMU to accomplish its purposes among the whole constituency of the church, not just the women and young people.

The committee thought that closer, friendlier relationships were needed with the Sunday School Board.

The committee acknowledged that the local church was "as yet a pastor-deacon-man led church" with differences of attitude and approach to problems. This conflict made necessary "a greater love for the Cause rather than self, individual, or organization. . . . A difficult situation puts woman at her best in witness and Christian social graces." To resolve these, a closer relationship to the church program was suggested.

The committee suggested a closer involvement of WMU leaders in foreign lands, whether missionary or native, in the planning of the WMU, SBC, program.

The committee suggested a closer relationship with the women's schools in each of the seminaries.

The committee believed that the professional WMU workers with children and youth must have greater status with the WMU Executive Board, and that the younger organizations of WMU must no longer be treated as second-class to the women's society.

The committee insisted that WMU members wanted the personnel in the national office to be paid fairly. They wanted a budget committee to help direct and enlarge the resources of the national organization. They suggested that WMU own its own building.

Looking at the internal structure of the national office, they called for enlargement of the staff, to include an editorial department and age-level specialists.

Most controversial of all was the proposal that WMU stop counting, reporting, and receiving credit for Cooperative Program contributions.

And finally, the committee urged WMU to confront the worsening racial crisis.

In short, the committee proposed that almost everything about the WMU program and national operations needed major changes but these: auxiliary status to the SBC, relations with the mission boards, and the community missions program.

In retrospect, the Survey Committee report seems tame. All of its proposals eventually came to pass, or continue as WMU dreams. The human factors made the Survey Committee a test of WMU's ability to handle controversy, for even in its polite tones, it implied a loss of confidence in the officers.

As soon as the Executive Committee meeting was over, Laura Armstrong wrote to Cora McWilliams, letting her know that their friendship was intact. McWilliams wrote back:

> I needed no assurance that our recent difference of opinion in any way affected our friendship, but I liked getting it! Long ago I knew we had built something not dependent upon how we think or what we do. . . . We can really see into the heart of each other and know that we shall find nothing there disloyal or untrue one to the other.

She admitted that she had never done anything so hard as to seem critical of Kathleen Mallory, "whom I love, admire, and in whose judgment I have much confidence."

> My love for you is very true. You have given me many hard responsibilities that have been conducive to my own growth . . . this last one was hard . . . , but I honestly tried to do the task as I thought you and Miss Mallory wanted it done. I have no regrets, only the sincerest prayer that Woman's Missionary Union may go on finely, rightly, true to her worthy purpose, and enjoy the continued blessing of our Lord. History will reveal your big contribution to its plans and purposes.

The committee members expected their report to be buried, and it physically was. But Armstrong and Mallory showed their strength by quietly proceeding to implement many of the changes. Three years later Mallory ended her 36-year tenure. Alma Hunt came to the office without having to break the seal on the envelope; she had innocently helped McWilliams with her clerical work four years earlier, never dreaming that she would be the one to implement many of the Survey Committee's plans.

A FELLOWSHIP OF KINDRED MINDS

The internal controversies of Woman's Missionary Union make a short chapter in WMU history. They have been almost invisible. Disagreements and intense discussions have constantly been on the agenda, but these have been handled with a style which can be explained only by the unique woman's, missions character of the organization. Also, the makeup of the governing bodies is effectively representative.

Ellis Fuller, president of Southern Baptist Theological Seminary, observed Kathleen Mallory under the lights of the Survey Committee controversy. He said, "Ladies, I wish that every preacher in the Southern Baptist Convention could have been here tonight. I didn't know that anybody in the world would ever dare to differ with Miss Mallory. I have heard that she runs Woman's Missionary Union. Now I know that she only helps."[100]

The first president of WMU set the pattern. Martha McIntosh was quiet and genteel, wearing a mask over her executive ability. Her peers commended her "womanly dignity and efficiency."[101]

The Texas Baptist state convention was discussing whether to permit women to take part in discussions before the body. One man thought that the women would get into fusses if they were allowed such privileges. Lou Beckley Williams (Mrs. W. L.), a Texas WMU president who had been at the 1888 founding of WMU, wanted to say: "I knew about the women through all of their organized life and knew that they had never had an unpleasant controversy in any of our meetings. I wonder if the brethren have not learned some good things from the women?"[102]

Avoidance of divisive controversy seems to have been one of the prevailing concerns of WMU. Annie Armstrong had more controversy than any other figure, and suffered more for it. "I am no fighter and I would be so thankful if I only could do the work without being put in prominent positions where, when persons want to make an attack on same, I have to be the target. . . . Trouble of this nature always causes me to succumb physically."[103]

One way she and her descendants in WMU have avoided controversy is to work behind the scenes. When Armstrong was commended by J. M. Frost for her leadership, she urged him never to say so in public. "We can go a certain distance and there have to stop and unless we have the support of our brethren the work does not assume the proportions it should. If I had to appear before the public as the one who was responsible for some measures which I have suggested and the Boards have carried out . . . I could not have borne it."[104]

WMU leaders succeeded in getting their ideas before the Convention without personally debating. They have relied on influential men in the denomination to carry the ball for them. Not until the administration of Alma Hunt did WMU officers freely work in give-and-take with men, even around the conference table. Mallory continued Armstrong's successful practice by asking men such as J. B. Gambrell, George W. McDaniel, M. E. Dodd, L. R. Scarborough, I. J. Van Ness, and the mission board secretaries to speak for her. In a case where she had to turn down a business deal with a man, she first asked Van Ness to save her the embarrassment. Then she decided to do it herself. "It seems to be easier for men to make explanations to men than it is for women to do so. Men are so incurably deferential to women that I never am sure that we women convince their mind, unless perhaps we are so unfortunate as to make an issue personal, and you know that women are naturally personal."

Van Ness had tried to help Mallory adjust to men's ways of doing business. She liked to have more prayer and lengthy discussions, making sure that every person had stated and restated feelings. Van Ness advised her, "I think perhaps you misunderstand the masculine which comes to the forefront in our commission meetings. I find myself and others coming into these meetings with the sense that our praying has been already done and that we must try then to exercise our best judgment. There is the masculine tendency when a thing is clearly stated and everybody understands it, not to talk anymore about it."[105]

Mallory lived through the significant changes in the way that women dealt with men. By the end of her tenure, "she could take the gloves off" in interagency combat, according to Duke McCall. He and other men who observed Mallory viewed her as sharp, shrewd, and tough, but treated her with the chivalry due a tiny white-haired lady of the Old South.[106]

Because WMU was growing ever closer to the everyday operations of the SBC as a whole, women leaders were of necessity relating to men more directly. Mallory confessed to some women, "Honey, I just ignore men." Her secretary learned that she kept her files of correspondence with women in a separate cabinet from the files of men. No wonder the younger WMU leaders considered that WMU's public relations image had slipped when she went out of office.[107] The style was not unique to Mallory. Her attitude toward working with men was widespread. Women leaders, it was believed, were a different breed from males.

Women have tried to learn to lead from their study of history. Heroines figure prominently in the culture of WMU. Beginning with Ann Hasseltine Judson, women missionaries have been studied and restudied. Henrietta Hall Shuck (Mrs. J. Lewis) and Lottie Moon are two whose stories never wear thin. A place of honor close behind them has been accorded to WMU leaders. Certainly women placed Annie Armstrong on a pedestal even if they knew all about her clay feet. They wept when she left office and even her nemesis, Fannie Heck, heaped praise on her.

Heck herself has been the most revered and idealized of WMU leaders; Minnie James wrote her biography after years of being fascinated by her. A copy of Heck's biography has been handed down to the presidents of WMU.

WMU has had remarkable stability in leadership through a century. Only 5 women have held the top administrative post. Only 15 women have served as president, and after serving they have continued in the organization as supraleaders. Through these admirable women, WMU's values in effective roles for women have been carefully transmitted.

As early as 1945 the serious study of women as leaders entered WMU's curriculum for adults. In 1968-69 when WMU instituted major changes in its church program for women, leadership styles and methods were constantly examined.

The early days of WMU were marked by strong dependence on parliamentary procedure. As late as 1962 *Royal Service* stated: "If there is one thing a WMS member knows besides missions it is parliamentary procedure. At meetings, local or associational—a parliamentarian with a copy of Robert's Rules of Order watches to see that the motion has been made and seconded correctly. It has been said that if three WMS members were cast on a desert island, they would immediately form a committee and elect a chairman, following Robert's Rules."[108]

WMU women have always had their idiosyncrasies about parliamentary procedure. In selecting national officers, a nominating committee has done the work behind closed doors. There has never been an embarrassing public competition for office. Presidents have usually been selected, according to oral tradition, by having the nominating committee pray, perhaps while holding hands, and then write the names of nominees on secret ballots. Sometimes the candidate is picked on the first ballot unanimously. Sometimes subsequent discussion and balloting are required.

In deliberations, the will of the majority has often been set aside or deferred out of concern for the feelings of the minority. I. J. Van Ness's explanations to Kathleen Mallory about men coming to quicker conclusions than women still hold true. WMU Board meetings last longer than any SBC agency's. Porter Routh commented after observing the 1944 WMU Annual Meeting on the dignity and decorum of the meeting. "They trust their leaders," he said, noting that there was little debate on recommendations.

In the 1920s WMU leaders began distributing fliers to national Annual Meeting attenders. "Please do not applaud. Abstain from conversation. Show reverence in sessions. Do not take photos." Timekeepers were appointed in every meeting after the first. As soon as electricity was available an electric "silence" sign was placed at the presiding chair to be switched on when the president wished. Since the 1960s an electric system of warning lights has been used to keep speakers on time. WMU took its meetings seriously. Leaders created a mood different from the rambunctious, even rowdy, atmosphere of the Southern Baptist Convention meetings.[109]

Often the main business of WMU conventions is inspiration. Beginning in the 1940s WMU meetings took on a flavor of pomp and circumstance that made masses flock to see them. Under the dramatic hand of Marie Mathis, national Annual Meetings of 1956-75 became stage spectaculars.

COMPELLING BELIEF

Marion Bates (Mrs. Edgar), a Canadian who was president of the Women's Department of the Baptist World Alliance, identified one characteristic which she felt distinguished Southern Baptist women: "They are warm, gospel-oriented. They still have the Bible read at meetings. They always turn to the Scriptures. I'm not saying that others don't, but when a body of women that big turns to the Bible, they have something going for them."[110]

The Bible has constantly been the centerpiece of WMU thought. In 1906 at the pinnacle of controversy over the WMU Training School, Lillie Barker began the meeting by reading John 15. Scriptural watchwords have been chosen almost every year. Memorization of Scripture passages has been stressed in children's organizations.

Devotion to knowing God's Word has brought the specialized viewpoints of belief into WMU thinking. Members have believed that women are especially suited for understanding the gospel. Ethlene Cox said in 1930: "Women have much in common with men, but woman also has mental and soul attributes peculiar to her alone. . . . This sixth sense of woman's is not something to be treated lightly, or laughed at, for it is God-given and intended to cleave to the heart of spiritual truths and life situations."[111]

Speaking on the appeal of Christianity to women, Mary Hill Davis (Mrs. F. S.), president of Texas WMU, said: "Woman's quick and blessed response to the call of love divine has been the cause of heaping of much opprobrium upon her devoted head. . . . Such an impeachment is to her eternal credit. . . . It is the glory of Christianity that women preponderate on all the occasions, and in all the forms of testimony to it. Has the gospel of Jesus Christ been a friend to women?"[112]

In WMU Bible studies and in public addresses of the officers, the attention Jesus gave to women has frequently been cited. *The Why and How of Woman's Missionary Union*, a methods manual in use through the 1930s, included an outline of the Gospels citing Jesus' ministries to women. These were suggested for study along with the study of WMU operations.[113]

Dorothy Sample, addressing a group of women concerned about whether the Christian faith would meet their needs in contemporary times, said, "Filter everything through Jesus."

In WMU theology, not the benefits of the gospel for women, but its obligations predominate. Lillie Barker's address of 1905 began with this statement:

> To woman, as well as to man, comes the imperative voice of duty, and from her, too, God expects obedience to the command, "Go ye therefore and teach all nations." . . . In view of the success that has crowned her efforts, the qualifications and scope that are hers and the promise, "Lo, I am with you always," . . . what may we not expect from women in the realm of missions? . . . What has been done by woman can again be done by woman. . . . Let us "Go Forward" believing that all things are possible to us through Jesus Christ our Lord.[114]

Marie Mathis, who was the first woman to preside as an officer of the Southern Baptist Convention, and who counseled with heads of state and Communist government ministers and came away saying, "I was not afraid," frequently quoted her favorite passage of Scripture. It was the order of the angel at the tomb of the risen Christ to the women: "Fear not . . . go quickly and tell" (Matt. 28:5-7).

WMU leaders have not usually been certified theologians. Their beliefs have been framed in their own searching. They have been aware of theological disputing but not actively interested in it. Kathleen Mallory and her good friend Alma Wright, southwide stewardship chairman of WMU, found that they were on opposite sides of the question about the second coming of Christ. One was a premillennialist. The other was a postmillennialist. They argued suavely for an hour, until they agreed that their work did not depend upon agreement about this point, just so they were both "pro-millennialist."[115]

The sure belief in a day of reckoning has been a beacon to WMU officers that contributed even to their creation of WMU. Jennie Snead Hatcher (Mrs. W. E.) said to the 1886 meeting of women at the SBC, the first one held "for women only": "Let us watch lest some outstrip us in the reaping while we stand idling, for when the day of garnering shall come, others will come bringing their sheaves with them while we will be left to regret our wasted lives."[116]

Ninety years later Carolyn Weatherford told the Brotherhood Commission: "We must resell ourselves on the importance of what we are doing. Unless we believe that what we are doing has value in terms of eternity, we might be doing something else."

These opening doors for women, never so numerous or so wide in the history of the world before, are God's call to us to work as we have never worked before. Past successes should only be stepping stones to future endeavors. Rewards await us yonder, work awaits us here. And, while so much work has been left undone we have no time to stop even for congratulations or praise.

Annie Armstrong
1890 Annual Report

Epilogue

14

The veil over the future

The veil over the future is one of God's tenderest mercies.

Annie Armstrong
1889 Annual Report

NNIE Armstrong had lifted only a corner of the veil over the future when she spoke those words in 1889. She could only go forward, confident that the same divine hand that had framed the promising past of WMU also held the future.

She spoke on the basis of one year of WMU history. Now WMU has a century of experience. The veil is a little higher now. The face and potentials of WMU have been revealed. Certain persistent characteristics have made history.

A CENTURY TO CELEBRATE

"Her-story" is fingerprinted with dozens of daringly new activities WMU helped shape. Many of the innovations were later adopted into the care of other hands. WMU played a key role in beginning the following among Southern Baptists:

    student ministries on college campuses
    Vacation Bible School
    theological education for women
    professional training in religious education
    professional training for missionary service
    opening the door for women to serve in church-related vocations
    promotion of tithing in SBC experience
    emphasis on systematic, regular giving
    first blacks on professional staffs
    camping as a means of religious education
    recognition of missions as a content area in religious education
    age-graded missions education in churches
    direct missions in one's own community

social work ministries in the denomination; introduction of ministry techniques such as literacy training

education and concerted action on community social problems

first church program publications in Spanish

first SBC, literature in Romanian, Korean, Japanese, Chinese

weekday church activities for children and youth

the financial system that now provides the major avenues of funding of home missions and foreign missions: the Annie Armstrong Easter Offering for Home Missions and the Lottie Moon Christmas Offering for Foreign Missions

use of nonsalaried volunteers in missions work

systematic prayer plan for daily devotions

education of missionaries' children

first women speakers at SBC meetings, first woman officer of SBC, first women on SBC committees.

In addition to these innovations, WMU has shared with other centers of Southern Baptist leadership a significant role in the following developments:

Cooperative Program, especially in its survival between 1925 and 1935; then in its continued promotion

acceptance of the principle of the unified church budget; the every-member canvass to subscribe the church budget; use of the envelope system

all-age, graded religious education system for churches

correlation and coordination of church programs

recruitment of candidates for professional missionary service

use of broadcast and film for Baptist promotion.

Without doubt much that is characteristic of Southern Baptist life is the work of Woman's Missionary Union. WMU has shown the ability to be innovative.

Success.—Among women's organizations, WMU has many distinctives. WMU is more conservative, larger, stronger, and less vulnerable to alteration than that of other denominations. The body of literature and records of WMU is more extensive than similar groups.

The most revealing fact about Woman's Missionary Union is not its own statistics but those of the mission boards of the Southern Baptist Convention. Their dominance in numbers of missionaries, dollars available, upward trends, and points of geography touched make them worthy of note. Each point of strength is directly linked to WMU.

Woman-led.—Although other activities in Baptist life involve many women, no other is significantly influenced by female leadership at decision-making levels. WMU, of course, is largely woman-led. In churches WMU is subject in large degree to policies and decisions of male leaders. At the national level WMU is self-determining. In between, at the associational and state levels, WMU leaders have varying degrees of opportunity to exercise their own approach to leadership.

Size.—Although WMU is a giant among women's organizations, it has always been relatively small within the Southern Baptist Convention. Its size has apparently been large enough to make a significant impact, but it is small enough to move rapidly and cohesively in time of crisis. On the other hand, WMU's size has been too small to make as great changes as the women have hoped for, and at all levels leaders have felt overworked from operating on a bigger scale than they have numerical strength to support.

Cohesiveness.—WMU has not been scarred by dispute and controversy. Neither has WMU been derailed from its original central and exclusive purpose of missions. Cohesiveness may be due to two factors: the strongly magnetic purpose of the organization and female leadership style. WMU spokeswomen have maintained that purpose is the key.

Opposition.—WMU has always enjoyed enough disapproval to keep members on the alert about survival and eager to win friends. Opposition has come because of the missions emphasis, the denominational cooperation emphasis, and the female leadership emphasis. Threats against any one of these points have tended to draw WMU to united defense.

Friends.—Opposition has been offset by allies who have encouraged WMU. These have without fail been the men best informed about and most sympathetic with missions and with the Southern Baptist denomination. Missionaries, both men and women, have been WMU's supporters.

Adaptability.—WMU has adjusted to the slowly widening admission of women to the Southern Baptist Convention, to years of retreat and years of advance in missions, and to drastically changed roles of women and children in society.

Stable Funding.—Although WMU at the national level has operated with strictest economy and even self-sacrifice, the organization has had the benefit of stable, consistent funding. WMU, SBC, has received only a small fraction of mission board funds at any time, but the allocation could be counted on. WMU's publishing sales, which became the main source of funds, suffered only one period of decline. The organization has been able to project its work on a reliable basis, without cutbacks, panics, or debilitating debts. WMU's survival has not been threatened by lack of money.

Laywomen.—WMU was the first, and remains the largest, body of organized laypersons in the SBC. Among these laypersons are an influential body of professional WMU workers and missionaries. The Southern Baptist Convention in session and its boards are by contrast essentially organizations of ordained clergy.

Governance.—WMU is the only element at the national level of the SBC which is controlled by a fairly democratic system of representation on its Executive Board. Among the church program organizations (Sunday School, Church Training, Brotherhood, and Church Music) WMU is the only one with a fully organized membership. WMU has a tight structure of associational officers who in many states compose the state WMU executive group. WMU uses the associational structure as a means of training and communicating.

Auxiliary Status.—The most controversial factor in WMU's makeup may be one of the most important. This is the auxiliary status which makes WMU at the national level (and in some states) able to make its own decisions. Although WMU has always used its independence to achieve interdependence, at several turning points WMU was able to play the role of "loyal opposition." Thus WMU provides a counterbalance to the SBC actions about missions.

A FUTURE TO FULFILL

These legacies from the past will undoubtedly guide WMU into the future. The future presents most of the same challenges that brought WMU into being a century ago.

Carolyn Weatherford, executive director of WMU, at the WMU Writers Conference in 1986 invited the women who would be writing the WMU magazines in the Centennial year to welcome tension and opposition. "Tension helps us to grow and be strong," she said. She predicted that WMU would continue to find its strength by pulling between tensions such as these:

dependence and independence
erudition and simplicity
modern methods and the same old story
frontiers and boundaries
quality and quantity
history and the future.

Divine Imperative.—WMU enters the future with its sense of divine mandate intact. Laborers Together with God continues as the watchword.

The women have believed it. They continue to believe they are building a sacred structure. They believe they are working under God's specific orders, laying each brick as directed. They believe they are working with each other only because God wills them to do so. They believe they are accountable to God for how they handle opportunity. They believe that Christ's commissions to make disciples of all nations apply personally to them. History is on their side in their belief that

Woman's Missionary Union will be divinely prospered.

Carolyn Weatherford spoke for current officers in saying, "We have no intention of changing the purpose of WMU. The more we change the more we are the same."[1]

With idealism ever fresh, WMU prepared to enter its second century by celebrating the first century, and by reaching for 2 million members, and by giving record sums to missions through the Lottie Moon Christmas Offering and the Annie Armstrong Easter Offering.

> *Has not time vindicated the wisdom of our organization? And are not our mission workers just as womanly while they are earnestly carrying out Christ's last commands, as in the days of yore? Let us "Go forward" into the new year with faith strengthened by a glimpse into our past God-directed history; with courage strong to bear the burdens of to-day, knowing that Christ is with us "all the days;" and with hopes high because we are a part of that plan of the ages which shall sooner or later usher in the kingdom of our Lord.*
> Annie Armstrong,
> 1903 Annual Report

Examine everything carefully;

hold fast

to that which is good.

1 Thessalonians 5:21

Bibliographic Data:
A Century of Sources

*A compilation from many authorities too numerous to
mention and for which acknowledgment is hereby made.*

Sketch and Constitution of the
Woman's Missionary Societies,
Auxiliary to SBC, 1888

Woman's Missionary Union's own archives in Birmingham are tremendous veins of history. Complete sets of official records and periodicals for a century tell the story of a sturdy organization. These records are largely unmined. From the beginning the officers took pains to preserve their records and publications to a remarkable degree.

Among the official records of WMU are the published Annual Reports or Minutes, available continuously from 1888. Executive Committee (later called Executive Board) minutes are available also in unbroken line from 1888. The more recent years of executive session minutes are restricted from current use.

In 1886, prior to the organization of WMU, Annie Armstrong and other founders began operating the Maryland Baptist Mission Rooms, a publishing venture. The publications of the Rooms are preserved in scrapbooks, as are the leaflet and booklet publications of WMU from 1888 onward. In 1906 WMU issued its first periodical, and it has continued to be issued without interruption under the name *Royal Service*. This magazine has been joined by a dozen other magazines and by more than 300 operating manuals, books, pamphlets, and other literature. The files of these compose an unequaled body of literature by and for women.

In addition to these official and published records, the WMU archives has preserved some of the officers' correspondence files. Memorabilia in the Birmingham offices of WMU range from photographs to dresses. Several of Annie Armstrong's notebooks, a scrapbook of Ethlene Boone Cox, correspondence containing recollections of some early WMU participants, the libraries of some officers, and other items indicate much about the formative influences in WMU.

Very few students and writers have availed themselves of the resources in WMU archives. While the holdings are not yet fully indexed, a professional staff is available to guide serious researchers.

From the WMU archives in Birmingham, a researcher should visit the Southern Baptist Historical Commission in Nashville. The library contains a good collection of old books on missions with reference to WMU. Various manuscript collections, such as the Amzi C. Dixon Papers and the W. O. Carver Papers, contain direct reference and background. The archives of the SBC Executive Committee, of the $75 Million Campaign, of the Cooperative Program, and of numerous SBC special committees show perspectives on WMU.

Significant collections of WMU data are found in the following historical collections: Southern Baptist Theological Seminary, Southwestern Baptist Theological Seminary, Virginia Baptist Historical Society, Samford University, Wake Forest University, Furman University, Baylor University. The archivists at each center were extremely helpful.

Southern Baptist Theological Seminary library holds the extensive records of the Woman's Missionary Union Training School/Carver School of Missions and Social Work. Among this collection are large scrapbooks dating from before the school's founding in 1907.

In the Southwestern Baptist Theological Seminary library are many trails leading back to the 1904 Woman's Missionary Union Training School which merged into the seminary. Southwestern holds many archival records from Texas Woman's Missionary Union and the Texas Baptist Historical Collection. Among the most interesting are the papers of J. B. and Mary T. Gambrell, the recollections of Mina Everett, and the $75 Million Campaign files of L. R. Scarborough.

Virginia Baptist Historical Society's wing of the University of Richmond library is a rich deposit of WMU lore. The early files of Virginia WMU are held there. Among the surprises discovered at the VBHS is the peace treaty between Annie Armstrong and Fannie E. S. Heck. This collection contains the largest file of WMU publications outside of Birmingham. Among them is a history of WMU written by Lillie Easterby Barker (Mrs. J. A.) which was not previously known. The papers of Blanche Sydnor White, an influential WMU executive, excellent historian, and employee of the historical society, contain many personal insights. Some of the papers of Olive Brinson Martin (Mrs. G. R.) are found here, with the remainder at the Freemason Street Baptist Church in Norfolk. Other WMU presidents represented in VBHS collections are Minnie Kennedy James (Mrs. W. C.) and Christine Burton Gregory (Mrs. A. Harrison). The VBHS owns the diaries of George Braxton Taylor, founder of the Sunbeam Band. A useful tool compiled by the VBHS is a partial index of the *Religious Herald*.

Wake Forest University library houses the North Carolina Baptist Historical Collections. Of chief interest is a trove of papers by and about Fannie E. S. Heck, including her deathbed diaries.

Baylor University's Texas Collection includes a helpful file concerning Marie Wiley Mathis (Mrs. R. L.) and the early diaries of Annie Jenkins Sallee, one of the first field workers of WMU and a missionary in China. Baylor's oral history program has preserved fresh insights of several women close to the top of WMU leadership.

The South Carolina Baptist Historical Collection at Furman University contains an autograph of Hephzibah Jenkins Townsend, the earliest known southern woman missionary organizer. Records and some correspondence of the state WMU are housed there.

Samford University's Special Collection contains the papers of Gaines S. Dobbins and the research of Hermione D. Jackson, historian of Alabama WMU. Other Baptist schools have data about their own historical connections with WMU and about local WMU heroines. Some that have been used and cited include William Jewell College, Judson College, and Meredith College.

Not only the Baptist university libraries, but also secular collections contain much about WMU. The Maryland Historical Society has the papers of the Franklin Wilsons and of Ann Jane Baker Graves, extremely important WMU founders. The Virginia Historical Society has a few items concerning Abby Manly Gwathmey in the Gwathmey Papers.

The University of South Carolina's Caroliniana Library has priceless papers about WMU's first president, Martha McIntosh, in the McIntosh and Coker-Stout Papers. Caroliniana also has good collections of WMU, Woman's Christian Temperance Union, and Woman's Club annuals.

At Coker College was found a rare privately published book by Kate Waller Chambers, donor of the Margaret Home.

Yale University Divinity School library's China Collections contain the Hartwell Family Papers. Hartwell women helped found WMU in four states.

The University of North Carolina manuscript library houses the papers of Jessie Daniel Ames. In these are found evidence of WMU's involvement in interracial movements of the 1921-47 era. Further information is at Atlanta University library. North Carolina also has papers relating to Fannie E. S. Heck's involvement in Raleigh Woman's Club and other civic affairs.

Duke University's manuscript collections include papers of several Baptists related to WMU, including Martha Foster Crawford.

The state libraries or archives of Virginia, Alabama, Georgia, Tennessee, and North Carolina yielded information about WMU personalities, their churches, and their secular organizations.

At the outset of research, contact was made with every major university library and major historical society library in the Southeast and Southwest. Many responded that they have local and regional WMU histories, some of them in manuscript form, on file. Likewise, all major

Baptist libraries have numbers of these. Most of these individual histories remain unexamined. All known relevant manuscript collections revealed in this inquiry were examined. However, probably more collections could be discovered through closer inspection.

Samford University has an unusually fine collection of microfilms of Baptist records, especially of the news periodicals produced in various states. Many of these are available for purchase through the Southern Baptist Historical Commission. Any serious study of WMU must include examiniation of such periodicals. From the 1870s, periodicals in Maryland, Virginia, and South Carolina regularly featured women's missionary information. As women became organized state by state, the Baptist newspapers invariably offered regular columns to the women. The publications most carefully examined in preparation of this book include the following: *Religious Herald* (Virginia); *Baptist Argus* (Kentucky); *Western Recorder* (Kentucky). For the earlier years of WMU, the following were consulted: *Baptist and Reflector* (Tennessee); *Alabama Baptist; Baltimore Baptist; Biblical Recorder* (North Carolina); *Baptist Courier* (South Carolina); *Baptist Standard* (Texas).

Important periodicals published by certain Baptist agencies include *Foreign Mission Journal* (later succeeded by the *Commission*) which for many years included frequent columns by and about WMU. Also, *Home and Foreign Fields*, published by the Sunday School Board, contained a page submitted by WMU. The Home Mission Board periodical (*Home Fields* and later *Home Missions*, now *MissionsUSA*) has included regular mention of WMU. *Kind Words*, a Sunday School paper published variously by the Home Mission Board and the Sunday School Board, was one of WMU's main news contacts with children.

Among the most significant periodicals in WMU development were two published by and for women. The *Baptist Basket* and the *Heathen Helper* have not been discovered or collected in continuous runs. Some issues are available at the Southern Baptist Theological Seminary, some are at the Foreign Mission Board, and others are at WMU archives. The Historical Commission is attempting to collect these on microfilm.

Contemporary women's studies and works on southern religion were studied as background. While these works generally ignored WMU, they have pointed the way to fresh views of WMU. It is to be hoped that serious scholars will now be able to find their way into the many trails of WMU interest.

Joan Jacobs Brumberg's *Mission for Life: The Story of the Family of Adoniram Judson* (New York: The Free Press, 1980) was helpful in its understanding of the impact of missions in women's thinking prior to WMU organization.

After research for *A Century to Celebrate* was near completion, Patricia R. Hill's excellent book *The World Their Household: The Ameri-*

can Woman's Foreign Mission Movement and Cultural Transformation, 1870-1920 (Ann Arbor: University of Michigan, 1985) came to hand. Hill proves the power of women's missions organizations in shaping missions and in shaping society. She concentrated her research on the women's organizations that directly employed and administered women foreign missionaries. WMU was not closely treated, because WMU did not directly appoint missionaries. Hill judged that the women's organizations lost their influence by the 1920s. WMU, by sharp contrast, did not gain its power until that era.

The classic work on women and missions has been R. Pierce Beaver's *American Protestant Women in World Mission: A History of the First Feminist Movement in North America* (Grand Rapids: William B. Eerdman's Publishing, Co., 1980), originally published as *All Loves Excelling* (1968). The updated book asserts that the women's missionary organization was the first feminist movement. Beaver also indicated that once the mainline women's organizations altered their purpose and lost their prerogatives in the 1950s, the support of missions in general deteriorated. Again, WMU's experience has run counter to the trend. With the exception of these mentioned, contemporary works on women's history and sociology are important for background and technique, not specifics about WMU.

Internally, WMU has written extensively about itself (see preface, pp. 9-13). Among the essential books touching WMU history are the following: Catherine B. Allen, *The New Lottie Moon Story* (Nashville: Broadman Press, 1980); Bobbie Sorrill, *Annie Armstrong: Dreamer in Action* (Nashville: Broadman Press, 1984); Annie Wright Ussery, *The Story of Kathleen Mallory* (Broadman Press, 1956); Mrs. W. C. James, *Fannie E. S. Heck* (Broadman Press, 1939); and others which are cited in footnotes.

In preparation for *A Century to Celebrate*, the WMU national office issued an appeal for church and associational WMU units to write their histories. When the last page of this book was written, these fascinating stories were still arriving at the archives in Birmingham. They await detailed scrutiny, but without doubt they confirm the local origins and applications of the nationwide program of WMU.

The Southern Baptist Foreign Mission Board and the Sunday School Board have enormous archives in which WMU appears prominently. Both of these agencies granted generous access to their records; and indeed WMU history is their history. The Home Mission Board records are more limited. Some are now in the hands of the Southern Baptist Historical Commission. In them, as in other Historical Commission collections, is much information about WMU.

An interesting interplay of personalities is revealed in the Nannie Helen Burroughs Papers (Library of Congress) and in the Una Roberts Lawrence Papers (Home Mission Board Collection, Historical Commission). Burroughs, Lawrence, and Blanche White carried on and pre-served a sizable correspondence full of stunning insights.

The oral history method was employed to a large extent. Alma Hunt, whose tenure as executive secretary spanned one-fourth of WMU's life, granted 85 hours of interviews. Because of the currency of many of Hunt's recollections, those interviews are largely restricted from ex-amination until another generation. However, Hunt will draw from her oral history *Reflections from Alma Hunt*, a book to be published by WMU in 1987. WMU leaders; all living presidents of WMU, SBC; as well as a number of longtime staff members of WMU, SBC; and of state WMUs were extensively interviewed.

Retired executives from Southern Baptist posts who granted inter-views include: Porter W. Routh, executive secretary-treasurer of the SBC Executive Committee; Duke K. McCall, who related to WMU at significant points when he was executive secretary of the SBC Executive Committee, next president of Southern Baptist Theological Seminary, then president of the Baptist World Alliance; James L. Sullivan, execu-tive secretary of the Sunday School Board.

WMU personalities who were interviewed, other than past national presidents and executives, include: Edith Stokely Moore, Frances Lan-drum Tyler (Mrs. W. C.), Ethalee Hamric, LaVenia Neal, Nicy Murphy, Becie Shewmake Kirkwood (Mrs. A. L.), Mary Essie Stephens, Edwina Robinson, Mrs. James Cobb, Hannah Hills, Ruth Provence, Annie Wright Ussery.

Several persons went to exceptional lengths to research topics on request of the author. These include Ruth Provence on the relationship between WMU and the WCTU in South Carolina; Evelyn Wingo Thomp-son on the life and work of Agnes Osborne and Charlotte Ray Osborne, earliest Baptist women publishers and journalists; Betsy Criminger Lowery on the Vacation Bible School movement; Mary Essie Stephens on the life of Sarah Jessie Davis Stakely (Mrs. Charles A.); Annie Wright Ussery on the life of Kathleen Mallory; L. Katherine Cook on the social impact of Texas WMU; Susan Shaw on WMU statistical studies. Lowery's findings will be published in the October-November-December 1988 issue of *Quarterly Review*.

A comprehensive view of WMU development on any front must include a look at the state WMU organizations which constitute the national organization. All but the youngest state WMUs have published their own histories. Some states have published as many as four sub-stantial volumes. A fairly complete collection is available in the national WMU archives. Several state WMUs have retained considerable manu-script collections either at their offices or nearby Baptist libraries. In cooperation with research for *A Century to Celebrate*, most of the states compiled chronologies of their major events and verified lists of their officers (see p. 442). Of their research, nothing was more challenging than discovering the given names of their deceased officers.

In sum, hundreds of separate manuscript collections, individuals, and published works have been consulted in research for this book. Those specifically used are cited in the notes. This bibliographic essay is included as a guide to future researchers in hopes that more detailed research and analysis on topics and individuals will soon commence.

ACKNOWLEDGEMENTS

A nationwide search of the magnitude deserved by Woman's Missionary Union's Centennial history required much assistance.

Numerous persons responded by mail to questions; others conducted special searches and interviews on behalf of the author; several persons responded to the appeal to place their WMU papers in the WMU archives. The gracious response of these persons is an indicator of the keen interest of many in the proper preservation and interpretation of WMU history.

The librarians, curators, and archivists of the institutions cited in "A Century of Sources" were without fail helpful in locating and granting access to documents.

Eljee Bentley, archivist of Woman's Missionary Union, performed a significant service in her preparation of the chronology of the organization. In abbreviated form her work is published as an appendix in this volume.

The extensive listing of officers, staff, and other key leaders was prepared by Carolyn Smith. Among WMU staff members who assisted in preparing statistical charts were Katherine Roberts, Margaret Rothe, Mary Hines, Jan Turrentine, and Barbara Massey.

Secretarial and clerical assistance in research, oral history transcriptions, and manuscript preparation were rendered by Montez Waid, Rebecca Thomas, Roberta Kleinstein, Judy Elliott, Margaret Ennis, Linda Wellborn, and others of the WMU staff.

The editorial team consisted of Laurella Owens, Kathryne Solomon, Deena Williams Newman, and Janell E. Young.

The author especially acknowledges the research and guidance rendered by Lee N. Allen, professor of history and dean of the Howard College of Arts and Sciences at Samford University, who is also her husband.

Preface

[1]*Western Recorder,* August 1, 1929. For John Broadus's statement, see *WR,* April 19 and May 10, 1888.

Chapter 1. Shaking the Treetops

[1]Mark 4:30-32.
[2]The teapot is on display at Fuller Baptist Church, Kettering, England.
[3]Alexis de Toqueville, *Democracy in America,* vol. 2 (New York: Vintage, 1945); Patricia R. Hill, *The World Their Household: The American Woman's Foreign Mission Movement and Cultural Transformation, 1870-1920* (Ann Arbor: University of Michigan Press, 1985).
[4]Joanna Bethune, *The Power of Faith Exemplified in the Life and Writings of the Late Mrs. Isabella Graham* (New York: American Tract Society, 1843).
[5]The idea that the women's missions organizations constituted a feminist movement was proposed by R. Pierce Beaver in *All Loves Excelling* (1968), 177-78, revised as *American Protestant Women in World Mission: A History of the First Feminist Movement in North America* (Grand Rapids: William B. Eerdmans Publishing Co., 1980). A more recent excellent study is Hill, *The World Their Household.* Both books concentrate on the women-run foreign missionary appointing boards. They give scant attention to Southern Baptist women, who did not appoint missionaries directly. Both Beaver and Hill assume that with the passing of the female foreign mission boards, the power of religious women waned. That seems to be true in the denominations of the women's mission boards. But those organizations declined just as Southern Baptist Woman's Missionary Union showed its real strength. Beaver correctly identified the loss of power in women's organizations as a cause for decline in mission success of their denominations. His thesis is further proved by Southern Baptists, whose missionary forces have continued to grow and to be fed by the success of Woman's Missionary Union.
Possibly a southern women's society predated the Boston Female Society. Martha McIntosh Bell, the first president of Woman's Missionary Union and a knowledgeable leader from 1872 onward, was told of a women's society in King and Queen County, Virginia, which had celebrated its centennial prior to 1900. She saw no written record of this group, however. See Martha McIntosh Bell, "Beginnings of Woman's Work for Missions," South Carolina Baptist Historical Collection, Furman University, Greenville, South Carolina.
[6]Albert L. Vail, *Mary Webb and the Mother Society* (Philadelphia: American Baptist Publication Society, 1914), 18-19. The Scripture verse is 2 Chronicles 15:7.
[7]Kathryn A. Greene, *The Eternal Now: A History of Woman's Missionary Union, Aux-iliary to South Carolina Baptist Convention* (Columbia: Woman's Missionary Union, Auxiliary to South Carolina Baptist Convention, 1980), 20-22. Townsend was a strongly independent woman who at one point moved out of her own house in protest of her husband's decision to follow the tradition of leaving the fortune only to the oldest son. She is buried among her slaves on Edisto Island behind the handsome church she built in 1818, now used by an all-black congregation. Some of her personal items and an original signature are at the South Carolina Baptist Historical Collection, Furman University. The ovens, made of a local building material called tabby, are still visible.
[8]Albert L. Vail, *The Morning Hour of American Baptist Missions* (Philadelphia: American Baptist Publication Society, 1907), 125-35.
[9]Vail, *Mary Webb and the Mother Society,* 48, 35. The Scripture passage referred to is 1 Timothy 2:9, King James Version. The Boston Female Society issued its circular letters through the *Massachusetts Baptist Missionary Magazine;* for example, March 1812, June 1815.
[10]Juliette Mather, *Light Three Candles: History of Woman's Missionary Union of Virginia, 1874-1973* (Richmond: Woman's Missionary Union of Virginia, 1973), 4; Blanche Sydnor White, *First Baptist Church, Richmond, 1780-1955: One Hundred Seventy-Five Years of Service to God and Man* (Richmond, 1955), 27.
[11]Blanche Sydnor White, *Our Heritage: History of Woman's Missionary Union, Auxiliary to the Maryland Baptist Union Association, 1742-1958* (Baltimore: WMU of Maryland, 1959), 11.
[12]Minutes and Constitution of the Fredericksburg Society are at Virginia Baptist Historical Society, Richmond.
[13]"Proceedings of the Baptist Convention for Missionary Purposes, May 1814" (Philadelphia, Printed by Ann Coles, 1814).
[14]Evelyn Wingo Thompson, *Luther Rice: Believer in Tomorrow* (Nashville: Broadman Press, 1982), 150-51.
[15]Hermione Dannelly Jackson, *Women of Vision* (Montgomery: Woman's Missionary Union, Auxiliary to Alabama Baptist State Convention, 1964), 6, 16.
[16]*Religious Herald (RH),* December 1, 1887.
[17]Blanche Sydnor White, "Highlights in History of Woman's Missionary Union, Auxiliary to Dover Association 1886-1949," White Papers, Virginia Baptist Historical Society. In this study of Richmond area churches, White identified 26 women's societies known during the years of Virginia's affiliation with the Triennial Convention (1814-45). She identified 26 more formed in a similar number of years of Southern Baptist affiliation. But churches and Baptists had become far more populous by then, so the trend had slowed significantly. A more meaningful comparison would be the 1830s (20 formed) with the 1840s (8 formed). If

women's societies did not prosper in Richmond, seat of the SBC Foreign Mission Board, then certainly they would have perished in outlying areas.

Fannie E. S. Heck, *In Royal Service: The Mission Work of Southern Baptist Women* (Richmond: Foreign Mission Board, 1913), 246-49, lists 72 women's and children's societies in the South prior to 1842. At least 50 others have come to this author's attention, without a formal search. No reports of women's organizations were collected, even informally, prior to the 1880s.

Among the earliest women's societies in more or less continuous existence, in addition to First Baptist, Richmond, are First Baptist, Savannah, Georgia (1813); First Baptist, Fredericksburg, Virginia (1814); First Baptist, Athens, Georgia (1819); and First Mt. Moriah, Greenwood, South Carolina (1832).

[18]Robert A. Baker, *The Southern Baptist Convention and Its People, 1607-1972* (Nashville: Broadman Press, 1974), 226-55. This is the best summary of Civil War and Reconstruction impact on Southern Baptists at large, though little reference is made to women.

[19]Whitsitt's address on the 50th anniversary of the SBC is in SBC Annual 1895.

[20]Heck, *In Royal Service.*

[21]Viola Klein, *The Feminine Character: History of an Ideology,* 2d edition (Urbana: University of Chicago Press, 1971). See the introductory essay by Janet Zollinger Giele.

[22]Joan D. Mandle, *Women and Social Change in America* (Princeton: Princeton Book Co., 1979).

[23]*RH,* February 9, 1871.

[24]Julia Toy Johnson (Mrs. J. L.), "A History of Woman's Missionary Union [of Mississippi], 1888-1913," Mississippi WMU Office Files.

[25]Lynn E. May, Jr., *The First Baptist Church of Nashville, Tennessee, 1820-1970* (Nashville: First Baptist Church, 1970).

[26]Rev. J. W. Joyner, *A History of the Baptists of Butler County, 1819-1957* (Georgiana, Ala.: [Baptist Historical Society of Alabama, 1957]).

[27]Fanna K. Bee and Lee N. Allen, *Sesquicentennial History, Ruhama Baptist Church* (Birmingham: Ruhama, 1969).

[28]Curry Jo Boesch, Ida Mae Thompson, and Committee, "History of Woman's Missionary Union, First Baptist Church, Lufkin, Texas," 1986, WMU Archives, Birmingham, Alabama; Theron Robert Ledford, *On Fire for Christ: First Baptist Church, Gainesville, Georgia, 1831-1976,* WMU Archives.

[29]*Texas Baptist,* November 9, 1876.

[30]Mrs. W. L. Williams in *Baptist Standard,* January 5, 1922. Also, *Golden Years: An Autobiography* (Dallas: Baptist Standard Publishing Co., 1921), 96.

[31]Roberta Turner Patterson, *Candle by Night: A History of Woman's Missionary Union, Auxiliary to The Baptist General Convention of Texas, 1800-1955* (Dallas: Woman's Missionary Union of Texas, 1955).

The Ladies General Aid Society merged with the WMU of Texas (founded 1880) in 1886. The resulting organization was known until 1919 as Baptist Women Mission Workers. Then it resumed the name of Woman's Missionary Union.

[32]Heck, *In Royal Service.*

[33]Minutes of Executive Committee, WMU, SBC (EC), May 1898.

[34]Gambrell to J. B. Pyatt, October 20, 1908. This is only one example of the long confrontation between the "missions plank" and the aid societies.

[35]Johnson, "History of Mississippi WMU."

[36]S. A. Chambers, "Woman's Work in the Church," manuscript prepared 1882 for the Alabama Baptist Convention, WMU Archives.

[37]*RH,* February 2, 1875.

[38]May, *First Baptist Nashville.*

[39]Jean E. Friedman, *The Enclosed Garden: Women and Community in the Evangelical South, 1830-1900* (Chapel Hill: University of North Carolina Press, 1985), 114-15; Ruth Bordin, *Woman and Temperance: The Quest for Power and Liberty, 1873-1900* (Philadelphia: Temple University Press, 1981).

[40]The account of the Woman's Union Missionary Society and the following description of Sarah Doremus are drawn from an excellent unpublished manuscript by Helen J. Tenney, "No Higher Honor: Centennial History of the Woman's Union Missionary Society of America 1861-1960," Tenney Papers, Archives of the Billy Graham Center, Wheaton College, Wheaton, Illinois.

[41]Even Adoniram Judson objected to having unmarried women missionary colleagues. The Triennial Convention did not consider male appointees' wives as missionaries, and even appointed at least one man whose wife was not a Christian.

[42]See full biographical sketch of Ann Graves in Catherine B. Allen, *Laborers Together with God* (Birmingham: Woman's Missionary Union, 1987). Rosalind Robinson Levering, *Baltimore Baptists, 1773-1973: A History of the Baptist Work in Baltimore During 200 Years* (Baltimore: Baltimore Baptist Association, [1973]). Further information about J. W. M. Williams and "First Female Church" in his autobiography, *Reminiscences of a Pastorate of Thirty-Three Years in the First Baptist Church, Baltimore* (Baltimore: J. F. Weishampel, Jr., n.d.). The matter of females in church government had split First Baptist Church, the more conservative members (including the Armstrongs and Leverings) forming Seventh Baptist Church. See also White, *Our Heritage.* The only clue to Ann Graves's Baptist baptism is in *The Baptist Visitor,* August 1868, which noted that Graves had been baptized several weeks earlier by J. W. M. Williams at First Baptist of Baltimore.

[43]Corinthia Williams, "Woman's Mission to Woman (Baptist)" (Lutherville, Md.: Maryland Baptist Historical Society, 1881).

[44]*RH,* February 24, 1870.

[45]Williams, "Woman's Mission to Woman."

[46]Constitution is in Minute Book, Woman's Mission to Woman, Maryland Baptist Historical Society.

[47]Bell, "Beginnings of Woman's Work for Missions."

[48]The Woman's American Baptist Foreign Mission Society was organized in Boston, April 1871. A parallel organization for the West was formed in Chicago in May. See *RH*, May 2, 1872, for John Pollard's claim that the Baltimore group would be an acceptable alternative to the northern groups. Pollard's sister-in-law, daughter, and niece would be founders of WMU. Regarding Evans, see *RH*, January 30, 1873, and February 27, 1873.

[49]Bell, "Beginnings of Woman's Work for Missions." The women's society at First Baptist of Newberry claimed to be the first south of Baltimore after the Civil War (Greene, *The Eternal Now*, 26). Quite likely it is the oldest in continuous existence. Societies were reported in Kentucky in 1868. Dixie Bale Mylum, *Proclaiming Christ: History of Woman's Missionary Union of Kentucky, 1878-1978* (Middletown, Ky.: Woman's Missionary Union of Kentucky, Auxiliary to the Kentucky Baptist Convention, 1978), 26-27.

[50]*Baptist Courier (BC)*, May 9, 1872; *RH*, April 25, 1872.

[51]Mather, *Light Three Candles*.

[52]*BC*, May 2, 1872; White, *Our Heritage*.

[53]Edwards had been gently reared and thoroughly educated by her pioneer preacher-teacher father. She had been married to a prosperous planter, a founder of the Southern Baptist Convention, who lost his fortune and his sanity in the Civil War. He had died in the state asylum, and she had been declared a pauper, living in one room of their house, teaching school. Franklin Wilson (husband of the Woman's Mission to Woman president) offered to finance the education of her son, J. Hartwell, for the ministry. The son became a well-known pastor in Blacksburg, Virginia. His mother made her home with him and was memorialized by the Blacksburg church in the Home Mission Board Church Building Loan Fund (Ellen Edwards to J. B. Hartwell, Hartwell Family Papers, Yale University Divinity School Library, New Haven, Connecticut; Hannah Lide Coker to Fanny Coker Stout, March 14, 1872, Stout Papers, South Caroliniana Library, University of South Carolina, Columbia, South Carolina; *BC*, August 28, 1902).

[54]Bell, "Beginnings of Woman's Work for Missions"; Greene, *The Eternal Now;* Minute Book of Woman's Mission to Woman, Welsh Neck Baptist Church, Society Hill, South Carolina. The society forwarded its funds through Baltimore at the beginning, later directly to the FMB.

[55]FMB Minutes, April 3, July 1, and October 7, 1872.

[56]Anna Thurmond Pate, *The Incense Road* (New Orleans: Bible Institute Press, 1939).

[57]Moss-James B. Taylor Correspondence and Moss-Henry Allen Tupper Correspondence, FMB Archives, Richmond, Virginia; Diary of Mrs. O. P. Moss, Archives of William Jewell College, Liberty, Missouri.

[58]Mrs. H. Lee Bruns, *History of the St. Louis Associational WMU, 1872-1985;* Eleanor Mare, *A Brief Chronicle of the Rise and Progress of Baptist Development in Saint Louis Association from 1800-1922* (Saint Louis Baptist Woman's Missionary Union and Benevolent Union, 1922); *Our Mission Fields*, AMJ 1913.

[59]William Heth Whitsitt Address delivered at the SBC Annual Meeting, 1895.

[60]Minute Book, Woman's Mission to Woman of Baltimore.

[61]Williams, "Woman's Mission to Woman."

[62]Mattie A. Heck, "Cloud and Sunshine," 1900, Fannie E. S. Heck Papers, North Carolina Baptist Historical Society, Wake Forest University, Winston-Salem, North Carolina.

[63]*RH*, November 14, 1878.

[64]SBC Annual 1879.

[65]Baker, *Southern Baptist Convention*, 239-44, 253.

[66]See reports of the respective boards in SBC Annuals 1877, 1878, 1879.

[67]T. P. Bell, "The Woman's Missionary Union, Auxiliary to the Southern Baptist Convention" (Address delivered at the Missionary Society of the Southern Baptist Theological Seminary, 1897); Early Leaflet Scrapbooks, WMU Archives.

[68]White, *Our Heritage*, 33; Minute Book, Woman's Baptist Home Mission Society of Maryland, Maryland Baptist Historical Society.

[69]*Western Recorder (WR)*, December 6, 1888.

[70]*Alabama Baptist (AB)*, March 4, 1886.

[71]*WR*, December 6, 1888.

[72]*Baltimore Baptist*, May 5, 1888.

[73]C. Vann Woodward, *Origins of the New South 1877-1913*, vol. 9, *A History of the South* (Baton Rouge: Louisiana State University Press and the Littlefield Fund for Southern History of the University of Texas, 1951).

[74]For example: *AB*, May 22, 1884; *RH*, September 17, 1877, July 24, 1884, December 6, 1888; *Foreign Mission Journal (FMJ)*, May 1885; *WR*, May 21, 1885.

[75]*Montgomery Advertiser and Mail*, January 1, 1880, quoted in Woodward, *Origins of the New South*.

[76]Annie Armstrong in Annual Report (AR), WMU, SBC, 1900.

[77]The author is indebted to Evelyn Wingo Thompson of Shelbyville, Kentucky, for her extensive research into the Osborne family and their two women's periodicals, *Heathen Helper* and *Baptist Basket*. Thompson is author of *Luther Rice: Believer in Tomorrow* (see note 14).

[78]*RH*, March 22, 1888.

[79]*Heathen Helper (HH)*, December 1882.

[80]*WR*, May 31, 1883; *Texas Baptist—Extra*, May 12, 1883.

[81]*Historical Sketch, Woman's Auxiliary*

(Waco: Waco Baptist Association, [1928]), 4; *Then to Now, 1904-1955: A History of Woman's Missionary Union, Auxiliary to Waco Association* (Waco, n.p., [1955]), 2; Frank E. Burkhalter, *A World-Visioned Church: Story of the First Baptist Church, Waco, Texas* (Nashville: Broadman Press, 1946).

[82]*RH*, February 16, 1871, and March 9, 1871, and following.

[83]*HH*, June 1883. The following account is from this source.

[84]*Baptist Argus (BA)*, March 16, 1898; *Texas Baptist—Extra*, May 12, 1883.

[85]*BA*, February 27 and March 16, 1898.

[86]*Baltimore Baptist*, April 17, 1884.

[87]*RH*, September 25, 1884.

[88]Annie Armstrong, "Women as Helpers in God's Kingdom" (Maryland Baptist Mission Rooms, 1900), WMU Archives.

[89]*RH*, September 25, 1884; *Baltimore Baptist*, May 15, 1884, gives text of speech on the necessity of women missionaries for women.

[90]*AB*, May 22, 1884; *Baltimore Baptist*, May 15, 1884.

[91]*AB*, May 22, 1884.

[92]Kate Ellen Gruver, *From This High Pinnacle: One Hundred Years with Georgia Baptist Woman's Missionary Union* (Atlanta: Woman's Missionary Union, Auxiliary to Georgia Baptist Convention, 1983), 34.

[93]*HH*, March 1885.

[94]*AB*, April 30, 1885.

[95]*FMJ*, May 1885; Catherine B. Allen, *The New Lottie Moon Story* (Nashville: Broadman Press, 1980), 142.

[96]*Baltimore Baptist*, May 14, 1885.

[97]Jane B. Watson, *Laborers Together: The History of Arkansas Woman's Missionary Union* (to be published 1988); J. P. Eagle, *A Brief Memoir of Mary K. Eagle* (Little Rock: Press of Arkansas Democrat Co., 1903); Mrs. W. D. Pye, "A Bouquet of December Roses," Arkansas WMU Office.

[98]All major state papers carried detailed accounts of the meeting; see *WR*, May 14, 1885.

[99]Ibid.

[100]*HH*, May 1885.

[101]*Baltimore Baptist*, June 25, 1885, and May 28, 1885. *RH*, June 4, 1885, and April 19, 1888. The pseudonymous article of 1888 said, "Now men think we will be out of our sphere if we meet in council with them, and yet they do not want us to meet in council by ourselves. In the name of common sense, do they want us to sit down and do nothing for God's cause, like so many of them have done for ages and are still doing?"

[102]*RH*, June 4, 1885.

[103]*Baltimore Baptist*, October 1, 1885.

[104]*WR*, May 20, 1886. A detailed account appears in an unsigned letter to Fannie E. S. Heck in WMU Archives, presumably prepared by someone in the Osborne family, perhaps Mrs. W. B. McGarity, about the role of *Heathen Helper* and *Baptist Basket* in the pre-1888 meetings of women.

[105]*Baltimore Baptist*, May 12, 1887; Mrs.

James Pollard, "Enlistment of State Forces and Organization of Woman's Missionary Union," Early Leaflet Collection, WMU Archives; *Missionary Talk* (Raleigh: North Carolina Woman's Central Committee of Missions), June 1, 1887.

[106]*RH*, July 28, 1887.

[107]SBC Annual 1887.

[108]*WR*, April 12, 1888.

[109]Evidence of the women's behind-the-scenes political efforts is a letter from Alice Armstrong to Professor H. H. Harris, February 29, 1888, asking him to explain the facts about the women's plans and to advocate them. She claimed that even J. William Jones, the opponent of 1884 and 1885, had favored the plans once they were explained to him. Letter in WMU files, Virginia Baptist Historical Society.

[110]Tupper to Ford, January 23, 1888, Tupper Letter Book, FMB Archives, Richmond, Virginia.

[111]Mattie Heck, "Cloud and Sunshine."

[112]*HH*, April 1888.

[113]*BC*, July 5, 1888.

[114]Agnes Osborne as secretary published her notes in *HH*, June 1888, while a fuller account was published in *Baptist Basket*, June 1888. Further details are found in *BC*, June 14 and July 5, 1888. Other state papers contributing significant details are *Baltimore Baptist*, May 24, 1888, and *RH*, May 24, 1888.

[115]*BC*, May 17, 1888. One of the most comprehensive reports on the SBC is in *Baptist Basket*, June 1888.

[116]William Owen Carver recalled the incident in his address to the 50th anniversary Annual Meeting of WMU (*RS*, Oct. 1938, 7). Carver had been a student in Richmond in 1888; later he became WMU's advocate in the realm of theological education. The account was also written in 1913 by Heck, *In Royal Service*, 126-77.

[117]Undated clipping, apparently from *RH*, May 1938. This was a recollection of J. J. Wicker, who became a member of the FMB. He wrote in 1938, when WMU returned to Richmond for its 50th anniversary.

[118]Susan Tyler Pollard, "Enlistment of State Forces."

[119]*Baptist Basket*, June 1888.

Chapter 2. We the Women

[1]*Western Recorder (WR)*, June 7, 1888.

[2]J. William Jones, quoted in *Alabama Baptist (AB)*, May 22, 1884.

[3]Annie Armstrong, Annual Report (AR), WMU, SBC, 1903.

[4]Annie Armstrong, AR 1892.

[5]Susan Tyler Pollard, "Enlistment of State Forces and Organization of Woman's Missionary Union, SBC," Early Leaflets, WMU Archives, Birmingham, Alabama. James Pollard had brought the motion at the 1887 Convention which led to the indirect approval given WMU by the Southern Baptist Convention of 1888.

[6]Constitutions and bylaws are printed in each year's Annual Report.

[7]*Religious Herald (RH)*, April 19, 1888; Hannah Reynolds in *Home and Foreign Fields*, October 1926.

[8]WMU Year Book 1912.

[9]A highly revealing study is James J. Thompson, Jr., *Tried as by Fire: Southern Baptists and the Religious Controversies of the 1920s* (Macon, Ga.: Mercer University Press, 1982), 137.

[10]AR 1918.

[11]AR 1919.

[12]WMU Year Book 1958-59.

[13]*Royal Service (RS)*, August 1965. Changes in statements of purpose are best tracked in the annual WMU Year Book. From the mid-1960s, the tasks were meticulously explained in in-house program design documents. Entitled "WMU Base Design" the documents have been updated every few years by staff, with input and approval by the WMU Executive Board and the staff of other church program agencies. The 1988 Base Design was approved by the Executive Board in 1986.

[14]Ralph Winter of Fuller Theological Seminary and acting director of the World Mission Center, Pasadena, California, as noted in Executive Board Minutes, WMU, SBC (EB), 1977.

[15]AR 1899.

[16]*Foreign Mission Journal (FMJ)*, June 1888; H. A. Tupper to Martha McIntosh, June 6, 1888. Tupper Letter Book, Foreign Mission Board (FMB) Archives, Richmond, Virginia.

[17]Executive Committee Minutes, WMU, SBC (EC), June 8, 1912; January 12, 1912.

[18]Mallory to Charles E. Maddry, September 27, 1944, FMB Archives.

[19]Alma Hunt Oral History, WMU Archives.

[20]Hunt to Baker James Cauthen, September 16, 1966, FMB Archives; Hunt to Arthur B. Rutledge, September 17, 1966, Hunt Papers, WMU Archives.

[21]Bobbie Sorrill, *Annie Armstrong: Dreamer in Action* (Nashville: Broadman Press, 1984), 161-69, 224, 259, 265-69.

[22]Catherine B. Allen, *Laborers Together with God* (Birmingham: Woman's Missionary Union, 1987), biographical sketch of Olive B. Martin.

[23]AR 1899; Annie Armstrong to R. J. Willingham, undated, apparently early 1900, FMB Archives.

[24]Armstrong to Willingham, undated, apparently May 1900, FMB Archives.

[25]EC, June 12, 1900; AR 1901.

[26]EC, June 17, 1903; *Christian Index*, May 21, 1903. Resolutions of Executive Committee of Baptist Women Mission Workers of Texas, 1905 Folder, BGCT Collection, Southwestern Baptist Theological Seminary (SWBTS) Archives, Fort Worth, Texas; Sorrill, *Annie Armstrong*.

[27]Marjean Patterson, *Covered Foundations: A History of Mississippi Woman's Missionary Union* (Jackson: Mississippi Woman's Missionary Union, [1987]), 14-15.

[28]EC, May, June, November 1889; AR 1890.

[29]See Treasurer's Report, AR 1907-11 and thereafter.

[30]*RS*, June 1916. Dixon was the daughter of the fundamentalist preacher A. C. Dixon. She was a graduate of Mt. Holyoke and did graduate study at Ratcliffe.

[31]Minutes, Secretaries and Field Workers Council, WMU Archives.

[32]AR 1914, 1915.

[33]AR 1939, 56.

[34]Hunt to Albert McClellan, July 15, 1966; Hunt Papers, WMU Archives.

[35]EB, August 14, 1957.

[36]EB, January 1976.

[37]Ivyloy Bishop Oral History.

[38]AR 1948, Tributes to Kathleen Mallory.

[39]Salaries are detailed in AR for 1907 through 1948, in treasurer's reports. FMB and HMB salaries are included in SBC Annuals for the same period; EC, January 25, 1951.

[40]Minutes of Board of Managers, May 11, 1936; EC, May 12, 1941.

[41]Alma Hunt Oral History.

[42]EC, November 1940; Ethlene Cox to Laura M. Armstrong, 1944, WMU Archives; Mallory to Carrie U. Littlejohn, August 27, 1943, Woman's Missionary Union Training School files, Southern Baptist Theological Seminary, Louisville, Kentucky.

[43]*Baptist and Reflector*, January 5, 1983, gives the story of Vaughtie B. Rowland, for 25 years the WMU and church media library consultant for the Hamilton County Baptist Association, Tennessee, one example of an associational WMU employee.

[44]Addresses of the headquarters were as follows: 1888, 10 East Fayette Street (building now marked with a plaque); 1892, 9 West Lexington Street; 1897, 304 North Howard Street; 1902, 233 North Howard Street; 1906, 301 North Charles Street (Wilson Building); 1909, 15 West Franklin Street.

[45]J. M. Frost Letter Book, 1906 March-May; Armstrong-Mrs. Charles Ammen, Armstrong-Eliza Broadus, Armstrong-Mattie Kerfoot Correspondence; Lillie Easterby Barker to Armstrong, March 21, 1896. Frost took a strong hand in the transition era.

[46]*Baptist Argus*, June 21, 1906; Heck to J. M. Frost, May 26 and May 29, 1906; Frost to Heck, June 21, 1906; Frost to Mrs. W. C. Lowndes, June 6, 1906.

[47]AR 1909.

[48]EC, February 19, 1920.

[49]AR 1920; *RS*, November 1920.

[50]Juliette Mather Oral History; AR 1921.

[51]*RS*, April 1922.

[52]Minnie K. James to I. J. Van Ness, October 9, 1921; Sallie Bailey Jones to I. J. Van Ness, November 7, 1921, Van Ness Papers, BSSB. See AR 1922-49 for BSSB contributions reflected in treasurer's report.

[53]Mallory to Sarah Joe Hurst Burney, April 25, 1947, Burney Papers, WMU Archives.

[54]AR 1947; Board of Managers Minutes, May 7, 1947; Kathleen Mallory retirement letter, WMU Archives.

[55]*RS*, October 1951.

[56]EC, January 25, 1951; AR 1952 and 1953.

[57]EC, January 1957; Hunt Letters, April 17, 1959, and February 26, 1960.

Chapter 3. The Minority Rules

[1]See biographical sketches of each of the WMU, SBC, officers in Catherine B. Allen, *Laborers Together with God* (Birmingham: Woman's Missionary Union, 1987).

[2]Mrs. T. L. Tomkinson, "The Art of Having Time," (Baltimore: The Mission Literature Department, SBC, n.d.).

[3]Mary Emily Wright, *Rise and Progress of Woman's Missionary Union* (Baltimore: Baptist Mission Rooms, 1899). Wright was president of WMU of Georgia and a recording secretary of WMU. The pamphlet would have been edited by Annie Armstrong. We can assume each fully subscribed to this philosophy of the powers of the state organizations.

[4]Annual Report (AR), WMU, SBC, 1889.

[5]Wright, *Rise and Progress*.

[6]Mrs. A. J. Aven, "History of Woman's Missionary Union of Mississippi," (Mississippi WMU, 1913).

[7]Juliette Mather, *Light Three Candles: History of Woman's Mission Union of Virginia, 1874-1973* (Richmond: Woman's Missionary Union of Virginia, [1973]), 39.

[8]Hermione Dannelly Jackson, *Women of Vision* (Montgomery: Woman's Missionary Union, Auxiliary to Alabama Baptist State Convention, 1964).

[9]Foy Johnson Farmer, *Hitherto: History of North Carolina Woman's Missionary Union* (Raleigh: WMU of North Carolina, 1952), 14. Farmer quotes a letter from Annie Armstrong to Fannie E. S. Heck, December 11, 1890, welcoming North Carolina into the Union.

[10]*Baptist Argus*, October 20, 1898.

[11]Armstrong's involvement in Oklahoma Territory and Indian Territory is carefully documented in Bobbie Sorrill, *Annie Armstrong: Dreamer in Action* (Nashville: Broadman Press, 1984), 137-38, 183-86. See also J. M. Gaskin, *Baptist Women in Oklahoma* (Oklahoma City: Messenger Press [Historical Commission, Baptist General Convention of the State of Oklahoma], [1986]), 94-101.

[12]Sorrill, *Annie Armstrong;* Allen, *Laborers Together with God.*

[13]Inez (Price) Taylor, *Facets of a Diamond: 75 Years of Illinois WMU History* (Springfield: Woman's Missionary Union, Illinois Baptist State Association, 1983), 7.

[14]*Encyclopedia of Southern Baptists (ESB)*, vol. 2, articles on New Mexico Baptist Convention and on WMU, Auxiliary to Baptist Convention of New Mexico.

[15]Robert A. Baker, *The Southern Baptist Convention and Its People, 1607-1972* (Nashville: Broadman Press, 1974), 361.

[16]Minutes of Executive Committee (EC), WMU, SBC, January 26-28, 1954.

[17]Minutes, Executive Secretaries' Meeting, May 10, 1952.

[18]Mrs. James Cobb (formerly Mrs. Charles M. Griffin) Oral History Interview by Hannah Hills, October 31, 1985; Nicy Murphy Oral History, July 22, 1985, and scrapbook.

[19]Hamilton to Catherine B. Allen, January 4, 1986; Interview with Nicy Murphy.

[20]*Royal Service (RS)*, May 1960 and August 1961.

[21]*ESB*, vol. 3, "Thirty Thousand Movement."

[22]Ibid., "Project 500."

[23]Alma Hunt Oral History.

[24]Ava James Papers, WMU Archives, Birmingham, Alabama.

[25]Alma Hunt Oral History Interviews; *RS*, March 1963.

[26]*RS*, March 1963.

[27]Helen Fling Oral History; Interview with Edwina Robinson, April 20, 1985; Ava James Papers.

[28]"Paul and Ava James State Missions Offering," leaflet, Ava James Papers.

[29]Executive Board Minutes (EB), WMU, SBC, January 1976.

[30]Carolyn Weatherford Oral History; Christine Gregory Oral History.

[31]Although the Choctaw-Chickasaw WMU has been said to be the oldest associational union, it is younger than the St. Louis WMU, formed 1872.

[32]Recollection by Mrs. J. S. Murrow quoted in Gaskin, *Baptist Women in Oklahoma.*

[33]AR 1939; Una Roberts Lawrence to Kathleen Mallory, July 31, 1926, and July 27, 1931; Lawrence Papers, HMB Collection, Historical Commission (HC), Nashville, Tennessee.

[34]E. P. Alldredge, *The New Challenge of Home Missions* (Nashville: Sunday School Board of the SBC, 1927).

[35]Una Roberts Lawrence, *Winning the Border: Baptist Missions Among the Spanish-Speaking Peoples of the Border* (Atlanta: Home Mission Board, SBC, 1935), 80-89; *Destellos del Rubi: Es Un Boceto de la Historia de la UFM del Estado de Texas* (San Antonio, n.p., 1957). Also, the author is indebted to Martha Thomas Ellis, longtime leader of Hispanic WMU work in the US, for her translation of *Sendas de Luz: Historia de la Union Femenil Misionera, Auxiliar a la Convencion Bautista Mexicana de Texas 1917-1967* (Dallas: Woman's Missionary Union of Texas, [1967]).

[36]Lulie P. Wharton, *Fruits of the Years: The Story of Woman's Missionary Union and Home Missions* (Atlanta: Home Mission Board, Southern Baptist Convention, 1938).

[37]Noemi Cuevas Jimenez to Catherine B. Allen, 1985.

[38]*RS*, April 1916; *Personal Service Guide*, WMU Archives.

[39]Alma Hunt Board Letter, April 4, 1962.

[40]Carolyn Weatherford Board Letter, May 13, 1975.

[41]Interview with Becie Kirkwood, May 20, 1986.

[42]Heck to Mrs. Black, April 25, 1898.

[43]AR 1914.

[44]AR 1914.

[45]AR 1925 and 1926; Kathleen Mallory–

I. J. Van Ness Correspondence, 1925 and 1926, Van Ness Papers, Sunday School Board, Nashville, Tennessee; SBC Annual 1924.

[46]Alma Hunt Oral History.

[47]Foreign Mission Board Reports in SBC Annuals contain statistics on WMU on foreign fields. For information about development of WMU abroad, see AR 1913-1953. Also see Blanche Sydnor White, *Saved to Serve* (Richmond: Rice Press, 1937). Ethlene Boone Cox, *Following in His Train* (Nashville: Broadman Press, 1938) includes a chapter on foreign WMUs. These sources are not in agreement about dates. A 1986 survey by the author contributed some new data, but a real study of these organizations has never been done.

[48]*Religious Herald (RH),* June 29, 1911.

[49]Blanche Sydnor White, *The Tie that Binds: A Brief History of the Women's Department of the Baptist World Alliance, 1911-1960* (Baltimore: J. H. Furst Co., n.d.); Ferne Levy, *God's Command—Our Response: A History of the Women's Department of the Baptist World Alliance* (n.p., [1985]).

[50]Marion Bates, interviewed May 16, 1985, by Dorothy Neal, Toronto, Canada.

[51]WMU's earliest contribution was $25 in 1925.

Chapter 4. Laborers Together

[1]Minutes of Woman's Missionary Union, WMU Archives, Birmingham, Alabama, contain account of the 1888 meeting as recorded by Agnes Osborne, secretary pro tem, from *Heathen Helper,* June 1888.

[2]Exodus 14:15.

[3]*Mosaics of Missions Methods* (Baltimore: Woman's Missionary Union, [1899]).

[4]Scrapbook of Early Leaflets, WMU Archives.

[5]Annual Report (AR), WMU, SBC, 1889.

[6]Heck Address in AR, 1912; Illustration in WMU Year Book 1912-13 and in AR 1913; Comment from diary of Rosa Hunter, WMU Archives.

[7]AR 1912, Heck Address.

[8]AR 1911.

[9]Statistics on standard achievement are reported in Annual Reports from 1914 onward.

[10]WMU's realistic view of the competing women's societies was seldom discussed outright. But it was detailed in the first *Manual of WMU Methods,* compiled by Kathleen Mallory and published for WMU by the Sunday School Board in 1917. Also, see letter from Kathleen Mallory to Selsus E. Tull December 16, 1916, including manuscript; Van Ness Papers, Box 5.7, Baptist Sunday School Board (BSSB), Nashville, Tennessee.

[11]Records of the WMU of Capitol Avenue Baptist Church, Atlanta, Georgia State Archives.

[12]Selsus E. Tull, Lansing Burrows, M. H. Wolfe, J. T. Henderson, J. B. Lawrence, *Church Organization and Methods: A Manual for Baptist Churches* (Nashville: Sunday School Board, 1917, published by action of the Southern Baptist Convention, 1916).

[13]Examples of WMU willingness to cooperate with the church treasurer: Annie Armstrong to E. S. Reaves, December 15, 1904, Tennessee WMU Office Files; *Alabama Baptist (AB),* January 9, 1890. Alabama WMU could not have gotten permission of the state convention to exist without promising to send contributions via the church treasurer.

[14]Spartan Association Minutes, 1921, quoted in Ellen Batson Watson, *A History of Woman's Missionary Union, Auxiliary to Spartan Baptist Association 1912-1968,* WMU Archives.

[15]Mallory to I. J. Van Ness, August 17, 1916; Van Ness to Mallory, April 20, 1917; Mallory to Van Ness, April 23, 1917; Box 6.8, Van Ness Papers, BSSB.

[16]Tull, *Church Organization and Methods.* Tull continued to campaign and WMU continued to resist him; Minutes of Executive Committee (EC), WMU, SBC, December 13, 1922.

[17]*Dimension,* July-August-September 1971; July-August-September 1972.

[18]See chapter 12 for discussion of the auxiliary-department relationships of state WMUs. This shift in WMU operating control was basically an outgrowth of the changing patterns of church finance.

[19]The former president of WMU, Sarah Davis Stakely (Mrs. Charles), unified the multiple women's organizations at First Baptist Church of Montgomery in 1915. All their records to date were placed in a bank vault. In deference to the aiders, the new Woman's Union temporarily omitted the word *Missionary* from their title. The strongbox of records is now in WMU Archives.

[20]Inez (Price) Taylor, *Facets of a Diamond: 75 Years of Illinois WMU History* (Springfield: Woman's Missionary Union, Illinois Baptist State Association, 1983), 36.

[21]*Royal Service (RS),* July 1942; Vaughtie B. Rowland, *Polishers of Diamonds: Seventy-five Years of Woman's Missionary Union Work in Ocoee Association, Oct. 1898-Sept. 1949 and Hamilton County Association, Oct. 1949-Sept. 1973* (Chattanooga: Hamilton County Baptist Association, 1973), 5.

[22]Mrs. George Westmoreland, *Through the Years with WMU: History of the Woman's Missionary Union, Auxiliary to the Atlanta Association of Baptist Churches from 1908-1936* (Atlanta: Baptist Woman's Missionary Union, [1936]), 73-74.

[23]*RS,* April 1941.

[24]Executive Secretaries Meeting Minutes, July 31, 1948; EC, January 19-24, 1952.

[25]EC, January 1960.

[26]EC, January 1964; WMU Year Book 1964-65.

[27]AR 1970.

[28]*World Comrades,* JFM 1923. The magazines in 1936 carried several 50th anniversary stories of Sunbeam history.

[29]SBC Annual 1889, FMB Report.

[30]Mrs. B. D. Gray, "Sunbeam Origins," manuscript for *Home Fields* [November] 1911, WMU Archives.

[31]EC, November 30, 1888; January 3, 1889.

[32]AR 1896.

[33]Hyde had a regular column in the *Baptist Courier*. Her correspondent of January 19, 1899, was Mrs. Montgomery of Clifton, South Carolina.

[34]Gambrell to Minnie Burke, March 18, 1908, Southwestern Baptist Theological Seminary Archives, Fort Worth, Texas.

[35]EC, January 1959 and January 1967.

[36]Broadus to Juliette Mather, 1931-32 collection in YWA Files, WMU Archives.

[37]Mrs. J. H. Eager, "The Dropped Stitch," Early Leaflets, WMU Archives.

[38]Characterization by Katherine Davis (Mrs. George E.) of South Carolina, seemingly an eyewitness account of the 1907 Annual Meeting, WMU Archives. Davis went on to be a primary leader of YWA work in South Carolina and throughout the South.

[39]Heck, "YWA: The Rally Cry for Young Woman's Auxiliary," Early Leaflets, WMU Archives; Minutes of Secretaries and Field Workers Conference, May 17, 1914.

[40]Note on postcard to Mather from Katherine Davis, May 24, 1924, WMU Archives.

[41]AR 1921; Margaret McRae Lackey, *Decade of WMU Service, 1913-1923* (Nashville: Sunday School Board, SBC, 1923), 99-101; Clarence Prouty Shedd, *The Church Follows Its Students* (London: Oxford University Press, 1938), 87-92.

[42]Juliette Mather, *Light Three Candles: History of Woman's Missionary Union of Virginia, 1874-1973* (Richmond: Woman's Missionary Union of Virginia, [1973]), 103.

[43]EC, January 1965.

[44]Juliette Mather Oral History.

[45]*Baptist Courier*, June 26, 1901.

[46]AR 1890.

[47]AR 1907; *Times-Dispatch*, Richmond, May 18, 1907.

[48]Fiftieth Anniversary Scrapbook containing 1938 Richmond newspaper clippings, WMU Archives; AR 1950.

[49]*RS*, October 1938; EC, October 2, 1907; May 1908.

[50]*Baptist and Reflector*, February 9, 1933.

[51]Mrs. John R. Crawford to Juliette Mather, April 25, 1938, RA Files, WMU Archives; AR 1909.

[52]Lawrence to Margaret Hutchinson, September 27, 1964, RA Files, WMU Archives.

[53]EC, May 6, 1925.

[54]EC, January 1927; Ethlene Boone Cox Address, Annual Meeting, 1930; AR 1939; EC, January 16, 1948, and January 1949.

[55]Ivyloy Bishop Oral History.

[56]Delegates were listed in Annual Reports.

[57]Alma Hunt Board Letter, April 24, 1952.

[58]EC, May 6, 1950.

[59]Full reports of the committee chaired by Robert E. Naylor are found in SBC Annuals 1953 and 1954. See also SBC Annual 1952 for original motions. In 1953 an attempt to stop the committee's work and leave all

initiative with WMU was made by John H. Buchanan, pastor of several WMU staff members in Birmingham. Some understood this to be WMU's wish. It may have been, for WMU wanted to risk no endorsement of Boy Scouts, as the "camel's nose under the tent," according to Ivyloy Bishop. See also EC, January 25-28, 1954; Robert E. Naylor to Catherine B. Allen, March 3, 1986.

[60]Recollection of Omer Shermer Alford (Mrs. John I.), then president of WMU of Georgia, May 9, 1985, WMU Archives. See also Naylor to Allen, March 3, 1986.

[61]Carolyn Weatherford to Alma Hunt, October 11, 1967. Weatherford was then executive secretary of Florida WMU. EC, 1969.

[62]Because WMU did not have enrollment records classified by male and female, it is impossible to know how many boys were transferred in 1970. Perhaps 15,000 to 20,000 would be approximately correct.

[63]*Our Mission Fields*, 1909 and following.

[64]AR 1964.

[65]W. L. Howse Papers, BSSB; Alma Hunt Interview; WMU Year Book 1968-69, 1969-70, 1970-71.

[66]AR 1966.

[67]AR 1909.

[68]AR 1966.

[69]EC, January 1970.

[70]AR 1967.

[71]Helen Fling Oral History.

[72]W. L. Howse Papers, BSSB.

[73]Recollection of Alberta Gilpin, executive director of Missouri WMU, June 10, 1985, WMU Archives.

[74]Mrs. R. Knolan Benfield, EC, May 30, 1971.

Chapter 5. Mites to Millions

[1]"Sketch and Constitution of the Woman's Missionary Societies, Auxiliary to SBC" (Baltimore: Executive Committee of Woman's Mission Societies, 1888).

[2]*Religious Herald (RH)*, March 2, 1876.

[3]Ann J. Graves to James B. Taylor, July 4, 1871; Graves to H. A. Tupper, March 1, 1872; Graves to Rosewell Graves, July 6, 1871, Goodman-Graves File, Foreign Mission Board Archives, Richmond, Virginia; Mrs. Eugene Levering, "Sketch of the Organization of the Woman's Missionary Union," 1938. Helen E. Falls, "Baptist Women in Missions Support in the Nineteenth Century," *Baptist History and Heritage*, January 1977, 26-36.

[4]Kathleen Mallory and Ethlene Cox, SBC Annual, WMU Report to SBC, 1932.

[5]*Heathen Helper*, May 1888; Inez (Price) Taylor, *Facets of a Diamond: 75 Years of Illinois WMU History* (Springfield, Illinois: Woman's Missionary Union, Illinois Baptist State Association, 1983), 9, 17, 18; Laura Mason, *Ye Are the Branches: A History of the Missouri Baptist Woman's Missionary Organizations*, (Jefferson City, Mo.: Woman's Missionary Union of Missouri, 1987); *Alabama Baptist (AB)*, January 20, 1887.

[6]*Baptist Courier (BC)*, April 15, 1880; *Missionary Interchange*, Missouri, undated. Quoted in Cora McWilliams, *Women and Missions in Missouri: A History of the Seventy-five Years of Organized Baptist Missionary Activity in Missouri, 1876-1951* (Jefferson City, Mo.: Woman's Missionary Union of Missouri, 1951), 207.
[7]Fannie E. S. Heck address, Annual Report (AR), WMU, SBC, 1893; Quoted by Ruth Alleyn (Alice Armstrong), *RH*, December 1, 1887.
[8]Annie Armstrong to R. J. Willingham, September 26, 1898, FMB Archives.
[9]*BC*, April 15, 1880.
[10]Account of the Ladies Missionary Society, First Baptist Church of Richmond, *Religious Herald*, May 31, 1900. John Stout conveyed money collected by Martha McIntosh to the Foreign Mission Board. J. W. M. Williams or Franklin Wilson transmitted the money of Baltimore Woman's Mission to Woman. *Baptist and Reflector*, June 16, 1892; Mary Gambrell to Mrs. J. E. Garrison, February 19, 1908, Southwestern Baptist Theological Seminary (SWBTS) Texas Baptist Collection, Fort Worth, Texas.
[11]SBC Annual 1888; *RH*, May 17, 1888.
[12]AR 1889; *Heathen Helper*, July 1888.
[13]Scrapbook of Early Leaflets, WMU Archives, Birmingham, Alabama.
[14]Plan of Work, AR 1889 and 1890.
[15]Minutes of Maryland Woman's Baptist Home Mission Society, Maryland Baptist Historical Archives, Lutherville, Maryland.
[16]SBC Annual 1904; AR 1912; Lansing Burrows, *How Baptists Work Together* (Nashville: Sunday School Board, 1911), 115-116; Victor I. Masters, *Baptist Missions in the South* (Atlanta: Home Mission Board, 1915), 153-154; *Our Mission Field (OMF)*, AMJ 1914.
[17]AR 1909 and 1910.
[18]Box value totals are reported in AR, financial tables, 1898-1941. Flier, "Boxes to Frontier Missionaries," giving full directions for process and a blank for missionary to fill out with the clothing data, Heck File, SWBTS.
[19]*Baptist Argus (BA)*, May 26, 1898.
[20]No formal records of Christmas-in-August participation are maintained. Chaplain Tiller's letter to Carolyn Weatherford is one random thank-you letter that came to the WMU office in Birmingham.
[21]Alma Hunt and Catherine B. Allen, *History of Woman's Missionary Union*, Revised Edition (Nashville: Convention Press, 1976), 49-50; *Birmingham Age-Herald* and *Daily News*, May 12, 1891.
[22]AR 1894. Heck was paraphrasing William Carey.
[23]The New Century Movement is summarized in these sources: SBC Annual 1900; AR 1901 and 1902. Armstrong to R. J. Willingham, June 5 and June 11, 1900, FMB Archives; Armstrong to F. H. Kerfoot, July 23, 1900, in transcriptions by Una Roberts Lawrence, WMU Archives; AR 1901; *BC*, May 30, 1901; *BA*, June 28 and August 16, 1900.
[24]Mary Emily Wright, *The Missionary Work of the Southern Baptist Convention* (Philadelphia: American Baptist Publication Society, 1902), 303-304; J. B. Lawrence, *History of the Home Mission Board* (Nashville: Broadman Press, 1958), 73-74.
[25]Home Mission Board (HMB) Minutes, March 3, 1900.
[26]AR 1901; *Royal Service (RS)*, October 1917; Leaflet by Annie Armstrong, "Women as Helpers in God's Kingdom."
[27]SBC Annual 1909 and 1910; Annie Armstrong Notebook transcribed by Una Roberts Lawrence, WMU Archives; *Baptist and Reflector*, November 29, 1917.
[28]*Home and Foreign Fields*, February 1919, gives a colorful example of a Texas meeting in which the women overpledged their goal. The Baptist Hall of Fame books are at Historical Commission (HC), Nashville, Tennessee, and Home Mission Board (HMB), Atlanta, Georgia. Among WMU leaders prominently mentioned: Amanda Tupper Hamilton of Alabama; Sarah Jessie Davis Stakely; Emma Amos of Georgia; Eliza Broadus of Kentucky; Mrs. W. P. Throgmorton of Illinois; Marie Buhlmaier of Maryland; Fannie E. S. Heck; Margaret M. Lackey of Mississippi; Mary Belle Wheeler of Tennessee; Fannie Breedlove Davis of Texas. Kathleen Mallory personally gave $500 in honor of her aunt and uncle.
[29]SBC Annual 1920.
[30]HMB Minutes, May 5, 1899; FMB Minutes, April 11, April 27, and May 20, 1899; *RS*, February 1928.
[31]*RS*, March 1919; AR 1919; Minutes of Executive Committee (EC), WMU, SBC, February 5, 1919.
[32]EC, December 7, 1921. Kathleen Mallory was quoting Rufus Weaver.
[33]AR 1920. Extensive data about WMU's involvement in the campaign may be found in the L. R. Scarborough Papers, SWBTS Archives.
[34]Minutes of Conservation Commission of the $75 Million Campaign, HC.
[35]AR 1923.
[36]Isa-Beall Neel, *His Story in Georgia WMU History* (Atlanta: Woman's Missionary Union, Auxiliary to the Georgia Baptist Convention, 1939), 118.
[37]T. B. Ray, *Southern Baptists in the Great Adventure* (Nashville: Sunday School Board, Southern Baptist Convention, 1934), 194.
[38]Good discussions of the difficulties are found in James J. Thompson, Jr., *Tried as by Fire: Southern Baptists and the Religious Controversies of the 1920s* (Macon, Georgia: Mercer University Press, 1982); and J. F. Love, *What Is the Matter with the Baptists?* (Richmond: Educational Department, Foreign Mission Board, 1926), 34-38.
[39]AR 1922.
[40]Lee N. Allen, *Woodlawn Baptist Church: The First Century* (Birmingham: Woodlawn Baptist Church, 1986).
[41]Merrie Pender Sugg Papers, Virginia Baptist Historical Society, Richmond, Virginia.
[42]*BC*, January 1, 1925. Ledger book is pre-

served in vault of South Carolina WMU, Columbia.

43"The Seven-Fold Appeal of the 1925 Baptist Program," leaflet, HC.

44Douglas J. Ginn, *Seventy Years History of Tennessee Woman's Missionary Union as I Saw It* (Nashville: Woman's Missionary Union, Auxiliary to the Tennessee Baptist Convention, 1958), 70.

45SBC Annual 1895.

46AR 1896.

47Foreign Mission Board (FMB) Minutes, January 5, 1915.

48FMB Minutes, June 28, 1915; AR 1916; AR 1917. Leaflet, "Willing-Hearted Giving" by J. F. Love and Kathleen Mallory; FMB Minutes, May 25, 1916; Article by Mrs. J. Marse Grant, undated, from *Biblical Recorder,* quoting account by Abbie B. Bonstell; J. F. Love said (1917 SBC Annual) that the women gave $60,000, though the records did not show that much; *RS,* November 1916.

49Love Resolutions, SBC Annual 1928.

50AR 1936.

51AR and SBC Annual 1932 and 1933.

52*AB,* April 27, 1933; AR 1933; EC, May 1933; SBC EC, May 1933.

53Juliette Mather Oral History; Mather to Carrie S. Vaughan, April 15, 1977, VBHS; Recollection by Mrs. W. D. Pye, Mallory File, WMU Archives; Recollection by Sarah Joe Hurst Burney (also an SBC Executive Committee member), Mallory File, WMU Archives. According to statistics in AR 1935, Virginia WMU gave $1.00 per adult member while promoting only the FMB debt, while all states supporting the Hundred Thousand Club gave 31 cents per adult.

54SBC Annual 1934; *RS,* July 1933; *Western Recorder* (WR), June 22, 1933.

55*RS,* April 1940 and August 1941; EC, January 1940; SBC Annual, 1942.

56SBC Annual 1944. *RS* in 1940 quoted Dillard and Wright, stressing women's supposed innate hatred of debt. Figures for WMU contributions can be derived from SBC Annuals which recorded overall debt contributions and from WMU AR. In 1938 reports WMU's percentage passed 60 and rose as high as 81 in 1942.

57EC, June 3, 1925.

58"The Calendar," First Baptist Church of Montgomery, November 29, 1925, cited in Lee N. Allen's history of the church. The other churches were Ensley and Southside of Birmingham; Parker Memorial of Anniston, Alabama; and First Baptist of Texarkana, Texas.

59Quoted in James Franklin Love, *Today's Supreme Challenge to America* (Nashville: Sunday School Board of the SBC, 1925), 21.

60The WMU proposal was passed by the January 1926 EC "after prayer." See *Home and Foreign Fields,* March 1926.

61EC, January 25, 1927.

62EC, June 13, 1928.

63EC, January 29, 1929.

64Albert McClellan, *The Executive Committee of the Southern Baptist Convention, 1917-1984* (Nashville: Broadman Press,

1985), 96.

65SBC Annual 1932, 27.

66EC, February 3, 1934; AR 1932 and 1934.

67W. O. Carver was one who violently objected to the Cooperative Program in 1931-33, calling it an "idol" and "repression." Carver to I. J. Van Ness, 1933, Van Ness Papers, SSB; Carver to Austin Crouch, February 20, 1931, Carver Papers, HC; John R. Sampey in *Baptist Standard,* April 27, 1933; WMU Year Book 1933-34.

68*RS,* October 1936.

69WMU's maneuvers involved not only Frank Tripp's aid, but also Mallory's pastor at First Baptist Church of Birmingham, John Slaughter. They were opposed by John Buchanan of Southside Baptist Church of Birmingham, whose majority plan was reported by a WMU staff member in his church.

70SBC Annual 1946, 47-48; Olive Martin to Carrie Littlejohn, January 8, 1947; Littlejohn to Martin, January 16, 1947, WMUTS Files, Southern Baptist Theological Seminary (SBTS).

71M. T. Rankin-Juliette Mather Correspondence, January 14, 1946, and March 21, 1947, FMB Archives; SBC Annual 1947, Business and Financial Plan.

72A. Hamilton Reid, *Baptists in Alabama: Their Organization and Witness* (Montgomery: Alabama Baptist State Convention, 1967), 309-10; Interview with Mary Essie Stephens, former executive secretary of Alabama WMU; Ethlene Boone Cox (Mrs. W. J.) to Alma Hunt, November 14, 1950, Cox Files, WMU Archives.

73AR 1950, Greetings from the Home Mission Board.

74SBC Annuals 1961 and 1962; Manuscript of Hunt's address in Hunt Friday Letters, WMU Archives; EC, January 1961.

75For example, Michael L. Speer to June Whitlow, November 1, 1973.

76AR 1974.

77*RS,* January 1936.

78Mrs. W. D. Pye, *Yield of the Golden Years: A History of the Baptist Woman's Missionary Union of Arkansas, 1888-1938* (Little Rock: Baptist Woman's Missionary Union of Arkansas, n.d.), 34.

79*Heathen Helper,* March 1885 and February 1888 as examples. *Baptist Basket* and *Heathen Helper* available on microfilm, HC.

80Quoted in Catherine B. Allen, *The New Lottie Moon Story* (Nashville: Broadman Press, 1980), 170, 161.

81SBC Annuals 1894 and 1895.

82Heck, *In Royal Service,* 210-211; EC, June 15, 1909; AR 1909 and 1910.

83AR 1912, 1913, and following; WMU Year Book 1912-13.

84Foy Johnson Farmer, *Sallie Bailey Jones* (Raleigh: WMU of North Carolina, 1949), 75; *RS,* October 1922; Leaflet, "How a Woman Can Tithe," revised by Alma Wright, undated.

85Blanche Sydnor White Correspondence gathered as research material by Carrie S. Vaughan for White's biography, *For Such a*

Time as This, VBHS.
[86]*RS,* June 1926; AR 1926.
[87]M. E. Dodd to W. O. Carver, May 25, 1932, Carver Papers. Dodd said that 118 Louisiana churches out of 318 with standard WMUs had failed to give in the last year. AR 1934; *RS,* August 1933 and June 1934; EC, April 21, 1943.
[88]*RS,* November 1938, 9.
[89]AR 1943; *RS,* January 1944, 4.
[90]*RS,* September 1943.
[91]WMU Year Books 1979-80, 1980-81, 1981-82.

Chapter 6. The Habit of Victory

[1]Full biographical data in Catherine B. Allen, *The New Lottie Moon Story* (Nashville: Broadman Press, 1980). The roommates were Julia Toy Johnson of Mississippi WMU and Jennie Snead Hatcher of Virginia WMU.
[2]*Foreign Mission Journal (FMJ),* December 1887.
[3]Minutes of the Woman's Missionary Society, Welsh Neck Baptist Church, Society Hill, South Carolina; Undated circular from McIntosh promoting the 1889 offering.
[4]*Baptist Basket,* April 1889.
[5]Annual Report (AR), WMU, SBC, 1892.
[6]AR 1906.
[7]Minutes of Executive Committee (EC), WMU, SBC, May 10, 1926; Juliette Mather, *Light Three Candles: History of Woman's Missionary Union of Virginia, 1874-1973* (Richmond: Woman's Missionary Union of Virginia, Baptist General Association of Virginia, [1973]), 88.
[8]EC, May 14, 1928; Foreign Mission Board (FMB) Minutes, February 8, 1928, April 5, 1928, June 1928, June 1929.
[9]EC, May 6, 1929.
[10]EC, May 9, 1931, and October 6, 1931.
[11]SBC Annual 1936; AR 1934 and 1935; Maddry's unpublished history of the FMB, FMB Archives, Richmond, Virginia.
[12]AR 1935; Mallory to Nelle Putney of Waichow, China, May 2, 1936, FMB Archives, is one example of WMU's communication with missionaries.
[13]FMB Minutes, June 11, 1936, and many other references beginning 1930.
[14]Blanche White to Charles E. Maddry, April 13, 1938, FMB Archives. This letter gives an example of how WMU firmly restricted $1,000 to appoint a new missionary to do "definite WMU work in the Good Will Center" in Jerusalem. White asked if Maddry were sending out a young woman "for a sort of BYPU job. If so, I'm not one bit interested, as you know, in spending WMU money for that. Anyhow, this money is not ours to designate, but belongs to the Southern Union (WMU, SBC) in the Mrs. W. J. Cox Fund."
[15]Mallory to Jessie Ford, FMB, January 23, 1940, FMB Archives.
[16]Maddry to Mallory, June 17, 1941; Mallory to Maddry, January 29, 1942; M. T. Rankin to Mallory, July 5, 1945, FMB Archives.

[17]Juliette Mather to M. T. Rankin, October 28, 1944.
[18]Rankin to Mallory, May 21, 1947.
[19]Mallory to Rankin, June 26, 1947, FMB Archives.
[20]SBC Annuals 1948 and 1949, FMB financial statements.
[21]AR 1951.
[22]Rankin to Olive Martin, January 8, 1952, WMU Archives, Birmingham, Alabama.
[23]Alma Hunt to Rankin, September 16, 1952, and Rankin response September 18; Hunt to Rankin, February 26, 1953, FMB Archives.
[24]EC, January 21, 1953; Hunt to Mrs. O. C. Hancock, August 31, 1956, Hunt Papers, WMU Archives; George W. Sadler to Mrs. Lester L. Knight, September 28, 1955, FMB Archives; Alma Hunt Oral History.
[25]FMB Minutes, October 1955.
[26]EC, September 6, 1956; FMB Minutes, October 1956; Cauthen to Marie Mathis, September 18, 1956, FMB Archives; George W. Sadler to Alma Hunt, October 1, 1956.
[27]AR 1967.
[28]Ethel Winfield to Blanche S. White, September 6, 1928, unclassified White Papers, Virginia Baptist Historical Society (VBHS).
[29]EC, October 2, 1928.
[30]Una Roberts Lawrence, *The Trail of Seed* (Atlanta: Home Mission Board, 1941), 17-18.
[31]Lulie P. Wharton, *Fruits of the Years: The Story of Woman's Missionary Union and Home Missions* (Atlanta: Home Mission Board, Southern Baptist Convention, 1938), 59.
[32]Lawrence, *The Trail of Seed,* 35-37; J. B. Lawrence, *History of the Home Mission Board* (Nashville: Broadman Press, 1958), 127-132; Wharton, *Fruits of the Years,* 57; Lawrence to Kathleen Mallory, November 6, 1934; Una Roberts Lawrence Papers, HMB Collection, Historical Commission (HC), Nashville, Tennessee.
[33]AR 1932.
[34]AR 1935.
[35]HMB Minutes, March 7, 1940.
[36]Hunt tribute to Lawrence, September 18, 1968, WMU Archives.
[37]Hilton Jones Crow, *God's Highway: Four Decades in Review* (Arizona: Woman's Missionary Union, Auxiliary to Arizona Southern Baptist Convention, 1968), 26.
[38]Armstrong to J. B. Lawrence, undated letter, Una Roberts Lawrence Papers, WMU Archives.
[39]*RS,* January 1969.
[40]Wilma Kirkham Reed and Elmin Kimbol Howell, Jr., *With These Hands* (Dallas: River Ministry Section, Baptist General Convention of Texas, 1982); Letter from Charles P. McLaughlin to author, November 25, 1986.
[41]Sarah Joe Hurst Burney to WMU 60th Anniversary Committee, April 17, 1947, 60th Anniversary File, Margaret Home Fund Files (1938), WMU Archives.
[42]"Houston's First Baptist Church" newsletter, December 2, 1948; November 24, 1949, November 30, 1950; and years follow-

ing, show example of one influential church's churchwide participation in the LMCO and week of prayer.

[43]Olive B. Martin (Mrs. George R.) to Alma Hunt, undated, early January 1951, Martin Files, WMU Archives; Mathis-Rankin Correspondence, FMB Archives, gives examples of her promotional ideas, opposition she overcame, and the FMB's warm appreciation.

[44]White Papers, VBHS, include several major documents tracing Virginia WMU's beliefs and practices on this question until the state acquiesced to the general plan in 1964.

[45]Mrs. Charles Herren Interview.

[46]EC, September 6, 1956; Hunt to state WMU executive secretaries, September 12, 1956, Hunt Letters, WMU Archives.

[47]Among critics were Reuben E. Alley, editor of the Virginia *Religious Herald*; C. R. Daley, editor of the *Western Recorder* of Kentucky; and Erwin L. McDonald, editor of the *Arkansas Baptist Newsmagazine.* Also Porter W. Routh in *Baptist Program* expressed his uneasiness about the offerings' growth. An extensive file of such published criticism from the early 1960s was kept in WMU Archives. Unfortunately, it is largely undated.

[48]AR 1951.

[49]EC, 1953.

[50]FMB Minutes, January 12, 1956.

[51]Hunt letter, October 22, 1971.

[52]Cauthen to Alberta Gilpin of Missouri WMU, March 2, 1972, FMB Archives.

[53]WMU News Release from Ridgecrest Baptist Conference Center, September 9, 1981.

Chapter 7. Come and Go

[1]Matthew 11:28; Mark 1:17; 16:15.

[2]*Woman's Missionary Friend,* September 1907, quoted in Patricia R. Hill, *The World Their Household: The American Woman's Foreign Mission Movement and Cultural Transformation, 1870-1920* (Ann Arbor: The University of Michigan Press, 1985), 149.

[3]Annual Report (AR), WMU, SBC, 1898.

[4]AR 1897.

[5]Helen Barrett Montgomery, *Western Women in Eastern Lands: An Outline Study of Fifty Years of Woman's Work in Foreign Missions* (New York: The Macmillan Co., 1910). This was the first general history of the women's missions movement.

[6]1888 account by Agnes Osborne.

[7]Elizabeth Dorean of Danville, Kentucky, to Juliette Mather, September 6, 1931, YWA Files, WMU Archives, Birmingham, Alabama.

[8]Mrs. L. S. Cole of Marks, Mississippi, "History of the Hebron YWA, Hebron Baptist Church, Newhebron, Mississippi," 1931, YWA Files, WMU Archives.

[9]Turner to Juliette Mather, 1931, YWA Files, WMU Archives. Turner was in a young women's group in Raleigh led by Fannie Heck.

[10]"Ma," apparently Harris, to Juliette Mather, 1931, YWA Files, WMU Archives.

[11]Foy Johnson Farmer, *Sallie Bailey Jones* (Raleigh: Woman's Missionary Union of North Carolina, 1949). Early WMU publications in Scrapbooks, WMU Archives, encourage prayer.

[12]Executive Committee (EC), WMU, SBC, Minutes, December 1891; AR 1892; *The Daily American*, Nashville, May 16, 1893.

[13]EC, December 19, 1907.

[14]Calendar for 1916 in J. S. Dill Papers, Historical Commission (HC), Nashville, Tennessee. Mrs. J. S. Dill was the author, and she claimed that this was the first calendar of its kind. Possibly this claim meant that it was the first so elaborately manufactured.

[15]Margaret McRae Lackey, *Decade of WMU Service, 1913-1923* (Nashville: Sunday School Board, Southern Baptist Convention, 1923), 78.

[16]Kathleen Mallory to J. E. Lambdkin, February 16, 1939, Holcomb Papers, Baptist Sunday School Board (BSSB), Nashville, Tennessee.

[17]Alma Hunt Oral History. Letters from Kathleen Mallory to the Foreign Mission Board (FMB) indicate that WMU maintained meticulous files and lists of the missionaries.

[18]*Royal Service (RS),* June 1965.

[19]Armstrong to J. M. Frost, August 31, 1895, Frost-Bell Papers, BSSB; AR 1901 and 1904.

[20]Sara Kanoy Parker (Mrs. A. L.), president of North Carolina WMU, June 1985.

[21]EC, January 1963.

[22]Helen Barrett Montgomery, *Prayer and Missions* (West Medford, Mass.: Central Committee of the United Study of Foreign Missions, 1924).

[23]AR 1910.

[24]A sketch of Heck written by her sister, unpublished, Heck Papers, Wake Forest University, Winston-Salem, North Carolina.

[25]Handwritten prayer in Heck Papers.

[26]Heck's journal while hospitalized, Heck Papers.

[27]Helen Fling, "Abiding in Him Through Prayer," *Star Ideals* (Birmingham: WMU, [1962]).

[28]*RS*, March 1968.

[29]Quoted in Joan Jacobs Brumberg, *Mission for Life: The Story of the Family of Adoniram Judson* (New York: The Free Press, 1980), 82.

[30]Ibid.

[31]FMB Minutes, July 31, 1848.

[32]Examples of FMB Minutes concerning single women in this period: November 5, 1849; December 3, 1849; June 20, 1851; July 9, 1851.

[33]*Western Recorder*, May 18, 1872.

[34]H. A. Tupper to Heck, no date; Tupper to McIntosh, 1883. Tupper Letter Books, FMB.

[35]FMB Minutes, July 1, 1878; November 4, 1878; November 17, 1878. After three years of ignoring applications of women, the Board could not turn the persistent Stein aside, but voted to "express the hope that

in the providence of God some way may be opened for her to carry out the apparently absorbing desire of her heart."

[36]FMB Minutes, November 19, 1881; January 3, 1882; November 28, 1882; January 2, 1883; February 5, 1883 are scattered samples. Cora McWilliams, *Women and Missions in Missouri: A History of the Seventy-Five Years of Organized Baptist Woman's Missionary Activity in Missouri, 1876-1951* (Jefferson City, Mo.: Woman's Missionary Union of Missouri, 1951), 60-61.

[37]FMB Minutes, April 1883; March 2, 1884; March 1886. Ruth McCown File, FMB.

[38]AR 1892 and 1905. As an example of a WMU group's support for a particular missionary, see *Alabama Baptist (AB),* March 3, 1898.

[39]James F. Love, *Missionary Messages* (New York: George H. Doran Co., 1922).

[40]AR 1946; SBC Annual 1947, WMU Report; Survey of issues of *RS,* 1946-47.

[41]AR 1946, Cornell Goerner Address; AR 1948, Rankin Address; *RS,* December 1953; Eloise Glass Cauthen (Mrs. Baker James) Interview; FMB Minutes 1943, reports of J. W. ["Bill"] Marshall.

[42]FMB Minutes, April 19, 1949.

[43]FMB Minutes, October 1957.

[44]FMB Minutes, March 15, 1904.

[45]Catherine B. Allen, *The New Lottie Moon Story* (Nashville: Broadman Press, 1980), 238.

[46]EC, May 22, 1911, May 15, 1912; AR 1913; AR 1915; FMB Minutes, May 28, 1914, November 4, 1915.

[47]*RS,* September 1922.

[48]AR 1930.

[49]Weatherford to Baker James Cauthen, Winston Crawley, and Keith Parks, May 8, 1978.

[50]Home Mission Board (HMB) Minutes, September 22, 1884; *Baptist Courier (BC),* 1884 (clipping not dated; a report of the South Carolina Central Committee); *Heathen Helper,* March 1884.

[51]*Heathen Helper,* November 1885; Marjean Patterson, *Covered Foundations: A History of Mississippi Woman's Missionary Union* (Jackson: Mississippi Woman's Missionary Union, [1978]), 14.

[52]Marie Buhlmaier, *Along the Highway of Service* (Atlanta: Home Mission Board, 1924); Minutes, Woman's Baptist Home Mission Society of Maryland, Maryland Baptist Historical Society. Una Roberts Lawrence, *Pioneer Women* (Nashville: Sunday School Board, 1929) is the only significant study of women home missionaries of the early era.

[53]SBC Annual 1901; Lawrence, *Pioneer Women;* AR 1902.

[54]Kate Ellen Gruver, *From This High Pinnacle: One Hundred Years with Georgia Baptist Woman's Missionary Union* (Atlanta: Woman's Missionary Union, Auxiliary to Georgia Baptist Convention, 1983), 114; HMB Minutes, May 22, 1901, June 7, 1901.

[55]HMB Minutes, March 4, 1902.

[56]*Baptist Standard,* March 12, 1936; L. Katherine Cook, "Texas Baptist Women and Missions, 1830-1900," and Mina Everett, "Recollections," both in *Texas Baptist History,* 1983; Roberta Turner Patterson, *Candle by Night: A History of Woman's Missionary Union, Auxiliary to the Baptist General Convention of Texas, 1800-1955* (Dallas: Woman's Missionary Union of Texas, 1955), 34, 39, 41-42.

[57]Kathryn A. Greene, *The Eternal Now: A History of Woman's Missionary Union, Auxiliary to South Carolina Baptist Convention* (Columbia: Woman's Missionary Union, Auxiliary to South Carolina Baptist Convention, 1980), 33; Minutes of the Woman's Missionary Union, Auxiliary to the Baptist State Convention of South Carolina, 1902-1916; AR 1905.

[58]HMB Minutes, November 30, 1938. Fairly detailed information on missionaries by their source of support is given in minutes through 1944.

[59]HMB Minutes, July 12, July 30, September 3, 1942, show how state WMU officials were able to negotiate support for women missionaries to serve in their states. The money was designated by WMU in the Annie Armstrong Offering.

[60]Survey by Irvin Dawson, director of Missionary Personnel Department, HMB, January 26, 1986.

[61]Margrette Stevenson, HMB, to Catherine B. Allen, February 2, 1984.

[62]EC, February 1-4, 1944; *Window of YWA,* March 1944 and June 1944; Arthur B. Rutledge, *Mission to America: A Century and a Quarter of Southern Baptist Home Missions* (Nashville: Broadman Press, 1969), 197; Foy Johnson Farmer to Laura M. Armstrong, August 14, 1943, WMU Archives.

[63]Sallie Bailey Jones (Mrs. Wesley N.), "A Sketch of the Woman's Missionary Union of North Carolina."

[64]*RS,* April 1962; EC, May 4, 1963, January 1964, January 1965.

[65]"The Margaret Fund," a single page, undated, printed statement identified as "Published by Woman's Missionary Union, SBC. Distributed free through state WMU offices," Box 551-434, FMB Archives.

[66]The chief biographical material on the Wallers, Stouts, and Chamberses is in two privately printed volumes: Kate Waller Chambers, *Recollections 1855-1924* (New York and London: G. P. Putnam's Sons, The Knickerbocker Press, 1931), and *Chronicles of a Worth-While Family; Chambers-Stout* (New York: The Knickerbocker Press, 1919). See also Lee N. Allen, *The First 150 Years: Montgomery's First Baptist Church, 1829-1979* (Montgomery: First Baptist Church, 1979), 145-46; *Heathen Helper,* June 1884, 2; *Montgomery Advertiser,* January 19, 1915; *Beacon,* First Baptist Church, Montgomery, Alabama, October 17, 1947. A substantial note was made of the death of John Stout in *SBC Annual,* 1895, 45.

The Chamberses lived in a lovely palatial home they named Crow's Nest where they freely entertained southern friends, missionaries passing through the port of New

York, and an endless stream of relatives. For many years prior to her death in 1915, Margaret Waller spent six months every year with the Chamberses. She was so beloved by her Montgomery friends that she was annually reelected WMU president in spite of prolonged absences.

[67]Frank R. Chambers to R. J. Willingham, August 31, 1904, Box 551-475, FMB Archives; Bobbie Sorrill, *Annie Armstrong: Dreamer in Action* (Nashville: Broadman Press, 1984), 258-259; *Christian Index*, May 25, 1905.

[68]Fountain Hamilton, the last resident, was totally orphaned. She was legally the ward of WMU, and the officers had to make every arrangement for her upbringing.

[69]Edith Campbell Crane, "The Margaret Home for Missionaries' Children," 12-page undated leaflet published by WMU (Baltimore), in WMU Archives; AR 1914; *RS*, December 1914, October 1926; Kathleen Mallory to Dear Friend, January 27, 1913, Willingham Correspondence, Box 551-468, FMB Archives.

Mrs. C. H. Richardson of Hartsville, South Carolina, was first housemother. The first children were the three sons of Mr. and Mrs. E. A. Nelson of Brazil. Mother Richardson, "Merson" for short, established a rigid schedule for the youngsters. On the spacious grounds were chickens and a cow furnished by members of WMU societies. An advisory board composed of one member from each state was assisted by a board of local women and an advisory committee of six local men.

[70]Ethlene Boone Cox, *Following in His Train* (Nashville: Broadman Press, 1938), 189-90; Minutes, Margaret Fund Committee, May 14, 1934, WMU Archives.

[71]Burney File, WMU Archives; LaVenia Neal to Rogers M. Smith, October 4, 1967, Margaret Fund Correspondence, WMU Archives; Executive Board, WMU, January 12, 1973; Alma Hunt to Executive Board Members, State Executive Secretaries, February 2, 1973, Margaret Fund File, WMU Archives.

An unidentified statement in the Burney File describes Burney as she attended an evening meeting of the WMU Executive Board. With golden hair and brilliant blue eyes she was startlingly beautiful in a long, cobalt-blue velvet gown, with pearls at her neck and a diamond sunburst pin on her shoulder. Employing excellent diction and beautiful terminology, her committee reports were eagerly awaited.

[72]Mrs. Ben S. Thompson to J. B. Lawrence; J. B. Lawrence to Mrs. Russell, June 18, 1937; J. B. Lawrence to Sarah Joe Hurst Burney, June 30, 1936, Lawrence Papers, HMB Papers, HC.

[73]Douglas J. Ginn, *Seventy Years History of Tennessee Woman's Missionary Union as I Saw It* (Nashville: Woman's Missionary Union, Auxiliary to the Tennessee Baptist Convention, 1958), 94; Clippings and correspondence in Margaret Fund-Mary B. Rhodes File, WMU Archives; Ethlene Cox to LaVenia Neal, August 31, 1954, Margaret

Fund Correspondence, 1950s, WMU Archives; Cox to Alma Hunt, January 4, 1950, Margaret Fund File, WMU Archives.

[74]Margaret Fund Policy (1956), Box 551-1149, FMB Archives; AR 1953. Cox to LaVenia Neal, August 31, 1954, Margaret Fund Correspondence, late 1950s, WMU Archives.

[75]The Margaret Memorial Scrapbook, compiled in 1935, contains the names of all who contributed to or were honored by the Margaret Memorial Offering (WMU Archives). On other gifts see leaflet in Burney Gifts Policy File, WMU Archives, and Ethlene Cox to Ethel Winfield, August 9, 1951, Margaret Fund Correspondence, late 1950s, WMU Archives.

Chapter 8. First Comes Knowledge

[1]Fannie E. S. Heck Address, Annual Report (AR), WMU, SBC, 1895.

[2]Virginia Lieson Brereton and Christa Ressmeyer Klein, "American Women in Ministry: A History of Protestant Beginning Points," in Rosemary Ruether and Eleanor McLaughlin, eds., *Women of Spirit: Female Leadership in the Jewish and Christian Traditions* (New York: Simon and Schuster, 1979), 301-24. Also, R. Pierce Beaver, *All Loves Excelling,* reissued as *American Protestant Women in World Missions: History of the First Feminist Movement in North America* (Grand Rapids: William B. Eerdmans, 1980). Also, Patricia R. Hill, *The World Their Household: The American Woman's Foreign Mission Movement and Cultural Transformation, 1870-1920* (Ann Arbor: The University of Michigan Press, 1985).

[3]*Royal Service (RS)*, July 1920.

[4]Mary C. Gambrell (Mrs. J. B.) to Mrs. J. A. Stanford, February 24, 1909, Gambrell Papers, Southwestern Baptist Theological Seminary (SWBTS), Fort Worth, Texas.

[5]Isa-Beall Neel, *His Story in Georgia WMU History* (Atlanta: Woman's Missionary Union, Auxiliary to the Georgia Baptist Convention, 1939), 15.

[6]Catherine B. Allen, *Laborers Together with God* (Birmingham: Woman's Missionary Union, 1987). A survey of women's club papers in several state archives and a study of the leading national and state personalities of WMU indicates that a number belonged to local study clubs. A few held minor offices in the state federations. Quote is from Heck's oft-quoted final message, AR 1915.

[7]Betty Friedan, *The Feminine Mystique* (New York: Norton and Company, Inc., 1963).

[8]*RS*, July 1920.

[9]AR 1891.

[10]SBC Annual 1918, FMB Report.

[11]AR 1893.

[12]Early Leaflets Collection and Scrapbooks at WMU Archives contain samples (it is believed) of the bulk of the publications of the Maryland Baptist Mission Rooms and its successors, including informational leaf-

lets about its own operations. Also a bit of history is given in SBC Annual 1901, HMB Report and SBC Annual 1902, HMB Report; AR 1899 and 1905. Further data in Lulie P. Wharton, *Ready Pens Proclaiming Missions 1886-1836*, published by WMU for the Golden Anniversary of Missions Literature. Biography of Amzi C. Dixon: Helen C. A. Dixon, *A. C. Dixon: A Romance of Preaching* (New York: G. P. Putnam's Son's, 1931), shows something of his closeness to WMU. Mrs. W. R. Nimmo, longtime secretary of the WMU Literature Department, was an intimate associate of his family. His daughter was employed by WMU 1916-18.

[13]Minutes of Executive Committee (EC), WMU, SBC, May 10, 1897. Papers of the Central Committee for the United Study of Foreign Missions, circa 1900, and of Abbie B. Child, NCC RG 27, Boxes 11 and 2, National Council of Churches Archives, deposited at Presbyterian Historical Society, Philadelphia. A letter to Abbie Child from Harlan Beach, educational secretary for the Student Volunteer Movement, June 29, 1900, refers to the SVM mission study classes for the last three years, implying that women were not well equipped to study missions. Child was the chairman of the women's meetings attended by Fannie Heck, and she also chaired the United Study Committee.

[14]Armstrong to J. M. Frost, June 10, 1898, Frost-Bell Papers, Baptist Sunday School Board (BSSB), Nashville, Tennessee.

[15]Heck to "Mother," April 24, 1900, Heck Papers, Wake Forest University; EC, March and February 1900.

[16]EC, November and December 1900.

[17]*Baptist Argus*, May 11, 1905.

[18]AR 1907, 1908, 1909, reveal the recommendations about mission study. Frost to Heck, April 4, 1908, BSSB Letter Books; Heck to T. B. Ray, April 11, 1908, Frost-Bell Papers, BSSB.

[19]Hill, *The World Their Household.*

[20]Mrs. W. S. Leake of Pearisburg, Virginia, to Miss Bennie, January 2, 1911, Virginia Baptist Historical Society (VBHS).

[21]AR 1942; Kathryn A. Greene, *The Eternal Now: A History of Woman's Missionary Union, Auxiliary to South Carolina Baptist Convention* (Columbia: Woman's Missionary Union, Auxiliary to South Carolina Baptist Convention, 1980), 159; Marjean Patterson, *Covered Foundations: A History of Mississippi Woman's Missionary Union* (Jackson: Mississippi Woman's Missionary Union, [1978]), 44; Juliette Mather, *Light Three Candles: History of Woman's Missionary Union of Virginia, 1874-1973* (Richmond: Woman's Missionary Union of Virginia, Baptist General Association of Virginia, [1973]), 77; Allen, *Laborers Together with God.*

[22]AR 1931.

[23]Orville A. Petty, ed., *Home Base and Missionary Personnel, Laymen's Foreign Missions Inquiry Fact-Finders' Reports,* vol. 7, Supplementary Series, Part 2 (New York: Harper and Brothers, 1933).

[24]Leachman Papers, WMU Archives, Birmingham, Alabama.

[25]AR 1948.

[26]AR 1935.

[27]*RS*, August 1955.

[28]AR 1962.

[29]Olin T. Phillips to Carolyn Weatherford, March 29, 1985.

[30]EC, May 29, 1906, June 13, 1906; SBC Annual 1906, Reports of HMB and SSB; AR 1907.

[31]Evelyn Wingo Thompson is studying WMU writers, editors, and journalists for an article to be published in *Baptist History and Heritage* after March 1987.

[32]EC, January 12, 1912; *RS*, June 1915 and June of each year through 1922.

[33]Blanche Sydnor White, *Highlights in History of Woman's Missionary Union, Auxiliary to Portsmouth Baptist Association 1885-1953*, White Papers, VBHS; Olive B. Martin (Mrs. George R.), "Summer Camping Program" and "The Purpose of Woman's Missionary Union Camps," VBHS.

[34]Recollection of Katherine Test Davis (Mrs. George E.), notes, WMU Archives.

[35]*RS*, August 1923; Southern Baptist Clip Sheet, Scarborough Papers, July 21, 1924, SWBTS. News story reports that the first camp was just held with 166 young women in 15 states. EC Minutes and Mather's reports in AR give consistent view of camp progress.

[36]Survey by author.

[37]J. M. Gaskin, *Baptist Women in Oklahoma* (Oklahoma City: Messenger Press, n.d.), 422.

[38]Correspondence of Juliette Mather with FMB staff; J. Ivyloy Bishop Oral History.

[39]Ibid.; Edwina Robinson Interview.

[40]AR 1952 and 1955. Mission Study Conference in Birmingham was repeated in 1954.

Chapter 9. Woman's Soft Hand

[1]Hugh A. Brimm, "The Social Consciousness of Southern Baptists in Relation to Some Regional Problems, 1910-1935" (ThD thesis, SBTS, 1944). Brimm was professor at the WMU Training School/Carver School of Missions and Social Work. Also, Samuel S. Hill, Jr., *Southern Churches in Crisis* (New York: Holt, Rinehart, and Winston, 1966). Also, John L. Eighmy, *Churches in Cultural Captivity: A History of the Social Attitudes of Southern Baptists* (Knoxville: University of Tennessee Press, 1972). The quotation is from James J. Thompson, Jr., *Tried as by Fire: Southern Baptists and the Religious Controversies of the 1920s* (Macon: Mercer University Press, 1982).

[2]Home Mission Board (HMB) Minutes, October 3, 1899.

[3]Executive Committee (EC), WMU, SBC, January 10, 1893.

[4]SBC Annual, HMB Report, 1900.

[5]See *Royal Service (RS)*, May 1915 and August 1919 for coverage of congress meetings. The congress issued annual volumes

of proceedings and membership lists.

6James E. McCulloch, ed., *The Call of the New South* (Nashville: Southern Sociological Congress, 1912).

7Mary P. Ryan, *Womanhood in America: from Colonial Times to the Present*, 3d ed., (New York: Franklin Watts, 1983, 209).

8*RS*, October 1915.

9Heck to Lulie Pollard Wharton (Mrs. H. M.), August 19, 1912, Personal Service Scrapbook, WMU Archives, Birmingham, Alabama; *A Manual of Personal Service.*

10Executive Committee, WMU, SBC, Policy, 1910-11.

11*RS*, September 1917; Annual Report (AR), WMU, SBC, 1911, Crane Report.

12Standard of Excellence printed in AR 1912.

13Heck to Wharton, August 19, 1912.

14*RS*, December 1922.

15*RS*, 1921.

16"Some Questions and Answers," Leaflet, Fall 1913, WMU Archives.

17EC, April 9, 1919.

18Marjean Patterson, *Covered Foundations: A History of Mississippi Woman's Missionary Union* (Jackson: Mississippi Woman's Missionary Union, [1978]), 84-85.

19*Our Mission Fields (OMF)*, October-November-December 1911.

20*RS*, December 1922.

21Personal Service Scrapbook, WMU Archives.

22Tenie Seale, "Personal Service Interpreted" (Virginia WMU, 1917). Virginia Baptist Historical Society (VBHS). Leaflet included 15 separate personal service suggestions for rural communities.

23Mabel Swartz Withoft, *Oak and Laurel* (Nashville: Baptist Sunday School Board, 1923).

24Kate Ellen Gruver, *From This High Pinnacle: One Hundred Years with Georgia Baptist Woman's Missionary Union* (Atlanta: Woman's Missionary Union, Auxiliary to Georgia Baptist Convention, 1983); Mary Lou Burnette and Carrie Sinton Vaughan, *For Such a Time as This: Biography of Blanche Sydnor White, 1891-1974* (Richmond: First Baptist Church, 1980).

25Cora McWilliams, *Women and Missions in Missouri: A History of the Seventy-Five Years of Organized Baptist Woman's Missionary Activity in Missouri, 1876-1951* (Jefferson City, Mo.: Woman's Missionary Union of Missouri, 1951), 170.

26Fannie H. Taylor, Leaflet, "From Mothers' Club to WMS," undated, WMU Archives.

27Kathryn A. Greene, *The Eternal Now: A History of Woman's Missionary Union, Auxiliary to South Carolina Baptist Convention* (Columbia: Woman's Missionary Union, Auxiliary to South Carolina Baptist Convention, 1980).

28*Home and Foreign Fields*, December 1919.

29Omer Shermer Alford to Catherine Allen, October 17, 1985.

30Rosalind Robinson Levering, *Baltimore Baptists, 1773-1973: A History of the Baptist Work in Baltimore During 200 Years* (Baltimore: Baltimore Baptist Association [1973]), 157.

31*RS*, February and March 1915, contain detailed suggestions for an industrial school at a cost of approximately $20 per year. The WMU office offered the loan of a book giving models of schools. These models were largely lifted from the City Mission Manual of Woman's Home Mission Society of the Methodist Episcopal Church South.

32Blanche Sydnor White, *Our Heritage: History of Woman's Missionary Union, Auxiliary to the Maryland Baptist Union Association, 1742-1958* (Baltimore: Woman's Missionary Union of Maryland, 1959).

33Robert A. Woods and Albert J. Kennedy, *Handbook of Settlements* (Philadelphia: New York Charities Publication Committee, Russell Sage Foundation, 1911). Also, Eleanor Hull, *Women Who Carried the Good News* (Valley Forge: Judson Press, 1975) indicates that the Christian Center movement rose among Northern Baptists, at the hands of women, between 1910 and 1920, the same time period in which Southern Baptist women developed good will centers.

34*RS*, April 1915; McLure to Heck, February 8, 1915, Heck Papers, Wake Forest University, Winston-Salem, North Carolina.

35From leaflets, Personal Service Scrapbooks, WMU Archives.

36*RS*, April 1919.

37Leachman's interesting papers are preserved in WMU Archives.

38AR 1924.

39Minutes of Secretaries and Field Workers Meeting, August 5, 1949, WMU Archives.

40Rees Watkins, *The House of Happiness: A Ministry of Love* (Richmond: WMU of the Richmond Baptist Association, 1981), 13, 31, 46.

41*RS*, October 1914, August 1951. The author is indebted to Betsy Criminger Lowery for her research on WMU and the Vacation Bible School Movement, which is slated for publication in the October-November-December 1988 issue of *Quarterly Review*.

42*OMF*, October-November-December 1913.

43WMU Year Book 1920-21.

44SBC Annual 1939.

45Fred Eastham in *RS*, March and June 1945.

46AR 1946; SBC Annual 1946.

47Inez (Price) Taylor, *Facets of a Diamond: 75 Years of Illinois WMU History* (Springfield, Ill.: Woman's Missionary Union, Illinois Baptist State Association, 1983), 23.

48*RS*, March 1941.

49AR 1942. By typographical error, the new terminology did not appear in the WMU Year Book until 1943.

50AR 1952.

51WMU Year Books 1949 through 1954 show Stokely's influence.

52AR 1951 through 1955.

53*RS*, August 1958; AR 1957.

54The fascinating story of Lillian Isaacs and her literacy ministry is found in Nell T.

Bowen, *John and Lillian Isaacs: Making the Word Known* (Birmingham: Woman's Missionary Union, 1985). See also *RS*, May 1960.

[55]Gruver, *From This High Pinnacle,* 117.

[56]Woman's Missionary Union Program Base Design.

[57]Alma Hunt to Albert McClellan, May 19, 1971, Hunt Papers, WMU Archives.

[58]Chandler to Blanche White, VBHS; Gross to Carolyn Weatherford, April 13, 1985.

Chapter 10. In Sympathy with All Righteousness

[1]Mrs. J. B. Cranfill gave a report of the temperance committee at the Texas WMU Annual Meeting in 1918: "Coincident with the advance of the sentiment for . . . Prohibition, is the increasing interest and conviction concerning Woman Suffrage. These great reforms are marching almost hand in hand" (Texas Baptist Annual, 1918), 53. J. B. Gambrell advocated woman suffrage as early as 1912 (*Baptist Standard*, Dec. 19).

The negative correlation between missions and suffrage is discussed by Ruth Bordin, *Woman and Temperance: The Quest for Power and Liberty 1873-1900* (Philadelphia: Temple University Press, 1981).

[2]A review of histories of the woman suffrage movement reveals no prominent WMU leaders in the forefront of the movement, although some of the suffragists were active Baptists. Elizabeth Cady Stanton, Susan B. Anthony, and others (eds.), *History of Woman Suffrage* (Rochester and New York, 1889-1922; 6 vols.) is the standard reference work, filled with reports of suffrage work in individual states. Other studies are represented by these: A. Elizabeth Taylor, "The Woman Suffrage Movement in Arkansas," *The Arkansas Historical Quarterly*, 15:1 (Spring 1956), 17-52; Lee N. Allen, "The Woman Suffrage Movement in Alabama, 1910-1920," *The Alabama Review*, 11:2 (April 1958), 83-99; Letha Evelyne Robinson Casazza, "A Study in Pressure Politics and the Amending Process with Reference to the Nineteenth Amendment," MA Thesis, Graduate School of American University, 1938. Casazza became president of WMU in the District of Columbia.

[3]An important study on this subject is Bill Sumners, "Southern Baptists and Women's Right to Vote, 1910-1920," *Baptist History and Heritage*, January 1977, 45-51.

[4]Leon McBeth, "The Role of Women in Southern Baptist History," *Baptist History and Heritage*, January 1977, 12.

[5]Written from Baltimore, August 16, 1900, FMB Archives, Richmond, Virginia.

[6]E. B. Teague articulated the opposition viewpoint eloquently in *Alabama Baptist (AB)*, February 7 and April 4, 1895. See also *Texas Baptist and Herald*, April 18, 1888; Texas *Baptist Standard*, April 18, 1895.

[7]Fannie E. S. Heck, *In Royal Service: The Mission Work of Southern Baptist Women* (Richmond: Foreign Mission Board, 1913),

349.

[8]Proceedings of WMU, Texas Baptist Annual 1920, 57.

[9]Mrs. W. B. McGarity, delivering temperance report. Proceedings of the WMU, Texas Baptist Annual 1920, 57.

[10]Annual Report (AR), WMU, SBC, 1924; *Royal Service (RS)*, September 1929.

[11]For example, *RS*, February 1924 and February 1928.

[12]Texas Baptist Annual 1922, 10-11.

[13]*RS*, June 1965.

[14]*Chattanooga Times*, May 16, 1928.

[15]AR 1891.

[16]Mrs. W. C. Golden, *Going Forward with Tennessee Woman's Missionary Union,* n.p., n.d., WMU Library.

[17]*RS*, January 1944 and June 1957.

[18]Quoted in *RS*, January 1944.

[19]At the Annual Meeting of 1917 WMU called on Congress to pass a pending bill to prohibit the manufacture and sale of intoxicants. They also petitioned the government to take precautionary measures to guarantee that any person who had authority over troops was not a user of alcoholic beverages (AR 1917).

[20]For general information on the course of Prohibition with specific reference to Southern Baptists (though not WMU), see A. C. Miller, "Prohibition," *Encyclopedia of Southern Baptists* (Nashville: Broadman Press, 1958), vol. 2, 1115-16.

[21]Minutes, Executive Committee (EC), WMU, SBC, March 31, 1926.

[22]Lee N. Allen, *Born for Missions: Birmingham Baptist Association, 1833-1983* (Birmingham: Birmingham Baptist Association, 1984), 82.

[23]Edith Stokely Moore Oral History.

[24]Bordin, *Woman and Temperance.*

[25]Dixon to Fannie Breedlove Davis, September 22, 1890, Fannie Breedlove Davis Papers, Southwestern Baptist Theological Seminary (SWBTS).

[26]Provence to Catherine Allen, October 14, 1985, with accompanying documentation of her study in South Caroliniana Library's WCTU collection.

[27]For example, January 1928. Annie Armstrong kept a scrapbook on Prohibition which was filled with WCTU imprints.

[28]Harriett B. Kells, president of Mississippi WCTU, to J. B. Gambrell, March 18, 1908, Mary T. Gambrell Papers, SWBTS.

[29]Inez Boyle Hunt, *Century One: A Pilgrimage of Faith* (Dallas: Woman's Missionary Union of Texas), 41.

[30]Ann J. Graves to H. A. Tupper, April 14, 1873, FMB Archives.

[31]*Baptist Argus*, May 26, 1898.

[32]Maud Reynolds McLure's mammy and her husband were honored at a 50th wedding anniversary party at Mount Ida Plantation so elaborate as to become legendary in Alabama. See J. S. Dill's biography of Isaac Taylor Tichenor.

[33]Kate Waller Chambers, *Recollections, 1855-1924* (New York: G. P. Putnam's Sons, The Knickerbocker Press, 1931), Alabama

State Archives, Montgomery, Alabama. US Census records show that Lottie Moon's family estate had its share of mulatto children.

[34]Heck, *In Royal Service,* 68-69.

[35]AR 1907.

[36]AR 1892 and 1895; EC, June 9 and September 2, 1892; *Washington Post,* May 12, 1895; Armstrong to Frost, January 26, 1897; SBC Annual 1986, HMB Report.

[37]WMU Archives collection of early publications includes several leaflets such as these. Armstrong to J. M. Frost, August 31, 1895, Frost Papers, Baptist Sunday School Board (BSSB), Nashville, Tennessee.

[38]AR 1893; EC, October 8, 1895; Armstrong-Frost Correspondence, Frost-Bell Papers, BSSB.

[39]*Baptist and Reflector,* May 4, 1899.

[40]Armstrong to Frost, January 26 and June 14, 1897.

Armstrong's tight ties to the development of the National Baptist Woman's Convention and Publishing Board are voluminously revealed in Armstrong-Frost Correspondence; in various HMB and FMB papers; in the minutes of the Woman's Convention, Auxiliary to National Baptist Convention; in Nannie Helen Burroughs Papers, Library of Congress; and in EC Minutes. The key period is December 1896 through 1906.

[41]Annual minutes of the Woman's Convention, 1901, 1902, 1905. For 1901 and 1905 the author did not examine originals but saw excerpts which Burroughs had copied out for WMU examination in the 1930s.

[42]HMB Minutes, May 22, 1901, and March 4, 1902; Annual Minutes of the National Baptist Woman's Convention, 1901, 1902.

[43]AR 1904; *The Nashville American,* May 14, 1904; Annual Minutes of National Baptist Woman's Convention, 1904.

[44]Texas *Baptist Standard,* April, May, and June 1904 issues give examples of the running dialogue about the race issue.

[45]Nannie Helen Burroughs, "The Dawn of a New Day in Dixie," in *Think on These Things,* rev. ed., (Washington, D.C.: privately published, 1956).

[46]Allen, *Born for Missions;* Allen's research into Southside and Woodlawn Baptist Churches in Birmingham; Annual Reports of Woman's American Baptist Home Mission Society; *RS,* April 1916.

[47]The author is indebted to Martha Brown of Nashville for her research on Nashville WMU. For history of Fireside Schools, see Grace May Eaton, et al., *A Heroine of the Cross: Sketches of the Life and Work of Miss Joanna P. Moore* (privately published [1934]).

[48]*RS,* February 1918; Mrs. L. H. Hammond, *Southern Women and Racial Adjustment* (The John F. Slater Fund, 1917). Lulie Pollard Wharton (Mrs. H. M.) participated in the survey.

[49]Jessie Daniel Ames Papers, University of North Carolina; Jacquelyn Dowd Hall, *Revolt Against Chivalry: Jessie Daniel Ames and the Women's Campaign Against Lynching* (New York: Columbia University Press, 1979), 90-95.

[50]AR 1921 and 1922.

[51]EC, February 9, 1922.

[52]Sample survey found in South Carolina WMU Collection, Furman University.

[53]EC, October 4, 1927.

[54]Leaflet in Early Leaflets Scrapbooks, WMU Archives. See John W. Storey, *Texas Baptist Leadership and Social Christianity 1900-1980* (College Station: Texas A and M University Press, 1986).

[55]In Arkansas, for example, 4 Southern Baptists were among 31 who signed the call, according to a study by Jane Watson. Full papers of the ASWPL are included in the Jessie Daniel Ames Papers, University of North Carolina. Other information in Records of Interracial Commission, Atlanta University.

[56]Helen Davis Gullick (Davis's daughter) to Catherine Allen, May 6, 1985. Davis was a regular participant in the Interracial Commission meetings.

[57]*RS,* June 1930.

[58]A thorough study is possible because each woman left extensive papers. The Burroughs Papers are in the Library of Congress. The Lawrence Papers are part of the Home Mission Board Collection housed with the Southern Baptist Historical Commission. The White Papers are at the Virginia Baptist Historical Society.

[59]Burroughs to Mallory, September 18, 1935; Lawrence to Burroughs, November 11, 1936; Burroughs to Lawrence, November 17, 1936, Burroughs Papers, Library of Congress.

[60]Burroughs to White, August 11, 1940, Burroughs Papers.

[61]Report of the Committee on Cooperation with Negro Women; EC, February 15, 1937.

[62]From WMU's 50th Anniversary Scrapbook, Richmond, newspaper clippings with bibliographic details not noted. Interestingly, WMU's $10,000 Negro fund was not mentioned in news clippings, indicating that WMU perhaps kept a low profile about it. Also see SBC Annual 1938.

[63]Laura M. Armstrong to Burroughs July 16, 1939, Burroughs Papers.

[64]Burroughs to Lawrence, June 29, 1935, Burroughs Papers.

[65]Burroughs to Lawrence, May 8, 1943.

[66]Recollection by Mrs. E. L. Dupuy of Martinsville, Virginia, at Virginia Baptist Historical Society (VBHS), quoted in Mary Lou Burnette and Carrie Sinton Vaughan, *For Such a Time as This: Biography of Blanche Sydnor White, 1891-1974* (Richmond: First Baptist Church, 1980), 63.

[67]VBHS; research material of Carrie S. Vaughan for her biography of White, *For Such a Time as This.*

[68]EC, September 25, 1940.

[69]Janice Singleton to Catherine Allen, October 30, 1985. Singleton was executive secretary of Georgia WMU and inaugurated interracial institutes in the state. While she

found WMU women able to carry on the interracial work graciously, other leaders had some unpleasant moments. Mary Christian, community missions chairman on the WMU, SBC, staff during the institutes, found that whites refused to attend the meetings, leaving the WMU officers all the work. Marjorie Jones McCullough, when a young woman helping with an interracial meeting in Louisiana, found that older WMU women would provide refreshments for the event, but refused to serve the blacks; young WMUers did serve.

[70]Statement by Mrs. Charlie Mae Pearson, in "Season of Prayer for State Missions" (Baptist Woman's Missionary Union of Georgia, 1970). A national officer of the Woman's Convention, NBC, Inc., and one of the original institute planners, Pearson became an employee of Georgia WMU, which then transferred her to the staff of the Georgia Baptist Convention so that she might qualify for retirement benefits.

[71]RS, September 1942.

[72]EC, March 17 and April 21, 1943; Ames Papers, University of North Carolina, including letter of White to Ames, June 24, 1943, and Mallory to McGill, May 10, 1943.

[73]Representative writings on the race issue in RS: March 1928, November 1936, July 1937, March 1942, May 1946.

[74]RS, March 1949 and February 1950 are examples.

[75]Mather-Marjorie Moore [Armstrong] Correspondence, FMB Archives; J. Ivyloy Bishop Oral History; EC, January 21-28, 1954, January 29, 1955, January 1957, February 3-8, 1958.

[76]Times-Picayune, New Orleans, May 14, 1930.

[77]RS, January 1958; Hunt to Executive Board, State Secretaries, and State Mission Study Chairmen, December 13, 1957.

[78]T. B. Maston in Home Missions magazine, September 1966.

[79]Examples are in RS, December 1963.

[80]Mary Essie Stephens Interview; Minutes of Virginia Interracial Committee, Virginia WMU Office.

[81]Edwina Robinson Interview, April 1, 1985.

[82]Hunt Oral History; Helen Fling Interview.

[83]Billie McMurry Emmons, Letters from Mother (Nashville: Broadman Press, 1967), 86.

[84]Hunt Oral History.

[85]Fling Interview; see Fling's address, 1965 Annual Meeting, printed in Booklet of Speeches to Pastor's Conference and WMU.

[86]Helen Fling Interview, Miami Herald, May 31, 1967.

[87]Hunt to Executive Board, June 15, 1968.

[88]Emmanuel McCall to Catherine Allen, November 22 and December 27, 1985.

[89]David Wilkinson, quoting Sid Smith, Ethnicity, March-April 1985, 7; Leroy Fitts, A History of Black Baptists (Nashville: Broadman Press, 1985), 308; Sid Smith, Ethnicity, May-June 1985, 1; Baptist Press release, March 13, 1986.

[90]Mrs. C. M. Pearson to Catherine Allen, March 6, 1986; Janice Singleton to Allen, October 30, 1985.

[91]Minutes of Missions Coordination Subcommittee of the Inter-Agency Council, 1977-78.

[92]Alma Hunt and Catherine B. Allen, History of Woman's Missionary Union, rev. ed. (Nashville: Convention Press, 1976), 148.

[93]EC, October 3 and November 7, 1917; RS, October 1917, February 1918; AR 1917, 1918; Baptist and Reflector, November 29, 1917; Watchman-Examiner, August 29, 1918; Home and Foreign Fields, September 1918.

[94]RS, December 1918 and February 1919.

[95]Numerous associational WMU histories remark in general ways about the gloom among women during the World War. These histories tell the stories of WMU ministries in countless military camps.

[96]RS, May 1943.

[97]Interview with Sue Saito Nishikawa (Mrs. Nobuo), executive director of Hawaii WMU, and one of Maddry's helpers.

[98]HMB Minutes, June 4, 1942; Argye M. Briggs, A Question Once Asked: A History of Woman's Missionary Union Auxiliary to the Baptist General Convention of Oklahoma (Oklahoma City: Woman's Missionary Union, Baptist Convention of Oklahoma, 1956); EC, September 22, 1943.

[99]RS, April 1943, January 1944, May 1943; EC, April 11, 1945; Letters from Blanche S. White to Virginia WMU presidents, 1942, concerning transportation difficulties.

[100]Guidance leaflet for the stay-home camps in WMU Archives.

[101]RS, April 1943; AR 1944.

[102]Hunt Oral History; Ayako Hino Interview.

[103]Proceedings for "Strategies for Peacemaking," a National Peace Convocation, Louisville, Kentucky, August 5-7, 1982, 25-27.

Chapter 11. Our Daughters as Cornerstones

[1]W. O. Carver, October 2, 1948, quoted in RS, December 1948, 22.

[2]Heathen Helper, March 1883, announced that Miss Morris of Missouri was attending lectures at Southern Baptist Theological Seminary (SBTS) preparing to go as a missionary. Religious Herald (RH), July 24, 1884, reported two women, one from Missouri and one from Kentucky, attended classes in 1883 and went to China. See also Baptist Argus (BA), March 16, 1905.

[3]Diary of Mina Everett, Southwestern Baptist Theological Seminary (SWBTS) Archives, Texas Baptist Historical Collection, also published in The Journal of Texas Baptist History, vol. 3, 1983. The 1889 date for Simmons's initial campaign is also established by Isla May Mullins, House Beautiful (Nashville: Sunday School Board, 1934), 13.

[4]Ibid. Also letter from Everett to Olivia Davis, October 19, 1931, Texas WMU Office

Files, Dallas.
[5]Annual Report (AR), WMU, SBC, 1895.
[6]Executive Committee (EC), WMU, SBC, November 12, 1895.
[7]Mary Hill Davis (Mrs. F. S.), *Living Messages: Official Addresses of Mrs. F. S. Davis, 1907-1931* ([Dallas]: Woman's Missionary Union of Texas, 1935), 116-17; Roberta Turner Patterson, *Candle by Night: A History of Woman's Missionary Union, Auxiliary to the Baptist General Convention of Texas, 1800-1955* (Dallas: Woman's Missionary Union of Texas, 1955).
[8]Mullins, *House Beautiful,* 13.
[9]Simmons to T. T. Eaton, W. W. Landrum, and E. Y. Mullins, November 22, 1901.
[10]Collection of correspondence among E. Z. Simmons, R. J. Willingham, E. Y. Mullins, and Annie Armstrong, February-March 1900. The seminary was already courting WMU for financial support. See Bobbie Sorrill, *Annie Armstrong: Dreamer in Action* (Nashville: Broadman Press, 1984), 115-17, 134-37.
[11]Annie Armstrong to R. J. Willingham, June 28, 1900, FMB Archives, Richmond, Virginia.
[12]EC, April 10, 1900.
[13]Diary of Annie Jenkins Sallee, 1900-1902, Sallee Papers, Baylor University Texas Collection, Waco. Jenkins returned to Texas as state WMU organizer in 1904-1905, went to China as a missionary, ran a successful school there, and married Eugene Sallee who became an executive of the Foreign Mission Board.
[14]AR 1903 and 1904; SBC Annual 1903.
[15]Carrie U. Littlejohn, *History of Carver School of Missions and Social Work* (Nashville: Broadman Press, 1958), 169. The student's daughter, Emily K. Lansdell, became president of Carver School.
[16]BA, April 28, 1904, and May 5, 1904.
[17]BA, April and May 1904; SBC Annual 1904; AR 1904.
[18]Baptist Standard (BS), August 24, 1904, September 8, 1904, September 22, 1904, September 29, 1904, November 10, 1904, December 15, 1904; Proceedings of Baptist Women Mission Workers (BWMW) 1904, 1905, 1906; Proceedings of Baptist General Convention of Texas 1904, 1905, 1906, 1907.
[19]Eunice Ruark, "Maryland Trained Women to Evangelize," *Baptist True Union,* March 20, 1986.
[20]BS, February 11, 1904.
[21]BA, July 14, 1904; *Home and Foreign Fields,* May 1918.
[22]Account by Rena Groover Shepard, *Royal Service (RS),* April 1957. The "Big Four" were legendary in training school culture. Although Clemmie Ford lived a rather quiet life (letter to W. O. Carver, June 6, 1938, Carver Papers, Historical Commission [HC], Nashville, Tenn.), the others achieved fame as foreign missionaries. Ella Jeter Comerford after a term working with Lottie Moon in China, married into another denomination. One account of the Big Four's living conditions is in *BA,* August 24, 1905.
[23]Emma McIver Woody (Mrs. S. E.) to

R. J. Willingham, April 1, 1905; E. Y. Mullins to R. J. Willingham, April 4, 1905; EC, April 11, 1905.
[24]Littlejohn, *History of Carver School,* 29. This book is the fullest history of the school and should be consulted for a detailed description.
[25]Mrs. W. J. McGlothlin to Mrs. A. C. S. Jackson with brochure attached, undated, probably fall of 1905; Tennessee WMU Office Files, Nashville.
[26]RS, September 1938.
[27]Full details in Sorrill, *Annie Armstrong.* Also see EC, 1905. Annie Armstrong to J. M. Frost, October 9, 1905, and April 1, 1906; Emma Woody to Virginia WMU, February 29, 1906.
[28]Eyewitness account written in manuscript by Katherine Test Davis (Mrs. George E.), YWA 25th Anniversary File, WMU Archives, Birmingham, Alabama.
[29]AR 1907.
[30]News Leader, Richmond, May 18, 1907.
[31]SBC Annual 1907; AR 1907.
[32]The women known as "the five founders" of the WMUTS were Heck, Eliza Broadus, Emma McIver Woody (Mrs. S. E.), Anna C. Eager (Mrs. George B.), and Maud Reynolds McLure. Heck not only championed the school at its founding, but she also was a consistent visitor, role model, and lecturer. The chapels in two successive buildings were named for her.

Eliza Somerville Broadus, the eldest daughter of John A. Broadus, a founder of Southern Seminary, was born in 1851. Educated by her father, she devoted herself to assisting him and to leading WMU. She was a member of the Kentucky Central Committee from its beginning in 1878 until her death in 1931 and was chairman 32 years. She took the initiative in establishing the WMUTS and channeling Kentucky's financial support to it.

Emma Woody continued as local chairman of the school's board of managers after WMU, SBC, established ownership. Her family had been tied to the early growth of Texas WMU. The wife of a prosperous doctor and the mother of small children, she had the task of securing a permanent building for the school. In this she was aided by another local board member and future chairman, Mrs. Trevor H. Whayne, and her husband, who was to serve the women as business agent in their property transactions.

Anna Eager, vice-chairman of the board of managers and the wife of a seminary professor, had been a founder of WMU, SBC, when she lived in Alabama in 1888. She was a leader in the Federated Woman's Club movement of Alabama (Lee N. Allen, *The First 150 Years: Montgomery's First Baptist Church, 1829-1979* [Montgomery: First Baptist Church, 1979]; Federation of Woman's Club Files, Alabama State Archives; *RS,* July 1933 and August 1925). Immediately upon arriving in Louisville when her husband joined the seminary faculty, she was swept into the training school movement. She was vice-chairman of the board until 1908, when she and Woody swapped roles. She continued as chairman of the board until 1920 when she became treasurer for five years. She taught the class on mission study methods.

[33]Biographical details from a 1940 sketch by her niece, Hannah Reynolds, secretary of Louisiana WMU. Also data sheet in Operation Baptist Biography Project and memorial service oration by Kathleen Mallory, 1938. The story of Mount Ida, which burned in 1956, from Ralph Hammond, *Antebellum Mansions of Alabama* (New York: Bonanza Books, 1951). Hammond says that Maud's wedding gown was the finest that money could buy. In 1939, in connection with the premiere of *Gone with the Wind*, the dress won second place in a southwide contest to find the finest antebellum wedding gown.

[34]Dixie Bale Mylum, *Proclaiming Christ: History of Woman's Missionary Union of Kentucky, 1878-1978* (Middletown, Kentucky: Woman's Missionary Union of Kentucky, Auxiliary to the Kentucky Baptist Convention, 1978).

[35]*RS*, August 1925; C. Vann Woodward, *Origins of the New South, 1877-1913*, vol. 9, *A History of the South* (Baton Rouge: Louisiana State University Press and The Littlefield Fund for Southern History of the University of Texas, 1951), 401.

[36]Several Founder's Day addresses by alumnae, WMUTS Files, SBTS; Louise Fletcher Papers, Virginia Baptist Historical Society (VBHS), Richmond.

[37]*Baptist and Reflector*, May 21, 1908.

[38]Mary Lou Burnette and Carrie S. Vaughan, *For Such a Time as This: Biography of Blanche Sydnor White, 1891-1974* (Richmond: First Baptist Church, 1980), 26, 27.

[39]Mullins, *House Beautiful;* Emma Leachman Founder's Day Address, October 1, 1937, Leachman Papers, WMU Archives.

[40]Carrie Littlejohn to Kathleen Mallory, March 31 and April 1, 1939, Mallory File, WMUTS Papers, SBTS Archives; Laura M. Armstrong to W. O. Carver, April 9, 1940, Carver Papers, HC.

[41]Examples of economy-mindedness are letters from alumnae president Wilma Bucy to Training School sisters, February 1932, WMU Archives.

[42]Frost to Heck, March 12, 1915, Frost-Bell Papers, Baptist Sunday School Board (BSSB); *RS,* December 1916, May 1917.

[43]Seventy-Five Million Campaign and Cooperative Program Commission Minutes, HC, show how the allocation formulas were reached. Some annual budgets are found in WMUTS Files, SBTS Archives. WMUTS funds handled by the WMU treasurer are shown in her annual report. The WMUTS financial reports began to be included in SBC Annuals in 1947. See also Ethlene Cox to Carrie Littlejohn, November 15, 1944, and April 2, 1945.

[44]Ellis Fuller to Laura M. Armstrong and

Kathleen Mallory, February 8, 1944, Armstrong Papers, WMU Archives; SBC Annual 1943.

[45]*RS*, November 1942; SBC Annual 1943; Cox to Littlejohn, September 26, 1945, and October 15, 1945.

[46]Cox-McCall Correspondence, Fall 1946; Cox to Littlejohn, September 27, 1946.

[47]Olive Martin to Littlejohn, January 8, 1947; Littlejohn to Kathleen Mallory, March 30, 1947.

[48]EC, January 25, 1949.

[49]Austin C. Dobbins, *Gaines S. Dobbins: Pioneer in Religious Education* (Nashville: Broadman Press, 1981); Gaines S. Dobbins to Nathan C. Brooks, Jr., January 8, 1959, Dobbins Papers, Samford University, Birmingham, Alabama.

[50]SBC Annual 1948, SSB Report. Also reference in Armstrong-Carver Correspondence, Carver Papers, HC. The SSB also gave grants to the training schools at SWBTS and New Orleans Baptist Thelogical Seminary "to enable them to maintain courses of study along the lines of work committed to the SSB."

[51]Baker J. Cauthen to J. M. Price, May 26, 1954, WMUTS Papers, Lansdell Files, SBTS Archives.

[52]Interview with Duke K. McCall, March 1, 1985; Emily K. Lansdell to WMUTS Trustees, February 7, 1952, WMUTS Files, SBTS Archives.

[53]Cox and Littlejohn, November 12, 1949, Cox Files, WMUTS, SBTS Archives.

[54]Carver's enlightened views about women are discussed by Catherine B. Allen, "Concerns Beyond Feminism," in John N. Jonsson, ed., *God's Glory in Missions* (privately published, 1985). Carver's statements concerning women's rights and responsibilities were by far the most progressive among Baptist leadership until the 1970s.

[55]AR 1952; EC, May 1952; *RS,* September 1952.

[56]M. Theron Rankin to Alma Hunt, March 2, 1953, FMB Archives.

[57]Porter Routh Oral History Interview, April 22, 1985.

[58]"Missionary Problems" File developed at CSMSW by Maxfield Garrott, 1952-53, FMB Archives; EC, January 1953 and January 1955.

[59]President's Report to the Trustees, June 11, 1957, WMUTS Files, SBTS.

[60]Lansdell to Cauthen, March 1 and 2, 1954, WMUTS Files, SBTS Archives.

[61]AR 1957, 1958, 1963.

[62]In an interview July 8, 1986, Herschel Hobbs stated that his committee wanted to find a solution that would give the Carver School Cooperative Program funds under the terms of the SBC Business and Financial Plan, yet leave initiative with WMU. However, he felt that some members of the Branch Committee, especially Carr P. Collins of Dallas, saw the school only in terms of dollars spent. See AR 1956 and SBC Annuals 1956 and 1957.

[63]Handwritten news release by Lansdell,

shortly prior to June 19, 1957, published in *Louisville Times*, June 19, 1957.

[64]Booz-Allen and Hamilton Report, Carver School Files, SBTS Archives.

[65]Leon McBeth, "The Role of Women in Southern Baptist History," *Baptist History and Heritage*, January 1977, 18-19.

[66]AR 1949.

[67]Mrs. W. L. Williams, *Golden Years: An Autobiography* (Dallas: Baptist Standard Publishing Company, 1921), 147.

[68]L. R. Scarborough, *A Modern School of the Prophets* (Nashville: Broadman Press, 1939).

[69]Minutes, District 17, Woman's Missionary Union, 1916-1930. District 17's scholarship girl, a Miss Evans, was the first unmarried woman to receive the master of missions degree at the SWBTS, 1920.

[70]AR 1924.

[71]1929 pamphlet of Baptist Woman's Missionary Training School Regulations; Mrs. B. A. Copass, "Woman's Missionary Training School of the Southwestern Baptist Theological Seminary," Brochure, apparently 1949.

[72]*RS*, March 1923; AR 1922, 1923, 1924; SBC Annual, Report of BBI, 1921.

[73]*Home and Foreign Fields,* April 1919.

[74]*RS*, May 1930; AR 1931.

[75]Copass to Ethlene Cox, October 12, 1937, Texas WMU Files, Dallas.

[76]Cox to Carrie Littlejohn, October 15, 1945, WMUTS Files, SBTS.

[77]Cox to Littlejohn, October 31, 1945; WMUTS Files, SBTS.

[78]"According to His Purpose," Booklet, Mary Hardin-Baylor College, 1945, WMU Archives.

[79]Annie Armstrong to J. M. Frost, March 21, 1896, Frost-Bell Papers, BSSB.

[80]AR 1927.

[81]Collegiate relations are documented in various state WMU histories: Hermione Dannelly Jackson, *Women of Vision* (Montgomery: Woman's Missionary Union, Auxiliary to Alabama Baptist State Convention, 1964), 90, 108; Kate Ellen Gruver, *From This High Pinnacle: One Hundred Years with the Georgia Baptist Woman's Missionary Union* (Atlanta: Woman's Missionary Union, Auxiliary to Georgia Baptist Convention, 1983), 147; Patterson, *Candle by Night*, 86-87; J. M. Gaskin, *Baptist Women in Oklahoma* (Oklahoma City: Messenger Press, n.d.); Foy Johnson Farmer, *Hitherto: History of North Carolina Woman's Missionary Union* (Raleigh: WMU of North Carolina, 1952); History of WMU District 9 (Texas), 1956; Minutes of WMU District 17 (Texas); Mrs. W. D. Pye, *The Yield of the Golden Years: A History of the Baptist Woman's Missionary Union of Arkansas, 1888-1938* (Little Rock: Baptist Woman's Missionary Union of Arkansas, n.d.), 79-80.

[82]Laura Mason, *Ye Are the Branches: A History of the Missouri Baptist Woman's Missionary Organizations* (Jefferson City, Mo.: Woman's Missionary Union of Missouri, 1987).

[83]Mary Essie Stephens Interview, June 4, 1985.

[84]Mylum, *Proclaiming Christ*, 176-177; Jane B. Watson, *Laborers Together: The History of Arkansas Woman's Missionary Union* (to be released March 1988).

[85]Manuscript of Mallory's eulogy for McLure is in Emma Leachman Papers, WMU Archives. Source of verse is unknown.

Chapter 12. In Union There Is Strength

[1]Annie Armstrong to James M. Frost, January 10, 1899, Frost-Bell Papers, Baptist Sunday School Board (BSSB), Nashville, Tennessee.

[2]Armstrong to Frost, September 3, 1895, Frost-Bell Papers.

[3]Susan Tyler Pollard, "Enlistment of State Forces and Organization of Woman's Missionary Union, SBC," Early Leaflets, WMU Archives, Birmingham, Alabama.

[4]Annual Report (AR) 1895.

[5]AR 1899.

[6]AR 1895.

[7]Armstrong to Frost, June 23, 1893; Armstrong to T. P. Bell, September 3, 1895, Frost-Bell Papers.

[8]Armstrong to Frost, June 25, 1898.

[9]AR 1906.

[10]Mallory to Una Roberts Lawrence, 1945, Lawrence Papers, Historical Commission (HC), Nashville, Tennessee.

[11]White to Burroughs, July 10, 1939, Burroughs Papers, Library of Congress.

[12]Laura Armstrong to White, March 7, 1944; White to Armstrong, March 11, 1944, WMU Archives.

[13]*Royal Service (RS)*, October 1945.

[14]Interviews with Duke K. McCall, Porter Routh, James Sullivan; Robert Naylor to Catherine Allen, February 13, 1986. Naylor said of Martin: "This Mrs. George Martin has not been surpassed in terms of strong leadership."

[15]Alma Hunt Oral History; White to Martin, undated, apparently 1956, Historical Collection, Freemason Street Baptist Church, Norfolk, Virginia.

[16]Cox to Hunt, November 14, 1950, Cox Papers, WMU Archives.

[17]AR 1974.

[18]McCall Interview.

[19]SBC Annual 1958.

[20]Hunt Oral History; Carolyn Weatherford Interview.

[21]Weatherford Interview.

[22]AR 1951.

[23]Offering allocations are listed in AR through 1963.

[24]Laura Mason, *Ye Are the Branches: A History of the Missouri Baptist Woman's Missionary Organizations* (Jefferson City, Mo.: Woman's Missionary Union of Missouri, 1987).

[25]L. H. Moore, *The History of Southern Baptists in Ohio* (Columbus: State Convention of Baptists in Ohio, 1979).

[26]Ibid.; Becie Kirkwood Interview, May 20,

1986.

[27]Hunt Oral History.

[28]Notes from 1962 discussion by Louise Berge Winningham, then executive secretary of Indiana WMU.

[29]Ibid.; Hunt Oral History.

[30]Kirkwood Interview.

[31]Murphy Interview, July 22, 1985.

[32]Weatherford to Hunt, January 3, 1968, Hunt Files, WMU Archives.

[33]Weatherford Interview.

[34]Porter Routh, Duke McCall, and Alma Hunt, all experienced observers of the denomination, agreed in interviews that the departmental trend is too young to analyze. Hunt said, "What will happen when the personalities who made the departmental agreements leave the scene? Will their successors keep faith with the assurances given WMU?"

[35]Lucy W. Peabody, "Woman's Place in Missions Fifty Years Ago and Now," *The Missionary Review of the World*, December 1927.

[36]Helen Barrett Montgomery, *Western Women in Eastern Lands: An Outline Study of Fifty Years of Woman's Work in Foreign Missions* (New York: Macmillan Co., 1910).

[37]Elizabeth J. Miller, "Retreat to Tokenism: A Study of the Status of Women on the Executive Staff of the American Baptist Convention" (mimeographed, 1970).

[38]R. Pierce Beaver, *American Protestant Women in World Missions: History of the First Feminist Movement in North America* (Grand Rapids: William B. Eerdmans, 1980).

[39]Weatherford Interview.

[40]*RS*, August 1941.

[41]Cora McWilliams, *Women and Missions in Missouri: A History of the Seventy-Five Years of Organized Baptist Woman's Missionary Activity in Missouri, 1876-1951* (Jefferson City, Mo.: Woman's Missionary Union of Missouri, 1951); *Heathen Helper*, January 1883.

[42]*Religious Herald (RH)*, July 4, 1878.

[43]*Baptist Standard*, May 26, 1904.

[44]*Home and Foreign Fields*, September 1918.

[45]"History of Woman's Missionary Union, Auxiliary to Union Baptist Association" (Houston), Southwestern Baptist Theological Seminary (SWBTS) Archives; Ledger of Clara Routy, first president of Collin County Associational WMU, 1905, SWBTS Archives; Lee N. Allen, *Born for Missions: Birmingham Baptist Association, 1833-1983* (Birmingham: Birmingham Baptist Association, 1984).

[46]Mrs. Albert Harris, "History of the Baptist Missionary Union in Erath Association, 1908-1958," SWBTS Archives.

[47]Mathis and Hunt to Associational Missionaries and Area Missionaries, February 6, 1961, Hunt Papers, WMU Archives.

[48]*AR* 1891.

[49]*Baptist Argus (BA)*, May 25, 1899.

[50]The New Century Movement is summarized in these sources: SBC Annual 1900; AR 1901 and 1902; Armstrong to R. J. Wil-

lingham, June 5 and 11, 1900, Foreign Mission Board (FMB) Archives, Richmond, Virginia; Armstrong to F. H. Kerfoot, July 23, 1900, in transcriptions by Una Roberts Lawrence, WMU Archives; AR 1901; *Baptist Courier (BC)*, May 30, 1901; *BA*, June 28 and August 16, 1900.

[51]SBC Annual 1901.

[52]SBC Annual 1907.

[53]Executive Committee (EC) Minutes, WMU, SBC, May 18 and June 5, 1912; Kathleen Mallory to R. J. Willingham, February 20, 1913; SBC Annual 1913; AR 1913; *RS*, October 1938.

[54]*Baptist and Reflector*, May 29, 1913.

[55]*Baptist World*, May 22, 1913.

[56]*RH*, May 17, 1900.

[57]*Christian Index*, May 17, 1904.

[58]*RH*, May 25, 1905; *Kansas City Star,* May 15, 1905.

[59]Diary entry for May 19, 1911, and undated portion, Sallee Papers, Baylor University Texas Collection, Waco.

[60]*Christian Index*, May 25, 1916. For other insights into the occasion, see *Watchman-Examiner*, May 25, 1916; Mallory's obituary address for McLure in Leachman Papers, WMU Archives; *RS*, July 1916; and Carrie U. Littlejohn, *History of Carver School of Missions and Social Work* (Nashville: Broadman Press, 1958).

[61]*Texas Baptist and Herald*, May 12, 1892; *Alabama Baptist*, July 14, 1892.

[62]*Baptist Basket*, October 1891.

[63]Fannie E. S. Heck, *In Royal Service* (Richmond: Foreign Mission Board, 1913). E. C. Routh, *Life Story of Dr. J. B. Gambrell* (Oklahoma City: Baptist Book Store, 1929); Una Roberts Lawrence, *Winning the Border: Baptist Missions Among the Spanish-speaking Peoples of the Border* (Atlanta: Home Mission Board, SBC, 1935).

[64]Gambrell to Mallory, February 22, and May 1, 1917; Gambrell Papers, SWBTS Archives.

[65]SBC Annual 1917; *Watchman-Examiner*, May 31, 1917; *Baptist and Reflector*, May 24, 1917.

[66]Mallory to Gambrell, August 31, 1917; Gambrell Papers.

[67]Gambrell to Mallory, September 29, 1917.

[68]Mallory to Van Ness and reply, August 31, 1917, and September 4, 1917; Van Ness Papers, BSSB.

[69]SBC Annual 1918.

[70]AR 1918.

[71]SBC Annual 1919. Approximately 16 percent of the 1919 messengers were women, among them all the officers of WMU.

[72]*RS*, August 1921.

[73]Mallory to Littlejohn, June 17, 1946, SBTS Archives, Louisville, Kentucky.

[74]*RS*, July 1922.

[75]AR 1921.

[76]*RS*, July 1922.

[77]Armstrong to George W. Sadler, November 27, 1941, FMB Archives.

[78]FMB Minutes, April 22, 1942.

[79]Fred A. Grissom, "Lay Leadership in the

Southern Baptist Convention," *Baptist History and Heritage*, June 1985.

[80]Porter Routh Interview.

[81]SBC Annual 1985.

[82]Routh Interview; Alma Hunt Board Letter, May 14, 1963.

[83]*Memphis Press Scimitar*, May 11, 1929; Unidentified clipping in Ethlene Boone Cox's Papers, WMU Archives.

[84]Catherine B. Allen, "Women's Movements and Southern Baptists," *Encyclopedia of Southern Baptists (ESB)*, vol. 4 (Nashville: Broadman Press, 1982).

[85]AR 1897.

[86]Dixon to F. H. Leavell, July 18, 1917, Van Ness Papers, BSSB.

[87]*Manual of WMU Methods*, 1917.

[88]EC, March 1, 1916; Minnie K. James-I. J. Van Ness Correspondence, Van Ness Papers, BSSB, April 1918; *Mission Messenger* of WBMU of Georgia, March 1918; Sue O. Howell, "Woman's Baptist Missionary Society of Oklahoma," undated leaflet.

[89]SBC Annuals 1924 and 1925; Papers of F. S. Groner concerning Committee on Correlating and Defining Work of Various Departments of Convention Activities, SWBTS; EC, January 30, 1924.

[90]EC, February 13, 1937; *RS*, April 1938; Dobbins Papers, Samford University.

[91]Laura Armstrong to Carver, May 6, 1939; Carver Papers, HC.

[92]SBC Annuals 1946, 1947, 1948, 1949; Littlejohn to Martin, October 21, 1947, WMUTS Papers, SBTS; Martin to M. T. Rankin, May 31, 1948, FMB Archives; Littlejohn to Martin, May 25, 1948, WMUTS Papers; Martin to Littlejohn, May 29, 1948; Littlejohn to Martin, June 3, 1948; Rankin to Martin, June 4, 1948; "Suggested Unified Southern Baptist Educational Program," 1946, Dobbins Papers, Samford University; Sarah Joe Hurst Burney, "Recollections of Mrs. George R. Martin," Martin Files, WMU Archives; Austin C. Dobbins, *Gaines S. Dobbins: Pioneer in Religious Education* (Nashville: Broadman Press, 1981).

[93]SBC Annual 1950; WMU Year Book 1949.

[94]Collins to Douglas Branch, January 10, 1956, and January 23, 1959; Papers of the Committee on Total Program, HC. Group was also known as the Branch Committee.

[95]Alford to Catherine Allen; James Sullivan Interview.

[96]SBC Annuals 1958, 1959.

[97]EC, February 3-8, 1958.

[98]Mathis to Porter Routh, June 27, 1961, Baptist Jubilee Advance Papers, HC.

[99]W. L. Howse, "Programming for Southern Baptist Churches and the Denomination by the Education Division," BSSB; Genevieve Howse (Mrs. W. L.) to Catherine Allen, October 22, 1985; Routh, McClellan, Sullivan Interviews; Alma Hunt Oral History; W. O. Thomason to Allen, December 18, 1986. A letter from Marie Mathis to W. L. Howse, January 1, 1969 (Howse Papers, BSSB), gives a personal insight into Mathis's opinion of Howse. She was privately giving him the news that she was leaving WMU's staff to resume the presidency. "I cannot express my sense of loss as I think of giving up 'my team' with you at the helm. I truly love every one of you and no difference of opinion ever changes that love and friendship. To be a part of the CPDG [Church Program Development Group, the program leaders who met 16 times a year] has been the best thing that ever happened to me. Remember this, won't you? And remember, too, that I shall continue to work with all of you. All you have to do is to tell me what to say and how to vote."

[100]Elaine Dickson Interview, November 1986. Howse Papers contain letter from Mildred McMurry (Mrs. William) giving WMU's initial favorable reaction to Howse's design of tasks.

[101]Executive Board (EB), WMU, SBC, January 18, 1963.

[102]EB, June 1962 and May 1963.

[103]Howse, "Programming for Southern Baptist Churches."

[104]Dickson Interview; Sullivan Interview; Hunt Oral History.

[105]See chapter 8 for a summary of WMU's interest in Brotherhood becoming missions oriented and able to assume responsibility for missions education for boys. Also, see AR 1966.

[106]AR 1960.

[107]AR 1966.

[108]Ibid.

[109]Hunt to "Co-Workers," May 1, 1971, WMU Archives; Alma Hunt to State Baptist Convention Executive Secretaries, June 18, 1971, Hunt Papers, WMU Archives.

[110]James L. Sullivan to Hunt, February 25, 1972; Hunt to Sullivan and Hunt to Albert McClellan, March 1, 1972, Hunt Papers, WMU Archives.

[111]Report of the Study Committee of Fifteen, December 21, 1973; Response of Woman's Missionary Union to the Report of the Committee of Fifteen, February 13, 1974, Allen Papers, WMU Archives.

[112]Porter Routh Interview; Jesse C. Fletcher, *Baker James Cauthen: A Man for All Seasons* (Nashville: Broadman Press, 1977).

[113]Albert McClellan, *The Executive Committee of the SBC 1917-1984* (Nashville: Broadman Press, 1984), 246. Also, see McClellan, "Bold Mission Thrust," *ESB*, 4:2125.

[114]EB, January 1976.

[115]Weatherford to Executive Board, September 19, 1977.

[116]Armstrong to Frost, May 15, 1896, Frost-Bell Papers, BSSB.

[117]Armstrong to Frost, March 21, 1896.

[118]Armstrong to Frost, February 12 and January 19, 1898. Numerous letters between 1896 and 1899 show how Armstrong relayed data from A. J. Rowland and O. F. Flippo, employees of the ABPS, to Frost.

[119]James M. Frost, *The Sunday School Board, Southern Baptist Convention: Its History and Work* (Nashville: Sunday School Board, [1914]).

[120]Quoted in AR 1917.
[121]Rankin to Olive Martin, June 4, 1948, FMB Archives.

Chapter 13. Louder, Please

[1]H. H. Harris, quoted in *Baptist Basket (BB)*, June 1889.
[2]Joan Jacobs Brumberg, *Mission for Life: The Story of the Family of Adoniram Judson* (New York: Free Press, 1980). See also Patricia R. Hill, *The World Their Household: The American Woman's Foreign Mission Movement and Cultural Transformation, 1870-1920* (Ann Arbor: University of Michigan Press, 1985).
[3]Fling Interview; Catherine B. Allen, *Laborers Together with God* (Birmingham: Woman's Missionary Union, 1987).
[4]Oral Memoirs of Hallie Jenkins Singleton, Baylor University Program for Oral History, 1978.
[5]*Religious Herald (RH)*, May 19, 1881.
[6]Quoted in Laura Mason, *Ye Are the Branches: A History of the Missouri Baptist Woman's Missionary Organizations* (Jefferson City, Mo.: WMU of Missouri, 1987).
[7]Alice Armstrong wrote as Ruth Alleyn, *RH*, May 14, 1885.
[8]*Western Recorder (WR)*, April 19 and May 10, 1888.
[9]Ada Bell, daughter of McIntosh, to Ruth Provence, August 15, 1962.
[10]Catherine B. Allen, *The New Lottie Moon Story* (Nashville: Broadman Press, 1980).
[11]*Mosaics of Mission Methods*, about 1899, Early Leaflets, WMU Archives.
[12]*BB*, June 1889.
[13]Quoted in Ethlene Boone Cox, *Following in His Train* (Nashville: Broadman Press, 1938).
[14]Annual Report (AR) 1898.
[15]Missouri Baptist *Woman's Missionary Interchange*, August 1887.
[16]*Royal Service (RS)*, June 1941.
[17]*WR*, September 8, 1898.
[18]Jennie Dixon to Fannie Breedlove Davis, September 22, 1890, Davis Papers, Southwestern Baptist Theological Seminary (SWBTS) Archives, Fort Worth, Texas.
[19]Everett, "Recollections" and L. Katherine Cook, "Texas Baptist Women in Missions 1830-1900"; *Texas Baptist History*, 1983.
[20]*Baptist Courier (BC)*, September 23, 1897.
[21]Executive Committee (EC), WMU, SBC, Minutes, December 10, 1895.
[22]EC, January 8 and March 12, 1895; Bell to Armstrong, February 26, 1895, Frost-Bell Papers, Baptist Sunday School Board (BSSB), Nashville, Tennessee.
[23]Armstrong to R. J. Willingham, January 5, 1900, Foreign Mission Board (FMB) Archives, Richmond, Virginia; Armstrong to J. M. Frost, October 4, 1905, Frost-Bell Papers.
[24]Armstrong to Frost, October 4, 1905.
[25]Allen, *Laborers Together*.
[26]Quoted by Wayne Flynt, "Women, Society and the Southern Church, 1900-1920," manuscript in Flynt's possession, Auburn University, Auburn, Alabama.
[27]Mullins to J. B. Gambrell, September 1, 1916, Gambrell Papers, SWBTS.
[28]Ibid.
[29]*Savannah Press*, May 1903.
[30]*Home and Foreign Fields*, July 1924.
[31]*Chips from Many Workshops*, Early Leaflets, WMU Archives.
[32]*RS*, October 1931.
[33]*RS*, January 1942.
[34]Littlejohn and Berta K. Spooner, secretary of Oklahoma WMU, in *Oklahoma City Times*, May 17, 1949.
[35]*RS*, September 1923.
[36]*Word and Way*, November 13, 1919; Mallory had been speaking at 11:00 A.M. on Sunday mornings as early as 1915. An early such experience was among Pawnee Indians in Oklahoma on Thanksgiving. An occasional, but not frequent, Sunday pulpit was offered her throughout her career (*RS*, Jan. 1916; EC, Nov. 5, 1919; Woodlawn Baptist Church records, Birmingham, Ala., Dec. 3, 1939). Also she was regularly invited to be commencement speaker for Baptist colleges.
[37]*Florida Baptist Witness*, December 4, 1919.
[38]AR 1936 and 1937; EC, December 1, 1926.
[39]*Biblical Recorder*, March 13, 1929.
[40]EC, October 12, 1921.
[41]Note fragment, dated February 19, 1954, White Papers, Virginia Baptist Historical Society (VBHS), Richmond.
[42]Emma Leachman's life story, unpublished, unfinished manuscript, Leachman Papers, WMU Archives.
[43]*Historical Sketch, Woman's Auxiliary, Waco Baptist Association* (n.p. [1928], Baylor University Special Collections); Matt Dawson Interview, October 1985.
[44]Mrs. George Westmoreland, *Through the Years with WMU, Auxiliary to the Atlanta Association of Baptist Churches 1908-1936* (Atlanta: n.p., 1936).
[45]Oral Memoirs of Hattie Jenkins Singleton.
[46]Walter Pope Binns, president of William Jewell College, to Hunt, Hunt Papers, WMU Archives.
[47]Annie W. Armstrong, "Women as Helpers in God's Kingdom" (Baltimore: Baptist Mission Rooms, 1900).
[48]Fannie Coker Stout, "Shall the Baptist Women of the South Organize for Mission Work?" Leaflet, Scrapbook No. 1, WMU Archives.
[49]AR 1893.
[50]Mina S. Everett, "Recollections," *The Journal of Texas Baptist History*, 1983.
[51]Mrs. T. A. Hamilton, "Woman's Baptist Mission Work: Its Origin and Object: History in Alabama" (Woman's Baptist Missionary Union of Alabama, 1906), Early Leaflets, WMU Archives; *WR*, August 1, 1929.
[52]"The Woman's Missionary Society as a Factor in the Evangelization of the World," reprinted from the Woman's Home and Foreign Missionary Society of the Lutheran

Church (Baltimore: WMU Literature Department, n.d., [after 1906]).

[53]*Alabama Baptist (AB)*, March 22, 1900.

[54]"Woman's Missionary Training School of the Southwestern Baptist Theological Seminary," SWBTS Archives.

[55]AR 1921.

[56]See *RS*, 1928 through September 1929, studies for WMS and YWA.

[57]AR 1890.

[58]*World Comrades*, May 1928; SBC Annual 1920.

[59]AR 1905.

[60]Carver, "Christ's Gift to Woman and His Gift of Woman to the Human Race" (address to WMU Training School Commencement, May 8, 1941), WMU Archives.

[61]Catherine B. Allen, "Concerns Beyond Feminism," in John N. Jonsson, ed., *God's Glory in Missions: In Appreciation of William Owen Carver* (Louisville: Nilses Publication, 1985).

[62]Survey of WMU Training School/Carver School of Missions and Social Work Alumnae, 1985, conducted by Catherine B. Allen in preparation for Alumnae Reunion, August 3-4, 1985.

[63]*RS*, September 1964.

[64]Robert J. Hastings in *RS*, September 1970. Alma Hunt in the epilogue to *History of Woman's Missionary Union*, which she wrote in 1963, made no mention of the woman's movement, for it had hardly begun. Again, co-writing in 1970, *A Dynamic Church: Spirit and Structure for the Seventies*, published in 1969, she made no mention.

[65]Mathis and Elaine Dickson, *The Woman's Missionary Union Program of a Church* (Nashville: Convention Press, 1966).

[66]Interview with Mathis and Hunt, *St. Louis Globe-Democrat*, May 31, 1971.

[67]Program Booklet, 1973 WMU Annual Meeting, Portland.

[68]Jessie Tillison Sappington (Mrs. Richard Lee), *From My Point of View on the Ordination Issue*, privately published, apparently 1978.

[69]Personal files of 1973 WMU Annual Meeting and SBC Annual Report 1973.

[70]Mathis to Executive Board, June 25, 1973, Hunt Letters, WMU Archives.

[71]AR 1974.

[72]Sappington, *From My Point of View.*

[73]Sarah Frances Anders, "Woman's Role in the Southern Baptist Convention and Its Churches as Compared with Selected Other Denominations," *Review and Expositor*, Winter 1975; Interview with Carolyn Weatherford.

[74]*RS*, September 1977; *Contempo*, August 1977.

[75]"Findings of the Consultation on Women in Church-Related Vocations," 1978. Papers of the consultation are at the Historical Commission and in WMU Archives.

[76]SBC Annual 1984.

[77]Typical letter sent by Weatherford to inquirers about WMU and Women in Ministry, shared with Executive Board, July 17, 1984.

[78]Jane B. Watson, *Laborers Together: The History of Arkansas Woman's Missionary Union* (to be published 1988); Mrs. W. D. Pye, "A Bouquet of December Roses."

[79]See Catherine B. Allen, *The New Lottie Moon Story* (Nashville: Broadman Press, 1980).

[80]Kate Ellen Gruver, *From This High Pinnacle: One Hundred Years with Georgia Baptist Woman's Missionary Union* (Atlanta: Woman's Missionary Union, Auxiliary to Georgia Baptist Convention, 1983); EC, January 8, 1895, April 9, 1895, November 13, 1894, November 9, 1897; T. P. Bell to R. J. Willingham, June 3, 1895, Bell Letter Book, BSSB; Armstrong to T. P. Bell, December 22, 1894, December 24, 1894; Armstrong to J. M. Frost, December 27, 1897; Armstrong to A. J. Rowland of ABPS, March 30, 1898; Rowland to Armstrong, March 31, 1898; Armstrong to O. F. Flippo, January 18, 1898; and other letters of this period; Frost-Bell Papers, BSSB; Armstrong-R. J. Willingham Correspondence, FMB, same period.

[81]Agnes B. Yost, *And Greater Works: The Woman's Missionary Union of the Raleigh Baptist Association 1886-1986* (Raleigh: Raleigh Baptist Association, 1986).

[82]Armstrong to R. J. Willingham, June 13, 1898, FMB Archives.

[83]Jeanne Madeline Weimann, *The Fair Women* (Chicago: Academy Chicago, 1981); E. M. Wherry, ed., *Woman in Missions: Papers and Addresses Presented at the Woman's Congress of Missions* (New York: American Tract Society, [1894]); James P. Eagle, *A Brief Memoir of Mary K. Eagle* (Little Rock: Press of Arkansas Democrat Co., 1903); EC, March 14, 1893.

[84]Edward M. Bliss, ed., *Ecumenical Missionary Conference New York, 1900*, vol. 1 (New York: American Tract Society, 1900).

[85]EC, October 30, 1910.

[86]EC, January 12, 1910; April 9, 1910.

[87]EC, December 7, 1910, June 12, June 28, October 11, and November 8, 1911; AR 1911, 1912; *OMF*, October-November-December 1911, January-February-March 1912; Sallee Papers, Texas Collection, Baylor University, Waco; Leaflets concerning the Jubilee, WMU Archives; Hill, *The World Their Household.*

[88]EC, March 6 and June 5, 1912, February 11, 1914.

[89]*RS*, December 1914, January 1915, November 1915; EC, December 1, 1915, February 2, 1916.

[90]J. F. Love, *The Union Movement* (Nashville: Sunday School Board of the SBC, 1918).

[91]Frost to Mallory, February 19, 1915, Frost Letter Book; Mallory to Frost, Frost-Bell Papers, February 17, 1915. See also AR 1915.

[92]*Home and Foreign Fields*, November 1917.

[93]AR 1919. *RS*, March 1919; Margaret McRae Lackey, *Decade of WMU Service 1913-1923* (Nashville: Sunday School Board, SBC, 1923).

[94]Papers of Bessemer Baptist Associational WMU, Samford University Special

Collections.

[95]The Heck-Armstrong dispute is best summarized in Bobbie Sorrill, *Annie Armstrong: Dreamer in Action* (Nashville, Broadman Press, 1984.)

[96]Bell to Frost, June 1898, Frost-Bell Papers, BSSB.

[97]Fragment of what was apparently a fuller document, found in 1893 folder of M. C. Tupper, Virginia WMU Files, Virginia Baptist Historical Society. This document was apparently drawn up in formal style and placed on file for future reference, for Armstrong referred to it in writing R. J. Willingham, August 26, 1898. However, it does not exist in the archives of any of the agencies involved, possibly destroyed out of sensitivity to the women and their friends. The process of this dispute is well documented in the Frost-Bell Papers and in FMB Archives, sources spelled out in Sorrill's *Annie Armstrong.*

[98]AR 1899.

[99]The envelope sealed by Mallory was opened in 1974. It contained a complete set of research and recommendations as well as the letter of Cora McWilliams to Laura Armstrong. Also, Ruth Provence, a member of the committee, made available her valuable files of research conducted in 1944. Edwina Robinson, the only other surviving member of the committee, confirmed its members' fears and hopes. Both Ruth Provence and Edwina Robinson completed long tenures as state WMU executive secretaries, helping to implement the recommended changes over the next 20 years.

[100]Notes from Frances Tyler (Mrs. Wilfred C.), WMU Archives.

[101]AR 1892; Fannie E. S. Heck, *In Royal Service: The Mission Work of Southern Baptist Women* (Richmond: Foreign Mission Board, 1913).

[102]Williams, *Golden Years: An Autobiography* (Dallas: Baptist Standard Publishing Co., 1921).

[103]Armstrong to Frost, November 18, 1896, Frost-Bell Papers.

[104]Armstrong to Frost, July 24, 1896.

[105]Mallory to Van Ness, December 16, 1925. Van Ness Papers, BSSB; Mallory to Van Ness June 17, and reply June 18, 1926.

[106]McCall and Routh Interviews.

[107]Edwina Robinson and Mary R. Godwin Interviews.

[108]*RS*, October 1962.

[109]Instructions to Delegates leaflets are available in some Annual Meeting files, WMU Archives.

[110]Bates Interview.

[111]AR 1930.

[112]Mary Hill Davis, *Living Messages* (Dallas: Texas WMU, 1935).

[113]Wilma Bucy, *The How and Why of Woman's Missionary Union* (Nashville: Sunday School Board of the Southern Baptist Convention, 1928).

[114]AR 1905.

[115]Annie Wright Ussery, *The Story of Kathleen Mallory* (Nashville: Broadman Press, 1956).

[116]*AB*, August 26, 1886.

Chapter 14. The Veil Over the Future

[1]Carolyn Weatherford Address to WMU Writers Conference, May 15, 1986.

ABBREVIATIONS

AB	*Alabama Baptist,* Birmingham, Alabama
ABPS	American Baptist Publication Society
AR	Annual Report, WMU, SBC
BA	*Baptist Argus*
BB	*Baptist Basket,* Louisville, Kentucky
BBI	Baptist Bible Institute (now New Orleans Baptist Theological Seminary)
BC	*Baptist Courier,* Greenville, South Carolina
BGCT	Baptist General Convention of Texas, Dallas, Texas
BS	*Baptist Standard,* Dallas, Texas
BSSB	Baptist Sunday School Board, Nashville, Tennessee (also SSB)
CSMSW	Carver School of Missions and Social Work, Louisville, Kentucky
CI	*Christian Index,* Atlanta, Georgia
CP	Cooperative Program
EB	Executive Board, WMU, SBC
EC	Executive Committee, WMU, SBC
FMB	Foreign Mission Board of the Southern Baptist Convention, Richmond, Virginia
FMJ	*Foreign Mission Journal,* Foreign Mission Board, Richmond, Virginia
GA	Girls' Auxiliary
HH	*Heathen Helper,* Louisville, Kentucky
HC	Historical Commission of the Southern Baptist Convention, Nashville, Tennessee
HMB	Home Mission Board of the Southern Baptist Convention, Atlanta, Georgia
NOBTS	New Orleans Baptist Theological Seminary, New Orleans, Louisiana
OMF	*Our Mission Fields*

RA	*Royal Ambassadors*
RH	*Religious Herald,* Richmond, Virginia
RS	*Royal Service,* Birmingham, Alabama
SBC	Southern Baptist Convention
SBTS	Southern Baptist Theological Seminary, Louisville, Kentucky
SWBTS	Southwestern Baptist Theological Seminary, Fort Worth, Texas
SSB	Sunday School Board of the Southern Baptist Convention, Nashville, Tennessee (also BSSB)
TS	Training School
VBHS	Virginia Baptist Historical Society
WR	*Western Recorder,* Middletown, Kentucky (previously Louisville)
WCTU	Woman's Christian Temperance Union
WMS	Woman's Missionary Society
WMU	Woman's Missionary Union
WMUTS	Woman's Missionary Union Training School, Louisville, Kentucky
YWA	Young Woman's Auxiliary

Mrs. Mary B. Barnes Mrs. S. Wilson Mrs. Harvey Hatcher Mrs. N. D. Chipley

Miss Ella Miller Mrs. J. K. Pace Mrs. A. Broaddus Miss Agnes Osborne

Mrs. John Phillips Mrs. S. Y. Pitts Mrs. John Stout Miss M. E. McIntosh

Mrs. C. A. Lofton Miss Evie Brown Mrs. F. B. Davis Miss Minnie Slaughter

Miss Minerva Alfred Mrs. O. F. Gregory Mrs. Jas. Pollard Miss A. W. Armstrong

Delegates Who Attended Organization Meeting

Delegates Appointed Whose Pictures Could Not Be Obtained

Mrs. S. A. Forbes, *Ark.*	Mrs. J. L. Burnham, *Mo.*	Miss Julia Blackman, *Tenn.*
Mrs. L. B. Telford, *Fla.*	Mrs. M. A. Hewitt, *S. C.*	Miss Ella Hill, *Tenn.*
Miss Allen, *Ky.*	Mrs. A. C. Ardrey, *Tex.*	

Delegates Appointed from Mississippi and Virginia

Mrs. A. M. Hillman, *Miss.*	Miss M. C. Tupper, *Va.*
Mrs. S. A. E. Bailey, *Miss.*	Mrs. W. E. Hatcher, *Va.*
	Mrs. R. Adam, *Va.*

Street-level room in Broad Street Methodist Church, Richmond, Va., where WMU was organized in 1888.

WMU headquarters building at 15 West Franklin Street, Baltimore, Md.

WMU leaders in 1902: *Top row, left to right:* Eliza Broadus, Ky.; Jane M. Ammen (Mrs. Charles), La.; Mary K. Oldham Eagle (Mrs. J. P.), Ark.; Mary Emily Wright, Ga. *Bottom row:* Annie Kate Woods (Mrs. W.R.), Miss.; Sarah Jessie Davis Stakely (Mrs. Charles), Ala.; Abby Manly Gwathmey (Mrs. W. H.), Va.

Student body and staff of Woman's Training School, Louisville, 1904.

First home of Woman's Training School on Fourth Street, Louisville, Ky.

Scrapbooks showing early missions literature.

Office employees in Baltimore headquarters in 1915.

WMU workers attending a $75 Million Campaign conference in Nashville, Tenn., July 2-3, 1919.

Fourth home of the Training School at 334 East Broadway, Louisville, Ky. Known as House Beautiful.

Marble lobby of House Beautiful.

Students and staff of WMU Training School, 1927-28.

Christmas scene in the chapel of WMU Training School.

Seven WMU Training School students calling the school to report that they had been appointed by the Foreign Mission Board for overseas service, April 1946.

Kathleen Mallory leading a Bible devotional period at Ridgecrest, August 1944.

Margaret Waller, the woman in whose honor the Margaret Home was named.

Sarah Joe Hurst Burney (Mrs. Frank), longtime chairman of the Margaret Fund.

Missionaries' children in front of the Margaret Home in Greenville, S.C., 1906.

Women attending WMU's 50th anniversary celebration in 1938.

Juliette Mather (*seated in center*) with WMU state young people's secretaries at the January 1947 meeting of the WMU Executive Committee.

Students and staff of WMU Training School, 1947-48.

Left to right: Juliette Mather, Margaret Bruce, newly-elected executive secretary Alma Hunt, Olive Martin, Ethlene Boone Cox, Frances Tyler, and Mary Edmundson Lee at WMU Annual Meeting in 1948.

1111 Comer Building, Birmingham, Ala., where WMU rented offices from September 1921 to September 1951.

Employees filling orders at WMU headquarters, the Comer Building.

Left to right: Madeline Dix Reeves (Mrs. W. P.), J.B. Lawrence, Angeline McCrocklin Grooms (Mrs. H. H.), Porter Routh, Kathleen Mallory, Alma Hunt, Theron Rankin, and Olive Martin at dedication of WMU headquarters at 600 North 20th Street, Birmingham, Ala., on January 21, 1952.

Ethel Winfield, Alma Hunt, Mildred McMurray, Martha Franks, and Margaret Bruce in front of 600 North 20th Street building, circa 1952.

Women attending the first WMU Conference at Glorieta, N. Mex., July 6-12, 1953.

Royal Ambassador Joint Committee meeting in Memphis, Tenn., to discuss the transfer of Royal Ambassadors from WMU to Brotherhood, circa 1955.

Left to right: Frances Tyler, Alma Hunt, Marie Mathis, and LaVenia Neal at WMU Annual Meeting in 1956.

Mrs. Robert Deneen leading a YWA conference at Ridgecrest, N.C., in 1957.

WMU, SBC, professional employees at a meeting around 1962. *Left to right:* Billie Pate, Laurella Owens, Doris DeVault, Margaret Bruce, Betty Brewer, Alma Hunt, Dorothy Weeks, Ethalee Hamric, Abbie Louise Green, Katharine Bryan (photo by Fon H. Scofield).

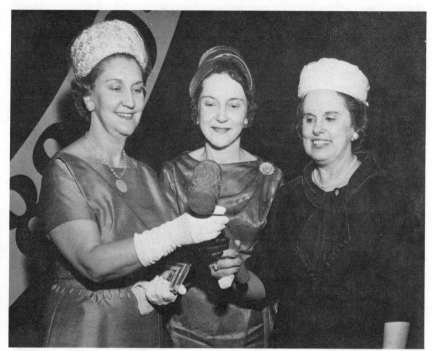

Marie Mathis (*right*) handing the presidential gavel to Helen Fling (*left*) as Alma Hunt (*center*) looks on (1963).

Stage at the 75th anniversary of WMU in 1963.

Girls celebrate the 50th anniversary of the Girls' Auxiliary organization in 1963.

K. Owen White, SBC president (*left*); Marie Mathis, second vice-president (*center*); and P. S. James, first vice-president (*right*) after their election in Kansas City in 1963.

Alma Hunt and Helen Fling (*both on right*) at the 50th anniversary celebration of Nigeria WMU.

Large replica of *World Comrades*, the magazine for Sunbeam and Girls' Auxiliary until May 1953 and for Royal Ambassadors until June 1946; *Tell*, the magazine for Girl's Auxiliary members; and *Tell*, leadership edition for GA leaders until October 1970.

WMU members reach for copies of some of the new magazines which first appeared in October 1970.

Ruby Snider (*left*), Marie Mathis (*center*), and newly elected executive secretary Carolyn Weatherford (*right*) in Dallas in 1974.

Helen Fling (*at podium*) brings a resolution before the Southern Baptist Convention in 1974.

Carolyn Weatherford with Foreign Mission Board executive secretary Baker James Cauthen and his wife, Eloise, at the WMU Annual Meeting in 1979 in Houston.

Christine Gregory, Southern Baptist Convention first vice-president (*left*); stands with Bailey Smith, president (*center*); and Don Kim, second vice-president (*right*) after their election in Los Angeles in 1981.

Acteens National Advisory panelists serve as first girl pages for the Southern Baptist Convention in Los Angeles in 1981.

Present and former WMU presidents stand together at the WMU Annual Meeting in 1981. *Left to right:* Dorothy Sample, Marie Mathis, Helen Fling, and Christine Gregory.

Dorothy Sample and Carolyn Weatherford stop to talk during a cities tour sponsored by the Home Mission Board.

Helen Fling (*seated on front row, left*), Marie Mathis (*seated on front row, right*), and Carolyn Weatherford (*standing on back row, left*) at an executive committee meeting of the North American Baptist Women's Union in 1982.

14,005 girls and leaders gather at the fifth National Acteens Convention in Fort Worth in 1984.

Former foreign missionary Marjorie J. McCullough at her election as WMU president in Atlanta in 1986.

WMU headquarters on New Hope Mountain in Birmingham, Alabama.

CHRONOLOGY OF
WOMAN'S MISSIONARY UNION
AUXILIARY TO SOUTHERN BAPTIST CONVENTION

*Prepared by Eljee Bentley, PhD.

1868   Ann Baker Graves (Mrs. John) invited women attending SBC meeting in Baltimore to meet for prayer concerning missions. She possibly conducted further such meetings in 1871 and 1872.

1871   Baptist women in Baltimore, organized as Woman's Mission to Woman, appealed to women to organize branches in each state for prayer and dissemination of missionary intelligence.

1872   SBC first encouraged the formation of women's societies for foreign missions.

FMB, for the first time since 1849, appointed single women: Edmonia Moon and Lula Whilden.

1873   Foreign Mission Board appointed Lottie Moon as missionary to China.

1877   SBC first suggested women be urged to cooperate in the work of home missions.

1878   SBC recommended that the mission boards organize central committees of women in each state, the committees to organize societies that should be auxiliary to state conventions of the SBC.

1882   Kentucky Central Committee began publication of *The Heathen Helper* and requested the cooperation of other state central committees.

1883   Women attending SBC in Waco, Texas, met together. Sallie Rochester Ford (Mrs. S. H.) presided and read Scripture. Martha Crawford (Mrs. T. P.) told of work in China.

1884   Women who met together during SBC in Baltimore resolved to meet annually during the SBC. Women convenanted to pray on the first Sunday morning of each month for the success of woman's missions work.

1885   SBC refused women delegates their seats and amended its constitution, changing *members* to *brethren*.

The women, at second annual meeting, sent their resolutions to be printed in the SBC minutes: (1) Women do not want a separate and independent organization; (2) Women want to work through the churches and to have representation in the SBC, through state conventions, as heretofore.

SBC recommended that state conventions, not mission boards, foster central committees.

1887   Maryland Baptist women opened the Mission Rooms, from which missions literature was published and distributed.

Woman's Mission Societies at their informal annual meeting requested each state central committee to appoint three delegates to the 1888 meeting.

---

*Comprehensive annals in WMU, SBC, archives, are fully footnoted. Sources are SBC Annual, the Annual Report of WMU, WMU Year Book, Minutes of Executive Committee/Board, and magazines of WMU.

1888	Women delegates from 12 central committees met at Broad Street Methodist Church in Richmond. Delegates from ten states adopted a constitution, forming the Executive Committee of the Woman's Mission Societies (Auxiliary to Southern Baptist Convention). Baltimore was chosen as headquarters and officers were elected.

Organization agreed to aid HMB in building a church and enlarging a cemetery in Cuba.

Woman's Executive Committee in consultation with the FMB initiated a special offering to send a missionary to China to relieve Lottie Moon.

FMB and HMB agreed to pay expenses of the Executive Committee, as all contributions were to go to the boards.

1889 State central committees were encouraged to push young people's work and to organize associational or district committees.

Women planned next year's work based on recommendations by FMB and HMB.

1890 Women changed organization name to Woman's Missionary Union, Auxiliary to Southern Baptist Convention (WMU).

Sending boxes of clothes and other necessary items to frontier and other needy home missionaries became part of WMU's plan of work.

WMU agreed to raise enough money to support all women foreign missionaries.

WMU's Executive Committee employed a clerk and purchased a typewriter.

1892 First week in January was observed as a week of prayer in connection with the Christmas offering. In 1926 the week was changed to the first week in December.

WMU's plan of work included work with foreigners and black women.

WMU participated in SBC's centennial of missions, raising money for a chapel fund and furnishing materials for Sunbeam Bands and for an August Children's Day in the Sunday Schools.

1893 WMU sent the Sunday School Board leaflets and mite boxes for Missionary Day in Sunday School. Beginning in 1904-1905, FMB and HMB each had its own day in SS, and WMU supplied literature for both.

1894 SSB presented recommendations to WMU and began contributing toward the expenses of WMU, continuing to contribute through 1947.

WMU voted at Annual Meeting to raise an additional $5,000 before August 1 to pay off the FMB debt. The women raised $5,397.

1895 Week of Self-Denial was observed the third week of March to relieve the HMB of debt. Until 1922 Self-Denial was the name of the offering, despite many efforts to change it to Thank Offering. By 1911 the first week in March was customary.

1896 WMU adopted Sunbeam work at the request of the FMB. George Braxton Taylor, with Anna Elsom, had begun Sunbeams in 1886.

Each state was assigned a specified amount toward the goals of $30,000 each for the two mission boards. This system of apportionment became standard practice, lasting until 1943. Apportionments for the Training School continued as long as WMU owned the school.

Southern Baptist Theological Seminary began using one of its missionary days to promote WMU work. In 1900 space was offered in its magazine.

1897   WMU began contributing toward the SSB's Bible Fund to furnish Bibles for missionaries. Contributions continued until 1932. WMU also sent boxes of clothing to Sunday School missionaries.

1898   WMU recommended that states have associational vice-presidents, each one in charge of the work in her association.

1899   Money was given through WMU to all three boards to be invested and to pay an annuity, thus establishing for all three an annuity plan.

WMU recommended that the churches adopt a graded system of missionary education with organizations for all age levels, beginning with Baby Bands.

1900   WMU established HMB's Church Building Loan Fund. In 1903 WMU undertook to raise $20,000, a memorial to I. T. Tichenor, to put the fund on a secure basis.

WMU, at the request of the SBC, helped lead the New Century Movement, an effort to induce every church and every member to make regular contributions.

WMU encouraged women to begin schools in mountain regions.

WMU corresponding secretary began traveling the states to promote the work and to visit home missionaries. The boards paid her travel expenses.

1901   Ownership of the Maryland Baptist Mission Rooms, founded in 1886 with Annie Armstrong as secretary, passed to the HMB and the SSB. It was later called the Mission Literature Department of the SBC. The operation, publication, and distribution of literature remained with the women.

Delegates to the WMU Annual Meeting were given badges entitling them to seats on the floor of the SBC.

WMU recommended a home department for every church to reach those who could not attend meetings. In 1904 WMU recommended that missionary home departments be merged with Sunday School home departments.

Annie Armstrong addressed the Woman's Auxiliary of the National Baptist Convention, which had organized with her advice in 1900. In 1902 WMU approved her work with the black organization.

WMU recommended that societies collect missions libraries and place missions literature in Sunday School libraries.

1903   Salary was approved for the corresponding secretary. Annie Armstrong declined to accept.

Emphasis on enlistment of young women was launched.

1904   WMU called attention to the mission society as an opportunity for Bible study.

WMU encouraged members to a careful study of proportionate and systematic giving. The practice but not study of giving had been recommended earlier.

1905   Using a gift of $10,000, WMU opened Margaret Home, a home for the children of missionaries who were overseas, in Greenville, South Carolina.

1906   WMU recommended that each state organization observe a week of prayer for state missions. As early as 1895 WMU had recommended that state central committees cooperate with their state boards or conventions, making all departments of state work their work.

HMB and SSB returned ownership of the Literature Department to the Maryland Baptist Union, who transferred it to WMU.

WMU issued its first periodical, the quarterly *Our Mission Fields,* to provide complete programs for the monthly meetings of societies.

1907   A more thorough and systematic study of missions was recommended for all age levels, through reading WMU and other Southern Baptist literature, and through special study classes. Recommended by name were two interdenominational courses.

WMU workers met for training and mission study at the annual conferences sponsored by the Young People's Missionary Movement.

The home for women attending classes at Southern Seminary in Louisville became the Woman's Missionary Union Training School.

Young Woman's Auxiliary (YWA) was the name adopted for young women's societies; also chosen were a badge, a motto, and aims.

WMU launched a vigorous enlistment and enlargement campaign with an enlistment day in October.

1908   WMU introduced its Calendar of Prayer, prepared by a committee appointed at the 1907 Annual Meeting.

Order of Royal Ambassadors (RA), with a constitution, motto, and pin, became the official name for missionary societies for boys. In 1913 WMU recommended that RAs be graded: juniors and intermediates.

WMU recommended that states sponsor local missionary institutes to train workers.

WMU elected the faculty for the WMU Training School at Annual Meeting, continuing annually until 1952.

1909   WMU purchased and occupied 15 West Franklin Street in Baltimore, renting out part of the space.

1910   WMU chose its first annual watchword. A Bible verse had been chosen the year before, but it had been called a motto. The first hymn of the year was selected in 1913.

WMU elected its first officer to work specifically with young people.

Personal service became a regular department of WMU work.

WMU's plan of work emphasized tithing.

1911   WMU recommended that a college correspondent be elected in every state.

Spiritual development of members was added as an aim of WMU.

WMU adopted Standard of Excellence for local organizations.

Edith Campbell Crane planned the program for the first women's meeting of the Baptist World Alliance (BWA). Out of that meeting came the Women's Committee of the BWA with Miss Crane as secretary.

State corresponding secretaries and field workers met together to discuss methods and policies. A year later they organized and adopted a constitution. They met annually through 1955.

WMU participated with women of other denominations in meetings all over the country celebrating 50th anniversary of woman's missionary work.

1912   WMU published its first Year Book, setting out the plan of work for 1912-13.

1913   Several state WMUs reported separate organizations for 12- through 16-year-old girls. Such organizations had been recommended at the Annual Meeting of 1909, and in that year *Our Mission Fields* provided separate program suggestions for them. In 1914 the name Girls' Auxiliary was adopted.

WMU began sending representatives to meet with the FMB each time an unmarried woman was interviewed for appointment.

WMU celebrated its Jubilate, or 25th, Anniversary in meetings and fund raising throughout the South.

WMU adopted an offical seal, designed by Emma Whitfield. In 1914 a pin used the design of the seal.

WMU recommended that societies in larger towns establish settlement houses. The model was the house in Louisville, authorized in 1912, where the Training School students got practical missions experience. In 1914 the name Good Will Centers was adopted for these houses.

WMU reported directly to the SBC in addition to reporting through the boards.

WMU's first book-length history, In *Royal Service* by Fannie Heck, was published.

YWAs were encouraged to begin Daily Vacation Bible Schools.

WMU recommended that larger societies be divided into circles, which would meet once a month, preferably the week before the society meeting. In 1917 circles were recommended for all societies.

1914   WMU recommended that societies organize groups for businesswomen who could not attend daytime meetings; these came to be known as Business Woman's Circles.

Efficiency commissions began reporting on better methods.

Royal Service, a monthly magazine, replaced *Our Mission Fields*.

WMU's plan of work included a declaration of sympathy with all that makes for the spiritual and physical uplift of the country. After 1923 the declaration with some changes was called Moral Standards, and was carried in the plan of work until 1949.

1916   Scholarships to children of missionaries were first granted from the Margaret Fund, established from proceeds of sale of the Margaret Home.

1917   WMU introduced correspondence courses for leaders of YWA, RA, GA, and Sunbeams.

Manual of WMU Methods, the first book-length manual, was published.

Cornerstone of House Beautiful, a new building for the Training School, was laid. The building was dedicated in May 1918.

1918   The Calendar of Prayer was incorporated into *Royal Service*.

WMU plan of work emphasized tithing and stewardship. Each woman was asked to sign a stewardship covenant and each society was to have a stewardship chairman. The plan called for Emergency Women, women who would give to meet emergency needs of the mission boards.

WMU issued mission study certificates and awarded seals to those who successfully completed study of specified books. By 1919 there were graded courses with awards offered for all age levels. An advanced course was planned for adults.

Christmas offering was named the Lottie Moon Christmas Offering (LMCO).

SBC reversed its decision of 1885, and admitted women as messengers.

1919   WMU cooperated in the $75 Million Campaign, pledging to raise $15,000,000 in five years for SBC work. Each state had a WMU campaign director; 838 associations and 14,491 churches had WMU campaign organizers.

WMU recommended that state WMUs sponsor camps for YWAs, GAs, and RAs. Many states had already had camps at summer assemblies.

WMU voted to oppose Baptist churches joining with those of other denominations under the leadership of a central organization.

1920   Soul winning was added as an aim of WMU.

White Cross work, preparing bandages and other supplies for use in Southern Baptist hospitals on the missions fields, was recommended.

Secretaries of Ministerial Relief and Annuities Board and Education Board spoke at the WMU Annual Meeting. Since WMU members had begun contributing to the work of these boards, boards contributed to the general fund of WMU. The Relief and Annuity Board contributed through 1946, Education through 1927.

1921   Student Activities Committee with representatives of the FMB, HMB, SSB, Education Board, and WMU recommended an SBC plan for student work. WMU began to issue "College YWA Bulletin."

WMU requested a quota of female representation on the SBC Executive Committee and boards. SBC voted to elect members on personal qualifications, regardless of sex.

WMU Advisory Committee for the Bible Institute at New Orleans (later New Orleans Baptist Theological Seminary) was appointed. This committee or a representative of the seminary reported at every WMU Annual Meeting until 1947. Reports were printed with the Annual Meeting minutes unti 1953.

Birmingham became the home of WMU. The staff moved into 1111 Comer Building in September.

1922   WMU began cooperating with the Commission on Interracial Cooperation as a means of personal service.

WMU Resolutions (plan of work) called for study of specific foreign and home missions books in connection with the weeks of prayer.

World Comrades, a quarterly publication for GAs, RAs, and Sunbeams, began publication.

1923   Grace McBride Circles of YWA began at Baptist hospitals. In 1927 their News Sheet was first published.

1924   First conventionwide YWA camp was held at Ridgecrest, North Carolina; the last was in 1970.

WMU in Annual Meeting voted to cooperate with the Woman's National Committee for Law Enforcement.

WMU appointed an advisory board to Southwestern Seminary Training School, which had been begun by Texas women as part of the seminary. A representative of the seminary reported at Annual Meeting until 1947; reports were printed with Annual Meeting minutes until 1953.

Kathleen Mallory traveled to the Orient. Annie Armstrong had been to Mexico in 1902; Mallory was the first WMU executive to visit overseas missions fields.

New grading system was established.

WMU encouraged societies to send relief boxes to aged, needy ministers.

1925   WMU had raised $16,713,100 on its pledge of $15,000,000 and continued cooperating with the SBC in a new program of funding denominational work, later known as the Cooperative Program.

The plan of work called for cooperation in church schools of missions.

State WMUs, receiving matching funds from the SSB, organized nearly 1,000 societies in rural churches.

WMU, Auxiliary to Southern Baptist Convention, was incorporated in Alabama.

WMU took greater responsibility for reaching Jews. A part of the reserve capital of the Literature Department was set aside for publications to be used in this witness.

1926   Tithing was the emphasis. The campaign to enlist new tithers was launched at the 1925 Annual Meeting. In 1926 WMU brought out tithing pins, seals, songs, and record cards. YWAs had a tithing story contest.

White Cross work was extended to Baptist hospitals in the United States.

1927   President and corresponding secretary of WMU were included in the committee to whom the SBC delegated promotion of the Cooperative Program.

1928   WMU celebrated its Ruby Anniversary by an intensified effort to organize more societies, enlist new members, and give more money. To pray for the work an Intercessory League of Shut-ins was organized. The league became a regular part of WMU work; its name was changed to Intercessory Prayer League.

Forward Steps, an individual achievement plan for members of Girls' Auxiliary, became an immediate success. A ranking system for RAs was already in use.

Executive Secretary of the SBC Executive Committee first spoke at Annual Meeting; his subject was the Cooperative Program.

WMU's first book-length manual for leaders of young people's missions organizations was published.

FMB published a book to be studied prior to the Week of Prayer for Foreign Missions. Similar books were printed until 1945. From 1930 a WMU committee planned each book and suggested writers.

WMU gave $500 to HMB in memory of Mrs. W. R. Nimmo, secretary of Literature Department, to fund literature in Spanish for Cuba WMU. This also served Spanish WMU in the United States.

1929   Ruby Anniversary resulted in 6,405 new organizations, bringing the total to 30,415. WMU enrollment passed the half million mark.

YWAs got their own monthly magazine, *The Window of YWA*.

Mrs. Cox addressed the SBC despite objections. She was the first woman invited to address the Convention.

HMB published a book to be studied prior to the Week of Prayer for Home Missions. Similar books were printed most years until 1945; from 1930 a WMU committee planned them and suggested writers.

1930   WMU asked the FMB to give priority to graduates of the WMU Training School when selecting missionaries. Since 1927 WMU had been allocating the LMCO for salaries.

Church Leadership Week was held at Ridgecrest, and WMU sent representatives to teach WMU work.

Part of the Lottie Moon Christmas Offering was allocated for WMU work on foreign fields. From 1933 this allocation was known as the Mrs. W. J. Cox Fund.

1931   WMU increased efforts to have every woman church member contributing to missions. WMU had been supporting the every member canvass since at least 1909. Beginning in 1934 recognition was given at Annual Meeting to churches in which every resident woman member contributed.

Personal service among the deaf, already being done by societies in Alabama, was recommended.

WMU gave nearly 50 percent of the total Cooperative Program contributions for the year.

1932   YWAs celebrated their 25th anniversary with simultaneous meetings throughout the Convention. Mrs. Cox spoke to all those attending via radio.

Local WMU's were encouraged to continue fostering Young Men's Brotherhoods, composed of those who were too old for RAs.

WMU appointed an Advisory Committee on Cooperation with the Woman's Auxiliary, National Baptist Convention.

1933   WMU adopted a plan to reduce the debt of the FMB and suggested that the SBC adopt a plan. The SBC adopted the Hundred Thousand Club, and WMU cooperated with the plan.

Corresponding secretary of WMU became a member of the SBC Executive Committee by virtue of her office.

1934   The name Annie W. Armstrong Offering for home missions was adopted.

Elizabeth Lowndes Scholarship was established. The first annual award to the outstanding Margaret Fund recipient was made in 1937.

1935   WMU adopted at Annual Meeting a recommendation of the Mission Study Committee: representatives of WMU and of the two mission boards should plan a cycle of graded, correlated mission study books. FMB published the first of what came to be known as the Graded Series. The HMB series began in 1943.

Focus Weeks began as promotional emphasis on WMU organizations.

1936   WMU presented $250 to establish Literature Department for the Woman's Auxiliary, National Baptist Convention, the first of what became an annual gift.

1937   Regular scholarships for "missionaries' kids" became allocations of the two missions offerings. WMU ceased a separate campaign for the Margaret Fund and concentrated on supporting MKs with prayer, guidance, and loving care.

1938   Among the special goals of the Golden Jubilee were gifts for the future development of the Training School and for work with black women and young people.

SBC committee appointed in 1937 recommended that representatives of the boards and of WMU meet annually to coordinate and correlate the activities suggested for the local church.

LMCO allocations for women's training schools on foreign fields were referred to as the Heck Memorial and were given preference over all other items except salaries and the Margaret Fund.

1939 WMU began sending small amounts of money for personal use, Burney Gifts, to Margaret Fund students.

WMU asked Brotherhood to take an interest in RA work, suggesting that church organizations study RA work in one program each year and furnish counselors when requested.

WMU cooperated in the Southwide Revival.

1940 WMU officers, designated the standing committee for WMU work, presented the WMU report to the SBC. Until 1937 the committee had been headed by a man. After 1939 the WMU officers were the committee.

In support of the campaign For a Debtless Denomination by 1945, WMU agreed to raise one-third of the total amount, exceeding the goal in 1943.

WMU laid the cornerstone for a new Training School building, occupied in the fall 1941.

WMU began annual promotion and funding of state or regional institutes to train black Baptist women.

1941 WMU promoted a church night for stewardship to take place before the every member canvass. This time of educating the church in giving was an annual event until 1962.

First annual WMU Year Book in Spanish was prepared by Esther B. Moye (Mrs. John), home missionary working with Texas Mexican WMU. Programs from *Royal Service* were translated and printed in the Texas Mexican convention's monthly magazine.

1942 Personal service was changed to community missions.

Business Woman's Circles held their first conventionwide conference at Ridgecrest.

1943 Because of the war, no Annual Meeting was held. WMU mailed its book of reports for 1942 and recommended local meetings to discuss the reports.

J. Ivyloy Bishop, first male staff member, was employed to work with RA.

1944 Because of wartime travel difficulties, WMU held its Annual Meeting at a time and place separate from the SBC.

LMCO funds were allocated to the American Bible Society.

WMU sponsored the first conventionwide Young Men's Mission Conference at Ridgecrest.

1945 Missionary Round Table was introduced, a plan by which WMS members shared in buying, circulating, and discussing books of missionary significance.

WMU encouraged members to send food and other supplies to European Baptists.

No Annual Meeting was held because of the war.

LMCO exceeded $1,000,000.

1946 *Ambassador Life* was published for RA.

All members of WMS, not just those in Business Woman's Circle, were invited to summer conference at Ridgecrest.

Missionary Education Council of Southern Baptist Agencies was formed by WMU, the mission boards, the SSB, the Brotherhood, and others.

1947 YWA celebrated 40th anniversary. A service at YWA Camp was broadcast.

1948   WMU celebrated 60th anniversary by reaffirming its moral standards and pledging to teach others to reverence God's Word and "His plan for the salvation of nations through individuals."

Women's Committee of BWA was revived with the president of WMU as chairman.

1949   The WMU Year Book included an SBC calendar, "Coordinated Denominational Activities." In 1948 the SBC had recommended better coordination; and in 1949 the Inter-Agency Council began its work, with WMU participating.

Annie Armstrong Offering allocations were made for WMU field workers among the Hispanic and Indians.

1950   WMU encouraged church WMU presidents to meet regularly with pastors and other church leaders in the church council or cabinet.

WMU's reported membership more than 1 million.

WMU magazines encouraged young people to send Christmas gifts to missionaries, calling the project Christmas in August.

1951   WMU purchased a headquarters building in downtown Birmingham, 600 North 20th Street.

WMU coordinated mission study plans with the new denominational Church Study Course.

First of a series of regional leadership training conferences for young people's leaders was held in Memphis.

State mission study leaders participated in a conventionwide Mission Study Institute, then conducted 400 institutes. Similar training was sponsored again in 1954.

1952   Prayer calendar in *Royal Service* began to list missionaries on their birthdays.

Special three-day training meeting of the Community Missions Council was held in Birmingham. State leaders then trained district, associational, and local chairmen. Similar training was given in 1955.

1953   A WMU conference was held at Glorieta Baptist Conference Center, New Mexico, as well as at Ridgecrest.

Tell, a monthly magazine for GAs, and *Sunbeam Activities,* a quarterly for Sunbeam leaders, replaced *World Comrades.*

Five thousand RAs met in Atlanta to celebrate their 45th anniversary.

WMU Training School became Carver School of Missions and Social Work.

State stewardship leaders were trained in Birmingham, then trained district, associational, and local leaders. Similar training was planned for 1956.

1954   WMU voted to transfer RA work to Brotherhood by 1957. In the interim a joint committee of WMU and Brotherhood promoted RA.

1955   At the BWA meeting in London the Women's Committee, which had reorganized in 1950, became the Women's Department.

The Texas Mexican WMU published the first issue of *Nuestra Tarea,* funded by the HMB.

1956   Aims for Advancement replaced the Standard of Excellence. The eight aims were world awareness, spiritual life development, Christian witnessing, sharing possessions, educating youth in missions, enlistment for missions, leadership training, and reporting advancement.

WMU Executive Board received the report of Booz-Allen and

Hamilton, management consultants it had employed to study WMU structure and operation.

WMU decided to promote churchwide giving through the Lottie Moon Christmas Offering and Annie Armstrong Offering.

1957   WMU transferred ownership of Carver School of Missions and Social Work to SBC.

Carver School and YWA celebrated their 50th anniversaries.

1958   WMU transferred ownership of the Good Will Center in Louisville, Kentucky, to the HMB, provided that the center be continued. In 1965 it was returned to WMU, then sold.

WMU adopted goals for the five years leading up to Baptist Jubilee Year of 1964.

At the request of the SBC, WMU promoted the 30,000 Movement for new churches and missions.

Aims for Advancement for associational WMU were introduced in the 1959-60 WMU Year Book.

1959   WMU adopted a new plan for training local leaders, offering courses by class and individual study for leaders of all organizations, not just those for young people.

WMU introduced Sunbeam Nursery for children from birth through three.

1960   WMU strengthened work with eight-year-olds, giving them the organizational name, World Friends, an emblem, motto, song, and materials.

Woman's Missionary Society (WMS) Manual was introduced. It launched a second plan of organization, one for churches needing more than one WMS.

WMU encouraged church organizations to be included in their church budgets.

1961   WMU transferred administration of the Margaret Fund to the two mission boards.

WMU and the HMB jointly employed a staff member to work with WMU in pioneer states.

Sunbeam Band celebrated its 75th anniversary.

WMU sponsored a conventionwide conference on residential camping and day camping.

1962   WMU Executive Board ceased to vote on LMCO and Annie Armstrong Offering allocations.

WMU changed its bylaws: state WMUs no longer sent delegates to Annual Meeting. Anyone present was eligible to vote.

WMU used the statistics gathered by the SSB from church letters rather than its own; membership was 1,496,926 in 96,558 organizations.

1963   Carver School of Missions and Social Work merged with Southern Baptist Theological Seminary.

WMU celebrated 75th anniversary. Goals for church and associational organizations included an anniversary prayer retreat.

GA celebrated 50th anniversary. A total of 21,533 girls and their leaders attended three national conventions in Memphis.

Braille Baptist carried features adapted from *Royal Service.*

WMU asked the HMB to find ways to involve more women in volunteer missions.

WMU staff met regularly with staff of SBC agencies and boards whose work affected the program of the local church.

1964   WMU celebrated the Baptist Jubilee, 150 years since the organization of the Triennial Convention, with prayer retreats and attention to Baptist ideals and history.

Alma Hunt's *History of Woman's Missionary Union* became available in Baptist Book Stores.

WMU membership peaked at 1,529,454 in 99,821 organizations.

WMU with the SBC began a five-year emphasis on A Church Fulfilling Its Mission, and provided curriculum to support the first year's focus on worship.

WMU spoke of its role in the church in terms of tasks: (1) teach missions; (2) lead members to participate in missions; (3) provide organization and leadership for special missions projects of the church; (4) provide and interpret information regarding the work of the church and denomination.

WMU defined mission study (teach missions) to include the missionary message of the Bible; Bible study was published in every issue of *Royal Service*, a practice that had been discontinued in 1948.

1965   The terms *mission action* and *mission action publications* were introduced.

WMU Year Book suggested an optional plan for organizing WMS, a society without circles.

During its 150th anniversary celebration, the American Bible Society thanked Southern Baptists for contributions made through allocations in the LMCO and AAO.

1966   WMU, Brotherhood, Sunday School, Training Union, and Music Ministry provided fully correlated curriculum, called the Life and Work Curriculum, for young people and adults.

WMU adopted an agency program statement that had been prepared in cooperation with the SBC Executive Committee. The SBC accepted WMU's statement.

Missionary Education Council, formed in 1946, dissolved; and the Missions Education and Promotion Conference was formed by staff representatives of WMU, Brotherhood, and the mission boards.

1967   WMU and Brotherhood with the help of the mission boards sponsored a world missions conference.

A church WMU Achievement Guide was introduced. Age-level and associational organizations continued to use Aims for Advancement for one more year.

Mission action replaced community missions and new publications were released: a survey guide, a projects guide, and five mission action group guides. WMS and YWA were encouraged to form mission action groups.

WMU agreed to produce and distribute North American Baptist Women's Union publication, *The Tie*, for five years (the first issue had appeared in 1961) and continued to do so until 1983.

1968   WMU presented new organizational plans and materials for the church and association.

Groups replaced circles in WMS; a group might specialize in prayer, mission action, or study.

WMU's Executive Board adopted a new name for the offering for home missions, Annie Armstrong Easter Offering (AAEO).

1969   Spanish-speaking women were invited to conferences conducted in their own language during WMU conference at Glorieta.

WMU, Brotherhood, the two mission boards, and the Vocational Guidance Department of the SSB sponsored Mission '70, a conference for students and other young people during the Christmas holidays.

WMU sponsored PACT, intercessory prayer for the Crusade of the Americas.

1970   All WMU leadership courses became part of the Church Study Course.

In October WMS, YWA, Girls' Auxiliary, and Sunbeams were replaced by Baptist Women (BW), Baptist Young Women (BYW), Acteens, Girls in Action (GA), and Mission Friends. The new organizations used the grouping-grading plan adopted for all church organizations.

New organizations had new manuals and new magazines: the monthly *Contempo* for BYW, *Accent* for Acteens, and *Discovery* for GA; the quarterly *Aware* for GA leaders, and *Start* for Mission Friends leaders. *Royal Service* became the magazine for Baptist Women. WMU officers had a new quarterly, *Dimension.*

Forward Steps and the YWA Citation were replaced by new plans for individual achievement: Missions Adventures for GA and Studiact for Acteens.

WMU work in the church was planned around a new statement of tasks: (1) teach missions; (2) engage in mission action; (3) support world missions through praying and giving; (4) provide and interpret information regarding the work of the church and denomination.

1971   WMU Focus Week replaced the age-level focus weeks.

1972   WMU language missions was moved to WMU headquarters from the HMB, which continued to fund it.

WMU and the HMB sponsored 15 national mission action workshops.

First National Acteens Conference (NAC) was held at Glorieta during WMU Week.

Burney Gifts to Margaret Fund students were discontinued.

WMU encouraged its members to participate in their church in Lay Evangelism Schools, a program of the HMB.

1973   WMU began a two-year emphasis on enlistment and enlargement using the theme Each One Bring One, Cultivate One. Giant Step goals were adopted.

WMU presented two Elizabeth Lowndes Awards, one to a child of home missionaries and one to a child of foreign missionaries.

1974   Membership and the number of organizations increased in the 1973-74 church year—the first increase since 1963-64.

1975   WMU celebrated the 50th anniversary of the Cooperative Program.

National Acteens Conference attracted 10,716 Acteens to Memphis.

WMU Year Book 1975-76 introduced expanded task statements: Teach missions included the spiritual development of members. Mission action included direct evangelism.

Preceding the SBC, WMU and the Pastors Conference held a joint session to begin their annual meetings.

1976   National BYW meeting, Kaleidoscope, preceded Annual Meeting in Norfolk, Virginia.

1977 WMU encouraged women to begin Big A Clubs for children in transitional communities and published curriculum for 52 weekly meetings. The Executive Board approved curriculum for a second year.

First Acteens National Advisory Panel was chosen.

WMU introduced a new campus organization, Campus BYW.

WMU launched its Annual Meeting and participation in Bold Mission Thrust with a Bold Mission Rally.

With the Baptist Book Stores, WMU began the Round Table Book Club.

WMU joined with Brotherhood, the SSB, FMB, and HMB to form the Missions Education Council.

WMU nonperiodical literature was merchandised only through Baptist Book Stores.

WMU encouraged churchwide missions activities, calling them Missions Night Out.

Executive Board adopted six objectives (priorities) for WMU as an agency.

1978 WMU cooperated with the SBC in the North Central Mission Thrust, undertaking a Bold Mission Prayer Partners Project.

WMU, along with boards and agencies of the SBC, sponsored a Consultation on Women in Church-Related Vocations.

Acteens began a volunteer missions program called Acteens Activators.

New publication for preschoolers, *Mission Friends Share*, was introduced.

Churches were encouraged to have churchwide prayer retreats for Bold Mission Thrust.

WMU and the HMB employed a WMU consultant to work in relationship with black Baptists.

WMU employed seminary students as interns.

WMU cosponsored a Convocation on World Hunger.

1979 Third National Acteens Conference was held in Kansas City in July with 11,500 registered.

1980 WMU launched a National Enlargement Plan, a three-year effort to organize WMU in more Southern Baptist churches.

WMU participated with Southern Baptist agencies in a Center for Study of Urban Ministry.

WMU encouraged members to see that their churches observed World Hunger Day.

More than 30 women from seven language groups came to WMU headquarters for a leadership training conference.

1981 WMU with the assistance of the HMB published materials in Chinese, Korean, Japanese, Romanian, and Basic English. Materials in other languages followed.

Black WMU leaders came to WMU headquarters for a special training conference. A similar conference was held in 1982.

First issue of *Our Missions World*, a monthly magazine in Basic English for use by the deaf and those whose second language is English, appeared in December.

1983 WMU adopted an enlistment goal of 2 million members by its Centennial, 1988.

WMU produced videotapes for purchase or rental.

The Baptist Nursing Fellowship was organized, with WMU providing a national office and staff.

WMU assisted the HMB in sponsoring Dayspring, an evangelism conference for women, at Ridgecrest. A western conference was held in 1984 at Fort Worth.

1984   WMU moved into new headquarters, a building designed and built by WMU at 100 Missionary Ridge south of Birmingham.

Fourth National Acteens Conference brought 14,005 to Fort Worth.

First home missions teleconference aired live from Birmingham to promote Week of Prayer for Home Missions. A similar teleconference promoted the week for foreign missions.

1985   WMU published missions-related products under the name New Hope. These products were designed for an audience wider than WMU membership and were not marketed exclusively through Baptist Book Stores.

ROSTER OF LEADERS
Prepared by Carolyn Smith

OFFICERS AND EXECUTIVE BOARD, WMU, SBC
(Executive Committee until 1954)

PRESIDENTS

1888-1892	Martha E. McIntosh (later Mrs. Theodore Percy Bell)
1892-1894	Fannie Exile Scudder Heck
1894-1895	Mrs. Abby Manly Gwathmey (William Henry)
1895-1899	Fannie Exile Scudder Heck
1899-1903	Mrs. Charles A. Stakely (Sarah Jessie Davis)
1903-1906	Mrs. John A. Barker (Lillie Easterby)
1906-1915	Fannie Exile Scudder Heck
1916-1925	Mrs. W. C. James (Minnie Kennedy)
1925-1933	Mrs. W. J. Cox (Ethlene Boone)
1933-1945	Mrs. F. W. Armstrong (Laura Dell Malotte)
1945-1956	Mrs. George R. Martin (Olive Brinson)
1956-1963	Mrs. R. L. Mathis (Marie Wiley)
1963-1969	Mrs. Robert Fling (Helen Long)
1969-1975	Mrs. R. L. Mathis (Marie Wiley)
1975-1981	Mrs. A. Harrison Gregory (Christine Burton)
1981-1986	Dr. Dorothy Elliott Sample (Richard H.)
1986-	Mrs. Glendon McCullough (Marjorie Jones)

EXECUTIVE DIRECTORS
(Corresponding Secretary was title until 1937; Executive Secretary 1937-1975; Executive Director after 1975.)

1888-1906	Annie Walker Armstrong
1907-1911	Edith Campbell Crane (later Mrs. Samuel T. Lanham)*
1912-1948	Kathleen Moore Mallory*
1948-1974	Alma Hunt*
1974-	Carolyn Weatherford*

ASSISTANT CORRESPONDING SECRETARIES

1906-1909	Elizabeth H. Poulson (Lizzie)
1911-1912	Nancy Lee Swann
1919-1952	Ethel Winfield

RECORDING SECRETARIES
(In 1902-1908 the constitution provided for two recording secretaries.)

1888-1892	Mrs. James Pollard (Susan Bancroft Tyler)
1892-1895	Mrs. Frank M. Ellis (Mary Anna Dow Briggs)
1895-1904	Ellen Webster Martien (Nellie)

NOTE:

Until the last decade the majority of married WMU officials were known in public life by their husbands' names. In some cases their birth names could not be discovered. In this roster, the officials are listed by the name they commonly used when in office. Other names (usually the maiden name but sometimes a marriage name) are shown in parenthesis, if they are known.

*Denotes Executive Committee/Board members who received salaries for most of their tenure; some others, for example, the other WMU representatives, received small payment plus travel expenses.

†Until 1930 the position did not carry Executive Board status.

1902-1906	Mary Emily Wright (later Mrs. J. Milnor Wilbur)
1904-1921	Mrs. A. C. Johnson (Cora Harlan)
1906-1908	Mrs. F. C. Wallis
1921-1938	Mrs. H. M. Wharton (Lulie K. ["Lucy"] Pollard)
1938-1957	Mrs. Wilfred C. Tyler (Frances Landrum)
1957-1963	Mrs. Robert Fling (Helen Long)
1963-1969	Mrs. J. R. Lobaugh (Elizabeth Casebolt)
1969-1975	Mrs. Roy E. Snider (Ruby Herrick)
1975-1981	Mrs. William Ellis (Carolyn Stratton)
1981-1986	Mrs. J. Frank Gilreath, Jr. (Betty Collins)
1986-	Mrs. Pattie Tate Dent, Sr. (Robert P., Sr.)

ASSISTANT RECORDING SECRETARIES

1908-1913	Mrs. F. C. Wallis
1913-1921	Mrs. H. M. Wharton (Lulie K. ["Lucy"] Pollard)
1921-1922	Mrs. Darby Brown (Mary Bestor Tartt)
1922-1941	Mrs. Sumter Lea, Jr. (Ethel Jones)
1941-1954	Mrs. J. Furniss Lee (Mary Edmundson)

TREASURERS

1888-1892	Mrs. John Pullen
1892-1894	Mrs. M.E. Oliver
1894-1895	Sarah Tyler
1895-1904	Mrs. W.C. Lowndes* (Elizabeth Chapman)
1904-1906	Ella V. Ricker
1906-1934	Mrs. W.C. Lowndes* (Elizabeth Chapman)
1934-1952	Mrs. W.J. Cox* (Ethlene Boone)
1952-1953	Mattie Morgan* (acting)
1953-1957	La Venia Neal*

VICE-PRESIDENTS

Elected presidents in states meeting requirements for representation on the Executive Board are recognized as vice-presidents. Since 1954 the Executive Board bylaws have required that a state WMU's president be its WMU, SBC, vice-president. However, states had been electing the same person to both positions for some years before that date. See state-by-state listing of vice-presidents, pages 443-52. State presidents who were not WMU, SBC, vice-presidents are listed on pages 458-59.

Alabama

1890-1897	Mrs. George B. Eager (Anna Banks Coor-Pender)
1897-1901	Mrs. Henry L. Mellen (Annie Grace Tartt)
1901-1911	Mrs. D. M. Malone (Hermione Brown)
1911-1912	Mrs. T. A. Hamilton (Amanda Tupper)
1912-1920	Mrs. Charles A. Stakely (Sarah Jessie Davis)
1920-1926	Mrs. William H. Samford (Kate Park)
1926-1931	Mrs. J. Carter Wright (Alma Worrill)
1931-1933	Mrs. R. T. Anderson (Mattie Haynes)
1933-1937	Mrs. H. T. McGehee (Ivah Belle Crawford)
1937-1940	Mrs. J. Furniss Lee (Mary Edmundson)
1940-l943	Mrs. Ida Rochester Ford Mitchell Stallworth (Fletcher B.)
1943-1947	Mrs. E. H. Hawkins (Erma Yoe)
1947-1952	Mrs. W. P. Reeves (Madeline Dix)
1952-1956	Mrs. Fred W. Kilgore (Clara Smith)
1956-1957	Mrs. Andrew M. Coltharp (Frances Jeffers)
1957-1963	Mrs. Albert J. Smith (Katherine Samford)
1963-1968	Mrs. Alex A. Hall (Nan Simpson)
1968-1973	Mrs. Joe W. Triplitt (Isabel Andrews)

1973-1978 Mrs. Lamar Jackson (Hermione Dannelly)
1978-1982 Mrs. James Lowry (Camilla Hamilton)
1982-1986 Mrs. Jerry W. Miller (Carolyn Downs)
1986-   Mrs. Thomas A. Leggett (Burma Reid)

Arizona
1929-1940 Mrs. W. C. Henderson (formerly Mrs. G. H. Woodson; Carrie Wilhoit)
1940-1943 Mrs. J. N. Campbell (Myrtle Copeland)
1943-1948 Mrs. Harold F. Hensley (Nancy Carolyn Bridgeford)
1948-1952 Mrs. John J. Casey (Genevieve Davis)
1952-1957 Mrs. Cecil M. Stewart (Lois G. Davis)
1957-1960 Mrs. Wiley Henton (Jo Vivian Marlow)
1960-1965 Mrs. H. E. Martin (Lena Tatum)
1965-1970 Mrs. R. Q. Kinney (Eula Murphy)
1970-1974 Mrs. Lloyd Fuller (Louise Burks)
1974-1978 Mrs. Cecil Secrest (Bertha Lackey)
1978-1982 Mrs. Harold McGhee (Beth Howell)
1982-1986 Mrs. Larry Gutshall (Carol Robinson)
1986-   Mrs. Jerry Day (Roena King)

Arkansas
1888-1889 Mrs. M. D. Early (Margretta Adelaide Dudgeon)
1889-1890 Mrs. W. A. Forbes (Sarah Holland)
1890-1899 Mrs. E. Longley (Fannie Thomas)
1899-1902 Mrs. James P. Eagle (Mary Kavanaugh Oldham)
1902-1908 Mrs. E. Longley (Fannie Thomas)
1908-1910 Mrs. W. T. Amis
1910-1912 Mrs. C. E. Witt (Genevieve Maynard)
1912-1913 Mrs. E. Longley (Fannie Thomas)
1913-1915 Mrs. J. G. Jackson (Dixie Farrior)
1915-1926 Mrs. John L. Hawkins (Lelia Files)
1926-1929 Mrs. W. D. Pye (Lila Westbrook)
1929-1932 Mrs. J. M. Flenniken (Addie Miears)
1932-1938 Mrs. C. H. Ray (Hattie Ann Neighbors)
1938-1941 Mrs. L. M. Sipes (Sallie Moore)
1941-1948 Mrs. J. E. Short (Esther Howle)
1948-1952 Mrs. F. E. Goodbar (Lottie Loewer)
1952-1957 Mrs. J. R. Grant (Grace Sowers)
1957-1964 Elma Cobb
1964-1969 Mrs. Roy E. Snider (Ruby Herrick)
1969-1974 Mrs. J. A. Hogan (Marie Kirkpatrick)
1974-1976 Mrs. George Tharel (Nathalie Sessums)
1976-1979 Mrs. James Sawyer (Mary Etheridge)
1979-1984 Mrs. Boyd Margason (Bonnie Lionberger)
1984-   Mrs. John McAlister (Katsy Cannefax)

California
1944-1946 Mrs. A. F. Whitehurst
1946-1947 Mrs. A. F. Crittendon
1947-1953 Mrs. Fred A. McCaulley (Ona Violet Harris)
1953-1955 Mrs. J. L. Brantley (Margaret Grogard)
1955-1959 Mrs. Everett E. Hill (later Mrs. Richard Mueller; Marguerite Lewis)
1959-1961 Mrs. Gordon C. Goodier, Sr. (Mayble Cole)
1961-1962 Mrs. Clyde B. Skidmore (Marjorie Skeen)
1962-1966 Mrs. Thomas L. Kilpatrick (Dorothy Leek)
1966-1968 Mrs. Harry King (Ruth Hammond)
1968-1972 Mrs. Clyde B. Skidmore (Marjorie Skeen)
1972-1976 Mrs. Paul S. Parker (Mildred Holland)
1976-1979 Mrs. J. M. Bailey (Reba Haydon)
1979-1981 Mrs. Augustine Salazar (Grace Peña)
1981-1985 Mrs. Robert Staver (Brenda Huffman)
1985-   Mrs. Burney Tate (June Hauser)

Colorado
1957-1959 Mrs. John J. Hamilton (Virjama Rose)
1959-1964 Mrs. E. E. Wheeless, Jr. (Alleen Witten)
1964-1965 Mrs. Nell Baggett Matthews (later Mrs. Kenneth Hoffman)
1965-1966 Mrs. E. E. Wheeless, Jr. (Alleen Witten)
1966-1969 Mrs. James R. Fish (Mary Ellen Totten)
1969-1973 Mrs. George E. Ray, Sr. (Tera Bitters)
1973-1978 Mrs. Charles Farr (June Kendrick)
1978-1983 Mrs. Charles Clayton (Margaret Day)
1983-   Mrs. Jimmie D. Burton (Mary Allen)

District of Columbia
1896-1899 Mrs. Charles A. Stakely (Sarah Jessie Davis)
1899-1901 Mrs. E. P. Pollard
1901-1904 Evy M. Dickinson
1904-1907 Mrs. C. F. Winbigler
1907-1909 Mrs. J. H. Wilson Marriott (Lulie Williams)
1909-1911 Mrs. George E. Truett
1911-1913 Mrs. Annie E. Grigsby
1913-1916 Mrs. Cline N. Chipman
1916-1922 Mrs. W. E. Mooney
1922-1925 Mrs. E. Hilton Jackson
1925-1927 Mrs. H. M. Watkins
1927-1933 Mrs. O. E. Howe
1933-1937 Mrs. Joseph N. Gary
1937-1940 Mrs. George A. Ross
1940-1944 Mrs. James G. Yaden
1944-1949 Mrs. Carleton M. Long (Dorothy Fisher)
1949-1954 Mrs. Will E. Ivie, Sr. (Nell Nall)
1954-1959 Mrs. Lawrence S. Casazza (Letha Robinson)
1959-1960 Mrs. Daniel doCarmo (Helen Gibson)
1960-1965 Mrs. Thornton Slough (Hilda Lipscomb)
1965-1968 Mrs. Carleton M. Long (Dorothy Fisher)
1968-1970 Mrs. Eugene Botz (Irene Keirns)
1970-1972 Mrs. Richard J. Sweetman, Sr. (Victoria Trillet)
1972-1973 Mrs. James Blalock (Polly Butler)
1973-1974 Mrs. John Templin (Helen Clark)
1974-1978 Mrs. James Blalock (Polly Butler)
1978-1983 Mrs. Clayton Teague (Ellen Sims)
1983-   Mrs. Aldon Nielsen (Vivian Lee)

Florida
1888-1889 Mrs. W. D. Chipley (Elizabeth ["Bettie"] Billups)
1889-1893 Mrs. L. B. Telford
1893-1910 Mrs. W. D. Chipley (Elizabeth ["Bettie"] Billups)
1911-1913 Mrs. C.A. Carson
1913-1916 Mrs. J.A. Mellon
1916-1926 Mrs. S.B. Rogers
1926-1927 Mrs. Brinson McGowan
1927-1930 Mrs. E.C. Bostick
1930-1936 Mrs. G.J. Rousseau (Christine McConnell)
1936-1941 Mrs. Robert Walden (Alta E. Eifler)
1941-1943 Mrs. Robert E. Lee (Theo Thomas)
1943-1948 Mrs. J.L. Rosser (Evelyn Craig)
1948-1954 Mrs. Roy L. Lassiter (Lelia Boring)
1954-1959 Mrs. George Q. Holland (Mary Belle Russell)
1959-1964 Mrs. J.H. Lockhart (Margaret Eckland)
1964-1969 Mrs. Clyde B. Lipscomb (Rosella Herman)
1969-1974 Mrs. August A. Lenert, Jr. (Cleota Bullock)
1974-1979 Mrs. A. D. Dawson (Tanna Temoshchuk)
1979-1984 Mrs. W. Mount Ely (Oma Dell Franklin)
1984-   Mrs. Don L. Wennerberg (Martha Leathers)

Georgia

1888-1889	Mrs. J. Stainback Wilson (Martha Eleanor Loftin)
1889-1890	Mrs. Harvey Hatcher
1890-1891	Mrs. R. M. Seymour
1891-1903	Mary Emily Wright (later Mrs. J. Milnor Wilbur)
1903-1906	Mrs. J. D. Easterlin
1906-1911	Mrs. E. G. Willingham (Mary Peoples)
1911-1932	Mrs. W. J. Neel (Isa-Beall Williams)
1932-1937	Mrs. Ben S. Thompson (Annie Lucy Newton)
1937-1942	Mrs. Frank Burney (Sarah Joe Hurst)
1942-1947	Mrs. Peter Kittles (Grace Evans)
1947-1952	Mrs. Paul S. Etheridge (Estelle Fitzgerald)
1952-1957	Mrs. John I. Alford (Omer Shermer)
1957-1961	Mrs. C. O. Smith (Esther Cutts)
1961-1966	Mrs. Ernest L. Miller (Agnes Jenkins)
1966-1970	Mrs. J. J. Clyatt (Josie Golden)
1970-1975	Mrs. I. W. Bowen III (Nell Tyner)
1975-1980	Mrs. Lindsey Barron (Genet Heery)
1980-1985	Mrs. Edwin Howard (Rachel Stringer)
1985-	Mrs. J. Lamar Branch (Edna Bedingfield)

Illinois

1911-1921	Mrs. W. P. Throgmorton (Catherine Baker)
1921-1927	Mrs. L. C. Biggs
1927-1928	Mrs. John Hathaway (Maude Wall)
1928-1930	Mrs. Frank B. Keen (Ethel Rea)
1930-1933	Mrs. L. F. Maynard (Addine Gregory)
1933-1936	Mrs. Harry Wilson (Elsie Smith)
1936-1939	Mrs. I. E. Lee (Beatrice Flannigan)
1939-1943	Mrs. H. R. Moore (Virginia Hull)
1943-1948	Mrs. J. F. Gill (Betty Ferguson)
1948-1950	Mrs. O. J. Carlock (Nell Hunsaker)
1950-1953	Mrs. R. W. Wallis (Prudence Douthit)
1953-1956	Mrs. Curtis Martin (Vivian Nattier)
1956-1960	Mrs. Paul Hays (Essie Gifford)
1960-1965	Mrs. Theron H. King (Frances Huntley)
1965-1970	Mrs. James M. Laughlin (Grace Gray)
1970-1973	Mrs. Frank Claybourne (Ruth Kell)
1973-1976	Mrs. Craig Ridings (Mary Helm)
1976-1980	Mrs. L. D. Patrick (Mickey Williams)
1980-1983	Mrs. W. T. Branon (Ann LaGrand)
1983-1987	Mrs. L. D. Patrick (Mickey Williams)

Indiana

1959-1960	Mrs. T. B. Rollins (Ruth Wyrick)
1961-1964	Mrs. Clarence Brock (Alena Bill)
1964-1967	Mrs. E. W. Springs (Frances Stovall)
1967-1969	Mrs. William R. Greene (Margaret Geary)
1969-1972	Mrs. R. P. Griffin (Sadie Bigham)
1972-1976	Mrs. Roscoe Kissel (Doris Swain)
1976-1980	Mrs. Donnie Cox (Cleo Youngblood)
1980-1983	Mrs. John Tarry (Sharon Pritchard)
1983-1986	Mrs. R. P. Griffin (Sadie Bigham)
1986-	Mrs. Larry Hazlewood (Nancy Powers)

Kansas-Nebraska

1949-1952	Mrs. J. D. Williamson (Nellie Gentz)
1952	Mrs. Mervin McGill
1952-1955	Mrs. Lloyd Burdette (Mary Ingram Morgan)
1955-1957	Mrs. R. L. Braden (Gladys White)
1957-1962	Mrs. J. R. Lobaugh (Elizabeth Casebolt)

1962-1967 Mrs. Don Kordis (Ethmer Gray)
1967-1968 Mrs. Byron Tracy (Alma Decker)
1968-1971 Mrs. Max Briggs (Norma Morgan)
1971-1976 Mrs. Carson Bates (Opal Jones)
1976-1979 Mrs. Tom Barber (Maxine Glenn)
1979-1983 Mrs. George Foster (Renoma Salmons)
1983-1987 Mrs. Martin Nolan (Jeanie Grise)

Kentucky
1888-1920 Eliza Sommerville Broadus
1920-1922 Mrs. Janie Cree Bose (later Mrs. J. H. Anderson)
1922-1928 Mrs. A. T. Robertson (Ella Thomas Broadus)
1928-1936 Mrs. Robert Pryor
1936-1937 Mrs. Eureka Whiteker (Prudence Sayers)
1937-1940 Mrs. M. H. Highland (Mary Ely)
1940-1943 Mrs. Charles Ison (Eleanor ["Ella"] McFatridge)
1943-1947 Mrs. W. H. Moody (Mellie Harp)
1947-1949 Mrs. George R. Ferguson (Odessa Lyons)
1949-1951 Mrs. Harold J. Purdy (Virginia Burdette)
1951-1955 Mrs. Encil Deen (Utha ["Sally"] Blackburn)
1955-1959 Mrs. H. C. Randall (Estelle Pittenger)
1959-1961 Mrs. Carl W. Liebert (Thelma Maloy)
1961-1965 Mrs. J. S. Woodward (Julia Powell)
1965-1968 Mrs. W. C. White II (Martha Waldington)
1968-1971 Mrs. J. S. Woodward (Julia Powell)
1971-1975 Mrs. William Ellis (Carolyn Stratton)
1975-1978 Mrs. Wayne Dehoney (Lealice Bishop)
1978-1981 Mrs. Horace T. Hambrick (Maribeth Porter)
1981-1985 Mrs. Ray Mullendore (Doris Jones)
1985- Mrs. Bryant Hicks (Peggy Greene)

Louisiana
1888-1891 Minerva Alfred (Minnie)
1891-1892 Mrs. M. C. Cole
1892-1894 Mrs. W. S. Penick
1894-1895 Mrs. C. C. McCloud
1896-1899 Mrs. G. S. Dodds
1899-1908 Mrs. Charles Ammen (Jane M.)
1908-1911 Mrs. F. M. Hollingsworth
1911-1914 Mrs. T. R. Falvy
1914-1915 Mrs. Charles Ammen (Jane M.)
1915-1916 Mrs. W. F. Weishaupt
1916-1919 Mrs. T. R. Falvy
1919-1923 Mary Georgia Barnette
1923-1930 Mrs. T. E. Stephenson
1930-1936 Mrs. H. M. Bennett
1936-1941 Mrs. Mary Lou Jenkins (Charles Edward)
1941-1947 Mrs. R. A. Everett (Maude)
1947-1953 Mrs. T. V. Herndon (Martha)
1953-1960 Mrs. F. D. Mabry (Charlotte Jones)
1960-1963 Mrs. Claude Kirkpatrick (Edith Kilgore)
1963-1965 Mrs. F. D. Mabry (Charlotte Jones)
1965-1967 Mrs. Stanley R. Barnett (Dorothy Freshwater)
1967-1973 Mrs. Carl Conrad (Frances Daigle)
1973-1978 Mrs. James O. McNair (Lucille Keith)
1978-1980 Mrs. Carl Conrad (Frances Daigle)
1980-1985 Mrs. A. D. Foreman III (Joyce Litton)
1985-1986 Mrs. Nelda Crotwell Seal (Lavelle)
1986-1987 Mrs. Woodrow Young (Marguerite Beeson) (interim)

Maryland-Delaware
1888-1892 Mrs. A. J. Rowland
1892-1898 Mrs. W. Judson Brown
1898-1902 Mrs. William B. Graves
1902-1905 Mrs. John Howard Eager (Olive May Board)
1905-1906 Mrs. James E. Tyler
1906-1910 Mrs. John Howard Eager (Olive May Board)
1910-1919 Mrs. E. B. Mathews
1919-1940 Mrs. Eugene Levering (Harriett Ellis)
1940-1943 Mrs. Wayland A. Harrison
1943-1945 Mrs. Wade H. Bryant (Lillian Martin)
1945-1949 Mrs. Arthur E. Whedbee (Catherine B.)
1949-1955 Mrs. Harry P. Clause (Mayme Slaughter)
1955-1957 Mrs. J. Winston Pearce (Winnie Rickett)
1957-1958 Mrs. E. E. Garland (Ruth Grey)
1958-1961 Mrs. Willis C. Hall (Virginia Conaway)
1961-1966 Mrs. W. P. Watson (Mildred Hodges)
1966-1968 Mrs. Samuel H. Jackson (Dorothy Churn)
1968-1973 Mrs. William L. Andrews (Frances Carter)
1973-1977 Mrs. Edward J. Templeton (Dorothy Allen)
1977-1980 Mrs. Elwood L. Ulmer (Emily Popp)
1980-1982 Mrs. William L. Andrews (Frances Carter)
1982-1986 Mrs. Walter Agnor (Bettye Willingham)
1986-   Mrs. Russell Morris (Brenda White)

Michigan
1960-1963 Mrs. James R. Culley (later Mrs. John M. Jones; Josephine Smith)
1963-1965 Mrs. Milton Hicks (Eula Patterson)
1965-1967 Mrs. Harry Harp (Harriette McDurmon)
1967-1969 Mrs. Emmitt Cross (Violet Roach)
1969-1970 Mrs. Jay Brown (Cecile Helen Grammar)
1970-1971 Mrs. Emmitt Cross (Violet Roach)
1971-1973 Mrs. Robert Hamilton (Hilda Pollard)
1973-1974 Mrs. Edward N. Sickafus (Mary Sue Gist)
1974-1978 Mrs. Charles Wilkinson (Amy Ratterree)
1978-1981 Dr. Dorothy Elliott Sample (Richard H.)
1981-1986 Mrs. Warren Harris (Ruth Cobble)
1986-   Mrs. Bill Bradford (Dolly Lawrence)

Mississippi
1889-1895 Mrs. Adelia Thompson Hillman (Walter)
1895-1899 Mrs. A. J. Aven (Mary Bailey)
1899-1901 Mrs. J. W. Bozeman (Julia Evans)
1901-1905 Mrs. J. A. Hackett (Emma Gardner)
1905-1908 Mrs. William Andrew McComb (May Willis)
1908-1910 Mrs. J. G. Hasselle
1910-1912 Mrs. William R. Woods (Annie Kate Whitfield)
1912-1915 Mrs. William Andrew McComb (May Willis)
1915-1920 Margaret McRae Lackey
1920-1934 Mrs. A. J. Aven (Mary Bailey)
1934-1943 Mrs. Ned Rice (Vira Neely)
1943-1944 Mrs. J. H. Street (later Mrs. Clifton J. Allen; Rosalind Shepherd)
1944-1946 Mrs. Webb Brame (Grace Stroud)
1946-1951 Mrs. Horace Sledge (later Mrs. J. S. Maxey; Wilma Bobo)
1951-1957 Almarine Brown
1957-1963 Mrs. J. T. Lyons (Jimmie Lou Turner)
1963-1969 Mrs. W. E. Hannah (Elizabeth King)
1969-1974 Mrs. Vernon May (Mae Lee Jenkins)
1974-1979 Mrs. Robert V. Smira (Frances Turner)
1979-1984 Mrs. Pattie Tate Dent (Robert P., Sr.)
1984-   Mrs. James Fancher (Ewilda Trenor)

Missouri
1888-1889   Mrs. S. Y. Pitts
1889-1896   Mrs. W. F. Elliott
1896-1915   Mrs. J. L. Burnham (Elize Martin)
1915-1916   Mrs. S. E. Ewing
1916-1918   Mrs. H. O. Severance
1918-1921   Mrs. R. T. Stickney
1921-1922   Mrs. C. E. Graham
1922-1923   Mrs. E. C. Henderson
1923-1934   Mrs. F. W. Armstrong (Laura Dell Malotte)
1934-1941   Mrs. George A. McWilliams (Cora Cowgill)
1941-1946   Mrs. T. W. McKee (Louise Enloe)
1946   Mrs. T. Shad Medlin (Josephine Riley)
1946-1952   Mrs. Fred B. Kinell
1952-1956   Mrs. O. R. Burnham (Lena Pearl Shaner)
1956-1960   Mrs. R. L. Crozier (Elizabeth Tillery)
1960-1964   Mrs. Bradley Allison (Eunice Powell)
1964-1969   Mrs. Homer E. DeLozier (Ferroll Woodford)
1969-1974   Mrs. Hughes Scherff (Viola Volkart)
1974-1976   Mrs. Fred Coble (Marilyn Harris)
1976-1981   Mrs. Donald Murphy (Lorene Hamblen)
1981-1986   Mrs. Tom Bray (Barbara Birt)
1986-   Mrs. Hubert Altis (Norma Hays)

New Mexico
1911-1912   Mrs. J. C. Kuyrkendall
1912-1914   Mrs. J. M. Milhuff
1914-1918   Mrs. E. B. Atwood
1918-1919   Mrs. R. H. Carter
1919-1924   Mrs. M. D. Schumaker
1924-1925   Mrs. W. C. Thomas
1925-1929   Mrs. T. W. Bruce
1929-1930   Mrs. E. W. Provence (Mary Eugenia King)
1930-1933   Mrs. O. E. Carman (Sally)
1933-1937   Mrs. R. I. Creed
1937-1944   Mrs. O. E. Carman (Sally)
1944-1947   Mrs. D. C. Setser (Mabel Short)
1947-1951   Mrs. R. L. Brunson (Margaret Browning Robinson)
1951-1953   Mrs. T. H. Rixey (Adrianne Hammond)
1953-1957   Mrs. F. A. Green (Ina Belle)
1957-1958   Mrs. Earl Hartley (Vora Lowe)
1958-1963   Mrs. M. K. Hall (Irene Stewart)
1963-1966   Mrs. J. S. Newman (Opal Cothran)
1966-1971   Mrs. Oliver D. Lambirth (Helen Lee Shepard)
1971-1974   Mrs. Earl Hartley (Vora Lowe)
1974-1978   Mrs. Clarence V. Thompson (Lynette Day)
1978-1982   Mrs. Oliver D. Lambirth (Helen Lee Shepard)
1982-1984   Mrs. E. G. Lambright (Pat Grissom)
1984-   Mrs. Dalton Edwards (Judith Perry)

North Carolina
1891-1892   Fannie Exile Scudder Heck
1892-1894   Mrs. J. A. Briggs
1894-1895   Fannie Exile Scudder Heck
1895-1899   Mrs. J. A. Briggs
1899-1906   Fannie Exile Scudder Heck
1906-1908   Susan Clark
1908-1913   Mrs. Wesley N. Jones (Sallie Bailey)
1913-1916   Blanche Barrus
1916-1938   Mrs. Wesley N. Jones (Sallie Bailey)
1938-1942   Mrs. J. Clyde Turner (Bertha Hicks)

1942-1945 Mrs. James S. Farmer (Foy Johnson)
1945-1946 Mrs. J. Clyde Turner (Bertha Hicks)
1946-1951 Mrs. James S. Farmer (Foy Johnson)
1951-1956 Mrs. Gordon Maddrey (Mabel Clair Hoggard)
1956-1961 Mrs. W. K. McGee (Velma Presslar)
1961-1966 Mrs. A. L. Parker (Sara Kanoy)
1966-1971 Mrs. R. Knolan Benfield (Emma Hartsell)
1971-1976 Mrs. Gilmer Cross (Bernice Apple)
1976-1981 Mrs. J. Frank Gilreath, Jr. (Betty Collins)
1981-1986 Mrs. Horace McRae (Beatrice McNeill)
1986-   Mrs. Hoyle Allred (Dorothy Purvis)

Northwest (Oregon-Washington)
1950-1963 Mrs. Sylvia Abeenes Wilson (William Henry)
1963-1967 Mrs. Felix B. Green (Dorris Bailey)
1967-1971 Mrs. Gilbert O. Skaar (Greta Lofman)
1971-1975 Mrs. Don Buckley (Billie Draper)
1975-1979 Mrs. William D. Walker (Lu DeBord)
1979-1982 Mrs. David C. Bandy (Nova Land)
1982-1986 Mrs. Gordon D. Green (Charlotte Couch)
1986-   Mrs. Adrian W. Hall (Nancy Unruh)

Ohio
1954-1957 Mrs. Gerald K. Ford (Virginia Cross)
1957-1960 Mrs. Henry Johnson (Frances Lucille Trew)
1960-1961 Mrs. E. O. Edwards (Lois Morgan)
1961   Mrs. Herbert Paper
1961-1964 Mrs. T. A. Benefield (LaVera Shankles)
1964-1965 Mrs. J. H. Simpson, Jr. (Vivian)
1965-1970 Mrs. C. E. Price (Mary Bishop)
1970-1974 Mrs. Howard R. Carpenter (Helen Stalion)
1974-1978 Mrs. Sidney B. Deskins (Ruby Rudd)
1978-1982 Mrs. Rodney Thorpe (Dorothy Hall)
1982-1986 Mrs. James Wolford (Akiko Naito)
1986-   Mrs. Ralph Turnbull (Betty Rhoads)

Oklahoma
1903-1904 Mrs. W. H. Kuykendall
1904-1905 Mrs. W. M. Anderson
1905-1906 Mary Prosser Jayne
1906   Mrs. Lindsay C. Wolfe (Cynthia Ellen Shumate)
1906-1908 Mrs. Thomas C. Carleton (Mary Heard)
1908-1910 Mrs. W. E. Dicken (Bertha Mildred Smith)
1910-1916 Mrs. W. A. McBride (Clara Amelia Murrow)
1916-1917 Mrs. W. E. Dicken (Bertha Mildred Smith)
1917-1920 Mrs. H. R. Denton (Emily Beadle)
1920-1927 Mrs. R. T. Mansfield (Elsie)
1927-1938 Mrs. George McMillan (Edna Susan Brown)
1938-1946 Mrs. H. B. Wilhoyte (Minna Gray)
1946-1949 Mrs. Morris S. Whitehead (Peggy Warren)
1949-1952 Mrs. Dan M. Reed (later Mrs. Charles Williams; Helen Carlin)
1952-1956 Mrs. C. A. Summers (Fern Hardy)
1956-1960 Mrs. Earl Stark (Veretta Bell)
1960-1964 Mrs. Laurence Mantooth (Margaret Beam)
1964-1968 Mrs. Sam Arnold (Willie Belle ["Billie"] Richmond)
1968-1973 Mrs. Robert Bazzell (Trula Frances Curb)
1973-1977 Mrs. Virgil Landers (Elva Lohner)
1977-1981 Mrs. Glen McClain (Mary Digmon)
1981-1985 Mrs. J. T. Robison (Jarene Caffey)
1985-   Mrs. H. D. Stephens (Susanne Edwards)

South Carolina
1888-1889   Mrs. Mattie A. Huiet (W. J.) (Huiet was incorrectly spelled Hewitt in WMU,
            SBC, minutes.)
1889-1891   Mrs. John Stout (Fanny Lide Coker)
1891-1892   Mary Lide Coker
1892-1895   Martha E. McIntosh (later Mrs. Theodore Percy Bell)
1895-1905   Mary Lide Coker
1905-1908   Mrs. J. D. Chapman (Janie Weston)
1908-1912   Mrs. A. L. Crutchfield (Elma Gwaltney)
1912-1913   Mrs. J. R. Fizer (maiden name Rossiter)
1913-1930   Mrs. J. D. Chapman (Janie Weston)
1930-1939   Mrs. J. B. Boatwright (Inez Acree)
1939-1950   Mrs. Charles M. Griffin (later Mrs. James S. Cobb; Gladys Morris)
1950-1955   Mrs. D. C. Bomar (Mildred Cone)
1955-1957   Mrs. James F. Burriss (Belle Gibson)
1957-1963   Mrs. Russell C. Ashmore (Nell Blakely)
1963-1968   Mrs. E. R. Eller (Frances Greer)
1968-1971   Mrs. Edward L. Byrd (Nora Brown)
1971-1976   Mrs. A. T. Greene, Jr. (Kathryn Abee)
1976-1981   Mrs. D. C. Bomar (Mildred Cone)
1981-1984   Mrs. C. O. Smith (Sarah Stephens)
1984-   Mrs. Milton Raffini (Irene Wheatley)

Tennessee
1888-1889   Mrs. Anson Nelson
1889-1890   Evie Brown
1890-1893   Mrs. Anson Nelson
1893-1894   Sarah E. S. Shankland ("Miss Lily")
1894-1896   Mrs. A. C. S. Jackson
1896-1898   Mrs. S. E. Nelson
1898-1902   Mrs. A. C. S. Jackson
1902-1915   Mrs. A. J. Wheeler (Mary Belle)
1915-1918   Mrs. Avery Carter
1918-1924   Mrs. Hight C. Moore (Laura Miller Peterson)
1924-1925   Mrs. W. J. Cox (Ethlene Boone)
1925-1939   Mrs. R. L. Harris (Emma Byrns)
1939-1947   Mrs. C. D. Creasman (Myrtle Robinson)
1947-1951   Mrs. Sam Holloway (Susan Anthony)
1951-1957   Mrs. M. K. Cobble (Lois Fuhrman)
1957-1961   Mrs. Roy W. Babb (Marguerite Skinner)
1961-1967   Mrs. Bradford Duncan (Amanda Hall)
1967-1971   Mrs. D. Isbell (Elizabeth McWhorter)
1971-1975   Mrs. Bob Peek (Willodene Gentry)
1975-1979   Mrs. Claude Jennings (Jewel Bennett)
1979-1980   Mrs. Robert Gay (Claudia Wilbourn)
1980-1982   Mrs. Glendon McCullough (Marjorie Jones)
1982-   Mrs. Jerry Trivette (Judy Needham)

Texas
1888-1889   Mrs. A. C. Ardrey
1889-1896   Mrs. Fannie Breedlove Davis (George Bowen)
1896-1900   Mrs. M. V. Smith (Cornelia)
1900-1904   Mrs. C. C. Slaughter
1904-1906   Mrs. George W. Truett (Josephine Jenkins)
1906-1931   Mrs. F. S. Davis (Mary Hill)
1931-1946   Mrs. B. A. Copass (Crickett Keys)
1946-1949   Mrs. Earl B. Smyth (Rosalind Kyser)
1949-1955   Mrs. R. L. Mathis (Marie Wiley)
1955-1961   Mrs. Clem Hardy (Ethel Cooper)
1961-1963   Mrs. Bert Black (Leila Withers)
1963-1964   (District Presidents)

1964-1968   Mrs. C. J. Humphrey (Ophelia Hatton)
1968-1972   Mrs. H. C. Hunt (Inez Boyle)
1972-1976   Mrs. Earl W. Johnston (Mauriece Vance)
1976-1980   Mrs. C. W. Coy (later Mrs. Elvis Egge; Huis Middleton)
1980-1984   Mrs. Earl W. Johnston (Mauriece Vance)
1984-   Mrs. J. Ivyloy Bishop (Amelia Morton)

Virginia
1889-1892   Mrs. William E. Hatcher (Virginia ["Jennie"] Snead)
1892-1894   Mary Caldwell Tupper ("Mamie")
1894-1895   Juliet Pollard (later Mrs. J. W. Wills)
1895-1903   Mrs. Abby Manly Gwathmey (William Henry)
1903-1906   Mrs. W. S. Leake (Harriet Alverda French)
1906-1920   Mrs. Julian P. Thomas (Mary Antoinette Pleasants)
1920-1921   Mrs. John F. Vines (Valeria Lawrence)
1921-1922   Mrs. George W. McDaniel (Martha Douglas Scarborough)
1922-1923   Mrs. Herbert B. Cross (Ruth Edna Graham)
1923-1925   Mrs. C. W. McElroy
1925-1931   Mrs. George R. Martin (Olive Brinson)
1931-1934   Mrs. A. S. Downes (Elizabeth Bloxom)
1934-1946   Mrs. George R. Martin (Olive Brinson)
1946-1956   Mrs. Lester L. Knight (Carol Roper)
1956-1964   Mrs. O. C. Hancock (Ada Hatcher)
1964-1971   Mrs. E. S. Stratton (Emma Mantiply)
1971-1975   Mrs. A. Harrison Gregory (Christine Burton)
1975-1978   Mrs. W. Peyton Thurmon (Mary Jane Cubbage)
1979-1983   Mrs. George B. Clarke (Jane Matthews)
1983-   Mrs. Robert F. Woodward (Jean Nelson)

West Virginia
1986-   Mrs. Russel Talley (Lynn Baker)

Western Arkansas, Indian Territory, Oklahoma
1891-1893   Mrs. May Moss (W. Ark.-Ind. Ter.)
1893-1896   Jennie S. Compere (W. Ark.-Ind. Ter.)
1896-1897   Mrs. A. G. Washburn (W. Ark.)
1896-1897   Mrs. S. A. Ewing (Ind. Ter.)
1897-1898   Mrs. L. W. Wright (W. Ark.-Ind. Ter.)
1898-1899   Mrs. W. H. Kuykendall (W. Ark.-Ind. Ter.)
1899-1902   Mrs. W. H. Kuykendall (Ind. Ter.-Okla.)
1902-1903   Mrs. M. Choate (Ind. Ter.)
1903-1904   Mrs. J. H. Scott (Ind. Ter.)
1904-1907   Mrs. Thomas C. Carleton (Mary Heard) (Ind. Ter.)

Western North Carolina
1894-1895   Lottie Price
1895-1897   Mrs. J. H. Tucker
1897-1898   Mrs. P. M. Hudgins

YOUTH SECRETARIES

(This position did not carry Executive Committee status until 1918.)
1910-1911   Mary K. Applewhite (later Mrs. J. Killian Yates), College Correspondent
1911-1917   Susan Bancroft Tyler (later Mrs. Curtis Lee Laws), College Correspondent
1916-1917   Mary Faison Dixon,* Young People's Secretary
1917-1918   Mary Faison Dixon,* Young People's Secretary and College Correspondent
1921-1927   Juliette Mather,* Young People's Secretary and College Correspondent
1927-1948   Juliette Mather,* Young People's Secretary
1929-1937   Pearle Bourne,* Associate Young People's Secretary
1939-1941   Elma Currin* (later Mrs. Walter Lee Robertson), Associate Young People's
            Secretary
1948-1957   Margaret Bruce,* Young People's Secretary

EDITORIAL/PUBLICATIONS SECRETARY

1948-1957 Juliette Mather*

MISSIONARY FUNDAMENTALS SECRETARY

1954-1957 Mrs. William McMurry* (Mildred Dodson)

WMU REPRESENTATIVES/FIELD WORKERS†
1922-1924 Blanche Sydnor White*
1926-1929 Mrs. Taul B. White
1926-1940 Mrs. R. K. Redwine (Beatrice Barnard)
1930-1939 Mrs. Taul B. White
1930-1941 Mrs. J. Carter Wright (Alma Worrill)
1939-1948 Mary Christian*
1941-1944 Mary Nelle Lyne*

MARGARET HOME/FUND CHAIRMEN†

1904-1906 Annie Walker Armstrong
1906-1907 Mrs. A. J. Orme
1907-1908 Mrs. T. W. Hannon (Emilie Littlepage)
1908-1914 Mrs. Julian P. Thomas (Mary Antoinette Pleasants)
1914-1915 Mrs. J. W. Vesey
1915-1922 Mrs. J. R. Fizer (maiden name Rossiter)
1922-1938 Mrs. Frank Burney (Sarah Joe Hurst)
1938-1941 Mrs. Herman M. Rhodes (Mary Baxter)

COMMUNITY MISSIONS CHAIRMEN†

(Title was Personal Service Chairman until 1942.)
1910-1924 Mrs. H. M. Wharton (Lulie K. ["Lucy"] Pollard)
1924-1929 Mrs. Peyton A. Eubank (Annie Barksdale)
1929-1932 Mrs. Una Roberts Lawrence (Irvin)
1932-1937 Mrs. P. B. Lowrance (Frances Acree)
1937-1941 Mrs. Eureka Whiteker (Prudence Sayers)
1941-1945 Mary Christian*
1945-1947 Mrs. Edgar Godbold (Lucie T. Yates)

STEWARDSHIP CHAIRMEN†

1929-1933 Mrs. George R. Martin (Olive Brinson)
1933-1944 Mrs. J. Carter Wright (Alma Worrill)
1944-1947 Mrs. Clyde V. Hickerson (Amy Compere)

MISSION STUDY CHAIRMEN†

1930-1947 Mrs. Una Roberts Lawrence (Irvin)

**PRINCIPAL/PRESIDENT, WOMAN'S MISSIONARY UNION TRAINING SCHOOL/
CARVER SCHOOL OF MISSIONS AND SOCIAL WORK†**

1907-1923 Mrs. Maud Reynolds McLure*
1925-1930 Mrs. Janie Cree Bose* (later Mrs. J. H. Anderson)
1931-1951 Carrie Uarda Littlejohn*
1951-1958 Emily Kilpatrick Lansdell* (later Mrs. J. B. Weatherspoon)
1958-1963 Nathan C. Brooks, Jr.
(President of Carver School ceased to carry Executive Board status in 1957, the year
WMU transferred the school to SBC.)

CHAIRMEN OF WMUTS/CSMSW LOCAL BOARD OF MANAGERS

1907-1908 Mrs. S. E. Woody (Emma McIver)
1908-1926 Mrs. George B. Eager (Anna Banks Coor-Pender)
1926-1931 Mrs. S. E. Woody (Emma McIver)
1931-1937 Mrs. Trevor H. Whayne

LOCAL EXECUTIVE COMMITTEE, BALTIMORE 1888-1921

1888 Mrs. James E. Tyler
1888 Mrs. J. J. G. Riley
1888-1889 Mrs. J. H. Brittain
1888-1889 Lily Graves
1888-1892 Mrs. F. M. Ellis (Mary Anna Dow Briggs)
1888-1892 Adelaide Wilson
1888-1892 Mrs. W. Judson Brown
1888-1903 Mrs. Oliver F. Gregory
1888-1906 Alice Armstrong
1889-1890 Mrs. A. Fuller Crane (Mary Clement Levering)
1889-1890 Mrs. A. C. Wroe
1889-1892 Mrs. Fannie Roper Feudge (formerly Mrs. Robert Davenport)
1890-1891 Mrs. William Harris
1890-1921 Mrs. William R. Nimmo (Elia Brower)
1891-1893 Mrs. James E. Tyler
1891-1899 Mrs. Chester R. Turnbull
1892-1893 Mrs. J. A. Smith
1892-1894 Mrs. N. R. Barnes
1892-1896 Mrs. James V. Pollard (Susan Bancroft Tyler)
1892-1896 Mrs. Edgar Y. Mullins (Isla May Hawley)
1893-1894 Nora Land
1893-1894 Belle Lowndes
1894-1896 Mrs. J. M. Keeler
1894-1896 Mrs. E. R. Singleton
1894-1903 Mrs. J. H. Wilson Marriott (Lulie Williams)
1896-1898 Elizabeth H. Poulson ("Lizzie")
1896-1900 Mrs. W. J. E. Cox
1896-1901 Mrs. Howard Wayne Smith
1897-1899 Mrs. William B. Graves
1898-1900 Mrs. E. E. Ayres
1898-1902 Mrs. J. Milnor Wilbur
1899-1900 Minnie Levering
1900-1901 Mrs. Philip S. Evans (Mary Levering)
1900-1902 Mrs. John Howard Eager (Olive May Board)
1900-1905 Mrs. James E. Tyler
1901-1902 Mrs. Joshua Levering
1901-1903 Mrs. T. P. Holloway
1902-1903 Mrs. Francis Biggs (Lenora Land)
1902-1904 Mrs. William B. Graves
1902-1905 Mrs. J. W. Millard
1903-1906 Mrs. Curtis Lee Laws
1903-1904 Mrs. H. A. Griesemer
1903-1904 Mrs. Thomas Cross
1903-1905 Mrs. A. C. Johnson (Cora Harlan)
1904-1906 Mrs. W. C. Lowndes (Elizabeth Chapman)
1904-1906 Mrs. H. Grady
1904-1921 Clara M. Woolford
1905-1906 Mrs. M. Brown
1905-1906 Mrs. R. B. Kelley
1905-1921 Mrs. A. J. Clark
1906-1908 Mrs. George H. Eyster
1906-1910 Mrs. Howard B. Weishampel
1906-1920 Mrs. Charles Z. Butler

1906-1921   Mrs. James W. Kirkman (maiden name Ness)
1906-1921   Bessie Potter
1907-1913   Mrs. Joshua Levering
1908-1909   Mrs. E. B. Mathews
1908-1920   Mrs. Frank Grady
1909-1910   Mrs. Charles T. Bagby
1910-1912   Mrs. H. M. Wharton (Lulie K. ["Lucy"] Pollard)
1910-1912   Mrs. E. Asbury Davis
1910-1915   Mrs. John Howard Eager (Olive May Board)
1911   Mrs. G. Morton Scott
1912-1913   Adelaide Wilson
1912-1921   Susan Bancroft Tyler (later Mrs. Curtis Lee Laws)
1912-1921   Mrs. A. J. Fristoe
1912-1921   Mrs. George H. Stevens
1913-1916   Mrs. W. S. Love
1913-1918   Mrs. William H. Baylor (Julia Phillips)
1915-1916   Mrs. George H. Whitfield (Laura Crane)
1916-1917   Mary Faison Dixon
1916-1921   Mrs. Oscar G. Levy (Ruby Bartholomee)
1918-1921   Mrs. E. W. Pickering
1918-1921   Mrs. J. Harry Tyler
1919-1920   Mrs. Joshua Levering
1920-1921   Ethel Winfield

LOCAL/RESIDENT EXECUTIVE COMMITTEE/BOARD, BIRMINGHAM 1921-1961
1921-1922   Mrs. William F. Johnson
1921-1922   Mrs. Sumter Lea, Jr. (Ethel Jones)
1921-1922   Mrs. G. W. Morrow
1921-1923   Mrs. W. P. McAdory
1921-1924   Mrs. B. A. Inglis
1921-1924   Willie Jean Stewart
1921-1929   Mrs. James G. Smith (Bessie Adams)
1921-1930   Mrs. T. G. Bush (Alberta Williams)
1921-1930   Mrs. J. E. Dillard (Lillian Cotton Madison)
1921-1930   Mrs. Charles A. Stakely (Sarah Jessie Davis)
1921-1937   Mrs. W. L. Rosamond
1921-1944   Mrs. Hugh McDonald
1921-1945   Mrs. W. T. Berry (Rebecca Cecil)
1921-1945   Mrs. J. T. Doster (Mary Senn)
1922-1925   Mrs. Darby Brown (Mary Bestor Tartt)
1922-1935   Mrs. R. A. Clayton
1922-1945   Mrs. Peyton A. Eubank (Annie Barksdale)
1924-1931   Mrs. R. T. Anderson (Mattie Haynes)
1924-1941   Nell Bates
1924-1945   Mrs. George Ross
1926-1929   Mrs. Ed S. Moore (Janie Morton Moore)
1929-1933   Mrs. J. A. Coker
1930-1933   Mrs. H. T. McGehee (Ivah Belle Crawford)
1930-1935   Mrs. E. P. Jones (Katie Snow)
1931-1933   Mrs. W. P. McAdory
1931-1933   Mrs. Ed S. Moore (Janie Morton Moore)
1933-1934   Mrs. J. W. Gillon, Sr. (Lucie Conner)
1933-1935   Mrs. L. R. Vines
1933-1937   Mrs. J. Furniss Lee (Mary Edmundson)
1933-1945   Mrs. R. T. Anderson (Mattie Haynes)
1935-1940   Mrs. R. S. Marshall (Mary Poole)
1935-1946   Mrs. Louis M. Smith (Mary Moore)
1935-1947   Mrs. George Lewis Bailes (Emilu Fox)
1935-1947   Mrs. W. I. Pittman (Renah)
1937-1947   Mrs. H. T. McGehee (Ivah Belle Crawford)

1937-1948	Mrs. Charles Burris (Rosa Wood)
1940-1941	Mrs. J. Furniss Lee (Mary Edmundson)
1942-1943	Mrs. Walter Lee Robertson (Elma Currin)
1942-1948	Mrs. C. P. Underwood (Emma Williams Donelson)
1946-1948	Mrs. E. R. LaSalle
1946-1948	Mrs. W. H. Prater (Eloise Montgomery; later Mrs. S. C. Southard)
1946-1949	Mrs. Charles G. Herren (Mildred Green)
1946-1949	Mrs. J. H. Hudgins (Jessie)
1946-1949	Mrs. B. L. Pearson (Betty)
1946-1949	Mrs. James W. Wood (Johnie Batton)
1947-1948	Mrs. B. C. Cowart (Louise Almon)
1947-1950	Mrs. J. I. Freeman (Gussie Vinson)
1947-1950	Mrs. H. H. Grooms (Angie McCrocklin)
1947-1950	Mrs. G. C. Illingworth (Susie Nabb)
1948-1950	Mrs. W. G. Hairston (Minnie)
1948-1951	Mrs. R. G. Brinson
1948-1951	Mrs. W. C. Drake (Hilda Hall)
1948-1951	Mrs. John R. Sampey (Ellen Wood)
1948-1951	Mrs. Louis M. Smith (Mary Moore)
1949-1952	Mrs. T. B. Richardson (Rosa Mitchell)
1949-1952	Mrs. John L. Slaughter (Margaret Hooker)
1949-1952	Mrs. L. M. Ward (Lula Holcomb)
1949-1952	Mrs. W. J. Weaver
1950-1951	Mrs. George G. Baker (Christy Chambers)
1950-1951	Mrs. William Hugh McEniry (Louise Hill)
1950-1953	Mrs. J. W. McIntosh (Katherine Wynn)
1950-1953	Mrs. W. H. Prater (Eloise Montgomery; later Mrs. S. C. Southard)
1951-1952	Mrs. Fred W. Kilgore (Clara Smith)
1951-1953	Mrs. J. I. Freeman (Gussie Vinson)
1951-1954	Mrs. W. B. Rogers (Marie Patrick)
1951-1954	Mrs. J. A. Timmerman
1952-1953	Mrs. James W. Wood (Johnie Batton)
1952-1954	Mrs. James D. Parker (Hazel Spurlin)
1952-1954	Mrs. John R. Sampey (Ellen Wood)
1952-1956	Mrs. Lamar Jackson (Hermione Dannelly)
1952-1956	Mrs. Carson C. Reeves (Neola Alday)
1952-1957	Mrs. Charles G. Herren (Mildred Green)
1952-1959	Mrs. Louis M. Smith (Mary Moore)
1953-1954	Mrs. W. T. Berry, Jr. (Dorothy Frances Kay)
1953-1954	Mrs. B. P. Bowden (Sunset Cleckler)
1953-1954	Mrs. Parks Redwine (Elizabeth Smith)
1953-1954	Mrs. Fred B. White (Ruby Arnold)
1953-1955	Mrs. H. L. Anderton (Elizabeth Chew)
1954-1955	Mrs. H. W. Peerson (Sue Ella Vincent)
1954-1957	Mrs. L. M. Ward (Lula Holcomb)
1954-1958	Mrs. Edgar M. Arendall (Sara Goode)
1954-1958	Mrs. H. H. Grooms (Angie McCrocklin)
1954-1959	Mrs. J. Orlando Ogle (Virginia Keith)
1955-1960	Mrs. J. I. Freeman (Gussie Vinson)
1955-1960	Mrs. W. E. Waterhouse (Glennie)
1956-1961	Mrs. Fred W. Kilgore (Clara Smith)
1956-1961	Mrs. H. A. Williams (Margaret Plunkett)
1957-1961	Mrs. Vernon G. Davison (Marjorie Winebrenner)
1958-1961	Mrs. W. B. Rogers (Marie Patrick)
1959-1961	Mrs. B. Lloyd Parsons (Merle Hill)
1960-1961	Mrs. Harold O. Smith (Susie White)

MEMBERS-AT-LARGE OF EXECUTIVE BOARD
1954-1955 Mary Christian
1954-1955 Blanche Sydnor White
1954-1956 Carrie Uarda Littlejohn
1954-1957 Mrs. W. C. Henderson (formerly Mrs. G. H. Woodson; Carrie Wilhoit)
1954-1958 Mrs. Walter Lee Robertson (Mary Currin)
1955-1956 Mrs. R. L. Mathis (Marie Wiley)
1956-1959 Mrs. Harry P. Clause (Mayme Slaughter)
1956-1960 Mrs. George R. Martin (Olive Brinson)
1956-1961 Mrs. D. C. Bomar (Mildred Cone)
1957-1962 Mrs. Wilfred C. Tyler (Frances Landrum)
1957-1962 Mrs. Louis Nagy (Cora Irene Pennick)
1958-1963 Mrs. R. K. Redwine (Beatrice Barnard)
1958-1963 Mrs. J. Wash Watts (Mattie L. Reid)
1959-1964 Mrs. John I. Alford (Omer Shermer)
1959-1964 Mrs. M. K. Cobble (Lois Fuhrman)
1960-1965 Mrs. Roy Johnson (Nelle Cowan)
1960-1965 Mrs. Ellis A. Fuller (Elizabeth Bates)
1961-1962 Mrs. Vernon G. Davison (Marjorie Winebrenner)
1961-1963 Mrs. W. B. Rogers (Marie Patrick)
1961-1964 Mrs. B. Lloyd Parsons (Merle Hill)
1961-1965 Mrs. Harold O. Smith (Susie White)
1961-1966 Mrs. Lawrence S. Casazza (Letha Robinson)
1961-1966 Mrs. Ralph Gwin (Nina Brice)
1962-1967 Eva R. Inlow
1962-1967 Mrs. W. K. McGee (Velma Presslar)
1963-1968 Mrs. Albert J. Smith (Katherine Samford)
1963-1968 Mrs. N. B. Moon (Floyce Orr)
1964   Mrs. William McMurry (Mildred Dodson)
1964-1969 Mrs. Joe W. Burton (Lula Grace Williams)
1965-1969 Mrs. J. Winston Pearce (Winnie Rickett)
1965-1970 Elma Cobb
1965-1970 Mrs. O. K. McCarter (Matrel Hill)
1966-1968 Mrs. Glenn Field (Aletha Taylor)
1966-1971 Mrs. Harold J. Purdy (Virginia Burdette)
1967-1972 Mrs. Stanley R. Barnett (Dorothy Freshwater)
1967-1972 Mrs. E. E. Wheeless, Jr. (Alleen Witten)
1968-1973 Mrs. Wayne Dehoney (Lealice Bishop)
1968-1973 Mrs. Charles R. Standridge (Doris Rippy)
1969-1973 Mrs. John Maguire (Clyde Merrill)
1970-1974 Mrs. Duke McCall (Marguerite Mullinnix)
1970-1974 Mrs. David Northcutt (Donna Davis)
1971-1975 Mrs. Gary McNeece (Paula Parker)
1972-1976 Mrs. Edward L. Byrd (Nora Brown)
1972-1976 Mrs. Huber Drumwright (Minette Williams)

HONORARY MEMBERS OF WMU EXECUTIVE COMMITTEE/BOARD
1920-1931 Eliza Sommerville Broadus (vice-president emerita)
1921-1936 Mrs. Julian P. Thomas (Mary Antoinette Pleasants)
1922-1943 Mrs. A. C. Johnson (Cora Harlan)
1933   Mrs. W. J. Cox (Ethlene Boone)
1934-1935 Mrs. W. C. Lowndes (Elizabeth Chapman)
1937-1962 Mrs. W. C. James (Minnie Kennedy)
1939-1943 Mrs. W. N. Jones (Sallie Bailey)
1939-1948 Mrs. H. M. Wharton (Lulie K. ["Lucy"] Pollard)
1948-1953 Kathleen Moore Mallory
1952-1965 Mrs. W. J. Cox (Ethlene Boone)

PRESIDENTS OF STATE WOMAN'S MISSIONARY UNIONS NOT REPRESENTED ON EXECUTIVE BOARD

Alaska
1949-1952 Mrs. Felton Griffin (LaVerne Taylor)
1952-1953 Mrs. John DeFoore (Telle Topp)
1953-1955 Mrs. B. I. Carpenter (Helen)
1955-1957 Mrs. John Dickerson (Alvilda Craft)
1957-1958 Mrs. John Jeffcoat (Raleigh)
1958-1959 Mrs. C. H. Terwilliger
1959-1960 Mrs. James Akin (Fern Hetrick)
1960-1961 Mrs. David Pree (Nadine Blankenship)
1961-1964 Mrs. James Akin (Fern Hetrick)
1964-1967 Mrs. Dyke Brandon (Phyllis Baergen)
1967-1969 Mrs. Bill Hansen (Margaret McDonald)
1969-1972 Mrs. Ray Hustead (Trudy Rackley)
1972-1975 Mrs. Dick Wight (Muriel Hixson)
1975-1980 Mrs. Bill Loew (Dorothy Isaacs)
1980-1981 Mrs. Leonard Nicholson (Orpha Thomas)
1981-1982 Mrs. Lewis McClendon (Alma McCutcheon)
1982-1987 Mrs. Barbara McCormick Young

Hawaii
1944-1947 Mrs. C. K. Dozier (Maude Burke)
1947-1948 Mrs. Homer McDonald (Clarabel Isdell)
1948-1950 Mrs. H. P. McCormick (Mary Reeks)
1950-1954 Itsuko Saito (later Mrs. Nobuo Nishikawa; Sue)
1954-1955 Mrs. Carter Morgan (Agnes McMahan)
1955-1957 Mrs. Ralph Means (Helen Turner)
1957-1958 Mrs. Sam Longbottom (Marian Cross)
1958-1959 Mrs. Arianwen Jones Prokopchuk
1959-1960 Mrs. Charles Meyer (Annie Sue Bishop)
1960-1961 Mrs. John Hausser (Katsuko ["Dixie"] Arakawa)
1961-1963 Mrs. Dan Kong (Mary Eleanor Braddock)
1963-1964 Mrs. Henry Holley (Bettie Haun)
1964-1967 Mrs. Charles Farr (Donna Strange)
1967-1971 Mrs. Kenneth Newman (Alice McCarter)
1971-1975 Mrs. Hubert Tatum (Peggy Gasteiger)
1975-1979 Mrs. Curtis Askew (Mary Lee Trenor)
1979-1981 Mrs. Roger Laube (Irene Chadburn)
1981-1984 Mrs. Curtis Askew (Mary Lee Trenor)
1984-   Mrs. Clifford Hoff (Margie Miller)

Minnesota-Wisconsin
1980-1984 Ruth Harris
1984-   Mrs. Kenneth McDonald (Ann Adams)

Nevada
1978-1981 Mrs. Adrian W. Hall (Nancy Unruh)
1981-1985 Mrs. Michael Gallagher (Florence Sanders)
1985-   Mrs. Jerry Johnston (Linda Glasscock)

New England
1983-   Mrs. Robert H. Brindle (Susan Braden)

New York
1969-1970 Mrs. Hartmon Sullivan (Maurice Pollard)
1970-1971 Mrs. W. W. Boisture (Mildred Copenhaver)
1971-1976 Mrs. Robert Fling (Helen Long)
1976-1977 Mrs. W. W. Boisture (Mildred Copenhaver)
1977-1983 Mrs. Robert F. Nesmith (Barbara Capell)

| 1983 | Mrs. David Leary (Bonita Benfield) |
| 1984- | Mrs. Roger Knapton (Mary Orsley) |

Northern Plains
1967-1971	Mrs. Dolores Scott Gilliland (Ray)
1971-1976	Mrs. Duane Steinkuehler (Pearl Jackson)
1976-1981	Mrs. Glenn Field (Aletha Taylor)
1981-1983	Mrs. Charles Crimm (Lottie Rutledge)
1983-1987	Mrs. Tom Sherrill (Lou Ramsey)

Pennsylvania-South Jersey
1970-1973	Mrs. Otha Winningham (Louise Berge)
1973	Mrs. D. B. Martin (Peggy Thornton)
1974-1979	Mrs. Ed Price (Mary Bishop)
1979-1982	Mrs. James Cravens (Ann Thomas)
1982-	Grady Cox

Utah-Idaho
1964-1969	Mrs. John Embery (Barbara Sullivan)
1969-1974	Mrs. Bruce Conrad (Bea McKown)
1974-1978	Mrs. Olan McAuley (Verdice Daniels)
1978-1983	Mrs. Medford Hutson (Dorothy Slaton)
1983-1985	Mrs. Bruce Conrad (Bea McKown)
1985-	Dr. Roberta Cox Edwards (Frank)

West Virginia
1971-1973	Mrs. Robert Gillespie (Shirley Mason)
1973-1975	Mrs. Lee Graham (Marjorie Weaver)
1976-1979	Mrs. John Caldwell (Velma Lee Brooks)
1979-1981	Mrs. Charles Irons (Joyce Francis)
1981	Mrs. Bynum Orr (Betty Watkins)
1981-1984	Mrs. Floyd Tidsworth (Mary Ida Campbell)
1984-1986	Mrs. Russel Talley (Lynn Baker)

Wyoming
| 1983-1985 | Mrs. Ernest Hastey (Donna Havner) |
| 1985- | Mrs. John Herrington (Triss Flat) |

EXECUTIVE DIRECTORS OF STATE WOMAN'S MISSIONARY UNIONS

In 1954-57 and since 1969 the professional executive directors in states qualifying for representation have been entitled to privileges of voting with the Executive Board on matters pertaining to the promotion of WMU in churches and associations. From 1957 until 1969 directors could attend meetings for promotion but could not vote. Prior to that time those holding the position were informally organized and exercised general leadership in WMU, SBC. The position has been variously known as executive secretary, corresponding secretary, organizer, and field worker. Some early state corresponding secretaries were not salaried, but still assumed major leadership.

Alabama
1893-1896	Mrs. I. C. Brown (Maryann Bestor)
1897-1909	Mrs. D. M. Malone (Hermione Brown)
1910-1912	Kathleen Moore Mallory
1913-1920	Laura Lee Patrick (later Mrs. Henry W. Munger)
1921-1922	Mary Northington
1923-1928	Mrs. Ida Rochester Ford Mitchell Stallworth (Fletcher B.)
1929-1930	Mary Nelle Lyne
1930-1933	Wilma Bucy
1934-1940	Mrs. Ida Rochester Ford Mitchell Stallworth (Fletcher B.)
1941-1954	Mrs. R. S. Marshall (Mary Poole)
1954-1984	Mary Essie Stephens
1984-	Beverly Sutton

Alaska

1957-1968	Louise Yarbrough
1968-	Judy Rice

Arizona

1928	Floy Hawkins
1929-1930	Clara Rock
1930-1934	Constance Morton
1936-1945	Mrs. G. D. Crow (Hilton Jones)
1945-1947	Mrs. Milton Cunningham (Marie Tatum)
1948	Mrs. Berta Keys Spooner
1948-1949	Mrs. Minnie Guyton
1949-1957	Mrs. Charles M. Griffin (later Mrs. James S. Cobb; Glady Morris)
1957-1969	Almarine Brown
1969-1972	Mary Jo Stewart
1973-1985	Beverly Goss
1985-	Mrs. Ruth McCay Wood

Arkansas

1888-1889	Mrs. M. D. Early (Margretta Adelaide Dudgeon)
1889-1896	Mrs. E. Longley (Fannie Thomas)
1896-1897	Mrs. C. B. Davidson (Mary Brantley)
1898-1903	Mrs. E. Longley (Fannie Thomas)
1903-1904	Mrs. J. W. Colquitt
1904-1909	Mrs. A. H. Reaves (Alice Black)
1909-1910	Mrs. E. Longley (Fannie Thomas)
1910-1914	Mrs. W. S. Farmer (Luna Green)
1914-1929	Mrs. J. G. Jackson (Dixie Farrior)
1929-1937	Mrs. W. D. Pye (Lila Westbrook)
1937-1949	Mrs. C. H. Ray (Hattie Ann Neighbors)
1949-1974	Nancy Cooper
1975-	Julia Ketner

California

1941	Mrs. J. O. Crow
1942	Mrs. Rex Looney (Catherine)
1943-1944	Naomi Ready
1945-1952	Mrs. W. C. Howell (Brooksie)
1953	Mrs. E. E. Steele
1954-1963	Clara Lane
1964-1971	Eula Stotts
1972-1974	Bernice Popham
1975-1979	Louise Scott
1981-	Dixie Hunke

Colorado

1956-1968	Nicy Murphy
1968-1970	Betty Lynn Cadle
1971-	Sydney Portis

District of Columbia

1872-1880	Mrs. G. M. P. King
1880-1895	Mrs. J. E. Dexter
1895-1906	Emily E. York
1906-1908	Mrs. William Allen Wilbur
1908-1909	Mrs. Calvert
1909-1910	Mrs. M. E. Highfield
1910-1913	Mrs. Randolph Zeph
1913-1915	Mary Durico
1915-1917	Mrs. Edward Richardson

1917-1921 Mrs. John E. Dawson
1921-1922 Mrs. R. R. Gassford
1922-1924 Elsie Phillips
1924-1930 Mrs. W. F. Brothers
1930-1938 Mrs. G. A. Jones
1938   Mrs. Mabel V. Mercer
1952-1965 Mrs. Carleton M. Long (Dorothy Fisher)
1966-1971 Mrs. Harold B. Tillman (Retha Stewart)
1971-1980 Mrs. Kathryn Stephens Grant (Worth)
1981-   Gloria L. Grogan

Florida
1881-1886 Mrs. N. A. Bailey
1886-1893 Mrs. L. B. Telford
1893-1911 Jennie L. Spalding
1911-1936 Mrs. H. C. Peelman (Charlotte Rinckenberger)
1936-1943 Mrs. David F. Boyd (Louise Smith)
1944-1967 Josephine Jones
1967-1974 Carolyn Weatherford
1974-1976 Bernice Popham
1977-   Vanita Baldwin

Georgia
1884-1888 Mrs. A. C. Kiddo
1888-1894 Mrs. J. Stainback Wilson (Martha Eleanor Loftin)
1895-1897 Mrs. J. B. Gambrell (Mary T. Corbell)
1897-1906 Mrs. J. D. Easterlin
1906-1913 Emma L. Amos
1914-1918 Evelyn Campbell ("Evie")
1918-1919 Susan B. Anderson
1919-1921 Mrs. Kate Coleman Wakefield (later Mrs. George Fiske)
1921-1922 Maude Powell
1922-1924 Laura Lee Patrick (later Mrs. Henry W. Munger)
1924-1935 Mrs. A. F. McMahon
1935-1939 Mary Christian
1939-1963 Janice Singleton
1963-   Dorothy Pryor

Hawaii
1954-1980 Mrs. Nobuo Nishikawa (Itsuko ["Sue"] Saito)
1981-1983 Mrs. Dan Kong (Mary Eleanor Braddock) (interim)
1985-   Mrs. Kenneth Newman (Alice McCarter)

Illinois
1915-1920 Mary Northington
1921-1922 Ren Lay
1922   Mrs. John Hathaway (Maude Wall)
1923-1924 Evelyn Quarrels
1924-1926 Aretta Beswick (later Mrs. C. A. Westbrook)
1927-1930 Annabel Wall
1930-1933 Sallie Thomas
1934-1943 Mrs. John Hathaway (Maude Wall)
1943-1944 Josephine Jones
1944-1950 Mrs. John Hathaway (Maude Wall)
1950-1954 Mrs. Irene Curtis
1954-1955 Mrs. John Hathaway (Maude Wall)
1955-1983 Helen Sinclair
1983-   Evelyn Tully

Indiana
1959-1966 Louise Berge (later Mrs. Otha Winningham)
1967   Martha Fellows (later Mrs. Ronald Robinson)
1968-   Margaret Gillaspie

Kansas-Nebraska
1946-1952 Mrs. Orbie R. Clem
1953-1956 Ida Polk
1957   Eva Berry
1957-1982 Mrs. Collins Webb (Viola Middleton)
1982-   Mrs. Yvonne Kelsoe Keefer (James)

Kentucky
1878-1891 Agnes Osborne
1891-1892 Mrs. Thomas H. Fearey
1892-1894 Mary P. Caldwell
1894-1897 Mrs. Hamet Carey
1897-1904 Mrs. B. G. Rees
1904-1910 Willie Lamb
1910-1912 Nona Lee Dover
1912   Margaret Webster
1912-1913 Clifforde Elizabeth Hunter
1913-1916 Mrs. Kate Coleman Hinkle
1916-1923 Mrs. Janie Cree Bose (later Mrs. J. H. Anderson)
1923-1924 May Gardner
1924-1934 Jennie Graham Bright
1934-1942 Mary Nelle Lyne
1942-1949 Mary P. Winborne
1949-1970 Mrs. George R. Ferguson (Odessa Lyons)
1970-1984 Mrs. Kathryn Jasper Akridge (William)
1984-   Mrs. Dolores Scott Gilliland (Ray)

Louisiana
1899-1911 Mrs. J. L. Love
1912-1915 Mrs. Charles Ammen (Jane M.)
1915-1929 Mary Georgia Barnette
1930-1954 Hannah Elizabeth Reynolds
1955-1986 Kathryn Ellen Carpenter
1986-   Mrs. Nelda Crotwell Seal (Lavelle)

Maryland-Delaware*
Woman's Mission to Woman, Baltimore and Maryland Branches 1871-1892/Woman's Baptist Foreign Mission Society of Maryland 1892-1912
1871-1878 Mrs. Ann Jane Baker Graves (John James)
1878   Mrs. Fannie Roper Feudge (formerly Mrs. Robert Davenport)
1878-1891 Lily Graves
No date   Mrs. J. W. M. Williams (Corinthia ["Kennie"] Read)
1891-1892 Belle Lowndes
1892-1893 Mrs. Chester R. Turnbull
1893-1894 Belle Lowndes
1894-1897 Mrs. E. R. Singleton
1896-1898† Mrs. Howard Wayne Smith
1898-1899 Mrs. H. M. Wharton (Lulie K. ["Lucy"] Pollard)
1899-1900 Mrs. James V. Pollard (Susan Bancroft Tyler)
1900-1905 Mrs. William B. Graves
1903-1905† Mary E. B. Platt
1905-1906 Mrs. Charles Z. Butler
1906-1907 Mrs. Philip H. Barnes
1907-1908 Mrs. J. Harry Tyler
1908-1912 Bessie Potter

†Dates overlapped—probably assistant corresponding secretaries.

Woman's Baptist Home Mission Society of Maryland
1882-1889 Mrs. J. H. Brittain
1889-1894 Mrs. M. E. Oliver
1894-1895 Mrs. J. F. Pullen
1895-1898 Edith Chapman
1898-1899 Mrs. Willoughby M. McCormick (Helen Cobb)
1899-1905 Ann W. Reins
1905-1906 Mrs. Norman G. Kelley
1906-1913 Mrs. Oscar G. Levy (Ruby Bartholomee)

Woman's Baptist State Mission Society of Maryland
1898 Mrs. John Kemper
1898-1909 Mrs. John E. Gault
1909-1910 Mrs. A. H. Pattison

Maryland-Delaware
1913-1921 Mrs. George Stevens
1921-1946 Mrs. Samuel R. Barnes (Kathryn Hays)
1947-1954 Marjorie Allen
1954-1978 Josephine C. Norwood
1979-1981 Betty Lynn Cadle
1982- Willene Pierce

Michigan
1958-1978 Frances Brown
1979-1984 Joyce Mitchell
1985- Marilyn Hopkins

Minnesota-Wisconsin
1981- Betty Lynn Cadle

Mississippi
1878-1885 Mrs. J. L. Johnson (Julia Anna Toy)
1886-1889 Mrs. Minnie C. Dameron
1890-1891 Mrs. Mattie L. Leavell
1892 Mrs. Nellie D. Deupree
1893-1896 Mrs. Rebecca P. Sproles
1897-1898 Mrs A. J. Aven (Mary Bailey)
1899-1911 Mrs. W. R. Woods (Annie Kate)
1912-1930 Margaret McRae Lackey
1930-1944 Frances Traylor
1944-1971 Edwina Robinson
1971- Marjean Patterson

Missouri
1883 Mrs. George Gammage
1886-1900 Mrs. J. L. Burnham (Elize Martin)
1900 Mrs. M. J. Breaker
1901-1915 Eleanor Mare
1915-1917 Aretta Beswick (later Mrs. C. A. Westbrook)
1917-1921 (District Field Secretaries)
1921-1936 Mrs. J. G. Reynolds (Mable Lyne)
1937-1947 Mrs. C. M. Truex (Madge Nicholson)
1947-1954 Eva Berry
1954 Mrs. T. W. McKee (Louise Enloe) (interim)
1954-1958 Hilda Beggs
1959-1973 Mary Bidstrup
1973- Alberta Gilpin

Nevada
1979-1985   Mrs. Adrian W. Hall (Nancy Unruh)
1986-   Cindy Still

New England
1985-   Beulah Peoples

New Mexico
1912-1914   Alma Harris
1915-1916   Mrs. E. B. Atwood
1916-1917   Mrs. M. E. Joiner
1917-1918   Mrs. W. M. Hayward
1919-1920   Beulah M. Fonville
1920-1922   Lilian May
1922-1924   Aretta Beswick (later Mrs. C. A. Westbrook)
1924-1925   Amy Goodman
1926-1928   Harriet K. Gatlin
1928-1929   Charlotte Burnett
1929-1930   Harriet K. Gatlin
1930-1935   Charlotte Burnett
1935-1961   Eva R. Inlow
1961-1977   Vanita M. Baldwin
1978-   Mrs. Aquilla Brown Smith (Lonnie)

New York
1976-1981   Gloria Grogan
1982-   Nona Bickerstaff

North Carolina
1886-1887   Sallie Bailey (later Mrs. W. N. Jones)
1888-1889   Mrs. J. A. Briggs
1900-1906   Mrs. W. N. Jones (Sallie Bailey)
1907-1910   Mrs. Hight C. Moore (Laura Miller Peterson)
1910-1911   Elizabeth Norwood Briggs (later Mrs. T. M. Pittman)
1911-1916   Blanche Barrus
1916-1921   Bertha Carroll (later Mrs. J. E. Hoyle)
1921   Mrs. W. H. Reddish
1922-1926   Mary Warren (later Mrs. Herman T. Stevens)
1926-1939   Mrs. Edna R. Harris
1939-1943   Mrs. W. D. Briggs (Helen Moring)
1943-1945   Mary Currin (later Mrs. Walter Lee Robertson)
1945-1946   Mrs. James S. Farmer (Foy Johnson) (acting)
1946-1954   Ruth Provence
1955-1968   Miriam Robinson
1968-1977   Sara Ann Hobbs
1977-   Nancy Curtis

Northern Plains
1968-1976   Nicy Murphy
1977-1983   Mrs. Dolores Scott Gilliland (Ray)
1985-   Mrs. Glenn Field (Aletha Taylor)

Northwest
1949-1961   Mrs. Roland Hood (Rhoda Davidson)
1962-1969   Mary Jo Stewart
1969-1971   June Mason
1972-   Sara Wisdom

Ohio
1956-1961   Beulah Wingo
1961-1976   Mrs. A. L. Kirkwood (Becie Shewmake)
1976-   Mrs. Helen M. Armstrong Allan

Oklahoma
1906-1907 Mrs. W. E. Dicken
1907-1908 Mrs. C. A. Porterfield
1908-1919 Sue O. Howell
1919-1921 Pearl Todd
1921-1945 Mrs. Berta Keys Spooner
1946-1947 Mrs. Bill V. Carden (Susan Adams)
1947-1948 Mrs. Berta Keys Spooner
1948-1963 Margaret Hutchison
1963-1980 Abbie Louise Green
1982-   Mrs. Frances Vance Grafton (Weldon)

Pennsylvania-South Jersey
1973-1975 Mrs. Otha Winningham (Louise Berge)
1976-1977 Bobbie Black
1978-   Peggy Masters

South Carolina
1882-1893 Martha E. McIntosh (later Mrs. Theodore Percy Bell)
1893-1904 Mrs. John Stout (Fanny Lide Coker)
1904-1912 Mrs. A. L. Crutchfield (Elma Gwaltney)
1912-1921 Mrs. J. R. Fizer (maiden name Rossiter)
1922   Mrs. J. D. Chapman (Janie Weston) (acting)
1923-1954 Vonnie E. Lance
1954-1973 Ruth Provence
1973-1985 Mrs. Douglas Hills (Hannah Brummitt)
1985-   Evelyn Blount

Tennessee
1882   Elizabeth J. Scovel ("Bettie")
1887-1889 Mrs. Frank Hollowell
1889-1890 Ella Hill
1890-1891 Mrs. Ebenezer Calvert
1891-1892 Sarah E. S. Shankland ("Miss Lily")
1892-1894 Mrs. R. C. Stockton
1894-1895 Mrs. J. T. Paris
1895-1896 Lucy Cunningham
1896-1898 Mollie M. Claiborne
1898-1902 Mrs. W. C. Golden
1902-1906 Mrs. A. C. S. Jackson
1906-1911 Mrs. B. H. Allen
1911-1913 Mrs. Harry Allen
1913-1923 Margaret Buchanan
1923-1953 Mary Northington
1953-1967 Mary Mills
1967-1984 Mary Jane Nethery
1984   Mrs. Glendon McCullough (Marjorie Jones) (interim)
1984-1985 Mary K. Hutson (interim)
1985-   Dr. Katharine C. Bryan

Texas
1880-1882 Mrs. O. C. Pope
1882-1883 Mrs. J. B. Link
1883   Lizzie Wallace
1886-1887 Mrs. S. J. Anderson
1887-1889 Minnie Slaughter
1889-1896 Mina Everett
1896-1897 Mrs. W. C. Luther
1897-1910 Mrs. J. B. Gambrell (Mary T. Corbell)
1910-1923 Mrs. A. F. Beddoe
1923-1938 Mrs. J. E. Leigh (Cornelia)

1938-1942 Mrs. E. F. Lyon
1945-1947 Mrs. R. L. Mathis (Marie Wiley)
1947-1980 Eula Mae Henderson
1980-   Mrs. Joy Phillips Fenner (Charlie)

Utah-Idaho
1969-1985 Mrs. Guy Ward (Gernice Cox)
1985-   Mrs. Bruce Conrad (Bea McKown)

Virginia
1876-1880 Mrs. Edwin Wortham (Ann E. McGruder)
1880-1885 Mrs. Charles H. Ryland (Alice Marion Garnett)
1885-1886 Annie G. Tupper
1886-1888 Mary Caldwell Tupper ("Mamie")
1888-1894 Juliet Pollard (later Mrs. J. W. Wills)
1894-1895 Daisy Hutson
1895-1898 Elizabeth Pollard
1898-1901 Mrs. H. A. Coleman
1901-1902 Mrs. I. M. Mercer ("Nannie")
1902-1906 Mrs. W. S. Leake (Harriet Alverda French)
1906-1921 Mrs. Julian P. Thomas (Mary Antoinette Pleasants)
1921-1924 Elizabeth Shepherd Savage ("Lizzie")
1925-1950 Blanche Sydnor White
1950-1957 Ellen Douglas Oliver
1958-1975 Carrie S. Vaughan
1975-   Kathryn E. Bullard

West Virginia
1971-1974 Mrs. Elmo Cox (Ola Shipp)
1975-1978 Delores Palmer (later Mrs. Tom Eggleston)
1978-1979 Mrs. Floyd Tidsworth (Mary Ida Campbell) (interim)
1979-   Maxine Bumgarner

Wyoming
1984-   Mrs. Michael Mullins (Andrea Jones)

PRESIDENTS OF STATE WOMAN'S MISSIONARY UNIONS NOT ALSO SERVING AS WMU, SBC, VICE-PRESIDENTS

Until the last 50 years the vice-presidents of WMU, SBC, representing a given state might be a different person from the president of that state's WMU. The following is a list of persons who served as state president while not also serving as WMU, SBC, vice-president. Also, the presidents of state WMUs formed prior to founding of WMU, SBC, are listed.

*The asterisk denotes a state president who also began to serve as vice-president of the national organization.

Alabama
1889-1895 Mrs. T. A. Hamilton (Amanda Tupper)
1896-1907 Mrs. L. F. Stratton (Lucy)
1907-1920* Mrs. Charles A. Stakely (Sarah Jessie Davis)

Arizona
1928-1940* Mrs. W. C. Henderson (formerly Mrs. G. H. Woodson; Carrie Wilhoit)

Arkansas
1883-1902 Mrs. James P. Eagle (Mary Kavanaugh Oldham)
1902-1910 Mrs. E. Longley (Fannie Thomas)
1910-1911 Mrs. H. C. Fox (maiden name Broadus)
1911-1914 Mrs. M. G. Thompson (Lena Bristol)

1914-1916 Mrs. W. T. McCurry (Mayme Smith)
1916-1919 Mrs. C. M. Roberts (Leola Rhodes)
1919-1922 Mrs. J. H. Crawford (Elizabeth McMillan)
1922-1923 Mrs. O. O. Florence (Laura Jones)
1923-1929* Mrs. W. D. Pye (Lila Westbrook)

California
1941-1942 Mrs. Cecil H. Colvard (Kate)
1943   Mrs. J. C. Arnold
1943-1946* Mrs. A. F. Whitehurst

District of Columbia
1888-1895 Mrs. M. M. Mason
1895-1897 Mrs. J. D. Smith
1897-1902 Mrs. S. P. Bliss
1902-1904 Mrs. Irene Buchanan
1904-1907 Mrs. Robert R. West
1907-1908 Mrs. Elizabeth Hinton Hoeke
1908-1916 Mrs. Charles G. Gould
1916-1934 Mrs. O. E. Howe
1934-1940* Mrs. George A. Ross

Florida
1894-1896 Mrs. T. D Crawford
1896-1897 Mrs. J. E. Oates
1897-1904 Caroline Palmer
1904-1905 Mrs. B. M. Bean
1905-1906 Mrs. M. B. Harrison
1906-1907 Mrs. W. C. Powell
1907-1911 Mrs. M. B. Harrison
1911-1923 Mrs. N. C. Wamboldt
1923-1925 Mrs. J. A. Mellon
1925-1929 Mrs. E. C. Bostick
1929-1936* Mrs. G. J. Rousseau (Christine McConnell)

Georgia
1884-1888 Mrs. J. Stainback Wilson (Martha Eleanor Loftin)
1888-1900 Mrs. R. M. Seymour
1900-1906 Mary Emily Wright (later Mrs. J. Milnor Wilbur)
1906-1911* Mrs. E. G. Willingham (Mary Peoples)

Illinois
1908-1909 Mrs. J. A. Leavitt (Lillie Lemon)
1909-1921 Mrs. W. P. Throgmorton (Catherine Baker)
1921   Mrs. W. B. Wilhoyte
1921-1925 Mrs. I. E. Lee (Beatrice Flannigan)
1925-1927 Mrs. W. A. Rhine (Lillie Boyd)
1927-1928* Mrs. John Hathaway (Maude Wall)

Kansas-Nebraska
1946-1952* Mrs. J. D. Williamson (Nellie Gentz)

Kentucky
1878-1881 Mrs. Leora B. Robinson
1881-1885 Mrs. M. B. Fontaine
1885-1887 Mrs. Ellen Carey
1887-1920 Eliza Sommerville Broadus†
1903-1909 Mrs. B. F. Proctor
1909-1910 Mrs. Loraine McGibbon Bramble
1910-1911 Mrs. E. B. Sayers
1911-1912 Mrs. J. W. Stevenson

1912-1914 Mrs. W. E. Mitchell
1914-1916 Mrs. E. T. Forsee
1916-1919 Mrs. Peter F. Smith
1919-1922 Mrs. C. W. Elsey
1922-1924 Mrs. L. L. Roberts
1924-1925 Mrs. J. M. Roddy
1925-1927 Mrs. John Stegar
1927-1929 Mrs. O. P. Bush
1929-1931 Mrs. L. C. Kelly
1931-1933 Mrs. C. F. Creal
1933-1937* Mrs. Eureka Whiteker (Prudence Sayers)

(†Kentucky had simultaneously a central committee chairman and a WMU president.)

Louisiana
1895-1898 Mrs. George S. Dodds
1899-1904 Mrs. Charles Ammen (Jane M.)
1904-1905 Mrs. Arthur Edward Reimer
1905-1908 Mrs. Charles Ammen (Jane M.)
1908-1911 Mrs. F. M. Hollingsworth
1911-1914 Mrs. T. R. Falvy
1914-1915 Mrs. W. F. Weishaupt (Myrtie Shively)
1915-1916 Mrs. T. R. Falvy
1916-1920 Mrs. W. F. Weishaupt (Myrtie Shively)
1920   Mrs. Rudolph Krause (interim)
1920-1921 Mrs. D. C. Freeman (Ola Creager)
1921-1929 Mrs. T. E. Stephenson
1929-1936 Mrs. H. M. Bennett
1936-1941* Mrs. Mary Lou Jenkins (Charles Edward)

Maryland-Delaware
1913-1929 Clara M. Woolford
1929-1932 Mrs. Wayland A. Harrison
1932-1936 Mrs. Eugene Levering (Harriett Ellis)
1936-1940 Mrs. Oscar G. Levy (Ruby Bartholomee)
1940-1943* Mrs. Wayland A. Harrison

**Woman's Mission to Woman, Baltimore and Maryland Branches 1871-1892/
Woman's Baptist Foreign Mission Society of Maryland 1892-1913**
1871-1887 Mrs. Franklin Wilson (Virginia Appleton)
1887-1891 Mrs. A. J. Rowland
1891-1897 Mrs. James V. Pollard (Susan Bancroft Tyler)
1897-1898 Mrs. George Tyler
1898-1899 Mrs. James V. Pollard (Susan Bancroft Tyler)
1900-1905 Mrs. John Howard Eager (Olive May Board)
1905-1913 Clara Woolford

Woman's Baptist Home Mission Society of Maryland
1882-1905 Annie Walker Armstrong
1906-1913 Mrs. A. C. Johnson (Cora Harlan)

Woman's Baptist State Mission Society of Maryland
1898-1910 Mrs. George H. Eyster
1911-1916 Mrs. James E. Tyler

Mississippi
1878-1886 Mrs. J. L. Johnson (Julia Anna Toy)
1886-1887 Mrs. A. H. Longino (Marion Buckley)
1887-1893 Mrs. Adelia M. Thompson Hillman (Walter)
1893-1896 Mrs. A. J. Aven (Mary Bailey)
1896-1899 Mrs. J. K. Pace

1899   Mrs. J. W. Bozeman (Julia Evans)
1899-1911 Mrs. J. A. Hackett (Emma Gardner)
1911-1914 Mrs. William Andrew McComb (May Willis)
1914-1916 Mrs. George W. Riley (Lilly Belle)
1916-1934* Mrs. A. J. Aven (Mary Bailey)

Missouri
1877-1886 Mrs. O. P. Moss (Caroline Thornton)
1886-1900 Mrs. W. F. Elliott
1900-1902 Mrs. G. W. Hyde (Eliza Gaw)
1902-1905 Mrs. H. B. Scammell
1905-1908 Mrs. J. H. Roblee
1909-1910 Mrs. J. S. Tustin
1910-1911 Mrs. J. H. Roblee
1911-1915 Mrs. E. T. Trueblood
1916   Mrs. John A. Guthrie
1918   Mrs. Patee Russell
1919   Mrs. B. F. Reese
1920-1921 Mrs. J. G. Reynolds (Mable Lyne)
1921   Mrs. E. C. Henderson
1922   Mrs. C. E. Graham
1923-1934* Mrs. F. W. Armstrong (Laura Dell Malotte)

New Mexico
1912   Mrs. G. T. Veal
1912-1916 Mrs. Minnie E. Lawing Pack
1916-1919 Mrs. William H. Long
1919-1924* Mrs. M. D. Schumaker

North Carolina
1877   Mrs. Jonathan McGee Heck (Mattie Callendine)
1886-1915 Fannie Exile Scudder Heck
1916-1936 Mrs. Wesley N. Jones (Sallie Bailey)
1936-1942* Mrs. J. Clyde Turner (Bertha Hicks)

Oklahoma
1902-1904* Mrs. W. H. Kuykendall

South Carolina
1882-1888 Mrs. John Stout (Fanny Lide Coker)
1888-1904 Mary Lide Coker†
1902-1907 Mrs. J. D. Chapman (Janie Weston)
1907-1911 Mrs. I. W. Wingo
1911-1912 Mrs. A. L. Crutchfield (Elma Gwaltney)
1912-1913 Mrs. W. J. Hatcher
1913-1930* Mrs. J. D. Chapman (Janie Weston)

(†South Carolina had simultaneously a central committee chairman and a WMU president.)

Tennessee
1882   Jennie Fish
1887-1889 Mrs. Anson Nelson
1889-1894 Mrs. G. A. Lofton (Ella E. Martin)
1894-1895 Mrs. R. C. Stockton
1895-1902 Mrs. A. C. S. Jackson
1902-1913 Mrs. A. J. Wheeler (Mary Belle)
1913-1918 Mrs. Avery Carter
1918-1920 Mrs. Hight C. Moore (Laura Miller Peterson)
1920-1922 Mrs. Albert E. Hill
1922-1923 Mrs. C. D. Creasman (Myrtle Robinson)
1923-1925* Mrs. W. J. Cox (Ethlene Boone)

Texas
1880-1895 Mrs. Fannie Breedlove Davis (George Bowen)
1895-1906 Mrs. W. L. Williams (Lou Beckley)
1906-1931* Mrs. F. S. Davis (Mary Hill)

Virginia
1874-1887 Mrs. J. B. Jeter (Mary Catherine)
1887-1892 Mrs. W. E. Hatcher (Virginia ["Jennie"] Snead)
1892-1893 Mary Caldwell Tupper ("Mamie")
1893-1897 Mrs. Abby Manly Gwathmey (William Henry)
1897-1898 Mrs. J. S. Dill (Kate Tichenor)
1898-1899 Daisy Hutson
1899-1901 Mrs. John A. Barker (Lillie Easterby)
1901-1902 Mrs. F. P. Robertson (Josephine Ragland Willis)
1902-1905 Mrs. John A. Barker (Lillie Easterby)
1905-1907 Mrs. T. P. Bagby (Fannie E. Scott)
1907-1909 Mrs. George W. McDaniel (Martha Douglass Scarborough)
1909-1911 Mrs. W. C. James (Minnie Kennedy)
1911-1912 Mrs. J. W. Wills (Juliet Pollard)
1912-1914 Lizzie Savage
1914-1916 Mrs. W. C. James (Minnie Kennedy)
1916-1921 Mrs. John F. Vines (Valeria Mabel Lawrence)
1921-1923 Mrs. H. B. Cross (Ruth Edna Graham)
1923-1925 Mrs. C. W. McElroy
1925-1929 Mrs. George R. Martin (Olive Brinson)
1929-1931 Mrs. Howard C. Gilmer (Lila Saul)
1931-1934* Mrs. A. S. Downes (Elizabeth Bloxom)

PROFESSIONAL STAFF

ALLAN, Helen M. Armstrong, editor, Mission Friends Materials 1969-76. ALLEN, Catherine Bryant (Lee N.), Sunbeam Band Department editorial associate 1964-65; editor, Sunbeam Band Materials 1965-66; WMU consultant in press relations 1966-70; Public Relations director 1970-74; assistant to the executive director—Public and Employee Relations 1974-83; associate executive director 1983-. ALSTON, Mrs. Clara G., production manager 1959-66.

BARBOUR, Louise,* media designer 1983-. BARNES, Victoria Overall (Robert S.),* travel coordinator and hostess 1978-79; Public Events director 1979-83; travel and meeting specialist 1983-.† BEECHNER, Mrs. Jackie Black, Circulation Group manager 1985-.† BENSON, Karen Wigger (Tommy), Communications Group manager 1986-. BENTLEY, Eljee Young (Arthur), Baptist Women Products editor 1978-83;† archivist 1983-. BISHOP, J. Ivyloy, Royal Ambassador secretary 1943-1953. BLOUNT, Evelyn, Youth Department supervisor 1973-74; Promotion Department director 1974-76; Field Services Department director 1976-79; assistant to Education Division director 1979-80; National Enlargement Plan director 1980-83; program development specialist 1983-85. BOCK, Betty, Young Woman's Auxiliary director 1966-69. BONHAM, Adrianne, Editorial Services Department director 1970-73; Adult Department supervisor 1973-74; editor, Baptist Women and Baptist Young Women Materials 1974-77; editor, Baptist Women Materials 1978; *Royal Service* editor 1979-81. BOWERS, Evelyn Bussey (Ben F.),* production manager 1966-74. BREWER, Betty (later Mrs. S. E. Kidd), Division of Girls' Auxiliary secretary 1955-57; Girls' Auxiliary Department director 1957-64. BROWN, Pam Hammett (Eddie), *Accent* editor 1977-83. BRYAN, Katharine, Girls' Auxiliary promotion associate 1961-65.† BRUCE, Margaret, Young People's Secretary 1948-54; Department of Youth secretary 1954-57; Woman's Missionary Society Department director 1957-65; Woman's Missionary Society director 1965-70; Baptist Women director 1970-73.

CABALLERO, Gladys (later Mrs. Milton Leach), editor, Spanish Materials 1978-79; Language WMU editor 1979-81. CABARCAS, Elina, Language WMU editor 1983; Spanish Materials editor 1984-. CARTER, Frances Tunnell (John), Acteens/Girls in Action Products editor 1983-85. CAUSEY, Carol, training designer 1986-. CHURCHILL, Sheryl (Mrs. James Lewis), Baptist Young Women consultant 1976-1984; Consulting Services Group manager 1984-. COLVIN, Rachel,* editorial associate 1948-56; art editor 1956-57; art associate 1957-60. CORUM, Betty Jo, Editorial Services Department director 1965-70. COWLEY, Audrey Evans (William A.), treasurer 1979-83; Financial Services Group manager 1983-84. CREASMAN, Myrtle Robinson (C. D.), stewardship director 1949-52.

DeVAULT, Doris, Division of Young Woman's Auxiliary secretary 1955-57; Young Woman's Auxiliary Department director 1957-65; coordinator of special services 1965-82. DIAZ, Doris, Language WMU consultant 1972-.† DICKSON, Elaine, promotion associate 1958-63; Woman's Missionary Society Department promotion associate 1963-65; assistant to the director of Promotion Division 1965-69. DOSSETT, Ellen, editor, Baptist Young Women Materials 1973-74. DUCKETT, Nancy Hasty (Truman), accounting specialist 1986-.

ELDER, Barbara, program development specialist 1985-. ELLIOTT, Bernice, promotion associate in pioneer areas 1961-73; promotion associate in new areas 1973-77. ELLISON, Edna Martin (J. Theodore), *Royal Service* editor 1986-.

FLING, Helen Long (Robert), promotion associate in new areas 1977-84. FLOWERS, James G., procurement specialist 1978-.† FOREHAND, Mary Anne, editor, Sunbeam Band Materials 1967-69. FOWLER, Ida Shirley (Jack),* Office Services supervisor 1976-78. FUSELIER, Aline (later Mrs. Philip Summerlin), Baptist Young Women director 1969-72; Baptist Women consultant 1972-77.

GARRETT, Carol Sisson (Danny),* public information specialist 1984-. GENTRY, Oneta, editor, *Tell*/GA Materials 1969-70; *Accent* editor 1970-77; *Dimension*/Products editor 1977-.† GILLILAND, Dolores Scott (Ray), marketing communication specialist 1983-84. GODWIN, Mary Rawlings (J.H.),* administrative assistant 1957-75. GONZALEZ, Carmen, Spanish Materials editor 1975-76. GORE, Anne Hooks (William R.), Financial Services Group manager, 1986-. GREEN, Abbie Louise, Sunbeam Band Department director 1959-63. GROGAN, Gloria, WMU consultant 1975-76.

HAMRIC, Ethalee,* editorial associate 1948-55; *The Window* editor 1955-57; editorial associate 1957-65; editor, Woman's Missionary Society Materials 1965-70; editor, General Administration Materials 1970-76.† HARRIS, Beth Anne, promotion specialist, 1987-. HELMBOLD, Dale (later Mrs. Terry Cutrer),* assistant editor, Acteens Materials and *Contempo* 1974-76. HICKS, Elizabeth Jones (Larry),* production director 1976-78. HILL, Stanley W., video specialist 1983-. HINES, Mary, Sunbeam Band director 1964-70; Mission Friends director 1970; Field Services Department director 1970-72; Children and Preschool Department supervisor 1972-74; Customer Services Section director 1974-.† HIX, E. Jane, Baptist Young Women consultant 1974-76. HOLLEY, L. Tom III, Literature and Supplies Department director 1976-83; Warehouse Unit supervisor 1984-. HUIE, Mary Lou Huggins (Clarence),* Subscription Fulfillment Department director 1976-83; Subscription Group manager 1983-85.† HURTT, Betty Dougherty (Claude), librarian 1977-.

JOHNSON, Ellen Hale (Tom),* assistant to Customer Services Division director 1976; travel and reception coordinator 1976-78. JONES, Marjorie (later Mrs. Glendon McCullough), Girls' Auxiliary Department director 1964-65; Girls' Auxiliary director 1965-69.

KELLY, Carrol, Baptist Women consultant 1978-80; assistant to Education Division director 1980-83; Communications Group manager 1984-85. KILNER, Ann (later Mrs. David Hughes), Baptist Young Women/Acteens Products editor 1981-83; Baptist Women/Baptist Young Women Products editor 1983-84. KIZER, Kathryn Willingham (Lawton E., Jr.,), *Start*/*Share*/Products editor 1981-.†

LOWERY, Betsy Criminger (Jeff),* circulation system specialist 1985-.†

MANN, Anne Leavell (later Mrs. J. B. Collingsworth), *Royal Service* editor 1982. MAPLES, Donna, Training Design Group manager 1984-85. MARQUEZ, Grace Ezell (Francisco), editor, Spanish Materials 1976-77; Editorial Department director 1977-78. MARTIN, Mickey, Girls in Action and Mission Friends consultant 1971-76; General Administration consultant 1976-.† MASSEY, Barbara, *Aware*/*Discovery* editor 1979-. MATHER, Juliette, Young People's Secretary and College Correspondent 1921-27; Young People's Secretary 1927-1948; editorial secretary 1948-54; Department of Publications secretary 1954-57. MATHIS, Mrs. R. L. (Marie Wiley), Promotion Division director 1963-69. McCLAIN, Cindy, Products editor 1986-. McINDOO, Ethel, Girls in Action/Mission Friends consultant 1981-. McMURRY, Mrs. William (Mildred Dodson), Mission Study director 1951-54; Department of Missionary Fundamentals secretary 1954-57; Promotion Division director 1957-62.

MERRELL, Betty Caughron (Ron D.), *Royal Service* editor 1983-85; Age-level Magazines Group manager 1985-. MITCHELL, Joyce, Interpretation Section director 1984-. MOORE, Patricia Ferguson, management information specialist 1983-.

NEAL, La Venia, treasurer 1953-57; Business Division director 1957-74; Treasurer 1974-79. NEWMAN, Deena Williams (Tom), publications coordination specialist 1983-84; Products editor 1984-.†

OSBORNE, Rosanne, editor, General WMU Materials 1968-69; editor, Baptist Women Materials 1969-73. OWEN, Jennifer Bryon (John), Products Group manager 1985-86. OWENS, Laurella, Young Woman's Auxiliary Department editorial associate 1957-65; editor, YWA Materials 1965-70; editor, Baptist Young Women Materials 1970-72; editor, Baptist Women Materials 1972-74; editor, *Royal Service* 1974-77.

PATE, Billie, promotion associate 1957-63; Young Woman's Auxiliary Department promotion associate 1963-65; Field Services Department director 1965-69. PERKINS, Margaret Thomas (William), WMU Associate for Black Church Relations 1978-.† POWELL, Lane Holland (Robert), editor, *Royal Service* 1977-78.

RITCHIE, Pat, Training Design Group manager 1986-. RIVES, Elsie, Division of Sunbeam Band secretary 1955-57; Sunbeam Band Department director 1957-59; editorial-promotion associate 1959-60. ROBERTS, Katherine,* general ledger accountant 1976-.†

SHIELDS, Bonnie Murray (Robert L. III),* assistant director—Employee Relations 1976-79; personnel director 1979-83; Staff Services Group manager 1983-. SIMONS, Karen Campbell (Tommy), promotion specialist 1985-86; Products Group manager 1986-. SMITH, Carolyn Mulvehill Roberts (Roy),* administrative assistant 1976-. SMITH, David, Distribution Group manager 1984-85. SMITH, Frasier, Distribution Group manager 1985-. SMITH, Karen (Bayne),* assistant director—Employee Relations 1974-76. SOLOMON, Marti, Acteens consultant 1979-. SORRILL, Bobbie, Field Services director, Children's Division 1968-1970; director, Church WMU Administration and Associational WMU Administration 1970-72; General Administration Department supervisor 1972-74; Education Division director 1974-83; associate executive director 1983-. SPRADLIN, Marsha, Baptist Young Women consultant 1986-. STOKELD, Susan, *Start*/Girls in Action/Mission Friends Products editor 1976-81.† STOKELY, Edith (later Mrs. Lyle S. Moore, Jr.), Community Missions director 1949-54; Division of Community Missions secretary 1954-55. SULLIVAN, Patricia Lemonds (Jon), Girls in Action and Acteens Materials editor 1976-77; Baptist Young Women/Acteens Products editor 1978-81.† SUTTON, Beverly, Acteens consultant 1975-79; Field Services Department director 1979-83; Interpretation Section director 1983-84.

TERRY, Anne Carr (Mack), personnel specialist 1983-. THARPE, Gertrude Addis (Edgar), Editorial Department director 1978-83; Publications Section director 1983-84. THOMAS, Betty, editorial-promotion associate 1962-63. TUCKER, Iva Jewel Burton,* editor, Girls in Action Materials 1970-76; editor, *Aware* and *Discovery* 1976-79. TULLY, Evelyn, Acteens director 1969-72; Acteens consultant 1972-74. TURRENTINE, Jan, *Accent* editor 1983-.

UNDERWOOD, Kathy, assistant editor, Girls in Action Materials and *Royal Service* 1974-76.

WALDREP, Montise, Financial Services Group manager 1984-86. WARD, Mary Ann (Mrs. Walter Appling), *Contempo* editor 1974-. WATTIER, Debbie Stewart (Mark), public information director 1980. WEBB, Lawrence E., Editorial Department director 1974-77. WEEKS, Dorothy, editorial associate 1953-57; *Tell* editor 1957; Girls' Auxiliary Department editorial associate 1957-65; editor, Girls' Auxiliary Materials 1965-67.† WHITLOW, June, Church WMU Administration consultant 1967-70; Promotion Division director 1970-73; Education Division director 1973-74; assistant to the executive director—Research and Planning 1974-1983; associate executive director 1983-. WILDES, Beth Sayers (William),* public information director 1980-83. WINTER, Jimmye Simmons (Charles), Girls in Action/Mission Friends consultant 1977-80; Baptist Women consultant 1980-85; promotion associate in new areas 1985-.

YARBROUGH, Lynn Butler (Kenneth A.), Training Design consultant 1981-83; Training Design Group manager 1983-84; Publications Section director 1984-. YOUNG, Janell Evans (John),* Art Section supervisor 1974-77; Art Department director 1977-83; senior artist 1983-.

*Indicates WMU employment prior to professional service.
†Indicates minor changes in job titles have occurred; latest title is used.

STATE WMU ORGANIZATION AND REPRESENTATION DATES

State	Founding Date[2]	Representation with WMU, SBC[4]	Order of Qualification for Representation
Alabama	Nov. 11, 1889	1890	13
Alaska	Aug. 25, 1949		-
Arizona	1928	1929	19
Arkansas[1]	1883	1888	1
California	1942	1944	20
Colorado	Nov. 21, 1955	1958	24
District of Columbia	1888	1896	15
Florida[1]	Jan. 12, 1894[3]	1888	1
Georgia[1]	1884	1888	1
Hawaii	Aug. 23, 1944		-
Illinois	1908	1911	17
Indiana	April 9-10, 1959	1959	25
Iowa	[1963][6]		-
Kansas/Nebraska	1946	1949	21
Kentucky[1]	1878	1888	1
Louisiana[1]	1895[2]	1888	1
Maryland/Delaware[1]	1871	1888	1
Michigan	1957	1961	26
Minnesota/Wisconsin	1983		-
Mississippi	1878	1888 (July)	11
Missouri[1]	April 8, 1877	1888	1
New England	Nov. 3-5, 1983		-
Nevada	Oct. 16-17, 1978		-
New Mexico	July 20, 1912[3]	1911	17
New York	Sept. 26, 1969		-
North Carolina	Jan. 8, 1886	1890	14
Northern Plains	Nov. 7, 1967		-
Northwest	April 1948	1950	22
Ohio	Feb. 23, 1954	1954	23
Oklahoma	1891	1891[5]	16
Pennsylvania/So. Jersey	Oct. 1970		-
South Carolina[1]	Jan. 10, 1875	1888	1
Tennessee[1]	Dec. 13, 1887	1888	1
Texas[1]	Oct. 3, 1880	1888	1
Utah/Idaho	Oct. 28, 1964		-
Virginia	Sept. 7, 1874	1889	12
West Virginia	Oct. 22, 1971	1986	27
Wyoming	Jan. 1, 1984		-

[1] Original states organizing WMU, SBC, May 14, 1888.
[2] Date of first statewide continuous organization, often called a central committee, after the state gained recognition in the Southern Baptist Convention.
[3] These states had several earlier organizations which did not form into one statewide until this date. They had previously affiliated with WMU, SBC.
[4] Date state qualified to be represented by a vice-president of WMU, SBC, and on the conventionwide WMU Executive Board.
[5] The West Arkansas and Indian Territory organization which was entitled to a vice-president in 1891 merged into the permanent Oklahoma organization in 1900 and again in 1906.
[6] Iowa is not a state convention, but a fellowship group is planning to organize into a convention.

MEMBERSHIP

Year[*]	Total Membership	WMS Total Membership	YWA Membership	GA Membership	RA Membership	Sunbeam Membership
1888						
1889						
1890						
1891	37,200[1]					
1892						
1893						
1894						
1895						
1896						
1897						
1898						
1899						
1900						
1901						
1902						
1903						
1904						
1905						
1906						
1907						
1908						
1909						
1910	111,473	59,201	12,402		1,526	44,344
1911	200,000[1]					
1912						
1913						
1914	225,000[1]					
1915						

Year*	Total Membership	WMS Total Membership	YWA Membership	GA Membership	RA Membership	Sunbeam Membership
1916						
1917						
1918						
1919	250,000[1]					
1920						
1921						
1922						
1923	148,108					
1924	269,906[4]					
1925	359,368	168,424				
1926	348,405	197,598				
1927	440,009[2]	26,218				
1928	523,736	311,255				
1929	531,394	314,237				
1930	624,659	338,598				
1931	651,690	425,027				
1932	563,830	284,045				
1933	581,442	282,114	64,425	84,906	41,865	108,132
1934	571,702	282,505	62,259	85,877		
1935	593,766	293,883				103,232
1936	595,852	297,594	64,269	82,237	42,644	109,108
1937	611,875	315,613	65,292	92,899	44,233	93,838
1938	705,399	361,159	77,423	109,416	47,745	109,656
1939	746,845	389,129	77,872	113,245	55,332	111,267
1940	753,246	399,003	78,839	109,416	56,332	109,656
1941	768,976	412,325	73,766	115,715	57,484	109,686
1942	748,465	404,144	65,260	113,686	57,827	107,548
1943	715,433	388,314	59,011	108,066	55,862	104,180

Year*	Total Membership	WMS Total Membership	YWA Membership	GA Membership	RA Membership	Sunbeam Membership
1944	719,186	381,655				
1945	739,360	400,464	58,861	115,385	59,488	105,162
1946	767,521	420,592	52,003	116,361	63,416	115,149
1947	806,051	438,324	55,942	120,953	67,047	123,785
1948	875,298	482,476	52,084	133,426	75,939	131,373
1949	942,988	517,265	54,608	141,541	85,009	144,565
1950	996,124	548,532	55,300	151,637	87,586	153,069
1951	1,067,582	596,838	58,346	160,026	90,649	161,723
1952	1,143,993	613,822			105,834	
1953	1,197,364	641,096	61,238	189,192	115,294	190,554
1954	1,281,936	667,527	70,312	206,709	127,262	210,126
1955	1,245,358	700,226	66,831	222,151		228,289
1956	1,267,850	720,521	65,681	230,119		231,107
1957	1,324,295	729,139	70,777	256,811		251,048
1958	1,395,974	739,108	73,620	268,104		258,763
1959	1,456,192	756,382	78,992	285,657		279,552
1960	1,484,589	742,901	80,996	290,462	311,386	
1961	1,496,634	752,556	83,035	308,682	325,908	
1962	1,489,352	752,961	72,734	320,477	350,754	
1963	1,512,840	762,656	77,874	330,035	342,275	
1964	1,509,484	765,770	86,291	330,699	346,694	
1965	1469,739	733,446	85,058	324,438	341,716	
1966	1,459,828	714,881	78,607	331,102	350,542	
1967	1,444,428	696,836	74,144	334,405	341,945	
1968	1,407,673	664,975	70,599	331,571	344,285	
1969	1,291,221	588,886	65,848	318,806	334,205	
1970	1,199,813	558,978	57,335	299,851	300,673	

Year*	Total Membership	Baptist Women Membership	Baptist Young Women Membership	Acteens	Girls in Action Membership	Mission Friends Membership
1971	1,140,506	499,488	47,159	157,469	244,263	130,015
1972	1,125,641	489,977	48,063	147,798	237,930	118,468
1973	1,102,432	483,455	53,692	138,355	229,226	118,431
1974	1,115,149	496,499	61,256	136,802	215,750	119,314
1975	1,133,587	497,056	62,420	139,315	225,541	127,226
1976	1,139,034	496,293	72,382	135,434	222,667	130,509
1977	1,118,085	494,310	72,015	131,995	212,462	124,823
1978	1,094,966	492,456	69,790	123,396	205,355	121,088
1979	1,086,785	494,273	71,155	115,944	202,857	121,454
1980	1,100,043	489,859	72,327	117,331	213,282	128,652
1981	1,114,461	490,735	72,870	118,197	219,088	136,033
1982	1,149,266	491,085	76,683	121,929	227,711	149,563
1983	1,175,354	500,893	79,708	125,542	227,781	158,643
1984	1,169,630	498,718	77,146	123,660	223,666	162,313
1985	1,165,240	502,606	75,899	119,007	220,897	163,895

Notes for Membership and Organizations Charts

*Each year's figures are drawn from reports dated with the subsequent year. Unless otherwise indicated reports are drawn from WMU Annual Report statistical tables or from Quarterly Review. Prior to the mid-1960s WMU collected its own statistics through internal channels. These were reflected in Annual Reports. Meanwhile, the SBC collected similar statistics. Seldom did the two sets of statistics match.

[1]Estimated enrollment according to unofficial statements by WMU officers.

[2]Figures prior to this year did not include all states. For the first time reasonably comprehensive figures, including such large states as Texas and North Carolina, are included. See WMU Annual Report 1927, 1929, and WMU Annual Report 1928, 1933.

[3]From WMU Report to the SBC or informal estimates of WMU officers. Data not reflected in WMU Annual Report tables.

[4]1925 SBC Annual states that nearly half of total WMU membership are young people.

[5]Totals represent more than the sum of bands and societies, due to irregularities in method of reporting.

ORGANIZATIONS

Year*	Number of Southern Baptist Churches	Churches Reporting WMU	Percent of Churches Reporting WMU	WMS—Number of Organizations	Total Number of WMU Organizations
1888	15,343			1,935	1,961
1889	15,894			1,690	1,835[5]
1890	16,091			1,924	2,308[5]
1891	16,654			2,134	2,258
1892	17,710			1,865	2,027[5]
1893	17,346			2,252	2,548
1894	17,803			3,130	3,578[5]
1895	18,143			3,674	3,808
1896	18,678			3,288	3,773[5]
1897	18,922			3,318	4,320[5]
1898	18,873			1,250	1,736
1899	18,963			1,255	1,744
1900	19,558			3,573	4,546[5]
1901	19,653			4,040	4,792[5]
1902	19,991			4,088	4,621
1903	20,431			3,646	3,986
1904	20,402			4,409	5,117
1905	21,802			7,047	8,203
1906	20,776			4,407	6,585
1907	21,266			4,161	6,855
1908	21,887			5,655	9,251
1909	22,438			6,168	10,053
1910	23,248			6,503	10,627
1911	23,676			6,654	10,563
1912	23,982			6,914	11,383
1913	24,171			7,181	12,098
1914*	24,338			7,913	13,424
1915	24,451			8,203	14,663

Year*	Number of Southern Baptist Churches	Churches Reporting WMU	Percent of Churches Reporting WMU	WMS—Number of Organizations	Total Number of WMU Organizations
1916	24,602			8,767	15,840
1917	24,883			8,998	16,198
1918	24,851	9,850	38	9,010	15,014
1919	25,303			9,967	16,964
1920	27,444			10,522	19,485
1921	27,634			10,677	20,878
1922	27,919			10,889	22,109
1923	27,611			10,615	22,326
1924	27,517			10,646	22,837
1925	24,341			10,623	22,944
1926	24,774	9,393[3]	38	10,739	23,908
1927	24,274			10,989	26,151
1928	25,705	13,541[3]	52	11,628	30,415
1929	24,010	13,010[3]	54	11,107	29,777
1930	23,731			10,940	30,020
1931	23,806			10,888	30,149
1932	24,035			10,459	31,549
1933	24,270			11,002	33,678
1934	24,360			11,053	32,863
1935	24,537			11,407	34,645
1936	24,671	13,544[3]	55	11,360	34,228
1937	24,844	2,503		11,423	34,594
1938	24,932	12,569[3]	50	12,326	38,597
1939	25,018	12,779[3]	51	12,648	39,720
1940	25,259			12,722	40,614
1941	25,603			12,995	41,719
1942	25,737			12,845	40,472
1943	25,790			12,387	38,695

Year*	Number of Southern Baptist Churches	Churches Reporting WMU	Percent of Churches Reporting WMU	WMS—Number of Organizations	Total Number of WMU Organizations
1944	25,965			12,651	39,667
1945	26,191			12,734	41,227
1946	26,401	12,224[3]	46	13,326	43,081
1947	26,764	14,043[3]	52	14,043	46,722
1948	26,822	13,338	50	14,812	49,613
1949	27,285	14,312	52	15,693	54,574
1950	27,788	15,294	55	16,451	56,874
1951	28,289	16,101	57	17,237	60,812
1952	28,865	17,157	59	18,219	65,125
1953	29,496			19,207	70,719
1954	29,899			19,896	75,637
1955	30,377			20,617	65,132
1956	30,834			21,612	65,681
1957	31,297	20,628	66	21,888	70,777
1958	31,498	22,022	70	22,467	73,620
1959	31,906	22,930	72	23,237	78,992
1960	32,251	23,406	73	23,556	91,184
1961	32,598	23,843	73	24,446	96,395
1962	32,892	24,158	73	24,640	96,558
1963	33,126	24,304	73	23,493	96,221
1964	33,388	24,320	73	24,156	99,821
1965	33,797	22,988	68		
1966	33,949	23,379	69	24,366	102,368
1967	34,147	23,316	68	24,235	102,037
1968	34,295	23,242	68	23,894	101,455
1969	34,335	22,935	67	23,731	99,005
1970	34,360	22,433	65	23,878	93,408
1971	34,441	21,631	63		86,859

Year*	Number of Southern Baptist Churches	Churches Reporting WMU	Percent of Churches Reporting WMU	WMS—Number of Organizations	Total Number of WMU Organizations
1972	34,534	22,376	65		82,516
1973	34,665	22,164	64		83,682
1974	34,734	22,444	65		85,599
1975	34,902	22,818	65		85,238
1976	35,073	23,021	66		86,035
1977	35,255	23,082	65		84,990
1978	35,404	23,451	66		82,048
1979	35,605	23,737	67		82,089
1980	35,831	23,999	67		83,308
1981	36,079	24,407	68		85,927
1982	36,302	24,942	69		91,008
1983	36,531	25,391	70		89,828
1984	36,740	25,517	70		92,709
1985	36,979	25,564	70		

Notes for Membership and Organizations Charts

*Each year's figures are drawn from reports dated with the subsequent year. Unless otherwise indicated reports are drawn from WMU Annual Report statistical tables or from Quarterly Review. Prior to the mid-1960s WMU collected its own statistics through internal channels. These were reflected in Annual Reports. Meanwhile, the SBC collected similar statistics. Seldom did the two sets of statistics match.

[1]Estimated enrollment according to unofficial statements by WMU officers.

[2]Figures prior to this year did not include all states. For the first time reasonably comprehensive figures, including such large states as Texas and North Carolina, are included. See WMU Annual Report 1927, 1929, and WMU Annual Report 1928, 1933.

[3]From WMU Report to the SBC or informal estimates of WMU officers. Data not reflected in WMU Annual Report tables.

[4]1925 SBC Annual states that nearly half of total WMU membership are young people.

[5]Totals represent more than the sum of bands and societies, due to irregularities in method of reporting.

CONTRIBUTIONS[23]
(as reported in WMU Annual reports)

	Lottie Moon Christmas Offering	Annie Armstrong Easter Offering	Other Foreign Missions	Other Home Missions	Sunday School Board	Christian Education[2]	State[3] Missions	Ministerial Relief (Annuity Board)
1888	$3,315 (3.85)[1]	$	$12,239	$ 7,014	$	$ 830	$ 2,866	$15,704
1889	2,660 (2.69)		16,057	12,057		1,658	4,011	12,590
1890	4,320 (3.96)		17,078	10,162		5,369	7,413	13,498
1891	4,985 (4.4)		18,776	15,229		5,658	18,726	275
1892	5,069 (4.3)		19,971	19,243		4,810	18,699	513
1893	3,569 (2.3)		32,456	26,284		2,079	15,155	144
1894	3,455 (3.2)		20,060	21,614		1,395	6,450	590
1895	4,502 (3.5)	5,000 (5.6)[1]	20,432	18,516		3,259	11,421	700
1896	3,708 (3.6)	211[3]	19,091	33,332		3,064	15,405	432
1897	4,356 (3.6)	484[3]	19,120	29,448		1,937	11,044	771
1898	4,493 (3.6)		17,140	35,636	1,024			
1899	5,310 (4.9)		18,843	36,697	3,263			
1900	6,356 (4.54)		25,402	45,204	6,305			
1901	6,088 (3.9)		25,713	20,550	9,024			

	Carver School	Margaret Funds	Other[19]	WMU[12] Specials	Total	Cooperative[14] Program	Place of Annual Meeting	Box Totals
			$			$		$
1888			3,799		$ 45,768		Richmond	
1889			23,543		72,575		Memphis	
1890			32,992		90,834		Ft. Worth	
1891			45,683		109,331		Birmingham	4,420
1892			38,117		106,421		Atlanta	6,776
1893			32,921		112,636		Nashville	8,225
1894			42,782		96,346		Dallas	11,327
1895			26,769		90,598		Washington	12,872
1896			28,949		104,191		Chattanooga	21,475
1897			28,000		95,159		Wilmington	5,445
1898					58,294		Norfolk	24,353
1899					64,113		Louisville	22,567
1900					83,267		Hot Springs	
1901					61,374		New Orleans	26,888

	Lottie Moon Christmas Offering	Annie Armstrong Easter Offering	Other Foreign Missions	Other Home Missions	Sunday School Board	Christian[2] Education	State[3] Missions	Ministerial Relief (Annuity Board)
1902	$ 7,534 (4.33)	$	$ 27,253	$19,510				
1903	10,957 (5.0)		25,898	19,295	256			
1904	11,787 (4.77)		35,991	24,870	443			
1905	14,016 (4.95)		39,662	30,698	418			
1906	17,522 (5.56)		45,197	37,392	304			
1907	21,272 (5.27)	10,488 (4.52)	53,472	28,866	517			
1908	26,300 (6.54)	13,572 (5.1)	61,215	42,619	1,561			
1909	27,921 (6.06)	17,199 (5.65)	68,720	40,170	1,380			
1910	25,284 (5.05)	18,591 (5.36)	97,932	59,291	1,341			
1911	28,943 (5.68)	19,899 (5.74)	98,957[7]	63,951	1,219			
1912	31,876 (5.49)	19,181 (5.08)	124,971	78,376	1,575			
1913	38,036 (6.10)	16,941 (4.35)	130,309	88,672	1,428			
1914	27,661 (4.71)	15,742 (3.65)	147,003	92,989	1,532			
1915	36,148 (6.73)	14,017 (3.30)	128,722	89,910	1,765			

	WMUTS/ Carver School	Margaret Funds	Other[19]	WMU[12] Specials	Total	Cooperative[14] Program	Place of Annual Meeting	Box Totals
1902	$	$	$		$ 54,777		Asheville	$33,354
1903					56,404		Savannah	34,121
1904		10,500			83,591		Nashville	38,952
1905					84,794		Kansas City	43,105
1906		3,187			103,602		Chattanooga	49,171
1907		1,836	8,673[4]		125,124		Richmond	29,586
1908	15,512	1,910	21,011[5]		183,700		Hot Springs	24,543
1909	15,945	1,428			172,764		Louisville	24,380
1910	11,966[6]	1,556			215,960		Baltimore	21,500
1911	12,148	1,389			226,508		Jacksonville	13,246
1912	10,725	1,254			267,957		Oklahoma City	13,057
1913	14,123	1,219			290,729		St. Louis	10,119
1914	15,805				300,733		Nashville	10,017
1915	32,785	14			303,360		Houston	11,742

	Lottie Moon Christmas Offering	Annie Armstrong Easter Offering	Other Foreign Missions	Other Home Missions	Sunday School Board	Christian[2] Education	State[3] Missions	Ministerial Relief (Annuity Board)
1916	$ 40,986 (7.92)	$19,820 (4.62)	$140,863	$ 91,507	$1,259			
1917	44,111 (8.08)	20,226 (4.26)	153,765	100,701	1,500			
1918	53,687 (6.34)	25,043 (3.52)	179,309	123,788	1,671			
1919	68,769 (6.18)	30,688 (2.73)	199,433	154,682	1,852			
1920	40,093 (1.72)	39,949 (2.51)	596,085	346,921	1,787	490,390	288,723	56,449
1921	28,616 (1.14)	21,102 (1.29)	804,034	480,793	1,644	786,862	407,297	107,856
1922	29,584 (1.63)	18,130 (1.45)	638,479	434,622	1,624	634,783	509,975	93,118
1923	42,206 (2.23)	23,011 (2.18)	596,156	387,168	1,355	629,555	338,287	96,573
1924	48,677 (2.54)	23,706 (2.19)	658,876	379,597	1,485	722,007	345,920	89,710
1925	306,376 (19.7)	27,632 (3.43)	413,679	331,393	1,650	542,795	297,667[11]	68,467
1926*	246,153 (10.8)	83,740 (12.06)	356,571	141,000	1,100	479,239	337,936	52,131
1927	172,457 (10.7)	89,061 (13.04)	601,774	191,970	1,650	496,719	539,805	72,149
1928	235,274 (16.16)	92,560 (14.2)	396,371	183,531	1,650	437,465	458,293	73,970
1929	190,131 (13.3)	78,639 (7.9)	574,828	372,713	1,650	727,203	504,850	76,439

	Carver School	Margaret Funds	Other[19]	WMU[12] Specials	Total	Cooperative[14] Program	Place of Annual Meeting	Box Totals
1916	$29,004	$ 788			$ 324,227		Asheville	$ 10,910
1917	53,855	1,474			375,631		New Orleans	10,905
1918	67,570	1,920			452,989		Hot Springs	11,009
1919	37,563	2,772	119,496		615,254		Atlanta	9,292
1920	50,848	3,459	486,673[9]	2,498[9]	2,403,876		Washington, D.C.	15,048
1921	70,481	6,606	654,106[9]		3,369,397		Chattanooga	38,615
1922	57,988	8,305	737,008[9]		3,163,616		Jacksonville	74,457
1923	63,870	6,600	585,523[9]		2,770,284		Kansas City	56,803
1924	55,969	7,200	698,018[10]		3,031,165		Atlanta	93,801
1925	58,084	15,874	877,575	31,674	2,972,865		Memphis	122,834
1926	31,402	9,705	391,076	20,900	2,150,952		Houston	71,030
1927	14,355	2,574	590,170	32,861	2,805,545		Louisville	95,449
1928	29,430	636	830,248	32,792	2,772,221		Chattanooga	
1929	28,578	24,297	910,688	10,151	3,500,167		Memphis	

	Lottie Moon Christmas Offering	Annie Armstrong Easter Offering	Other Foreign Missions	Other Home Missions	Sunday School Board	Christian[2] Education	State[3] Missions	Ministerial Relief (Annuity Board)
1930	$200,800 (16.4)	$ 92,645 (18.78)	$440,438	$155,473	$1,650	$535,304	$515,955	$67,211
1931	170,725 (16.57)	99,577 (21.65)	428,788	171,273	1,650	509,244	536,384	51,547
1932	143,331 (17.8)	77,355 (21.41)	390,014	182,970		431,547	469,928	51,974
1933	172,513 (19.6)	68,198 (19.97)	296,402	166,616		312,340	344,928	39,462
1934	213,926 (27.0)	100,256 (27.37)	246,265	82,871		232,230	293,997	35,423
1935	240,455 (26.5)	106,565 (23.83)	275,441	80,070		275,295	324,869	35,345
1936	292,402 (22.6)	118,360 (23.30)	257,992	81,393		235,387	334,180	36,401
1937	290,220 (26.9)	135,364 (25.88)	299,867	92,283		284,011	359,792	37,987
1938	315,000 (28.13)	147,792 (27.25)	263,628	101,344		322,169	368,661	40,333
1939	330,425 (29.14)	159,190 (27.51)	308,399	115,730		354,416	414,645	51,695
1940	363,746 (30.9)	167,905 (28.02)	273,580	119,429		358,716	432,208	60,513
1941	449,162 (30.46)	206,168 (27.75)	255,955	93,149		354,813	485,776	64,293
1942	562,609 (37.8)	239,730 (27.56)	247,012	122,207		425,787	594,397	71,099
1943	761,270 (33.6)	312,762 (29.06)	219,915	105,966		423,451	698,512	82,418

	WMUTS/ Carver School	Margaret Funds	Other[19]	WMU[12] Specials	Total	Cooperative[14] Program	Place of Annual Meeting	Box Totals
1930	$24,223	$22,342	$519,908	$ 11,627	$2,587,576		New Orleans	$106,166
1931	17,310	612	505,661	37,364	2,530,135		Birmingham	
1932	15,645	28,878	402,948	2,680	2,197,271		St. Petersburg	
1933	11,499	28,703	425,697	812	1,867,169		Washington, D.C.	62,980
1934	10,273	27,508	352,062	12,495[12]	1,607,306		Ft. Worth	73,348
1935	8,998	29,325	361,430	178,009[12]	1,915,803		Memphis	
1936	11,236	28,854	395,548	180,618[12]	1,972,370		St. Louis	88,457
1937	10,738	28,718	432,828	193,978	2,165,787		New Orleans	66,597
1938	14,790	29,777[14]	515,176	238,335	2,357,003		Richmond	86,861
1939	32,814	22,000	603,168	222,076	2,614,556		Oklahoma City	94,053
1940	29,696	24,161	560,242	164,245	2,556,443		Baltimore	108,292
1941	31,376	25,522	619,110	207,985	2,793,310		Birmingham	
1942	29,098	25,843	744,745	223,727	3,286,252		San Antonio	
1943	27,991	27,577	832,854	299,040	3,791,755		No Annual Meeting	

	Lottie Moon Christmas Offering	Annie Armstrong Easter Offering	Other Foreign Missions	Other Home Missions	Sunday School Board	Christian[2] Education	State[3] Missions	Ministerial Relief (Annuity Board)
1944	$ 949,844 (40.83)	$ 401,080 (31.45)	$ 323,744	$113,991		$ 571,981	$ 891,112	$105,214
1945	1,201,962 (40.59)	468,802 (27.84)	354,519	197,029		1,201,887[17]	2,798,481[18]	125,488
1946	1,381,049 (21.29)	529,047 (32.51)	681,300	320,708		250,727	1,506,278	184,046
1947	1,503,010 (28.30)	558,678 (32.66)	633,637	348,545		273,359	1,415,431	182,266
1948	1,669,683 (30.33)	654,433 (32.71)	1,015,972	291,604		353,684	1,672,408	309,480
1949	1,745,683 (28.29)	690,230 (33.69)	1,273,632	377,787		415,046	1,935,249	338,478
1950	2,110,019 (29.97)	704,437 (33.09)	908,500	443,665		444,708	2,058,954	330,538
1951	2,668,051 (32.71)	874,788 (38.59)	524,058	255,405		524,565	2,143,015	346,559
1952	3,280,373[15] (35.17)	991,484 (34.54)	1,868,477	895,968			764,871	
1953	3,602,555[16] (34.41)	1,119,865 (36.69)	51,394	26,289			1,094,969	
1954	3,957,821 (35.38)	1,212,435 (37.59)					734,286	
1955	4,628,691 (36.19)	1,256,255 (35.44)					823,837	
1956	5,240,745 (36.91)	1,574,891 (36.53)					929,603	
1957	6,121,585 (39.12)	1,741,860 (36.16)						

Year	WMU Carver School	Margaret Funds	Other[19]	WMU[12] Specials	Total	Cooperative[14] Program	Place of Annual Meeting	Box Totals
								$
1944	$31,292	$26,817	$ 855,941	$ 402,440	$ 4,673,455	$2,277,902	Oklahoma City	
1945	30,582			8,848	6,387,599	2,600,193	No Annual Meeting	
1946	36,223	10,887	1,608,100	8,955	6,517,322	3,469,589	Miami	
1947	41,722	11,202	1,834,398	1,015,525	7,817,775	3,660,001	St. Louis	
1948	36,928	10,643	1,092,881	87,373	8,005,089	4,562,800	Memphis	
1949	35,063	10,920	2,187,880	6,731	9,016,667	4,888,511	Oklahoma City	
1950	37,487	10,550	2,110,571	70,927	9,230,354	5,453,491	Chicago	
1951	35,705	10,928	2,221,401	32,882	9,637,358	5,570,806	San Francisco	
1952	31,025	10,563	96,287	27,922	7,966,970		Miami	
1953	35,895	12,057	68,954	23,076	6,035,053		Houston	
1954	39,082	11,084			5,954,707		St. Louis	
1955	49,306	11,378			6,769,467		Miami	
1956	51,730	10,064			7,807,034		Kansas City	
1957	61,428	11,176			23,194,705		St. Louis	

	Lottie Moon Christmas Offering	Annie Armstrong Easter Offering	Other Foreign Missions	Other Home Missions	Sunday School Board	Christian[2] Education	State[3] Missions	Ministerial Relief (Annuity Board)
1958	$ 6,762,449 (41.90)	$1,676,354 (33.81)						
1959	7,706,847 (43.82)	2,126,085 (37.18)						
1960	8,238,471 (44.99)	2,226,166 (34.78)						
1961	9,315,755 (46.44)	2,553,723 (39.05)						
1962	10,323,592 (46.05)	2,891,184 (41.16)						
1963	10,949,857 (44.14)	3,049,284 (40.23)						
1964	11,870,649 (44.96)	3,193,954 (38.40)						
1965	13,194,357 (46.31)	3,573,146 (35.72)						
1966	13,760,147 (45.51)	4,033,080 (36.84)						
1967	14,664,679 (46.28)	4,088,470 (33.92)						
1968	15,159,207 (45.17)	4,682,555 (37.59)						
1969	15,297,559 (44.15)	5,045,783 (38.63)						
1970	16,220,105 (45.37)	4,966,985 (41.29)						
1971	17,833,810 (47.01)	5,345,551 (38.57)						

	WMUTS/ Carver School	Margaret Funds	Other[19]	WMU[12] Specials	Total	Cooperative[14] Program	Place of Annual Meeting	Box Totals
1958	$44,081	$10,469			$25,739,444		Philadelphia	
1959		2,545			29,135,896		Portland	
1960		9,211			31,364,236		Dallas	
1961		10,935			34,661,074		Miami Beach	
1962		9,289			38,394,823		Norfolk	
1963		9,204			42,581,351		Kansas City	
1964		16,480			48,201,833		Atlanta	
1965		15,500			54,768,750		Houston	
1966		14,032			61,179,372		St. Louis	
1967		15,364			69,324,086		Los Angeles	
1968		15,751			74,786,670		New Orleans	
1969		14,678			80,675,879		Pittsburgh	
1970		14,619			89,690,075		Kansas City	
1971		15,344			8,832,264		Chicago	

	Lottie Moon Christmas Offering	Annie Armstrong Easter Offering	Other Foreign Missions	Other Home Missions	Sunday School Board	Christian[2] Education	State[3] Missions	Ministerial Relief (Annuity Board)
1972	$ 19,664,973 (46.39)	$ 6,059,603 (40.46)						
1973	22,232,757 (46.07)	6,884,357 (40.57)						
1974	23,234,094 (45.15)	8,130,142 (41.89)						
1975	26,169,421 (45.03)	8,491,653 (83.96)						
1976	28,763,810 (45.58)	9,631,013 (39.28)						
1977	31,938,553 (46.15)	10,642,798 (40.64)						
1978	35,919,605 (43.64)	12,282,228 (40.33)						
1979	40,597,113 (36.69)	14,171,637 (41.18)						
1980	44,700,340 (40.84)	16,479,032 (34.82)						
1981	50,784,173 (41.21)	18,539,913 (39.24)						
1982	54,077,464 (40.07)	20,709,206 (40.32)						
1983	58,025,337 (41.43)	22,650,542 (39.82)						
1984	64,775,764 (45.85)	24,914,311 (40.68)						
1985	66,862,114	26,890,137						
	$785,545,250	$271,483,669	$19,516,834	$9,709,743	$58,990	$15,067,744	$29,980,882	$3,479,819

	WMUTS/ Carver School	Margaret Funds	Other[19]	WMU[12] Specials	Total	Cooperative[14] Program	Place of Annual Meeting	Box Totals
1972		$ 14,869			$ 8,493,352		Houston	
1973		18,781			9,835,478		Louisville	
1974					10,473,849		Miami Beach	
1975					11,880,413		St. Louis	
1976					13,224,065		San Francisco	
1977					14,008,345		Kansas City	
1978					15,081,084		Atlantic City	
1979					16,783,004		Dallas	
1980					17,807,259		Detroit	
1981					18,768,513		Miami Beach	
1982					19,857,513		Houston	
1983					20,358,019		New Orleans	
1984					21,201,709		Denver	
1985					93,752,251		Dallas	
	$1,651,242	$831,661	$27,371,611	$3,788,545	$1,168,485,990	$30,483,292		$1,798,146

[1]Percentage of Foreign/Home Mission Boards' total receipts for year.

[2]Includes college endowments, operating contributions, and building funds.

[3]Most states reported contributions under "Other Home Missions." Included in "Other."

[4]Tichenor Memorial (Home Mission Board) Church Building Loan Fund.

[5]Includes gift from Sunday School Board to Tichenor Memorial.

[6]Five shares of stock in State Mutual Life Insurance Company not included in cash figure.

[7]Includes $6,814 for Jubilee Offering.

[8]Includes $10,000 from Sunday School Board.

[9]Includes Judson Centennial, hospital, and orphanages.

[10]Includes $33,399 bequest.

[11]Includes gifts to Sunday School Board.

[12]Includes paying campaign debt.

[13]Includes $22,000 annual designation from week of prayer for Margaret Fund.

[14]Included in total spread among various causes, but also reported separately.

[15]California, Georgia, North Carolina, and Tennessee, reporting 9 months only.

[16]California, Georgia, Illinois, Kentucky, North Carolina, South Carolina, and Tennessee reporting 12 months. All others reporting 9 months.

[17]Includes $793,259 endowment from Texas.

[18]Includes $694,127 endowment from Texas.

[19]Includes funds for orphanages, hospitals, undesignated, etc.

[20]No contributions made through Cooperative Program included in this report.

[21]Figures for 8 months only (May 1, 1925, through Jan. 1, 1926).

[22]Cooperative Program no longer recorded separately by WMU.

[23]Contribution figures are taken from Minutes of WMU Annual Meetings and are for previous fiscal year. All amounts are rounded off to the nearest dollar.

WOMAN'S MISSIONARY UNION, SBC, OPERATING REVENUE

Fiscal Year Ending	1889	1890	1891	1892	1893	1894	1895	1896	1897	1898	1899
Periodical Sales[1]											
Literature Sales											
Investment Income											
Royalties											
Sale of Properties											
Other Revenue											
Foreign Mission Board[2]	200	250	600	700	857	798	892	910	930	955	1,027
Home Mission Board	200	250	600	700	575	600	700	700	750	800	850
Sunday School Board							200	200	200	200	200
Education Board											
Annuity Board											
Gifts for Margaret Home											
Gifts for Margaret Fund											
Gifts for WMU Training School[3]											
Gifts for Training School Scholarships											
Gifts for WMU Building											
TOTAL	400	500	1,200	1,400	1,432	1,398	1,792	1,810	1,880	1,955	2,077

Fiscal Year Ending	1900	1901	1902	1903	1904	1905	1906	1907	1908	1909	1910
Periodical Sales[1]											
Literature Sales								2,494	4,304	5,610	5,926
Investment Income							10	21	15	134	1,074
Royalties											
Sale of Properties											
Other Revenue							2	1,402[5]			
Foreign Mission Board[2]		1,123	1,300	1,400	1,650	1,600	1,950	1,950	3,050	4,250	4,650
Home Mission Board		950	1,300	1,400	1,650	1,600	1,950	1,950	3,050	4,250	4,650
Sunday School Board		400	400	400	400	400	400	400	400	400	400
Education Board											
Annuity Board											
Gifts for Margaret Home					10,000[4]	500	3,875	2,015	1,449	2,033	2,694
Gifts for Margaret Fund											
Gifts for WMU Training School[3]									35,888[6]	14,920	8,515
Gifts for Training School Scholarships											
Gifts for WMU Building											
TOTAL		2,473	3,000	3,200	13,700	4,100	8,187	10,232	48,156	31,597	27,909

Fiscal Year Ending	1911	1912	1913	1914	1915	1916	1917	1918	1919	1920	1921
Periodical Sales[1]					5,836	6,779	7,534	9,279	10,329	14,770	21,610
Literature Sales	6,255	6,479	6,562	3,376	2,170	2,321	2,794	1,644	2,404	3,007	4,272
Investment Income	1,029	1,357	895	954	1,717	3,254	4,378	4,247	3,599	7,017	5,698
Royalties											
Sale of Properties					1,200[9]	16,200[9]	4,515[9]			6,400[9]	
Other Revenue			60[7]	100[8]	480	480	465	100	620		
Foreign Mission Board[2]	4,800	4,600	4,050	5,600	4,750	5,900	7,560	8,400	9,000	10,800	13,200
Home Mission Board	4,800	4,600	4,050	5,600	4,750	5,900	5,000	5,600	6,000	7,200	8,800
Sunday School Board	400	400	400	400	400	400	400	400	400	600	600
Education Board											800
Annuity Board					14						800
Gifts for Margaret Home	1,539	1,637	1,800								
Gifts for Margaret Fund						788	1,474	1,920	2,772	3,459	6,606
Gifts for WMU Training School[3]	11,939	10,725	13,962	15,805	21,654	22,878	47,803	59,193	27,705	35,345	51,681
Gifts for Training School Scholarships						6,126	6,051	8,377	9,857	15,502	18,800
Gifts for WMU Building											
TOTAL	30,762	29,798	31,779	31,835	42,971	71,026	87,974	99,160	72,686	104,100	132,867

Fiscal Year Ending	1922	1923	1924	1925	1925[12] (8 months)	1926	1927	1928	1929	1930	1931
Periodical Sales[1]	24,610	32,739	35,281	41,956	29,262	47,037	51,605	54,843	58,108	57,831	56,918
Literature Sales	4,464	4,045	5,755	6,031	5,004	7,693	7,826	8,347	7,540	7,701	6,859
Investment Income	7,067	3,788	7,802	8,678	4,409	8,476	9,195	9,226	10,710	10,769	11,918
Royalties											
Sale of Properties	17,000[10]										
Other Revenue	1,200[11]	2,830	3,012	2,400	1,600	2,400	2,400	2,400	2,400	2,400	2,400
Foreign Mission Board[2]	18,000	18,000	18,000	19,800	13,200	19,800	19,800	19,800	22,800	22,800	22,800
Home Mission Board	12,000	12,000	12,000	13,200	8,800	13,200	13,200	13,200	15,200	15,067	13,000
Sunday School Board	800	800	800	800	534	800	800	800	800	800	800
Education Board	800	800	800	800	534	400					
Annuity Board	800	800	800	800	534	800	800	800	800	800	1,400
Gifts for Margaret Home											
Gifts for Margaret Fund	8,305	6,600	16,743	18,279	9,705	19,988	23,791	24,404	27,349	19,324	19,186
Gifts for WMU Training School[3]	38,916	47,591	40,740	32,956	22,688	16,519	15,621	24,899	23,878	18,686	16,510
Gifts for Training School Scholarships	19,073	16,280	15,229	16,875	8,152	11,632	12,867	11,981	11,690	10,060	11,507
Gifts for WMU Building											
TOTAL	153,035	146,273	156,962	162,575	104,422	148,745	157,905	170,700	181,275	166,238	163,298

Fiscal Year Ending	1932	1933	1934	1935	1936	1937	1938	1939	1940	1941[15]	1942
Periodical Sales[1]	52,806	51,791	60,533	63,508	65,632	71,480	77,638	84,764	89,028	97,796	104,556
Literature Sales	5,553	5,906	9,701	7,456	7,771	8,482	9,812	16,320	10,867	13,163	14,517
Investment Income	9,938	5,906	3,066	8,149	8,622	9,021	8,383	8,536	13,195	3,759	3,411
Royalties											
Sale of Properties											
Other Revenue	2,400	2,400	1,098	1,136	1,346	1,428	1,210	1,302	1,393	1,750	5,176
Foreign Mission Board[2]	22,800	22,800	21,000	21,000	21,000	21,000	24,000	24,000	24,000	24,000	24,000
Home Mission Board	11,300	10,800	10,800	10,800	10,800	10,800	15,000	15,000	15,000	15,000	15,000
Sunday School Board	800	800	3,200	3,200	3,200	3,200	3,200	3,200	3,200	3,200	3,200
Education Board											
Annuity Board	2,100	800	800	800	800	800	800	800	800	800	800
Gifts for Margaret Home											
Gifts for Margaret Fund	16,959	15,675	14,721	16,029	17,293	16,256	25,147	24,861	26,718	26,628	28,077
Gifts for WMU Training School[3]	16,191	16,154	21,982	19,105	23,636	19,801	25,230	117,812[13]	96,470[14]	27,864	29,975
Gifts for Training School Scholarships	7,852	7,486	5,690	7,583	6,683	10,354	7,758	9,359	11,796	8,972	8,673
Gifts for WMU Building											
TOTAL	148,699	140,518	152,591	158,766	166,783	172,622	198,178	305,954	292,467	222,932	237,385

502

Fiscal Year Ending	1943	1944	1945	1946	1947	1948	1949	1950	1951	1952	1953
Periodical Sales[1]	117,872	139,664	163,912	197,329	224,836	313,247	330,649	363,203	422,237	496,945	629,306
Literature Sales	17,716	19,563	29,588	36,654	37,852	41,952	74,227	89,768	106,933	127,844	156,603
Investment Income	3,301	3,302	3,409	3,147	3,220	2,881	3,565	5,819	4,763	5,243	5,433
Royalties			147	172	243						
Sale of Properties										57,595[17]	
Other Revenue	6,117	8,643	9,191	8,286	746			2,773			
Foreign Mission Board[2]	24,000	24,000	32,000	32,000	32,000	40,000	46,000	46,000	46,000	60,000	60,000
Home Mission Board	15,000	15,000	20,000	20,000	20,000	26,800	31,000	31,000	31,000	40,000	40,000
Sunday School Board	3,200	3,200	3,200	3,200	3,200						
Education Board											
Annuity Board	800	800	800								
Gifts for Margaret Home											
Gifts for Margaret Fund	26,817		30,362	43,493	47,439	53,630	51,383	48,252	43,010	45,913	87,961
Gifts for WMU Training School[3]	36,528	62,429[16]	34,973	24,005	23,146	22,758	22,965	24,627	24,036	27,168	39,082[18]
Gifts for Training School Scholarships	10,186		8,416	7,855	8,475	6,745					
Gifts for WMU Building						29,027	92,428	78,237	81,181	27,717	
TOTAL	261,537	276,601	335,998	376,141	401,157	537,040	652,167	689,679	759,160	888,435	1,018,385

Fiscal Year Ending	1954	1955	1956	1957	1958[20] (9 months)	1959	1960	1961	1962	1963	1964
Periodical Sales[1]	684,771	740,769	829,088	863,533	640,730	917,020	1,046,047	1,111,656	1,142,250	1,234,193	1,247,500
Literature Sales	175,524	205,252	235,435	346,598	190,054	316,909	410,194	449,099	436,121	568,775	571,446
Investment Income	14,010	20,576	27,965	25,059	17,068			52,909	40,599	54,562	56,763
Royalties	491	376	294	364				4,935		485	394
Sale of Properties											
Other Revenue									5,931	4,595	4,505
Foreign Mission Board[2]	60,000	60,000	60,000	60,000	45,000	60,000	60,000	60,000	60,000	60,000	60,000
Home Mission Board	40,000	40,000	40,000	40,000	30,000	40,000	40,000	40,000	40,000	40,000	40,000
Sunday School Board											
Education Board											
Annuity Board											
Gifts for Margaret Home											
Gifts for Margaret Fund	67,378	62,064	68,701	63,174	54,545[21]	9,211	10,935	9,289	9,204	16,899	16,500
Gifts for WMU Training School[3]	51,381	51,771	61,428	44,081[19]							
Gifts for Training School Scholarships											
Gifts for WMU Building											
TOTAL	1,093,555	1,180,808	1,322,911	1,442,809	977,397	1,343,140	1,567,176	1,727,888	1,734,105	1,979,509	1,997,108

Fiscal Year Ending	1965	1966	1967	1968	1969	1970	1971	1972	1973	1974	1975
Periodical Sales[1]	1,305,328	1,350,985	1,537,799	1,561,138	1,461,700	1,335,555	1,618,705	1,562,221	1,815,879	1,884,437	2,131,605
Literature Sales	571,987	483,088	531,183	720,561	567,247	697,995	538,519	425,678	492,436	575,802	706,244
Investment Income	76,590	90,646	107,862	137,631	168,834	196,161	194,749	149,600	147,619	190,519	216,800
Royalties	457	1,801	1,183	474	1,644	137	18				
Sale of Properties											
Other Revenue	10,684		6,500	1,363	597	3,500			24,548[22]	4,093	321
Foreign Mission Board[2]	60,000	60,000	60,000	60,000	60,000	60,000	60,000	60,000	60,000	71,250	75,000
Home Mission Board	40,000	40,000	40,000	40,000	40,000	40,000	40,000	40,000	40,000	40,000	51,250
Sunday School Board											
Education Board											
Annuity Board											
Gifts for Margaret Home											
Gifts for Margaret Fund	14,032	15,364	15,751	14,677	14,619	15,344	14,869	18,781	4,601		
Gifts for WMU Training School[3]											
Gifts for Training School Scholarships											
Gifts for WMU Building											
TOTAL	2,079,078	2,041,884	2,300,278	2,535,844	2,314,641	2,348,692	2,466,860	2,256,280	2,585,083	2,766,101	3,181,220

Fiscal Year Ending	1976	1977	1978	1979	1980	1981	1982	1983	1984	1985
Periodical Sales[1]	2,400,393	2,926,579	3,043,930	3,071,838	3,185,962	3,740,764	3,923,633	4,526,552	4,929,000	5,380,209
Literature Sales	853,669	716,791	747,000	753,498	966,723	1,180,264	1,266,904	1,361,749	1,541,622	1,619,531
Investment Income	199,074	255,633	279,808	370,105	513,319	702,425	870,039	763,980	729,736	704,414
Royalties					15,615	11,880	3,559	25,650	35,302	24,842
Sale of Properties								398,300	295,000	81,438
Other Revenue	12,193[22]	15,544[22]	12,217[22]	9,997[22]	16,023[22]	8,146		31,931	507,786[23]	159,005
Foreign Mission Board[2]	75,000	75,000	168,750	200,000	200,000	200,000	200,000	200,000	200,000	200,000
Home Mission Board	55,000	55,000	88,750	100,000	100,000	100,000	100,000	100,000	290,607[24]	341,647[24]
Sunday School Board										
Education Board										
Annuity Board										
Gifts for Margaret Home										
Gifts for Margaret Fund										
Gifts for WMU Training School[3]										
Gifts for Training School Scholarships										
Gifts for WMU Building								533	51,619	163,186	138,700
TOTAL	3,595,329	4,044,547	4,340,455	4,505,438	4,997,642	5,943,479	6,364,668	7,459,781	8,692,239	8,649,786

506

Notes

[1] Early sales of periodicals were included in literature sales.
[2] From 1893 through 1901 the Foreign Mission Board reimbursed offering expenses in addition to their regular contribution.
[3] Gifts for WMU Training School include contributions, investments, and earnings, and some Cooperative Program allotments which were recorded in WMU's financial reports. Additional support for the school was provided from other sources.
[4] In 1904 the original gift was made by a "Christian mother" to begin the Margaret Home for missionaries' children.
[5] In 1907 the Maryland Union Association gave to WMU $1,402 for the foundation and maintenance of a Missionary Literature Department.
[6] The 1908 donations for the WMU Training School include $20,588 given by the Sunday School Board. Donations in this and subsequent years include gifts from states, the student body of the school, the alumnae of the school, the Louisville Campaign Fund, additional gifts from the Sunday School Board, and other special gifts and collections.
[7] In 1913 a special gift of $60 was received for the Literature Department.
[8] In 1914 a special gift of $100 was received for the Literature Department.
[9] Indicates sale of Margaret Home properties.
[10] Indicates sale of Baltimore property.
[11] In 1922, $1,200 was received from the Sunday School Board for rent. Each year thereafter until 1934, $2,400 was recorded as rent income. After 1934 this amount is recorded as a contribution from the Sunday School Board.
[12] In 1925 the fiscal year was changed to correspond with the calendar year.
[13] In 1939 donations for the WMU Training School included $37,089 received from states for the Maud R. McLure Memorial Building Fund and $50,000 Golden Jubilee Gifts for the Fannie E. S. Heck Memorial.
[14] The 1940 donations for the WMU Training School included $70,750 for the Maud R. McLure Memorial Building Fund.
[15] The 1941 records also contain a recapitulation of the income and offsetting expenditures during 1938, 1939, 1940, and 1941 for the building fund. Total income of $399,189 includes memorials and other gifts and income from investments.
[16] Includes gifts for Margaret Fund, Training School, and Training School scholarships.
[17] Proceeds from sale of property in Birmingham
[18] Beginning in 1953 the financial reports reflect change of name from WMU Training School to Carver School of Missions and Social Work.
[19] On May 27, 1957, WMU voted to transfer control of Carver School of Missions and Social Work to the Southern Baptist Convention, giving property and cash to the school, and endowment and trust funds to the Southern Baptist Foundation.
[20] In 1958 the fiscal year was changed from calendar year to October through September.
[21] After 1958 WMU transferred the primary Margaret Fund activity to the mission boards. WMU continued to receive donations for certain Margaret Fund projects through 1973. Certain restricted Margaret Funds continue to be reflected in Investment Income.
[22] Includes refunds from the Annuity Board for nonvested annuities paid by WMU.
[23] Includes $497,495 revenue from the National Acteens Conference.
[24] For 20 years prior to 1984 the Home Mission Board reimbursements were not shown as income. This 1984 figure includes HMB provisions for staff jointly employed with WMU.

MAGAZINE CIRCULATION[1]

	Our Mission Fields/Royal Service[2]	The Window	Ambassador Life[3]	World Comrades	Tell	Sunbeam Activities	Total
1906	10,000						10,000
1916	30,000						30,000
1922	57,000			9,000			66,000
1926	71,859						71,859
1930	73,332	6,038		15,597			94,967
1936	76,554	9,527		18,989			105,070
1946	191,229	22,604	24,628	58,828			297,289
1953	225,303	30,665	48,991		83,446	14,982	403,307
1956	300,000	36,000	68,000		114,000	29,466	547,466
1966	492,696	69,511			300,284	54,205	916,696
1969	404,937	67,550			323,406	52,718	848,611

	Dimension	Royal Service	Contempo	Accent	Aware	Discovery	Start	Share	Nuestra Tarea[4]	Our Missions World	Total
1971	36,362	331,712	46,603	188,510	50,442	242,033	31,076				926,738
1972	30,804	324,180	39,716	160,152	45,404	224,579	25,980		3,850		854,655
1976	36,872	337,346	54,773	142,978	42,630	215,616	26,932		4,150		861,257
1983	44,216	324,346	57,449	130,122	41,809	215,876	29,453	12,100	4,344	751	860,466
1986	41,377	323,474	61,478	118,264	38,839	209,087	30,924	14,388	4,634	898	843,363

[1]Figures represent annual paid circulation.
[2]Our Mission Fields was renamed Royal Service in 1914.
[3]Ambassador Life was given to Brotherhood Commission in 1957.
[4]The Home Mission Board placed Nuestra Tarea, founded in 1955, under WMU management in 1972. Statistics prior to 1972 are not available.

508

INDEX

512

McCall, Duke K., 281, 354
McCall, Emmanuel, 256-57
McClellan, Albert, 317, 318
McCullough, Glendon, 108
McDaniel, George W., 266, 354
McGarity, Ray Osborne (Mrs. William B.), 283, 333
McIntosh, Martha E. (later Martha Mc- Intosh Bell), 26, 41, 42, 45-46, 68, 91, 92, 94, 118, 148, 161, 175, 180, 191, 289, 327, 338, 253. *See also* Bell, Martha M. (Mrs. T. P.)
McLure, Maud Reynolds (Mrs. Thomas Ed- ward), 213, 221, 224, 227, 259, 270-72, 276, 306
McMurry, Mildred Dodson (Mrs. William), 90, 198, 199-200, 209, 254, 255, 256
McWilliams, Cora Cowgill (Mrs. George A.), 309, 310, 351-52
Maddry, Charles, 151, 209, 260
Mallory, Kathleen, 54, 65, 72, 88, 128, 161, 204, 226, 259, 260, 261, 262, 270, 275, 292, 314, 331, 351, 352, 357; during debt and depression era, 128, 130, 132, 149, 291; editor and writer, 98, 197, 206, 240; frugality of, 60-61, 64-65, 209; and race issue, 248, 249, 250, 251, 252, 253; on relationship of WMU to SBC, 307, 308; relationships with SBC leaders, 96, 131, 323-24, 347, 353-54, 355; service on interagency groups, 105, 125, 126, 136, 198, 308, 315; speaker, 306, 333; sup- porter of mission boards and offerings, 135, 137, 151, 152, 153, 156, 158-59
Margaret Fund, 135, 186-88, 241
Margaret Home, 53, 186, 270, 290
Martin, Olive Brinson (Mrs. George R.), 56, 89, 131, 144, 154, 161, 207, 249, 275, 280, 292, 293, 310, 315, 347-48
Maryland Baptist Mission Rooms, 46, 47, 62, 167, 191
Maryland WMU, 75, 76, 255
Maston, T. B., 247, 255
Mather, Juliette, 105, 109, 131, 161, 184, 205, 206, 208, 334
Mathis, Marie Wiley (Mrs. R. L.), 208, 256, 311, 319, 348, 356, 357; on auxiliary sta- tus, 293, 296, 297, 302-3; and coopera- tive denominational planning, 73, 112, 140, 309, 317, 320-21; and missions offerings, 154, 161; and overseas wom- en's work, 87, 89; reliance on prayer, 170-71; on role of women, 340, 341
Membership (WMU) patterns, 59, 84-86
Mexican Baptist Convention of Texas, WMU, 79
Michigan WMU, 74, 76, 171, 296
Ministers' Wives Conference, 300
Minnesota-Wisconsin WMU, 76
Mission action, 100, 215, 230-33, 235, 319
Mission boards of SBC, 49, 53, 116. *See also* Foreign Mission Board; Home Mis- sion Board
Mission Friends, 115
Mission Literature Department, SBC, 193, 195, 203

Mission Service Corps, 185
Mission study, 49, 189-210; books, 199, 200; churchwide, 201-3; cooperative cur- riculum planning with Brotherhood, 198, 200-201; literature and periodicals, 191- 94, 203-9
Mission support, 121-22, 165-88
Missionaries, WMU support of, 165-69, 173-83, 185-88
Missionaries, volunteer, 184-85
Missionary calling, WMU responsibility for nurturing, 175-79, 183
Missionary families, ministries to, 121, 185-88
Missionary Round Table, 199
Missionary wife, role of, 179
Missions Challenge committee, 201, 321, 322
Missions Education Council, 199
Mississippi WMU, 69, 76, 79, 182, 194, 255
Missouri WMU, 76, 218, 245, 255, 286, 294, 295
Montgomery, Helen Barrett, 298, 346
Moon, Edmonia, 26, 174
Moon, Lottie, 38, 46, 129, 141, 147-48, 149, 174, 178, 285, 326, 327, 344, 345, 354
Moore, Alice (Mrs. Dewey), 89
Moore, Pauline Willingham (Mrs. John Allen), 56
Moss, Caroline Thornton (Mrs. Oliver Perry), 27, 175, 300, 327
Moye, Esther B., 80, 205
Mullins, E. Y., 226, 264, 268, 330-31
Murphy, Nicy, 184, 296, 297

National Baptist Convention, 241, 291
Naylor, Robert E., 108
Neal, LaVenia, 342
Neel, Isa-Beall Williams (Mrs. W. J.), 126, 127
Negro Americans. *See* Blacks
Nelson, Martha J. ("Mattie"), 58, 180, 182, 266
Nevada WMU, 76, 294
New Century Movement, 123, 303
New England WMU, 76, 297
New Hope (publishing arm of WMU), 202- 3, 232
New Mexico WMU, 71, 72, 79
New Orleans Baptist Theological Semi- nary, women's training school, 283-84
Newton, Louie, 131
New York WMU, 74-76
Nimmo, Elia Brower (Mrs. William R.), 58, 79, 204
Nishikawa, Itsuko Saito (Mrs. Nobuo), 77
North American Baptist Women's Union, BWA Women's Department, 89, 90, 255
North Carolina WMU, 70, 175, 195, 202, 214, 232
North Central Mission Thrust, 76
Northern Baptists, 25, 27, 31, 70-72, 242, 245
Northern Plains WMU, 76
Northington, Mary, 329

Requirements for Church Study Course Credit

The Church Study Course is a Southern Baptist educational system consisting of more than 500 short courses for adults and youth combined with a credit and recognition system. Credit is awarded for each course completed. These credits may be applied to one or more of the 23 subject areas.

Complete details about the Church Study Course system, courses available, and diplomas offered may be found in a current copy of the Church Study Course Catalog and in the study course section of the Church Materials Catalog. The Church Study Course may be obtained in two ways: (1) Read the book and participate in a 2½-hour study; (2) Read the book and write a brief summary of each chapter. (Have written work checked by an appropriate church leader.)

To receive credit, use Form 725, "Church Study Course Enrollment/ Credit Request," available from your state Baptist convention office or the Awards Office, 127 Ninth Avenue, North, Nashville, TN 37234. A record of awards will be maintained by the Awards Office. Twice each year copies will be sent to church for distribution to members.

Credit for this course may apply toward the Woman's Missionary Union Leadership Diploma for WMU Officers, Acteens Leaders, Girls in Action Leaders, and Mission Friends Leaders.